Natural and Supernatural

Natural
and Supernatural

A History of the Paranormal from
Earliest Times to 1914

Revised Edition

by
BRIAN INGLIS

PRISM · UNITY

This revised edition published in 1992 by
PRISM PRESS
2 South Street
Bridport
Dorset DT6 3NQ

Distributed in the USA by
AVERY PUBLISHING GROUP INC.
120 Old Broadway
Garden City Park
NY 11040

Published simultaneously in Australia by
UNITY PRESS
6a Ortona Road
Lindfield
NSW 2070

First published in 1977 by Hodder and Stoughton Limited, Sevenoaks, Kent

ISBN 1 85327 074 1

Printed by the Guernsey Press Limited, Channel Islands

Contents

Introduction

A WRITER WHO PLANS TO PROVIDE A DETACHED HISTORICAL SURVEY ordinarily does not need to state his aim; it should be manifest in his selection and interpretation of the facts. But the supernatural presents a problem, because one man's facts are another man's superstitions. 'Till we have a new light,' Renan wrote in his *Life of Jesus,* 'we shall maintain the principle of historical criticism that a supernatural relation cannot be accepted as such that it always implies credulity or imposture'; and the great majority of historians, whatever their personal opinions, have since followed his example. By taking the evidence for the supernatural seriously, therefore, a writer immediately identifies himself as a partisan. And as I am, in one sense, a partisan, perhaps the simplest way to declare an interest, and at the same time to give an idea of the aim and scope of this book, is to describe how it came to be written: as the culmination of a protracted wrestling-bout with two adversaries, the present-day equivalents of Bunyan's seedy giants, Pope and Pagan – Pope representing accumulated layers of superstition derived from fantasy, legend, myth, folklore and religious dogma; Pagan representing the dogmas and evasions of materialist science, refusing to credit what it cannot quantify.

When I was growing up in Ireland between the wars, the supernatural was still a force, at least in the countryside. People might no longer really believe in leprechauns or banshees, but they would not have been greatly astonished to encounter them, and they certainly accepted that there were forces unknown to science, apparently directed by 'powers' capable of benevolent or malevolent actions. Few Irish farmers would have dared to cut down or plough up a thorn bush, because the thorn enjoyed the powers' protection. And although my family and friends, being Anglo-Irish, regarded such beliefs as rather childish superstitions, this did not prevent us from having even sillier superstitions of our own. To sit down to dinner thirteen at the table would have been unthinkable; if salt were spilt, or the new moon seen through glass, the appropriate ritual had always punctiliously to be carried out to avert bad luck. We also accepted that certain houses were haunted. But in England, when I went to school there, although the tradition of haunted houses was firmly established, we were not expected to believe in it. Outwardly, at least, our teachers were sceptical; and most of us fell into line. I doubt whether any of us, teachers or boys, would have volunteered to spend the night alone in a room supposed to be haunted; but the proposer of the stock school debating society motion 'This House does not believe in ghosts' could be confident of a massive majority.

We were conditioned, in short, to be intellectual sceptics: to assume that the supernatural was only superstition. And a sceptic I would probably have remained but for coming across a copy of J. W. Dunne's *Experiment with Time,* with its description of dreams in which he had seen future events; and then hearing about Professor J. B. Rhine's experiments at Duke University in which some individuals, asked to guess which card was going to turn up next, had scored consistently higher than chance expectation. Not that I thought of these as supernatural. Dunne's mathematical hypotheses were abstruse; but his analogy – that we travel through life like passengers on a train sitting with their backs to the engine, able to see only what is past; the future being already there ahead of us, to be glimpsed sometimes in dreams – seemed natural, and quite plausible, even if its implication, that events might be predestined, was disturbing. Similarly there seemed no reason why extra-sensory perception, as Rhine called it, should not operate through a system analogous to radio waves, enabling certain individuals to communicate with each other, or to pick up information about what was happening at a distance. Orthodox scientific thinking in the 1930s, however, flatly rejected these hypotheses. Dunne, admittedly, was acceptable up to a point: as future events stem from past causes, it was not inconceivable that we might dream of something that was about to happen on the strength of information we had obtained, perhaps unconsciously, about forces already at work – in the sense that a rattle in a car might have warned us of an impending accident. Rhine's experimental results, though, were brushed aside as explicable only by statistical error, coincidence, or deception. The limits of the human mind's transmitting capacity were established; telepathy or clairvoyance could be ruled out.

At this stage I began to question science's dogmas. That future effects derive from past causes sounded reasonable, but it could not satisfactorily account for Dunne's experiences, let alone for countless examples of dreams or visions of the future in history and literature.

History and literature also abounded in cases of other kinds of extra-sensory perception, now becoming known as ESP. Might it not be that scientists were simply doing what they had so often done?

> They all laughed
> When Christopher Columbus
> Said he thought the world was round
> They all laughed when Edison recorded sound.

And from time to time my belief in ESP was reinforced – casually rather than dramatically: by seeing J. B. Priestley's play on the Dunne theme, *Time and the Conways*; by having a couple of 'Dunne dreams', as they came to be known, myself; most of all by reading or hearing about episodes which were easier to explain by ESP than by the alter-native proposition that they were illusions or inventions. And when, in the early 1960s, research for a book on unorthodox forms of medicine revealed to me just how closely linked they had been with ESP, I de-cided to join the Society for Psychical Research.

The Society had been founded eighty years before, with the aim of investigating scientifically certain phenomena which orthodox scien-tists tended to shun: thought-transference, clairvoyance, prevision, hypnotism, hauntings, spiritualist manifestations, and so on. Although in its publications it was always careful to emphasise that it did not hold or express corporate views, most of its members thought of them-selves, as they still do, as taking a rational view of the whole subject. The very term 'supernatural' made them shudder because, as one of the Society's founders, Frederic Myers, explained, it had come to be 'associated with arbitrary interference with law'. They tried 'super-normal' as an alternative; then for a while 'metapsychical'; and at the time I joined 'paranormal' was the front runner. It still is; but it has yet to settle into easy colloquial usage – and where it is used, it is often hardly distinguishable in its implications from supernatural. But what-ever term happened to be fashionable the basic assumption, and one which appealed to me, was that the absence of an explanation for cer-tain phenomena did not necessarily mean that they flouted natural laws. It might simply be that the code of laws needed revision.

Sympathetic though I had been, I had no idea of the quantity, quality and range of the evidence for ESP, experimental and anecdotal, which had been collected. As Sir George Thomson – Professor of Physics and Nobel prizewinner – had observed in 1955, it would cer-tainly have won acceptance 'if what is claimed were not such a funda-mental upsetting of systems of thought'. Unless there were 'a gigantic conspiracy involving some thirty University departments all over the world, and several hundred highly respected scientists', the psychologist Professor Hans Eysenck commented in 1957, 'the only conclusion the unbiased observer can come to must be that there does exist a small number of people who obtain knowledge existing either in other people's minds, or in the outer world, by means as yet unknown to science'. The great majority of scientists, however, never saw the evidence. If they read about it at all, it was usually in such works as Professor C. E. M. Hansel's *ESP – a Scientific Evaluation,* a barbed onslaught on the integrity as well as the competence of psychical researchers published in 1966, which led the *New Scientist*'s reviewer to announce 'parapsychology is dying'.

Parapsychology, however, was not dying. As things turned out, it was just beginning to revive. Discouraging though the prospect appeared in Britain, it was less gloomy elsewhere. In 1963 Professor L. Vasiliev's *Experiments in Mental Suggestion* had been published by Leningrad State University; and the English translation which appeared the following year showed that the Russians, who after the Revolution had appeared implacably hostile to parapsychology as a bourgeois deviation, had been allowing experiments with telepathy, some of which had been strikingly successful. In the United States, too, the American Association for the Advancement of Science, which had steadfastly rebuffed the psychical researchers, at last repented; in 1966 it accepted the Parapsychological Institute as an affiliate. And the following year an investigation was held in Germany the significance of which, though it created no great stir at the time, is now obvious. It was the case of the Rosenheim poltergeist.

'Poltergeist' – noisy or rackety ghost – was the name given to a particular type of haunting which had been reported from all over the world. Its characteristic was mischief; it was as if invisible Pucks or Til Eulenspiegels were taking a perverse delight in rapping and banging, throwing cutlery or crockery about, and knocking pictures off walls. Their activities were better documented than other types of haunting because they tended to stay around for a time, so that investigators could be brought in to check that it was not simply some naughty child creating the disturbances. The Rosenheim poltergeist was even more co-operative than most, in this respect. Its activities were in a lawyer's office in the town of Rosenheim in Bavaria; they went on day after day; and they took place during working hours. In addition to the usual effects, too, there was interference with the office's electrical and telephone systems. As a result it was possible to set up elaborate monitoring apparatus which revealed that the fault did not lie with the equipment or the power supply – or with a practical joker. The circuits were being interfered with, but not by any human hand.

A continual succession of telephone calls, for example, was being put through to the local 'speaking clock'; yet the office instruments were not being used, and could not have been in use, because the calls were registering more rapidly than they could have been dialled. Eventually two scientists, Dr. F. Karger of the Max Planck Institute and a Munich physicist Dr. G. Zicha, in collaboration with the parapsychologist Professor Hans Bender of Freiburg, traced the manifestations to the presence in the office – but not the active physical intervention – of a girl secretary. It had been generally admitted in the natural sciences, the physicists wrote in their report, that no special physical laws needed to be postulated for the interaction of man with matter. But these phenomena broke the rules. Since they only occurred in connection with a particular person, the physicist was now presented 'with the unforeseen possibility of making physical discoveries by investigating man'. For this reason, they felt, such phenomena must be of interest to him: and their clarification must, in turn, 'have repercussions on our knowledge of man's being'.

Some of the most highly regarded physicists in Europe, a century before, had been psychical researchers: Fechner, Weber and Zöllner in Germany, Schiaparelli in Italy, Lodge and Crookes in Britain, Flammarion in France. They had ceased to be so highly regarded when their orthodox materialist colleagues realised that they accepted the reality of psychical phenomena. But now, a century later, physics and materialism were in the last stages of protracted divorce proceedings. Physicists could no longer confidently claim that the kind of phenomena reported in the Rosenheim case were contrary to natural laws. They could, however, still insist that it would be unwise to place reliance on tests carried out in the inadequately controlled conditions of a lawyer's office; the effects must be reproduced in a laboratory.

There matters rested until on October 18th, 1974, *Nature* published a report by Hal Puthoff and Russell Targ, two physicists working in the Stanford Research Institute in California, of experiments which had compelled them to accept that 'a channel exists whereby information about a remote location can be obtained by means of an as yet unidentified perceptual modality' – to put it colloquially, by clairvoyance. It was the second sign (the acceptance of parapsychology by the Association for the Advancement of Science had been the first) that the scientific Establishment was under pressure. *Nature*, as an editorial self-consciously explained, 'although seen by some as one of the world's most respected journals, cannot afford to live on respectability'; and even if the Stanford experiments were not absolutely fool-proof, they could not be dismissed as 'magic tricks'. But they were thus dismissed; and understandably, as the subject who had been tested was the young Israeli, Uri Geller.

By the time the report appeared Geller had made an international impact with what he claimed were feats of clairvoyance and psychokinesis. But in his public performances on the stage or on television he did the kind of things conjurors had long done for a living – guessing what picture had been contained in a sealed envelope, bending spoons or latchkeys; and many members of the Society for Psychical Research shared the view of sceptics that he was simply an accomplished prestidigitator. Eventually, however, further laboratory tests conducted in American universities, in Toronto, in London and elsewhere, some of them monitored by professional magicians, began to assuage these doubts. In the meantime, too, a number of other individuals had presented themselves for investigation and shown themselves capable of similar – and in the case of the New Yorker Ingo Swann, some even more remarkable – feats. After the long years of frustration, parapsychologists began to wonder if the break-through were in sight.

By this time the problem referred to by Sir George Thomson – the fact that acceptance of psychic phenomena entailed such a fundamental upsetting of systems of thought – though still an obstacle, was not quite so formidable as it had been earlier. It was not just that the course which physicists had been taking had lured them a long way from the assumptions upon which the scientific objections to ESP had initially been based: so that, as Arthur Koestler put it in *The Roots of Coincidence*, 'the seemingly fantastic propositions of parapsychology appear less preposterous in the light of the truly fantastic concepts of modern physics'. Perhaps still more influential was the lesson of Professor Thomas Kuhn's *The Structure of Scientific Revolutions*, illustrating how dependent scientists have been on the maintenance of a shared set of assumptions, a paradigm; their aim traditionally being 'to force nature into the preformed and relatively inflexible box that the paradigm supplies'. Normal scientific research, Kuhn explained, is directed only to 'the articulation of those phenomena and theories that the paradigm already supplies'; phenomena which do not fit the paradigm 'are often not seen at all'. Kuhn was not complaining about this; the scientist, he felt, was right to stick to his last. Perhaps on this account, scientists listened to him; his thesis attracted unusual interest. And though it did not make scientists any better disposed to parapsychology, it did make them less dogmatic in their rejection of the paranormal. Instead of 'it's all nonsense', they could simply say 'it is not our affair'.

When a deeply sceptical friend sent me a copy of Kuhn's essay, to justify his refusal to take an interest in the subject, I had already started on this book; and Kuhn's theme offered a way out of the dilemma posed by the rejection of the supernatural. What I have done is work within a hypothetical paradigm, writing on an 'as if' assumption – the events being related *as if* they may have occurred. On this assumption, it has been possible to select evidence for inclusion on the same basis as any other history; the criterion being the quantity, and still more the quality, of the testimony.

A rather stricter standard, though, has to be applied than would ordinarily be required, because the supernatural has been intertwined with superstition and fraud. Here, a remark made by Professor Flournoy of Geneva, one of the shrewdest of the earlier psychical researchers, is relevant. Compelled by what he had witnessed in his careful investigations to abandon his original outright scepticism, he enlisted a couple of guides: Hamlet, and the astronomer-mathematician Laplace. Realising that there were more things in heaven and earth than he had dreamed of, Flournoy was no longer prepared to say that anything was impossible. But at the same time he accepted Laplace's view that the weight of the evidence needs to be proportioned to the strangeness of the facts; the more unfamiliar the phenomena, the more contrary to common experience and to common sense, the greater the reluctance should be to credit reports of them. An admirable principle, I thought, to follow.

It has not been quite so simple. The temptation has been to ignore or dismiss what is manifestly contrary to common experience and to common sense; not simply because it has upset my own preconceptions, but also out of regard for Dante's admonition that 'we should conceal, as far as possible, those truths which resemble lies, because they wrong us, without our being responsible for them'. We all of us tend to have a 'thus far, and no farther' point; for somebody to ask us to take seriously what lies beyond it may arouse our mistrust. Augustus de Morgan, first Professor of Mathematics at University College, London, was confronted with this dilemma after his scepticism had been confounded by what he had witnessed at seances in the early 1850s. People like himself, he wrote, were reproached 'for not accommodating their narratives to the swallow of their hearers'; it was intimated to them that they should present something less incredible, if they wanted to be believed. But this, he felt, would be dangerous. The same principle should apply as in court cases. If counsel said to a witness, 'Do you expect the jury to believe . . .?', it was the duty of the judge to interrupt: 'Brother Buzfuz, the witness is to mind his *truth*: the jury will take care of the *credibility*'.

Historical credibility being primarily derived from the reputation of the source, I have been guilty of persistent name-dropping. For every case here described there are dozens of others as good or better; and as Walter Prince remarked, introducing his collection *Noted Witnesses for Psychical Occurrences,* a description of, say, a vision has no less validity if it is vouched for by William Moggs of Sheboygan, Wisconsin, than by Abraham Lincoln or Garibaldi. But at least, Prince claimed, the reader has a better chance to judge the evidence for himself if he knows something about the individual. Few people, for example, would pay much attention to a story about a man and his wife who, in 1765, heard heavy footsteps one night in a locked room, and recognised them by the sound as those of a friend who, they later discovered, had died precisely at that hour; but when it is disclosed that the teller of the tale was the founder of modern botany, Linnaeus, it takes on a rather different complexion.

Admittedly this is not a justification which commends itself to scientists. Science, the young H. G. Wells asserted, 'produces its facts; history at best produces reputable witnesses to facts'; and the tendency has been to reject anecdotal material as an irrelevance. Yet in practice science *does* accept the evidence of reputable witnesses, provided that evidence falls within the paradigm. Until the early years of the nineteenth century, for example, scientists refused to accept that meteorites existed; consequently anybody who claimed to have seen or found one was dismissed as a liar. But as soon as meteorites gained acceptance, earlier witnesses could be rehabilitated ('When the improbability of a fact is the chief objection to the belief in its reality,' the science-populariser Eusebe Salverte explained, 'the evidence which attests it regains all its value if the improbability is proved to be only apparent'). It remained necessary to scrutinise the credentials of such witnesses, in case they might have some reason for inventing a meteorite, for instance a priest wishing to frighten his flock, or a showman to attract customers; but so long as a witness's reputation merited it, his evidence could become retrospectively acceptable.

Granted the hypothetical paradigm – granted that the story may be told *as if* the events described, or at least some of them, could have happened – it is surely legitimate to claim the same status for witnesses of supernatural events. But to justify this claim it is necessary to concentrate attention on those phenomena to which the ordinary rules of historical evidence can be applied; the phenomena, in fact, on which psychical research has chiefly concentrated. They fall into two main categories: perception other than through the recognised five senses (ESP); and the action of mind, or any non-physical entity, on matter (psychokinesis, or telekinesis). ESP has itself been broken down into sub-categories: telepathy, or thought-transference (communication between minds); clairvoyance, or second sight, along with clairaudience, voices in the inner ear, and clairsentience, psychic intuitions (perceptions of events, or things); precognition, or prevision (perception of the future); retrocognition (perception of the past). But I have ordinarily

used whatever term was in use in the period, with explanations where
necessary; and I have differentiated psychic 'seeing' or 'hearing' from
ordinary seeing and hearing by inverted commas.

There are also a few manifestations which do not fit readily into
either of the two main categories, or which overlap them: for example,
hauntings, dowsing, and automatic writing. And I have included mes-
merism/hypnosis, partly because the process by which it came to be
transferred from the supernatural to the natural classification is so
instructive, partly because its intimate links with paranormal phenomena are by no means severed. But, reluctantly, I have left out psychic
healing, except where it is inextricably intertwined with the subject
under discussion, as in the section on mesmerism. Although healing
miracles are by far the most commonly reported manifestation of the
supernatural, it is virtually impossible to be certain that individual
cures are not explicable by natural causes; even if, say, it were recorded
that a man had grown a new limb to replace one lost in an accident,
it could plausibly be attributed to a genetic freak, a throwback to the
process by which lizards grow new tails.

It may seem less easy to justify the absence of any consideration,
except in passing, of some of the more celebrated magical cults such
as the Cabala; but though there is a mass of evidence, and scores of
books, about how they operated through rituals, incantations and so
on, there is hardly any evidence that the magic actually worked, and
such as there is is usually reliable only as a guide to contemporary
fantasies. Much the same applies to the exploits of the great magicians,
from Zoroaster to Crowley. As Charles Richet wrote in his introduction to his *Thirty Years of Psychical Research*, half a century ago,
'those who may expect to find in this book nebulous discussions on
human destiny, on magic, or on Theosophy will be disappointed. I
have endeavoured to write on science, not on dreams.'

The other obvious omission is the story of the years between the
first world war and the present. The year 1914 happens to be the
most convenient natural break, bringing to an end as it did the first
phase of scientific psychical research. The second phase, which can
be said to begin with Rhine's experiments, was for forty years to be an
exercise in frustration, with psychical researchers elaborating on and
refining experimental techniques and occasionally obtaining remarkable results, but unable to make any impression on orthodoxy. And
the latest period, so full of interest, is too close to be comfortably contained in a history.

Tribal Communities

Chapter One
Beliefs and Practices

THE EVIDENCE ABOUT THE SUPERNATURAL IN TRIBAL COMMUNITIES HAS to be treated with particular caution, for two reasons. One is that although, in its historical perspective, it is the earliest available to us, most of it has been collected in the past hundred years; tribal customs have therefore often been affected directly or indirectly by contact with civilisation. Ordinarily this would be more than compensated for by the fact that it has been possible, and to a limited extent still is possible, actually to investigate the communities instead of having to rely on archaeological remains and unverifiable chronicles, as we do in the case of those civilisations which have not survived. But here, the second complication arises. The majority of investigators – the overwhelming majority, in the case of professional anthropologists – have equated belief in the supernatural with superstition. They have studied and reported tribal beliefs and practices; but only rarely have they attempted to assess whether the beliefs may be justified, or whether the practices can work.

Mana

Living among the Melanesian islanders in the 1870s the missionary R. H. Codrington found that they believed in a force they called *mana*, which they thought of as natural, but which to him was supernatural. It was not the first description of such a belief; in his study of the Peruvian Indians Clements Markham had mentioned that they thought all substances had their *mama* (as they called it). But it was Codrington's account which focussed attention on the subject; and soon, variations were being reported from tribal communities all over the world.

There were problems, however, of interpretation. Tribesmen found it hard to explain what was often to them an abstraction; and even if they could explain, their language might not be adequate to convey their meaning. Translations into European languages created further distortions, and anthropologists bickered among themselves about what precisely, or even imprecisely, *mana* or the equivalents might mean. In *La Force Magique*, published in 1914, Pierre Saintyves did his best to define it.

It is by its nature material, yet invisible and impalpable, and comparable to a colourless flame or an imperceptible wind. It is, moreover, intelligent and, without being a spirit, has a spiritual nature. It might be defined as a kind of material fluid devoid of personal intelligence but capable of receiving, incorporating and reflecting the impression of all ideas and spirits . . . a kind of impersonal spirit without ideas proper to it, in which the intentions of men and of spirits can be incorporated so that they can fulfil their aims.

The abstract idea of *mana*, though – like the abstract idea of the supernatural itself, in Europe – was usually intertwined with a belief that it was operated by spirits; sometimes themselves abstractions, sometimes the equivalent (though again, translations at best tended to be rough and ready) of fairies, ghosts, angels, demons or gods. And nearly all tribal communities believed in and practised magic. Some individuals, the belief ordinarily was, were endowed with the ability to exploit *mana*; or more commonly, to induce the spirits to exploit it, either by invocation, or by exercising the kind of power over them which Aladdin had over the slave of the lamp. The aim was to control or direct the forces of nature in order, as Codrington explained, 'to make rain or sunshine, wind or calm, to cause sickness or remove it, to know what is far off in time or space, to bring good luck and prosperity, or to blast and curse'.

Mana, the force; spirits capable of using it; humans able to get the spirits to work for them: these were the three elements of the supernatural which were found in some form or other virtually everywhere. Often this included forces which, like thunder and lightning, Europeans had come to accept as natural. But there were two phenomena which in European eyes were unquestionably supernatural: the faculty of obtaining information by second sight, for use in divination; and the ability to influence events or objects by mental, or psychic, power.

Divination
The belief that information could be acquired other than through the five senses was found in all tribal communities. The information could emerge spontaneously; either in dreams – the Zulus used dreams to guide them to herds of game; the Malays, to show them where to fish – or in waking visions. Of these, the most commonly reported were apparitions of people who had just died. Among the Maoris of New

Zealand an apparition was regarded almost as a formal notification of death; so much as that in one case described by Caesar de Vesme in his *Primitive Man* – the first serious attempt at a general survey of the supernatural in tribal communities, published in 1930 – a Maori woman was permitted to marry again on the strength of an apparition of her absent husband; a decision which was to lead to complications when, a few weeks later, the original husband returned.

Spontaneous dreams and visions, though, could not be relied upon to come up with the answers to all the tribe's problems; and the practice of inducing clairvoyance was general. In some tribes, it was assumed that anybody could do it, as the missionary bishop Henry Callaway reported in his pioneering work *The Religious System of the Amazulu*, published in 1869 – 'perhaps the most accurate record,' his obituarist in the *Dictionary of National Biography* thought, 'of the beliefs and modes of thought of an unlettered race in the English tongue'. It was the more important because Callaway had studied the tribes before civilisation had made much impression on them. Among black men, he had found, there was

a something which is divination within them. When anything valuable is lost, they look for it at once; when they cannot find it, each one begins to practise this inner divination, trying to feel where the thing is; for, not being able to see it, he feels internally a pointing which tells him, if he will go down to such a place, it is there, and he will find it. At length he sees it, and himself approaching it; before he begins to move from where he is he sees it very clearly indeed, and there is an end of doubt. The sight is so clear that it is as though it were not an inner sight, but as if he saw the very thing itself and the place where it is.

According to Andrew Lang, the Zulus had a poetical name for the faculty; they called it 'opening the gates of distance'.

The ability to induce clairvoyance and telepathy casually in this way, though, was uncommon. Usually some ceremonial procedure was required; an invocation of *mana* or the spirits. Among the Melanesians, Codrington reported, 'almost every man of consideration' knew how to make the correct approach; but a few individuals were believed to have particularly effective ways of setting about it and they tended to acquire professional status. In most tribes, divination was left to such specialists. They were variously described: as medicine men in the Americas, witch doctors in Africa, shamans in Asia. But though they had other functions, their chief task was to exercise their powers of second sight. The term 'witch doctor', the Rev. Joseph Shooter claimed from his experience of the Kafirs in the 1850s, was consequently misleading; by avocation he was really a seer, or prophet. Callaway agreed, but preferred the term diviner.

A diviner was usually recognised, and selected – if necessary, conscripted – when in his youth he showed signs of possessing psychic powers. As de Vesme described it:

> He has perceived, in a dream or otherwise, some event happening at a distance; has read inexplicably the thoughts or the past of some other man; has had the premonition of some fact he could not normally have known; has cured a sick man by touching him or by some suggestion. Inert objects have been displaced around him without his touching them; or mysterious sounds have been heard, and so forth; or perhaps some other person has seen him appear by telepathic communication.

Before qualifying, an aspirant was expected to go through an initiation period, which might be protracted (in some cases, as long as ten years) and arduous. Sometimes it would begin by his behaving as if deranged, and eventually rushing off into the bush, or jungle, there to live for a time in solitude. Or he might be banished by the tribe to lead an ascetic existence, the assumption being that the ability to withstand hunger, extremes of temperature, solitude, even torture, was necessary to chasten the body, and thereby liberate the spirit, so that it would be free to collect the information required. This might be accomplished through the diviner entering into what appeared to European observers to be a state of abstraction, or trance, for a time; and then, on coming out of it, describing what he had 'seen' while free to 'travel', where the game or the stolen cattle or the enemy tribe were to be found. Or in the trance state his own spirit might leave him, so that other spirits could possess him and talk through him, using him as a medium to convey their information (though as what they said could be in strange languages or sometimes be simply garbled, somebody else might have to be called upon for an interpretation).

Some diviners were able to achieve dissociation (as psychologists came to describe the trance state) at will; some required assistance, in the form of plant drugs (the fly agaric mushroom in Siberia, the peyotl cactus in Mexico, tobacco in both North and South America) or rhythm – drums, music and dancing, to take the diviner 'out of himself'. The dance itself might become part of the divination; among the Azande of Sudan, Edward Evans-Pritchard reported, 'a witch doctor does not only divine with his lips, but with his whole body. He dances the questions which are put to him'. Evans-Pritchard's houseboy, who became a diviner, explained that the dance stirred up the 'medicine' (magic) within him, providing him with the answers.

A variety of devices were used to assist divination. To make contact with the spirits, a diviner might fashion objects to represent or symbolise them. In Papua a figurine would be put on the lap or shoulder of the diviner in his trance, to make sure that he was possessed by the right spirit, which would then speak out through him. A similar method was employed in Northern Rhodesia. 'Usually the diviner, in a state of possession, communicates with the spirits *via* the figure,' Barrie Reynolds reported in his study of Barotse magic, 'whispering to it and listening to its equally secretive reply.' Such objects were like radio tuning devices, designed to put the diviner's dissociated mind on the required wave-length for psychic communication; the forerunner of what has come to be known as psychometry, where a medium touches or holds an object belonging to a client, the better to pick up psychic messages from, or information about, him or the object's past owners.

In his *Voyage Round the World 1800–4* John Turnbull described how in Tahiti stolen goods were recovered by applying to a diviner who was able to 'show the face of the thief reflected in a calabash of clear water' – a forerunner of the fairground clairvoyant's crystal ball. 'Scrying' with the help of water, smoke ('pictures in the fire'), glass, or even polished fingernails, was found in use all over the world; as was another technique still familiar through its use by water-diviners. Sometimes this type of divination was accomplished with bare hands, as it was by the Navajo's 'hand tremblers'. The trembler held out his hands in front of him until they began to shiver, the process acting as a kind of direction-finder by which the diviner ascertained where, say, a missing flock had strayed. More commonly, though, the diviner would employ some device, which appeared to do the trembling itself. In the 1880s Frank Swettenham watched Malays using a rattan rod which would begin to vibrate in an odd fashion when it was brought close to the object of a search. Later, the anthropologist C. G. Seligman described how a Melanesian diviner held a branch out in front of him, his arms stiffly extended at the elbows; the branch, moving to and fro, 'pulls him in the direction of the thief'. Konde diviners carried the horns of an antelope in the same fashion: the proximity of a thief, Frank Melland observed, drove their arms up and down like a pump handle. In other communities, a pendulum was preferred. B. H. Hodgson, who studied Indian tribes in the early part of the nineteenth century, described how when a spirit was thought to be giving trouble, the diviner set out leaves, each with the name of a spirit attached to it, and held a pendulum over them until by its movements it indicated the spirit responsible. The Malays used a lemon suspended from a thread: William Skeat described in his *Malay Magic* how when the questions were getting 'warm', the lemon would begin to swing, the belief being that the more vigorous its movements, the greater the emphasis which it was trying to convey.

Another device which Evans-Pritchard found employed by the Azande worked on a principle rather similar to the spiritualists' ouija board; it consisted of a table and a piece of wood which slid over it, answering questions according to whether it slid, or stuck. A variation on this practice was the use of a stick, lightly moistened with goat's blood, which the operator would rub his hand up and down, putting questions, the degrees of friction supplying him with the answers.

Magic

At this point, powers of the kind which a diviner employed to obtain information cease to be readily distinguishable from those which he used to make *mana* or spirits work for him. The piece of wood that was used for divination, for example, was assumed to be psychically or demonically 'charged' with a fetish, or spirit, so that it had a kind of life of its own which might manifest itself in various ways. At initiation ceremonies in Japan, according to Adolf Bastian, a sieve would be invested with a demon; when it was handed to an initiate it would proceed to 'twist his body into the most strange and wonderful positions'. Travelling through the Middle East in the seventeenth century, Thomas Shaw was assured that a certain iron bar 'upon command would give the same noise as a cannon, and do the like execution'; often no command was required, the object after being charged was assumed capable of injuring or killing anybody who touched it. Few European observers, however sceptical, were inclined to test the validity of such claims.

The ability to exercise psychic control over matter was usually described as magic. It is admittedly an unsatisfactory term; but the alternatives, witchcraft or sorcery, are also misleading, because they were ordinarily used about magic employed for evil purposes; whereas the tribal diviner used it, or at least was expected to use it, for the benefit of the tribe. The assumption was that certain individuals possessed the power to influence matter at a distance (or the knowledge how to summon spirits for that purpose); to materialise, or dematerialise, objects; or to use them as weapons, as when they 'pointed the bone' at somebody, causing him to fall ill and die. Sometimes it was believed that the weapon actually left the magician's hand and entered the victim's body; sometimes the gesture sufficed. This was a grey area, in which European observers found difficulty in separating the physical from the psychical elements in magic.

Much the same problem arose over the common claim that a magician could transform himself into somebody else, or into an animal; that he could vanish and reappear instantaneously at some distant place – translocation; or that he could be in two places at once – bilocation. Observers were often unable to say whether it was the magician's body, or simply his spirit, which was supposed to be transformed, or to do the travelling. Still, in some tribal communities it was assumed that magicians could actually raise themselves off the ground by mental power. Fr. Paul Lejeune, a French Jesuit missionary in Canada in the 1630s, was assured that levitation was a common occurrence; two centuries later Australian aborigines told A. W. Howitt that magicians had been expected to be able to convey themselves by air.

Speaking in unknown tongues was another of the magician's accomplishments; and the ability to display strength, skill or endurance far beyond the normal. He should be able to break free from bonds, and run or dance without stopping for hours at a time. Here, the difficulty for observers lay in distinguishing between supernatural and superhuman feats. But there was one particular form of endurance which was frequently encountered, and was not easy to explain naturally – except as deception: the ability of magicians to endure extremes of temperature, and in particular, to carry red hot coals in their mouths or hands, or to walk over and through fire. Ceremonies of this kind were reported from many parts of the world; from Pacific islands, Japan, Malaya, India and Trinidad. Nor was it only magicians who had this power. Trial by ordeal was also a common practice. A suspect would hold a heated bar of iron or put his hand in boiling water for a prescribed period of time. If he were guilty, the assumption was, he would be burned or scalded; but innocence would ensure incombustibility. If his hand remained unmarked, he was acquitted.

One other supernatural element was commonly reported; effects which were attributed to the spirits, rather than to the magician, though they could be an accompaniment of his magic. When the North American Indians held meetings to obtain advice, the spirits were expected to announce their arrival by making certain signs. The teepee with the medicine man inside it would begin to rock, as if caught in a gale (though even the fiercest gale could not ordinarily shift it); lights, or fire, would be seen over it; strange sounds or voices would come out of it, or sometimes out of the empty surrounds. Similar manifestations could also occur at the whim of the spirits; sometimes casually, sometimes as if with malice. In the first of the classical compendiums of anthropological knowledge, *Primitive Culture,* Edward Tylor noted that 'the elf who goes knocking and routing about the house at night, and whose special German name is the poltergeist', was known to the Dyaks, Siamese, Singhalese and Esthonians. Andrew Lang and de Vesme provided further examples. In Java, poltergeists were so common that there was even a term in the language to designate them, distinguishing them from other spirits.

Chapter Two
Natural or Supernatural

BY CONTRAST WITH THE SOURCE MATERIAL ON SUPERNATURAL BELIEFS and practices, which testifies to the importance of divination and magic in tribal society at every level, the evidence for their effectiveness is scrappy and anecdotal, because the great majority of observers during the past two hundred years have assumed that such beliefs are superstitions, and that the magic is sleight-of-hand. There was an earlier period, though, when travellers were more open-minded. They observed that the diviner, entering his trance, often behaved in the way men traditionally did in Europe when possessed by an evil spirit. The convulsions, the strange tongues, the displays of manic strength resembled those familiar since biblical times. It seemed not at all improbable that the devil would be at work among the heathen, to keep them under his control. If there were any supernatural element in the magic, this would account for it.

The Possessed

So when Marco Polo, on his journey to China, saw shamans whip themselves up into a frenzy in order to answer the questions which tribesmen had come to ask them, it disturbed but did not surprise him. Nor, two centuries later, did it surprise the Catalan friar Ramon Pané, on Columbus's second expedition to Hispaniola, when he watched medicine men go into similar frenzies there in order to 'learn many things by revelation', which they then passed on to the chiefs of their tribes. Wherever the later Spanish priests and missionaries went in the Americas, and found medicine men acting like men possessed, they took for granted that it was the devil's work. Nothing could be more probable, they felt, than that he had hit upon this simple way of keeping the natives in his clutches. By giving the medicine men magical powers, he could prevent them from losing their reputations, and perhaps loosening his own grip on their tribes. 'They can see and predict anything,' the seventeenth-century zoologist and botanist, Francisco Hernandez, wrote of the Mexican diviners. 'For instance, whether enemies are going to attack them the following day; or whether the weather will continue favourable; or to discern who has stolen from them some utensil, or anything else.'

The devil might also work magic on his own account. In the Province of Popayan in Peru, according to the Spanish chronicler Cieza de Leon, when an Indian chief wished to become a convert to Christianity he was possessed by devils, who carried him through the air; the chief bitterly complaining, the devils whistling and shouting. They would leave him for a time, but when he was sitting with a glass of wine in front of him, the Christians who were with him saw the glass raised up in the air, and put down empty, 'and a short time afterwards the wine was again poured into the cup from the air'. The invisible devils also hurled stones around, until dispersed by the saying of a mass.

Although the missionaries might accept that the devil could exercise supernatural powers, not all of them were convinced that he was responsible for what they witnessed. The French Jesuits in Canada in the seventeenth century wrote despatches describing their experiences which R. S. Lambert, in his carefully-documented survey of supernatural phenomena in Canadian history, described as comparing favourably with the work of a modern psychical investigator. Regarding the medicine man as the main obstacle to conversions, they did their best to detect fraud. But they met with little success. Fr. Lejeune, head of the mission to the Hurons of Quebec, was challenged in 1634 to attend a seance by a young convert to Christianity who had lapsed because he felt that the medicine man's magic was more powerful than Lejeune's. The medicine man entered alone and naked into a teepee; it began to shake; and after a time sparks were seen to come out of the top. Lejeune did his best to convince himself that the light must have been smuggled in, and the tent shaken by brute force; but he could not deny that its movements were of a kind that were hard to account for in human terms. As the convert reminded him, he had himself tested the pole, and been unable to move it; yet he had seen it 'sway to and fro, and even bend down from the top, though it was taller than a man'. The shaking, too, had gone on for a length of time which, Lejeune had to admit, would have exhausted any ordinary man.

Other missionaries were similarly impressed. A medicine man told Fr. Pijart that Fr. de Brebeuf was ill,

Fr. Pijart laughed at this old man – it not being three hours since he had left Fr. de Brebeuf at the House of St. Joseph in very good health. The magician answers him 'Thou wilt see whether I am a liar. I have told thee enough.' In fact Fr. Pijart, having returned the same day to St. Joseph, two good leagues distant, finds Fr. de Brebeuf attacked with a heavy fever, a pain in the stomach and headache, and with all the symptoms of a severe illness; at the moment when the magician had spoken, no savage had been warned of it.

Although some of his colleagues remained convinced that trickery must be the explanation, Fr. de Brebeuf was himself reluctantly impressed. Obviously, he felt, the medicine man's powers could not come from God.

But that all they do is the product of deception or imagination hardly accords either with the reputation they have acquired, or with the length of time they have practised their profession. How comes it that their tricks have never been exposed through all these years, and that their trade has been so well rewarded – if they have never succeeded except through sheer imagination? There is, therefore, some ground for thinking that the devil does sometimes lend them a helping hand, revealing himself to them for temporal profit, as well as for their eternal damnation.

Other European observers were prepared to accept the possibility that supernatural phenomena might exist in their own right, neither gods, devils nor spirits being involved. The seventeenth-century French traveller and writer, Jean Regnard, described how a servant, left in Lapland and wondering what his master was doing, consulted a Lapp diviner and wrote down everything he was told; his master, when he returned, had to admit that it was correct, even down to the fact that he had, on a certain day, 'slept with a girl'. When the sceptical Professor Scheffer of Uppsala decided to investigate second sight, a Lapp who was anxious to become a Christian confessed to him tearfully that he could not help getting his visions, which came to him whether he wanted them or not and to demonstrate, described in accurate detail Scheffer's journey north. Taken prisoner by some North American Indians in 1759, Alexander Henry wrote a detailed and workmanlike account of his experiences among them, including seances in which the teepee was duly shaken, and disembodied voices were heard. He studied the process with care, 'on the watch to detect the particular contrivances by which the fraud was carried on. But such was the skill displayed in the performance, or such my deficiency of penetration, that I made no discoveries.'

Anthropology
But travellers' tales of this kind, though common enough, were rarely

presented in a form which encouraged confidence that the witness had not allowed himself to be deceived; and any chance that such investigations might become more systematic was spoiled by the growing influence of scientific materialism. By the eighteenth century not merely had belief in diabolic possession begun to disappear, but it had come to be assumed that if somebody suffered from the traditional symptoms, it was an indication that he must be insane; and it was absurd to imagine that a lunatic had access to information beyond the reach of a normal man's senses – even if clairvoyance were accepted as a scientific possibility. By the time Charles Darwin went on his voyage on the *Beagle*, primitive magic did not even arouse curiosity: only contempt. In 1836 Darwin was taken to a ceremony on the Cocos Islands, where some Malay women dressed up a large wooden spoon in garments, to carry it to a graveside, where 'they pretend it becomes inspired at the full of the moon, and will dance and jump about'. Held by two of them, it duly convulsed, dancing to the song of surrounding children. The Malays, his host assured him, believed that its movements were spirit-induced; Darwin dismissed it as 'a most foolish spectacle'.

This attitude, soon to be widely shared by anthropologists, could not have been adopted at a worse time if there were anything worth investigating in magic, because over the next hundred years colonialism was to sweep through most of the old pre-civilised communities, disrupting and transforming them. Often, too, it was the magician who was the first victim, because whether or not he could work magic, his tribe believed he could, and that made him a threat in the eyes of colonial officials; he would be imprisoned, or even executed, and the fact that his magic was so feeble compared to the white man's guns quickly sapped his authority. In Rhodesia Melland, who realised that the subject was worth investigating, found himself thwarted by his duty as a magistrate to stamp it out. When Andrew Lang came to survey the evidence for his *The Making of Religion*, published in 1898, he was unable to find a single serious study of the subject in the English language; and only one, Adolf Bastian's 'meagre tract', as he described it, in German. And in the United States in this period only the ethnologist Daniel Brinton publicly expressed doubt whether the prevailing scepticism was justified. He cited as one example an episode in the career of Colonel John Mason Brown. In the course of an expedition to look for a lost tribe, Brown had been met by some of its warriors, sent by their medicine man who had 'seen' Brown coming, and 'heard' why he wanted to find them. Although trickery could be held responsible for many such episodes, Brinton commented, 'there is something more than these vulgar arts now and then to be perceived. There are statements supported by unquestionable testimony, which

ought not to be passed over in silence.' But that was as far as he would
go: 'I cannot but approach them with hesitation. They are so revolting
to the laws of science, so alien, I had almost said, to the experience of
our lives.'

Inevitably, therefore, such evidence as there is from this crucial
period comes not from professional anthropologists but from explorers,
missionaries, traders, and colonial officials. There is plenty of it, but
most has to be set aside not because it is necessarily untrustworthy, but
because it is now impossible to tell in the case of, say, most stories in
Wide World magazine, with its abundant source material, whether the
writer can be relied upon or not. Nevertheless there remain a few reports from travellers, missionaries and colonial officials whose reputation was such that their descriptions of what they saw and heard were,
and still are, acceptable. Their accounts of supernatural phenomena
deserve to be treated with respect, even if they must also be treated
with caution.

Clairvoyance

For a while, it continued to be missionaries who were most interested in the diabolic element (as they still assumed it must be) in tribal
divination and magic. By the middle of the nineteenth century, though,
most Catholic missionaries had acquired a measure of scepticism, and
were no longer disposed to attribute the diviner's outpourings to evil
spirits. In his *Esquisses Senegalaises*, published in 1853, Fr. P. Boilat
described how he had carried out his functions for six years clinging
to the belief that what the native diviners did was simply lying and
trickery. Then he and some colleagues decided to expose a diviner
who used what to them seemed a particularly suspect method, asking
anybody who came for guidance to formulate a question in his mind
and then 'spit it out' into a heap of sand. When Boilat complied, and
spat, the diviner had to admit he could not pick up the question; but
this impressed Boilat, who had deliberately not formulated one. So he
mentally asked a question which was very much on his mind. 'You
will receive the papers you are expecting from your country,' the
diviner replied, 'in fifteen days.' This proved correct, as did the answers
given to the other missionaries; and Boilat eventually accepted that the
diviner's powers could be genuine, albeit from the devil.

In *Fleurs Noires et Ames Blanches*, published half a century later,
Fr. Trilles described an even more striking demonstration. A Yabikou
diviner told him that he was planning to meet the other witch doctors
of the region the following day, at an old abandoned village which
Trilles knew to be four days' march away. Would the diviner, Trilles
asked, do him a favour and ask one of his converts, who lived in
another village near the one where the witch doctors were to gather, to

'come at once, and bring me the cartridges of the shot gun which I gave him to keep?' The witch doctor agreed, and proceeded to go into his trance; Trilles keeping an eye on him to check that he did not slip off anywhere, until he came out of it the following day. Three days later the cartridges were duly delivered. Trilles asked the bearer whether he had seen the witch doctor; 'No,' he replied, 'but I heard him during the night; he called me from outside my hut, and told me that you wanted these at once.'

Protestant missionaries were less open to conviction; and many explorers, traders and officials dismissed divination without a thought. But a few, from first-hand experience, were impressed in spite of themselves; among them David Leslie. Leslie had been brought out to South Africa as a boy, in the middle of the century; and though he was only thirty-five when he died, he had by that time built up a reputation not just as a hunter and trader, but as the friend of Zulu chiefs and an acknowledged expert on Zulu affairs, a man noted, *The Natal Mercury* observed, for his 'remarkable sagacity and shrewd sense'. Among reports and articles which he had written, published in book form after his death, one described how in spite of his ingrained mistrust of magic and diviners he had eventually been forced to concede that some of their performances were 'absolutely marvellous'. He had experienced so many examples himself that he had 'sometimes half-fancied that they had a familiar spirit – a Puck, or a Robin Goodfellow, which kept them *au courant* on matters hidden from mortal ken, and brought them intelligence of everything which had happened, and was going to happen, within a radius of hundreds of miles'. On one occasion, arriving at a Kafir village, he decided without premeditation to spend the night there. Annoyed to find accommodation difficult to get, owing to the presence of a celebrated woman diviner, he challenged her to demonstrate her powers. He would recognise them, she told him, when he left the territory without either a companion or even a hoof of cattle. 'By a coincidence, as strange as it was unpleasant, her words came true'; on his way out of the territory with a large herd one of his servants was killed by a charging buffalo; another was snatched from a stream by a crocodile; and the rest fled, presenting him with no option but to leave without the cattle he had bought.

Leslie was still more impressed by another diviner who told him precisely what was happening to all eight of his native hunters, scattered up to two hundred miles away; how one had killed four elephants; another had been killed; another had died of fever, 'and so on through the whole, the men being minutely and correctly described, their success or non-success equally so'. He wrote the divination down at the time; 'to my utter amazement, it turned out correct in every particular'.

Experiences of this kind, though frequently reported by men who lived and worked among tribal communities, proved unacceptable as evidence for clairvoyance. Nobody suggested that Leslie had invented the stories; but a few years later, Dudley Kidd pointed out in *The Essential Kafir* that Leslie should have known the country and the people well enough 'to see that a diviner has sources of knowledge open to him over a far wider area than mentioned'. Leslie had, in fact, tried to make it clear that the hunters were too scattered for the diviner to have up-to-date information unless he had been forewarned that he was going to be consulted: and he could not have been forewarned, as Leslie had not known himself until an hour before the seance. Still, Leslie could not hope to prove conclusively that the witch doctor had not somehow anticipated his coming.

In a few cases the theory that divination worked by local knowledge, coupled with hunch, is even harder to sustain. De Vesme cited an account by Dr. R. W. Felkin, who was with Stanley's 1899 expedition to rescue the beleaguered Emin Pasha from Lado. Felkin was told one day by a local diviner that he had seen two steamers arrive at Mescheraer-Rak, some five hundred miles away, the night before. An Englishman had disembarked, carrying papers from 'the great Pasha in Khartoum' – General Gordon. Although Felkin immediately recognised the Englishman from the description, he did not take the information seriously, particularly as the diviner claimed he had obtained it by 'visiting' Mescheraer-Rak. But a month later, the Englishman, with the letters from General Gordon, arrived and confirmed the accuracy of this diviner's account.

To explain such mysteries, the 'bush telegraph' – a relay of men with tom-toms, beating out information in code – was usually invoked. But had there been such a link the sceptical Felkin would have known about it. In any case, there were many stories of divination where not even the bush telegraph could have provided an explanation; such as an episode described in detail in the *Frankfurter Zeitung* by a German army medical officer, Dr. Schultz. He was in the veldt with Ernest Marcis, editor of a Pretoria Afrikaner journal, who was convalescing after an illness; and, for amusement, they decided to have their fortunes told by a Kafir diviner, whom neither had met before. Not content to listen to a vague exercise in fortune telling, Schultz demanded answers to particular questions concerning his family, living and dead, of a kind which he was sure that nobody could have known but himself.

The Kafir told me everything without the least error and then, without any question being put, he told me of events in my life which were very unpleasant to me, and finally announced that I should return to the land whence I had come. This was far from my thought, for I had decided to establish myself at Pretoria as a doctor . . . but the prediction came true.

Clairvoyance of this kind continued to be reported from Africa. In *The Sixth Sense* Joseph Sinel described how his son, who lived among the tribesmen of the southern Sudan, had found that 'telepathy is constant'. They always knew where he was and what he was doing, even when he was far away. On one occasion when he got lost men came out, as if sensing his plight, to collect him; on another, when he had picked up an arrow tip and brought it back with him, two natives came to ask him if they could examine it. Laurens Van Der Post found that the villagers in the Kalahari could tell in advance which of the 'bush pilots' would be flying the aircraft which periodically used their landing strip – 'Red Nose', 'Shining Face', or 'Hippo-belly' – though there was no radio communication. And when a Kalahari bushman killed an eland – regarded as a notable achievement – the camp immediately knew of it 'by wire', as one bushman described it, evidently under the impression that the white man's telegraph also worked by telepathy. Before they reached the camp with the eland, Van Der Post would hear the sounds of the song which was used to celebrate on such occasions.

Similar stories were reported from other parts of the world; particularly from North America. Among the American Indians, divination was a standard procedure; and white men often resorted to a medicine man for information. Again, this could be attributed to local knowledge; but in the mid-nineteenth century L. John du Bay, who lived almost all his life among the Indians, assured Chief Justice Larrabee of Wisconsin that in his experience their predictions could not be so easily accounted for. Waiting for a friend one day, he had asked a medicine man when to expect him. The following day, the reply was, it was going to be cloudy; but just before sunset, the sky would begin to clear, and if at that time he looked at the clear patch he would see his friend. The weather turned out as predicted; the clear patch emerged, but no friend. Du Bay began to tease the medicine man, who told him to be patient, as in five minutes he would see his friend arriving. In five minutes, his friend could be seen.

Attempts to verify the knowledge provided in divination experimentally were few; but one test was conducted in the 1890s by Frank Swettenham, a British magistrate in Malaya, later to be Governor of the colony. He had been recommended to consult a diviner after he had had some property stolen; and the man told him to write down the names of all the suspects on pieces of paper. Taking care not to allow anybody to see the names, Swettenham folded up the pieces into pellets, so that he himself did not know which name was in which. A wooden bowl full of water, covered by cotton so that it resembled a drum, was given to two men to hold, and the diviner threw the pellets on to it, one by one, until the bowl reacted to one of them by twisting uncontrollably in the men's hands. Asked by Swettenham to repeat the procedure, they did; there was the same reaction to what turned out to be the same pellet. Swettenham was unable to discover whether the bowl's verdict was correct, because no proof was forthcoming that the man indicated was in fact the thief; but he was impressed, in spite of himself, by the procedure. 'I asked the men who held the bowl why they made it turn around at that particular moment, and they declared that they had nothing to do with it, and that the vessel twisted itself off their fingers against their inclination.'

In a lecture delivered in Ballarat in 1914 David Unaipon – described in the Melbourne journal which reported it, the *Harbinger of Light*, as 'a Christianised and highly-educated brainy Australian native' – described how the aborigines used smoke signals not, as travellers had reported, as a kind of code, but to attract attention, so that the communication could then be made by telepathy.

He might want to give his brother, who might be twenty miles away, a message; so he would set to and make a smoke signal, and then sit down and concentrate his mind on his brother. The column of smoke would be seen by all the blacks for miles around, and they would all concentrate their minds, and put their brains into a state of receptivity. Only his brother, however, would get into touch with him, and he (David) could then suggest to his brother's brain the message which he wished to convey.

Although he had not done it himself, Unaipon knew that travelling clairvoyance was also practised by some aborigines; they went off into a trance, 'and said their spirit travelled to see where their friends were'. On one occasion, wanting to know what a friend was doing five miles away, he had obtained the information by this means; and when he checked it a few days later, his friend corroborated what the clairvoyant had said.

Investigating the aborigines forty years later Ronald Rose, too, was assured that smoke signal messages were not in the smoke itself. 'When we see smoke we think, and often we find clearness,' he was told. The smoke was of a different kind from that which rose from a camp fire, but this was simply to alert the receiver, so that he would get to thinking: 'I am thinking, too, so that he thinks my thoughts.'

Telepathic communication, Rose found, was very much a part of the aborigine way of life. If somebody died, his relatives would 'know' immediately, however far away from them he might be; they would 'see' the dead person, or realise he was dead from some feeling, their explanation being that their 'totem' had told them what had happened. In his *Living Magic*, published in 1957, Rose described how he decided to test their psychic ability with the help of a pack of Rhine's 'Zener cards'. Lizzie, a woman of over seventy, was able to score consistently, guessing the cards correctly far more often than chance expectation. In the first series she could have been expected to have guessed about three hundred and forty right out of one thousand seven hundred. In fact she scored four hundred and eighty-eight; and the odds against achieving that total are astronomical. Other aborigines also did well, though none came near to Lizzie's performance. Years later, when a further series was undertaken, at the age of seventy-nine Lizzie still obtained scores of millions to one above chance level. And taken as a whole, the aborigines' scoring was sufficiently high to have established, in any other research field except extra-sensory perception, that an element other than chance must be involved. Although Rose did not feel that his method of testing was really suitable – future researchers, he hoped, would find more effective techniques – the results, he felt, at least gave aboriginal magic a less ephemeral character than it had before.

Perhaps the strongest evidence for the existence of a clairvoyant faculty, though, came not from tests which European observers conducted, but from the fact that in many parts of the world the tribes themselves imposed tests for clairvoyance on those who aspired to become diviners. Zulu youths, Bishop Callaway noted, had to prove themselves capable of finding hidden objects; and similar procedures, such as putting something under one of a number of inverted pots and inviting the aspirant to tell which pot it was, were reported from other parts of the world. The tests were sometimes of a kind which even the most skilled conjurer could not easily have accomplished by sleight-of-hand; and it is difficult to imagine that the tribal elders would have allowed young members of the tribe to delude them with amateurish tricks.

Magic

If the evidence for second sight lacks precision, the evidence for magic can be expected to be even less satisfying; and so it proves. For a variety of reasons, of which the possibility of trickery is only one, there are many problems in evaluating samples of psychokinesis. The great majority of cases of magicians translocating or doing other similar feats were not checked – or even checkable. As Endicott noted, the anthropologist in Malaya could not even discover whether an alleged werewolf, or weretiger, was supposed to be a man who physically turned into a wolf or a tiger, or an animal which a man's spirit periodically possessed; let alone whether either of those alternatives actually happened.

It was also impossible to tell whether the arrival of rain after it had been invoked, or the death of somebody after a spell had been put on him, was 'on account of ' or simply 'after'. What might be magic, too, was often accountable for, in theory at least, by muscle power, not necessarily consciously applied; a possiblility which sceptical observers tended to fall back on whenever other explanations proved unsatisfying. In 1918 D. R. McKenzie watched a Konde diviner, who had been asked to find some property which had been stolen, put 'medicine' (magic) into a figurine made from a block of wood. The figurine was then handed to a strong man; soon, it began to shake so violently that he could hardly hold it, and by following in the direction which appeared to be tugging, the onlookers were led to a house, whose owner thereupon confessed to the theft. Unable to accept the possibility that any supernatural force might be at work, McKenzie hazarded the explanation that the diviner had a picture in his mind of how the figurine would behave, which 'tended to become a physical fact'; the proceedings coming to a halt 'in obedience to a previously-formed decision, of which the operator is, in most cases, not consciously aware'.

A few eye-witness accounts of performances of magic, though, sound as if they were the product of careful observation; such as the report of a seance in 1879 by Sir Cecil Denny, Bart., who had joined the Canadian Mounted Police as a young man and made a reputation for himself as a cool and level-headed officer. Ordinarily, medicine men went into the teepee alone, when calling up the spirits; but Denny managed to obtain permission from one of them to sit in with him, hoping to find out how the trick was done. After a time he heard an invisible bell ringing, above his head.

> Presently, the teepee began to rock, even lifting itself off the ground a foot or more behind me. When it is remembered that a large Indian tent consists of dozens of long poles crossed at the top and covered with buffalo hides, it will seem that it is nearly impossible to lift one side – for no wind can blow them over.

Denny slipped out to check for collusion, but nobody was in sight and when the tent began to rock again, its sides actually lifted high enough for him to *see* nobody was there. Yet all the time, the medicine man never stirred. Denny returned to his camp 'thoroughly mystified'.

Russian investigators were similarly puzzled, a few years later, when they were investigating Siberian shamanism. In seances, Waldemar Bogoraz found, pots and other utensils might be flung around as if by an invisible hand; sometimes snow from outside would be sprayed over the company; and voices, which the shaman insisted came from the spirits, were heard from all parts of the hut, sometimes from outside it. Earlier researchers had argued that this must be accomplished by ventriloquism; and Bogoraz hit upon the idea of using a phonograph. A machine, he reasoned, could not be fooled like the human ear; it should be possible to detect from it whether the shaman himself was making the sounds. The recordings showed that he was not. There was a marked difference between his voice, at a distance from the machine, and the voices of the spirits, which perversely sounded as if the spirits had stationed themselves at the mouth of the receiver, and were talking directly into it.

Bishop Weston of Zanzibar was taught an even ruder lesson, when he went to investigate a poltergeist there, aiming to show the credulous natives that it had no power when boldly confronted by a man of God. He entered the hut which was reputed to be haunted, making sure that he was alone. While he was there, he saw 'large pieces of earth violently plucked from the walls, and thrown into the air'. Some were thrown out of the door; one, apparently thrown at him, struck him on the head. He had entered sceptically; what he saw changed his mind. As he explained on his return, assertions that there were no spirits around might be made 'here in England'; but in a country like Zanzibar, 'where everyone believes in the existence of spirits, and one may say the atmosphere is saturated with the belief, the case is very different'.

A few other eye-witnesses have left accounts of the effects of magic on inanimate objects. A Zulu diviner's sticks, Callaway reported, appeared to jump up on to a patient's body, as if to assist in the diagnosis by pointing to the affected part; and half a century later, Melland saw Konde diviners relying on the same procedure to indicate the whereabouts of a witch or a thief. The botanist William Brigham, working in Hawaii half a century ago, touched one of the heavy wooden sticks which had been charged by local magic and received what seemed like an electric shock, severe enough to make his head swim. And Laurens Van Der Post described how when he took a camera team to film some Kalahari rock paintings, a succession of incomprehensible breakdowns prevented any film being taken. First the magazine, a new one, jammed. The same thing happened with a second; and again with a third. There had been other indications that, as their guide had explained, they were unwelcome to the guardian spirits in that particular region; but these could have had a natural explanation. So could one, or even two, jammings of a magazine. For three to jam, though, was outside all experience. And when the cameraman returned from the camp where he had gone to clear the magazines and to pick up spares, it was to no purpose; the jams continued. Eventually a steel swivel, a part ordinarily considered so safe that no spare was carried, also went wrong. The sound equipment, too, would not work, though no fault could be found. There was nothing for it, Van Der Post realised, but to leave the place, their mission inadequately accomplished.

Levitation of human beings, as distinct from objects, though quite commonly claimed as part of a magician's repertoire, was rarely witnessed by Europeans – or if they saw it, they might be unwilling to risk their reputations by reporting it. But Fr. Papetard, Superior of the French African missions in the 1870s, claimed that he had more than once seen magicians levitating to the height of two or three feet, and walking as if they were bouncing along the tops of tufts of grass; missionaries from many other pagan regions, he claimed, could attest similar feats. And Monsignor Alexandre Le Roy, who worked for many years as a missionary in Africa before becoming Super General of the Fathers of the Holy Ghost, though he was sceptical about magic – and even about diabolic possession: the best exorcism, he thought, 'as well as the cheapest, would be a strong purgative' – conceded there were some cases

in which the most sceptical must acknowledge himself nonplussed. For example, the one possessed (they are most often women) disappears from her home during the night and on the next day is found high up in a big tree, tied to a branch by fine bindweed. When a sacrifice is offered, and the bonds that have held her have fallen, she glides down the length of the trunk like a serpent. For several minutes she remains elevated above the ground and speaks fluently in a language of which she hitherto did not know the first word.

The conjuror Harry Kellar, too, who prided himself on his ability to detect tricks of any kind, had to admit that he had been baffled when on a world tour in the 1870s he had watched a Zulu witch doctor cause the head of a warrior's knobkerry to explode and then, as the warrior lay apparently knocked unconscious on the ground, had waved burning grass over him until, 'to my intense amazement, the recumbent body slowly arose from the ground and floated upward in the air to the height of about three feet, remaining in suspension and moving up and down, according as the passes of the burning grass were slower or faster'.

The commonest reports of magic, though, describe practices which come in the borderland 'superhuman' area, where individuals have been observed to perform feats of such striking skill or endurance that they cannot easily be naturally explained; such as those described by Peter Furst, Professor of Anthropology at the State University of New

York. He watched 'Ramon' cross over the top of a falls, with a sheer drop of hundreds of feet below him; after performing a ritual, he 'proceeded to leap – "fly" might be a more appropriate term – from one rock to another with arms stretched sideways, often landing but a few inches from the slippery edge'.

In the superhuman category, too, there are innumerable accounts of incombustibility; such as Fr. Lejeune's description of an Indian ceremony held near Quebec, to which he and some French travellers were invited in 1637. The medicine men had handled red-hot stones; 'you may believe me – since I speak of a thing that I saw with my own eyes – they separated the brands, drew the stones from the midst of the fire, and holding their hands behind their backs took them between their teeth, carried them to the patients, and remained some time without loosening their hold'. Examination showed that there was no sign of burning; 'and not only these persons, but even the sick were not burned. They let their bodies be rubbed with glowing cinders without their skin appearing in the least affected.'

The standard argument, that magicians had some way of insulating themselves, was easier to apply to fire-walking ceremonies, where only the soles of the feet would require protection. But shortly before the turn of the century a couple of accounts were published which made it difficult to accept this as a satisfactory explanation. Challenged by a Raratoa magician to do what he and his flock were doing, the New Zealand magistrate Colonel Gudgeon and three companions had courageously removed their shoes and stockings and, accepting only the protection of the magician's *mana*, walked across an 'oven' of heated stones. Although Gudgeon was in no doubt about the temperature – 'my impression as I crossed the oven was that skin would all peel off my feet' – all that he felt when he was across was 'a tingling sensation not unlike electric shocks'. Yet there could be no doubt of the heat of the 'oven'; one of the party – who 'like Lot's wife, looked behind him, a thing against all the rules' – had been badly burned.

The other test was made by a doctor, T. N. Hocken. Hocken brought along a thermometer and hung it six foot above the pit, with a view to estimating the precise heat; but though capable of taking readings up to 400°F. it would quickly have burst, he reported, had it not been for the fact that the solder melted before that temperature was reached. Hocken's chief concern, though, was to examine the feet of the fire-walkers. Their soles, he found, were not leathery, but soft and flexible. Nor were they covered with any insulating substance, a fact he established with the help of various tests, including the application of his tongue. Trickery might have been used in the past, he conceded; but it certainly could not account for what he had seen.

These were only two of many such investigations, in many parts of the world; and even if at the time they failed to make any dent in the prevailing scepticism, they were not effectively rebutted. Although the evidence for other forms of magic was by contrast slight, too, in one respect it can now be seen to be stronger than it looked. There is one curiously consistent source of testimony to the reality of the powers of magicians in the confessions of former magicians who were converted to Christianity. They would not forswear their former belief that the spirit phenomena had been genuine.

In his *History of the Supernatural*, published in 1863, William Howitt gave an example provided by a German missionary who had lived among the American Indians, and who had been baffled by a medicine man's tent-shaking. Hearing thirty years later that the medicine man had become a Christian, the missionary thought that at last he would be able to find out how the trick had been done; but no. 'Believe me,' the medicine man told him, with evident sincerity, 'I did not deceive you; I did not shake the lodge; it was shaken by the power of the spirits.' Nor, he insisted, had he employed 'a double tongue' – ventriloquism. 'I only repeated what the spirits said to me. I heard their voices. The top of the lodge was full of them, and before me the sky and wide lands lay expanded; I could see great distances around me; and I believed I could recognise the most distant objects.'

Early Civilisations

Chapter Three
From Shaman to Priest

REVIEWING THE HISTORICAL SOURCE MATERIAL FROM TRIBAL COM-munities, a hypothesis presents itself which, though speculative, may help to explain both how shamanism (the blanket term which anthropologists adopted) came about, and why it disintegrated. At some stage in his evolutionary progress man discovered that he could exploit *mana*. But the process by which he became conscious of his power happened to be precisely the process by which he was depriving himself of the ability to utilise it: consciousness, reason, memory were taking over from instinct. To tap the psychic forces, therefore, individuals had to be found who still had access to *mana*, either naturally, or through their ability to go into a trance, in order to practise divination or work magic. In time, such individuals became harder to find; and for those who were found, it became harder to dissociate. They had to use aids; drugs, rhythm, divining instruments, rituals, codes. And eventually systematised divination and magic took over, the process becoming mechanical rather than inspirational; as in the case of the Zunis of Mexico. According to Ruth Benedict their emphasis became exclusively on ritual, conducted with absolute precision. 'If the procedure is correct, the costume of the masked god traditional to the last detail, the offerings unimpeachable, the words of the hours' long prayers letter-perfect, the effect will follow according to man's desires.' But if it were found that a feather, part of the traditional costume, had been taken from an eagle's shoulder, rather than from the breast, that alone would nullify the effect of the entire ceremony.

Granted a progressive decline in the ability to tap psychic powers, this would explain how they came to be at first reinforced and eventually replaced by ritual and routine. Allowance has to be made, though, for the possibility that some communities may have discovered ways to reverse the trend. Archaeologists have revealed the existence of monuments the secrets of whose construction nobody has been able to fathom. How were the huge blocks of stone excavated, transported over great distances, carved with astonishing precision, and sited with apparently cosmic accuracy? Were divinatory and telekinetic forces harnessed for the purpose? The available evidence is insufficient to provide an answer; but the possibility cannot be ruled out.

And there is another problem. Watching African diviners throwing bones or pieces of carved wood on to the ground, and answering questions according to the pattern which they made when they fell, the French explorer Henry Junod decided that the answers were provided by their vivid imaginations, playing on the pattern; not from 'the mathematic evidence'. Similarly many practising clairvoyants today, using cards or even tea-leaves as aids, claim that the aim is chiefly to spark off imagination's flow. The fact that the great bulk of the evidence from early civilisations points to reliance upon mechanical divination may consequently be misleading. The Chaldeans and Egyptians, for example, retained many tribal beliefs and practices. They accepted that there was a spirit world with gods – superior beings who could be asked for advice (which their statues sometimes provided by nodding); spirits of the dead, who might be encountered by the living; and evil spirits (including poltergeists: a surviving papyrus describes one who was heard to 'wail, groan and laugh dreadfully', causing terror and nightmares; made rappings and knockings; and 'Practised stealthy theft'). It was also taken for granted that dreams and omens could be used for divination. But the assumption was that they needed to be interpreted, and the manuals of interpretation suggest that the method was largely mechanical.

So, apparently, were the techniques of divination. Again, caution is needed in reviewing the evidence because by this time it was in written form, and although this adds a welcome new dimension to the historical record, the writing was done for the priestly authorities and may bear as little relation to everyday life as, say, the prayer book does today. Still, it comes as no surprise to find that divination was systematised. Evidently the same process had been at work, though more gradually, as that which a century ago divested medicine men and witch doctors of their authority when they came under colonial rule. Where tribes were merging into, or being submerged by, states, they had to accept the authority of the rulers under whose domination they came. A recommendation from the shaman's voices or visions could no longer be unquestioningly obeyed; it had first to be ascertained whether the authorities would object. In such circumstances the authority of the shamans was eroded. Trance divination, too, became suspect, because it could offer impracticable and even dangerous advice. So into the shaman's place stepped the priest: still a diviner, still a magician (or claiming to be), but working for the authorities, and relying on a great range of rote interpretations instead of inspired divination. If a bird were seen to fly in one direction it meant one thing; if in a different direction, something else. It was all laid down in the instruction manuals. The entrails of sacrificial animals provided simple answers: by their condition – if diseased, that spoke for itself; or by association – 'if the cystic duct be long, the days of the rulers will be long' (though there were presumably also qualifications; it could have been unwise to intimate to a ruler that the entrails predicted his days would be short).

The shamanist initiation period was preserved; but it was to enable the candidate to learn the necessary formulae and rituals, not to liberate his psychic faculties. As there was a risk that the priesthood would lose its mystique if the formulae and rituals were too widely known, they were shrouded as far as possible in secrecy, and the emphasis was placed on meticulously correct observances which only a priest would know. There was consequently no further need for dissociation. Whether spontaneous or induced, the trance state was actually unwelcome, as it might interrupt the orderly flow of the prescribed rites. Instead of being chosen, as shamans were, because of signs that they had psychic powers, priests came to be recruited by co-option, becoming a caste.

Chapter Four
The Old Testament

SHAMANISM, HOWEVER, DID NOT GO DOWN WITHOUT A STRUGGLE, dramatically portrayed in the Old Testament. It will never be possible to sift fact from folklore, legend and myth, in these chronicles; but even so sceptical a commentator as Professor Edmund Leach has conceded in his *Genesis as Myth* that there must be a measure of valid historical material, increasing in the later stages. This is of no help, unfortunately, in deciding which episodes are historical and which are not. Still, the descriptions of psychic phenomena can be regarded, if not as evidence of what actually happened, at least as a record of what the chroniclers believed had happened – and assumed was still happening, in their own day. And as such, it is remarkably consistent with what has become known about shamanism in primitive communities.

Moses

Because the events recorded were to lay the foundations of two religions, Jewish and Christian, dominated by priesthoods, the tendency has been to ignore or gloss over the fact that the unifying thread running through the Old Testament is shamanism's fierce and protracted struggle *against* priesthoods. The prophets were shamans: Moses, indeed, is the archetype of shamanism. His vocation is made clear to him by signs and wonders – the bush that burns but is not consumed by the flames; by clairaudience – the voice of the Lord sounding as if it came from the midst of the bush; and by the discovery he can work magic – his rod is changed into a serpent, and back into a rod again. Overruling his protest that he is 'of a slow tongue', the Lord says 'I will be thy mouth' – in other words, he will be possessed, and Aaron his brother will interpret, if required. Gradually Moses gathers confidence, defying Pharaoh and worsting Pharaoh's magicians; they can turn rods into serpents too, but only by sleight-of-hand, and their serpents are worsted and eaten by his and Aaron's. And in the flight from

Egypt various shamanic phenomena make their appearance: pyrotechnics – the pillar of fire to guide them; divination – the water found at Horeb; materialisation – the manna in the wilderness; and many more.

Moses, then, and the other prophets were in the shamanist tradition. But they enjoyed one advantage over the tribal witch doctor; they had the confidence born of the assumption that they were the Lord's spokesmen and executors. The Lord was not yet regarded as the *only* god; there were rivals, and pretenders. But the Israelites were brought up to believe that he was the only *true* god; and his prophets were his instruments, in the service neither of the tribe nor of the ruling authorities, but of the Lord.

Divination remained their chief function; but not so much to ascertain what was happening or what was about to happen, as to transmit the Lord's will about what ought to happen. Sometimes it was given in general terms, commanding obedience: sometimes it took the form of particular instructions, as when the Lord told Noah to build an ark of gopher wood, and gave precise details how it was to be proportioned. The prophets might be possessed, the Lord speaking through them; or they could receive his instructions by clairvoyance or clairaudience; or his spirits might pass messages to them. Some spirits were unidentified, like the one whose passing made the hair of Job's comforter Eliphaz the Temanite stand on end; but the general impression was that they were the Lord's servants. This did not mean that they could be trusted; the Lord had no compunction about employing spirits to lie, in order to sow confusion, as he did by getting one of them to speak through the mouth of a prophet to lure Ahab to his death. Satan, too, when he put in his first appearance as Job's tempter was acting on the Lord's behalf, or at least with the Lord's sanction, to see how far Job could be trusted; it was not until later that he came to be regarded as an adversary. The spirits most often encountered, though, were angels, appearing either in dreams, or as materialised beings. Abraham would hardly have offered food to the angels who came to visit him in his tent on the plains of Namre if he had not assumed them to be men of flesh and blood; still less would Lot have felt compelled, in order to save the angels who visited him in Sodom, to offer his virgin daughters instead to the Sodomite mob to appease its lust. At other times angels appeared in visions, or in dreams. Jacob, sleeping at Bethel, saw them on the ladder stretched between earth and heaven, and heard the Lord telling him that the land on which it rested would be his, and his children's. And sometimes, to provide reassurance that a dream or a vision was to be trusted, a sign was given. In Gideon's case, there had to be a succession of signs, so mistrustful was he. First, fire sprang up from an altar to consume a sacrificial kid. Then, at his request, a fleece left overnight on the ground was covered in dew, yet the ground remained dry. Finally, he craftily asked that the fleece should remain dry while the ground became covered in dew; and this too was granted him. Yet still, to clinch it, the Lord had to persuade him to go down into the midst of the Midianite host. There, Gideon heard a soldier describing to a companion his dream of a cake of barley tumbling down into their camp, and knocking down a tent; to which the companion replied that the cake could only be the sword of Gideon, 'for into his hand hath God delivered Midian, and all his host. And it was so.'

Sometimes the signs took a new form; written instructions appeared. The tablets which Moses brought down from Sinai 'were the work of God, and the writing was the writing of God'. At Belshazzar's feast there 'came forth fingers of a man's hand, and wrote over against the candlestick upon the plaster, *Mene, Mene, Tekel Upharsin*'; and the king 'saw the part of the hand that wrote'. The dead Elijah's warning of an impending plague, too, was given in writing. Or the message might be given through the prophet while he was possessed. Describing to Solomon the plans for a new Sanctuary, David explained 'the Lord made me understand in writing, by his hand on me'.

The great advantage the prophets enjoyed was that their access to information from the Lord – whatever channel it came through – enabled them to humiliate diviners who had to rely on rote, as Joseph did when he heard Pharaoh's dream about the seven fat kine being eaten by the seven lean kine, and correctly interpreted it as presaging seven years of plenty, followed by seven years of famine; Pharaoh's description of Joseph as 'a man in whom the spirit of God is' was a recognition of the superior merit of the inspirational diviner. But some rivals used inspirational methods for purposes other than the Lord's; and they had to be stamped out. 'There shall not be found among you,' Moses laid down, 'any one that maketh his son or his daughter to pass through the fire, or that useth divination, or an observer of times, or an enchanter, or a witch. Or a charmer, or a consulter with familiar spirits, or a wizard, or a necromancer; for all that do these things are an abomination unto the Lord.' Divination and magic as such were not abominable; only when they were practised without the Lord's authority. 'Guardian angels' were authorised familiar spirits. What was considered wicked about the materialisation of Samuel by the witch of En Dor was that Saul had asked for it; not the fact that a spirit had given advice – the spirit of the Elijah was to do that, to warn Jehoram of an impending plague. In the same way, the use of a divining instrument, denounced by Hosea – the people had taken to divination 'as the spirit of whoredom has caused them to err' – was not objectionable provided it was in the Lord's service. The term 'rod' often appears in this context apparently referring to an implement which might be described as a combination of divining rod and magician's wand. Rods were employed by Jacob to select the best cattle; Moses smote the rock at Hebron with his rod, at the Lord's bidding, to obtain water for the people; 'thy rod and thy staff', the psalmist sang, praising the Lord as his shepherd, 'they comfort me'. 'Urim' and 'Thummin', crystals carried by the prophets, were also for divination.

How highly regarded the inspirational element was can be judged from the fact that though the prophets were expected to remain in the Lord's service, they were not expected to lead moral lives. If Abraham had simply led an exemplary life, Mrs. St. Clair Stobart surmised in her study of biblical psychic phenomena, 'we should probably never have heard of him'; but his divinatory ability was so useful that his deceptions and his concubines could be condoned, as was the persistent dishonesty of Jacob. So long as the prophets were shamans – advisers and executors rather than rulers – there was some check on them, as Micaiah found when his clairvoyant advice was so unwelcome that Ahab had him imprisoned and put on the bread and water of affliction. But sometimes prophets were made rulers because, like Joshua, they were found to be 'in the spirit' or because, like Jehu, they were picked out by divination as men who would do the Lord's bidding – which did not necessarily make them good rulers. Having accomplished what his own self-interest and the Lord's instructions dictated by killing off all Ahab's descendants, Jehu obtained the Lord's promise that his heirs down to the fourth generation would rule in Israel; and thereafter behaved as if he no longer needed 'to walk in the law of the Lord God'. Lusting after Bathsheba, David used his authority to arrange for her husband Uriah the Hittite to be killed; and many of the lesser known prophets had ugly records. Occasionally they received their desserts; but often they were indulged because the Lord needed them – or, put the other way round, because the Israelites needed a diviner-magician with real powers.

There seemed hardly any limit to what a prophet could do when the hand of the Lord was on him. He could perform superhuman feats of strength or endurance of the kind for which Samson became renowned. Or he could become incombustible: Isaiah had a live coal placed on his lips by a seraphim, to take away his iniquity; Shadrach, Mesach and Abed-nego survived unscathed in Nebuchadnezzar's burning fiery furnace, so hot that the men who put them into it were killed, yet 'the princes, governors and captains, and the king's counsellors, being gathered together, saw these men, upon whose bodies the fire had no power, nor was an hair of their head singed, neither were their coats changed, nor the smell of fire had passed on to them'. The prophets, like the Indian medicine men, could also summon up fire: Solomon

obtained it as a benediction for his achievement in setting up the
Temple, and Elijah to help him in his contest with the priests of Baal.

Elijah and Elisha

This contest, Mrs. Stobart thought, has some claim to be the first
controlled psychic experiment in history. Worried by a protracted
drought, Ahab had the idea of getting the magicians from the rival
factions, the Lord's and Baal's, to compete against each other in a
display of their powers, the winner then to bring rain. The four hundred
and fifty priests of Baal, hoping to become possessed, 'cried aloud and
gashed themselves after their manner with knives'; but they failed to
meet Elijah's challenge, to call down fire from heaven. When it came
to Elijah's turn, he was clearly determined that nobody should subsequently accuse him of trickery. He had a trench dug round the altar,
filling it with water, and pouring barrels of water not only on the
sacrificial bullock, but on the wood that was to burn it; yet 'the fire of
the Lord fell, and consumed the burnt sacrifice, and the wood, and
stones, and the dust, and licked up the water that was in the trench'.
The display over, he went on to the more serious business of ending
the drought; and a small cloud duly rose out of the sea, no bigger than
a man's hand. Still in his trance state, Elijah was so elevated that,
girding up his loins, he was able to run back to Jezreel faster than
Ahab could ride there in his chariot.

Elisha displayed similar powers, having taken the sensible precaution, when Elijah asked what he would like as a parting gift, of
replying 'a double portion of thy spirit'. As soon as Elijah had been
carried up to heaven, Elisha began trying it out, smiting the waters of
Jordan with Elijah's mantle to divide them; making brackish water
drinkable; putting a curse on some children who had called him
'Baldy' (they were eaten by she-bears); arranging that the widow's
cruse should remain full, however much oil she used; and causing an
iron axe-head, which had fallen into the river, to float. Elisha could
also translocate himself, to any destination; and he could listen to conversations in distant places. When the king of Syria found his secret
plans were being disclosed to the Israelites, and wondered who the
spy was in his entourage, a servant assured him, 'None, my Lord, O
King; but Elisha the prophet, that is in Israel, telleth the king of Israel
the words that thou speakest in thy bedchamber.'

The account of Elisha's career, though, brings us back to earth.
What was attributed to him had been too often attributed to earlier
prophets for comfort; it begins to sound like the repetition of legend.
Yet it illustrates what Professor Mircea Eliade described as 'the perfect
continuity of paranormal experience from the primitive right up to the
most highly evolved'; and the general implication of the Bible story,

that the prophets kept their grip on Israel because they had psychic powers, remains plausible. Why, then, was that grip eventually lost?

One reason stands out: the misery to which the Lord and his prophets condemned the Lord's chosen people. It was not simply that so many of the Lord's acts and the prophets' interpretations were arbitrary, tyrannical, and cruel; they also continually promoted disputes with neighbouring communities which led to violence, to destruction, and exile. The Israelites did not even have the consolation of believing they would be rewarded by an after-life in heaven. They were sustained only by the fear that, bad as things were, if the Lord became offended with them their lot would become even worse. And they had been left in no doubt about the Lord's ruthlessness. When the Philistines captured their tribal fetish, the Ark of the Covenant, and set it up in the house of their own fetish idol Dagon, 'early on the morrow, behold, Dagon was fallen upon his face to the earth before the ark of the Lord'; and when they set Dagon up again, the next morning not merely had he fallen as before, but his head and his hands had de-materialised. Some men of Bethshemesh, who peered into the Ark, were killed; so was the unlucky Uzzah, whose only crime was that, seeking to steady it when the cart it was on was shaken by the oxen, he touched it; for to touch it meant death.

The Israelites were only likely to put up with the tribulations which they had to suffer so long as the prophets retained their psychic powers; and sometimes, as in Eli's time, 'there was no open vision' – no channel of clairvoyant or clairaudient communication. When the Lord called out, only the child Samuel heard. And later, under Roman rule, to be an inspirational prophet became as risky as to be a witch doctor under British colonial rule. The prophets became priests, settling into routine; and the feats achieved by men when the hand of the Lord was upon them became only a memory – though an inspiring one.

Chapter Five

Greece

IN HIS *Supernormal Phenomena in Classical Antiquity* E. R. DODDS, Professor of Greek at Oxford University, and a former President of the Society for Psychical Research, recalled that many interesting ideas on the subject had been presented by the classical scholars who had been involved in the Society's foundation; but later, this serious interest had given way to the attitude common to popular works on occultism, with its 'jejune and obviously second-hand ancient material, torn from its context of thought and interpreted in the light of the author's pre-possessions'. Only those familiar with the background, Dodds felt, could appreciate just how careful it is necessary to be in assessing the evidence; hardly any of it first-hand, and little even at second-hand of a kind which can be treated as historical. And there is the further problem that potentially the most valuable source of information about magical practices, the Eleusinian mysteries, have remained mysteries to this day. Nevertheless a useful purpose could be served, Dodds suggested, by examining the surviving evidence to see whether the phenomena described are consistent with those from other periods of history. If they were strikingly different, it would be easy to argue that each age is the victim of its superstitions.

The Iliad and the Odyssey

All the traditional shamanist features appear in Homer: the difference from the Bible is mainly in attitudes to them. In the Old Testament there is ordinarily a distinction, even if it is not always clear-cut, between what can be accounted for by natural causes and what should be attributed to divine intervention. The Lord is careful to make his will known, either directly or through his prophets. Homer's gods, however, intervene so casually and continually that natural and supernatural are hopelessly intertwined. A peal of thunder may be a sign of Zeus's wrath; a patch of mist may have been sent by a god to cloak

the flight of some favourite in danger of death. The chronicler of the
Book of Kings wrote that 'a certain man drew a bow at a venture', to
slay Ahab; Homer would have made some god responsible for directing, or diverting, the arrow's flight. When Socus's spear cuts through
Ulysses's shield it is Athene, on behalf of the Danaans, who does not
allow it 'to penetrate his bowels'; when Teucer aims an arrow at Hector
it is Zeus, on behalf of the Trojans, who breaks the cord of his bow.

When intervening in man's affairs, Homer's gods do not require the
services of a diviner. To ensure that her favourite Ulysses gets a hearing, Athene simply possesses a herald, and calls the meeting to order
through him. As a consequence seers, though respected, play a minor
role compared to that of the Old Testament prophet, their function
being chiefly to explain why the gods have been behaving in unpre-
dictable or undesirable ways. They can rarely forecast what is going
to happen, except in general terms, because the gods are constantly
and capriciously upsetting each other's plans. So little standing has
Calchas that he cannot even rely on Apollo, to whom he owes his gift,
for protection: he has to obtain a safe-conduct from Achilles before he
dares to explain that Agamemnon has offended the gods, for fear
Agamemnon will kill him. Homer politely describes Theoclymenus, the
diviner-in-residence at Ulysses's court, as 'godlike', but as Eliphas Levi
observed he is little more than a parasite 'purchasing a not too friendly
hospitality from the suitors of Penelope by a useless warning, and
prudently withdrawing before the disturbance which he foresees'. And
it is the fate of the most celebrated of all the diviners of the era,
Cassandra, that although her predictions invariably turn out to be
correct they are never heeded. As for magic, if the *Iliad* alone of the
two books had survived the ancient Greeks might be classified as the
sole people in history who did not use it; and even in the *Odyssey*, where
Circe and others are shamans, the assumption is that they are gods, or
quasi-gods.

The Oracles
By the fifth century B.C. a new element had come to permeate
Greek belief: the idea of Fate, or Destiny. The gods had not entirely
changed their ways; but they accepted, as the chorus in Aeschylus's
Agamemnon put it,

> . . . that always
> Events and causes hold
> Sequence divinely ordered,
> And next by last controlled.

Fate was bound up with certain moral principles, so that punishment must follow misdeeds unless certain steps were taken to avert the consequences. It had consequently become legitimate, and sometimes appeared essential, to find out what the fates had in store. Dreams were watched with care, and acted upon; when Orestes heard that his mother Clytemnestra had dreamed that she had given birth to a snake which had drawn blood as well as milk from her breasts, he had no difficulty in deciding.

> I must transmute my nature; be viperous in heart and act
> The dream commands it: I am her destined murderer.

Dreams were also sometimes artificially induced for divination by what appears to have been a form of hypnotism. But the standard procedure was a visit to an oracle, there to put questions to the sibyls.

The oracles, Frederic Myers claimed in his essay on the subject, must originally have been shamanist, the resident diviners chosen because they could induce a trance to obtain the required information. Describing how the Cumae oracle functioned when Aeneas visited it after the fall of Troy, Virgil provided what could still serve as a textbook case history of dissociation and possession: the sibyl's bosom began to heave, her heart to thump, her hair to become dishevelled; when she went into convulsions, her body appeared to elongate; and finally, the voice of Apollo broke through to give his message. Sometimes such messages would be clear, if vague; 'wars do I see, grim wars, and the Tiber foaming with blood'; sometimes they would be enigmatic; but essentially they were inspired. The inspirational technique, though, was not employed in all oracles. Occasionally they were simply places where portents could be easily observed – thunder, or the flight of birds; scrying could be used, or lots cast. The original purpose was to enable individuals to ascertain their fate (and to try to escape or mitigate it by the observance of certain rituals, ranging from human sacrifice, as when Agamemnon appeased the gods by offering up Iphigenia, to putting locks of hair on a grave, as Orestes did on Agamemnon's). But in time, people began to consult oracles on everyday matters – a trend which Xenophon, who took the oracles seriously and consulted them when he felt the need for advice, regarded as blasphemous. People living nearby began to bring domestic problems for solution. Two millennia later, excavations at Dodona were to turn up tablets upon which inquiries had been registered; and among them were requests from a householder who wanted to know if certain blankets and pillows had been stolen or simply mislaid, and from a husband asking if he were the father of the child his wife was about to bear.

The best known stories about the oracles' pronouncements come from Herodotus; among them his account of what happened when the Lydian, Pactyas, fled to Cymae after leading an unsuccessful revolt against Cyrus. When the Persians demanded that Pactyas should be handed over to them, the Cymeans sought the advice of the local oracle; and it recommended compliance. Aristodicus, who had hoped for a different answer, asked again; and when he had the same reply, he vented his irritation by pulling down some birds' nests in the sanctuary, a blasphemy which provoked a supernatural voice to denounce him for his wickedness. Taken aback, Aristodicus remarked that the oracle had not shown the same concern for the unfortunate Pactyas as it had for the birds; to which the oracle ominously replied that it had made its recommendation only because, if Pactyas were handed over, it would be an act of impiety for which the Cymeans would receive such condign punishment that never again would they approach an oracle with so disgraceful a question. Chastened, the Cymeans got out of their difficulty by allowing Pactyas to escape, doubtless hoping that, to spare them from the Persians' wrath, he would be caught elsewhere; as he was.

The oracles appear to have specialised in double-talk, notably in the advice which, according to Herodotus, led Croesus to his ruin in 546 B.C. Uncertain whether to allow Cyrus of Persia to continue to build up his forces, or to try to destroy them by a swift pre-emptive assault, Croesus had sent agents to each of the best-known oracles, with instructions to ask what he would be doing at a certain hour on a certain day (an unusually well-controlled test, even by modern standards, as the envoys would not themselves know the answer). The Delphic oracle replied:

> The savour of the hard-shelled tortoise, boiled in brass with the flesh of lamb, strikes on my senses. Brass is laid beneath it, and brass is put over it.

Croesus had, in fact, cut up a lamb and a tortoise, and boiled them in a brass kettle. Lavishing gifts on the Delphi establishment, he asked if he should attack Cyrus. Back came the reply:

> When Croesus has the Halys crossed
> A mighty Empire will be lost.

Encouraged, Croesus attacked, and was defeated, so it was the mighty Lydian Empire that fell.

Such ambiguities enabled the oracles to maintain their reputation for infallibility, but only at the cost of losing their usefulness. The impression left from Professor H. W. Parke's detailed research into them is that equivocation became their standby; and occasionally they were actually suborned – not surprisingly, as the temples could be, and sometimes were, sacked if the oracle did not give satisfaction. Early in the fifth century B.C. the Spartan Cleomenes managed to get the oracle at Delphi to say his rival Demaratus should be deposed. The story of the plot leaked out; and the reputation of Delphi and, by association, of oracles suffered.

Socrates

The earliest evidence for divination of a kind which can reasonably be called historical are Plato's descriptions of the daemon of Socrates. In the sixth century B.C. Epimenedes had gone into prolonged trances and, on coming out of them, described conversations he had had with the spirits, in which he obtained their advice on such matters as how to ward off a threatened plague; and by Plato's account Socrates used the same device. In his case, though, he was in communication with a single spirit, which he thought of as his 'daemon', a pagan guardian angel from whom he took advice. Its voice would break into his thoughts, even into his conversations; or to consult it, he would go into a trance, sometimes lasting for hours – once for a day and a night – in which he remained as if rapt in contemplation. And he relied upon it to the last. 'I would like to tell you of a truly wonderful circumstance,' he told his judges at his trial.

Hitherto the divine faculty of which my voice is the source has constantly been in the habit of opposing me even about trifles, if I were going to make some slip or error in any matter . . . but it has made no sign of opposition within when I was leaving my house this morning, or when I was on my way to court, or while I was speaking, at anything I was going to say; and yet I have often been stopped in the middle of a speech . . . What do I take to be the explanation of this silence? I will tell you. It is the intimation that what has happened to me is a good, and that those of us who think that death is an evil are in error.

The nature of Socrates's daemon has invited conjecture ever since. 'We may surmise,' Plutarch suggested, 'that what reached him was not a voice or a sound, but the silent voice of the daemon, touching the intelligence of his soul'; Plutarch's assumption being that spirits, having intelligences of their own which penetrate those of men who are capable of reception, 'need neither the names nor the words which men use in speaking to one another, to put across their ideas'. And some recent commentators have argued that the daemon is most easily explained in terms of unconscious inhibitions. 'Voices', though, of the kind Socrates claimed he heard have been reported throughout history; that he should have heard them was surprising only because they had not usually been associated with men of his intellectual calibre – as he was himself aware. As a rule, he admitted, the gods only communicated with people 'either in sleep, when the intellectual faculties are restrained, or in an abnormal state through disease or some kind of ecstasy'. This meant that the medium might be unable to make sense out of their messages; 'while the person remains in the state of madness, it is not his business to interpret the apparition he sees or the cries he himself makes; the old saying is true, that it belongs to the sane man, alone, to do and know his own business'. Nevertheless mania should not necessarily be regarded as an evil. 'The greatest blessings come by way of madness, if it is heaven sent,' Socrates told Phaedrus; 'it was when they were mad that the prophetesses at Delphi and the priestesses at Dodona achieved so much for both states and individuals in Greece; when sane they did little or nothing.' Breaking out in this way, he felt, was also a method of relieving the possessed individual of his troubles; and it could open the way for the muses to take over. The authors of great poems 'do not attain to excellence through the rules of any art; they utter their beautiful verses in a state of inspiration'.

Here, then, was an early attempt to explain the bizarre phenomena of mediumship. They were a form of madness designed not to humiliate but to elevate man, by providing him with the power of divination; by purging and purifying him; or by giving him the gift of poetic inspiration. And just as certain individuals were the gods' instruments, because the madness could descend on them, so certain spirits were chosen by the gods as their messengers. There were other categories, among them the spirits of the dead: when the corporeal element was heavy, Socrates suggested, it dragged the soul back to earth where it 'haunts, as men say, monuments and tombs'; and as a result shadowy apparitions were sometimes seen, reflecting the fact that souls had not yet been fully separated from bodies. But these were distinct from the daemons which acted as guardians and as messengers from the gods. The problem for a man of intellect was how to facilitate communication. Socrates felt he had been lucky in being able to listen occasionally to his daemon; but anybody really proficient in such intercourse was a daemonic man, 'compared with whom experts in arts and handicrafts are but journeymen'. He therefore recommended people who desired to obtain what was beyond human wisdom to study divination. Anybody who discovered ways by which the gods give indications to men respecting human affairs, he told Xenophon, would 'never fail of obtaining the gods' advice'.

Hearsay also credited Socrates's daemon with providing premonitions: as in the tale that although he twice warned Timarchus, with whom he was drinking, not to leave the house, Timarchus slipped out and killed a man, for which he was eventually executed. Episodes of this kind, Frederic Myers felt, must be considered doubtful; but what was clear was that Socrates's daemon gave him advice, positive and negative, which he found to be always right and wise, and occasionally of a kind which implied knowledge not available to him through his ordinary senses.

Aristotle

The idea that the gods used spirits as their emissaries could account for Socrates's voices, but it was difficult to believe that spirits were responsible for the kind of second sight or prevision which was casually encountered in dreams. Socrates's contemporary Democritus suggested that such images might be transmitted to the human mind not by divine intervention, but simply by emanations which flowed out from animate or inanimate sources, and in certain circumstances could be picked up in sleep. The idea attracted Aristotle, leading him to modify his own early acceptance of spirits, and to suggest that just as water, when stirred, continues to move even though the motive force has ceased, 'it may well be that a movement, and a consequent sense perception, should reach sleeping souls' – dreams often being the channel, because people are more open to impressions when asleep. This would also explain why prophetic dreams often came to a commonplace individual – such a mind is 'not given to thinking but, as it were, derelict or totally vacant, and when once set moving is borne passively on in the direction taken by whatever moves it' – or to people whose minds were deranged. Such dreams, Aristotle argued, could not be inspired by the gods, because they would not give the power of foreseeing the future to inferior people. The more likely explanation was that every dreamer must occasionally be right about his future, just as every gambler must occasionally pick a winner; and that as the future must to a considerable extent be implicit in the present, small changes taking place in a man's body could give notice of diseases which will follow later – 'clearly these beginnings must be more evident in sleeping than in waking moments'. Coincidence, too, could account for the apparently prophetic nature of many dreams. Dream divination could not be dismissed as incredible; but the lack of anything to account for it, Aristotle felt, justified mistrust.

Chapter Six
Rome

De Divinatione

Aristotle, then, was moving towards scepticism about divination; and three centuries later Cicero, in his essay on the subject, presented scepticism's first manifesto, in the form of a dialogue between himself and his brother Quintus, Quintus accepted the traditional Hellenic view of the gods and their mode of communication with men. All people, at all times, he pointed out, had accepted that there could be foreknowledge of future events. Nor was it strange that it so often presented itself in dreams, or in frenzies such as those of the sibyls: 'when the soul of man is disengaged from bodily impediments and liberated, either relaxed in sleep or in a state of ecstasy, it beholds those wonders which, when obscured by the veil of the flesh, it cannot see'. That the future could be foretold from omens such as the entrails of sacrificial animals, he admitted, was a little harder to accept. The original assumption had been that each time an animal was about to be sacrificed, the gods would ensure that its entrails were so prepared as to ensure the correct prediction. The Stoics, however, arguing that the gods could not be expected to concern themselves with such trivia, had decided that the state of the entrails must have been planned ahead by Fate. But this, too, seemed far-fetched to Quintus; he preferred to believe that some form of divine energy, permeating everything, could effect the necessary adjustments to the entrails at the right moment – 'for by very trifling exertions nature can alter, or refashion, or diminish many things'. A truly serviceable gift, this divinatory power, Quintus claimed, 'and one by which our mortal nature most nearly approaches the power of the gods'.

That people had always believed in divination, Cicero replied, was simply because people had always been gullible; and the arguments Quintus had used in his desperate attempt to explain the principle of divination by artificial means – 'the inspection of entrails, the observation of thunderstorms and prodigies, and the auguries of those who deal in signs and omens' – was an example of the contortions which intelligent men had to fall back on to justify such ludicrous beliefs. The notion that nature, to oblige diviners, would alter sacrificial entrails was too absurd, Cicero felt, to be taken seriously.

About the inspirational method of divination he was hardly less scathing. He dismissed the Delphic oracle as having become contemptible, and derided the sibylline books – originally used, according to tradition, by the Cumaean sibyl, and in the sixth century brought from her oracle to Rome, there to be consulted in times of crisis. The verses in these books, he pointed out, could not have been composed by the sibyl in a state of ecstasy; and where they were not impenetrably obscure they were ambiguous. And although these were criticisms not so much of the natural, or inspirational, method as of the failure to maintain it, Cicero made it clear that he did not accept the reality of divination in any form. Even those oracular forecasts which had come true, he argued, could usually be seen on examination to have been couched in terms which could be claimed as true, whatever the outcome, as in Croesus's case – or in Hamilcar's. Besieging Syracuse, Hamilcar had dreamed that he would dine in the town the following day. This had naturally encouraged him to order an assault; but in the preparations for it, his Carthaginian troops came into conflict with their Sicilian allies; the Syracusans seized the opportunity to launch an attack of their own, in which Hamilcar was captured; and his dream was thus ironically fulfilled.

Quintus had insisted that interpretation was a different issue. It did not matter how many false interpretations, or even false prophecies, had been made; 'I will even declare without hesitation that a single case of presage and prediction, all the points of which are borne out by subsequent events, and that definitely and regularly, not casually and fortuitously, would suffice to compel an admission of the foreknowledge of future events'. But there had never in fact been a case of this kind, Cicero replied, which could not be given a natural explanation. Some prophecies had worked out because they were derived from intuition and knowledge; but as Quintus had himself admitted, this was not, strictly speaking, divination. In other instances coincidence could be responsible. And often, in the case of portents, natural forces were at work. The wind blew doors open; and if the statue of a god was seen to 'perspire', the moisture might well be what 'we see sometimes on plaster during the prevalence of a south wind'.

Some familiar stories of divination, Cicero was prepared to admit, sounded impressive; such as cases collected by Chrysippus, who had gone into the evidence with care. Chrysippus had related how two travellers arrived at Megara, where one went to stay with friends.

During the night he 'saw' his travelling companion in danger at his inn; jumping up to help, he realised that he had been dreaming and returned to bed. He then had a further dream, in which his friend was murdered, and his corpse thrown into a dungcart; and investigation the next morning showed the information from the dream had been correct. 'But the main part of these dreams happened to strangers,' Cicero protested; 'some of them may be mere fiction; by whom are they vouched for?' And those who believed in them reduced the chance of getting them accepted as genuine by also crediting, or at least not repudiating, grotesque stories of other unaccountable happenings. Did Quintus really believe that Romulus's staff had survived a fire unscathed? Or that Attius Navius's razor blade could slice through a whetstone? 'Such fables as these should not be admitted into philosophical discussion.' As for the tale of the sacrificial bull which Caesar offered up, and was found to have no heart, 'believe me, you are betraying the city of philosophy while defending its castles. In trying to prove the truth of the auguries, you are overturning the whole system of physics.'

The Decline of the Oracles

With only slight changes, *De Divinatione* might have been written by a nineteenth-century sceptic following Voltaire and Hume. In a sense, it was itself a striking divinatory exercise, rehearsing precisely the arguments that were to become so familiar nearly two thousand years later. But his thesis suffered from the weakness of many later exercises in scepticism: it was based on the premise that the supernatural, if it existed, must be bound up with gods and spirits, and that consequently if the gods and the spirits were to be jettisoned in rationalism's cause, the supernatural must go overboard with them. It did not occur to Cicero that such phenomena as divination and psychokinesis might be natural realities upon which people had built supernatural beliefs and fantasies; and that some beliefs and fantasies might be swept away without prejudice to the acceptance of the phenomena.

This was understandable, because divination had become systematised: and the systems employed, based on the interpretation of omens, portents and auguries, had become hopelessly confused and corrupted – as, indeed, the more discerning of commentators often complained. Strabo, a student at the time Cicero wrote *De Divinatione*, was to express regret at the trend: 'among the ancients both divination in general and oracles were held in greater honour, but now great neglect of them prevails, since the Romans are satisfied with the sibylline books and with the Tyrrhenian prophecies obtained by means of the entrails of animals, the flight of birds, and omens from the sky'. And in the middle of the first century Curtius Quintus, the biographer of Alexander the Great, diagnosed the cause of the decay. In the past, men or women had been singled out by the gods as channels of communication with men;

> and as a sign that it is no human wisdom and art which reveals the divine will, Apollo speaks through the mouth of feeble girls and women. The state of inspiration is by no means one of specially heightened powers. The human being's own powers – his own consciousness – are as it were extinguished, in order that the divine voice may be heard all the louder. The secret communicated by the god resembles a load oppressing the breast it visits; it is a clairvoyance from which no satisfaction accrues to the mind of the seer. The seer or sibyl is accordingly not herself capable of revelation.

Because the seer or sibyl could not interpret the god when the meaning was obscure, Curtius explained, it had become necessary to employ specialists for that purpose. Naturally they had tended to be chosen from among the cult of dedicated believers that oracles attracted; in time, from their families; and this was the point at which the diviner's art and the priesthood, which originally had nothing in common, 'first enter into their momentous connection'.

The designation 'priest' was loosely applied, but more and more it tended to mean a functionary at a temple, shrine or oracle who performed set rituals, and if called upon for divination used mechanical means. Occasionally an oracle would win a reputation for being exceptionally perceptive, perhaps because one of the priests there was supplementing the code with inspirational divining, perhaps simply by luck; and then for a while it would become fashionable. Following Croesus's example, the Emperor Trajan sent a wrapped and sealed packet to the oracle at Baalbek, which happened to be in favour; and it enhanced its reputation by sending back the package with the seals still intact, accompanied by the oracle-god's interpretation – a blank sheet of paper; which was what Trajan had sent. But in such cases it was always possible that the story had been put about by the oracle's staff for promotional purposes; or that a way had been found to remove seals intact, and later replace them, as Lucian alleged. Lucian's lively scepticism meant that he was not the most detached of critics; but there was plenty of other evidence that the continuing decline in the repute of oracles was justified, such as a report Myers cited from Oenomaus, in Hadrian's time. Visiting the oracle of Apollo at Colophon he obtained a reply to his question which would have sounded more impressive had he not known that the same answer had been given to the commercial traveller who had gone in ahead of him; and when he asked 'where shall I go now?', and the oracle told him to 'draw a long bow and knock over untold green-feeding ganders', he departed in disgust. 'Who in the world,' he asked, 'will inform me what these untold ganders may mean?'

The decline in the oracles' reputation left the field open to the 'prophets without a temple': magicians, soothsayers and, as Juvenal noted, astrologers; he contrasted silenced Delphi with the prestige that astrologers had begun to acquire in the eyes of Roman matrons. The testimony of sceptics and believers alike testifies to the morbid interest Romans had in the supernatural, in any of its manifestations. other historians; the trouble is that it is rarely possible to separate The evidence about them is abundant in the pages of Suetonius and out history from the legends. Belief in omens and portents encouraged writers to accept reports which sounded appropriate to the occasion; for example, Suetonius's descriptions of the apparition of superhuman size and beauty, playing a reed pipe, which prompted Caesar to cross the Rubicon; and of the rash of warnings of his impending assassination – the soothsayer's 'Beware the Ides of March'; the report that a herd of his horses had been seen shedding tears; and his wife's dream about his death, followed by the bursting open of her bedroom door of its own accord when she awoke. Rarely are there any confirmatory accounts which would justify crediting such stories; and even at the time, they excited the ridicule of rationalists like Pliny. In his *Natural History,* published in A.D. 77, he mocked the cult of omens – 'the admonitions of thunder, the warnings of oracles, the predictions of soothsayers, and things too trifling to be mentioned as sneezing and stumbling'; a particularly ludicrous example being the episode when the Emperor Augustus, on the day he was nearly assaulted by his soldiers, recalled that he had, that very morning, tried to put his left shoe on his right foot. And Pliny related with relish the fate of Hermotinus, who had claimed that at any time he could release his soul from his body to travel wherever it wished, so that it could report back to him from a distance 'many things that only someone present at them could know of'. As this was an information service which his enemies found disconcerting, they took advantage one day of the fact that while his soul was away, his body was left in a comatose condition; they seized it, and burned it, 'so depriving his soul, on its return, of what might be called its sheath'.

Pliny the younger was more cautious. In a letter to the consul Licinius Sura he posed the eternal dilemma of the man who does not regard himself as gullible, and is reluctant to be thought credulous, but who cannot help wondering whether there may not be something in stories he has heard, some from reputable sources. He had been particularly intrigued by a tale he had heard about Athenodorus the philosopher who, finding that a house was up for rent cheaply in Athens because it was supposed to be haunted by a man with clanking chains, had rented it. The ghost appeared, beckoning him; and Athenodorus accompanied it out of the house, marking the spot to which it pointed. The next day he informed the magistrates; the ground was dug up; a skeleton was found of a man in chains; and after it was given a decent burial, the house was haunted no more.

Should such tales be believed? Pliny was uncertain; but, asking Sura for his views on the subject, he expressed his own view that they were not all simply illusions.

What particularly inclines me to believe in their existence is a story which I heard from Curtius Rufus. When he was in humble circumstances and unknown in the world, he attended the Governor of Africa into that province. One evening as he was walking in the public portico there appeared to him the figure of a woman of unusual size and of more than human beauty. As he stood there, terrified and astonished, she told him that she was the tutelary power that presided over Africa, and had come to inform him of the future events of his life. He should go back to Rome to enjoy high honours, return to the province of Africa, vested with proconsular dignity, and there he should die. Every circumstance of this prediction actually came to pass.

Plutarch was of a like mind. 'It has been claimed,' he wrote in his life of Dion,

that no man in his senses ever saw a ghost, that these are the delusive visions of women and children or of men whose intellects are impaired by some physical infirmity, and who believe that their distressed imaginations are of divine origin. But if Dion or Brutus, men of strong and philosophic minds, whose understandings were not affected by any constitutional infirmity, if such men could place so much faith in the appearance of spectres as to give an account of them to their friends, I see no reason why we should depart from the opinion of the ancients.

But to Lucian, even more than to Cicero, the supernatural was nothing more than a compound of delusion and fraud. It was pitiful, he felt, that men should credit such stories as that of the man who was visited by the spectre of his dead wife, complaining that he had not burned all her belongings, as he was pledged to do, and showing him where one of her shoes which had eluded his notice was hidden. Occasionally, Lucian admitted, people might indeed believe they had

seen a spirit; but if they did it was because they had been duped by
hoaxers like Alexander of Abunoteichos, who faked a god with the
help of a tame serpent and a human head made out of linen, to represent Aesculapius.

Theurgy

The most striking accounts of divination and magic in the classical
era are to be found not in the standard histories and commentaries,
but in the works of writers who were involved in two spiritist cults:
Theurgy and Christianity.

Theurgy had been derived, or so it was believed, from Pythagoras,
but infused with Platonic ideals. In his *Laws*, Plato had recommended
the death sentence for anybody using 'spells, charms, incantations or
other such sorceries' for purposes of mischief, from which it could
be inferred that they could legitimately be used for worthy purposes.
As Emperors tended to assume, often rightly, that if magic were
found to work it would be directed against them, Roman law ceased
to make the distinction; the practice of magic was banned. But the
frequency with which edicts appeared renewing the prohibition and
strengthening the penalties suggests that the law must have been
ineffective; partly, doubtless, because rulers and men in authority
under them were not above employing a magician themselves; and
partly because the Empire was too far-flung for such regulations to
be successfully enforced.

Like all systems of magic, theurgy picked up accretions from a
variety of sources, including Old Testament shamanism; some of its
magicians were men in the tradition of Moses and Elijah, such as
Jesus's contemporary Apollonius of Tyana. His destiny, according to
Philostratus, had been marked out for him at birth by signs and wonders; swans had assembled to greet it, clapping their wings. At the
age of sixteen he had acknowledged his vocation, henceforth abstain-
ing from meat and preaching poverty ('O God! Grant me few
possessions and no wants!'); and he had then begun to perform
miracles of healing, and to display powers of second sight. Passing
some men on their way to execution, he insisted that the confession
of one of them had been extracted by torture, and urged that he
should be put last on the list for execution, as a reprieve was on its
way – as it turned out to be. Another time he was out walking and
discoursing at Ephesus, when his voice fell and eventually he became
silent

> as if he had lost the thread of his discourse. Then, fixing his eyes
> steadfastly on the earth, and advancing three or four steps, he cried
> out 'Strike the tyrant! – Strike!' (this he did, not like one who

guessed what was passing from seeing its image in a mirror, but from literally seeing it, as it were promoting it). All Ephesus was astonished at what they heard (for every one was present at this disputation). But Apollonius, stopping for some time, like those who wait the issue of a doubtful action, at length cried out 'Keep up your spirits, O Ephesians! For this day the tyrant is killed. And why do I say this day? At this very moment, while the words are in my mouth, I swear it by Minerva, the deed is done.'

It was feared he had gone off his head; but in due course messengers arrived who confirmed that the manner of the death of Domitian, and the hour it took place, corresponded exactly.

The evidence for Apollonius's miracles, which included transloca-tion from the court of the Emperor to another place many miles away, was derived from Philostratus's biography, written a century after his death; and although the writer had access to records left by Apollonius's contemporaries, the book could be dismissed as hagio-graphy. To Christians, particularly, this was welcome as the miracles were too close for comfort to those presented in the gospels. Philostratus, they claimed, was simply a neo-Platonist propaganda-monger, a view which was to persist: the picture of Apollonius had been 'artificially assembled by a pagan philosopher', Alexander Bruce claimed in *The Miraculous Element in the Gospels,* published in 1886, 'to take the wind out of Christ's sails by showing He is not unparalleled'. And al-though Gibbon had dismissed this hypothesis, as a sceptic he, too, was not disposed to give any credence to Philostratus. Yet the book does not sound hagiographical in the sense that, say, the gospels do. It was written to show that Apollonius had been a remarkable man who attracted strange happenings; not to make him out to have been the Messiah. And some episodes carry conviction, however improb-able the event described; notably in the description of Brahman magic which Apollonius witnessed on a visit to India. After ritual purification he went with the Brahmans to a temple where 'with staves uplifted they struck the earth, all together, which made it heave and swell like the waves of the sea; by this, they were elevated to the height of almost two cubits above it'. But he was careful to make the point that although the Brahmans had the power to levitate, it was not displayed 'for the purpose of exciting admiration'; of this, he insisted, the Brahmans disapproved. Centuries later, Western ob-servers were to send back similar accounts of the ability of Brahmans to levitate, and of their disapproval of boasting about it.

Apuleius
How the theurgists were popularly believed to operate was to be

described in the second century A.D. by Apuleius. Introducing his translation of Apuleius's *The Golden Ass* Robert Graves pointed out that it was taken seriously even by St. Augustine who, though dubious, regarded Lucius's transformation into an ass as a subject for legitimate speculation; such transformations of men into beasts or birds, it was feared, were within a sorcerer's capability. The plot had in fact been borrowed from an earlier source; Apuleius was letting his fancy roam in a traditional traveller's tale. But Apuleius's *Discourse on Magic,* in which he defended himself from a charge of practising it, was actually delivered in court before Claudius Maximus, the Roman Proconsul for Africa; and even if Apuleius touched it up, as surely he would have done to make his forensic achievement all the more striking, Graves felt there was no reason to doubt that it gave a reasonably accurate account of the accusations made against him, reflecting contemporary assumptions about the nature of magical practices.

Apuleius was charged with having infatuated a middle-aged widow, to persuade her to marry him, by various arts, including incantations, charms and potions. He was known to have owned a fish, supposedly charged with magic significance; a piece of wood, fashioned into the likeness of a god, or spirit; and a magic mirror. Unfortunately for posterity, it was in Apuleius's interest to mock his prosecutors by concentrating upon the everyday, rather than the magical, uses to which such possessions could be put. Socrates had recommended people to observe themselves in mirrors, he recalled; Demosthenes had actually practised his speeches in front of them. Only as a second line of defence did Apuleius occasionally refer to magical practices, and then with the aim of showing that, though he personally had no experience in such matters, there was nothing inherently sinister about them. To the accusation, for example, that he had bewitched a boy with incantations in the hope of exploiting his psychic powers, his first line of defence was that the boy's convulsions, which formed the basis for the charge, were epileptic; but he also took the opportunity to produce a string of historical examples of the use of boys' clairvoyant capabilities for worthy purposes. When Fabius, having lost some money, consulted the magician Nigidius, Nigidius had put a boy into a trance, and the boy was able to describe how it had been stolen; adding that some of it was buried, some had been spent, and that one coin was actually in Cato's pocket, which to Cato's embarrassment was found to be correct. Were such things possible? Apuleius cagily admitted that he did not know. But if they were, there could be no doubt about the respectability of their source – Plato. Like Plato, he believed.

that there are certain divine powers which are intermediate in kind and in place between the gods and mankind, and that these powers are responsible for all divinations and miracles. And I am further of the opinion that the human mind, and especially the uncontaminated mind of a boy, may be lulled to sleep, and so estranged from the body as to become oblivious of the present, being either summoned away from it by the agency of charms, or else enticed by the allurements of sweet odours; and that so, all remembrance of what is done in the body having been banished for a time, it may be restored and brought back to its original nature, which no doubt is divine and immortal, and thus, being as it were in a kind of trance, may presage future events.

Neo-Platonism

In the middle of the third century theurgy, thanks to the movement that was to be known as neo-Platonism, became an intellectual and moral force in Rome under the inspiration of Plotinus. Plotinus was in no doubt that divination and magic were realities; he practised them himself. According to his pupil Porphyry he enjoyed second sight; once, when Porphyry in despair planned to commit suicide, Plotinus divined his despair and came round in time to stop him. And when Olympus of Alexandria tried to crush Plotinus by magic, he found the experiment turned against himself. The spirit of Plotinus had such power that assaults bounced back on anybody who made them; his assailant's limbs contracted, and he 'doubled up like an empty bag'.

Plotinus was no charlatan. A model of ascetic integrity, he regarded his powers as an intimation that man might aspire to become godlike, and that consequently they must be used only for worthy ends and in self-defence. They showed, he felt, that all life was linked.

Reflection tells us that we are in sympathetic relation to each other; suffering, overcome, at the sight of pain; naturally drawn to forming attachments; and all this can be due only to some unity among us.

Again, if spells and other forms of magic are efficient even at a distance to attract us into sympathetic relations, the agency can be no other than the one soul.

A quiet word induces changes in a remote object, and makes itself heard at vast distances – proof of the oneness of all things within the one soul.

The power of magic, Plotinus explained, was derived from being able to exploit this reigning sympathy within nature; 'the magician draws on these patterns of power, and by ranging himself also into the pattern is able tranquilly to possess himself of these forces with whose nature and purpose he has become identified'. The ability to make beautiful music, even, was a form of sorcery; though one which 'raises no question'.

But it is from the works of Porphyry, and his pupil Iamblichus, that the most revealing descriptions of magical ideas and practices have survived from this era. Myers's sketch of Porphyry's career shows him to have been a man of intellectual integrity with the courage to relinquish ideas he had passionately held when they ceased to satisfy him. A Syrian, educated by the Greek philosopher Longinus, he had produced a new edition of the *Iliad* and the *Odyssey*, and in the process become disturbed by doubts about the validity of the faith derived from such legends. This led him on to a study of oracles and divination, which was to culminate in the first serious attempt to investigate the process by which the gods, or the spirits, communicated to man through mediums or sibyls. His 'Letter to the Egyptian Anebo' – Iamblichus – was couched in the form of a request for information, but it clearly derived from a lively Socratic curiosity rather than from ignorance of the subject. Why, he asked, did divination come in so many diverse ways?

For we frequently obtain a knowledge of future events through dreams, when we are asleep; not being, at that time, in tumultuous ecstasy, for the body is then quiescent; but we do not apprehend what then takes place, in the same manner as when we are awake. But many, through divine inspiration, predict future events when they are in a wakeful state, and their senses active.

The multiplicity of ways of attaining the trance state also roused Porphyry's curiosity. Some people entered it on hearing cymbals, or drums; some by drinking water; some by inhaling vapour; some by taking potions; some by making incantations; some by scrying; some by sacrifices. Why, he wondered, were there so many different routes? Iamblichus's view was that the diversity of methods used to obtain divination, from the convulsions of sibyls to the consultations with entrails, simply represented different ways by which man had sought to open up channels to allow the divine information to flow. Intellectual development was all very well, but truth came from the gods; and priests ought to dedicate their lives to establishing such communication.

With the help of mediums, usually 'rather young and simple persons', Porphyry and Iamblichus began spiritist experiments. It was often difficult, they discovered, to bring about dissociation and possession for the first time; but once it had been accomplished it became much easier – sometimes too easy; some unwanted spirit would come butting in, aggressively, and take over. They found it possible to call up a particular spirit for questioning; its answers would be relevant, though not necessarily accurate; certainly not to be relied upon. The spirits appeared to have wills of their own, even consciences; 'Close the sitting!' one of them advised. 'I am going to speak falsehoods!' The reason, Porphyry surmised, must be something wrong with the circumstances: perhaps the spirits became susceptible to human influences, and ceased to be free agents.

As a rule the medium went into a trance state: apparently fast asleep, but voices would come through, not sounding like the medium's own, and sometimes speaking in strange languages. Darkness appeared to enhance the effects; bright lights would often herald the arrival or departure of spirits, and occasionally forms seemed to materialise. In their possessed state, the mediums could undergo changes; 'sometimes their bodies seem to grow in height', Iamblichus observed, 'sometimes in breadth; sometimes they hover in the air'. And not merely did entranced mediums cease to feel pain – 'though transfixed with spits, they do not perceive it; others that are struck on the shoulders with axes, and have their arms cut with knives, are not conscious of what is being done to them' – they could also be 'thrown into fire, and pass through fire', without suffering injury.

Scattered and shaky though most of the evidence is for the reality of pyschic experience in classical antiquity, it carries some conviction, with Socrates in the early stages and the neo-Platonists at the end; and even if the rest of the accounts cannot be relied upon, at least they answer Professor Dodd's question; the phenomena reported were the same as in any other age. Only one, he thought, was missing: he could find no mention of poltergeists. But the manifestations usually associated with poltergeist-*type* hauntings are there in abundance in classical antiquity: lights, and fires, and objects moving – like the armour clashing around in the temple of Hercules, which warned the Spartans of their impending defeat by Epaminondas. In a pioneering survey on classical divination which appeared in 1914, W. R. Halliday had claimed that there was no evidence of the use of the techniques of the dowser; but this was because Halliday, like most of his contemporaries, identified dowsing with the use of a forked hazel twig, the method generally used in his time. A few pages earlier, he had actually mentioned Lucian's reference to divination with a pendulum, or a wooden image. At Hieropolis, the image of the god used to intimate that it was about to provide information by stirring and sweating on its Temple pedestal; when it was lifted up, it would take charge, directing those who were carrying it, sometimes moving from one shoulder to another, and answering questions put to it by driving forward, for 'yes', and backward, for 'no'.

Where shamanism survived, in fact, its traditional manifestations continued; fire-walking processions in Cappadocia, for example, in which temple virgins, entranced, walked barefoot over burning coals. But with priests and augurs unwilling or unable to attain the state of possession, and with increasingly savage laws against the practice of magic, it is not surprising that supernatural phenomena were less frequently reported, except when they could be attributed to the gods: and as the charge of sorcery or necromancy was a simple way for a ruler to dispose of rivals, critics or wives, the evidence produced at trials is not to be trusted. Still, it is occasionally revealing. In the fourth century a group of Greeks were arrested for conspiring against the Emperor Valens; and at their trial one of the exhibits was a table made out of wood from Delphi. 'We made it, that confounded little table,' one of them confessed, 'under strange rites and spells, and at last we got it to work.' The way they had got it to work was to put a metal dish on it, round the rim of which were inscribed the letters of the alphabet. One of the group 'bowed himself over the table', holding a thread from which a ring was suspended: 'the ring, darting out and striking at intervals the particular letters that attract it, makes out heroic verses, in accordance with the questions put, as complete in mode and measure as those uttered by the Pythoness'. When the ring was asked who would succeed Valens, it replied 'T . . . H . . . E . . . O . . .'; at which point the conspirators, satisfied that this must be their preferred candidate, the virtuous Theodorus, took the experiment no further. One of them, however, was indiscreet enough to tell the story; it was relayed to the Emperor; and Valens had them all executed, along with Theodorus. Perhaps this purchased Valens a lease of life, as he reigned a further seven years. But when he was killed in his turn, his successor was Theodorus's son – Theodosius.

The fact that divination had forecast his ascent to the throne did not leave Theodosius any better disposed to it. The Theodosian code not merely confirmed that anybody engaging in magic would render himself liable to capital punishment: the death sentence could be passed even if the seance had been held in private, and for purposes of divination only – the first time in Roman law that magic and divination had been put on the same footing. Even possession of an amulet could render the wearer liable to the same penalty. But Theodosius was a devout Christian, the friend of St. Ambrose, Bishop of Milan. He may have been swayed by the hostility to spiritism which had developed in the now dominant Christian Church.

Christianity

Chapter Seven
The New Testament

THE CHRISTIAN CHURCH HAD GROWN FROM SHAMANIST ROOTS; AND as described by the gospel writers, Jesus is the most accomplished diviner-magician of them all. His destiny has been marked out for him in Joseph's precognitive dream even before he was born; his birth is heralded by many signs and wonders, notably the star in the east which the Magi – themselves shamans – correctly interpret; and his baptism represents a recognition of his vocation, prompting him to undergo the traditional apprenticeship of self-denial – forty days and forty nights in the wilderness wrestling with the temptations of the flesh for fear that they would impede his spiritual development. After subduing sensual lusts, however, Jesus is subjected to another form of temptation. Spiritual rebirth, he finds, has endowed him with psychic powers. Having the ability to convert a stone into bread, or to translocate himself to the top of a mountain or the pinnacle of the temple, he is tempted to use them for self-satisfaction, or self-aggrandisement. At first he is hesitant about using them at all. 'Mine hour is not yet come,' he tells the importunate woman when drink runs out at the Cana wedding feast; but he allows himself to be persuaded to do the kindly thing, and turn the water into wine. Later he uses his powers with more abandon: calming the sea, walking on the water, feeding the five thousand with five loaves and two fishes, and performing countless cures. Only in the region where he has grown up, and where his family still live, is he unsuccessful. In the face of local scepticism, 'he can do no mighty work'.

Attracted by these powers, Jesus's disciples had a further inducement to stay with him: the promise of a continued life after death. In Greek mythology some humans had been carried up after death to live on in the abode of the gods; but the Greek gods had been choosy. Jesus offered the prospect of a life after death to anybody, however humble, who followed him. And he clinched this pledge by his resurrection. While he lived supernatural manifestations had continued to testify to his, or his god's, powers. He had shown precognitive knowledge of his impending arrest and execution, and of episodes connected with it, like Judas's treachery and Peter's spinelessness under questioning ('before the cock crow, thou shalt deny me thrice'); and at the moment of his death the veil of the temple was rent in twain, from top to bottom. But such signs would hardly have sufficed to convince the disciples had Jesus not afterwards appeared in their midst, and demonstrated that he had materialised by eating broiled fish and honey, and allowing Thomas to put his finger into the wound in his side left by the spear.

At this point it has to be stated that for none of these psychic manifestations is there a shred of historical evidence. Not merely were the gospels written half a century or more after the events they recorded; they were written with a deliberate propagandist purpose, to confirm that Jesus really had been the Christ – the Messiah promised by the prophets. They consequently presented him as a miracle worker who had fufilled all the earlier expectations and forecasts. It is, of course, still possible to argue that even if the gospels cannot be accepted as an historical source, they could hardly have been written unless there had been a Jesus with some shamanist powers to create the beliefs; in which case, as the parapsychologist Louis Anspacher urged, he can and ought to be studied as a psychic personality, 'the most powerful medium and perhaps the greatest psychic sensitive who has ever walked down the aisles of history'. Due weight has to be given, too, to the experience of the anthropologist M. J. Field, who realised from her field-work in Ghana how similar the New Testament record was to her own experience, suggesting that on a psychic level the disciples were part of 'an age-old, worldwide pattern persistently exhibited' – in other words, the New Testament record is not incongruous, anthropologically speaking. Nevertheless there is no way of knowing which, if any, of the supernatural manifestations recorded in the gospels and the Acts of the Apostles occurred.

The belief that they *had* occurred, though, remains of profound historical importance. The effects of Jesus's resurrection was to confirm disciples in the expectation that they, too, would be resurrected, as he had promised, and thereafter dwell in heaven: lending moral support of a kind that no faith had enjoyed before. Humiliations, torture and even death could be viewed with relative equanimity, granted the prospect of eternal bliss thereafter. On earth, too, disciples were given a reassurance that they were the elect of the Lord. He had assured them that they would be able to heal the sick, cast

out devils, speak with tongues, pick up serpents or drink poison
without coming to any harm. And at Pentecost,

> suddenly there came a sound from heaven as of a rushing mighty
> wind, and it filled all the house where they were sitting. And there
> appeared unto them cloven tongues like as of fire, and it lay upon
> each of them. And they were all filled with the Holy Spirit, and
> began to speak with other tongues, as the spirit gave them utterance.

They were not drunk, Peter explained to the bewildered onlookers.
They were fulfilling the words of the prophet that the spirit would
pour forth; 'your sons and daughters shall prophesy, your young men
shall see visions, and your old men shall dream dreams'.

St. Paul

Epidemics of psychic hysteria of this kind had been reported before; in their Bacchic frenzies Dionysius's followers had been given
to prophecy. But Pentecost appeared to offer something more; an
instantaneous transition from man to shaman. Self-discipline was still
required; worldly goods were to be put away, and worldly ambitions,
and the lusts of the flesh. But it was no longer necessary to undergo
the traditional apprenticeship of self-denial and self-mortification. By
materialising on earth, and allowing himself to be crucified, Jesus
had redeemed men from the sins of his forefathers, enabling them
to become possessed by God through the holy spirit, and to enjoy
psychic powers, simply by embracing the faith.

It was the lesson of Pentecost which gave the early Christians their
sense of a common identity, and a common purpose; and in the Acts
they can be seen flexing their new shamanist muscles. Natural and
supernatural elements constantly overlap and interact. Ordered by an
angel to go far out of his way into a desert to find and baptise an
Ethiopian, Philip the Evangelist is miraculously carried back to the
region of Caesarea so that he need waste no time before resuming his
mission; and an angel liberates some of the disciples from prison so
that they can preach in the temple, to the embarrassment of the prison
officers, who find the cells still locked and guarded, but empty. And
the most influential of the new-style shamans emerges: Saul. His
conversion is attended by the traditional signs: a great radiance; a
voice – 'Saul, Saul, why persecutest thou me?'; a trance; and the appearance of the Lord in a vision to a disciple, Ananias, telling him
to go to the street called Straight in order to welcome Saul (who himself would see what was to happen in a precognitive vision) into the
Christian fold. Paul, as he was henceforth known, needed no apprenticeship: he soon found he had psychic powers, worsting a hostile

magician in combat by depriving him for a time of his sight, and performing miracles – including, apparently, materialisations ('from his body were brought unto the sick handkerchiefs, or aprons, and the diseases departed from them'). When Paul and Timothy tried to depart from Bythinia, 'the spirit suffered them not'; and he was later reluctantly compelled to obey the spirit's insistence that he must stay on in Corinth, and risk the consequences of stirring up the wrath of the Jews there by testifying in their synagogue.

The Acts, like the gospels, were a propaganda exercise, so that what is related in them of Paul's early career cannot be relied upon. The Epistles, though, and particularly those to the Corinthians, describe his own experiences, and give his own views, revealing him to be a dedicated spiritist, relying on his daemon. He thought of it not as a spirit, but as *the* spirit – the holy spirit, revealing the word of God to him. When he went to Jerusalem in the middle of the first century A.D. to tell Jesus's followers there that they were wrong to insist that converts must submit to the Jewish rite of circumcision, Paul did not argue with them: according to his account in the Epistle to the Galatians he simply told them that he *knew* they were wrong. 'I certify you, brethren, that the gospel which was preached of me is not after man. For I neither received it of man, nor was I taught it, but by the revelation of Jesus Christ.'

For Paul, then, Christianity was shamanist, relying on inspiration rather than doctrine: 'if you are led by the spirit you are not under the law'. But thanks to Jesus's intervention, there was no longer any need to rely on shamans: any Christian could take advantage of the holy spirit's gifts. To some, Paul explained, the spirit might bring wisdom, or faith; to some, the gift of healing: 'to another, the working of miracles; to another, discerning of spirits; to another, divers kinds of tongues; to another, the interpretations of tongues'. Some individuals might even begin to live a spiritual existence: Paul described one of his acquaintances as having so much spirituality that he had attained to the third heaven while still on earth; 'whether in the body, I cannot tell; or whether out of the body, I cannot tell,' Paul remarked, 'God knoweth'. But all such manifestations were to be valued. When somebody received the gift of tongues, what emerged might sound unintelligible, but it could still be meaningful if it were interpreted. Above all, Paul added – anticipating the neo-Platonists – what mattered was the attitude in which the spirit was invoked, and utilised. Its gifts would serve no good purpose unless suffused with love for others; 'though I have the gift of prophecy, and understand all mysteries, and all knowledge; and though I have faith, so I could move mountains, and have not charity, I am nothing'. That being understood, Paul felt, it was right to welcome spirit possession; 'wherefore, brethren, covet to prophesy, and forbid not to speak with tongues'.

Paul's advice revealed the existence of a problem. Suppose the voices were *not* endowed with charity? He and Timothy had already suffered as a consequence of the jealousy of rivals, as on the occasion in Thyatira when 'a certain damsel possessed with a spirit of divination' followed them around; her employers, who had been making a lot of money out of her, hauled Paul and Timothy before the magistrates, and they were flogged and imprisoned. Yet what she had been saying was not inherently diabolic; 'these men are the servants of the most high God, and show unto us the way of salvation'.

It was at this point that a growing conviction began to harden among Christians into a certainty; that there was an anti-Christ – Satan, or the devil – with a contingent of evil spirits capable of masquerading as the holy spirit, and performing the full repertory of miracles. In Greek mythology it had been the gods themselves who had given lying advice to humans, or materialised for their own lascivious purposes; and in the Old Testament, Satan had needed the Lord's permission to play Job's tempter. But the notion had grown that Satan and his spirits were acting in their own right. When Jesus reminded Peter, 'Satan hath desired to have you' he went on to say not that he had refused the request, but that he had managed to stop Satan by prayer.

Jesus had dealt with Satan's evil spirits by a kind of psychic shock treatment; and Paul followed his example by exorcising the evil spirit in the woman of Thyatira. It could be identified as an evil spirit because of the woman's profession; as a paid clairvoyant, she was obviously not eligible to receive her information from the holy spirit. Satan, in other words, was crafty enough to make those he possessed utter the most impeccably Christian sentiments, if it suited his purpose. 'Beloved, believe not every spirit,' John the Evangelist warned in his first Epistle General: 'But try the spirits whether they are of God; because many false prophets are gone out into the world.' As a simple test John suggested that the holy spirit could be distinguished from a false prophet by putting a simple doctrinal question: 'Every spirit that confesseth not that Jesus Christ is come in the flesh, is not of God; and this is that spirit of anti-Christ.' But Satan, being crafty, could surely answer such questions to the satisfaction of the listeners. 'The sin against the holy spirit' had initially been the sin of refusing to listen to its promptings; but how could any ordinary Christian be sure he was being prompted by the holy spirit, when it might be the devil in disguise?

Chapter Eight

The Early Fathers

UNTIL THE END OF THE SECOND CENTURY CHRISTIANITY REMAINED inspirational. The missionary bishop Irenaus reported from Lyon that many of his flock had prophetic gifts and spoke 'in all kinds of tongues'; and in his petition on behalf of the Christians to Marcus Aurelius the philosopher Athenagorus described their prophets as men who 'being out of themselves and their own thoughts, did utter forth whatsoever by the impelling power of the spirit is wrought in them', God making use of their organs 'even as men do of a trumpet, blowing through it'. But the inspirational element was becoming suspect, because of the difficulty of holding the Church together. The career of Tertullian illustrated the problem. A passionate believer in unity, a rooter-out of heresy, he nevertheless believed in direct communication with God; and 'the idea of a free-lance, self-appointed proclaimer of the truth', as Paul Johnson has put it, 'was, in the end, incompatible with a regular priesthood, charged with the duty of protecting the canon'. When the Montanists were declared heretics, Tertullian denounced them; but eventually he was to join them because he could not continue to endorse an orthodoxy which denied any independent role to the spirit, and insisted that 'all communication with the deity should be through the regular ecclesiastical channels'.

How far even the Montanists had moved from the Christianity of St. Paul is revealed in one of Tertullian's accounts of his community, in which he described a woman who conversed with angels, and sometimes with the Lord: 'she both sees and hears mysterious communications; some men's hearts she understands'; and she claimed frequently to encounter a spirit so material that she could actually grasp it by the hand. What was significant was that Tertullian should have regarded the woman's faculties as unusual. And in more orthodox circles, such inspiration was unwelcome. Inspired prophecy was a threat to order and discipline partly because the prophet had no control over the content of the messages delivered through him; partly because a prophet might pretend to be in the control of the holy spirit when in fact he was propagating heresy. As a result, tracts began to appear with such titles as *Proof that a prophet ought not to speak in a condition of ecstasy*. Possession which took the form of convulsions, in particular, came to be looked on as diabolic; in the fourth century, Cyril, Bishop of Jerusalem, warned that this was how Satan came down,

> like a wolf upon a sheep, ravening for blood and ready to devour. His presence is most cruel; the sense of it most oppressive; the mind is darkened . . . he perverts the tongue and distorts the lips. Foam comes instead of words; the man is filled with darkness; his eye is open, yet his soul sees not through it.

In time, divination as such became suspect. For a while Christians had accepted the genuineness of the oracles: the sibyls 'spake many great things', Justin Martyr claimed, 'with justice and with truth' – a view shared by many of the early fathers, who believed that the oracles had foretold the coming of Jesus. But when the Christians began to make converts throughout the Empire, pagan rivals became a nuisance; and the belief grew that inspirational utterances not clearly identifiable – both by the piety of the medium and by the orthodoxy of the message – as coming from the holy spirit must be considered as the work of a demon; the term which, ironically, came to be used to describe an evil spirit, because of its pagan associations. As soon as the Christians acquired political power they took care to stamp out such oracles as remained.

Divination came to be regarded as respectable only when it occurred spontaneously in circumstances where diabolic intervention was improbable, and where the information obtained was of a kind which the devil could not have had an interest in transmitting; as when, towards the end of the fourth century, Bishop Ambrose of Milan went into a trance as he knelt at the altar and, to the astonishment of the congregation, remained motionless for two or three hours. When he came out of it, he explained that St. Martin of Tours had died, and he had been at the funeral; he then carried on the service from the point where he had left off. When it was found that Martin's funeral had taken place at the time, and as described, this could be held to have been a divine dispensation to Ambrose. Had he not been a bishop, though, and had his 'journey' served a more secular purpose, he would have been more likely to be denounced as a sorcerer.

The same process could be observed in connection with other supernatural phenomena. For a time, Christians had regarded their magic as powerful enough to be confidently pitted against that of pagan competitors; as in St. Jerome's story of the fourth-century hermit Hilarion, who introduced the monastic system into Palestine, and was eventually canonised. Consulted by the Christian owner of a stable of horses used in chariot-racing, whose entries to the Gaza races were always being defeated through the crafts of the local magistrate, Hilarion provided some holy water to be used for scrying – or perhaps as a fetish – to counter whatever magic it was that the magistrate might be employing; the magistrate's chariot duly ran as if the horses were being curbed by an invisible hand, and the Christian chariot surged to victory. But the use of magic for purposes of that kind came to be frowned on. God, it was argued, was capable of taking his own measures, should the need arise.

St. Augustine

The assumption that the supernatural must be divine or diabolic was, however, resisted by one of the early fathers of the Church. God was assuredly almighty, Augustine agreed, 'for no other reason except that he can do whatever he wishes'. Nor were his interventions unnatural; a divine portent 'is not contrary to nature, but contrary to what is *known* of nature'. But the fact that God could and did make his presence felt was not to be taken as implying that he must be responsible for everything which happened contrary to what was known of nature. The condition of ecstasy, for example – in which, though a man's eyes were open, he could not see with them, but instead might 'see' visions, or spirits, or events taking place at a distance – could follow some spiritual experience; but it could also be a symptom of mental disorder. Augustine had encountered a man who had periodically been attacked by manic fits, requiring the attention of the local priest who lived twelve miles away. The sufferer would invariably 'know' when the priest was setting out to come to see him, and would keep up a running commentary on his progress along the route, which appeared to be accurate. This clairvoyance had been attributed to diabolic possession; but Augustine was prepared to accept that it might simply be the madness that gave him clairvoyant powers, and they duly disappeared when he recovered.

Dreams, too, Augustine believed, could provide information beyond the reach of the senses; and one which he recorded was the precursor of many of its kind. A youth had been compelled to pay a debt incurred by his father, who had died, though he was sure his father had paid it. One night he dreamed that his father came to him, and showed him where he would find the receipt; he found it, and was able to get the money back. And an even more remarkable dream story was related by a man whose veracity Augustine felt he could

vouch for. He had asked a specialist on the subject to help him eluci-
date certain passages from Plato; and the specialist had refused. The
student had consequently been surprised when the man appeared
that night, and gave him the information he required. The next time
they met, however, the man flatly denied that he had been round. He
admitted, though, that he *dreamed* that he had gone to the student,
and talked to him; 'thus one may see and hear in a vision,' Augustine
observed, 'that which another has seen or felt in a dream'.

Augustine also accepted that there were certain individuals who,
like the Carthaginian diviner Albicerius, had second sight of a kind
they could demonstrate in tests. Told that something had been lost –
Augustine being careful not to provide any more information –
Albicerius stated that it was a spoon, named its owner, and indicated
where it would be found. Asked what was in the mind of one of
Augustine's students, Albicerius quoted a verse from Virgil, which
was correct. It was not necessary, Augustine felt, to attribute such
gifts to the devil simply because they were not being used in the
service of the Lord; and there were many other manifestations which
could be regarded simply as showing that man had not yet fathomed
all life's mysteries. He was in no doubt that some places were haunted
by the spirits of the dead, and that those spirits could be conjured up
by the living. And although he did not believe that a man could
actually be changed into an animal, like Lucius in *The Golden Ass*,
he was prepared to accept that spirits could materialise, and

when the senses are dulled or deadened can, in some inexplicable
manner, be presented to the senses of others in corporeal form.
Thus, while this body lies somewhere still alive, but with the senses
more strongly bound than during sleep, the phantom of his imagination, incorporated so to speak under the form of some animal, appears to the senses of other people.

Chapter Nine
The Middle Ages

IN HIS ATTITUDE TO THE SUPERNATURAL AUGUSTINE WAS FAR AHEAD of his time. Not until Prospero Lambertini, thirteen hundred years later, was any churchman to discuss the evidence so shrewdly – and so modestly. 'If anyone can trace the causes and modes of operation of these visions and divinations and really understand them,' he remarked, 'I had rather hear his views, than be expected to discuss the subject myself.' Influential though his writings were to be, little attention was then paid to his views on this subject, because they did not suit the new needs of the Church. Visions and prophecies were becoming still more unfashionable because Christianity was systematising itself, as Judaism had done; but even more thoroughly, to meet the requirements of a Church which was becoming also a formidable temporal power. As a hierarchy of popes, bishops, priests and deacons established itself, worship became codified into ritual and formal prayers; and issues which had earlier been referred to the holy spirit, as Paul had recommended, were dealt with by priests relying not on prophetic inspiration but on what the evangelists and their later interpreters laid down. The pentecostal element which had given birth to Christianity did not merely go into abeyance; it came to be treated as a menace to good order and discipline.

Henceforth, the Church taught that what did not come from God must be treated as in all probability coming from the devil; a categorisation which for close on a thousand years meant that the evidence about supernatural phenomena would be at best suspect, and usually worthless. On the one side there were innumerable hagiographical accounts of miracles performed by holy men; on the other, countless reports of the consequences of magic and witchcraft which were clearly fantasies – particularly towards the end of the Middle Ages, when popular superstition about witchcraft became charged with paranoia, and the witch hunts began.

There are, however, some stories which do not immediately excite incredulity. Perhaps owing to Augustine's influence, perhaps because spontaneous divination in dreams occurred too frequently to be automatically reprobated, clairvoyant dreams were allowed to enjoy a measure of toleration as neither divine nor diabolic; as when Dante was forewarned in a dream of the death of Beatrice, and Petrarch, of the death of Laura. Spontaneous clairvoyance might also, it was conceded, serve a secular purpose. When Dante's sons Jacopo and Piero were unable to find some of his cantos which they were collecting after his death for publication, he appeared to Jacopo in a dream to show him where the copies lay mouldering in a secret recess.

If a man were rich and powerful enough he might even enjoy a reputation for second sight, provided he did not allow the suspicion to arise that he was using it to the detriment of some even more powerful rival. In 1385 the chronicler Jean Froissart happened to be staying with the Count de Foix, Governor of the Languedoc, at the time of the struggle for independence by the Portuguese. On the day the decisive battle of Aljuberota was fought, according to Froissart, the Count knew all about it; 'the whole days of Sunday, Monday and the following Tuesday he was in his castle of Orthes, and made such poor and melancholy meals that not one word could be drawn from him'. On the Tuesday evening he called for his brother and told him what he had seen, adding, 'never has the country of Béarn suffered so severely for these hundred years past, as it has now at this battle in Portugal'. Within ten days, the truth was known. 'Is he a wizard, then?' Froissart asked. Raymond, Lord of Carosse, he was told, had a familiar spirit which kept him informed of all that was going on in the world; and the Count, being Raymond's close friend, obtained his knowledge from that source.

Had Raymond been brought up on a charge of necromancy it would have been useless for him to claim that his source was not diabolic. It was, however, conceded that there was one aberrant species of demon, concerned not so much to seduce Christians from their allegiance as simply to make nuisances of themselves. The descriptions often show spirits behaving in what was to become the standard poltergeist manner. The inhabitants of a village near Bingen on the Rhine were plagued in A.D. 858 by bangings, showers of stones, and a voice which purported to tell the guilty secrets of members of the community; and in the twelfth century Giraldus Cambrensis described in his tour of Wales how he had come across two houses in which 'foul spirits have held intercourse with men', making their presence known by throwing lumps of dirt around, as if to express contempt rather than to hurt anybody. In one of the houses they damaged clothes, no matter how carefully they were locked away; 'but what was stranger still, in Stephen's house the spirit used to talk with men, and when people bandied words with it, as many did in mockery, it taxed them with all the things they had ever done in their lives which they were least willing should be known or spoken about'.

Fifty years later William of Auvergne, Bishop of Paris, described similar hauntings, also making the point that considering the barrage to which they were subject, the people involved were surprisingly rarely hurt. This protection did not, however, apply to people assailed by the victims of a different category of demon, which specialised in making the life of holy men and women in monasteries a misery. They were often reported as being the victims of vicious physical assault, like St. Christine of Sommeln, whose invisible assailants banged her head on the wall, slashed her, and spattered her with 'deluges of indescribable filth'.

The decision whether effects which could not be accounted for by any natural cause should be attributed to God, through the agency of the holy spirit, or to the devil, through the agency of his demons, was ordinarily still made on the basis of an assessment of the character of the individual to whom the event occurred and of the results, good or evil, flowing from it. Thus there would be no difficulty accepting as divine the experiences of St. Patrick, as related in the fragment of autobiography attributed to him. After he had been carried away as a youth into slavery in Ireland, he was employed for six years as a herdsman; and in this capacity he underwent the equivalent of a shamanist apprenticeship, by which his spiritual powers were roused 'so that I used even to remain in the woods and in the mountains; before daylight I used to rise to prayer, through snow, through frost, through rain, and felt no harm; nor was there any slothfulness in me, as I now perceive, because the spirit was then fervent within me'. In that condition he became psychic, receiving intimations of impending escape from slavery. One night in his sleep he was informed 'Behold, thy ship is ready'. He thereupon fled, allowing the Lord to direct him some two hundred miles to the coast where he found the ship about to sail. The captain at first refused to take him on board; but the crew, though heathen, 'knew' that they must bring him along with them – a favour which he was to repay after they reached land; when their food ran out, he led them to a herd of swine.

Where a member of the Church appeared to be of impeccable sanctity, too, it was conceded that he might be the recipient of grace in certain tangible, or at least perceptible, forms, most of them familiar from shamanist times. Homer had described how the body of Patroclus had been miraculously preserved from decay; and when the names of men and women were put forward to the Vatican for beatification, the fact that their corpses had shown no sign of putrefaction was one of the most encouraging indicators. Still better was for the corpse to produce the odour of sanctity; a fragrance which was sometimes also reported of the living (Thomas Aquinas, it was claimed, smelled of frankincense). But the most striking ways in which the holy could demonstrate their spirituality were by levitation, and by incombustibility.

Most of the evidence is suspect, for obvious reasons. The Church needed miracles to reassure the faithful – particularly in the fourteenth and fifteenth centuries, when the reputation of the Papacy was at its lowest. 'Men of extraordinary sanctity seemed naturally and habitually to obtain the power of performing them,' Lecky commented in his *History of Rationalism*; 'nothing could be more common than for a holy man to be lifted up from the floor in the midst of his devotions, or to be visited by the virgin, or an angel.' And as the accounts of the miraculous are as stereotyped as those of witchcraft, the tendency has been to dismiss them as the overripe fruits of a prolonged propaganda campaign. There is some evidence, though, that sceptics have been too readily dismissive. Lecky's assumption, for example, that such flights were common (in which he was followed by Edward Tylor, who called it 'a usual attribute of Christian saints') was to be challenged in 1928 by Olivier Leroy, whose research among the records revealed that fewer than one in every two hundred saints in the Christian calendar had been credited with levitation. And the evidence about those few who were, he was able to show, could not always be attributed to the development of posthumous legends. Thomas Aquinas's biographer, a contemporary, claimed to have seen him levitated on a number of occasions; and there were other reasonably well-attested examples. Savonarola's prophecies and levitations had been well-known, hailed as proof of the genuineness of his divine mission while he was in favour; they were hastily cited as proof that he was in league with the devil when he was charged with heresy.

Leroy also deployed a mass of evidence in his *Les Hommes Salamandres*, showing how individuals were continually being called upon to display their ability to resist intense heat, usually in ordeals, and often in the presence of many witnesses. In 1062 a cleric who had become Bishop of Florence by lavish bribery received a challenge from Peter Aldobrandini; when Peter had walked over hot embers along a narrow passage between two fiercely burning bonfires, and his clothes showed no sign of scorching, it was accepted that he had proved his point, and the bishop was deposed – Peter afterwards being canonised. Nearly two hundred years later, in a testimonial to the sanctity of Giovanni Buono, two monks described how they had seen him demonstrate his belief in God's protection by stepping into a fire and shuffling about in it, 'as if washing his feet in a brook', for as long as it would take to say 'half a *Miserere*'. When they examined his feet, they found no trace of burns.

A new variety of miracle was reported for the first time after the death of Francis of Assisi. 'Great joy!' Brother Elias wrote to tell the Provincial of France:

> Great joy, even a new miracle. From the beginning of ages there has not been heard so great a wonder, save only in the Son of God, who is Christ our God. For a long while before his death, our Father and Brother appeared crucified, bearing in his body the five wounds which are verily the Stigmata of the Christ; for his hands and feet had as it were piercings made by nails fixed in from above and below, which laid open the scars and had the black appearance of nails; while his side appeared to have been lanced, and blood often trickled therefrom.

According to Francis's friend and biographer Thomas of Celano, the stigmata had appeared for the first time two years before, and could still be seen on his dead body. In his lifetime Francis had refused to allow his stigmata to be publicised, fearing that they might be regarded with superstitious rather than religious awe; and the tradition established itself that miracles of this kind were best allowed to take place in the privacy of the cell, except where an established tradition like the liquefaction of the blood of St. Januarius was retained by popular demand.

To be credible, miracles had to be spontaneous. They were not to be invoked, except in spiritual self-defence, and then only by the approved methods: the use of holy water, or the sign of the cross, to ward off the attentions of a demon. Amulets and charms were banned; but in their place it was permissible to have a holy medal, a relic of some saint or martyr. Protective magic, in other words, was permissible so long as it was undertaken within the usages and ritual of the Church. But to practise magic arts, or to induce divination by any means such as scrying, was a sin punishable by excommunication, even for the clergy; in the fifth century Bishop Sophronius was charged with scrying, though his object was to discover the identity of a thief. And with the extension of the Church's hold over governments, civil penalties were introduced – fines, corporal punishment and death. The Church passed sentence; the secular arm carried it out.

That divination and magic were assumed to continue, in spite of the dangers, is clear from the continuing efforts of the authorities all over Europe to stamp them out. Charlemagne published many edicts specifying the practices to be condemned: necromancy; the manufacture of images to stick pins into, or to burn; recipes for love-potions; the invocation of demons; the summoning of storms or droughts; the use of spells or incantations; and divination by various means. Whether such practices existed on any substantial scale is difficult to assess. Recent studies of medieval witch hunts, such as those of Norman Cohn and Richard Kieckhefer, leave the impression that eventually attempts to enforce the laws were the consequence of superstitious terrors, rather than the existence of any real threat; terrors reflected even in a gentle devotional tract like *The Cloud of Unknowing*, published in England late in the fourteenth century.

In *The Cloud*, pentecostalism has been watered down to an injunction to approach God through feeling, rather than intellectually, 'by love he can be thought and held, but by thinking never'. The intention to love God, the anonymous author insists, is sufficient; the only aid he is prepared to offer being the use of a short word, like 'GOD', or 'LOVE', to help 'to suppress all thought'. But what seekers after God must *not* do, he insists, is strain as if to see or hear spiritually, or 'to smell and taste and feel and so on inwardly in the same way', because 'at once the devil is able to deceive them with false lights and sounds, sweet odours and tastes'. Thus far, the author is simply providing a mild warning against occult practices and spiritist credulity. But when he goes on to discuss spiritism, he reveals himself as the victim of the Church's conditioning. Demons, he explains, can always be recognised, for a reason which he has heard from practitioners of necromancy,

to whom the fiend has appeared in physical form. In whatever likeness he appears he has never more than one nostril, which is great and wide, and he will gladly turn it up so that a man can see through to his brain. And his brain is nothing else than the fire of hell, for the fiend cannot have any other brain. And if he can make a man look he wants no better. For when he looks he goes mad forever. But your experienced practitioner knows this well enough, and can so order things that he suffers no harm.

Demonology of this kind was to grow still crazier as individual demons began to acquire identities of their own in the literature. Belial, alias Berith, alias Bolfry, ordinarily appeared crowned, riding on a red horse; Cassimilar appeared as a dog, winged like a griffon; Malphas as a crow; Purson as a man with the face of a lion, riding on a bear. What they all had in common was the power to foretell the future, and to enable men to perform magic feats, such as becoming invisible or turning base metals into gold. And the assumption was that all diviners and magicians must either be working with demons, or have mortgaged their souls for demonic power. The published information about divination and magic from official sources consequently became progressively more grotesque. As the prosecutor had to rely, in framing his charges, on what had been published about witchcraft, he would use torture to make the accused confess to a set of standard accusations; and as the torture ordinarily was applied until they confessed, or died, what they said simply echoed the authorities' fears and fantasies. Only a few accounts have been preserved of magical practices which sound as if an actual ceremony is being described; as in one left by the eleventh-century Byzantine philosopher Michel Psellus of a seance where a basin of water was used, which looked no different from any other basin of water, but was inhabited by a resident demon which had the ability

> by the virtue which is infused into it of being able to compose verses, which renders it eminently apt to receive the prophetic spirit. For this sort of demon is capricious, earthbound and subject to enchantment; and as soon as the water begins to give out sounds, manifests its satisfaction to those who are present by some words, still indistinct and meaningless, but later, when the water seems to boil and spill over, a faint voice murmurs words which contain the revelation of future events.

Catharine of Siena; Joan of Arc

Infuriatingly opaque though the evidence about the supernatural is in this period, there are well-attested case histories of two women with psychic powers.

From the correspondence of St. Catharine of Siena, from her *Dialogues* (written, she maintained, not by herself but at the Lord's dictation, 'she being the while entranced'), and from what was written about her (not all of it adulatory; in her brief but crowded public life she undertook projects which made her enemies, such as her visit to Avignon to persuade Pope Gregory to return to Rome in 1376), a coherent portrait emerges, and the psychic element is consistent within it. As a child Catharine had visions and dreams, foretelling her destiny. Her father, who had wanted to marry her off, relented when one day he saw her apparently radiating light from her body. After three years' withdrawal from any contact with the world Catharine was told by the Lord, with whom she believed herself to be continually in communication through clairaudience, that she must go out and begin to rescue souls; and one of the ways in which she was able to fulfil this purpose was by clairvoyance, which often enabled her to detect what people were doing or thinking even if they were determined to disguise it from her. When one of her converts became involved in a plot against the government, the conspirators holding 'prayer meetings' in a Siena church as their cover, she divined what was happening: 'Is it thus that you change the house of God,' she asked him, 'into a work-shop for treason?' Francesco Malevolti, a young aristocrat whom she had rescued from a life of dissipation, allowed himself to relapse; she warned him that he could do nothing without her knowing about it, and that he ought to confess. 'When I heard her tell me precisely all that I had done and said,' Malevolti recalled, 'confused and shamed, and without an answer, at once and heedfully I fulfilled her command.' Such information, he realised, could reach her only from the Lord or the devil; and if the devil were responsible, why would he transmit the information to Catharine, and thereby lose his hold over the man he was trying to seduce?

Sometimes in her trances Catharine appeared to those with her to be irradiant; sometimes a fragrance wafted from her. By her own account, given to her confessor, her body on one occasion bore stigmata; but she would not display them, praying that only the pain of them would remain as evidence, because otherwise they might excite super-stitious reverence of a kind she, like St. Francis, mistrusted. And on another occasion, while she was rapt in one of her frequent ecstasies, her clothes were set alight by a candle flame; but the nun who rescued her reported that no damage had been done either to her body or to her clothes.

The quality as well as the quantity of the source material about Catharine's supernatural attributes makes her case unusual for its time; but it does not compare, historically, with the available evidence about Joan of Arc, half a century later. Much of what was written about Joan by contemporary observers, detractors and admirers has survived, as well as the detailed records of her examinations after she was cap-tured, of her trial in 1431, and of the legal process by which she was rehabilitated twenty years later. These documents have been frequently sifted by biographers and historians from a variety of points of view; and on one issue all but the most hardened sceptics have agreed. 'No man,' as Anatole France put it, 'can suspect her of falsehood.'

By her own account, Joan first 'heard' voices, which she assumed were from God, when she was about thirteen. Later she had visions in which she saw the Archangel Michael, who introduced her to St. Margaret and St. Catharine of Alexandria (herself reputedly a miracle worker; when she was sentenced to be broken on the wheel, it was the wheel which had broken). The saints, Joan claimed, could manifest themselves to any of her senses; she could hear them, and touch them, and they gave off a fragrant odour. But she was not possessed. She re-tained her ordinary faculties; she could interrupt whatever she was do-ing to consult with them, and report what they said if they interrupted her while she was involved in some task or discussion. Constantly they advised her what she must do. It was they who told her to go to Robert de Baudricourt to persuade him to lead her to the Dauphin; and she won over the Dauphin, according to his confidant Jean Dunois, by telling him 'matters so secret and hidden that no mortal except himself could know them save by divine revelation'.

Joan's voices provided her with a kind of travelling clairaudience. When they told her that she would find a sword in the Church of St. Catherine of Fierbois, behind the altar, she wrote to the clergy there; a search behind the altar revealed a rusty sword. The voices were also precognitive. The best known examples of her prophetic ability are the least convincing; her forecast of a change of wind, which enabled Dunois to sail across the river at Orleans, might have been peasant intuition; and her statement at her trial that before seven years were past the English would lose a greater stake than they had at Orleans, though correct – they lost Paris in 1436 – was hardly explicit. But some of her prophetic utterances resist any natural explanation, except farfetched coincidence. Her forecast to the Dauphin of how she was going to be wounded by an arrow or bolt at the siege of Orleans was recorded in writing by a Flemish diplomat a fortnight before she was actually wounded in the way she had described.

The information which has survived about Joan's psychic powers, therefore, is more detailed, better attested, and more convincing than about any earlier individual in history. The allowances which ordinarily have to be made for information extracted in the court proceedings are not here required; if she had been prepared to lie, either voluntarily or under duress, she would certainly not have taken the line she did. Her apologia, still in existence, in the *procès verbal*, impressed Frederic Myers because of its resemblance to that of Socrates.

> in its resolute insistence on the truth of the very phenomena which were being used to destroy her. Her answers are clear and self-consistent, and seem to have been little, if at all, distorted by the recorder. Few pieces of history so remote as this can be so accurately known.

From the Renaissance to the Age of Reason

Chapter Ten
Alchemy

DURING THE TWELFTH CENTURY A SCHOOL OF TRANSLATION WHICH
had been established at Toledo began to make Arabic works available
to Europeans; and some of them dealt with the supernatural. In Islam,
it was largely a tabooed subject. Mahomet himself had been a prophet
in the shamanist tradition. He would hear what sounded like a tolling
bell which sent him into a trance, during which he would receive
revelations. Sometimes angels would appear to him and talk with him:
the Koran was dictated to him in this manner. Later authorities were
to embroider these stories, describing how God had communicated
to him; and the familiar tales of signs, wonders and miracles were
linked with him. Mahomet himself, however, mistrusted ecstasy as a
route for his disciples; and although some sects preserved shamanist
practices orthodox Muslims, like orthodox Christians, eventually
settled for routine ceremonies and rituals. But among the works the
Moors brought with them to Spain were Hermetic tracts, expounding
shamanist ideas derived from Plato and the neo-Platonists, from the
Pythagoreans, Egyptians and Babylonians; and eventually in the mid-
fifteenth century the *Corpus Hermeticum* was translated, on the orders
of Cosimo de Medici, to become the occultists' Bible.

Alongside and intertwined with the Hermetic tradition was the
Cabala, Jewish in origin, shrouded in secrecy – it was supposed to
have been passed on down the generations only by word of mouth –
with magical theories and practices also derived from shamanism;
and alchemy, basically chemistry, but chemistry of a kind which
allowed for the possibility that subjective, spiritual or magical influences might be a component. The discovery that two inert substances,
brought together, could react explosively to produce a third had promoted the belief that experiment, guided by inspiration, would lead
to the discovery of a catalyst, the philosopher's stone, capable of
transmuting base metals into gold, or manufacturing an elixir of life.

These were the alchemist's fantasies; most of his actual work was conducted on what would now be regarded as orthodox lines. It was consequently possible for orthodox Christians, even divines, to take up alchemy without incurring the authorities' displeasure. When Michael Scot brought back translations of alchemical works from Toledo early in the thirteenth century their publication did not jeopardise his career as adviser to Frederick II; nor did the alchemical studies of Albertus Magnus, later in the century, harm his career or reputation (though later, both retrospectively came to be regarded as magicians). The formulae and laboratory instruments of the alchemist were not repugnant to the Church in the way that spiritism and necromancy were; and to rulers the prospect of a cheap source of gold, which always appeared to be just around the corner, was perennially attractive.

How far the psychic element in the Hermetic tradition could be put to practical use eludes discovery. Books on the subject, and they have been numerous, have tended to concentrate on the mathematical formulae, the symbols, the incantations, and anything which can be found which purported to describe the processes involved. But the two opposed meanings of the Cabalist term 'abracadabra' succinctly express the difficulty of getting at the realities. Written down, in various arrangements of the letters, 'abracadabra' served an incantatory function designed to stimulate or concentrate psychic forces; but it came to be colloquially a synonym for gibberish – as, divorced from its context, it must often have been.

The closer alchemists came to describing the psychic or magical element, the more guarded they became; excusing themselves, as Roger Bacon did, by claiming that it was desirable 'to hide the discoveries of the wise from a multitude unworthy to possess them', but doubtless chiefly concerned to preserve professional secrets – and in some cases, to avoid being accused of witchcraft. The writings of Scot, Albertus, Roger Bacon, Raymond Lully and others, though some of them claimed to have witnessed the conversion of base metals into gold (or themselves to have effected that conversion) contain no trustworthy evidence of any such achievement.

In 1531, however, the first of a three-volume work on occult philosophies was published which heralded an impending change. Cornelius Agrippa had been in the service of the Emperor Maximilian, first as a secretary and later as a soldier, before he began to study Cabalist lore; and to interest himself in the wider aspects of magic. As he told Abbot John of Trittenheim, a sympathetic listener, the fact that so much of the information was wrapped around in secrecy, and suspect because of its links with necromancy and sorcery, was no reason why magic should not be reconciled with Christianity. If Christianity had taken Aristotle to its bosom, why not the new neo-Platonists, too? His primary task, therefore, would be to try to find

> why magic itself – though formerly by the common consent of all ancient philosophers it was regarded as the first step upward, and was held always in the highest veneration by the wise men and the priests of old – should have become from the beginning of the growth of the Catholic Church hated and suspected by the holy fathers, at length exploded by the theologians, condemned by the sacred canons, and at last proscribed by every sort of law.

Agrippa's study of the subject led him to believe that those who had written on it in the preceding three centuries 'have either supplied idle matter without any connecting system, or else have published superstitions not to be received by honest men'; and he had determined to 'vindicate against the ill words of calumniators and restore that ancient magic, studied by all the wise, purged and freed from the errors of impiety, and adorned with its own reasonable system'. Agrippa's three books – the first setting out what was known about ancient magic, the second describing the mathematical principles involved, and the third discussing the relationship of magic to religion – were themselves heavily laden with idle matter and superstitions of earlier writers, many of them hardly above the level of the witches' recipe in *Macbeth*; but they did represent a serious effort to explain the occult in rational terms. The powers of the spirit, Agrippa felt, must be diffused through everything, everywhere, through the celestial bodies as well as the world, its inhabitants, its animals, and its inanimate properties. That was why the alchemist could influence herbs, or metals; and why, if he could master the process, he could convert base metals into gold. It was also why people could communicate even when at a distance.

> The form of things, though by their own nature they are conveyed to the senses of men and animals, can, however, while they are in the air, receive a certain impression from the heavens, by means of which, as also by the fitness deriving from the recipients' disposition, they may be transmitted to the senses of one recipient rather than another. Hence it is possible naturally, without any kind of superstition, and through the mediation of no other spirit, for a man to convey such thoughts to someone else in a very short time, however far apart they may be from one another.

Philosophy and religion could not be complete, Agrippa held, unless they took this power into consideration.

Agrippa's contemporary Paracelsus had similar ideas, but a deeper insight. Like Agrippa, he thought that belief in the Cabala involved no repudiation either of Christianity – it was 'beholden to God, in alliance with him, and founded on the words of Christ' – or of science, provided that the magician or alchemist had learned how to control the forces involved, which required training and dedication; the magi being 'holy men in God who serve the forces of nature', rather than sorcerers serving their own ends. Given the training and the purpose, Paracelsus believed, dreams could be correctly interpreted, future events forecast, and buried treasure found; 'by the magic power of the imagination', too, 'a person on this side of the ocean may make a person on the other side hear what is said on this side'. Such feats might also be achieved by sorcery; but in that case the information provided could not be relied upon, because 'you will be led by that spirit which tells you nothing but lies'.

Agrippa and Paracelsus, then, were both seeking to establish divination and magic as natural. But they found themselves up against formidable opposition. The Church, assailed by reformers – Luther nailed his theses to the church door in Wittenburg in 1517 – was no longer disposed to be tolerant of alchemy, still less of magic. Agrippa's aim might be to reconcile magic and Christianity; but it could be made to sound as if it were an attempt to water down the supernatural element, and by extension, God's role. Greatly though he admired Agrippa, Abbot John had realised the danger: 'speak of things public to the public,' he had warned, 'but of things lofty and secret only to the loftiest and the most private of your friends. Hay to an ox, and sugar to a parrot; rightly interpret this lest you, as some others have been, be trampled down by oxen.' It was too late; the oxen, led by the head of the Franciscan Order in Burgundy, were ready to stampede. On the threshold of a successful career – he had been elected Regent by the University of Dole, and had just married an eligible and beautiful wife – Agrippa was compelled to uproot himself, becoming for the rest of his life a wanderer, until he died in 1535. Paracelsus was similarly hounded from city to city (though more on account of this unorthodox views about medicine and his truculence in expressing them) until his death six years later.

Nostradamus; John Dee

Although Agrippa won the reputation of being a magician, there is no reliable account of what, if anything, he actually did. But some of his successors left evidence of their psychic activities: notably Nostradamus and John Dee.

Michael Nostradamus, born in 1503, had seemed set for a conventional career as a physician in Provence until the plague carried off his wife and children; disheartened, he too became a wanderer. In the course of his travels he found he was clairvoyant; and in 1555 he published *Centuries*, quatrains describing events which were going to take place in France and elsewhere in Europe over the next few hundred years. In the tradition of the Cabala, Nostradamus used various devices such as anagrams and 'abstruse and twisted sentences' to leave his meaning 'cloudy rather than plainly prophetic'; and this has left room for endless interpretations, often too ingenious for comfort. Nevertheless, as James Laver showed in his analysis of them, the number of palpable hits is astonishing.

Some prophecies were fulfilled within his lifetime:

> *Le lyon jeune le vieux surmontera*
> *En champ bellique par singulier duelle*
> *Dans cage d'or les yeux luy crevera*
> *Deux classes une, puis mourir, mort cruelle.*

(The young lion shall overcome the old in warlike field in single fight. In a cage of gold, his eyes will be pierced, two wounds in one, then die a cruel death.)

In 1559 King Henri II was jousting with Montgomery, the Captain of his Scots guard, when the splintered shaft of Montgomery's lance penetrated the king's cage-like helm, beneath its gilt visor, wounding him in the eye and throat. Ten days later he died; and Nostradamus's quatrain was recalled. Echoes of Nostradamus's quatrains continued to be heard in ways which defied rational explanation:

> When Innocent shall hold the place of Peter
> The Sicilian Nizaram shall see himself
> In great honours, but after that shall fall
> Into the dirt of civil war.

When in 1644 Innocent X became Pope, Mazarin, a Sicilian, had just succeeded Richelieu; and Nizaram was an anagram of his name. Four years later, when Mazarin appeared to be firmly in control, civil war – the Fronde – broke out, compelling the Court to flee from Paris. But the most celebrated of Nostradamus's predictions relate to the French Revolution, an event he actually dated. One quatrain ran:

> *De nuict viendra par la forest de Reines*
> *Deux pars, vaultorte, Herne la pierre blanche*
> *Le Moyne noir en gris dedans Varennes*
> *Esleu Cap, cause tempeste, feu, sang, tranche.*

(By night will come into Varennes through the forest of Reines two married people, by a circuitous route, Herne, the white stone the Monk in Grey, the elected Capet; and the result will be tempest, fire, blood, slice.)

On June 20th, 1792 Louis XVIII (Louis Capet: Nostradamus used 'Cap' elsewhere as an abbreviation), the first king of France to hold his throne through the vote of an Assembly, left Paris (dressed in grey) with Marie Antoinette (in white) and their family, to try to get through to the émigré army awaiting them to the east of Rheims. They went by a roundabout route through Varennes; and there they were stopped. The flight did more than any other action to discredit Louis, and set in train the events which were to lead to the 'slice' of the guillotine which ended both their lives.

Remarkable though Nostradamus's prophecies were, however, little is known – other than that he became entranced – of how he set about producing them. The only Cabalist from this era who left records of his divinatory methods which have survived was John Dee: astrologer to Queen Elizabeth, and also her special agent, employed to find out what was being plotted on the Continent: 'my noble intelligencer', the Queen called him; 'my ubiquitous eyes' (strangely, his code name was '007', chosen by Ian Fleming four hundred years later for James Bond).

A mathematician and astronomer, Dee had been influenced in his youth by Cornelius Agrippa. He accepted the existence of a sixth sense which could emerge spontaneously, in dreams, in visions, or simply in intuitions; and he believed that it could be tapped, using the techniques of the Cabala. One of them, with which he experimented, was the use of a divining rod, or a pendulum. He was careful to insist that this was not witchcraft; 'some persons,' he explained to Lord Burleigh, 'have super-normal powers not of a magician, but of a peculiar and scientific quality.' Had his services not been in demand by the Queen, this might not have protected him; as it was, he was left to conduct his experiments, and to prove that 'he did most miraculously have the divining power' (or so the woman who looked after him in his old age assured John Aubrey), 'with his divining rod he brought back to many people silver and other objects which had been missing, sometimes for years'.

In the 1580s Dee began to experiment with a different technique. 'I had sight offered me in crystal,' he noted in his diary, 'and I saw.' He did not 'see' very much; he was later to admit 'you know I cannot see or scry'. But what he saw was enough to fire him with the idea of employing someone who could scry on his behalf; and he found Edward Kelley, who could communicate with the spirits – a Greek peasant woman, and several others – and report what they told him in answer to Dee's questions. Untrustworthy though Kelley was, one of the methods Dee adopted precluded cheating; he persuaded the spirits to answer in a code which Kelley did not know, and which Dee himself had laboriously to decipher. The spirit utterances, which Dee meticulously recorded, were rarely illuminating; and though they could be 'merry and naughty', which intrigued Dee, they bored Kelley. He left his employer to try his hand at alchemy, claiming to be able to transmute other metals into gold; and Dee was unable to find another scryer. Still, the research the two men did together, unproductive though it proved to be, was a serious scientific attempt to explore the processes by which divination functioned.

Chapter Eleven

Miracles

THE SIXTEENTH-CENTURY CABALISTS PRESENTED A DUAL THREAT TO the Church: they were either diabolists, working for the anti-Christ, or rationalists, whittling down divine authority. Where it could, it continued to persecute them. For fifteen years Giordano Bruno, a Dominican friar who had become fascinated by the teachings of the neo-Platonists and of the Cabala, roamed Europe expounding his ideas in lectures and in salons, insisting among other arguments that magic was a natural operation whose character would eventually be understood; but in 1592 he fell into the hands of the Inquisition in Venice and after seven years' imprisonment in Rome he was burned at the stake. His career, however, had shown how easy it was by that time for a scholar to find sanctuary even if his views were anathema to the authorities (and to students; his contempt for Aristotle was unfashionable and unpopular) and his manner arrogant and tactless; although he was always soon in trouble wherever he went, he was able to move on to find new patrons. The Church, deprived of its hold over heretics, had to fall back on making the most of its own miracles for propaganda purposes; presenting them as much more spectacular than anything the Cabalists could boast. The evidence consequently remains suspect. But it cannot simply be ignored, on this account, as two writers who tried to sort out the historical from the hagiographical were to show: Olivier Leroy, in France; and the Rev. Herbert Thurston, S.J., in Britain, in a series of papers collected and published posthumously in 1952 as *The Physical Phenomena of Mysticism*.

Thurston's attitude was summed up in his comment that 'no Christian would question, in the abstract, God's power if it pleased Him to make a new leg or arm grow in the place of one that had been amputated; but in the concrete, we might reasonably demand the production of very unexceptional evidence before a miracle so unexampled in all recorded history could expect to gain credence'. The chief weakness of much of the evidence, Thurston felt, was that hagiographers had paid insufficient attention to what had *not* been written about saints, by their contemporaries. The levitations of St. Francis of Assisi, for example, and of St. Dominic, were famous; but the first accounts of them had not appeared until many years after their respective deaths; was it really conceivable that their intimate friends and fellow-workers, who had testified to their other miracles during their lifetime or immediately after their death, would not have mentioned levitation, if they believed it had happened?

St. Teresa of Avila

This did not mean, Thurston was careful to insist, that later hearsay evidence was necessarily false. But it did mean that 'we cannot appeal to such cases if we wish to convince a sceptical opponent of the truth of the phenomena'. So he set himself a task similar to that performed by the *Promotor Fidei*, or Devil's Advocate. And in connection with levitations he came to the conclusion that the evidence before the Reformation was generally inadequate, except in the cases of Edmund of Canterbury and Catharine of Siena. In the sixteenth century, however, with St. Teresa of Avila, it took on a new complexion. Her levitations had been reported by a number of eyewitnesses. Sister Anne of the Incarnation had been standing near where Teresa was praying, in daylight, when Teresa

> was raised about half a yard from the ground without her feet touching it. At this I was terrified and she, for her part, was trembling all over. So I moved over to where she was and I put my hands under her feet, over which I remained weeping for something like half an hour while the ecstasy lasted. Then suddenly she sank down and rested on her feet and turning her head round to me, she asked me who I was, and whether I had been there all the while. I said yes, and then she ordered me under obedience to say nothing of what I had seen.

As Anne had obeyed, her testimony was not given until informations were taken thirteen years after Teresa's death; but a number of witnesses independently produced comparable examples. A bishop recalled how Teresa had been levitated just after she had received communion from him through an aperture in the choir wall; he had seen her desperately clutching at the grille to try to stop herself floating up. On another occasion, she had grasped at some mats covering the floor, and rose with them still in her hands.

The most convincing account of St. Teresa's levitations, though, is her own. Ecstasy, she explained in her *Life*, would come on her irresistibly, before she had time to collect her thoughts. Sometimes she would try to stop it: either when she felt it coming on in public, for fear of embarrassment; or when she was alone, for fear of delusions. Occasionally she was able to make some slight resistance, though it was like wrestling with a giant. But at other times

> it was impossible to resist at all; my soul was carried away, and almost always my head with it – and now and then my whole body as well, so that it was lifted up from the ground.
>
> This has not happened to me often. Once, however, it took place when we were all together in Choir, and I, on my knees, on the point of communicating. It was a very sore distress to me, for I thought it a most extraordinary thing, and was afraid it would occasion much talk; so I commanded the nuns – for it happened after I was made prioress – never to speak of it. But at other times, the moment that I felt that our Lord was about to repeat the act (and once, in particular, during a sermon; it was the feast of our House, some great ladies being present) I threw myself on the ground. Then the nuns came round to hold me; but still the rapture was observed . . .
>
> I confess that it threw me into great fear, very great indeed at first; for when I saw my body lifted up from the earth, how could I help it? Though the spirit draws it upwards after itself, and that with great sweetness if unresisted, the senses are not lost; at least, I was so much myself as to be able to see that I was being lifted up.

Teresa's contemporary St. Philip Neri – whom several witnesses, including a cardinal, watched when he rose almost up to the ceiling – also described how it felt; it was 'as if he had been caught hold of by somebody and wonderfully lifted above the ground'. But this was reported by one of his colleagues; whereas there is a copy of Teresa's account of her feelings in her own handwriting, submitted to the Inquisition's censors seven years before her death, and accepted by them, which it certainly would not have been had they felt any doubts about her.

St. Joseph of Copertino

A weakness of the eye-witness's testimonies about St. Teresa's levitations is that they all came from people who believed in her. This cannot be held against the evidence for the levitations of Joseph of Copertino.

As a youth, Joseph had been thought soft in the head; and though his piety was not in question, confirmed as it was by the unremitting vigour with which he flagellated himself, he could not persuade the

Capuchins to accept him, and had to settle for the Copertino Franciscans. In the 1630s he began to exhibit psychic powers. He could read the thoughts of penitents, so that he knew when they were holding back confessions which they ought to be making; and he began to levitate. At a service to celebrate the Feast of the Nativity – one of the congregation deposed –

suddenly he gave a sob, then a great cry, and at the same time he was raised in the air, flying from the middle of the church to the high altar, where he embraced the tabernacle. Now, from the middle of the church to the high altar, the distance is about forty feet. A most wonderful thing is that the altar being covered with lighted candles, Brother Joseph flew and alighted among those candles and threw down neither a candle nor a candlestick. He remained thus about a quarter of an hour, kneeling and embracing the tabernacle, and then came down without being helped by anybody and did not disturb anything.

So far from regarding Joseph's levitations as proof of his sanctity, and exploiting them as miracles, his superiors found them embarrassing – as indeed they sometimes were: on one occasion when he was floating in mid-air before the altar where the Sacrament lay, his sandals fell off. Joseph himself was apologetic about his fits of 'giddiness', as he described them; and he submitted to punitive disciplinary measure. At various times he was banned from participating in masses where the public might be present, from choir practices, from processions, even from refectory meals; and he was investigated by the Inquisition. But his levitations continued. The presence of an image of the Virgin seemed to render him particularly susceptible, fifteen flights being recorded; but his ecstasy could be inspired by a casual remark. When a priest, while they were out walking, happened to say to him, 'Brother Joseph, what a beautiful heaven God has made!' Joseph soared into a tree, where he remained for half an hour kneeling, the branch on which he was perched gently swaying, as if a bird had alighted on it (when he came out of his trance, he was helpless; he could not get down until a ladder had been fetched). And on several occasions he was able to carry up somebody else with him, by the hand or by the hair, on his 'flights'.

These testimonies were collected in Joseph's lifetime, or immediately after his death; and the witnesses included a number of men of standing, including Pope Urban VIII (granted an audience at the Vatican, Joseph was so moved that he took off in the middle of it and remained aloft until ordered by his Superior to come down). The High Admiral of Castile, Spanish Ambassador to the Papal Court, who went to see

Joseph in Assisi, watched him fly to a statue of the Immaculate Conception over the heads of the bystanders and back again (to the stupefaction of the Ambassador's wife, who had to be revived with smelling salts). The Lutheran John Frederick, Duke of Brunswick, was standing by the door of a chapel where mass was being said when Joseph was lifted into the air, carrying the Host with him; thereby causing the Duke to abjure his faith and to become a Catholic. And shortly before Joseph died, doctors called in to operate on him noticed when they cauterised the wound that the patient, so far from being in pain, was 'rapt in ecstasy' and 'actually suspended in mid-air', where he floated for a quarter of an hour.

The evidence for the levitations of Joseph, therefore, is unusually varied; strong enough to impress even the man who in the twentieth century was to play the part of Devil's Advocate for the Society of Psychical Research, Dr. E. J. Dingwall. Making all possible allowances for exaggeration, Dingwall conceded, it was not easy to ignore such a remarkable range of testimony, particularly that which came from lay sources. And there are other accounts of levitation from the period which are also hard to dismiss because of the quality rather than the quantity of the evidence; such as the case of the Spanish-Jewish theologian Fr. Francis Suarez, S.J., testified to by only a single witness, Fr. Jerome da Silva. Asked by the Rector of the University of Salamanca to take a message to Suarez, da Silva found him entranced

> in a kneeling position in front of the crucifix, his head uncovered, his hands joined, and his body in the air lifted three feet above the floor on a level with the table on which the crucifix stood. On seeing this I withdrew, but before quitting the room I stopped bewildered, and as it were beside myself, leaning against the door-post for the space of three Credos. Then I went out, my hair standing on end like the bristles of a brush.

When Suarez realised that da Silva had seen what had happened, he begged him not to speak of it to anybody except their confessor; and the confessor agreed it should not be reported. But he asked da Silva, who was in poor health and unlikely to live, to write down what had happened; and the account, written at the time, was revealed after Suarez's death in 1671.

Reports of this kind, as Leroy observed, though they may conceivably be the result of illusion or fraud, cannot be dismissed as the product of legend or popular rumour; nor can some of the testimony about other kinds of miracles in beatification procedures. Among the most frequently reported were visions of men seen by friends at the time of their death – several people 'saw' St. Philip Neri in their rooms when he was dying in his own: clairvoyance – a cardinal described how St. Philip, who 'saw my secret sins before I had confessed them', had explained to him that the knowledge had come to him in prayer; the odour of sanctity – a curious feature being that the sweet perfumes described were often connected with the onset of a fatal illness, and that they lingered on in their cells after death; incorruptibility – the corpse resisting putrefaction; irradiance, or luminosity; incombustibility; and the stigmata.

With the stigmata, the Church found itself confronted with a new problem: how to be sure that they were not counterfeit. And it is at this point that the reliability of the evidence begins to become even harder to assess, not simply because of doubts about the honesty of the stigmatics, but also because of doubts about the purity of the motives of those who investigated them, particularly in two notorious cases where nuns were accused of having cheated: Magadalena de la Cruz, deposed and disciplined after confessing to deceit during an illness in 1543; and 'the holy nun of Lisbon', Maria de la Visitaçion, discredited half a century later.

Maria was still in her early thirties when elected Prioress of the convent of Annunciation, and the appearance of the stigmata confirmed her reputation for sanctity; in 1587 they were examined by the General of the Dominicans, who pronounced them indisputably genuine; and the following year Maria was given the honour of blessing the Armada before it set sail. But when the Inquisition investigated her, by the rough and ready method of scrubbing her hands in soapy water, the 'wounds' were attributed to paint. Maria was sentenced to perpetual imprisonment with a variety of disciplines, of which one of the less painful was having to lie on the refectory floor, before and after meals, for the nuns to step over her on their way in and out.

'That some instances of alleged stigmatisation are simply fraudulent,' Thurston conceded when he first wrote about the case, 'is not to be disputed,' and he cited Maria and Magdalena as 'two notorious religious impostors'. Had he lived to revise the essay he would surely have modified that statement, in view of the doubts which he later began to feel about the Inquisition's part in the affair. So long as Maria had remained in favour with Philip II her sanctity had not been questioned. But the shattering of the Armada left Philip's position in Portugal more precarious, and Maria was known to favour the independence party there. The Spanish Inquisition was under Philip's direct control, and nothing in his record suggests that he would have had any scruples about using it to destroy Maria's reputation. And if Maria had been cheating, she would hardly have been so stupid as to try to deceive the Inquisitors, when all she needed to do was tell them that the stigmata could not be summoned at will. Why, then, did she confess? Presumably because she must have known what awaited her if she did not confess. Hypocritical, even blasphemous, practices did not involve any denial of the Faith. The culprit might have to face the severest ecclesiastical penalties; but there would be no risk of being handed over to the secular arm, to be burned in an *auto da fé*. It is an early cautionary tale: a warning that the motives of investigators of psychic phenomena need to be checked with the same care as the motives of those by whom the phenomena are produced.

For reasons which were to become clear centuries later, the stigmata were in any case an unreliable indicator of either sanctity or supernatural powers; and surveying all the phenomena, Thurston felt that the evidence in their favour was most convincing in connection with levitations. For the other miracles a variety of natural explanations were theoretically possible; but only mass hallucination could account which showed discretion: the quiet elevation, say, of a monk at prayer. Joseph overdid it, and was clearly an embarrassment to them; the stories about him gain credence from the fact that they were not even be cited as evidence of the miraculous in beatification testimonies. This would not, and did not, prevent the Church exploiting them on the side, as it were. But the authorities clearly preferred the kind of account which showed discretion: the quiet elevation, say, of a monk at prayer. Joseph overdid it, and was clearly an embarrassment to them; the stories about him gain credence from the fact that they were not the kind which would have been invented to promote his beatification.

For the same reason, Thurston argued, reports of supernatural effects which were not of a kind which would impress observers as evidence of spirituality are more impressive as evidence than, say, bodily incorruptibility; and there was one manifestation 'which no devout client would be likely to invent in order to demonstrate the sanctity of the particular object of his veneration'; elongations, of the kind Iamblichus had mentioned. In the reports presented for the purpose of securing beatifications there are several references to them, notably the case of Sister Veronica Laparelli, who died in 1620. A number of witnesses testified that in her trances, she appeared to grow taller; a yardstick had been taken to her, on one occasion, and shown a difference of ten inches. Far from this helping her cause it was singled out by the Devil's Advocate not merely as incongruous and improbable, but as serving no edifying purpose. Yet such elongations continued to be reported, along with other distortions which, as described, sound as if some invisible force were pulling or twisting the body out of its normal shape.

Protestants and Puritans

The Protestant attitude to the supernatural had been foreshadowed

towards the end of the fourteenth century in one of the Twelve Conclusions adopted by the British Lollards: that

> exorcisms and hallowings, made in the Church, of wine, bread and
> wax, water, salt and oil and incense, and the stone of the altar, upon
> vestments, mitre, cross and pilgrims' staves, be the very practice
> of necromancy, rather than of the holy theology. This conclusion
> is proved thus. For by such exorcisms creatures be charged to be of
> higher virtue than their own kind, and we see nothing of change in
> no such creature that is so charmed, but by false belief, the which
> is the principle of the devil's craft.

What the Lollards were asserting was that God was perfectly capable of looking after his own, without the intervention of a priest
acting as a medium and pretending to be able to exercise magic
powers which he did not possess. They did not, however, dispute that
the devil enjoyed supernatural powers which his demons could supply
for the benefit of witches and necromancers; and the early Protestants
took the same stance. Visitors to the castle at Wurtzburg were shown
a black stain left by an ink bottle which Luther had thrown at the
devil, in exasperation; Luther's assumption being that the devil could
not merely tempt people into sin, but could give them the power to
see distant events, or to fly through the air. The Protestants, however,
rejected the use of counter-magic. Traditional rituals such as con-
secrations or the sign of the cross were banished, along with holy
water and the relics of saints. As Thomas Hobbes was to explain in
Leviathan, the mistake had been to invest such things with power.
'To *consecrate*,' he argued, 'is in Scripture to offer, give or dedicate,
in pious and decent language and gesture, a man or any other thing,
to God, by separating it from the common use.' But the change was
only in the *use*; not in the thing consecrated. The Catholic Church
pretended that an actual change occurred in the thing; but this was
'no other than a conjuration or incantation' enabling the priests to
pretend, 'conrtary to the testimony of men's sight and all the rest of
his senses', that a change of nature had occurred which had not in
fact occurred.

But if counter-magic were rejected, it was a short step to casting
doubt on the existence of magic of any kind, including witchcraft;
and this led to a more critical scrutiny of the states of mind associated
with the supernatural: trances, possession, ecstasy. The Dutch
physician Johan Weyer, often credited with being the founder of
modern psychiatry, began the process in 1563 by suggesting that dissociation and possession could be a form of mental illness; and a century later the Anglican clergyman Meric Casaubon added ecstasy to

this category, arguing that it was simply a species of epilepsy. Although neither Weyer nor Casaubon could be described as sceptics – Weyer believed in diabolic possession; Casaubon accepted that spirits might be involved in divination – they reflected the trend towards the rejection not merely of the devil and all his works, but of the supernatural.

Scepticism put down roots most quickly in England, as revealed in an aside in Izaak Walton's biography of John Donne in 1640. Walton described how Donne, who was in Paris, had a vision of his wife, who was in London, with a dead child in her arms. There could be no doubt of the authenticity of the story; a messenger who had been despatched back to London to find out if all was well had returned to Paris to confirm that on the day, and at about the hour, of the vision, Donne's wife had been delivered of a still-born son. Yet Walton admitted that the fact he recorded the story would cause some surprise, 'for most of our world are at present possessed with an opinion that visions and miracles are ceased'. Although he tentatively suggested an explanatory analogy – that if two lutes are strung and tuned to equal pitch and one is played upon, the other will answer with a faint but audible harmony – he clearly did not expect many of his readers to accept that a parallel 'sympathy of souls' existed. And in *Leviathan* in 1651 Hobbes bluntly stated the sceptics' case. There was no need to believe anecdotal evidence for divination; 'if a man pretend to me that God has spoken supernaturally, and I make doubt of it, I cannot easily perceive what argument he can produce to oblige me to believe it.'

Where the miraculous was not actually dismissed, it could sometimes be secularised; a process illustrated in John Evelyn's diary. On October 8th, 1672 he had dinner at Lady Sunderland's and saw 'Richardson the fire-eater'.

He devoured brimstone on glowing coals before us, chewing and swallowing them; he melted a bearer-glass and ate it quite up; then taking a live coal on his tongue he put it on a raw oyster, the coal was blown on with bellows till it flamed and sparkled in his mouth, and so remained until the oyster gaped and was quite boiled; then he melted pitch and wax with sulphur, which he drank down as it flamed; I saw it flaming in his mouth a good while. He also took up a thick piece of iron, such as laundresses use to put in their smoothing boxes, when it was fiery hot, held it between his teeth, then in his hand and threw it about like a stone, but this I observed he cared not to hold very long.

This last observation is the only sign Evelyn gave that he suspected some form of sleight-of-hand was involved, rather than incombustibility. But he clearly did not regard these 'and divers other prodigious feats' as either divine or diabolic. It had become possible to treat phenomena formerly held to be supernatural as natural; as marvellous, but not miraculous.

The Dissenters

The supernatural continued to keep its hold, though, in some sections of society, particularly among the dissenting sects. They repudiated all the paraphernalia of church magic, but they assumed that God and his angels could speak directly to man. The communication could be through dreams and visions, as in *The Pilgrim's Progress*; or, in answer to prayer, God would provide the information required by helping the right decision to form itself in the supplicant's mind, as if intuitively, because he had opened his mind up to the holy spirit. Sir Thomas More had described the process: praying for the recovery of his daughter, it came 'incontinent' into his mind that what she needed was a clyster. Meditative prayer was a technique which Protestants could use without feeling tainted by Popish superstition. 'Commit thy works unto the Lord,' the Bible had recommended, 'and thy thoughts shall be established'; and for some members of the clergy divination by prayer became standard practice, whenever they had an uncomfortable decision to take.

Some dissenters used aids to divination, the commonest being the Bible; if it were opened at random, and a finger placed on the page, the text would supply the answer. Lots were sometimes drawn, or thrown, in conjunction with prayer, to decide vexed issues; in 1649 the Army Council used them to decide which regiments should be sent to subdue the Irish, the assumption being that God could settle the issue by this means (Puritans believed that the devil, too, could influence the dice; giving runs of luck to susceptible individuals to lure them into becoming gamblers). Pentecostal sects also emerged. The founder of the Society of Friends, George Fox, came to realise his vocation in the 1640s through visions and voices and compelling intuitions; and they acquired the nicknames by which they came to be known, 'Quakers', or 'Shakers', from the convulsions which were often a feature of their meetings when the holy spirit was invoked. This 'great experiment in corporate mysticism', as Evelyn Underhill described it, represented a return to the ways of the early Church, and it produced the same manifestations; members of congregations would dissociate, and begin to talk in strange voices, often in strange languages, sometimes becoming clairvoyant – the leader of the French sect, Jean Cavalier, was converted to the movement by a clairvoyant experience.

Secular magic and divination, too, managed to survive in rural areas in Britain. Sorcerers remained common, Robert Burton noted in his *Anatomy of Melancholy*, 'cunning men, wizards, and white witches, as they call them, in every village, which if they be sought unto will help almost all infirmities of body and mind', with the ability to 'make fire that shall not burn, fetch back thieves or stolen goods, show them absent faces in a glass, make serpents lie still, staunch blood, salve gouts'. And in spite of witch hunts, and the spread of rationalism, they were still to be found two centuries later – in nearly every town, according to Robert Southey; 'though the laws are occasionally put in force against them, still it is a gainful trade'. Keith Thomas has suggested the possibility in his *Religion and the Decline of Magic*, that magic continued to be employed around the parish pump only because, though bogus, it provided so many people with a livelihood (the example of the legal profession, he unkindly noted, being a reminder 'that it is always possible for a substantial social group to support itself by proffering solutions to problems which they themselves have helped to manufacture'). But though this must have contributed, it is not an entirely adequate explanation, as payment was often by results. The standard fee charged by Ethelreda Nixon of Suffolk was twenty-five per cent of the value of such goods as she was able to recover; an unprofitable enterprise unless her method worked.

Chapter Twelve

Witchcraft

ON ONE ISSUE CATHOLICS AND PROTESTANTS WERE IN AGREEMENT. The devil could possess people; or they could sell their souls to him in return for the use, during their lifetimes, of his powers. Where possession was involuntary it might be treated by exorcism. But where the demons could not be expelled, or where a compact had been made with the devil, there could be only one verdict; death.

The mass of evidence available from the detailed records of the witch hunts of the sixteenth and seventeenth centuries could reasonably be expected to provide valuable information about magical practices. In fact, for the same reasons as in the Middle Ages, the evidence is utterly unreliable. The witch hunts were essentially heresy hunts, the hunters being more concerned to secure confessions than to investigate the methods the alleged witches used. As the confessions had still to be tailored to fit the hunters' requirements the accused were required to confess they had flown to sabbat meetings, to have sexual orgies with demons, and feast on the flesh of babies – or other similar stereotypes. The vast majority of those who confessed still did so because they were tortured until they agreed to say whatever the inquisitors wanted them to say, knowing that if they then withdrew their confessions, they would be tortured again. Doubtless there were a few people who had the illusion that they had flown to sabbats and copulated with incubi; but the real source of the information about witchcraft in these trials, as Norman Cohn put it, were still the 'inquisitors, bishops and magistrates, who used and abused the inquisitorial procedure to obtain all the confirmation they needed'.

As material for any survey of occult practices in the era, therefore, the records of the witch hunts are of little value. Reports of cases of what was assumed to be diabolic possession, though, could occasionally be more revealing, where they relate what the investigators claimed actually to have witnessed; as in a case reported in 1591 by a magistrate at Louviers, near Rouen. A local girl, Françoise Fontaine, suffered periodically from fits, and had to be restrained. When she was brought before him, in the presence of his clerk, her gaoler, and a number of other witnesses, she suddenly rose off the floor; and then was dumped down and hauled around the room as if some invisible hand was dragging her. The magistrate tried to read the gospel, with a view to exorcising the demon responsible; but

> all at once the body of the said Françoise was raised off the floor, three or four feet high, and borne horizontally, face upwards, along the court, without anything to support her. When we saw the said body making straight at us, thus suspended in mid-air, it threw us into such fright that we withdrew into the office of the court, locking the door behind us and reading the Gospel of St. John down to the end. But the said body kept following us through the air up to the office, against the door of which it struck with the soles of its feet, and then was carried back through the air, with the face upmost and head foremost, out of the court; which gave such a fright to the gaoler, his servants, our archers and many prisoners who were present, with several inhabitants of Louviers, that they fled.

Françoise made no attempt to take advantage of the confusion to escape, eventually being discovered lying on the ground by the prison door. She was carried to a church, five or six people being required to hold her, so that the curé could administer the sacrament; but before he could do so 'she was again snatched off the floor, higher than the altar, as if she had been taken up by the hair'.

Like Jerome da Silva's, this is a description which reads convincingly, even if it hardly measures up to strict historical specifications. In some of the witchcraft trials, too, where it was the victim of witchcraft rather than the witch whose supernatural activities were reported, the accounts could be reasonably realistic; such as those given by eye-witnesses in the case of Richard, 'the Surrey demoniac', who was seen in the 1680s to levitate during epileptic fits. Members of the aristocracy, too, could report supernatural happenings – or even experience them – without risk, at least in Britain, of their being tried for witchcraft. The Rev. Robert Woodrow, a collector of ghost stories, vouched for the fact that when the Countess of Dumfries was 'under a very odd kind of distemper' she frequently flew 'from one end of the room to the other and from one side of the garden to the other'; and Joseph Glanvil recorded a levitation which had been witnessed by a group which included Robert Boyle's cousin Lord Orrery, two bishops and the healer Valentine Greatrakes. The butler of a household near Orrery's, who lived in fear of being carried way by the spirits, was perceived to rise from the ground, whereupon Mr. Greatrakes and another lusty man clapped their hands over his shoulders, one of them before, the other behind, and weighed him down with all their strength, but he was forcibly taken up from them; for a considerable time he was carried in the air to and fro, over their heads, several of the company still running under him, to prevent him from receiving hurt if he should fall.

Loudun; Salem; St. Médard

The most detailed and convincing source material about the supernatural in this era is provided in accounts of epidemics of mass hysteria. These had been common in medieval times, notably in outbreaks of the dancing mania; but later they had been reported chiefly from closed communities, as when the children in an Amsterdam orphanage began in 1561 to behave in strange ways, speaking in tongues, demonstrating clairvoyance, and climbing up and down the walls like cats. The best-known, and best-attested, outbreak of this kind was in the small Ursuline convent of Loudun, in the 1630s; orchestrated and conducted by the Prioress, Sister Jeanne des Anges. Her attractive face and her hunchback were mirrored in a split personality: the outwardly devout, pious nun alternating with the erotic fantasist who succumbed to fits in which she blasphemed, howled, ground her teeth, and displayed her limbs: as did her nuns. When an inquiry was held the investigators reported a variety of what they took to be diabolic manifestations. Fr. Jean-Joseph Surin, appointed to exorcise the demons, claimed that Jeanne had discovered secret things, or read his thoughts, more than two hundred times; M. de Nion said that on many occasions he had seen her carried off her feet and suspended in the air at a height of two feet; and the Abbé Leriche saw two of the other nuns levitate during their exorcism. Confirmatory evidence was also presented by witnesses who were not immediately concerned with the exorcising process. The King's brother, Gaston d'Orléans, decided to try an experiment of his own: he silently 'willed' the demon which possessed one of the sisters to compel her to kiss the exorcist's right hand, which she promptly did. And a doctor, François Pidoux of Poitiers, noted the curious way in which some of the nuns while in the possessed state were capable of rising to their feet from a lying position without bending their bodies; it was as if they were being pulled up by invisible strings.

Although the evidence about the Salem epidemic in the early 1690s contains much that has to be ascribed to the prevailing fantasies about witchcraft, embedded in it are descriptions of manifestations familiar in scores of accounts of poltergeist hauntings; rappings and bangings; objects moving, or floating through the air, or being hurled as if by an invisible hand, or disappearing and reappearing elsewhere. There were also a few accounts which carry conviction because they were not in the stereotype; notably the descriptions by witnesses of the superhuman strength of an ordinary (one of them described him 'very puny') man, who among other feats used to demonstrate that he could put his forefinger into one end of a heavy gun-barrel, lift it, and hold it out straight in front of him, though strong men could with difficulty hold it up with both hands. And four witnesses testified to having seen Margaret Rule, who was a victim, not a suspect, raised from her bed (as one of them put it),

> wholly by an invisible force, a great way towards the top of the room where she lay. In her being so lifted she had no assistance from any use of her own arms or hands or any other part of her body, not so much as her heels touching her bed or resting on any support whatsoever. And I have seen her thus lifted when not only a strong person hath thrown his whole weight across her to pull her down, but several other persons have endeavoured with all their might to hinder her from being so raised up.

The most carefully collected and attested evidence about an epidemic of this kind relates to the outbreak which followed the death of the Jansenist François de Paris in 1727. At the time, healing miracles were reported and attributed to him; and his burial place at St. Médard became a place of pilgrimage. This was not unusual; but four years later, a pilgrim had a fit in front of the tomb, and this triggered off an epidemic. For a time the behaviour of the *convulsionnaires*, as they came to be known, was taken to be part of the healing process; but some of them began to attract attention by displaying strange powers. Catherine Bigot's head turned from left to right and back so quickly, for example, that her features became a blur. Visitors, many of them sceptical, came away convinced that supernatural forces were at work.

Among those convinced was Carré de Montgeron, a magistrate, a freethinker and something of a roué, who had a spiritual upheaval as a result of what he witnessed, and devoted the rest of his life to collecting and presenting the evidence to show that the phenomena were genuine. Hoping to win over Louis XV, who on Jesuit advice had ordered the closure of the St. Médard cemetery, Carré presented him with a copy of his first volume; as a result Carré was sent to the Bastille, and later into exile in the South of France. There, he produced two more volumes; and the evidence is the stronger for the fact that it does not depend on his own accounts, as he went to great pains to obtain attestation from other people who had been eye-witnesses.

The closure of the cemetery, he was able to show, had resulted in no dimunition of the number of unaccountable happenings; in fact they spread through Paris, becoming progressively more remarkable. A man suffering from dropsy, enormously heavy, rose three or four feet in the air. In 1733 M. Fontaine – a secretary in the royal household, and not a Jansenist – was having dinner in respectable company when he suddenly 'felt himself forced by an uncontrollable power to spin on one foot at a prodigious rate, without being able to stop, for more than an hour'; yet at the same time he was able to read a devotional book. Then '*la Salamandre*', the incombustible Marie Souet, made her appearance. Ten respectable citizens, two of them priests, testified to the fact that in a trance, with her head on one footstool and her feet on another, she had remained suspended above a fire of great violence for thirty-five minutes, during which the sheet in which she was wrapped remained unburned, though the flames were actually lapping around it. Another woman had displayed similar powers, being able repeatedly to plunge her head into flames.

A number of *convulsionnaires* seemed to be impervious to blows. Sister Margot of the Cross could be struck as hard as anybody liked, and it had no effect. Gabrielle Moler, twelve years old, could be thumped with heavy mallets, jabbed at with sharp-pointed poles, and sliced at with shovels without a mark appearing on her. To prove it was no trick, any spectator who wished could join the assault; and Carré was able to produce a signed testimony to her powers by twenty-one witnesses, 'of great distinction', including 'milord Edouard Drumont de Perth' the Comte de Nouvion, magistrates, army officers and ecclesiastics. Gabrielle, too, was incombustible; as were her clothes – though if she wished she could let her shoes burn in the fire, while wearing them, to show there was no deception.

Most of the phenomena associated with shamanism were also reported: visions, voices, clairvoyance (some of the *convulsionnaires* were able to read blindfold), speaking with tongues, and levitation (Mlle. Thevenet was seen at times floating at a height of seven or eight feet, people who tried to hold her down being hauled up with her). And the witnesses included Dominicans and Jesuits, bitterly hostile to Jansenism, who did not attempt to deny the reality of what they had observed, preferring to blame it on the devil. Even Diderot was impressed at the number and standing of the witnesses, hundreds of whose testimonies were preserved in the archives; a collection of a kind, he felt, which would 'challenge the incredulity of the most stubborn'. Further epidemics were to be reported from time to time – such as an outbreak in Namur in 1772, when children in a hospital began to have fits; some going into weird convulsions; some becoming paralysed; some behaving unaccountably, climbing and descending walls apparently without effort, and playing with fire without burning, the spectacle watched by crowds of inquisitive and incredulous spectators; but none were to be recorded with the meticulous attention Carré had given not just to the phenomena, but also to the credibility of the witnesses.

Chapter Thirteen

Ghosts

FOR BOTH THE CATHOLIC AND THE PROTESTANT CHURCHES, GHOSTS presented a problem. It had been difficult to sustain Tertullian's view that they were demons masquerading as the spirits of the dead: if they had been demons, after all, they would surely have haunted to better purpose, aiming to seduce rather than to terrify. An alternative, and for the Church much more lucrative, proposition was that ghosts were spirits awaiting judgment; allowed, perhaps, leave of absence from Purgatory to remind their relations and friends that a few more masses would have to be offered up to get them to heaven. To Protestants, this was simply a ruse to keep parish priests – and the Vatican, through the sale of indulgences – in funds. But whatever the explanation, ghostly visitations continued to be reported, often in the likeness of the dead. Everybody talked about ghosts, the Swiss writer Lewes Lavater noted in his treatise on them in 1572; and Shakespeare showed how much a part of the English scene they were. They could be useful, a seventeenth-century commentator claimed, 'in detecting the murderer, in disposing their estate, in rebuking injurious executors, in visiting and counselling their wives and children, in forewarning them of such and such courses, with other matters of like sort'. It was assumed, in other words, that ghosts had, or at least could have, a social function; they could appear like Hamlet's father to try to secure redress for past wrongs, or like Banquo as a warning of the wrath to come. And belief in them survived; partly because they were so commonly reported, partly because the stately homes of the aristocracy were as likely to be haunted as the cottages of their workers. As the far from credulous Joseph Addison put it in the *Spectator* in 1711, even if he were not disposed to accept the general testimony, he would have felt bound to accept it from living persons 'whom I cannot distrust in other matters'.

Only one kind of ghost, though, presents useful historical source material: the poltergeist. Between ghost and poltergeist no clear line can be drawn; but the chief characteristics of poltergeists were that they were usually heard – through bangings or rappings, or in some cases, voices – rather than seen; that they had personalities, as well as identities – often troublesome, sometimes actively malicious; that they were associated with psychokinetic activity – objects moving, falling, or flying through the air; and that they were persistent, remaining active for days or weeks. Occasionally it actually proved possible to establish communication with them. In the 1520s Adrian de Montalembert, almoner to King Francis I, was called in as adviser to a monastery haunted by the spirit of a nun who in her lifetime had decamped with some of its treasures and led a fast but brief life on the proceeds. When asked questions, the 'nun' would reply by means of raps indicating 'yes' or 'no'; and with the help of this system, her ghost was laid. 'I have heard these rappings many times,' Montalembert claimed in 1528; and they had provided him with information on matters of importance which no mortal creature could have known.

Because poltergeist activity tended to be persistent, it was often possible to document it with the help of witnesses; and some of the investigations were thorough, notably in the case of the poltergeist which infested the home of a Geneva pastor, the Rev. Francis Perreaud, in 1612. Noises were heard, pots and pans thrown around the kitchen, and eventually the spirit began to speak in a just intelligible voice, retailing malicious gossip, singing bawdy songs, exchanging banter with the maid, and chucking things about – though never doing any actual damage. Perreaud's sober account so impressed Robert Boyle when he was working in Geneva in the 1640s that he had it translated into English, remarking to the translator that although he had previously been sceptical about such matters, reading the book and meeting the author had at length 'overcome all my settled indisposedness to believe strange things'.

The first English poltergeist to attract more than local attention came to be known as 'the phantom drummer of Tidworth'. In 1661 a beggar was arrested in Wiltshire and charged with making himself a public nuisance by playing his drum; first to get alms and then, by continuing to play, to get people to offer him more alms to leave the neighbourhood. A local magistrate, John Mompesson, sent the man to gaol, and brought the drum back to his home at Tidworth. There it proceeded to play on its own; its tattoo being accompanied by other noises, and sometimes by physical effects. Mompesson's children were lifted up in their beds; shoes and other objects were flung around (one striking the Rev. Mr. Cragg, though without hurting him: 'a lock of wool could not have fallen more softly'). Often the 'drummer' played malicious little tricks, like hiding a gentlewoman's Bible in some

ashes. One of the people who came to witness the manifestations asked
it questions, telling it to knock three times if its owner had set it to
work, 'which it did very distinctly'. Perhaps with the hope of securing
an uninterrupted night's sleep, he asked it to give confirmation by five
knocks, and then stop, 'which it did, and left the house quiet all the
night'. Joseph Glanvil wrote an account of the drummer's activities,
and was himself a witness of some of them. The drumming had ceased
by the time he came to the house; but he heard strange scratchings;
experienced a bed moving under his hand, 'as if something within had
thrust it up'; and felt the whole room shaking. When he asked the
spirit 'in the name of God, who is it, and what would you have?' he
was given the reply, 'Nothing with you'.

Glanvil was a Fellow of the Royal Society; and his careful psychical
research won the respect of Boyle, who in 1677 wrote to encourage
him, making the point that although nineteen out of twenty stories of
witchcraft or magic might be spurious, any single account of a supernatural phenomenon, 'being fully proved and duly verified, suffices to
evidence the thing contended for; and consequently to invalidate some
of the atheists' most plausible arguments'. Glanvil, therefore, was careful to emphasise the trouble that had been taken to investigate the
'drummer' as scientifically as the circumstances permitted (the spirit
was fickle, declining to perform when some representatives of the
King arrived). One night the investigators strewed ashes over the room
where it was apt to manifest itself, 'in the morning, they found in one
place the resemblance of a great claw', and 'some letters in another
which they could make nothing of'. Fraud, Glanvil insisted, could be
ruled out; 'it is not to be conceived how tricks could have been performed upon so many, so jealous, and so inquisitive persons as were
witnesses'.

In any case, the only person in a position to have staged so elaborate
a hoax was the respectable Mompesson; and what conceivable grati-
fication, Glanvil asked, could he have obtained? He had 'suffered by
it in his name, in his estate, in all his affairs, and in the general peace
of his family'; and, final indignity, he had afterwards been branded as
an impostor – as, indeed, had Glanvil himself. In the preface to a later
edition of his book Glanvil described how people had begun to write
letters telling him it was being put about that Mompesson and he had
'confessed all to be a cheat and a contrivance'; so many letters, in fact,
that he had been 'haunted almost as bad as Mr. Mompesson's house'.
He had arranged for the new edition, to scotch this fabrication by re-
printing the alleged confession along with a letter from Mompesson
saying that it was 'a most damnable lie' – invented, Mompesson
assumed, by people who wanted to suppress belief in either God or
the devil. It was to be the first of many similar smear stories about men

who became involved in the investigation of psychic phenomena.

Accounts of poltergeists were remarkably similar all over the world, though often it was obvious that the witnesses had never heard of this kind of haunting before. The commonest feature, apart from the noises, were showers of stones; and again and again, it was to be recorded that although the stones fell all around people in a room, and sometimes hit them, it was rare for anybody to be seriously hurt. In Elizabethan times Reginald Scot had described how spirits 'throw down stones upon men, but the blows thereof do no harm to them whom they hit'; a century later Richard Chamberlain, Secretary to the Province of New Hampshire, recalled a haunting attested by respectable New England citizens, where he had been assailed by stones, some hitting him quite hard but others 'lighting gently on me'.

In some cases the effects took a less violent, more personalised form; such as the haunting of the rectory at Epworth, the home of Dr. Samuel Wesley, father of the evangelist. 'An author who in this age relates such a story,' Southey was to remark in his biography of John Wesley a century later, 'and treats it as not utterly incredible and absurd, must expect to be ridiculed; but the testimony upon which it rests is far too strong to be set aside because of its strangeness.'

The hauntings began in December 1715 with a sound like wood being planed, or clockwork being wound up. At first it seemed to come from a corner of the nursery, high up near the ceiling. Later there were rappings and bangings, and rumbling noises as if heavy objects were being moved around. Sometimes objects were seen to move: a hand-mill 'whirled about very swiftly'; a trencher danced a little jig. The spirit appeared to have a physical presence, too. Door latches would be lifted or rattled by an invisible hand; one of the daughters felt something brushing past her; and once when the Rev. Samuel Wesley tried to get into his study he was violently thrust back.

At first Mrs. Wesley thought it was the children playing tricks; but the rappings were often heard at family prayers, when the children and the servants were assembled, coming from all over the place. They were at their noisiest during prayers for King George; as the first Jacobite rising had been defeated only a few months before, the family came to the conclusion that 'Old Jeffery', as they called him, must have been a Jacobite. Although he would answer the children, if they rapped, by rapping back the same number of times, the family do not appear to have thought of asking him questions; and eventually, when Samuel Wesley went away on a visit in the new year of 1716, the haunting ceased. Old Jeffery was heard and felt no more.

A great variety of explanations were to be put forward for the Epworth ghost. Joseph Priestley, who interested himself in the subject, thought the servants were to blame; Coleridge argued that the family were hallucinated; Southey attributed the episode to the devil; and other writers were convinced that the children must have been responsible. But the correspondence among the family – not at all hysterical; puzzled, rather, and amused – confirms the impression that the sounds were not made by any of them; and the proposition that it was all a family joke is not credible. It would have been pointless, unless there had been visitors to play it on; and the only outsider involved, who testified to the reality of the ghost, was a clergyman friend.

In John Wesley's narrative, a reference to an earlier episode relating to his father provides a slender clue.

The year before King William died my mother did not say amen to the prayer for the king. She said she could not; for she did not believe the Prince of Orange was king. He vowed he would never cohabit with her till she did. He then took his horse and rode away, nor did she hear anything of him for a twelvemonth. He then came back, and lived with her as before. But I fear his vow was not forgotten before God.

If psychic forces can be derived from explosive human situations, Old Jeffery might have been the outcome of that earlier crisis.

The Epworth affair had not been forgotten when, nearly half a century later, it was superseded as a supernatural talking point by a London ghost, destined to become the most celebrated of all in the remarkable gallery of British hauntings. In 1759 'Mr. and Mrs. Kent' came to lodge in Cock Lane near Holborn in London in a house belonging to a clerk, Richard Parsons. William and Fanny were not, in fact, Mr. and Mrs. – he had been married to her elder sister, who had died, and as the law stood they could not wed; but Fanny was having a child by William. In his absences on business, she asked Parsons' daughter Elizabeth to share her bed; and one morning, they reported that they had been kept awake by banging noises. After a row with Parsons over some money he owed them, the Kents left; and shortly afterwards Fanny died of smallpox. But the noises continued, and neighbours were brought in to listen to them. As no other cause could be found, Fanny's spirit seemed the most likely culprit; and John Moore, assistant preacher at the church to which Parsons was clerk, was called in. With Parsons, he devised a scheme to question the spirit by means of a code; the spirit replying with a knock for 'yes', two knocks for 'no' and a scratching sound to express irritation.

The Cock Lane ghost soon achieved notoriety. 'It tells whether a watch, when held up, be white, blue, yellow or black,' Oliver Goldsmith reported; as well as giving 'several other marks of sagacity'. But it had its shortcomings. Not merely did it sometimes fall into error;

it turned out on occasion to be a deliberate liar. It accused William Kent of having poisoned Fanny, which the doctor who had attended her dismissed as impossible; she had been unable to take any nourishment, except what he had given her, for two days before her death. When sceptics came to listen, too, nothing was heard. 'As the ghost is a good deal offended by incredulity, the persons present are to conceal theirs,' Goldsmith sardonically commented; 'Otherwise they must hear no ghost.' When Samuel Johnson, along with 'many gentlemen eminent for their rank and character', came to watch a test seance, they sat in the girl's bedroom for over an hour, hearing nothing; after they had retired downstairs they were summoned up again because the rapping had begun, but it had ceased before they got back to her room. Nor did the spirit rap, as it had promised to do, when they went to the vault where Fanny was buried. 'It is therefore the opinion of the whole assembly,' Johnson wrote in his report, 'that the child has some art of making or counterfeiting particular noises'; and not long after, she was detected trying to make the noises in her bed with the help of a small piece of wood.

The explanation of the affair now appeared obvious. Parsons, furious at being pursued for debt, had thought up the ghost and exploited it with his family's help to get his own back on William Kent. Brought to trial, he was sentenced to two years in gaol and three appearances in the pillory; the Cock Lane ghost became for several months the staple of ballad writers, playwrights, satirists and cartoonists; and it continued to be remembered as a hoax that went sour. 'If one phantom is more discredited than another,' Andrew Lang was to remark in his essay on the subject, 'it is the Cock Lane ghost,' and to this day it is often cited as the classic example of a psychic fraud. There are features, though, which make the fraud diagnosis implausible. To begin with, the haunting began before there was any dispute between Parsons and his lodgers. The rappings, too, though they ceased if sceptics were present, were heard by people who could not have been party to a conspiracy, and who testified that the sounds they heard were not made by Elizabeth. Her parents could not have been responsible, as the phenomena were reported when she was taken to other houses to be tested. At the Missiter household, for example, where she was eventually caught cheating, Elizabeth had already passed some stringent tests in which her hands and feet had been held; and to Missiter and a fellow-investigator, the raps had sounded as if they were coming out of one of the walls of the room. Only when Elizabeth was spreadeagled, with her hands and feet tied down, had the rappings ceased. As an additional check Missiter had hit upon the idea of telling her that she and her parents would be punished if the rappings did not return; and then, sending her to bed without – or so she was left to think – any precautions to prevent her cheating. In fact, he had arranged for her to be spied on through a peep-hole, and it was by this means that she had been detected smuggling the piece of board into her bed. The noises which she made with its help, though, were so different from those which had been heard before 'that it was very apparent this method of operating was a fresh contrivance'; the sound, too, came from the bed, and not from another part of the room, 'as it used to'.

Mrs. de Morgan – wife of the mathematician, and a keen psychic investigator – a century later suggested a different explanation; that the girl, having been told she would be punished if the ghost did not come, naturally 'took the best means she could of producing the effect of his ghostly presence, by tapping on the board with her fingers'. The possibility remains, therefore, that the Cock Lane ghost was not a hoax; and for this, there is an additional piece of evidence of a kind which, as poltergeists had not yet been recognised in their own right, went unremarked at the time. Elizabeth was highly strung: she was subject to fits, which came on around the time of the rappings; and other kinds of characteristic poltergeist phenomena were reported from the times when she was staying away from her family. While she was in the house of a local comb-maker, a loose curtain ring was seen to spin on its rod; when she was helping in the kitchen, knocking of such violence was heard from the wooden panel above the fireplace that her hosts feared the hammerer would 'have broke it all to pieces'. Such manifestations were later constantly to be related, in hauntings, to highly-strung children.

The Cock Lane episode did not merely discredit everybody who had believed that there was a ghost. Some of the obloquy fell on those who had taken the trouble to investigate it, Charles Churchill taking the opportunity to lampoon 'Pomposo' Johnson for his part in the affair. Yet as quoted by Boswell, Johnson displayed a detached common sense on the subject which was unusual in his time. He drew the distinction between what might be produced by the imagination, and what the imagination could not produce. The imagination could account for a voice (he had once himself believed he heard his dead mother call 'Sam').

But if a form should appear, and a voice should tell me that a particular man had died at a particular place, and a particular hour, a fact which I had no apprehension of nor any means of knowing, and this fact, with all its attendant circumstances, should afterwards be unquestionably proved, I should, in that case, be persuaded that I had had supernatural intelligence imparted to me.

In his *Life of the Earl of Roscommon*, Johnson had earlier cited an example from Aubrey. As a boy, the future earl had been larking about one day when suddenly he was heard to say, 'My father is dead'; which turned out to be correct. The age in which they lived, Johnson observed, was 'little inclined to favour any accounts of this kind, nor will the name of Aubrey much recommend it to credit'. Nevertheless Johnson felt that such stories ought not to be rejected; and he offered advice which had been given by another writer, 'do not wholly slight them, because they may be true; but do not easily trust them because they may be false'. Still, he realised there was no point in trying to convince anybody who did not believe of the reality of a supernatural experience, such as seeing an apparition. In the most familiar of his aphorisms on the subject he remarked how wonderful it was that though five thousand years had elapsed since the world was created, it was still undecided whether or not there had ever been an instance of the spirit of any person appearing after death: 'all argument is against it; but all belief is for it'. To this he added, not long after, a further comment, which is less familiar. Whether in theology or in philosophy, he believed, the issue was 'one of the most important that can come before the human understanding'.

Chapter Fourteen

Second Sight

ANOTHER WAY IN WHICH THE SUPERNATURAL ELEMENT CONTINUED to appear in everyday life in the seventeenth and eighteenth centuries was in visions, voices and premonitions. In the Highlands and Western Isles of Scotland, second sight was taken for granted. As Johnson's reference showed, John Aubrey had come to be regarded as having been too credulous about the supernatural in his *Miscellanies,* a reputation which has clung to him ever since; but his accounts of second sight were not materially different from those produced soon afterwards by Martin Martin of Skye, physician and traveller, following conscientious research into the subject.

The commonest form, Martin related in his *Account of Second Sight,* was a sudden brief vision of something, or somebody, in connection with an impending death. Often the vision was symbolic; say, a shroud. Martin was not content simply to record the tales he was told; endlessly he asked probing questions. If more than one person was present when somebody saw a vision, did the others? Not necessarily, he was told; but if the one who saw it touched other people, they might then see it too. Animals could also be affected; a horse whose rider saw a vision might shy at it. The faculty, Martin found, was distributed throughout the Western Isles; and he became convinced that it must be genuine because the seer was usually illiterate and poor. He stood to make nothing out of it, as the gift was never exploited for money; and so far from its bringing him any prestige, the islanders considered it not quite respectable. As for the suggestion that the visions might be due to the local whisky, it was well known that a drunk man never had the second sight. 'Can it be reasonable,' Martin asked, 'to imagine that all the islanders who have not the second sight should continue together, and offer violence to their understandings and senses, to force themselves to believe a lie, from age to age?'

John Frazer, Dean of the Western Isles, was similarly converted.

In a treatise written in 1707, giving many examples, he expressed the opinion that the faculty was worthy of scientific consideration: 'that such representations are made to the eyes of men and women is to me out of all doubt; and that effects follow, answerable thereto, as little questionable'. And in 1763 the Rev. Donald MacLeod collected about forty examples of second sight from men whose veracity he could rely upon, and published them over his pen name, 'Insulanus'. The majority were premonitions of death, but there were lighter-hearted episodes. A man who had been away from Skye for some time on a sea voyage, and was returning to his family unannounced, decided to test his mother-in-law's reputation as a seer; and he concentrated on 'sending' her a haunch of venison which he was bringing to her as a present. When he arrived, she told him that they had begun to despair for his life until she had suddenly 'seen' him, holding something in his hand which looked like flesh.

Johnson would have liked to find out more about second sight on his visit to the Western Isles ten years later; but the seers, he found, did not speak English. He was interested, though, to find that everybody in the islands (except ministers from the mainland) accepted its existence; and also by the fact that it was, as he put it, a faculty rather than a power, neither voluntary nor constant; 'the appearances have no dependence upon choice; they cannot be summoned, detained or recalled'. What most impressed him, as it had Martin, was that

> by pretension to second sight, no profit was ever sought or gained. It is an involuntary effect in which neither hope nor fear are known to have any part. Those who profess to feel it do not boast of it as a privilege, nor are considered by others as advantageously distinguished. They have no temptation to feign; and their hearers have no motive to encourage imposture.

As well as the anonymous seers of the Western Isles, there were also a few individuals throughout Europe, some of them celebrated, who had second sight. The best known was Henri IV, who expressed his macabre certainty that he was going to be assassinated in his coach in the course of the coronation ceremonies for his second wife. 'Oh, this cursed coronation,' he told Sully, who recorded it in his memoirs, 'it will cause my death'; as it did. In his book on visions and premonitions Goethe's friend Johann Jung-Stilling – physician, professor of political economy and student of the supernatural – gave many more examples, some of them well-attested, and others engagingly convincing, like the experiences of Dr. Christopher Knape, a court apothecary in Berlin. While he was an apprentice, in 1768, Knape dreamed the winning numbers of the State lottery; and made a little money on them.

Eight years later, he dreamed them again; but a noise which woke him up distracted him momentarily, and he could only recall with certainty the first two of the five numbers involved, so that though his hazy recollection of the others turned out to be correct, his caution in buying only a few tickets meant that he made but twenty dollars, instead of a thousand. The following year, however, he dreamed that a number was going to come up; and he decided to put his shirt on it. Two hours before the lottery was due to be drawn, he received his money back; all the tickets for that number had already been sold, so that although it duly came up, he won nothing (thereby establishing a precedent: divination, whether spontaneous or induced, was rarely to make anybody's fortune; either something would happen to prevent a bet from being laid, or the information could turn out to have been subtly misleading).

Jung-Stilling also gave examples of retrocognition; glimpses into the past which could not readily be accounted for naturally. In 1705 Duke Christian of Saxe-Eisenburg had a vision of one of his forbears, the Princess Anna of Saxony, who had died while under suspicion of infidelity to her husband, a former Duke, more than a century before. She assured Christian she was innocent, and begged him to effect a reconciliation. Checking on her story, Christian found it to be true; and as if to intimate that his research had been appreciated Princess Anna and her husband both appeared to him, and in his presence were reconciled.

Scrying

Divination by scrying was also used whenever somebody was found who had the art of seeing visions in a crystal ball or similar device. In his memoirs Saint-Simon described how the sceptical Duc d'Orléans, hearing of a child who could scry by looking into water, decided to test her by asking what was happening at a house nearby, having previously sent a servant to check; and her description turned out to be accurate. He then asked her to tell him what would happen when Louis XIV died. The child, who knew nothing about the Court, reported what she 'saw' – the king's bedroom – sufficiently clearly for Orléans to be able to recognise the people, and to note the absence of four members of the royal family who could be expected to be present. It was eight years before the king died; and then, as Saint-Simon had reluctantly to concede, the girl's vision was shown to be correct; the missing four had died in the meantime.

There are also scattered accounts of dowsing, usually with the diviner's rod – the forked twig still often employed today. It was in use by miners in Germany in the early sixteenth century, to find underground deposits of metal; later by tin prospectors in Cornwall and by the Baron de Beausoleil, looking for seams of precious ore in France. In 1692 Jacques Aymar, a peasant from the Lyon region, showed how it could be put to a different purpose. He undertook to find three men who had murdered a Lyon wine merchant and his wife; and with the help of his divining rod, he tracked them southwards along the Rhône Valley, pointing out to the pursuers where they had stayed and even, on one occasion, the bottles from which they had drunk. Eventually his rod led the posse to the gaol in the town of Beaucaire. Applied to the prisoners, one by one, it singled out a young hunchback; though the man protested that he was innocent, witnesses along the road back to Lyon confirmed that he had indeed been employed by the other two as their servant, and he was executed. The search for the others was resumed; but the rod eventually intimated that they had fled the country.

Experiments at Lyon showed that it was not only for Aymar that the rod would work; some members of the professions tried it with success. Aymar's fame spread to the capital, and he was invited there in 1693 by the Prince of Condé, to undertake more rigorous tests, some of them from members of the Academy of the Sciences. It proved to be a humiliating experience. For a while, the rod continued to work; but the information it provided began to be unreliable, and the investigators finally pronounced it 'a pure illusion and chimerical invention'. Aymar returned to Lyon; and though he continued to obtain results with the rod, he could not re-establish his reputation. It was the first of many occasions when a dowser, confident of his ability to pass tests (for if Aymar had been a fraud, he would hardly have been so foolish as to undertake them), has found that his rod let him down; either by not working or, worse, by giving wrong answers.

Swedenborg

The most remarkable eighteenth-century clairvoyant was Emanuel Swedenborg, whose reputation as a mathematician, philosopher, astronomer and economist was already established when in the 1740s, he began to have visions in which he held converse with spirits – angels, as he thought. They looked and sounded to him, he explained, like ordinary people; but he was aware that they existed only in his mind, because they were not heard by anybody else. The reason, he decided, was that 'the speech of an angel or a spirit finds entrance first into a man's thoughts, and reaches his organs of hearing from within'. They spoke in his language, too, because it was not really they who spoke; it was he himself, interpreting them.

Swedenborg's writings on his other interests, which continued, showed that his spiritism was not due to any softening of the brain; and though his description of his spirits – who began to include celebrities, Virgil, Luther and many more – has to be accepted on trust, there is independent evidence for the reality of the clairvoyant powers which he believed they provided. Hearing that he talked with spirits the Queen of Sweden asked him if he had seen her dead brother; and when Swedenborg said he had not, flippantly said 'if you should see him, remember me to him'. A week later, Swedenborg whispered a message in the Queen's ear; 'only God and my brother,' she admitted, shaken, 'can know what he has just told me'. Later witnesses were to confirm that the Queen spoke of the occasion with extraordinary conviction. On another occasion, vouched for by Jung-Stilling, Swedenborg became abstracted in the course of a conversation. When he recovered, he announced that the Emperor Peter III had just died in prison, and described the manner of his death – strangled by the conspirators who had put his wife, Catherine, on the Russian throne. If those present cared to make a note of it, Swedenborg suggested, they could check; they did, and he was right.

Writing to his friend Charlotte von Knobloch in the late 1750s, Kant gave two further examples: one of them an echo of the story familiar from earlier times. The widow of the Dutch envoy to Stockholm received a bill from a silversmith for a debt her husband had incurred. Certain that her husband would not have left it unpaid, she consulted Swedenborg. He in turn consulted the spirit of the dead husband; and the husband appeared to his widow in a dream to tell her where she would find the receipt, in a concealed drawer where he had kept his secret correspondence.

'I am not aware that anybody has ever perceived in me an inclination to the marvellous,' Kant noted defensively, 'or a weakness tending to credulity.' He had nevertheless been impressed by what he had heard of Swedenborg's powers of second sight; and particularly by the example vouched for by several respected citizens of Gothenburg. Arriving there one day from England, Swedenborg had gone to the house of William Castel, where about fifteen guests were assembled.

About six o'clock in the evening Baron Swedenborg went out, and returned to the company pale and disturbed. He said that at that moment there was a terrible conflagration raging in Stockholm, and that the fire was increasing (Gothenburg lies 300 miles from Stockholm). He was uneasy and frequently went out. He said that the house of one of his friends, who he named, was already laid in ashes; and his own house was in danger. At eight o'clock, after he had again gone out, he said joyfully 'God be praised, the fire is extinguished, the third door from my very house!' This information occasioned the greatest excitement in the company, and the statement was carried to the Governor the same evening . . . on Monday evening there arrived in Gothenburg a courier who had been despatched by the merchants of Stockholm during the fire. In the letters brought by him the conflagration was described exactly as Swedenborg had stated it.

There could be no doubt, Kant insisted, about the authenticity of the story. He had asked a British friend who was going to Sweden shortly afterwards, Joseph Green, to look into it; and Green had been able to verify it from the lips of those who had been present. That such things could happen puzzled and disturbed Kant, with his reputation as a rationalist to maintain. To protect himself he adopted a device which was later to come into common use. 'It will probably be asked,' he had written in his letter to Frl. von Knobloch, 'what on earth could have moved me to engage in such a contemptible business as that of circulating stories to which a rational man hesitates to listen'; and in a letter a few years later, in 1766, he revealed how he had contrived to escape ridicule. He had decided, he wrote, 'to do the ridiculing myself'; his method being to expose and mock the flaws in individual accounts of the supernatural, which was not difficult because of their frequent absurdities, and also because of the unintelligible theories attached to them. Nevertheless he felt bound to make 'the common, though queer, reservation that while I doubt any one of them, still I have certain faith in the whole of them taken together'. There must, he decided, be spiritual beings who exist in space, yet remain penetrable by material beings: 'an acting power in space, but not a *filling* of it'. It would be proved in time

– I do not know where and when – that in this life the human soul stands in an indissoluble communion with all the immaterial beings of the spiritual worlds; that it produces effects in them, and in exchange receives impressions from them, without, however, becoming humanly conscious of them, so long as all stands well.

Mesmerism

Chapter Fifteen
The Growth of Scepticism

THAT KANT SHOULD HAVE FELT THE NEED TO TAKE SUCH PRECAUTIONS showed how prevalent scepticism about the supernatural had become, at least in academic circles. It was a trend which had already made its impact even on the Catholic Church, threatened not only by enemies but by candid friends – Galileo and Descartes; its influence can be seen in Prospero Lambertini's *De Canonisatione*, the most carefully-reasoned study of miracles that had yet appeared.

Prospero Lambertini
Lambertini, Archbishop of Bologna at the time, had been *Promotor Fidei*, Devil's Advocate; he knew the subject intimately from the viewpoint both of the Catholic, willing to accept miracles and anxious to show them to be God's work, and of the cynic, well aware how easily the pious and credulous could be deluded or delude themselves. To the Cartesians he replied that if they believed in an omnipotent God, as they claimed, they must accept that having laid down the laws of nature, God could also break or circumvent them; and this could be accomplished in three ways. Phenomena might be above nature, reversing natural processes – as when a dead man came to life again; or against nature, suspending natural processes – as in the Israelites' crossing of the Red Sea; or beyond nature, altering natural processes – as in the changing of the water into wine at the Cana wedding. In addition, the supernatural could stimulate and reinforce the natural, giving apparently superhuman power.
Lambertini, however, was careful to insist that apparently supernatural happenings often had natural explanations; before claiming that anybody had risen from the dead, it was necessary to exercise care to make sure that he had really died, as there were trance states very similar to death. And 'natural' might include certain faculties which had yet to be explained but ought not necessarily to be regarded as

miraculous. Fools, even animals, might have 'knowledge of things to come, things past, present events distant in space, and the secret places of the heart'; perception was possible other than through the five senses without God or the devil being directly involved. He accepted, too, that there might be apparitions of the living or the dead, of no divine significance. Whether an event was, or was not, supernatural, Lambertini was saying, could only be settled by careful evaluation of the evidence; and then still further sifting would be needed to decide whether or not it was the result of divine intervention. The more bizarre the phenomenon, the more important it appeared to him to be mistrustful; but mistrust should not be allowed to override well-attested evidence, as in the case of Joseph of Copertino. When Joseph's name was put forward for beatification early in the century, Lambertini as Devil's Advocate had strenuously and successfully opposed it. Half a century later, when he had become Pope Benedict XIV, the case came up before him again; and this time he felt compelled to concede that the 'famous upliftings from the ground and prolonged flights' had been vouched for by so many eye-witnesses of unchallengeable integrity that he could not withhold his consent.

By this time, Joseph had a more respectable successor. The miracles of Alfonso Liguori, founder of the Redemptorist Order, were unusually well authenticated as the proceedings for beatification began almost immediately after his death. Three canons and members of the congregation testified that when he was in Amalfi in 1750, he had levitated while preaching a sermon; and fellow members of his Order described how they had seen him floating when he was rapt in prayer in his cell. Even when, towards his death, he became a cripple in a wheel chair he still occasionally shot up into the air, on one occasion knocking his head against the chin of Fr. Volpicelli, who happened to be bending over him at the time. At their next meeting, a witness noticed that Volpicelli was careful to keep at a safe distance; wisely, as the levitation was repeated. Liguori's most celebrated miracle took place in 1774 when, preparing to celebrate mass, he went into a trance and on coming out of it two hours later, said he had been at Pope Clement XIV's deathbed in Rome. This caused some amusement to those present. 'We were all tempted to burst out laughing,' Sister Agatha Viscardi was to recall. But then those who were in attendance at the bedside of the dying Pope Clement described how they had not only seen, but talked to Alfonso; he had led them in prayers for the dying.

The Decline of Magic

In its investigations and assessments of the miracles of this kind the Church, following Lambertini, began to adopt a more rigorous scientific attitude. But it was not rigorous enough to satisfy Protestants.

By this time they were adopting a more aggressively hostile stance. They were no longer simply casting doubt on the evidence for the supernatural; they were beginning to doubt whether the supernatural existed – even that it could exist.

Discussing this development in his *Religion and the Decline of Magic* Keith Thomas has pointed out that the environment was becoming more amenable to man's control, with better economic organisation and improved techniques of food production and distribution. The growth of advertising, much of it devoted to the recovery of lost or stolen goods, and of insurance also reduced dependence on divination and magical techniques for discovery and recovery. Nevertheless Thomas felt that the improvement in man's ability to control his environment was less a cause than an effect of the decline; men emancipated themselves from their old beliefs without necessarily having the technology to replace them, 'because magic was ceasing to be intellectually acceptable, and because their religion taught them to try self-help before invoking supernatural aid'. Protestantism and scepticism therefore became irrationally linked. Protestantism 'unintentionally acted as a screen for rationalism', as Leslie Stephen put it in his history of English eighteenth-century thought, while rationalism 'naturally expressed itself in terms of Protestantism', a process facilitated in Britain by the fact that the clergy were chiefly recruited from the younger sons of the nobility and gentry, who were apt to regard their parishes literally as their 'livings', and were more likely to be infected by the scepticism of their brothers and their friends than by mysticism.

Towards the end of the century works were beginning to appear in which it was denied that there ever had been any miracles, in the sense of an event which upset the laws of nature. 'It is harder to believe that God should alter or put out of its ordinary course some phenomenon of the great world for once and make things act contrary to their ordinary rule,' John Locke remarked in his commonplace book, 'than that this is some fallacy or natural effect of which man knows not the cause, let it look ever so strange'. Even Protestant divines were ready to deny the authenticity of the New Testament miracles. It was surely inconceivable, Thomas Woolston argued in his 1720s *Discourses*, that Jesus should have countenanced the revellings at Cana, 'much less promoted them by the change of a large quantity of water into wine for the use of a company who were already drunk with it'. The Gospel miracles commonly believed in, he feared, implied 'improbabilities, incredibilities and the grossest absurdities, very dishonourable to the name of Christ'. Charged with blasphemy, Woolston died in gaol; but his views were frequently to be echoed by Protestants anxious to rid their Church of any taint of superstition.

The growing influence of scientists, reflected in Charles's grant of a charter in 1662 to the Royal Society – Fellowship of which was to be regarded until quite recently as about the highest honour to which a British scientist could aspire – also came to be thrown on scepticism's side. This was ironical, as its two most distinguished members, Boyle and Newton, were alchemists. Yet it was their discoveries which, more than anything else, promoted the belief that in time all mysteries and miracles would be naturally explained; or at least shown like gravity to behave so consistently that even if not explained, they could be classified as obeying natural law. From this, however, it proved to be an easy step to making a distinction between natural phenomena, which were real, and the supernatural, which were compounded of myth, legend, mysticism (henceforth regarded as anti-rational) delusion, hallucination and fraud.

David Hume

Scepticism's first manifesto appeared in the middle of the eighteenth century: David Hume's essay on miracles. Hume did not attempt to disguise that his aim was polemical, rather than scientific; he was out to undermine the arguments of Christianity's apologists in order 'to silence the most arrogant bigotry and superstition and free all of us from their impertinent solicitations'. To that end, he boasted, 'I flatter myself that I have discovered an argument of a like nature which, if just, will with the wise and learned be an everlasting check to all kinds of superstitious delusion, and consequently will be useful as long as the world endures'.

Hume defined a miracle as 'a violation of the laws of nature'; and his basic argument was that 'as a firm and unalterable experience has established these laws, the proof against a miracle, from the very nature of the fact, is as entire as any argument from experience can possibly be imagined'. Men must die, he claimed; lead cannot float in the air; fire consumes wood. It was not a miracle that a man should die suddenly, because that often happened; but it would be a miracle if a dead man should come to life,

> because that has never been observed, in any age or country. There must therefore be a uniform experience against every miraculous event, otherwise the event would not merit that appellation. And as a uniform experience amounts to a proof, there is here a direct and full *proof*, from the nature of the fact, against the existence of any miracle.

Hume did not go so far as to argue that miracles were impossible. He simply claimed that there was not to be found, in all history, any event attested by a sufficient number of men 'of such unquestioned good sense, education and learning, as to secure us against all delusion in themselves; of such undoubted integrity, as to place them beyond all suspicion of any design to deceive others'. And to illustrate his point, Hume cited the miracles associated with St. Médard, which had continued to be reported almost up to the time he was writing. Never, he thought, had so many been ascribed to a single cause. 'What is more extraordinary, many of the miracles were immediately proved upon the spot before judges of unquestioned integrity, attested by witnesses of credit and distinction in a learned age'; and they had not been refuted, in spite of the fact that the civil magistrates and the Jesuits had a common interest in refuting them. Yet all this testimony, Hume insisted, was insufficient to counter 'the absolute impossibility of the miraculous nature of the events' in the eyes of reasonable people.

What this amounted to was that as Hume's philosophy did not permit him to deny miracles on *a priori* grounds, he had had to find some other way to discredit them; and he had lit on the expedient of arguing that uniform experience provided the disproof. But his citation of St. Médard was a double-edged weapon: it could just as easily be cited as showing that experience had *not* been uniform. Such was the craving, though, among scientists and rationalists for any theory that would release them from Christianity's bondage that Hume's argument was constantly to be brought up as if, in some way, he had managed to prove that the supernatural could not exist, because natural law was sacrosanct. And very soon 'natural law' came to be regarded not as a goal towards which scientists and philosophers would lead mankind, but as a set of rules which had already been laid down, and could not be altered. Anomalies were not to be permitted to alter the law; not, at least, until they became intellectually insupportable, when the law would be quietly amended or extended to admit them.

On September 13th, 1768, a thunderclap was heard by villagers from Lucé, in France, followed by a whistling sound; and several crofters saw an opaque body describing a curve through the air before falling in a meadow. It turned out to be a stone, too hot to touch; and the Abbé Bachelay, breaking off a piece of it, sent it the Academy of the Sciences for identification. Lavoisier and some colleagues who believed thunderbolts were an occult superstition reduced the stone to powder and after various tests claimed they had proved that it did not fall from the sky: 'The opinion which seems to us the most probable and agrees best with the principles accepted in physics, is that this stone was struck by lightning'. When Ernst Chladni, founder of the science of acoustics (and inventor of the euphonium), later ventured to dispute this judgment, he was ridiculed by his colleagues, the Swiss meteorologist Deluc saying that if he saw one fall at his feet, he would admit he had seen it, but still say, 'I don't believe it'. And it was with this Humean attitude of mind – powerfully reinforced by the writings of Voltaire, to the point where, in Goethe's words, 'incredulity has become like an inverted superstition' – that Franz Mesmer and his followers had to contend.

Chapter Sixteen
Franz Mesmer

NOT ALL SCIENTISTS ACCEPTED THE ASSUMPTION THAT MIRACLES COULD not happen. A few were prepared to accept that undiscovered forces might be at work which would eventually be tracked down, and perhaps help to explain some supernatural phenomena. The Cabalist tradition included the idea of a 'fluid' analogous to gravity, or magnetism, permeating the atmosphere: a thesis which attracted Franz Mesmer while he was a medical student at the University of Vienna. In his inaugural dissertation, written in 1766, he propounded the theory that the sun, moon and stars influenced not merely each other in ways like the movement of the tides, 'but affect in similar manner all organised bodies through the medium of a subtle fluid, which pervades the universe, and associates all things together in mutual intercourse and harmony'.

Paracelsus and Van Helmont had held the same belief, relating the fluid to magnetism; and this had fused with the tradition of a healing force, divinely transmitted, which could be used to cure the sick by the laying on of hands. Some healers employed magnets to try to strengthen the healing flow; among them Fr. Hehl, S.J., Professor of Astronomy at the University. Experimenting, Mesmer found that the technique appeared to have effects which could be demonstrated. He could influence the rate of the flow of blood, for example, from a patient who was being bled by advancing or withdrawing the magnet. But a magnet, Mesmer found, was not essential. He could obtain the same results by pointing his forefinger at the patient, or using some object which he had 'magnetised' – with what he thought of as animal, rather than mineral, magnetism – by making passes over it with his hands; procedures resembling those used by tribal magicians, 'pointing the bone' or charging objects with *mana*, and having similar effects. His patients seemed to lose all control of their limbs, even of their identities.

Some went into convulsions; some dissociated, speaking in strange voices; some sank into catalepsies or comas. This, he assumed, must be part of the healing process; and his patients, though out of their minds during the process, were not disposed to worry so long as they felt better after it.

Mesmer was too successful, and too tactless, for his own good. Orthodox colleagues exploited a case in which he had claimed a cure when, they claimed, there was no cure (or the patient relapsed) to hound him out of Vienna. In Paris, however, where he settled in 1778, his treatment soon became so fashionable that he adopted a more flexible technique, using an oak tub filled with 'magnetised' water, with rods in it which patients could pick up for themselves and hold. And along with the reports of apparently miraculous cures there came descriptions of a variety of unaccountable by-products of the treatment: freedom from pain, and perception without the use of the five senses. Patients who appeared to be fast asleep, with their eyes shut (or open, with only the white showing), could 'see' what was going on around them, or follow the gestures of the magnetiser, even if he was in another room. Professor E. Seifert of Magdeburg was later to recall how, as a young man, he had asked Mesmer for a demonstration; and Mesmer indulged him by leaving the room and making his 'passes' at his patient through a wall. By placing himself in a doorway where he could see both men, the sceptical Seifert was able to satisfy himself that the patient really did react.

That subjects in the trance state could pick up information in this way came as no surprise to Mesmer; on his theory of animal magnetism, it was predictable. In a paper published in 1779, he re-stated his thesis. All the heavenly bodies, the earth, and life on it, he argued, were interconnected. A fluid 'so continuous as not to admit of a vacuum, and incomparably subtle' existed, its properties subject to mechanical laws 'with which we are not yet acquainted'. Like magnetism, it could be tapped, concentrated, stored and communicated at a distance. And when the nature of the fluid was better understood, he surmised, it would explain much that had been baffling in the past: the laying on of hands; visions; oracles; the action of mind on mind, and of mind on matter; animal migrations; and communication at a distance – 'there are few, however ridiculous, however extravagant they may seem, that may not be regarded as remnants of truths primitively recognised.' But this was not an aspect of his discovery, or rediscovery, which particularly interested him. He was chiefly concerned to popularise animal magnetism as a way to treat illness, and the first essential, to his mind, was to persuade the medical profession that it was an effective way.

The Franklin Commission

Although orthodox medicine was as predictably hostile in Paris as it had been in Vienna, Mesmer was in luck; he managed to convert Charles D'Eslon, physician to the Comte d'Artois, brother of Louis XVI; through him, Marie Antoinette became interested in animal magnetism; and it was apparently through her influence that in 1784 the king set up a Royal Commission of Inquiry into the subject, its members being drawn from the Academy of the Sciences.

It was the first scientific investigation of its kind, and in terms of the calibre and reputation of the investigators perhaps the most high-powered ever. Benjamin Franklin, then the United States Ambassador to France, was nominally in charge; supported by the astronomer (and future mayor of Paris), Jean-Sylvain Bailly; Dr. Guillotin, inventor of the humane killer (as he believed it to be) that bears his name; the botanist, Laurent de Jussieu; Lavoisier; and others as well known in their day. Investigation of D'Eslon's practice left them in no doubt that his method produced results. Their report described how patients went into convulsions which seemed to be catching, as other patients, not being magnetised, also succumbed. It was as if the patients were

entirely under the government of the person who distributes the magnetic force. They may appear to be in a state of extreme drowsiness; his voice, a look, a sign arouses them. It is impossible not to recognise, in these effects, an extraordinary influence acting upon patients.

But though the influence might sometimes be beneficial, convulsions might be dangerous; and Bailly had proved by tests that neither magnetism nor electricity was involved. 'There is nothing to show the existence of this magnetic fluid,' the report concluded; 'and since it is non-existent, it can have no salubrious effects.' Good or bad, the effects were principally due to the artificial stimulus given to the patients' imagination. The members of a committee from the Royal Society of Medicine were also unimpressed; they dismissed the case for animal magnetism as 'absolutely destitute of proofs'.

These were not quite such damning verdicts as they were clearly intended to be. In his reply, D'Eslon pointed out that he had never been in any doubt that the agent which had the biggest share in creating animal magnetism's effects 'might indeed be none other than the imagination itself, whose power is as extensive as it is little known'. To the commissioners, though, the crucial issue was whether there was, or was not, a fluid capable of being transmitted in the form of a 'fluence' (the old English term comes closest to describing how the early mesmerists regarded the process) acting on and through patients even when they were not aware of it. And in some of the tests, the subjects did remarkable things. One was able to play cards with his eyes closed and his eyelids held down; another, a hatter, showed no sign of pain when subjected to normally painful procedures. The committee, however, felt confident that these were tricks. 'Played picquet well, and recognised the cards with facility,' the report observed, but added, 'Query: by touch?' As for the hatter's ability to put up with the pins being stuck into him without wincing, this surely must be collusion.

The report would have been unanimously dismissive had it not been for Jussieu. A meticulous researcher – his botanical work was to provide the basis for a system of classification of plants which has lasted to this day – he had noticed something which had escaped his colleagues' attention; that patients sometimes reacted to a rod, or a finger, pointed at them from a distance of six feet even when they could not see it. One patient became aware she was being magnetised in this way, though her back was turned; others were seized with convulsive movements when a finger was moved behind them, the movements continuing while the finger action lasted. These observations, Jussieu conceded, might not sound very striking, but he had only mentioned those which seemed to him to have established a connection sufficient 'to compel the admission of the possibility of the existence of a fluid or force which is exercised by man on man, and which sometimes produces a perceptible effect'.

The Lyon School

Jussieu's plea for further research was rejected by his colleagues. The Academy of Medicine laid down that summer that 'no physician shall declare himself a partisan of animal magnetism, either in his practice or by his writings', under the penalty of being struck off the register; a penalty imposed even on the influential D'Eslon. But though the Academies could enforce their authority in Paris, they had less control in the provinces; and hardly had their edict been promulgated than fresh evidence to support Jussieu's contention came from Chastenet de Puységur, a former President of the Lyon Medical Society. Puységur's interest in physics – shared by many doctors of the time, hoping as they were to find some more rational basis for treatment – had led him to investigate magnetism and, more sceptically, animal magnetism. To his astonishment one of his patients, Victor, came under his control to such an extent that not merely did he do whatever he was told to do by words or signs; he obeyed unspoken commands. The wish alone sufficed, Puységur wrote to tell his brother. Victor would behave as he was willed to behave, talk as he was willed to talk; and if willed to stop talking, he would 'stay his thoughts, his phrases, in the middle of a word'. Yet this was not because he was stupid – though stupid he certainly was in ordinary life. His personality changed. 'It is the dullest witted peasant of the district'; but 'when he is in a trance, I do not know anyone more profound, more sensible, more clairvoyant.'

This clairvoyance, Puységur found, enabled Victor to diagnose his own or other people's disorders; a faculty which Puységur began to exploit. To Mesmer, convulsions had been part of the therapeutic process. But if diagnosis and treatment could be conducted without them, Puységur felt, so much the better. He proceeded with Victor's help to treat the local peasantry, with success. His standing in the community gave him protection; and though his colleagues were sceptical, one, J. H. Pététin – like himself a past President of the Lyon Medical Society – also did some experiments, which succeeded far beyond his critical expectations. Pététin found among his patients a woman who, when magnetised, could 'see' what was on a card placed on her stomach, and 'taste' foods by touch. To convince his friends that she was not using any deception, Pététin would ask her to tell them what they had in their pockets or purses, which she was able to do, even to the extent of describing the contents of letters. A doctor arrived with a concealed bottle of white wine, to test her: not merely did she correctly guess what it was, she told him it came from Condrieu, which he had not known, and provided sundry correct details about the donor.

Although Puységur had described Victor as clairvoyant, neither he nor Pététin thought of their somnambulists as possessing a supernatural faculty. Puységur believed in animal magnetism; Pététin thought that some electrical force was involved; but both assumed that thought-transference and eyeless vision in the trance state would be accounted for in natural terms. And by this time, other researchers, notably Tardy de Montravel, had come up with similar evidence. In spite of orthodoxy's ban research might have continued to spread, but for the events of 1789. 'Nothing short of the cannon of the Revolution could have silenced the discussions on magnetism,' Guillaume Figuier was to recall; 'but at the time, all this hubbub subsided, in Lyon as elsewhere, not because magnetism was forgotten, but because its adherents were scattered.' Mesmer's connections with the Court would have settled his fate had he not taken himself off to Switzerland, there to live out the rest of his life in semi-retirement; but the guillotine impartially claimed many of his patients and his opponents, including Lavoisier and Bailly. Guillotin himself was lucky to escape, as was Puységur, both being gaoled; and animal magnetism went into the shadows.

The Revival of Animal Magnetism

With Napoleon on the French throne, it ceased to be politically hazardous to dabble in mesmerism; and a young curator at the Paris *Jardin des Plantes*, Joseph Deleuze – impressed by what he had read, and still more impressed by what he experienced when he was himself mesmerised – began careful experiments, recording everything that happened when he put subjects into a trance. As orthodoxy was still contemptuous, however, he did not care to publish his findings. It was not until 1808 that the first sign of a thaw came with the publication of Pététin's *Electricité Animale*. Pététin had no longer anything to lose; he was dead. As he posthumously explained, he had decided that his case histories of a number of his patients who could 'see' or 'taste' objects with their fingertips, or other parts of the body, would carry more conviction if he could not be accused of having sought publicity for himself by reporting them. When Puységur's memoirs came out the following year he, too, stressed that he did not expect all that he had recorded to be believed. The important thing was to experiment. The fact that no acceptable theory had been produced to account for the facts was no reason, he insisted, for rejecting them: 'had we been obliged, in order to recognise the well-known phenomena of electricity, of the magnet, and of galvanism, to wait till we should agree as to their causes, there is reason to believe that we would today have neither lightning rods, nor compass, nor Voltaic pile'. Was there a magnetic fluid? He did not know; but there was certainly something. 'Increase the number of experiments and you will come upon a theory; else you will lose your time.'

Four years later Deleuze decided that his time had come; he must publish his results, putting them in a historical perspective. His *Histoire Critique du Magnétisme Animal* was chiefly concerned to establish the reality of the mesmeric trance state, and to describe how subjects behaved in it. What they did could best be accounted for, he thought, by the assumption that they were in a condition of induced somnambulism, but amenable to the mesmerist's verbal or visual instructions. In a few cases, though, he had found that his somnambulists developed faculties which could not be naturally accounted for. They could 'see' a concealed object, and diagnose their own or other people's disorders; occasionally they would have prophetic visions. The information provided was not always correct; but it had been accurate enough, often enough, to convince Deleuze that there must be a magnetic fluid (he left out the 'animal', and from this time on the supporters of Mesmer tended to do the same) giving some additional power of perception.

By this time, researchers in other parts of Europe were beginning to present corroborative evidence whose full range and significance were not to be grasped until the publication, a century and a half later, of the four-volume survey, *Abnormal Hypnotic Phenomena* edited by Dr. E. J. Dingwall, including contributions on Germany, Italy, Russia and elsewhere, as well as on France, showing how all over Europe there had been a surge of interest in the subject towards the end of the Napoleonic wars; showing, too, that although individuals obtained different results, phenomena such as eyeless vision, thought-transference and other unexplained forms of perception, were everywhere encountered. In 1814 a Dutch lawyer, Pieter van Ghert, described how he had found a boy who, when magnetised, could 'read' with his fingertips; and a girl who, when asked about people or places he knew, appeared to be able to 'visit' them in her trance and tell him about them, not always correctly, but sometimes with complete accuracy. Four years later Dietrich Kieser, a Professor and Privy Councillor at Jena, published an account of experiments he had made with an epileptic boy who could detect colours by touch, even with the soles of his stockinged feet, and describe correctly things which were being done in another room. In Baden Dr. Franz Durr magnetised Wilhemina Koch, daughter of the Court Artist, and asked her to describe the contents of an opaque sealed envelope. He did not know what they were himself; but she correctly pronounced that the message was, 'Trust in God. He will help thee.' And in Langenberg Adolf Köttgen, a silk manufacturer, did a series of tests of this kind with a girl, Maria, who suffered from fits (epileptics were often taken to magnetisers, as it had come to be believed that the treatment could succeed where orthodox methods notoriously were useless). Köttgen enlisted friends to act as referees, to prevent any deception. Words written by one of them were carefully wrapped up, sealed, and given to a friend who, not knowing what they were, brought them to Köttgen. Maria, magnetised, painfully spelled out *'Kunst-und-Musikalienhandlung'*. When the missive was brought back, still sealed, to the writer, he said that Maria had been very nearly right; what he had actually written was *'Buch-und-Musikalienhandlung'*. So he had; but when the seal was broken, and the paper opened up, it was found that some of the melted sealing wax had seeped through on to the paper, obscuring the first letter 'B'.

Similar accounts came from other countries. In Sweden Pehr Cederschjold, later Professor of Obstetrics at the Stockholm Medical School, watched a magnetist at work while he was on a visit to Denmark, and later began to experiment for himself. His first patient, 'Miss N' displayed eyeless vision; blindfold, she could describe people, tell him what he was doing, even read from a book. Far from being impressed, Cederschjold (who wanted to use magnetism in treatment) did a series of tests designed to provide some natural explanation; but when 'Miss N' was able to 'read' a book placed on her stomach while her head, swathed in a cloth, was turned in another direction, he was 'forced to throw rationalism overboard, and cease doubting what I saw with my own eyes'.

The fact that Cederschjold conducted his research into animal magnetism in a critical frame of mind, stressing its limitations as a form of treatment and warning of the risk of patients' deceptions, did not save him from the wrath of more orthodox colleagues. When he first applied for a Professorship in 1815 he was denounced by the leading Swedish scientist of the time, Jons Jacob Berzelius, for 'frothy ideas' which had led to his being regarded by many 'as a fool and a mountebank, rather than as a man of skill' – a verdict so manifestly unfair that it was repudiated even by a rival contender for the Chair. Perhaps in the hope of finding material with which to justify his mistrust of animal magnetism, Berzelius began to investigate it for himself. A year later, chastened, he admitted that although much more research needed to be done; 'many circumstances lead me to believe that the magnetised subjects have a perception of what is happening both within them and outside, by means which are still not known, whilst the use of the ordinary senses seems to be in abeyance'. But such retractions were unusual.

That researchers into animal magnetism received protection and encouragement was often due to court patronage, as it had originally been in France. In 1815 King Charles of Sweden provided the money for Cederschjold to study animal magnetism in Germany; and the same year, a commission which had been set up in Russia by the Tzar reported that on the available evidence, a case had been made for further research. The research should be undertaken, the report recommended, by members of the medical profession only; and this was to precipitate the first of many divisions of opinion among the mesmerists themselves.

Georg Parrot, a Professor of Physics, at once objected. Doctors were notoriously credulous; and a force which probably had electricity or magnetism as a component clearly needed physicists to understand it. Jeremias Lichtenstaedt, practising as a doctor in St. Petersburg, replied that the object of magnetising people should be to cure them of diseases. For this purpose, it was not necessary to put them into a somnambulist state; and if they were put into it with a view to investigating, say, eyeless vision, it might set back their treatment. He did not dispute that eyeless vision occasionally occurred; but he feared that research into this aspect might bring animal magnetism into disrepute, jeopardising its much more valuable role in healing.

These issues – to whom research should be entrusted, and whether the evidence from it should be suppressed if it looked like being too unpalatable for orthodoxy to accept – were to become a source of continual controversy in connection not only with mesmerism, but with other forms of research into territory outside the boundaries orthodoxy laid down as natural. There was the further complication in the case of mesmerism that even if it were agreed that the medical and the clairvoyant aspects were best kept separate, the distinction was proving impossible to maintain; for reasons which were revealed in a survey presented by Professor D. Veliansky of the Imperial Academy of St. Petersburg. Veliansky drew up a table showing the six stages, or depths, of the induced trance state. In the first, magnetic readiness, the patient was aware of what was going on. In the second, magnetic half-sleep, he retained some awareness, but not full control. In the third, magnetic sleep, he lost contact with external reality. In the fourth, somnambulism, he was entirely at the magnetiser's command. In the fifth, clairvoyance, he could 'see' into his own body and recommend a course of treatment. And in the sixth, he might achieve a state comparable to that which mystics had tried to describe: a feeling of community with nature, liberating him from the bonds of time and of space, and giving him the ability to describe not merely what was happening behind his back, or when blindfolded, but also to 'see' what was going on at a distance. It was as if part of him had detached itself from his body, and could visit other places; 'travelling clairvoyance', as it came to be known. As a doctor, Veliansky was naturally interested in the fifth stage; but it was precisely at this stage that orthodox medical science began to jib. If clairvoyance were incorporated into standard practice, it would be more difficult to persuade orthodoxy to take mesmerism seriously; and travelling clairvoyance would be even harder for orthodoxy to swallow.

In a memoir which remained unpublished until after his death, Deleuze was to recall how he had agonised over this issue before publishing his history in 1812. It had taken him years of research to convince himself that some of the phenomena he had encountered were genuine; and he could not expect his colleagues to be convinced by his evidence unless they were prepared to experiment along the same lines themselves. But he knew they would not experiment if his account frightened them off. He had therefore toned down, or omitted altogether, some of the more startling evidence he had collected. He had also refrained from theorising, contenting himself with presenting a simple explanatory analogy: 'we know that if we place side-by-side two stringed musical instruments that are in unison, and twang the strings of the first one, the corresponding strings of the second sound of their own accord. This physical phenomenon is like that which takes place in animal magnetism.' But it had been to no purpose; his colleagues proved to be 'actually more averse to examining a particular modification to the order of things which they accepted, than they would have been to adopt a system subversive of their doctrines'.

The Abbé Faria

Up to this point, although animal magnetism had spread out through Europe, it had made little impression except on the researchers themselves and their patients. For the great majority of scientists and doctors the entire process – not just eyeless vision and travelling clairvoyance, but also the convulsions and catalepsies, the freedom from pain and the somnambulism – was spurious, in the same category as levitation, ghosts, and similar superstitions. As for members of the public, they would have been unlikely to come into contact with a magnetist unless, in despair over the failure of orthodox medical remedies, they sought one out.

In the years of Napoleon's exile in St. Helena, however, a Portuguese priest, the Abbé J. C. Faria, was giving public demonstrations in Paris, not unlike those which were later to become familiar in theatres and music halls, putting members of the audience into the somnambulist state, and demonstrating his control over them. He did not use the standard method – making passes over them with his hands. He would simply say, quietly but authoritatively, 'sleep', and susceptible subjects would become somnambulist. This did not endear him to the other mesmerists; in any case they regarded public performances with suspicion. The behaviour of some of Faria's magnetised subjects on the stage, too, was such that sceptical members of the audience understandably suspected collusion. Eventually an actor – either on his own account or for a fee – volunteered to go up on the stage, to behave as if magnetised, and then to disclose that he had only been pretending to be in the somnambulist state. Other subjects, perhaps embarrassed at having been made to look foolish while under Faria's control, had the excuse to say that they had only been pretending, too; and Faria was discredited.

This struck an Irish doctor working in Paris, Richard Chenevix, as unjust. He had previously dismissed mesmerism; what led him to doubt his own cynicism was the illogicality of the popular assumption that, because Faria had allowed himself to be cheated, he must himself be a cheat. Faria, he was later to recall, was

> in the frivolous French metropolis called a charlatan, which made me suppose he was not so; and the event proved I was right. He was, indeed, poor; he exercised his art for money; he gave public lectures at three francs a ticket . . . but till the period of his death, I remained acquainted with the Abbé Faria, and never knew a man to whom the epithet impostor was less applicable.

Faria has, in fact, a right to be credited with being the first man to discover and utilise the simple method of inducing the trance state which, half a century later, was to become standard as 'hypnotism'; and also for pointing out the implication that there was no need to assume the existence of any magnetic fluid. The fluence might be simply mental. But he, too, occasionally encountered clairvoyance. Some subjects, he found, could 'see' what was happening in their bodies, and recommend remedies for their own disorders; or speak foreign languages which they did not know (as other researchers in different parts of Europe also reported); and one of his somnambulists could 'see' and 'hear' what was happening in a different part of Paris. But his work went for nothing, even among his fellow mesmerists; one of them, Alphonse Teste, was to say twenty years later that when Faria died in 1819, it was 'with the finest reputation for charlatanry that any man ever had, or, I would add, better merited'.

It was easy to deride Faria as a mountebank, and to dismiss his serious research as tainted by his exploitation of mesmerism as a source of income. No such criticism could be made of the researches of M. de Bruno, published in the year of Faria's death; they had been carried out before the Revolution while de Bruno was a member of the Comte d'Artois's circle, and had remained unpublished in de Bruno's lifetime. His case histories, painstakingly recorded thirty years earlier, displayed many of the features which had since become familiar, along with a few interesting variations. One of his patients could easily be put to sleep when he magnetised her; but annoyingly, her head would then begin to move, slowly but jerkily, until she fell out of the chair, even if it were a deep armchair.

At last, a thought struck me; that her head always leaned towards the side on which I was. I changed my position gradually, and what was my astonishment to find that her head, like a veritable compass-needle, followed the curve I slowly made round her at a distance of five or six feet. It stopped when I stopped, always leaning towards me . . . In vain, I went to a greater distance, the effect was the same. I left the room, went different directions . . . my 'compass' always showed, with the utmost exactitude, the point of the horizon at which I stood.

De Bruno had been able to confirm the accuracy of the 'compass' with the assistance of her doctor, who watched her while he went out of the house, the two men subsequently comparing notes. There must be some fluence passing between magnetiser and patient, de Bruno decided; but not everybody was gifted with the necessary sensibility, nor was it always present in the same individual in the same degree at all times, although it could be improved by practice.

Chapter Seventeen
The Second Inquiry

THE MOST IMPORTANT DEVELOPMENT, OF THIS PERIOD, PROVED TO BE the experiments which the young Baron J. D. Du Potet de Sennevoy was beginning to conduct. Du Potet had been a dreamy youth, much thrashed for his inattention to his studies; by his own account, animal magnetism had fired his imagination, giving him the energy to become a medical student; to introduce himself to Puységur, Deleuze and Faria; and in 1820 to obtain the permission of H. M. Husson of the Hôtel-Dieu hospital to carry out experiments with patients. Having found a good subject, Mlle. Catherine Samson, he gave Husson a demonstration; and Husson was impressed. But how could Du Potet convince other doctors, who had no reason to trust him, that Catherine and he were not in collusion? The real test, Husson suggested, would be for Du Potet to show he could mesmerise Catherine without her knowing that he was doing it. Du Potet hid in a closet; at a given signal, he began making his mesmeric passes through the partition to where Catherine was sitting; she immediately began to show signs of drowsiness; and soon she was in a state of somnambulism. A week later the experiment was successfully repeated for Professor J. C. Recamier. 'Are you convinced?' Du Potet asked him. 'No,' he replied, 'but staggered.'

Another observer who remained unconvinced was Dr. Alexandre Bertrand. Bertrand had become interested in animal magnetism through Deleuze, but had decided from his own experience that Faria's interpretation was correct: that suggestion, rather than animal magnetism, was the key. He realised that this theory could not account for all the reported phenomena; but this did not disturb him, because everything he encountered in his own practice appeared to him to have a natural explanation. A few of his somnambulists, for example, had the faculty of diagnosis as if by second sight. One of them was able to tell him what was the matter with his patients because she experienced their symptoms and their pains in her own body; sometimes she discovered disorders he had failed to diagnose. Another had an inner 'voice' which prompted her; when Bertrand asked her what was the matter with a patient he saw arriving, her 'voice' informed her, correctly, that he had been shot through the mouth, though no wound was visible. Bertrand, however, declined to believe this was due to animal magnetism. It was more probable, he felt, that patients were picking up clues naturally. But how, in that case, to account for Catherine becoming entranced when she did not know that Du Potet was mesmerising her? A possible explanation struck Bertrand: that she must have guessed, or sensed, what was being done, and behaved as she thought she was expected to behave. To try to prove his point, he persuaded Husson to set up the experiment again, and to go through the whole procedure in Du Potet's absence – Bertrand believing that she would become magnetised by force of habit when she expected to be. She was not. It remained to see if she could be magnetised by Du Potet at a time when she would *not* be expecting it; and she duly became entranced.

The explanation, Bertrand decided, must be that a form of induction occurred, as in electrical operations: a train of thought in the mind of the mesmerist could set off a similar train in the subject's. And only once, in his research, was he given any reason to doubt whether this was an adequate explanation. In a treatise on somnambulism in 1823 he described how he had taken the ring off the finger of one of his patients, when her eyes were shut and her back to the witnesses, and handed it to one of them, 'Mme. R.'; his expectation being that when he asked his patient who was holding it, she would be able to read his thoughts by induction, and reply 'Mme. R.' But when he asked her who had the ring, his patient named a doctor who was present, indicating with a gesture that it would be found in his pocket. Telling her she was wrong, Bertrand turned to the witnesses for confirmation; only to find that she had been right. The doctor, perhaps suspecting that there might be collusion between her and Bertrand, had waited until Bertrand's back was also turned, and then taken the ring from Mme. R.; thereby making the result of the experiment even more impressive. Still, it was not wholly destructive of Bertrand's theory. His subject might have picked up a stray thought from somebody else in the room. And though induction would hardly have accounted for travelling clairvoyance, let alone pre-vision of future events, he did not come across them in his research.

For most scientists, however, the issue was not whether magnetised subjects had some form of perception other than that provided by their five senses; it was simply whether the trance state existed. And by his enthusiasm, Du Potet had broken down the barriers which had been keeping some of them from undertaking research. Among those induced to experiment was Dr. E. J. Georget, author of a pioneering work on the physiology of the nervous system, in which he had expressed strictly materialist views. He was reluctantly convinced by demonstrations that patients really did become somnambulist; and he began to encounter subjects who in the somnambulist state appeared to acquire an additional sense. One was able consistently to detect which of a number of glasses of water he had magnetised.

Although many orthodox doctors and scientists remained as hostile as before – in 1823, the physiologist Baron Anthelme Richerand bluntly asserted that most of what had been described by earlier researchers was invention – it was becoming harder to attribute the evidence to a desire for notoriety, or to deliberate deception. Laplace thought it unphilosophic to deny the phenomena 'simply because they cannot be explained in the actual state of our knowledge'; according to Chenevix, he conceded before his death in 1827 that the testimony in favour of animal magnetism, 'coming with such uniformity from enlightened men of many nations who had no interest to deceive, and possessed of no possible means of collusion, was such that, applying to it his own principles regarding evidence, he could not withhold his assent'. The physicist Ampère and the naturalist Cuvier were similarly persuaded. And in 1825 Deleuze re-emerged in support of the cause, with a manual of practical instruction.

By this time, Deleuze's reputation as naturalist, philanthropist, translator and man of affairs was securely established, in spite of the mistrust which his earlier acceptance of animal magnetism had engendered (even his obituarist in the *Biographie Universelle,* who had no sympathy for this aberration and mentioned it only in passing, was to comment that it had not diminished the esteem which his character inspired). Deleuze dedicated his book to Puységur, who had just died; 'without you, magnetism would have been forgotten after Mesmer as it was after Van Helmont. No one would have engaged in it if the most active charity had not given you the courage to sacrifice your time, to despise criticism, and finally to brave all obstacles to establish a truth.' It was true, Deleuze had to admit, that the magnetisers must be on their guard against deception – or self-deception: 'I have seen men, otherwise well-informed, become the dupes of their visions'. And there were other problems, he had found. The results were most striking when the phenomena emerged spontaneously rather than when they were sought after; clairvoyant powers varied 'prodigiously', not merely as between individuals, but in the same individual at different times; in some cases, the powers suddenly vanished altogether (on one occasion, to his embarrassment, a young man, 'who for several days had exhibited the most extraordinary clairvoyance' had ceased to manifest it the moment he was asked to demonstrate it in front of witnesses); and somnambulists who became puffed up with their own success 'ordinarily lose the most important faculties'. Allowing for all this, though, Deleuze still felt that the evidence for the existence of the 'higher phenomena', as they were coming to be called, was convincing; and he urged Bertrand, whose work he admired, not to be too dismissive. If he had seen what Deleuze had seen, he would not lightly reject evidence simply because he had not himself encountered examples.

Deleuze had no hope of convincing the opposition. 'Our adversaries,' he complained, 'condemn us without examination.' But it happened that a massive new dictionary of medicine was being published in Paris, twenty-one volumes in all, spaced out over several years; and the task of writing a section on animal magnetism, to be published in 1825, had been entrusted to a man who had been expected to demolish it, Professor L. Rostan of the Salpêtrière Hospital in Paris. Before he came to write the section, however, Rostan had been converted. With a colleague, he tested a somnambulist; and they had found that he could tell what time was shown on a watch held at the back of his head, even when they twiddled the hands around in such a way that they did not themselves know what time was indicated; which suggested that he was 'seeing' the dial, rather than reading their thoughts. As a result, the dictionary included not only the results of Rostan's research, but his hypothesis to account for such phenomena : there must, he argued, be a force which could be directed by the will of the operator and could pass, like ordinary magnetism, through solid objects.

The fact that animal magnetism should have been noticed at all, let alone defended, enraged its critics; but there was nothing they could do about the article (until the second edition, when it was excised). And when a young researcher, Dr. P. Foissac, proposed to the Academies of the Sciences and of Medicine that it was time the subject was again investigated, whether by chance or by his own design the man the Academies appointed to advise on the proposal was Husson. He recommended that the proposal should be adopted; and in 1826, the Academies felt compelled, though not without vehemently expressed misgivings, to appoint another commission. Still, they could ensure an apparently safe majority of sceptics to control the proceedings. Even Husson was at first excluded, though he was subsequently co-opted.

The 1831 Report

Two books were published that year which foreshadowed problems ahead for the mesmerists, whatever course the committee's deliberations took. Bertrand's second work, *Animal Magnetism in France*, showed that he had not shifted from his earlier position, and his theory of induction to account for eyeless vision was one which the movement's critics could exploit; here was a mesmerist writing a book on animal magnetism to say that animal magnetism did not exist! Bertrand, how-

ever, had too great a respect for his predecessors to cast doubt on their
ability or integrity simply because he had not obtained the same results
from his research as they had. Dr. Amédée Dupau of Montpellier,
in his survey of animal magnetism, had no such inhibitions.

Dupau was the first of a line of critics who, in the guise of candid
friends, tried systematically to undermine confidence in any research
which did not present results which fitted their own specifications. He
accepted that there was a magnetised state, which he took to be physiological; but he dismissed eyeless vision, thought-transference and the
rest of the higher phenomena as the product of deception on the part
of the subjects and gullibility or excessive enthusiasm on the part of
the mesmerists (thereby providing himself with an excuse, when he
was asked how, having done no research himself, he could be so dogmatic. He explained he had been careful not to, in case he should lose
his own detachment). Dupau's critical method was simply to look for
possible flaws in the evidence: Rostan's somnambulist might have been
able to see the watch held behind his head in a mirror, for example;
or his correct guesses of the time could be attributed to coincidence.
And Dupau pounced upon a cautionary statement which Rostan had
made; that the presence of sceptics at a test sometimes appeared to
spoil the prospects of getting results. How could Rostan reconcile this
with the fact that he himself had been a sceptic? Was it not simply an
excuse for failure in test conditions?

The advantage of Dupau's method was that there was no need for
him to prove that the earlier researchers had been deceived, or had
deceived themselves. It was enough, for his purpose, to show how they
might have been deceived, or have deceived themselves. It was a weakness, though, that in no case could he produce convincing evidence that
deception of either kind had actually occurred. He claimed, indeed,
that he knew Catherine Samson to have been an impostor, and promised to provide the proof later; but the proof was never forthcoming.
Nevertheless Dupau's line of attack was to cause endless trouble. The
need to try to find ways to make experiments fraud-proof was to tor-
ment researchers from this time on.

The believers in the existence of higher phenomena suffered another
reverse in 1826, of a kind that was later to become familiar. One of the
somnambulists Georget had used in his Salpêtrière demonstrations
published a confession that she had imposed upon her investigators.
She offered no proof and, as she was a mental patient, she might have
been seeking notoriety; but Georget's critics demanded that his study
of the physiology of the nervous system, which he was known to be
revising, should contain a retraction of the views he had expressed
favourable to animal magnetism. Georget did not live to see the revision completed; but after his death in 1828 it was found that he had

left a note with his will reaffirming his belief in the existence 'in us and out of us, of an intelligent principle, differing entirely from anything material'. He had decided, though, in view of what might be said or implied if he made this statement in his lifetime, that it should only be published 'when my sincerity can no longer be doubted, nor my intentions suspected'.

By this time, the Commission had got down to work; and the expectations of its sceptic members were confounded. In 1829 those of them who believed that the trance state itself was spurious were to be given the most striking demonstration of its reality so far: a woman suffering from a tumour of the breast was magnetised and the tumour was removed by a surgeon, the patient showing no signs of feeling pain. Fears the mesmerists had that somnambulists might be inhibited by test conditions turned out to be unfounded. Foissac's subject, Céline, showed that although entirely ignorant of medical matters, she could tell the members of the Commission what was the matter with three patients; and the remedies she prescribed, not of a kind she could have been expected to know about, were adjudged reasonable. In one case, where the patient was being treated with mercury for what had been diagnosed as a venereal infection, she intimated that it was the remedy and not the disorder which was causing the patient's symptoms. Her advice was ignored; but when shortly afterwards the patient died, a post-mortem revealed that Céline had been right and the doctors wrong.

A problem for the Commission, however, was that ordinarily only a death, leading to a post-mortem, could show whether a clairvoyant's vision of internal organs had been right; and the verdict might not be accepted as conclusive even then. Perhaps for this reason, the Commission were willing to accept demonstrations of phenomena which could be more easily checked, such as eyeless vision. There were several failures in tests; but two somnambulists could distinguish objects, play cards without touching them, or read lines from a book opened at random. To make sure that Paul, a student who was one of Foissac's subjects, was really unable to see with his eyes, and that there could be no collusion, the investigators took it in turn to press down his eyelids with their fingers: a fresh pack of cards was produced and shuffled, yet Paul could effortlessly name the cards turned up. 'Reading' was more of an effort for him, and he made a few mistakes; but he was often able to get the general, and sometimes the exact, wording.

The commissioners were converted. In their report, presented by Husson to the Academies in 1831, they admitted they could neither decide what force was involved nor define precisely what the somnambulist state was: but they felt it could safely be assumed to exist when it gave rise to 'new faculties which have been designated by the terms clairvoyance, intuition, interior prevision', or when it produced great changes in the physiological condition of the patient 'such as insensibility on the one hand, or a sudden and considerable increase of power on the other, when this state cannot be ascribed to any other cause'. It had been demonstrated that the state had been induced 'under circumstances in which the magnetised subjects could not see, and were wholly ignorant of the means employed', when the mesmerist was out of sight, or when he was in another room with the doors between him and his patients closed. Although the commissioners felt that more evidence was required, they unanimously concluded that the facts they had collected were of sufficient importance 'to lead them to think that the Academy ought to encourage research into magnetism, as a very curious branch of psychology and natural history'.

At last the way ahead seemed clear. Deleuze was able to add a footnote to a new edition of his manual, claiming the existence of animal magnetism was no longer in question. 'No more doubt,' Du Potet exulted, 'no more uncertainty. Magic is rediscovered.' Animal magnetism, he felt, had been shown to be a real force; through its agency, magic began – 'that is to say, extraordinary phenomena begin to astonish us'.

Dreams, Visions and Poltergeists

While the struggle to secure recognition for animal magnetism was being won – or so it appeared – in France, there had been no comparable campaign in other countries; though in Germany several scientists of established reputation had pronounced themselves convinced, including the apostle of physiognomy, J. C. Lavater; Professor Dietrich Kieser (whose somnambulist, an epileptic eleven-year-old boy, could accurately describe when magnetised what was going on outside in the street, though it was out of his sight); and the botanist Gottfried Treviranus (who according to Coleridge evaded discussion of the subject by saying, 'I have seen much which I would not have believed on your telling; and in all reason, therefore, I can neither hope nor wish that you should believe on mine').

Schopenhauer believed there must be some form of communication between humans of the kind there was between animals, displaying itself in dreams, and in the way that 'the thoughts of the mesmerist pass to the somnambulist'; Hegel agreed, accepting the reality of thought-transference – 'the magic tie' – and clairvoyance: 'the intuitive spirit oversteps the confines of time and space; it beholds things remote, things long past, and things to come'. But it was not so much the quantity or quality of the evidence for animal magnetism that carried conviction, Jung-Stilling remarked, as the ability and integrity of the men who had provided it. When so many distinguished academic figures assured him that they had tested somnambulists and had satisfied themselves that books could be 'read' or pictures 'seen' without the use of eyes, he felt he had to accept that they were telling the truth, however improbable it sounded. They were not deceivers, he knew; many of them were friends and former colleagues. And it simply was not possible that all of them had been letting themselves be deceived.

But it was not necessary to rely on the evidence from animal magnetism to accept the reality of the higher phenomena. Jung-Stilling's book on science and spiritism, published in Nuremberg in 1808, re-stated the old theory of the spirit being able to liberate itself from the body in trance states, so that it could roam, and even become visible to people at a distance by materialisation. And Goethe, an admirer of Jung-Stilling ('one found in him a sound common sense, which rested on feeling and therefore was determined by the affections and passions; and from this very feeling sprang an enthusiasm for what was good, true and just'), became convinced as a result of personal experiences of clairvoyance: among them one which was unusual in that it involved a two-way psychic traffic. On the road to Weimar with a companion, Goethe encountered his friend Frederick, who was supposed to be in Frankfurt, incongruously wearing Goethe's dressing gown and bedroom slippers. Finding that his companion had seen nothing, Goethe realised it had been a hallucination, and began to fear for Frederick's safety. When they got to Weimar, however, they found Frederick installed. He had arrived there soaked by a storm, he told them, and had put on Goethe's clothes and gone to sit in front of the fire. Nodding off, he had dreamed about encountering Goethe on the road; the words with which Goethe had greeted him in the dream were those which he had actually spoken on the road. In his autobiography, too, Goethe was to recall an instance of precognition. Leaving his beloved Frederika in Sesenheim in 1771 he had a vision of himself riding back into the town in a grey coat fringed with lace, a kind he had never worn; and it had given him the conviction that he would see her again. Eight years later, he rode back to Sesenheim; and 'although it was not my will which had made me assume the costume', he was wearing a grey coat, fringed with lace.

Disapproving of what he regarded as Goethe's frivolous interest in the occult, George Henry Lewes was to make the point that Goethe had not mentioned this episode in his correspondence at the time; and most of the stories of precognition suffer from this defect. But a couple were reasonably well attested. In his memoirs Clement Carlyon vouched for an account which he had heard from a Cornishman, Williams, of an episode in 1812. In a dream, Williams was in the lobby of the House of Commons when he saw a man in a dark brown coat with peculiar buttons shoot the Chancellor of the Exchequer. Williams woke his wife and told her; fell asleep again, and had the same dream. He felt that he ought to send a warning, but friends dissuaded him. Eight days afterwards the news came of Spencer Perceval's assassination in the Commons' lobby; and later Williams saw a print in a shop, purporting to picture the scene, in which the assassin was dressed precisely as in the dream.

The most celebrated example of precognition in this period, though, was related by the French writer Jean-François La Harpe. At a dinner held in Paris just before the Revolution, attended by a distinguished company of courtiers and Academicians, the general feeling was of enthusiasm for the constitutional changes which, it was felt, could not be long delayed. Only the Marquis Cazotte remained abstracted. He had a reputation for second sight; and the others, chaffing him about his silence, pressed him for a forecast on what was going to happen. Eventually, he was induced to tell those present, one by one, what their fate was going to be when the Revolution came. Condorcet would succumb to poison, which he would take to cheat the executioner. Malesherbes, Bailly, and others would die on the scaffold; as would the Duchess of Gramont and, he feared, the highest in the land. 'And I?' La Harpe – a freethinker – asked. 'Do you not give me any place in this?' 'Something at least as wonderful will happen to you,' Cazotte replied. 'You will have become by then a Christian.'

The story of Cazotte's prophecy was found among La Harpe's papers when he died, a convert to Christianity, in 1803; and it was published three years later. Sceptics inevitably rejected it; and even those who were prepared to accept the possibility of precognition were unhappy about this sample, which seemed too elaborately detailed to be genuine. In the 1820s, however, the story found a champion in Mme. de Genlis, who as mistress of Philippe 'Égalité' Orleans had been one of the social set involved; she swore that she had many times heard La Harpe tell the story even before the Revolution broke out. Years later the publication of the memoirs of the Baroness Henriette d'Oberkirch provided even more effective confirmation. She had concluded them in 1789 with the outbreak of the Revolution, remarking on the 'dreadful omens', and referring to 'the many persons who heard the Cazotte prophecies'. She herself had heard of them from St. Petersburg through her friend the Grand Duchess Maria Fedorovna; and the Grand Duchess had heard of them from La Harpe himself. Recollection may have embroidered the details; but this contemporary reference makes it hard to reject the prophecy as an invention.

According to La Harpe, Cazotte predicted that he, too, would die on the scaffold. During the Terror he was arrested and imprisoned. 'Note old Marquis Cazotte,' Carlyle recalled; 'he is doomed to die; but his young daughter clasps him in her arms, with an inspiration of eloquence, with a love which is stronger than very death; the heart of the killers themselves is touched by it; the old man is spared.' All to no purpose, Cazotte insisted. He had 'seen' that he would be re-arrested on the orders of the mayor, brought before the Tribunal, and sentenced to death: 'My hour is come'. A fortnight later, he was arrested, brought before the Tribunal and sent to the guillotine.

Only a lucky chance saved Tom Paine from the same fate; a gaoler put the mark indicating that he was in the next execution batch on the wrong side of his cell door. But then, only a lucky chance – the fact that he stayed with William Blake on his way to France – had enabled Paine to reach Paris. Like Swedenborg, Blake believed that his spirits – his 'celestial friends', as he called them – provided him with information and inspiration; his 'Milton' and 'Jerusalem' were written from their immediate dictation, 'twelve or sometimes twenty or thirty lines at a time, without premeditation and sometimes against my will'. When Tom Paine was waiting to leave for France to take his seat in the Convention, Blake warned him to depart at once, as Pitt's agents were on their way to arrest him; and they arrived soon after Paine had left.

From this period, too, comes an account of psychic perception which carries conviction not because it is substantiated but simply because it sounds genuine. Johann Zschokke, German by birth, Swiss patriot by adoption, and a man generally admired for his integrity, described towards the end of his life how he had occasionally found on his first meeting with strangers, 'as I listened silently to their discourse, that their former life, with many trifling connected circumstances, or frequently some particular scene in that life, has passed quite involuntarily, and as it were dream-like, yet perfectly distinct before me'. Eventually he decided to put this to the test, and in a friendly family circle related what he had 'seen' of somebody who had just left the room, and whom he had never met; and was told he had been literally correct. Zschokke never quite got over the feeling that some day he would put on the same act, and find he had got it all wrong; but the faculty never let him down. As an example, he cited the case of an encounter at an inn with a group who were mocking Lavater, Mesmer and others: particularly one young man, whose former life suddenly flashed across Zschokke's mind.

He promised, if I were correct in my information, to admit it frankly. I then related what my vision had shown me, and the whole company were made acquainted with the private history of the young merchant: his school years, his youthful errors, and lastly with a fault committed in reference to the strong box of his principal. I described to him the uninhabited room with whitened walls where to the right of the brown door on a table, stood a black money box, etc. A dead silence prevailed during the whole narrative, which I alone occasionally interrupted by inquiring whether I spoke the truth. The startled young man confirmed every particular and even, what I had scarcely expected, the last mentioned. Touched by his candour, I shook hands with him over the table and said no more.

So diffident was Zschokke about his faculty that he was not even prepared to assert that it was clairvoyant: 'I shall not say another word of this singular gift of visions, of which I cannot say that it was ever the slightest service. It manifested itself rarely, quite independently of my will, and several times of persons whom I cared little to look through.'

Zschokke also left an account of some experiments in divination. When he came to Switzerland he found a few people there 'endowed with the mysterious natural gift of discovering, by a peculiar sensation, the existence of subterranean waters, metals, or fossils'. Among them were the Abbot of a monastery in the Canton of Lucerne and a woman whom the Abbot had tested by watching her go where he knew there was underground water, and finding that she was able to tell him not merely where the water lay, but its quality. Careful observation compelled Zschokke, in his turn, 'at length to renounce the obstinate suspicion and incredulity I once felt on this subject'. And Zschokke's was only one of a number of such investigations. In his autobiography Arthur Young described how in 1801 he went with his agricultural board to watch a diviner being tested in Hyde Park by Sir Joseph Banks, the botanist who had accompanied Captain Cook on his exploration of the Pacific. There was one failure, 'but in the four trials I watched, in which I knew he could not be acquainted with the direction of the pipes, he succeeded completely'.

The first half of the nineteenth century also provided a number of detailed accounts of poltergeist activity; perhaps the best known case in Europe being the haunting of Prince Hohenlohe's castle in Silesia, described by Justinus Kerner. It had begun when his friend Charles Kern and Councillor Augustus Kahn were staying there in 1806, with bangings and showers of what appeared to be lime. They suspected a practical joke, an explanation which proved inadequate when objects began to fly around though there was nobody to throw them, and candle snuffers rose from a table before falling to the floor. Friends who came to stay had the same experience; Captain Magerle actually cut with his sabre at what he thought must be his attackers, but succeeded only in damaging the furniture. On one occasion Kahn was about to shave when the brush, razor and soap flew towards him, falling at his feet. With a servant, John, he witnessed a beer jug raise itself and pour its contents into a glass, which was lifted and emptied; 'Lord Jesus,' John exclaimed in horror, 'it swallows,' and no trace of beer was found on the floor. Then the phenomena ceased. 'I am still as unable as ever to account for those events,' Kahn wrote, 'and I am content to submit to the hasty remarks of the world, knowing that I have only related the truth, and what many persons now alive have witnessed, as well as myself.'

In England a publisher put out a narrative in 1800 which, he claimed, was 'one of the most extraordinary and best-authenticated of any ever yet laid before the public on a similar subject': the narrative being provided by a staid citizen of Bristol, Henry Durbin. Hearing rumours of diabolic activity in a house in Lawford's Gate, Durbin had gone to it with the idea of unmasking the hoaxer; only to find it was no hoax. There were knockings and bangings, and objects moved when nobody was near them (a table was turned upside down, and a chamber pot rolled down the stairs when nobody was above to roll it). A young girl had marks on her flesh as if she were having pins stuck into her, or being pinched – as she was: disembodied fingers were seen doing the pinching. Asked if it would reply to questions the spirit agreed, and made scratching noises, sometimes getting correct answers even to questions set in Latin, or about events at a distance. This haunting had, admittedly, taken place nearly forty years earlier. But Durbin's account had been written at the time, and it was attested by sceptics as well as by members of the clergy. Nor could it be alleged that Durbin had any pecuniary or other interest in its publication. Because of the mockery he had suffered when he had tried to persuade people that the manifestations were genuine, he had declined to allow the narrative to be published until after his death.

One of the children, Durbin had noted, was sometimes 'pulled towards the ceiling' and would remain suspended for a time in the air. Recalling this in 1820, James Heaton described a similar case in Plymouth, to which several witnesses testified on oath. An eleven-year-old girl, when she had a fit, 'ran up the side of a wall to the ceiling, where she remained immovable on her feet for several minutes, her clothes being unaltered in their usual position'; and when sitting in a chair, she would be whirled around like a top. But the most detailed account of a haunting in this period came from Canada, nine years later. An Ontario farmhouse suddenly found itself under siege, its windows being continually smashed by bullets; but the bullets were not being fired from guns. The trajectory suggested that they had been lobbed through the glass, though there was nobody outside to lob them. Even when the windows were boarded up bullets still came in, making no holes in the board. Respected local citizens, asked to investigate, assumed they would be able to detect trickery; but the spirit appeared to take a malevolent delight in hazing them, concentrating its attention on anybody who expressed scepticism about its existence. When, in the presence of some thirty witnesses, the local

Methodist minister marked some of the bullets and stones and threw them into a river, they were promptly returned to the farmhouse – wet. When they were put into a leather bag, the bag mysteriously emptied itself. These and other manifestations – furniture moving, objects displaced, and even guns going off, though nobody was ever hurt – were seen, described and vouched for by numerous witnesses, who clearly had never heard of such things, let alone believed in them, before.

Chapter Eighteen
Counter-attack

WITH SO MUCH EVIDENCE TO GO ON, THE MEMBERS OF THE FRENCH Academy might have been expected to accept the recommendation of their committee, and encourage research into animal magnetism. The reaction of the meeting to which the committee reported, however, was hostile. When the motion that the report should be printed, ordinarily passed as a formality, was proposed, a member pointed out that if the report's facts were correct 'they would upset half our knowledge of physiology'; and it would be dangerous to allow the press to get hold of them. It was therefore agreed that the report should be noted, but not printed, pending the results of further research; and such was the hostility displayed that it was not undertaken – not, at least, under the auspices of the Academy. When in 1836 it was disclosed that a dentist, Dr. M. J. Oudet, had used mesmerism to extract a tooth painlessly, he explained that he had tried to keep it a secret because he knew his medical colleagues had their minds made up, and he was not anxious to make trouble for himself. But then the press had got hold of the story. To prove he was not a charlatan, he gave a demonstration show-ing that not merely could a tooth be removed, but that the patient could be pricked with a pin and have a finger held in a candle flame without showing any sign of discomfort, let alone pain. The outcome confirmed Oudet's morose expectations. The opponents of mesmerism fell back on two explanations: either the patient must have suppressed all indications of suffering by will-power; or she had somehow managed to cheat, presumably with Oudet's collusion, and had not really been operated on, pricked or burned at all. When they were reminded of the case of the woman whose breast tumour had been removed, a Paris surgeon, M. Lisfranc, declared that the man who operated on that occasion must have been an impostor or a dupe.

At this point a young physician with more enthusiasm than experi-ence, Dr. J. Berna, challenged the Academy of Medicine to examine two somnambulists he had discovered who could demonstrate the higher phenomena; and a committee of nine was set up for the purpose. Oudet was a member, but none of them had served on the earlier commission, and the rapporteur, J. F. Dubois d'Amiens, had already made his hostility public. One of the somnambulists was unable to provide even a sign of the eyeless vision and thought-transference Berna had brought her to display; and the other was only partially successful. Dubois's report intimated that the commission had been afforded no proof that the subjects were in a state of somnambulism; that insofar as one of the subjects had been able correctly to give answers to questions about what was happening when she was blindfold, these were 'plausible surmises'; and that such evidence as there was of clairvoyance had merely encouraged them to suspect her honesty. 'We do not attempt to decide whether the more numerous and varied facts supplied by other magnetisers would lead to a different conclusion,' their conclusion was; 'but it is certain that if other magnetisers exist, they do not openly appear, and they have not ventured to challenge the sanction or reprobation of the Academy.'

In vain, Husson protested that the commission had not been asked to pronounce on magnetisers in general, only on the wretched Berna. By a big majority the Academy accepted the report; one of its members, Dr. C. Burdin, backing his confidence that the magnetisers had been routed by depositing three thousand francs with a lawyer, to be given to the first person who could display eyeless vision.

Mlle. Pigeaire

The challenge provoked one of the crucial tests in the history of mesmerism. It was taken up by Dr. J. Pigeaire of Montpellier who had found that one of his daughters became clairvoyant when magnetised; she could tell him when he could expect visitors, and who they would be; she could read with her eyes closed, or when blindfold; and she could guess the identity of objects concealed in snuff-boxes. Colleagues from the university who witnessed these feats pointed out to Pigeaire that although they were willing to accept them as genuine, scientists elsewhere would not, unless stricter precautions were taken. In further tests the blindfold was reinforced, under the supervision of Professor Lordat, with a raised border designed to fit the contours of her face, 'very thick, and coated with plaster to intercept every ray', and sealed with sticking plaster round the edges. But still, Mlle. Pigeaire was able to 'read' using her fingers; and, as one acute witness noticed, she rested them only on the beginnings of words. There was no question of her reading by feeling the type.

Here was the opportunity, Pigeaire felt, to win the prize and convince the Academy. Two of its members, asked to do a preliminary screening investigation in Montpellier, pronounced Mllc. Pigeaire's faculties genuine; and in the summer of 1838 she and her father came to Paris for the decisive tests. On arrival they found that instead of her usual reinforced bandage, the committee had provided a mask which would be offset from her face, so that they could watch her eyes. Her father protested that this was out of the question; she was accustomed to doing tests with her eyes bandaged. Bandages, the committee argued, could not provide complete security against her cheating. As no compromise could be reached, the experiments were abandoned; and in what purported to be a factual account of them, the *Gazette Medicale* claimed that the commission had actually detected Mlle. Pigeaire cheating. 'Are there any among you, gentlemen,' Pigeaire protested to the Academy,

> who can suppose that a father or a mother, who believe themselves principled, would educate their child in deceit and falsehood, and would make her play a part which would be as despicable as without object, and so difficult to maintain? Or that we would remain for ten months in a state of complete illusion about so many phenomena observed by so many different people? Or that we could occasion the illusion in so many others who had previously been sceptical about the existence of phenomena?

The Academy, however, made no move to correct the *Gazette*'s version; and after the investigation of another somnambulist, presented by Dr. Adolphe Teste, had proved unproductive, the Academy took the opportunity to say that animal magnetism would join perpetual motion and squaring the circle as matters with which it would henceforth decline to concern itself.

John Elliotson

Animal magnetism had not succeeded in attracting as much interest in Britain as it had on the Continent. In 1792 Dr. J. Bell had written a brief survey of the subject describing his own experiences, which had included a subject who could read in the dark, and another who was a travelling clairvoyant. And from time to time a mesmerist would attract attention locally by public performances; but only Richard Chenevix had attempted any systematic research into the subject. Although Chenevix had been chiefly concerned to show that mesmerism – as it came to be more commonly called in Britain – could be used to treat illness, in his demonstrations in the 1820s he had shown that, like Puységur, he could make somnambulists stop talking, or walking, by 'willing' them to stop. He had been able to convince a few colleagues, but he could not convert the medical establishment; and when he died, the President of the Royal Society (of which Chenevix had been a member), while praising his ability and industry, regretted that he had recently latterly indulged 'in speculations wholly unworthy of being noticed in this place'.

The first serious attempt to survey mesmerism for British readers was *Isis Revelata*, a two-volume work by J. C. Colquhoun, which appeared in 1836. A barrister and Sheriff of his county, Colquhoun wrote from the viewpoint of a historian rather than a propagandist; but the book aroused some controversy and a few months later Baron Du Potet was invited to London, where he gave some demonstrations – described by, among others, Lady Louisa Molyneux. 'We have been tempted today to go to the Magnetism,' she wrote to tell the diarist Creevey in 1837, 'a most disagreeable sight.' Presumably she was referring to the, by this time, standard method of demonstrating the reality of the trance state: subjecting the subjects to pinches, pricks and burns to show they felt no pain. But she was impressed by the fact that the subjects were obviously not trained performers, as had been alleged: 'It is impossible to see the poor people of all ages – some quite children, out of the hospitals – under the influence, and suppose they have been taught to impose upon you.'

Some of the demonstrations were given at University College Hospital; and they were attended by one of the hospital's founders, Professor John Elliotson. Although still a young man, he had already made his name as a clinician and as an innovator (notably by introducing Laennec's stethoscope into hospital practice; it excited the derision of his older colleagues, one of them dismissing it as 'hocus pocus'); and he had been interested in Chenevix's work, but had not followed it up. As the magnetised subjects were patients from his hospital, Elliotson was in a good position to endorse Lady Louisa's belief that they had not been trained to put on an act. Impressed, he began to undertake research on his own account.

Elliotson was a pragmatist. He accepted only what could be demonstrated; and he rejected, sometimes with derision, what he regarded as superstitions. Believers in the prophecies of the sibyls, the ecstasies of the Dervishes, or 'the pretended miraculous cures of all ages', such as those of St. Médard, he dismissed as 'ridiculous enthusiasts'. And he found the higher phenomena unacceptable.

When we are requested to believe that persons perceive objects of sight through dead walls; perceive objects of hearing and sight, smell and taste with their bellies and fingers or toes; know what is going on at a distance, what will happen in regard to persons and places with which they have no connection, know the history of persons whom they never heard of before, but who are put *en rapport* with them by contact, speak languages they never learned, display scientific knowledge which they never acquired, and make anatomical and pathological observations in their own frames and those of others, the matter is too wonderful for belief.

But he was prepared to be convinced by what he saw with his own eyes; and experiments with patients and in particular with two sisters, Elizabeth and Jane Okey, satisfied him that there was a trance state, and that in it, subjects had certain faculties which they did not have in their ordinary waking state. Elizabeth felt no pain in her 'delirium' (as Elliotson described the active trance state), even when people who doubted the reality of her anaesthesia stuck pins into her; 'she used to take red-hot coals out of the fire and wonder, as she held them, why people cried out and desired her to throw them down'.

One of Elliotson's patients, he had found, would be drawn in whatever direction he moved, though her eyes were closed; if placed so that her feet could not move, she would actually bend towards him, at an angle where ordinarily she would have fallen over, and remain at that angle for an hour or more. In the Okeys, 'the susceptibility of traction of different parts was often extreme. When they were not aware of it, we have by movements of the hands behind their backs at the distance of many yards, drawn their limbs or body just as we wished.' He could even get them to lift their arms in this way, though each arm was attached to an eighty-pound weight. But to Elliotson, this did not mean that they were exhibiting the higher phenomena. It was simply that they had 'one or more of the intellectual faculties or external senses highly exalted beyond their usual pitch'; a theory which, he assumed, would also account for their ability to go into the trance state when handed a piece of metal which had been 'magnetised' by mesmeric passes.

It was this assumption, that they could recognise metal imbued with animal magnetism, which was to be Elliotson's undoing. To most of his colleagues, mesmerism was either fraudulent, or, if there were anything in it, a public danger. The fashionable London surgeon of the time, Sir Benjamin Brodie, denounced it in the *Quarterly* magazine in 1838 as resting 'on the most dangerous of all foundations, that of a debasing superstition, a miserable amalgam of faith and fear'. Brodie did not deny that the process produced effects. But these, he claimed, were the result of a disordered state of the nervous system, artificially aroused. He flatly refused to believe that the patient in the mesmerised state did not feel pain; the only new principle of pathology involved, he argued, was that 'it seems to be in the power of almost anyone, under the influence of excitement or a strong moral determination, to sustain bodily suffering without any outward expression of what he suffers'.

The patients who had been pricked or burned or operated upon, in other words, had been lying when they said the procedures had been painless. As for the higher phenomena, they were 'pure and unsophisticated delusions and collusions'; an opinion echoed that summer by another London surgeon, John Leeson, who wrote to the *Lancet* to say that he had been watching Elizabeth Okey, and although her performances were certainly surprising, they had nothing to do with animal magnetism. Her trance state was a fake, her skill consisting of the ability to detect the correct coin by detecting minute variations of heat produced by Elliotson's hands. And when this interpretation was challenged, the editor of the *Lancet*, Thomas Wakley, offered to set up a small committee to investigate.

In addition to being the outstanding medical editor of his time, perhaps of any time, Wakley was politically a radical; and radicalism was often linked, as in his case, with rationalism and scepticism. He did not take Leeson's hypothesis seriously; but it offered him a rational excuse to intervene, in order to demonstrate that the magnetised nickel was detected neither by its warmth nor by clairvoyance, but simply by deception. When Elliotson handed him the magnetised nickel, so that they could watch the effect it had on Elizabeth Okey, Wakley contrived to slip it to a colleague, who moved away from the group. Wakley then pretended to touch Elizabeth with the nickel. When she duly had a paroxysm, went into her trance and became cataleptic, he disclosed that he had not used the nickel; his colleague producing it in confirmation.

Wakley could not have known it, but Bertrand had made a similar test. He had magnetised a note, and asked a friend to place it on a somnambulist's stomach when he was a hundred leagues away, to find whether she could 'read' it, while they were that distance apart. She could; but she was also able to read a note which he had only pretended to magnetise. But whereas Bertrand had been satisfied that he had shown magnetism was not an essential ingredient of what he took to be a process of induction, Wakley assumed that he had 'perfectly conclusive' proof, as he told the readers of the *Lancet*, 'of the fact of general imposture against the girl'; he did not consider that any further investigation 'would ever be necessary'. The University College Hospital authorities imposed a ban on the use of mesmerism in treatment, and Elliotson resigned. Mesmerism, it seemed, was as comprehensively discredited in Britain as it had been in France.

James Braid

Three years later, however, another mesmerist arrived in London to give demonstrations: a French business man, Charles Lafontaine. Lafontaine had been introduced to animal magnetism by a circle of people in Brussels, who played it as a party game; and he had found that a girl in the group could describe not merely the contents of his pockets (which he thought she might have discovered by some ruse), but what he had written on a piece of paper in another room (it was a compliment, she hazarded, in some embarrassment; and when pressed, she had told him that he had written 'you are so pretty', which was correct). Intrigued, he had begun to experiment for himself along the usual lines, coming across one subject, a daughter of the playwright Mme. Felix de la Motte – who when magnetised had eyeless vision, and could read his thoughts; and another, an artist, who though he was not drinking himself appeared drunk when Lafontaine drank wine. Lafontaine gave demonstrations on 'pin and needle victims' – as the *Lancet* described them, in reference to his visit; it was a reproach to the nation, an editorial complained 'that such persons are capable of practising their devices amongst us for a single month. When will the age of humbug, credulity and folly end?' And among those who went to watch was a sceptical Scots surgeon, James Braid; hoping, as he was later to recall, to find 'the source of fallacy in certain phenomena I had heard were exhibited'.

Instead, Braid found the real source, as he believed, of the phenomena. There was no need, he decided after some experiments, to think in terms of animal magnetism, or even of a fluence. The trance could be induced simply by holding a bright object a little above the subject's eye line, and getting her to stare at it. This, he contended, meant that the trance was a physiological reaction. It was comparable to the blinking of somebody's eyes if a mock blow was aimed at him: the physical process worked on the mind, heightening sensitivity; the mind then worked on the body, producing the succession of responses, convulsions, catalepsy, immunity to pain.

The main reason for the fierce opposition to mesmerism, Braid felt, had been the extravagant claims of those mesmerists who had 'contended for the reality of clairvoyance in some of their patients, such as seeing through opaque bodies, and investing them with the gifts and graces of omniscience, mesmeric intuition and universal knowledge – pretensions alike a mockery of human understanding, as they are opposed to all the known laws of physical science'; and to the end of his life Braid was to maintain that he had never come across the higher phenomena. In fact he had; a difficulty which he got around simply by insisting they had a natural explanation, on the lines that Elliotson had earlier put forward. Patients in the trance state, Braid conceded, were sometimes capable of describing what was going on out of their range of vision. Some of them, he had found, could actually tell the shape of an object held at an inch and a half from the skin at the back of the neck. But this was not because they could 'see' the object; 'it is from *feeling* that they do so'. In the hypnotic state the 'extremely exalted sensibility' of the skin enabled them to tell what shape an object was; 'this however, is not *sight*, but *feeling*'. The same exalted state accounted for their movements in obedience to the hypnotist's signals, even when he stood at some distance behind them; 'enabling them to discern the currents of air, which they advance to, or return from, according to their direction' – a theory which Braid felt he had proved when 'a patient could feel and obey the motion of a glass funnel passed through the air at a distance of *fifteen feet*'.

Here, then, seemed a way to settle the vexed issue of mesmerism. On the one hand, Braid's theory would be acceptable to those who, like Brodie, had accepted that something happened but had insisted there must be a physical explanation. On the other, it would acquit Elliotson and the Okey sisters of deception, because it was easy to show – as Braid had discovered for himself – that though a patient might initially be hard to hypnotise (as Braid called his method) it later usually became a simple matter to induce the trance by a word, or a gesture; so Elizabeth's trance could easily have been set off by the fact that, as Wakley had noted in his account, the word 'nickel' had actually been spoken at the time. But the publication of Braid's *Neurypnology* in 1843, settled nothing; it merely divided the disputants into three camps – those who continued to believe in animal magnetism; those who continued to reject it; and those who, following Braid, accepted that there was a trance state resembling somnambulism, but insisted that no fluid or fluence was involved, and that the higher phenomena were simply a by-product of heightened sensory perception in the trance.

This happened to accord well a new line being taken by historians of science, notably Eusebe Salverte in France and Sir David Brewster in Britain. They did not repudiate Hume's dogma about miracles, but they adopted a different attitude to them; concentrating less on dismissing them as fables, and more on showing that, as Salverte put it in his *Occult Sciences*, 'the apparent miracles and magical operations of the ancients were the results of real scientific knowledge, more or less advanced, which the thaumaturgists for the most part had secretly transmitted from one period to another; at the same time, with the greatest care concealing that knowledge from all other men'. By showing how the tricks had been staged, Salverte hoped to be able to scrape off the remaining barnacles of superstition which still, he felt, impeded progress towards a truly scientific historical approach.

His method, though, led him into speculations as tortuous, and sometimes as far-fetched, as the superstitions he was hoping to eradicate. Although a man of great ability and undisputed integrity – he had sacrificed alluring career prospects rather than work for the restored Bourbons after 1815 – Salverte's rigorous devotion to the scientific truth, as he saw it, led him to make the same kind of speculative rationalisations in his search for natural causes as the Christian hagiographers, similarly convinced that Divine Truth was in their possession, had made in the opposite direction when they were searching for their favoured explanations. Where, for example, the hagiographers had been disposed to dismiss the miracles of Apollonius of Tyana as inventions designed to cast doubt on the uniqueness of Jesus, Salverte felt compelled to sustain Apollonius as a reliable reporter, who had accurately described what he had seen, without realising it was all a show staged by the cunning prestidigators. The reason Apollonius felt the earth being agitated under his feet 'like a boisterous sea' when the Hindu procession approached the temple, Salverte suggested, might well have been that the earth was actually behaving in that way. The sound of the procession approaching had doubtless tipped off the workmen underground, employed to await its arrival. At the correct moment, they would be ready to raise a movable stage, covered with earth, 'an operation readily effected by the aid of a mechanism, very easily understood'. In the improbable event of so elaborate a mechanical hoax having been invented, though, the 'magic' could hardly have been kept a closely guarded secret if gangs of workmen had had to be employed to work the tricks.

In his determination to demolish the evidence for clairvoyance, too, Salverte sometimes innocently produced arguments which could equally be used to show clairvoyance existed; such as his commentary on an episode described by Lavater. Lavater had proposed a simple test which a friend of his, a sceptic, could employ. He should go back to his home in Geneva and, at four specified times of day, make a note of what he was doing; the clairvoyant would try to 'see' him at those times. The first two reports turned out to be correct; the other two, wrong. 'In an earlier age,' Salverte remarked, 'credit would have been given for the first two trials, and their fortuitous success would have been deemed confirmatory of a supernatural power'; the two wrong guesses, he felt disposed of the clairvoyance notion. Yet two correct guesses out of four could well be claimed as evidence for clairvoyance.

Although Salverte's ideas were advanced simply as hypotheses, they came to be accepted as historical by those who wanted to believe in natural explanations, by the same process as the speculations of hagiographers had come to be accepted as historical by generations of the faithful. There was a measure of rough justice in this, in that the Church, which for so long had encouraged the process, now found itself faced with the need not merely to counter Salverte, with his ingenious rationalist explanations for the miracles of the New Testament (which the English translation discreetly omitted) but also the more extreme versions accepted by the school of Hermann Reinarius, displaying Jesus and the disciples as a band of itinerant rogues who sent somebody in advance to procure individuals who would sham halt, or blind, or dead, so that Jesus could 'cure' them miraculously and profitably; the 'resurrection' being accounted for by the need, after Jesus's crucifixion, to find some way to carry on the fraud. But the method, though stimulating in terms of controversy, was wildly unhistorical; and it was this defect which was to mar the work of the rationalists when they came to deal with the history of mesmerism, as Claude Burdin and Dubois d'Amiens did in their survey of animal magnetism in 1841.

Their method was to select from the evidence after the manner of a counsel for a prosecution, exposing all its weak points (nobody, for example, had been able precisely to define the somnambulist state; therefore, they argued, it could not be proved to exist) and proposing alternative explanations (history was full of stories of men who had been stoically indifferent to pain; therefore it was impossible to be certain that any operation had really been painless). They stressed the impossibility of making cheat-proof blindfold tests, citing the Pigeaire case as an example. And they made much of the inability of clairvoyants to produce results consistently in test conditions, the implication being that they never would if the correct precautions were taken against deception.

This approach, Burdin and Dubois could argue, was healthy even if their hypotheses were not necessarily correct; for it would compel mesmerists to conduct research in future with more care. But their book contained a clear intimation that however careful the researchers, their work would not convince sceptical critics. Where Burdin and Dubois could not fault an individual experiment, they did not hesitate to fall back on the possibility that there had been collusion between researcher, witnesses and subject to produce faked results. If the researcher were living they could not, as a rule, make this allegation outright; but they could argue that as there was no proof that there had *not* been collusion, the experiments were worthless, which amounted to much the same thing. And this confronted researchers with a problem which was to prove virtually insoluble, because of the difficulty of setting up a collusion-proof experiment. If independent assessors were invited to monitor a test of, say, clairvoyance, and pronounced themselves satisfied that it had been genuine, by so doing they would lose their independent status. For if they now accepted it, might not they have been in secret collusion with the experimenters from the start?

Chapter Nineteen

The Zoist

THERE WAS ONLY ONE WAY TO COUNTER SCEPTICISM OF THIS KIND: TO produce such a mass of evidence that it would be overwhelmed. But it was also important to show that mesmerism was potentially an asset; and as Elliotson had realised, its greatest value would be in giving immunity from pain.

Elliotson had not allowed his experience with Wakley to dishearten him; and he had been fortunate in the possession of friends who thought he had been shabbily treated, Charles Dickens among them. They became friendly in the late 1830s; and demonstrations of mesmerism not only made Dickens 'a believer against all my preconceived opinions', but encouraged him to practise mesmerism himself on his wife and her sister and sometimes on friends; to his wife's alarm he treated the attractive wife of a Swiss banker of a nervous tic and managed to get rid of it. 'I know that, under God,' Dickens wrote to tell his protégé John Overs in 1841, recommending him to see Elliotson, 'there does not live a man in whose hands you would have as much reason to hope for a perfect restoration to health'; if his own or his wife's life were in peril, Dickens went on, 'I would trust it to him implicity.' And Dickens' biographer John Forster was to recall that for nearly thirty years Elliotson's name was 'a synonym with us all for unwearied, self-sacrificing beneficial service to everyone in need'. It would consequently have been easy for Elliotson to abandon the attempt to secure recognition for mesmerism, and concentrate upon using it in his own practice. But he was not prepared to give up. In 1843 he founded the *Zoist*, a monthly magazine devoted to mesmerism and to other unexplained phenomena; much to Wakley's indignation. Periodically the *Lancet* continued to fulminate against the mesmerists: all those connected with the *Zoist* were 'lepers', and doctors who practised mesmerism, traitors – though as the progeny of mesmerism would turn out to be its natural enemies, 'they must in no long time utterly destroy their loathsome dam'.

Elliotson contented himself with sardonically re-printing the *Lancet*'s comments in the *Zoist*; but in 1846, he had a welcome occasion on which to preach his heresy in one of orthodoxy's temples: it fell to his turn to give the Harveian oration to the Royal College of Physicians, an opportunity which, though there were hostile mutterings, he declined to let pass. In the past, he reminded his audience, some of the College's most distinguished Fellows had been derided for their unorthodox opinions, notably Harvey himself; and some of the most important advances in medicine, such as quinine and vaccination, had also met with mockery. 'Let us never forget these things,' he pleaded; 'never allow authority, conceit, habit or the fear of ridicule to make us indifferent, much less to make us hostile, to truth'; and though he did not refer to mesmerism by name, he recommended members to interest themselves in a body of facts which were not only of importance in physiology and pathology, 'but of the very highest importance in the prevention of suffering under the hands of the surgeon, and in the cure of disease'. And as, at that time, anaesthetics had still not come into use in surgery, it was here that mesmerism had its most promising prospect.

James Esdaile

In the long history of science's resistance to new procedures which do not happen to fit orthodox theories, none is more depressing than the refusal of the medical profession even to examine mesmerism's possibilities as a pain-killer. The more successful the demonstration, the more ingenious had the sophistries become. When in 1842 a Nottingham surgeon amputated a patient's leg, using mesmerism, and the patient did not move a muscle throughout, Dr. Marshall Hall assured the Royal Medical and Chirurgical Society that this was proof the patient *must* have been an impostor; if he had been genuinely insensible to pain, the muscles in his other leg would have twitched. And with doctors and medical journals so hostile, the development of mesmerism as an adjunct to surgery in Europe was effectively blocked. But in India James Esdaile, a Scots surgeon working for the East India Company in Calcutta, had an unusual opportunity, when he became interested in the subject in the 1840s; he was able to experiment with mesmerism, and then introduce it in his practice, without disturbing his employers. The Company's managers were concerned primarily with the profitability of their enterprise; anything which helped their employees to recover rapidly after surgery, and return to work, was to be encouraged. And the employees, Hindu or Muslim, had no objection to pain-free operations.

When Esdaile reported the satisfactory results of the first seventy-five operations which he had carried out with the help of an assistant he had trained to mesmerise the patients, the Calcutta Medical Board did not even acknowledge his letter; and the local press, alerted to the existence of a charlatan in their midst, began a campaign of vilification against him, one editor asserting that the patients were 'a set of hardened impostors'. Again, though, Esdaile was lucky. The East India Company happened also to be the Government of India. The Deputy-Governor of Bengal ordered an investigation; a committee was appointed; and although the doctors who were members declined to commit themselves to accepting that mesmerism was responsible, they were unable to deny that the mesmerised patients underwent their operations without showing any sign of pain. This was good enough, the Deputy-Governor decided, to justify putting Esdaile in charge of a small experimental surgical unit, to continue his research. It was so successful that in 1847 he was formally appointed surgeon to the Government of India. His critics looked forward to the impending arrival of a new Governor-General, Lord Dalhousie, to overturn the appointment. They were to be disappointed. After an investigation, Dalhousie settled the issue in 1848 by publicly congratulating Esdaile on his work.

The Clairvoyants

In Britain in the meantime there had been occasional examples of the higher phenomena; and in 1845, Elliotson, previously inclined to doubt them, encountered an 'exquisite case of the highest kind, for the first time, and its truth I will now as fearlessly maintain as I originally did the production of simple sleep'. His somnambulist, 'the perfection of integrity', could tell him what friends of his, whom she did not know, were doing at any given time; and she often made predictions which came true. From that time on the *Zoist* began to carry more accounts of clairvoyance, spontaneous or induced; and though most of the material consisted of anecdotes, there were some quite well-documented accounts of experiments, such as one which had been carried out in Plymouth.

A controversy there between believers and sceptics had resulted in 1846 in a challenge, more amicable and restrained than the earlier contests in France. Both sides put up five pounds, the arrangement being that the believers would provide the clairvoyant – a youth, Thomas Laycock – and that the sceptics would provide the supervision. Aware, presumably, of the controversy over whether Mlle. Pigeaire and other somnambulists could have seen through or under their blindfolds, the Plymouth sceptics adopted a new method: they put adhesive tape horizontally over Laycock's eyelids, and then another layer vertically from cheeks to forehead, with one scrutiniser watching from the side to ensure that there was no rumpling of tapes, and another looking up from below to ensure there was no peeking. Nevertheless, Laycock, confronted with a piece of paper, correctly stated that the words 'Plymouth and South Devon Savings Bank' were printed on it in red ink; and when presented with a chemist's advertisement he 'screwed up his features and limbs crying "Oh, the nasty stuff, the filthy salts, how I hate them" '. When the tests had been satisfactorily completed it was found that his eyelashes were so firmly stuck together that it was with difficulty they could be parted; and the sceptics, confounded, passed over the money, four pounds going to charity and the remaining pound being awarded, by common consent, to Laycock.

Another series of experiments was reported by a retired cavalry officer, Major William Buckley, using an ingeniously simple technique. Confectioners' shops at that time used to stock walnut shells containing cracker-mottoes; and it occurred to Buckley that here was a ready-made device for ensuring that neither he nor his subjects could know the motto which each walnut, in a freshly purchased consignment, would contain. Yet some of his mesmerised subjects were able to produce correct, or nearly correct, answers. Finding that they obtained better results when they were not closely supervised, Buckley and fellow-researcher, Surgeon W. A. Mott, devised a way to allow them to do the tests in their own time; the newly purchased walnuts were put into a flexible bag with a combination lock, enabling the mesmerised subjects to make their guesses without the need to watch their every move, because only Mott knew how to open it. 'If the greatest delicacy is not observed in these experiments,' Buckley observed, 'they fail'; but he felt entitled to claim that the clairvoyance of his subjects had been tested 'as carefully, as watchfully, and as severely as the nature of the subject will warrant'.

The *Zoist* also carried reviews of books about research into mesmerism in this period; and the books themselves revealed how interest in the subject was being rekindled by researchers throughout Britain. A few were by men who had become interested professionally, like William Newnham, surgeon and psychologist, who had begun to write with the object of demolishing the pretensions of the mesmerists, but had been impressed first by the range of the evidence (on his count, by 1845, nearly one thousand five hundred works had been published on the subject in France and Germany); and later by his own research with a somnambulist, a factory girl from Bolton who, when mesmerised, could tell his guests all about what was happening in their homes, sometimes to their embarrassment. But some of the most careful research at the time was being done by amateurs; prominent among them, members of the clergy.

The attitude of the Churches to mesmerism had in general been one of distaste. A few priests had become convinced, as Faria had, that there was nothing inherently evil about it; preaching in Notre Dame in 1846 Fr. J. B. Lacordaire argued that for man to have the power to see through opaque substances, to prescribe healing remedies, and to know of things of which he was previously ignorant, represented a divine gift. And the following year, the Holy Office pronounced that animal magnetism, although unlawful if used for wicked purposes, was not unlawful *per se*. But for the most part, Catholics had viewed it with mistrust, as a regression to diabolism. Protestants by contrast had tended to be sceptical; and those who became interested often emphasised, when they came to write about it, that they had initially hoped to expose the mesmerists as fraudulent. When the clergy became involved, though, they were often in a good position to undertake research, having time on their hands and ready access to the raw material in the form of members of their congregation. They were a varied team: the mild George Sandby, the rector of a small Suffolk parish; the cosmopolitan Chauncy Townshend, a poet, who had lived for many years on the Continent; and one of the most remarkable men of the era, William Scoresby, whaler, polar explorer, cartographer, zoologist, author and Fellow of the Royal Society, who had taken orders after he had established himself as (according to the *Dictionary of National Biography*) 'the foundation stone of Arctic Science'.

Sandby was chiefly concerned to defend mesmerism from the aspersions of its critics: as he admitted he himself had been until he had seen its effects on patients. He had taken the trouble to follow up allegations made by sceptics, and in *Mesmerism and its Opponents*, in 1844, he showed how unscrupulous some of them had been – for example, in spreading the rumour that the Okey sisters had gone to the bad: one of them, he found, was most respectably married; and both had secured the good opinion of all who had known them.

Scoresby and Townshend had both carried out experiments of their own; Townshend with, among others, 'Anna M.' He could give instructions to Anna, Townshend claimed, while she was mesmerised, which she would faithfully carry out later even when it was an inconvenience; as on an occasion when he had told her to come round to his house later in the day – she felt compelled to leave a dinner party, though she could give no explanation for her action except that she just could not help herself. He could also mesmerise Anna from his house when she was in her house, a quarter of a mile away. Another of his subjects, 'E.A.' could 'see' in any direction when mesmerised, 'as if his head were one organ of visual perception'. These results, Townshend admitted, were not consistent; and he had tried to find why there was sporadic interference with perception. The weather, he thought, was one factor ('E.A.' did well when it was fine, but poorly when there were storms around). But the chief problem was psychological. 'The more I wish,' 'E.A.' complained, 'the less I can do'; the will, in other words, was a hindrance rather than a help.

It was characteristic of Scoresby that he should have felt moved to investigate a subject which, as he noted, so many people regarded with suspicion and scepticism, 'some with horror and scorn', because the quality of the evidence for it impressed him. It was characteristic, too, that he should describe his findings with the same scrupulous care that he had always shown in his reports about the flora and fauna of the Arctic seas. In order to get an idea of the range of susceptibility to mesmeric influence he had tried it on about seventy people, getting a significant response from two out of three. They did not, he admitted, provide him with any evidence either for travelling clairvoyance or for pre-vision. But he often came across what might be either thought transference, or some unexplained community of sensation between mesmerist and subject. 'Amelia O.', for example, when in a trance, could tell him what he was tasting, though he was on the other side of a partition. When he tasted a biscuit, she even knew the type (because, she told him, she was very fond of them herself). She and a few other subjects would also react when he pinched or pricked himself as if they were being pinched or pricked in the same part of their bodies. His most striking experiment was with 'Miss H.' He found that he had only to breathe on an object, and it would affect her. If she touched it, she would go into a trance and then carry out whatever mental command he had given through the object. By this means, he could magnetise the sofa in which she was going to sit, and she would be unable to get up; or he could draw an imaginary circle on the floor and when she was in it, she would be unable to leave, however anxious she might be to do so.

It happened that among those who read Scoresby's book, published in 1849, was James Esdaile, in India. Up to this point, Esdaile had not concerned himself with research into the higher phenomena, though he had occasionally come across them. Now, he thought, he would try Scoresby's experiment. After putting his hands on the knobs of an armchair, and breathing on them, he asked a mesmerised subject to sit on it, having mentally ordained that he would be unable to take his hand off the knobs. Rising to leave, and putting his hands on them to lever himself up, the subject found to his intense astonishment that he could not let them go. He was stuck so fast, in fact, that his fingers could not be prised open until Esdaile had performed mesmeric passes over him.

Alexis Didier

In this period the most comprehensive dossier of higher phenomena, as displayed by a mesmerised subject, related to Alexis Didier, a French youth whose specialities were eyeless vision and travelling clairvoyance. When magnetised by his manager J. B. Marcillet, a retired army officer, Alexis could tell visitors what they had been doing, where they had come from, what their dining rooms looked like, how many servants they had, and so on. M. Séguier, for example, for forty years President of the Paris Law Courts and notorious for his scepticism, went unannounced to ask Alexis to describe to him where he had been at two o'clock that afternoon. Alexis 'saw' him at work in his study, which might have been a fair guess; but then went on to describe the contents of the study, accurately except for a description of a small bell on his desk which Séguier knew had not been there. When Séguier reached home that evening, he found the bell; his wife had placed it on his desk in his absence. Lord Frederick FitzClarence, who called in on a visit to Paris, put an even more difficult question: he asked Alexis what he and a friend of his had been doing two days before. According to Marcillet's account, vouched for by FitzClarence, Alexis promptly replied that he could see the two men

> going to the St. Lazare in a carriage; there you take the train and travel to Versailles; you then get into another carriage, which conveys you to St. Cyr. You visit the military school; it was the other gentleman who proposed this excursion, he having been educated there . . . you return to Versailles; I see you both enter a pastry-cook's. Your companion eats three little cakes: you take something else.

Lord Frederick, astonished, said, 'You are right; I ate a small piece of bread.'

Many of Alexis's clients, too, tested him in such a way that a correct reply could not reasonably be attributed to advance information gleaned about them or their homes. Victor Hugo brought along a package he had prepared, which he was careful not to allow out of his hands. Alexis, touching it, correctly described its contents as a piece of light green paper which Hugo had found in a pamphlet in his home, on which the word 'politique' was written. The British consul in Le Havre selected a fragment of a Japanese idol to bring with him to a session; Alexis described the precise circumstances in which he had picked it up from the wreck of a Japanese ship on the Californian coast. E. Prévost, an official at the Mont de Piété, found that one of his staff had absconded with some funds: Alexis was able to tell him that the man had gone to Belgium to gamble with the money, describing his itinerary in detail, and concluding with the depressing information that by the time he was arrested, all the money would have been squandered, which proved to be right.

Like many earlier clairvoyants Alexis found difficulty in performing before hostile sceptics, such as Sir John Forbes, one of Queen Victoria's doctors. Yet though the results of a test session were poor by Alexis's normal standards, Forbes unwittingly presented him with a testimonial. When he watched Alexis play écarté, not merely with bandaged eyes but also with a partition between him and the cards, the performance was 'decidedly better than might have been expected of a blind man', and Forbes had to fall back on the argument that the card-playing was not as good as could be expected of a man who could really 'see' without using his eyes. But Alexis had never claimed that his eyeless vision was as reliable as his sight. On the contrary, he freely admitted that his clairvoyance was neither constant nor reliable; 'he fails in a crowd,' Dickens wrote to tell Lady Blessington, 'but is *marvellous* before a few'. For his clairvoyance to work, he needed to be in rapport with his questioner: as W. H. Parsons, a friend of Elliotson who watched Alexis doing tests in Brighton in 1849, confirmed. Elliotson had feared that Alexis and Marcillet might turn out to be just another pair of prestidigitators on the make; and Parsons was on the look-out for signs of trickery. What he saw impressed him, but also convinced him 'of the extraordinary, and as yet unaccountable power which scepticism has in obstructing the faculty'. It was enough, he thought, for a determined sceptic to hold an object in his hand to nullify the clairvoyant's power to work with it; though this, he admitted, 'is precisely the line of argument which unbelievers call begging the whole question'.

The most convincing testimony to Alexis's powers came from Jean Robert-Houdin, a professional magician who liked to show that he could do by sleight-of-hand anything that clairvoyants claimed to do by second sight. In 1847 he watched Alexis go through his standard routine; and being unable to detect how he could have done it by a trick he came back for a second session with a number of tests he had devised himself. He brought along his own pack of cards which he did not allow out of his hands, selecting cards from it in a way that ensured nobody could see which one would come up except himself; but Alexis guessed them correctly; he brought his own book, for Alexis to 'read' from a selected page, and though it was not even opened, Alexis got the passages right. It was utterly impossible, Robert-Houdin admitted, 'that chance or skill could ever produce such remarkable effects'; they had left him in no doubt that Alexis really must be clairvoyant.

'Upon my word, he astonished me,' the poet Samuel Rogers remarked, after visiting Alexis in Paris: Alexis had minutely described his London home, even down to the fact there was a picture of a man in armour by the drawing-room window. 'Still I cannot believe in clairvoyance,' Rogers added; 'because the thing is impossible.' But if it were not clairvoyance, what could it be? The most commonly offered explanation was that Alexis had a spy system to procure advance information on impending visitors. But frequently he did not know who the visitors were going to be. Chauncy Townshend, for one, took care not to disclose his identity: yet Alexis was able to describe not only his London home, but a house he had been visiting in the Lausanne, describing the pictures hanging on the walls, and noting that one of them had a warped frame. Even if Marcillet and Alexis had managed to find out in advance that, say, FitzClarence was coming, they could not have known what he was going to ask. To have covered all the possible ground for all their visitors (there were as many as four sessions a day) would have needed an international spy network far beyond their resources, as well as leaving them open to blackmail; as soon as an agent's income dried up, he would be tempted to supplement it by threatening to expose the fraud. Had Marcillet and Alexis been cheating their clients, they could hardly have avoided exposure, at some point; yet they were never exposed.

Reichenbach

Experiments of a different nature which the *Zoist* reported were being conducted in the 1840s by Baron Carl von Reichenbach. Having acquired a fortune as an industrialist in Moravia, Reichenbach was using it to gratify his taste for research into chemical compounds (he was the discoverer of creosote and paraffin); and in the process, he became absorbed in the quest for answers to other outstanding scientific problems, magnetism among them. Experimenting in Vienna with iron magnets, he found that some of the neurasthenic patients of a Vienna surgeon were able to see a kind of luminosity coming from the poles. To try to make sure that this was not the result of suggestion, Reichenbach arranged for the magnet to be brought close to one of the patients without her knowledge; yet she could still sense its presence. She could also sense the presence of a crystal in the same way. There must be some force related to magnetism, Reichenbach decided, in all substances – the odic force, as he called it, or odyle – which certain people, 'sensitives', were able to detect.

Tardy de Montravel had reported in 1787 that some patients could see light streaming from the magnetiser's fingers, or from magnetised objects; and some of Deleuze's subjects had told him that they saw luminosity round him, especially around his head and hands. Here, then, lay the prospect of an advance towards an understanding not merely of mesmerism, but perhaps also of other signs and wonders so often recorded by chroniclers in the past: auras, and strange lights, and the haloes traditionally associated with saintliness. Reichenbach, however, had determined on a strictly scientific, materialist approach. It was the mechanics of luminosity and of sensitivity to magnets which interested him, not the 'swarms of miracles' associated with mesmerism; when he came across a sensitive who could report what was happening three rooms away, he attributed it to hyperacuity of hearing. Yet in spite of this, and the wealth which provided him with the means to set up experiments, he found it impossible to induce physicists to co-operate in the research. Only one academic figure of any standing came to see what Reichenbach was doing: Berzelius. In a report he wrote in 1846 for the Swedish Academy of Sciences (which, as he was its Secretary and its most distinguished member, could hardly be re-jected), he argued that there was a need for research: 'There is clearly something in it'. He could not deny that the evidence sounded fishy:

> Yet in many fields it is true that experience often produces circum-stances which seem incomprehensible, and only too easy to condemn as misunderstanding or frauds. This is not the right way. It is just as necessary to demonstrate what one believes to be false actually is so, as to show that what we think true actually is in fact the truth; and the real scientist does not shun either duty.

Angélique Cottin

The *Zoist* also carried items of historical or contemporary interest about a great variety of supernatural phenomena. In the 1840s they were particularly abundant, and one of them was unusually well-attested – the best vouched-for case of its kind in history: the story of Angélique Cottin, a fourteen-year-old from the village of Bouvigny in the Department of the Orne.

On January 15th, 1846, the heavy oak table at which Angélique – a girl described as 'dull, and of small stature' – and other girls sat mak-ing gloves began to make unaccountable movements; and it soon be-came clear that they were associated with Angélique. Furniture began to back away from her, when she approached, as if shunning her. She could not sit down, as the chair would retreat from her 'at a prodigious speed', even when men were employed to try to hold it. When she was put to shelling beans, the beans began to dance around. Clearly, she must be possessed. The local curé, however, happened to hold ad-vanced views on the subject. He could not dispute the reality of the phenomena; but he felt they needed scientific investigation, in case she required not exorcism but medical treatment. A local landowner, M. de Farémont, decided to take Angélique under his care; and he wrote the first of what was to be many detailed descriptions of the phenomena.

He was careful to check for deception; but he soon realised that there could be no question of her accomplishing the movements of objects by physical force. The only contact between her and a heavy bin was a movement of her petticoat, which seemed to belly out towards it as if attracted to it; yet the bin was 'instantly lifted to a height of three or four inches above the ground', and 'continued to rise in that fashion four or five times a minute'.

The explanation, Farémont decided, must be that in some way, Angélique had become charged with electricity; and she became known as 'the electric girl'. To her parents, who were poor, this seemed a fine opportunity to earn some money by putting her on exhibition in nearby Mortagne; and while she was there she was again investigated, more systematically. The suspicions of a local doctor, Beaumont Chardin, were aroused by the movements of her dress; all displacements of objects, he noticed, seemed to be effected by contact with what she was wearing. But it was easy to satisfy himself that she was not using her feet or any contraption. If she went to sit down in a chair, her skirt would float out towards it, and the chair would shoot back as if repelled by some powerful force; as did heavy tables at her approach. And whatever the cause might be, as the local pharmacist noted, there was one point on which there was agreement. The effects had been witnessed and attested by a great number of respectable people, and they were convinced that Angélique had no confederates. There could be no question of fraud.

The decision was therefore taken to send Angélique to Paris for investigation by the Academy; and there she was seen by Dr. Tanchou, who had been asked to carry out a preliminary investigation. While she was with him, a cold breeze played around her; a chair he was holding was forcibly wrenched from his hand when she sat down; a dining table was more than once displaced 'by the mere touch of her dress'; and

a large and heavy sofa upon which I was seated was pushed with great force against the wall the moment the girl came to seat herself by me. A chair was held fast upon the floor by strong men, and I was seated on it in such a way as to occupy only half the seat; it was forcibly wrenched away from under me as soon as the young girl sat down on the other half.

At this stage, Tanchou took the sensible precaution of calling in the astronomer and physicist, François Arago; a radical and a free-thinker, known for his conviction that there were no phenomena of this kind for which a natural explanation could not be found. With three colleagues, Arago watched while the same performance was repeated;

tables and stands slid away when Angélique approached; a chair on which she tried to sit seemed to fling itself violently against a wall, though they were trying to hold it down; and when one of them sat on a small sofa, it too shifted away when she came to sit down beside him.

No scientist in France had a higher reputation than Arago; when he endorsed Tanchou's findings, the Academy had no choice but to set up a formal committee of inquiry. As they had found that paper was attracted to Angélique's hands and that pith balls, suspended on thread, were set in motion by them, the assumption was that she must in some way become charged with static electricity; and with this in mind, they confronted her with appliances of various kinds designed to ascertain whether the force involved was electrical, and if so, how it worked. The tests were unproductive. Between February 19th and 24th there was so little to report that Tanchou recommended that they should be discontinued. It would be prudent, he felt, to return to doubt, and await fresh proofs. As the original report presented by Tanchou and Arago had not been confirmed by the subsequent investigation, the decision was taken to deem it null and void. Angélique went home; and the manifestations apparently did not reappear.

The Paris Poltergeist

The most curious of all the manifestations of the period was reported from Paris in 1849; remarkable not just for what happened, but for the source of the report – the *Gazette des Tribunaux*, the official organ of the French police. An article in its issue for February 2nd recounted what had been happening since work had begun to open up a new street between the Sorbonne and the Panthéon. A little house, hardly more than a cottage, stood near where the new street was to run; and every evening, it was assailed by 'a hail of projectiles', as if it were under siege.

Whence come these projectiles, which are paving stones, fragments of the demolished walls near, and stones entire which from their weight and the distance they are hurled, are clearly from no mortal hand? This is just what, up to this moment, it has been impossible to discover. In vain has a surveillance been exercised, day and night, under the personal direction of the Commissary of Police, and able assistants. In vain has the Head of Security been continually on the spot. In vain have they let loose, every night, watchdogs in the adjoining enclosures. Nothing has been able to explain the phenomena, which in its credulity, the public has attributed to mysterious means. The projectiles have continued to rain down with great noise on the house, launched forth at a great height above the heads of those who have placed themselves in observation on the roofs of the small surrounding houses, and seeming to come from a great distance, reaching their aim with a precision as it were, mathematical, and without deviating from the parabola evidently designed for them.

But the *Gazette*'s hope that an explanation would be found was not, apparently, fulfilled.

Chapter Twenty
Mid-century

By 1850, THEREFORE, A MASS OF EVIDENCE HAD ACCUMULATED FOR THE existence of a great variety of forces as yet unrecognised by science, and awaiting verification and explanation; and in spite of all the setbacks, the most promising opening for research still lay in the use of mesmerism to explore the higher phenomena. There was by this time a precedent; homeopathy was managing to establish itself as an alternative form of medicine in spite of the uncompromising hostility of the medical profession, and it was doing so largely because its practitioners had managed to win the support of a sufficient number of men and women of intellectual and social standing. It remained possible this might happen with mesmerism. In *A Tale of the Ragged Mountains* Edgar Allan Poe, remarking on the discovery that a mesmerist could put patients into a trance even when they were unaware of his presence, noted 'it is only now, in the year 1845, when similar miracles are witnessed daily by thousands, that I dare venture to record this apparent impossibility as a matter of serious fact'. Some converts, like Victor Hugo and George Sand, had been convinced by personal experience with clairvoyants; others, like Harriet Martineau, by the effects of mesmeric treatment, which led her to deplore 'the far-fetched calumnies' with which so many doctors assailed mesmerism, 'as if they were in conflict with powerful truth, and they knew it'. And Thomas Arnold, headmaster of Rugby, expressed the view that the quantity and quality of the evidence put mesmerism 'beyond question'. Refusal to accept it, he felt, was an attitude 'far more dangerous to our Christian faith, than any belief in the facts'; facts which, though they might be 'mere wonders in our present state of knowledge', might later become the principles of a new science.

Gregory and Mayo
One advantage the mesmerists had, in popularising their ideas, was

that anybody could experiment. As the title of a pamphlet *The Mesmeric Mania of 1851* was designed to indicate, experimenters were to be found everywhere in Britain, at fashionable parties, in college common rooms, even in schools. The author, John H. Bennett, accepted Braid but disapproved of the excesses, as he thought them to be, of mesmerism; they had led, he feared, to the same kind of hysteria that had brought about the dancing mania in medieval times. That year, however, among the many books to appear on the subject in Britain, two were published which could not be dismissed as the products of hysteria, and which revealed that mesmerism was making inroads even into the heart of academic orthodoxy; one by William Gregory, Professor of Chemistry at the University of Glasgow – a bio-chemist with an international reputation, who had introduced Liebig's work in Britain; the other by Herbert Mayo, who had been Professor of Physiology at King's College, London.

Both surveyed the evidence with due caution, admitting the problems. Not all people were 'sensitives'; not all sensitives could produce clairvoyance at will; those who could, could not produce it consistently, or in a hostile atmosphere; and what they 'saw' was not necessarily an accurate representation of the reality. And neither of them was prepared to be dogmatic about the nature of the forces involved. 'I am quite content,' Gregory wrote, 'that any theoretical suggestions I have made should be thrown aside as quite unimportant, provided only the facts be attended to; because I consider it too early for a comprehensive theory and because I believe that the facts are as yet very partially known.' Even allowing for this, Gregory felt, the potential value of mesmerism was enormous, not only for medical treatment, but to trace missing people and lost or stolen goods.

In his *Letters on Animal Magnetism* Gregory's main object was to show that if, at last, mesmeric phenomena were to be recognised as genuine, this recognition could not exclude the higher phenomena. They only manifested themselves, he admitted, in a very few subjects; he himself had rarely encountered them. But friends, acquaintances and correspondents whom he could trust, experimenting in their own homes, had provided him with abundant evidence for community of sensation, for thought-transference, and in particular for travelling clairvoyance. The Rev. Andrew Gilmour of Greenock had a servant girl who, when mesmerised, could tell him what he was tasting, or where he was pinching himself, even if he were in another room; and could describe accurately what his mother or friends were doing in their homes. When he asked friends to take note of what they were doing in a day's time, at a certain hour, and then wrote to them describing what the servant, mesmerised, had 'seen', they would write back confirming its accuracy. Although Gilmour was baffled, and disturbed, he had felt he could not deny the evidence of his own senses, or any longer 'question the veracity of hundreds of upright and honourable men, who are far too clear-sighted to be imposed upon themselves, and much too honest to try to deceive others'.

Such examples, and there were many more of them, were cumulatively convincing precisely because the people involved in the research were not professionals. With a working team like Marcillet and Alexis, sleight-of-hand, coupled with a spy system, was at least a possible explanation; but not with these Scots servant girls. They could hardly have deceived even the most gullible of their investigators; and many of the investigators, clearly, were far from gullible. Nor was it conceivable that it was the investigators themselves who cheated. All of them were men of standing in their communities, whose reputations would have been ruined if they had been detected in any deception. And what possible motive could they have had? Unlike Marcillet and Alexis they had nothing material to gain from the production of the higher phenomena; on the contrary, in their professions they might jeopardise their prospects by becoming known to be involved with mesmerism. By their own accounts some of them would have preferred to use mesmerism simply as a healing force; particularly the clergy, in mental or emotional disturbances of the kind to which they were often called upon to minister. The higher phenomena often came as an unexpected intrusion which they felt in honesty bound to report, but did not welcome.

It was consequently absurd, Gregory felt, for those who followed Braid to accept somnambulism and a limited range of physiological effects, while dismissing the higher phenomena. And it came particularly ill, he felt, from those who had previously rejected mesmerism totally to lay down the law on the subject. 'I have often heard persons who now regard those phenomena as established not only deny them,' he commented, 'but assert with confidence that they were mere humbug and imposture.' Had they apologised, when they found they were wrong? They had not; neither had they learned humility. This kind of sceptic

had disdainfully rejected the evidence of many persons of good character and abilities, as well qualified as himself, perhaps better qualified, to observe such facts, and had accused them of imposture; he now finds, not only that they were innocent of that offence, but that they were remarkably accurate in the account they gave of the phenomena. But here he stops. He admits the facts, for example, of the artificial production of genuine somnambulism, or of insensibility to pain; but he rejects (as decidedly as he formerly did those facts), those further phenomena of animal magnetism, such as sympathy; thought reading; community of senses, of taste, smell etc.; the control exercised by the operator over the will and imagination of the subject; and all the forms of clairvoyance. In short he repeats, deliberately and recklessly, his former error.

Mesmerism, Gregory believed, could explain much that had previously been obscure, particularly in connection with magic and witchcraft: a point which Mayo also emphasised. If a mesmerised subject could 'see' without the use of his eyes, it became much easier to understand how people could 'see' ghosts, or have visions; and this in its turn, he felt, had important implications for humanity. From regarding visions, premonitions and such as an indication of witchcraft, society had come to accept them as a symptom of mental disorder; a step in the right direction, but one which all too often led to a fate almost as ugly – incarceration in a lunatic asylum. Sensory illusions, Mayo claimed, 'are not insanity, neither do they menace that disorder'; on the contrary, if properly understood they might be the means of providing the mind with an invaluable source of information. Mesmerism could also lead to a better understanding of 'the whole family of spasms', associated with disease from infancy to senility – convulsions, epileptic fits, St. Vitus's Dance, catalepsy and hysteria; perhaps even the spasmodic twitching of a water diviner's hazel twig.

The issue, Mayo pointed out, was not simply whether a dowser could, or could not, detect the presence of an underground spring. The nature of the force responsible for the movements of the hazel twig deserved examination in its own right, he argued; and he described the work of some researchers who had been pursuing this line of inquiry. In 1822 the Comte de Tristan had conducted over one thousand five hundred experiments in the Loire valley, observing that the movements of the hazel rod differed according to the individuals holding it: for some, it moved down; for others, the rod turned round and round in the fulcrum formed by their fists. Elementary though such observations were, they were original; nobody had thought to examine that aspect of dowsing before. Tristan had also found that the rod would not act if silk were interposed between it and the hands of the dowser; a line of inquiry which had been followed up in the 1840s by a Scots friend of Mayo, George Fairholm, testing a dowser. In place of the hazel twig, Fairholm had persuaded her to try a similarly-shaped piece of iron wire; and it worked satisfactorily. When he coated the part which she held with sealing-wax, nothing happened; but if she touched the wire at all, even if only with the slightest of contacts, it would react.

There must be some undiscovered force at work, Mayo surmised, to help account for convulsive movements. If it could be found, the divining rod 'will be a credit to the family of superstitions, for without any reduction, or slipping, or trimming, it may at once assume the rank of a new truth'. But Mayo was not sanguine.

Alas! the trials which await it in that character! What an ordeal is before it! A new truth has to encounter three normal stages of opposition. In the first, it is denounced as imposture; in the second – that is, when it is beginning to force itself into notice – it is cursorily examined, and plausibly explained away; in the third, or *cui bono* stage, it is decried as useless, and hostile to religion. And when it is fully admitted, it passes only under a protest that it has been perfectly known for ages – a proceeding intended to make the new truth ashamed of itself, and wish it had never been born.

William Benjamin Carpenter

In view of this accumulation of evidence in favour of mesmerism and allied phenomena, how could orthodoxy sustain its resistance? The main reason was that the difference of opinion among the mesmerists gave orthodoxy its opportunity. The fundamental split was over the higher phenomena. Although Braid had witnessed extraordinary feats of writing or drawing without the use of the eyes, of overhearing conversations in distant apartments, and of recalling past events, these to him were all simply a reflection of the heightening of sensory awareness under hypnosis. When Esdaile objected that this could not account for the way in which a blind man had been able to follow his unspoken suggestions, Braid brushed the objection aside; the blind man's hearing, doubtless improved by his loss of sight, must have enabled him to sense Esdaile's every movement, even his breathing, and by this means, guess what Esdaile was willing him to do.

This division between the mesmerists and the supporters of Braid militated against the chances of their gaining acceptance even for those aspects of the trance state about which they agreed; a split which took the same course, and had the same effect, in the United States. Mesmerism had been slow to catch on there in spite of the fact that Lafayette, an enthusiast, had introduced it as early as 1788, recommending it to George Washington; and that later it had attracted the interest of Henry Clay and Daniel Webster. But in 1836, Charles Poyen, who had picked up a knowledge of it in the West Indies, gave a lecture on the subject in Boston, and in the presence of some Harvard professors, mesmerised a girl so that she could have a tooth extracted without giving any sign of pain. Although the academics remained unimpressed, individual researchers began to explore the possibilities. Some of them reported clairvoyance, the most celebrated performer being a blind girl, Loraina Brackett. While she was on a visit to

Providence, Rhode Island, a local doctor, George Capron, found that when mesmerised she could move around as freely as if she had full use of her sight, 'read' from a book held behind her head, identify objects concealed in boxes, and describe what was happening at a distance; and when she went on to New York, Capron's account was confirmed by Colonel W. L. Stone. He and others had mocked the story of her abilities, he admitted in the *New York Commercial Advertiser*, of which he was owner-editor. As they found that she was able to read the contents of a sealed package, though none of those present had known what it contained, 'we shall laugh at it no more'. In the early 1840s, too, Dr. William B. Fahnestock of Pennsylvania made careful and detailed investigations of travelling clairvoyance; and Dr. Robert Collyer found that some of his New York patients could detect what he was doing (or tasting) behind their backs. But Collyer assumed like Braid that this was due to heightened sensory awareness, and when in the late 1840s, mesmerism began to attract wider attention under the new name of 'electro-biology', a term coined by a lawyer, J. Stanley Grimes, Grimes's contention was that there was no magnetic fluid, no higher phenomena, only a mental force acting electrically to influence the nervous system; and his theory and practice of 'electro-biologising', usually for convenience abbreviated simply to 'biologising', were not substantially different from Braid's.

The split among mesmerists was seized upon by one of the scientists in Britain to have been convinced of the genuineness of the trance state. If hypnosis (or electro-biology) could be presented as a natural physiological process, there would no longer be any need to deny that it existed; and in an appendix to a new edition of his textbook on physiology in 1846 William Benjamin Carpenter, Professor at the Royal Institute in London, conceded that there were certain effects which could not be disputed: coma, or insensibility, enabling surgical operations to be painlessly performed; somnambulism, identical to sleep-walking, except that it was artificially induced and that the somnambulist could be made to follow the will of the inducer; and excitation of the muscular system, enabling people to perform feats ordinarily beyond their capacity. (Carpenter had seen a man of low muscular development take a twenty-pound weight, which ordinarily he could barely lift, and twirl it round his little finger, having been assured by the hypnotist that it was as light as a feather.)

Coming from Carpenter, who was making his name as orthodoxy's most trenchant spokesman, this might have appeared to represent mesmerism's break-through. It was to have the opposite effect, because Carpenter went on to develop Braid's notion of hyper-sensitivity or hyperacuity of the senses to explain away the higher phenomena. There could be no question of clairvoyance or thought-transference; it was simply a matter of subjects picking up minute sensory clues, like currents of air wafted towards them when the mesmerist pointed his finger at them behind their backs. Carpenter also managed to insinuate that the mesmerists, as distinct from the hypnotists, were not to be trusted – 'Manifesting his strong and deep rooted hostility,' as the *Zoist* sourly put it, 'without the manliness of the open foe,' he was able to widen the breach between the two, leaving mesmerism still as suspect as before.

So far as orthodoxy was concerned, there was no need to pay any attention even to Carpenter's contention that surgery could be painlessly performed with the patient mesmerised. It came just too late; in 1846, ether and laughing gas were coming into use as anaesthetics in the United States; and that winter, Robert Liston performed the first operation in Britain with ether – ironically at University College Hospital. Very soon, chloroform was in standard use, rendering it unnecessary for surgeons to contemplate hypnosis as an alternative. This did not make them any less contemptuous of mesmerism's power to suppress pain. In 1850, Dr. Marshall Hall, who had earlier claimed that the patient who had had his leg amputated eight years before had only pretended that the operation had been painless, told the Royal Medical and Chirurgical Society that the patient had since confessed to the deception. When Dr. John Ashburner obtained an affidavit from the patient denying that he had ever made any such confession, and reiterating that he had felt no pain, Hall replied that he had had the information from a gentleman he regarded as 'the most honourable and truthful of men', and that as this most honourable and truthful of men had told him that *he* had the story from 'a person in whom he had full confidence', Hall still believed it. Accepting Hall's version, the Royal Medical and Chirurgical Society declined to allow Ashburner a hearing; a verdict which won the *Lancet*'s approbation as 'impartial'.

The following year, Esdaile returned to Britain. Before his retirement he had performed thousands of minor operations, with an assistant to mesmerise the patients, and three hundred operations involving major surgery; yet there had not been a single fatality which his rivals could attribute to the technique. On the contrary, his mortality rate was far lower than theirs. The medical journals in Britain, however, would not publish his account of his work; and when he eventually found an obscure paper whose editor consented to print it, it appeared in a garbled version. He had made no money out of his surgery, as he had refused to engage in private practice; and when he died a few years later, his achievements had obtained no recognition in the medical press.

Hypnotism and 'electro-biology', therefore, fell into a limbo: accepted by some orthodox scientists, but taken to be a curiosity, an anomaly, of no particular significance. Mesmerism remained excluded, on the occult side of the frontier. This might not have greatly worried the mesmerists; they were used to it. But now they were confronted by a rival operating from occult territory: Spiritualism.

Spiritualism

Chapter Twenty-one
The Forerunners

WHATEVER MIGHT BE THEIR DIFFERENCES OF OPINION ABOUT THE nature of the force with which they were dealing, most mesmerists had believed that animal magnetism, like magnetism, would eventually be shown to be natural. Few of them had thought that the higher phenomena had anything to do either with God – except, perhaps, in his general role as Creator – or with the devil. There had, however, been individuals and cults who believed that the force was spiritist: some because of their religious beliefs, others because what they saw and heard convinced them that spirits must be involved, particularly in the transmission of information. In the Scandinavian countries a Swedenborg sect had developed after his death in 1772; and its members began to use mesmerism to facilitate contact with the spirits of the dead. In his 1785 essay on animal magnetism, Tardy de Montravel had suggested spirits were involved in clairvoyance and thought-transference; and Deleuze had devoted a section of his history of animal magnetism to those mesmerists who believed that the action was produced by spirits. But it was not until 1829 that a case history was presented which could be regarded as presenting the spiritist case; the description by Dr. Justinus Kerner of Weinsberg of his patient, Friederika Hauffe.

The Seeress of Prevorst

As a child in Prevorst Friederika had seen visions, had premonitions, and talked to invisible beings; and after her marriage, when she had begun to suffer from an undiagnosed illness, the spirits used to come back to her in what she described as her magnetic sleep, a self-induced trance into which she fell every evening. Suffering from extreme debility – all her teeth dropped out – and malnutrition, she was brought to Kerner, who had established a reputation for his work on the chemistry of blood poisoning (and also as a song writer and poet;

he was a man of diverse talents). What Kerner must do, she told him when she arrived in 1826, was listen to what she would say in her magnetic sleep, because the spirits would prescribe for her. Kerner at first refused; it was her reliance on so dubious a source, he argued, that had given rise to her symptoms. But when his own remedies failed he gave way, and began to record what she said in, or about, her trance experiences.

On Christmas Day, Mme. Hauffe began to complain about a spirit, a man with a terrible squint, who kept disturbing her sleep. Kerner recognised the man from her description; he had died suddenly some years before, and there had been some suspicion that he had been involved in a dubious financial transaction for which another man had been blamed. The spirit was worried, Mme. Hauffe explained, about a document which had not been found after his death. The spirit knew where it was, on a desk in a certain room; and Mme. Hauffe was able to describe the document, its contents, the room, and the man who was working there so precisely that Kerner recognised the office and the man, Judge Heyd. A search brought the missing document to light. 'Even if incredulity must attribute everything to suggestion or a plot,' the judge wrote, confirming Kerner's account, 'the following remain inexplicable':

The fact that only I knew that I was sitting at work in an unusual position on the last day of the Christmas holidays.

The fact that quite accidentally and contrary to regulations, a chest was open in the room ... closed except to myself and my assistant.

The accurate determination of the position of the document, which was not found in its correct numerical order.

The indication of the small and long-standing bending of the corner of the paper of the document in question.

The upshot was that a widow was able to clear her wronged husband's name; and the man with the squint, though he continued to appear in Mme. Hauffe's sleep, troubled her no more.

As Mme. Hauffe had known nobody except Kerner in Weinsberg, and on account of her illness had had no opportunity to enter into collusion with anybody to set up the story, Kerner began to take her visions more seriously during the two remaining years of her life. For those who, like himself, could not see and talk with the spirits, she showed him various ways they had of attracting attention, 'sighing, knocking, noises as of the throwing of sand on gravel, rustling of paper, etc.' They were also able to move objects. Kerner could sometimes hear the knockings; he saw gravel and ashes falling in her room;

and once a stool rose gradually off the floor, and then as gradually fell again. Mme. Hauffe could also 'read' documents which he placed on her stomach, 'it often appears to me that I am out of my body,' she explained, 'and then I hover over it'. In this state her body appeared to become elastic; and when Kerner placed his fingertips to hers, she became attached to him as if by magnetism, so that she could easily be lifted off the ground.

Inevitably the fame of the 'Seeress of Prevorst' began to spread; and doubts were cast on the truth of the stories. Kerner, who had his reputation to protect, invited doctors and scientists to come and see for themselves. Among those who did and were impressed was Gotthilf von Schubert, who in his work on natural history speculated on the possibility that such interaction of the human body with inanimate objects might relate to old beliefs in magic which ascribed certain qualities and forces to stones; and Kant's disciple C. A. von Eschenmayer, Professor of Philosophy at Tübingen. So when Kerner's book on the seeress appeared, and was an immediate success, Kerner had a reply ready for those critics who dismissed it as the product of imagination or deception. 'When the seeress was alive,' he asked,

and those things were talked of, did any of those who now write volumes of refutation ever take the trouble to come and see her, and examine her for themselves? No: they sat still at their desks, and yet considered themselves better able to pronounce on these facts than the calm, earnest and profound psychologist, Eschenmayer, who examined everything on the spot, and in person, and thought nothing of taking a journey in the depth of winter for the purpose. So only, on such subjects, can truth be elicited.

Mme. Hauffe was not an isolated case. In 1839 Heinrich Werner of Stuttgart published an account of an eighteen-year-old girl, 'R.D.', who talked to a guardian spirit she called Albert. On one occasion R.D. 'saw' her younger sister in peril; she despatched Albert to the rescue; Albert warned her father; and her father – she told Werner – arrived just in time to stop her sister falling out of a window into the street below. Out of curiosity Werner wrote to her father, to find out whether there was anything in the story. In reply, the father described how he had been in his office that day, when he was assailed by a feeling of intense disquiet. He decided to go home, and arrived while a rope was being used to lift wood to the top of his house by means of a windlass. He rushed up to the attic, to find his daughter leaning out of the attic window, trying to clutch the rope; and he had caught her just as she had lost her balance.

There were other intimations in this period of the existence of what seemed to be psychic intelligences; some of them from witnesses like Elliotson, who refused to take spirits seriously but who was to recall that one of the Okey sisters in her trance thought she was in communication with a negro; she could be seen to 'whisper as if to someone with her; then to pause, as if receiving an answer; and then to answer the question'. The French mesmerist J. J. A. Ricard, who in the early 1840s ran a journal and wrote books on the subject, gave many examples of what he called 'spiritist somnambulists'; and in 1848 Alphonse Cahagnet began to bring out his *Arcanes de la vue future devoilés*, full of similar cases. A Swedenborgian, Cahagnet, had come to the conclusion that the best way to propagate the master's message was to look for subjects who in the trance state could converse freely with the spirits; and his case histories, being propagandist, need to be taken with some reserve. Yet even Frank Podmore, surveying the historical evidence from a mistrustful standpoint – he dismissed the manifestations of the Seeress of Prevorst, for example, as 'systematic trickery, often of a puerile character' – was to concede that in all his researches into mesmerism and spiritualism he had found no records which reached a higher evidential standard than Cahagnet's; 'nor any in which the writer's good faith and intelligence are alike so conspicuous'.

Paradoxically it was Cahagnet's faith which had prompted him to search for the higher evidential standards. To prove that spirits were responsible he had to find a way to eliminate the possibility that either guesswork or thought-transference was involved; and to do this, when he found a good clairvoyant subject like Adèle Maginot, who could 'see' relations and friends of his clients, he would ask the clients to bring with them the names of people that they did *not* themselves know. A local pastor accordingly asked one of his servants to provide him with the name of a deceased friend of hers; and she gave him 'Jeanette Jex'.

He came armed with this name. Adèle replied, 'I see a woman who is not tall. She may be between thirty and forty years of age; if she is not hump-backed, she must be crook-backed for she carries herself very badly. I cannot make her turn round. Her hair is auburn, approaching to red; she has small grey eyes, a thick nose. She is not good-looking. She has a prominent chin, a receding mouth, thin lips; her dress is countryfied. I see that she has a cap with two flat bands, rounded over the ears. She must have suffered from a flow of blood to the head. She has had indigestion. I see she has a swelling in the abdomen on one side, and in the glands of one breast. She has been ill a long time.'

The pastor gave the description to his servant; and she reported that it was correct 'as regards stature, age, dress, carriage, the disease, and the deformed figure'.

Spiritism, then, was already established in Europe before the middle of the century (the English term, 'spiritualism' was also in circulation: in his book on mesmerism Chauncy Townshend applied it to people who believed in spirit forces). And in the United States, as in Europe, mesmerists had from time to time reported spirit intervention. When in 1844 a Massachusetts doctor, Lyman B. Larkin, used mesmerism to try to cure his servant girl, Mary Jane, of fits, she claimed she encountered spirits: a good fairy, who told her useful things, and a sailor boy, who taught her obscene language. Her behaviour when she was possessed, quiet or profane, depended upon which spirit it was that possessed her. While she was in these trance states Larkin would sometimes hear loud knockings from the furniture, which was also 'often moved about violently by unseen hands'. Heavy weights were lifted from place to place; a kitchen flat-iron appeared suddenly in the living room, and when told by Mrs. Larkin to depart, vanished again, to be found later back in the kitchen, though the doors between the rooms had been closed. In spite of the verdict of a local minister and his wife, who came to investigate and pronounced that what they had seen was 'supra-mundane', Mary Jane was arrested on a charge of necromancy and sentenced to six months' solitary confinement. Larkin escaped more lightly; his punishment was to be banned from the church until he publicly confessed his guilt, which he did, though privately continuing to maintain that the spirits had indeed been responsible.

In the same year Andrew Jackson Davis of Poughkeepsie had a vision in which he spoke with the spirits of Galen and Swedenborg. He was eighteen, a leather-worker's son, with only a rudimentary education; a few months before, when he had been mesmerised, he had found that he could 'see' with his eyes bandaged; and following his encounter with the spirits, the faculty burgeoned. While he was in a trance, he explained, solid objects appeared to become transparent; he could see through walls; 'the broad sweep of the earth, for many hundred miles, came before my vision'. In his trances, too, he poured out lectures on philosophical and scientific subjects, spirit-dictated, which were to be published in a string of books. Turgid though works like his *Principles of Nature* were, they displayed a range of knowledge which, as the professor of Hebrew at the University of New York put it, would have done honour to any scholar of the age. Yet Davis was all but illiterate. More strikingly, perhaps, than any other individual in history, Davis had the ability to 'know' without ever having consciously acquired the knowledge.

Chapter Twenty-two
The Psychic Cloud

THEN, IN 1848, REPORTS BEGAN TO CIRCULATE ABOUT WHAT HAD BEEN happening in a house at Hydesville, near Rochester N.Y. It had not had the reputation of being haunted before the Foxes – father, mother and two daughters, Margaret, aged fifteen, and Kate, twelve – had moved in that winter; but now, sounds were heard, rappings, bangings or scrapings as if furniture was being shifted around. Kate challenged the 'ghost', as they took it to be, to answer when she snapped her fingers; and it rapped. Margaret took up the game (as the children, delighted with themselves, regarded it); and their mother asked questions, which elicited that the raps came from the spirit of the man who had lived in the house and had been murdered there, his body being buried in the cellar. Neighbours were called in; and one of them had the idea of extending the range of information which could be collected by calling over the letters of the alphabet, the spirit being asked to rap when appropriate. By this means, simple 'yes' and 'no' were supplemented by whole sentences, providing further gruesome details about the murder. An attempt to find the corpse, however, was thwarted by the discovery that the ground under the cellar was water-logged; the search had to be abandoned.

Neighbours flocked to the house to listen; a committee was set up to investigate, and depositions collected. Some of the investigators were sceptical; but none, after hearing the sounds, had any suspicion that the Fox family were responsible. To both parents, the affair was a nuisance and an embarrassment; and, sitting in the living room with the watchers, how could the children be responsible for rappings and bangings heard from other parts of the house, let alone for making correct answers to the questions put to the ghost? That the noises might be linked to the presence of the children was not realised until their mother took them away; then it was found that the noises continued in houses where they were staying. Suspicions were naturally aroused. Margaret and her elder, married sister, Leah – who though not psychic herself had realised that her sisters could be exploited as a commercial proposition – were called upon to submit to an investigation by a committee set up at a meeting of Rochester citizens. And it was at this stage that it first became clear how difficult it was to conduct such an inquiry in a way which would convince anybody but the people directly involved in it. The committee pronounced that the tests showed the raps were audible, and that Margaret could not have produced them physically. Dissatisfied, the meeting demanded a second investigation, which produced a similar verdict. Obviously the precautions had not been strict enough! A third committee was appointed; this time composed of women so that the sisters could be stripped and searched to find what mechanical devices they had on them. But this committee, too, reported that even when the sisters were made to stand on pillows, 'with a handkerchief tied around the bottom of their dresses tight to the ankles', the rappings were still distinctly heard around the room, on the walls and the floor. The meeting broke up in confusion.

By this time the Fox sisters had begun to produce new effects. People at seances with them felt themselves touched as if by an invisible hand; objects in the vicinity unaccountably moved; musical instruments played though nobody was playing them. Similar reports were beginning to be circulated about other mediums. E. W. Capron – a relation of the mesmerist who had treated Loraina Brackett, and himself interested in trances – had begun to investigate; and in his *Modern Spiritualism*, the most sensible of the early accounts of the period, he was to describe some of early seances. Usually they were held in the dark, the spirits intimating they preferred it that way; but occasionally they would tolerate light, and on one occasion, following rappings,

the table moved on the floor with nobody touching it – moved to the distance of a foot or more and back, in various directions. At our request, the table (which was a very light one) was held down on the floor so that it required the whole strength of a man to move it from its position. We also held one side and requested, if there was power to do it, that it would be drawn away from us; this was done, and our strength was not sufficient to hold it.

Later, in darkness, the table tilted over on one side and remained tilted, though they did their best to push it down.

That tables could move during poltergeist hauntings was by this time well-established: that they could be induced to move was a novelty – though a few years later the German theologian Franz Delitzsch, who detested spiritualism, was to reveal that table-moving had been practised by a Jewish sect early in the seventeenth century. If certain magical formulae were repeated, a critic had complained in 1614, 'the table springs up, even when laden with many hundredweight'; and that this was not simply anti-semitic propaganda was revealed the following year when a Jewish writer defended the practice, provided it was done reverently to the accompaniment of psalms; 'there can be no devil's work suffered when God is remembered'. The Fox sisters appeared to have rediscovered the secret; from this time on, table movements were commonly reported.

In 1850 the sisters were brought to New York to give seances. That they were professionals, giving public performances, aroused the suspicions of the Rev. Rufus Griswold, magazine editor and author, and he invited them to his home to be investigated by, among others, Charles Dana, of the *American Encyclopedia*; the historian and diplomat George Bancroft; John Bigelow, editor of the *New York Evening Post*, later U.S. Minister in France; the poet William Cullen Bryant; and Fenimore Cooper. At the first seance the girls were nervous and for some time nothing happened. But eventually, rappings were heard from all round the room, the spirits answering some questions correctly; and George Ripley, reporting the investigation for Horace Greeley's *Tribune*, had to admit that the girls could not have produced the sounds. Investigating on his own account, Greeley too accepted that whatever the origins of the rappings, 'the ladies in whose presence they occur do not make them'.

By this time almost every known form of supernatural manifestation was being reproduced by other mediums, including speaking with tongues and automatic writing or drawing. In eight weeks Mrs. Amelia J. Williams of Washington, who had never had any instruction in drawing, executed over a hundred extremely detailed pictures, mostly of plants and flowers, each picture 'even when it embodied every variety of shading,' Capron claimed, being drawn 'so rapidly that even the most experienced draughtsman could not equal the facility displayed'. As Conan Doyle put it in his *History of Spiritualism*, it was like 'some psychic cloud descending from on high, and showing itself to those persons who were susceptible'. A few of the people affected had, in fact, already known spirit visitations; including the Shaker communities, of which there were over fifty. For some years past, they could now reveal, their meetings had occasionally been taken over, as if by a kind of mass possession, by spirits who had identified themselves as members of a Red Indian tribe; but as the Shaker elders were sure that they would be put away in lunatic asylums if this became known, they had been careful not to let it be disclosed. And as spiritualism spread, mediums were often surprised to be told that they had been possessed by a Red Indian 'guide' who provided the initial link, summoning up the spirits of dead parents or friends, as requested. It was as if the Red Indians, passionate believers in the existence of spirits, had thereby acquired a standing in the spirit world.

The 'psychic cloud' also included the first poltergeist in the United States to be carefully investigated and documented. In March 1850 furniture began to move unaccountably in the rectory at Stamford, Conn., where the Rev. Dr. Eliakim Phelps lived with his family. For weeks on end knives, forks, spoons, nails, blocks of wood and other objects were hurled around; often when visitors were present – as one of them described:

The contents of the pantry were emptied into the kitchen, and bags of salt, tin ware and heavier culinary articles were thrown in a promiscuous heap upon the floor, with a loud and startling noise. Loaves of delicious cake were scattered around the house. The large knocker of the outside door would thunder its fearful tones through the loud resounding hall, unmindful of the vain but rigid scrutiny to which it was subjected by incredulous and curious men. Chairs would deliberately move across the room, unimpelled by any visible agency. Heavy marble-top tables would poise themselves upon two legs, and then fall with their contents to the floor, no human being within six feet of them.

The manifestations were most common when one of the family, a boy of eleven, was present; and this naturally led to speculation that he might be playing tricks, perhaps with the help of his brothers. But after the family had moved from Stamford, bringing the infestation to an end, the exasperated father wrote to his friend Asa Mahan – the first President of Oberlin College – to explain how objects had endlessly been seen to move

from places and in directions which made it certain that no visible power existed by which the motion could be produced. For days and weeks together, I watched these strange movements with all the care and caution and close attention which I could bestow. I witnessed them hundreds and hundreds of times, and I know that in hundreds of instances, they took place where there was no visible power by which motion could have been produced. Scores of persons, of the first standing in the community, whose education, general intelligence, candour, veracity and sound judgment none will question, were requested to witness the phenomena, and, if possible, help us to a solution of the mystery. But as yet, no solution has been obtained. The idea that the whole was a 'trick of the children' – an idea which some of the papers have endeavoured, with great zeal, to promulgate – is to everyone who is acquainted with the facts, as stupid as it is false and injurious. The statement, too, which some of the papers have reiterated so often, that 'the mystery was found out' is, I regret to say, untrue. With the most thorough investigation which I have been able to bestow on it, aided by gentlemen of the best talents, intelligence and sound judgment, in this and in many neighbouring towns, the cause of these strange phenomena remains yet undiscovered.

But an isolated poltergeist, though it caused a sensation for a time, could not for long compete for attention with the Fox sisters, by this time giving seance after seance. The usual procedure was for individuals to bring their questions, which might be about anything from the location of lost property to the solution of a mathematical problem, the spirits answering by raps or tiltings of tables; and although a few people who came to seances remained unconvinced, nobody could offer any explanation of how the girls did their tricks (except, what was really no explanation at all, that they had machinery concealed about their persons: searches had shown that they did not). But in 1851, after three years in which the girls had been subjected to numerous tests without anybody being able to detect them in any deception, three professors of the new Buffalo School of Medicine who had attended some of their seances produced an explanation of how the raps were made. If the girls' knees were held, the professors had found, the rapping sounds ceased. Clearly, they must be able to make the sounds by dislocating, and relocating, their knee joints.

> The displacement occasioning the knockings is sufficient to remove the ridge of bone which divides the two articular surfaces of the upper extremity of the tibia from its situation in the sulcus between the condyls of the femur and to carry it, more or less, upon the surface of the outer condyl. This movement gives rise to the first sound, and the return of the bone to its place causes the second sound.

Slater Brown, whose *Heyday of Spiritualism* has at last provided a reliable guide through the intricacies of the Hydesville affair and its repercussions, has unearthed the *Cincinatti Inquirer*'s version of the Buffalo professors' report, attributing the raps to

> the physiological defect of the membraneous system. The obtuseness of the abdominal indicator causes the cartilaginous compressor to coagulate into the diaphragm, and depresses the duodenum into the flandango. Now, if the taps were caused by the vogation of the electricity from the extremity, the tympanum would also dissolve

into the spiritual sinctum and the olfactory ossificator would ferment ...

and so on. But such ridicule had no effect. It did not matter that the Buffalo professors were unable to explain how the sisters managed to 'pop' their knee joints (as a result, toe joints, easier to 'pop', were soon commonly substituted for knee joints as an explanation); nor, assuming they could 'pop' joints in any part of their anatomies, how they were capable of making them give forth a variety of sounds ranging from hammer blows to the sawing of wood: nor, assuming they could make such sounds, how they could transmit them by ventriloquism (contrary to natural law) around the walls of a room; still less, how they could make tables move, or objects float without touching them. It was enough, for sceptics, that a plausible-sounding explanation had been provided; and it was soon reinforced when Mrs. Culver, the sisters' aunt-in-law who had quarrelled with their parents, claimed that Kate had confessed to her that they used trickery, and shown her how they did it. Although Capron, who analysed the confession, showed that much of it was sheer invention on Mrs. Culver's part, the story of the Fox sisters' 'exposure' was to continue to be retailed and accepted for some years to come.

Judge Edmonds
By 1851, though, the Fox sisters' act was only one of many. All over the United States mediums were being found who could produce raps and movements of objects; and groups were forming who, though they had no recognised medium, found that by simply sitting around a table, and waiting, they could conjure up manifestations. An account of the period, impressive in its obvious sincerity, was to be given by John Worth Edmonds, a New York judge. Edmonds first attended a seance in January 1851, at a friend's invitation. He had become interested in the philosophical questions posed by death; but he was certain that spiritualism could not provide the answers. Hoping to discover by what devices the phenomena were produced, he began to investigate them systematically; only to find that far from yielding up their sordid secrets – perhaps along the lines of the Buffalo professors' explanation – they eluded him by becoming progressively more bizarre and inexplicable. That spring, his experiences at a well-lit seance (seances in the dark had often been found to produce phenomena more easily; but they were unsatisfactory for an investigator) finally convinced him that his scepticism had been misplaced. The table did not simply move; it levitated, swaying backwards and forwards even when they tried to stop it; 'so we all drew back and by the light of these two burning lamps we saw the heavy mahogany table suspended

in the air'. At the next seance the phenomena were even more extra-ordinary. As he stood in a corner, apart from the rest of the group, he felt a hand thrust into his pocket, and when he pulled out his handker-chief he found that six knots had been tied in it. A bass viol was put into his hands and played upon; his chair was pulled from under him; and one of his arms was gripped as if by a hand from which he could not extricate himself. Baffled, he continued his investigations, jotting down notes of what happened at every seance so that when he re-turned home he could write out a full account 'with as much minute-ness and particularity as I had ever kept record of a trial before me in court'. To exclude any possibility of fraud – the risk of cheats cashing in having been greatly increased by the publicity which the Fox sisters attracted – 'no cavil was too captious for me to resort to; no scrutiny too rigid or impertinent for me to institute; no inquiry too intrusive for me to make'. But after two years' work, every conceivable objec-tion that he could raise had been answered; and he felt that he must avow that fact. He was aware that to do so might jeopardise his career; but he felt an obligation to publish his findings because that was what he certainly would have done if they had fulfilled his original sceptical expectations.

By the time Edmonds published his account in the summer of 1853, the news that he was investigating spiritualism had inevitably leaked out, and had excited some derision. It had an unexpected conse-quence: the former Governor of Wisconsin, Nathaniel Tallmadge, who had previously been sceptical, decided that the subject must be worth investigating if Edmonds, 'a man of unimpeachable integrity', had been impressed. In 1852 he went to a seance with the Fox sisters: a table moved when nobody was near it, and then levitated six inches off the floor while he was sitting on it; below the table, sweet music came from bells and a guitar; and a message materialised on a piece of paper from his old friend John C. Calhoun, a former Secretary of State, who had died in 1850 – 'I'm with you still', in Calhoun's hand-writing.

Tallmadge and Edmonds found they had another bond: both had daughters who were psychic. Although Tallmadge's fourteen-year-old girl had never learned music, when under the influence of Beethoven (as her spirit mentor claimed to be), she could play the piano well. Edmond's daughter Laura had a convent school smattering of school-girl French, and no other language; but when a Greek visitor arrived with an introduction to Edmonds, she went into a trance, informing him in fluent Greek that in his absence his son had died, which proved to be correct. And as friends were present, Edmonds knew that he could not have imagined the episode.

In this period, spiritualists were often attacked, sometimes physically, and driven from their homes or their jobs by newspaper or pulpit campaigns; a student, Fred Willis, was expelled from Harvard for mediumship, though he had made no attempt to practise it in public. But Edmonds was protected to some extent by his standing in the community and by his reputation: even those journals which mocked the spiritualists did not try to cast doubt on his intelligence or integrity. He continued as judge of the New York Appeal Court, in which capacity the *Evening Mirror* conceded that 'whatever may be his faults, no one can justly accuse him of lack of ability, industry, honesty or fearlessness. No one can doubt his general saneness.' And other men of integrity were to add their own testimony. In his abolitionist journal *The Liberator*, William Lloyd Garrison reported that he had felt invisible hands at a seance, patting him and pulling at his clothes; and when a stick which had been placed on the floor had wriggled over to him like a snake, before rising to present him with its handle, he was unable, hard though he tried, to pull it out of the 'hand' that was holding it. But whatever small chance such phenomena might have had of attracting the attention of scientists was spoiled by the spirit element. The notion of unexplained forces was disturbing enough; the possibility that they were operated by intelligences, and still worse, by the spirits of the dead, was intolerable. It was not even as if the messages that the spirits passed were illuminating. Edmonds might be convinced that Swedenborg was communicating with him: but the spirit was even more prolix than Swedenborg on earth. Spirit communications tended to be at best worthy: more often they were stupefyingly trite.

The Hydesville ghost did not give birth to spiritualism, which had long anteceded it (as had almost all the phenomena then and later associated with seances); but it did provide the initial impulse which generated Spiritualism with a capital 'S': a new Pentecostal faith based on the belief that through mediums, it was possible to enter into communication with the dead – or rather, with those who had departed this bodily life to begin another life in the spirit. And the fact that it became identified with religion meant that it aroused even more savage antipathy than mesmerism: from Catholics and Protestants on the one side, and on the other not just from sceptics, rationalists and scientists, but from people with no preconceived objections, who felt that it was an affront to common sense.

Mrs. Hayden

The British were introduced to Spiritualism by Mrs. W. R. Hayden, the wife of a former owner-editor of a New England newspaper, who came to London in 1852 and quickly confirmed the reputation she had won in America. Her seances were restrained; raps were usually the only phenomena reported. Spirits announced their identity with the help of a roll-call from the alphabet, rapping at the appropriate letter; then gave information designed to establish to the questioner that they were genuine, and answered questions. The most celebrated of her early converts was Robert Owen who in 1853 published a book about his experiences, *The Future of the Human Race*. It was subtitled 'on a great, glorious and peaceful revolution, near at hand, to be effected through the agency of departed spirits of good and superior men and women'; but as the spirit whose goodness and superiority had most impressed him was Queen Victoria's father, the Duke of Kent, a notorious martinet whose career as Governor of Gibraltar had ended in humiliation when mutinies threatened the safety of the Rock, it was difficult to take the communications seriously. Besides, Owen was in his eighties, and had been out of public life for many years.

Harder-headed observers, though, were also impressed. The explorer Galla assured Sir David Brewster that Mrs. Hayden had told him names of people and places in Africa which nobody but himself could have known; and some clients left records of visits to her which show that they had been careful to satisfy themselves that she could not have had prior access to the information she gave them. The actor Charles Maine Young, who went to see her without giving advance notice, found that she was able to tell him – among other things – where he was proposing to stay the following night. Surprised, he decided to ask her about a problem which was disturbing him: would a threatened legal action over a legacy be brought to court? Not wishing to disclose the nature of his worry, he asked if he might put a question mentally. Mrs. Hayden agreed; and when he put it, she told him that the answer was 'No'. This did not satisfy him; it might have been a guess. Could she just give a single word, he asked, to show she really had a clue to his thoughts? The word, she replied, was 'will'.

The most detailed descriptions of Mrs. Hayden's seances were provided by Augustus de Morgan and his wife Sophia. Mrs. de Morgan had been taken to a seance with Mrs. Hayden in New York, and the raps had brought her messages from old friends of hers who had been dead for years; although the content was banal – 'we long to hold you in our arms' – she was impressed, because she was certain that nobody present could have known about the friends. So when Mrs. Hayden came to London, Mrs. de Morgan persuaded her husband to attend a demonstration. As the first holder of the Chair of Mathematics at University College, London, and the Secretary of the Astronomical Society, Augustus had an academic reputation which he was determined not to forfeit; he was careful to stipulate that the seance should be in their own home, and that the medium should come alone. His first concern was with the rappings themselves, to satisfy himself that

Mrs. Hayden did not make them by some device. They were 'clean, clear, faint sounds, such as would be said to *ring*, had they lasted', making the kind of noise 'which the ends of knitting needles would make, if dropped from a small distance on to a marble slab, and instantly checked by a damper of some kind'. Mrs. Hayden was seated far enough from the table for her feet as well as her hands to be in view: she could not, he realised, be making the raps herself. The next step was to check the source of the information they provided. When he was asked if he would like to put a question to the spirit of his sister-in-law, who had come through (she had been dead for seventeen years) he asked if he might put it mentally. In a letter he wrote to a friend, describing the seance, he explained that he decided to ask his sister-in-law if she remembered a letter she had once written to him, and what was the subject? 'With the help of the alphabet and the raps, I got that word, letter by letter – CHESS.'

The possibility remained that Mrs. Hayden was cleverly picking up clues involuntarily given by the sister. George Henry Lewes, at that time owner-editor of the *Leader*, had decided that this must be the explanation; and to prove it, he introduced carefully prepared hesitations at the appropriate letters, when he read them out at a seance; the raps obligingly co-operated and among other items of information from the spirits, revealed that the ghost of Hamlet's father had seventeen noses, and that Mrs. Hayden was an impostor. But a fairer test, which de Morgan applied, was not to speak at all. When the raps informed him of the presence of the spirit of his father who had died in 1816, he put a large table, on which was a brightly lit lamp, between himself and the medium; and he concealed the alphabet card behind a book, running his finger down the letters, leaving it to the raps to choose when to sound. They spelled out the first six letters of a periodical which only his father would have known about. Although de Morgan was not still disposed to accept that he had been in communication with the spirits of his father or his sister-in-law, he was 'perfectly satisfied', he explained, 'that something, or somebody was *reading my thoughts*'.

Mrs. Hayden was occasionally tricked, as she was by Lewes. But she was never herself detected in any deception; and such evidence as there is about her does not suggest that, as hostile critics claimed, she was simply an adventuress. Conan Doyle was to recall the verdict of an unnamed British observer who described her as young, intelligent, and candid; 'she disarmed suspicion by the unaffected artlessness of her address, and many who came to amuse themselves at her expense were shamed into respect'. Her subsequent career was also to tell in her favour. Returning to America, she qualified as a doctor – not an easy accomplishment then, for a woman; found employment with the

Globe Insurance Company, apparently on the strength of her psychic diagnostic abilities; and according to the neurologist Joseph Rodes Buchanan, who was interested in psychic aspects of medicine, became 'one of the most skilful and successful physicians I have ever known'.

For a while, though, professional mediums remained a rarity in Britain. Seances were ordinarily conducted by groups of people, none of whom claimed mediumistic powers; they were usually prompted simply by curiosity to find out if raps could be invoked. The procedure involved sitting round a table in darkness, or near darkness, for half an hour or an hour before anything happened – if anything happened. As in America, there were soon reports of tables moving. Sometimes tables shifted along the carpet; sometimes they turned; sometimes they tilted, tilting coming to be regarded as an alternative to raps, as a means of answering questions. 'On Thursday evening June 16th,' the Rev. N. S. Godfrey of Leeds recorded in 1853, 'my wife, my curate and myself sat down at a quarter past nine p.m. and placed our hands upon a small round mahogany table'; to their astonishment, the table, which in an earlier session had failed to respond at all, began to react not, as they had thought it would, with raps, but with movements. As with mesmerism, the accounts given by clergymen are valuable precisely because they are so often naïve. The Rev. E. Gillson's family circle had also expected to be answered by raps; 'to their great consternation, when a question was proposed, the table deliberately lifted up its foot and replied.' Whatever caused tables to move, it was not conscious expectation on the part of sitters; nor is it conceivable that in so many respectable family circles there was always a conjuror, or a joker, rapping or shoving or tilting. By the spring of 1853 table-tilting had become the fashionable social pastime, even in the royal residence at Osborne, where the table moved for Victoria and Albert. Under Lady Ely's hands it fairly rushed about, convincing Victoria that it was no trick, or illusion: magnetism, she thought, or electricity must be responsible.

'I have no doubt,' Sir David Brewster noted on April 25th, 'that there are *thousands* of tables turning every night in London, so general is the excitement on the subject.' It was very much in Brewster's interest, if magnetism or electricity or any other known natural force was involved, that he should be able to identify it. Like Carpenter, he had come round to accepting hypnotism on the strength of Braid's physiological interpretation; but there is a hint in what he wrote after attending a demonstration at Dr. John Ashburner's London home in 1851 that he was finding some of the phenomena hard to account for on that basis. 'I saw things,' he admitted, 'that confounded me.' The following year he had brought a clairvoyant to Oxford to demonstrate before a group which included Samuel Wilberforce and William

Whewell, the Master of Trinity – 'an arch-sceptic', according to Lord Carlyle, who described the proceedings in a letter to Macaulay. 'About twelve of us in turn put our hands upon her eyes, and in every instance, she read without mistake, one, two or three lines from books taken at random.' They were all convinced, Carlyle admitted, 'except Whewell, who has very resilient eyes himself, which he thinks can see through everything'.

Although Brewster might be compelled to accept clairvoyance, however, he could not stomach the notion of spirits being involved; after hearing the explorer Galla praising Mrs. Hayden, his comment was 'the world is obviously going mad'. Yet here were the spirits – or, at least, some force with the ability to manifest a measure of intelligence – moving tables; a process which could not simply be dismissed as occultist nonsense, because so many intelligent and sceptical people were witnessing it. Even Macaulay, who had been the cynical host at a seance round the table in his chambers, had to admit 'there certainly was a rotary motion', adding that he could not confidently say in this case, 'as I say in cases of clairvoyance, there must be deception'. The only other possibility, he thought, was that the Bishop of Oxford, Samuel Wilberforce, might have done the pushing. But Wilberforce, though he, too, was sure that somebody had been cheating, was not himself the cheat. Recalling the occasion years later, he was to claim table-turning to be the work of the Evil One 'only so far as all frauds are, and this was rather a clumsy one' – which he would hardly have written if he himself had been the perpetrator.

Chapter Twenty-three
Table-turning Tested

BY THE SUMMER OF 1853 SO MUCH INTEREST HAD BEEN AROUSED THAT a table-tilting demonstration – or *conversazione*, as it was described, perhaps to poke fun at the spirit communicators – was held in the Manchester Athenaeum; and Braid, who attended, admitted that the tables did move, and that conscious trickery could be ruled out. It was becoming increasingly difficult for scientists to ignore such evidence – on the Continent as well as in Britain, as the naturalist and explorer Baron Alexander von Humboldt, science's elder statesman, admitted. 'The facts are undeniable,' he assured General Bertrand that June; 'it now becomes the task of science to explain them.' And on June 30th, Faraday disclosed in a letter to *The Times* that he had undertaken experiments with this aim in view.

Michael Faraday was in his sixties, his international reputation long since secure. The Royal Institution, in which he had been the dominant figure for nearly forty years, had been set up with the aim of 'diffusing the knowledge and facilitating the general introduction of useful mechanical inventions and improvements'; and if spirit power worked, it would have a potential far beyond that of steam. He was also a deeply religious man, to whom the idea of communicating with the spirits might have been expected to appeal. But from his private correspondence it is clear that he had embarked on the investigation simply because he detested what he regarded as a revival of superstition. People who had been taken in by it had been pestering him for an explanation; his aim was to restore sanity by 'turning the tables on the table-turners'. In his letter to *The Times*, too, he was careful to emphasise his personal distaste; 'I should be sorry that you suppose I thought this necessary on my own account'. Of the various possibilities which had been put forward to account for table-turning, he explained, he had ruled out one in advance: the idea that any supernatural agency could be at work. He could consequently ignore the spirit rappings. His concern was to find if a table's movements could be produced by human agency, without deception. To do this, he had fitted a table with a movable top which would register fingertip pressure on a dial; and as he explained in *The Times* (and in greater detail in the *Athenaeum* magazine two days later), he had been able to demonstrate not only to his satisfaction, but to that of the group concerned in the test, that although they believed they were pressing down on the table with their fingertips, they were assisting it to turn by 'quasi-involuntary muscular action'. Anybody who wished to pursue the subject further, he suggested, should study Carpenter's theory.

Faraday's experiment was hardly more relevant to the elucidation of the mystery than the Buffalo professors' had been two years before. That fingertips pressing down on a movable surface could lead to sideways pressure, without the people involved being aware of it, hardly required an instrument to reveal; in any case, it could not begin to account for the movements – by this time continually being reported, as a correspondent pointed out in a letter to *The Times* – of dining-room tables so heavy that the groups seated around them found it hard to move them by combined conscious muscular effort.

Again, accounts provided by the clergy were revealing. They were locked in controversy, at this stage, over whether the force was divine or diabolic; the title of Godfrey's pamphlet – *Table Turning Tested And Proved To Be The Result Of Satanic Agency* – being derived from an experiment he had undertaken; when he had placed a Bible on a table, it instantly stopped moving, though it would not stop for other books. Whatever the source of the movements of tables, as described in such tracts, it could not have been muscular pressure; as Gillson pointed out, taking Faraday to task, his group had actually been unable to move their table by combined muscular force, yet when no pressure at all was being put on it, it began to make violent movements. The Rev. R. W. Dibdin, too, emphasised the absurdity of crediting unconscious muscular pressure with the movements of *his* table which weighed almost a hundredweight. Again: had professional mediums been involved, such evidence could be discounted. But as the clergy ordinarily held their seances with wives, curates and domestic servants, they could not all have been duped, let alone all have been part of a spiritualist conspiracy. Scientists and sceptics, though, were unlikely to read their pamphlets. If Faraday's hypothesis was to be challenged, it would have to be by scientists.

De Gasparin; Thury; Hare

Table-turning had been quick to catch on in the other capitals of Europe. On the day Brewster noted in his diary that thousands of tables were turning in London, he had just met the Prussian Ambassador, Baron Bunsen, for breakfast; and while they were discussing 'the great subject of talk here', a letter had arrived from the King of Prussia saying the royal family had been trying it there, too; and other letters from Berlin described successful tests. In France at the time, according to the philosopher Pierre Bersot, everything else was forgotten.

In an intellectual country whose drawing rooms were generally famed for the lively conversations therein held, one saw during several months Frenchmen and Frenchwomen, who have so often been accused of being light-headed, sitting for hours round a table, stern, motionless, and dumb; their fingers stretched out, their eyes obstinately staring at the same spot and their minds stubbornly engrossed by the same idea, in a state of anxious expectation, sometimes standing up when exhausted by useless trials, sometimes, if there was a motion or a creaking, disturbed and put out of themselves, while chasing a piece of furniture that moved away. It was a beautiful period, a period of first enthusiasm of trust and ardor that would lead to success.

The enthusiasm for table-turning was not shared by the Catholic Church, which saw Spiritualism as a threat; and it appears to have been the Church's hostile reaction which prompted Count Agenor de Gasparin to investigate the subject. He had grown up in France, establishing his reputation as a scholar, a politician (he represented Corsica in the Chamber of Deputies) and a liberal, campaigning against slavery and against what he regarded as the obscurantism of Ultramontane Catholics. His loyalty to Louis Philippe had led him to leave France after the Revolution of 1848; but in Switzerland, where he settled, he continued to work for his liberal causes. Clerical denunciations of spiritualist phenomena as the work of the devil decided him to show that if they existed, they were not the work of the devil, or of spirits of any kind.

The preliminary stage of his investigation consisted of informal seances with his family and friends, designed simply to find how best to obtain raps or movements. Some individuals, de Gasparin found, appeared to exercise an injurious influence on the proceedings; while they were members of the circle, nothing would happen. But by trial and error a suitable circle was assembled; obtaining responses which, though not consistent, were frequent enough for serious testing to begin on September 20th, 1853. The table – a strong one, capable of bearing a man weighing eighty kilos – was linked up to a balance in such a way that any changes of weight would be registered; de Gasparin's assumption being that the pressure of fingertips on the table could only increase its weight so that any decrease registered on the balance must be the work of some other force. Forming a circle with hands touching round the table, the group 'willed' it to answer questions, which it did by raps, or shifts of position, or by 'lifting a leg'. Perhaps because some of his children were in the circle, he found that the best results were obtained when the proceedings were conducted with gaiety, high spirits, even frivolity: the table would respond by doing a kind of dance, 'beating the measure with one foot, or two'. On September 26th it not merely responded to the circle's touch: it continued to move even after they had taken their hands away from it, following them around until the chain formed by their hands was inadvertently broken, when it stopped. This did not quite satisfy de Gasparin. When he published the results, he knew, critics would argue that the motion must have been imparted earlier by their combined muscular force, transmitted while their hands were still on the table. 'It was necessary, therefore, to produce rotation from a condition of complete repose'; and on September 29th, they did.

The table being motionless, as well as ourselves, the chain of hands separated from it, we began to turn slowly at a short distance above its edge. After a moment, the table made a slight motion; and each person endeavouring by his will to incite the portion underneath his fingers, we drew the body of the table after us.

– thus demonstrating, de Gasparin felt, the existence of some psychic force.

In *Des Tables Tournantes*, published in 1854, he described the tests in detail, showing how the balance had enabled him to check the force involved, amounting at times to an upward pressure of over four kilos. It must emanate from the people involved, he claimed, and be capable of being directed by their will. As his reputation ruled out the possibility of a hoax, and as he was too rich to have been tempted to rig the results for gain, the only other possibility was that he had been the victim of deception by members of his family; and this was hard to sustain as he had employed outside observers to keep a watch, to check what was happening under the table, and to ensure that no physical pressure was being illicitly applied. And although it could be argued that as de Gasparin was not a scientist, he was not qualified to undertake such experiments, this could not be held against one of the observers: his friend Professor Marc Thury, Professor of Physics at the University of Geneva, whose study of table-turning appeared the following year.

There were only two choices, Thury had decided, for a scientist confronted with such phenomena. He must either refuse to have anything to do with them, on the ground that they were too puerile to merit serious attention; or examine them dispassionately to separate the true from false. Having decided to investigate, in other words, a scientist must set aside his preconceptions. And on the basis of the experiments he had observed at de Gasparin's he had been compelled to reject Faraday's hypothesis and to postulate, instead, the existence of a fluence produced by the mind which could be emitted outside the body, at the direction of the will, so that it could act even on inert substances: a force for which he proposed the name 'ectenic'.

Thury, however, carried this theory a stage further than de Gasparin, on the strength of episodes in the home of a friend, 'M.N.' – 'a man I wish I could name, as his science and his character are known to all'. Following a seance in the 'M.N.' household, in which a table had been willed to move, one of the children who had been involved was having a piano lesson when a strange sound came out of the instrument, which began to shake, and then to move. The next day, 'M.N.' came to watch the lesson; the sound was heard again; and the piano, which weighed about three hundred kilos, was seen to rise a little on its two front feet. For safety's sake, 'M.N.' decided to transfer the lessons to a different piano in another room. It performed the same movement, and the piano stool on which the boy was sitting suddenly shot backwards at great speed.

Inspecting the pianos, Thury found that it would have needed far greater strength than the boy possessed to move them. Assuming that the ectenic force was responsible, was it possible that the boy had willed the movement? Admittedly it was entirely contrary to the boy's predeliction, well known to his associates, for regularity and order. But some people, Thury pointed out, have dual personalities, as illustrated in dreams, 'an unconscious desire for what is not consciously wanted'. This, he felt, could be the explanation. The ectenic force might be operated by an unconscious desire, rather than by the conscious will. This was no more than speculation, Thury admitted, and it might seem over-subtle. But it was bad logic to affirm that there could be no other wills than those which were already known. 'Whether they wish to or not, savants must learn by means of their errors to suspend their judgment upon things which they have not sufficiently examined.'

Thury's was a notable contribution to more than the search for an explanation for table-turning (as, in deference to Faraday's experiment, it was henceforth generally to be known, although tables rarely turned). Savants, however, were capable of learning from their errors only if the new theory could be incorporated into the assumptions they already held; and Thury's did not. There was, however, one other possibility: that a scientist would be able to provide experimental proof of the ectenic force of a kind his colleagues would be unable to reject; and this prospect engaged the attention of Dr. Robert Hare, a former Professor of Chemistry at the University of Pennsylvania. He was in his seventies, but he had never lost the relentlessly inquiring turn of mind which had led him nearly half a century earlier to perfect an oxy-hydrogen blow-torch, and to devise a number of ingenious refinements of Galvani's gadgetry. Reading of Faraday's table-turning experiments, Hare realised that they did not provide conclusive proof that table-turning was fraudulent – as he, too, assumed it must be. Instead of tests to find whether people might move objects by unconscious muscular pressure, Hare decided, he must test them to find whether they could move objects when muscular pressure of any kind, conscious or unconscious, could *not* be exerted. With this in view he constructed an apparatus designed to make it possible for a medium to register psychic or ectenic pressure on a weighing machine, but to rule out any possibility of physical pressure being applied. Basically it consisted of a wooden board supported on a fulcrum about a foot from one end, the other being attached by a hook to a spring balance. So long as precautions were taken to ensure that the medium could not lift the end nearest to him, it followed that any physical pressure which he exerted would have to be downwards – which would lift the far end. If, therefore, the spring balance showed that the far end was being lowered, muscular force, conscious or unconscious, could be ruled out. To double assurance, Hare elaborated on this procedure, using a glass bowl of water in which a colander was suspended in such a way that the medium, putting his hands in the colander, could not exert any pressure on the bowl – or, consequently, on the board below. By this means, Hare was able to measure the force mediums were able to exert without allowing them even to touch the board. One medium managed to register a pressure the equivalent of eighteen pounds weight; and when another, a boy, was tested, the machine registered the equivalent of over forty pounds before the whole apparatus collapsed.

Hare's scepticism was routed; and what he had witnessed convinced him that spirits must be responsible. It remained to convince his colleagues; and in 1854 he arranged to bring the boy to Montreal for a meeting of the American Association for the Advancement of Science. Perhaps the collapse of the apparatus had not, after all, simply been an accident; for on the steamer which they used for part of the journey a spirit began to play up. The door of their state-room locked itself while they were inside, and the key could not be found until the spirit had been invoked. It explained that the key was in the bottom of Hare's carpet bag. But the key of the carpet bag was also missing. The spirit, called again, said it was at the bottom of his trunk. When the trunk had been unpacked, the key of the carpet bag was found; and the key of the state-room door was at the bottom of the carpet bag. Suspicious though Hare was of the boy, he could not see how he could have played that particular trick. And there were others for which the boy could not have been responsible. After Hare had put his shaving utensils into the carpet bag and locked it, they suddenly descended on him in a shower, 'all falling, apparently, from above and around him'.

Hare was evidently under the impression that his scientific standing would ensure him a respectful, if not a cordial, reception for his description of his research and his experiences. He was howled down, the Association formally recording a resolution that the subject was unworthy of its attention; and the professors of Harvard later united to condemn him for his 'insane adherence to a gigantic humbug'. It could not be humbug, Hare insisted, on the medium's part. If fraud were involved, 'it is my own character only that can be in question'. He continued to experiment, designing a method by which metal could be de-materialised and translocated under laboratory conditions; a visitor in 1858 was shown two hermetically sealed glass tubes and two pieces of platinum, which Hare put into a box and locked; after an hour's wait, the medium said there was a present for the visitor in the box (which had been lying in front of him); and when it was opened, the two pieces of platinum were inside the still sealed glass tubes. But by this time Hare was an object of derision among his old colleagues; his findings were ignored.

In Europe, too, the orthodox preferred to listen to Faraday and to Michel-Eugène Chevreul, Director of the Museum of Natural History in Paris. Chevreul was already internationally known for his work as a chemist (which had led, among other things, to the discovery of margarine). Years before, he had had a number of experiences of a kind which he might reasonably have thought psychic. In 1814, he had seen a wraith in his study; months later (communication in France being disrupted by the war), he heard that an old friend had died, leaving him a library of books, and on comparing the dates, Chevreul found that they had coincided. But he had not let himself be deluded. 'Had I been superstitious,' he told a friend, 'I might have thought I had seen a real apparition.' Now, he thought he could disclose another youthful aberration – he had learned about divination with the help of a pendulum from 'the respected M. Deleuze'. He could safely confess this because research into the subject had convinced him that the movements of a pendulum 'bob' were simply the result of 'the development in us' (as he described it in a letter to André Ampère), 'of a muscular action which is not the product of will, but the result of a thought carried over to a phenomenon of the outside world'. And in *De la Baguette Divinatoire et des Tables Tournantes*, published in Paris in 1854, he explained how the same principle could be applied to explain the movements of the divining rod, and of tables during seances. Man's unconscious mind was flexing his muscles, as it were, to answer the questions which his conscious mind put. It was a significant contribution, because it would explain why people had not realised that they themselves were manipulating the pendulum, or the rod, or the table; hence the attribution of their movements to outside forces – spirits. It also left open the possibility that the unconscious mind might, on occasion, know more than the conscious mind, which would give divination a rationale. But Chevreul's theory, like Faraday's, was plausible only if the movements of tables were consistent with the use of muscular force. It could not account for the movement of tables too heavy to be pushed, let alone of tables which moved without being touched. Here Chevreul had nothing to offer because, as he admitted, he had done no research into table-turning. He was merely extrapolating from his earlier research with the pendulum. And by this time Faraday had himself admitted that he had never troubled to attend seances – indeed, had taken credit for not attending them. 'In this day of boasted progress,' he told a lecture audience, 'to take such superstitions seriously is a disgrace to the age'; man lowered himself to the level of the beasts if, in his credulous folly, he investigated phenomena 'which reason would not for a moment allow and which, in fact, are utterly absurd'.

The Mesmerists

By virtue of their experience in such matters the mesmerists might have been in a position to expose the fallacies in the Faraday/ Chevreul theory; but on the issue of Spiritualism, they were hopelessly split. In Britain, Townshend took the line implicit in the title of his 1853 report on his investigation, *Mesmerism Proved True*; but Elliotson was horrified. By this time, he had recovered from his humiliation at Wakley's hands. When Thackeray's *Pendennis* was published in 1850 it contained the dedication

> To Dr. John Elliotson,
> My dear Doctor – thirteen months ago, when it seemed likely that this story had come to a close, a kind friend brought you to my bedside whence, in all probability, I never should have arisen but for your constant watchfulness and skill . . .
> As you would take no other fee but thanks, let me record them here on behalf of me and mine.

The readiness of some physiologists to accept Braid had meant that the gap between the mesmerists and orthodoxy was no longer so pronounced; and Elliotson, though he accepted the higher phenomena, had continued to insist 'we have no miraculous faculties' – as he put it in the *Zoist* in 1850 – 'nor can anything we do be miraculous'. But the action of mind on matter, to Elliotson, fell in that category. Spiritualism to him was 'gross wickedness'. Spirit rappings, the *Zoist* explained, were made by judicious kicking of table legs, and an illustration showed how the movements of tables were accomplished: one leg was put over the other, using the lower knee as a fulcrum to provide the required leverage.

The American mesmerists were similarly divided. Some, like Grimes, reacted violently against Spiritualism; others tried to explain away the phenomena in terms of a natural force acting in some as yet unexplained fashion. John Bovee Dods, the most energetic propagator of electro-biology, suggested 'a redundancy of electricity congregated upon the involuntary nerves'; Joseph Rodes Buchanan presented 'nervaura', which he thought of as a force linking electricity to the human mind; and Reichenbach's odic force was another contender. In the circumstances, Carpenter's theories of unconscious muscular pressure and Braid's of sensory hyperacuity had no difficulty in remaining acceptable. Carpenter took care to make the most of Faraday's blessing; in the autumn issue of the influential *Quarterly* magazine, under the pretext of reviewing a clutch of books on the subject of mesmerism and Spiritualism, he expounded it again – taking the opportunity, as the review was not signed, to give a puff for his own *Human Physiology*, which he claimed was employed as a textbook 'in almost every medical school in the country and in the United States'. The explanation of all the phenomena, he insisted, was simply that 'the entire concentration of the attention upon any object of consciousness, whether a sensory impression, an idea, or an emotion, *most wonderfully increases its intensity*'.

Carpenter offered no real evidence for this theory, but the fact that it provided a possible explanation of the phenomena in natural terms led scientists and sceptics to embrace it. One physicist, however, disclosed his real feelings: Jean Bernard Foucault, who, the year before, had constructed the first gyroscope. 'If I saw a straw moved by the action of my will, I should be terrified,' he remarked. 'If the influence of mind upon matter does not cease at the surface of the skin, there is no safety left in the world for anyone.' It might not be a scientific attitude; but at least it was honest.

Chapter Twenty-four
Daniel Dunglas Home

OF THE SCORES OF MEDIUMS WHO WERE THROWN UP IN THE FOX sisters' wake, one proved to be outstanding. Daniel Dunglas Home's record as a psychic remains unparalleled, not just for what he could do – or, as he always insisted, what the spirit forces could do through his agency – but for the way he did it, and for the extraordinary range of testimony about the things he did from America, Britain and many European countries. They were witnessed on hundreds of occasions by kings and conjurors, scientists and socialites, priests and policemen; and although among the witnesses there were many who would have been delighted to trip him – often they came to seances with that very much in mind – he was never detected in any trickery. The testimony is such that if it described a skill of which man might be naturally capable, it could not for a moment be questioned. But in Home's case, what happened was often so weird, so unbelievable, that with few exceptions only those who were actually witnesses could bring themselves to believe it, and influential though they were, they could not establish its credibility. Yet on the 'as if' assumption – that is, the assumption that such manifestations can occur – the evidence for them provided the most comprehensive and convincing dossier there had ever been.

Home was born in Scotland in 1833: the illegitimate son, he was led to believe, of one of the members of the aristocratic family (he pronounced his name as the earls did: Hume). Adopted by an aunt when he was still a baby, he was brought out to the United States; and as a child growing up in Connecticut he began to have visions, foreshadowing the death of his closest friend, and of his mother. When he was seventeen, Hydesville-style raps began to be heard in his vicinity, and furniture to move around him; and his aunt, who thought the devil must be in him, showed him the door. But other people, Home found, were glad to avail themselves of his growing powers of clairvoyance and of healing. He began to give seances; and his reputation reached the ears of two seasoned investigators of spiritualism, William Cullen Bryant and Professor David Wells of Harvard. After testing him in a well-lit room, they reported that a table had moved 'in every possible direction, and with great force, when we could not perceive any cause of motion'; when Wells sat on it, it rocked for some time with great violence, 'and at length it poised itself on two legs, and remained in this position for some thirty seconds, when no other person was in contact with it'. In the whole exhibition, 'we were constrained to admit that there was an almost constant manifestation of some intelligence which seemed, at least, to be independent of the circle'. As they had been given every facility to inspect the room and the table during the occurrences, they felt bound to conclude their testimony with 'this one emphatic declaration – *we know that we were not imposed upon nor deceived*'.

In 1852 Home was reported as levitating for the first time; and according to the description left by one of the witnesses, some of those present who tried to hold him were also lifted up with him a foot from the floor. By his own account, he also began to have out-of-the-body experiences in which he was conducted by a spirit guide, or guardian angel. Often there were materialisations: hands, which could be touched, were seen to lift and carry objects. The editor of the Hartford *Times*, Frank L. Burr, described how sitters saw a hand – 'very thin, very pale, and remarkably attenuated' – writing on some paper with a pencil.

The hand afterwards came and *shook hands* with each one present. I felt it minutely. It was tolerably well and symmetrically made, though not perfect; and it was *soft* and slightly *warm*. IT ENDED AT THE WRIST.

This proved to be one of the last seances Home was to hold in America. He was a consumptive; doctors in New York advised him that if he stayed in America, his lung condition would grow worse; and in the spring of 1855 he sailed for Britain, bearing introductions to some Swedenborgians. One of them, Dr. J. Garth Wilkinson, was the London correspondent of the New York *Tribune*, a man whose range of understanding and imagination, Emerson declared, was comparable only to Lord Bacon's. In his *Evenings with Mr. Home and the Spirits* Wilkinson described how in a room lit by a lamp, a large round table levitated; an accordion floated into his hand, and began to play; and a bell was brought to him by a disembodied hand. He had tried to hold it, but 'I had no sooner grasped it momentarily than it melted away, leaving my hand void, with the bell only in it'.

Home's fame began to spread. Sir Edward Bulwer Lytton came to a seance, and was impressed; as were the Brownings. What she had seen, Elizabeth wrote to tell her sister, was 'wonderful and conclusive'. Robert described Home as 'a well-grown young man of over the average height ... his face is rather handsome and prepossessing, and indicative of intelligence' and apart from little-boy mannerisms in the worst taste, there was 'nothing offensive or pretentious in his demeanour'. And what Browning had seen baffled him. The table had reared up, yet the table cloth, a lamp and ornaments on it had not slid off. A hand had appeared, moving around, rising and sinking; and another hand had taken a wreath off the table and placed it on Elizabeth's hand. He had felt touches, 'a kind of soft and fleshy pat'. After an interval, the table had been levitated in light good enough to inpect it; 'I looked under the table, and can aver that it was lifted from the ground, say a foot high, more than once' – Home's hands being plainly visible above it. 'I don't in the least pretend to explain how the table was uplifted altogether,' Browning concluded: nor could he account for the pluckings at his wife's clothes, or the playing of an accordion which nobody was touching.

A month later, though, Browning was telling a different story; 'the whole display of "hands", spirit utterances etc. were a cheat and imposture'. He had not been to any more seances: it was simply that in retrospect what he had seen appeared incredible (to him; not to Elizabeth, who remained convinced Home was genuine, much to Robert's fury). And Sir David Brewster was to follow a similar course. His initial reaction to table-turning, expressed after his breakfast with Bunsen, had been 'of course it is nonsense, and there must be some trick in it'. Later, he had accepted the Faraday/Carpenter view, explaining it as 'an involuntary action of the fingers'. Then, at the invitation of Lord Brougham (whose political career was long since over, but who still took a keen interest in a variety of social issues), he came to seances in William Cox's Jermyn Street hotel, where Home was staying, and in the house of a London solicitor, John Rymer. There could be no question of involuntary finger propulsion; tables rose in the air and musical instruments played when nobody was touching them. According to Cox, Brewster admitted that this 'upset the philosophy of fifty years'; and he assured Lord Dunraven, whom he encountered on the steps of the Athenaeum, that the manifestations were 'quite inexplicable by fraud, or by any physical laws with which they were acquainted'.

Flattered, Home wrote to a friend in America to describe what had happened; the account found its way into some newspapers there; and eventually the story filtered back to London, where it was published in the *Morning Advertiser*. But by that time Brewster had had the chance to reflect; and he wrote to the *Advertiser* repudiating the opinions attributed to him. He could not, he admitted, account for some of the 'mechanical effects', as he now described them, which he had seen. But he had seen enough 'to satisfy myself that they could all be produced by human hands and feet, and to prove that some of them, at least, had such an origin'. When Cox and others who had been present wrote reminding him that this was not what he had said at the time, he replied that

> rather than believe that spirits raised the table, *I will conjecture* that it was done by the agency of Mr. Home's feet. Some time after this experiment, Mr. Home left the room and returned; probably to equip himself for the feats which were to be performed by the spirits beneath a large round table covered with copious drapery, beneath which nobody was allowed to look.

This was too much for Thomas Adolphus Trollope – a better-known author, at this stage, than his brother Anthony. Trollope had been to a number of seances, including one with Brewster; and he wrote from his home in Florence to the *Advertiser* to say that he had been convinced that whatever the origin of the phenomena, it was certainly not fraud, machinery, or juggling on Home's part. Brewster had been urged by both Home and Rymer to look under the table; and he recalled that Brewster 'did look under it'; that 'while he was so looking, the table was much moved'; and that while he was looking, and while the table was moving, 'he avowed that he saw the movement'.

The issue of who was lying might never have been settled had not Brewster's daughter, in a memoir of him which she had published after his death in 1868, unwittingly included a letter he had written at the time of the seances in which he disclosed that he had, in fact, been invited to make an inspection under the table. He went on to describe what he had witnessed.

> In a short time the table shuddered, and a tremulous motion ran up all our arms; at our bidding these motions ceased, and returned. The most unaccountable rappings were produced in various parts of the table; and the table actually rose from the ground when no hand was upon it. A larger table was produced, and exhibited similar movements.

An accordion gave off a single note, otherwise the attempt to make it play was a failure. But

> a small hand-bell was then laid down with its mouth on the carpet,

and, after lying for some time, it actually rang when nothing could have touched it. The bell was then placed on the other side, still upon the carpet, and it came over to me and placed itself in my hand. It did the same to Lord Brougham.

These were the principal experiments; we could give no explanation of them, and could not conjecture how they could be produced by any kind of mechanism. Hands were sometimes seen, and feet; the hand often grasps another and melts away, as it were, under the grasp.

'The hero of science,' the *Spectator* commented, 'does not acquit himself as well as we could wish or expect.' It was not difficult to understand why. Brewster had made his reputation largely by his ability to explain the supernatural in natural terms; he must have realised that to admit himself baffled by Home would have been a let-down. Worse, it would have left him open to the charge of giving aid and comfort to Spiritualism; and that might have jeopardised his prospects. So he had chosen to smear Home. Four years later, he had enjoyed his reward when he was appointed to be Principal of Edinburgh University, a post which he had held till his death.

The Social Lion

Home had gone to stay in Florence before the Brewster controversy erupted; he was soon being lionised by the international set there; and he did not return to England for some years. It was a confused period for him. There were some spectacular demonstrations – 'I certainly saw, under circumstances where fraud, or collusion, or prearrangement of machinery, was impossible,' Hiram Powers, the leading American sculptor of the day, was to recall ' – in my own house or among friends incapable of lending themselves to imposture – very curious things. That hand, floating in the air, of which all the world has heard, I have seen.' But there were periods when the spirits informed Home that they were going to withdraw their support: once, for a whole year, in which he joined the Catholic Church. When they returned, however, he resumed his seances, breaking with the Church; and in 1857 finally established himself socially, as well as psychically, by levitating a table while Prince Murat, a sceptic, held its feet, and Napoleon III, himself an amateur conjuror, watched from above. 'Nothing can give you an idea of what I have experienced,' the Empress Eugénie wrote to tell her sister. She and the Emperor had both felt her dead father's materialised hand, which they recognised from a characteristic defect. Further seances produced even more spectacular results: a disembodied hand appeared, took a pencil, and wrote 'Napoleon' – in, the Emperor declared, Bonaparte's writing.

One thing had been lacking for Home: an assured income. He had always refused to accept payment for seances, and though there was no shortage of friends and admirers to provide hospitality, he only achieved independence when in 1858, he met and married a goddaughter to the Tzar Nicholas (Alexandre Dumas was best man, and Alexei Tolstoy one of the groomsmen). By the time Home returned to England, the following year, his social standing had been transformed, and he was pounced upon by Mrs. Milner-Gibson, wife of the President of the Board of Trade, to give weekly seances at her town house. They were attended by many celebrities: Lytton; Robert Chambers, editor of the *Encyclopedia*; Edwin Arnold; Monckton Milnes; Landseer; and droves of peers and peeresses. 'It is two o'clock in the morning. I have just left Home' – Alexei Tolstoy, on a visit to London, wrote to tell his wife – 'and in spite of the pain it gives me to be away from you I don't regret my journey to London, for this seance has been *overwhelming*.' A table had placed itself on top of another table; a bell had floated round the apartment, ringing.

The piano played with no one near it; a bracelet unclasped itself from the arm of Mrs. Milner-Gibson, and fell on the table, where it lay surrounded by a luminous appearance. Home was raised from the ground; and I clasped his feet while he floated in the air above our heads. Hands touched my knees and laid themselves in my hands; and when I sought to retain one *it dissolved in my grasp* ... a cold wind passed round the circle very distinctly, and perfumes were wafted to us.

Up to this point the attitude of the press to Home had been hostile. From the start, he had been subjected to vilification and malicious rumour in the scandal sheets; in the serious journals he had been largely ignored. In August 1860, however, the new *Cornhill* magazine published a factual and sober account of some seances by a writer who remained anonymous, in the *Cornhill* convention, but whose identity was later disclosed: Robert Bell, one of the most respected literary figures of the period. Not all of the seances were with Home: one had been with two ladies, with results so bizarre that Bell felt embarrassed to describe them. A small round table, supported by a single pillar with claw legs, had moved so violently that they had been unable to restrain it; and it had moved away from them down the room.

Using the leg of the large table as a fulcrum, it directed its claws towards the ottoman, which it attempted to ascend by inserting one claw in the side, then turning half-way-round to make another step, and so on. It slipped down at the first attempt, but again quietly resumed its task. It was exactly like a child trying to climb up a height.

Before the seance with Home, Bell had been agreeably impressed by his manner – 'he is yet so young that the playfulness of boyhood has not passed away' – and by his modesty. The seance's first effect was the sound of music coming from an accordion, though nobody was playing it. This might have been an illusion, Bell admitted; on that issue, his testimony was worth nothing. But with respect to fraud he could speak more confidently. It could not have been fraud, he knew, because when he himself took up the instrument with one hand, 'with the full light upon it, similar strains were emitted, the regular action of the accordion going on without any visible agency'. Later, Home had levitated. His feet had been illuminated only by the embers of a fire and gas lamps in the street; but the light was sufficient to see the medium, and to touch his foot, as he floated by overhead.

We watched in profound stillness, and saw his figure pass from one side of the window to the other, feet foremost, lying horizontally in the air. He spoke to us as he passed, and told us that he would then return the reverse way and re-cross the window, which he did.

The account carried conviction for two reasons: the restraint with which it was written (Bell began by quoting the German biologist Treviranus's reply when Coleridge had asked him about the phenomena of animal magnetism: 'I have seen what I would not have believed on your testimony, and what I cannot, therefore, expect you to believe upon mine'); and the fact that it was accompanied in the *Cornhill* by a note from Thackeray: 'as editor of this magazine, I can vouch for the good faith and honourable character of our correspondent, a friend of twenty-five years standing'. Thackeray might have added that he was in a position personally to vouch for the phenomena; he had been to a seance with Home in New York, and again in London. Although he did not avow his belief that they were genuine in the *Cornhill*, he was prepared to do so in private conversation. In *Last Winter in Rome*, Charles Weld was to describe how he had met Thackeray at dinner just after the *Cornhill* article had appeared. When some scientific men reproached him for printing it, Thackeray had replied, 'It is all very well for you, who have probably never seen any spiritual manifestations, to talk as you do; but had you seen what I have witnessed, you would hold a different opinion'; and he had gone on to describe how in circumstances where trickery was impossible he had seen a large and heavy dinner table, covered with decanters, glasses and dishes, rise two feet off the ground. Nobody who had read *Vanity Fair* or its successors could regard Thackeray as a man easily imposed upon; Home himself, at the end of his career, named him as the most sceptical man he had ever met. That so sympathetic an appraisal should appear in the *Cornhill* was the first intimation to scientists that Spiritualism had not been demolished by Faraday and Chevreul.

Prompted by Bell, Sir Emerson Tennant asked Faraday if he would attend a Home seance. Faraday replied that he would, provided certain conditions were fulfilled. Most of them would have been acceptable: for example, that the seance should not be held in darkness (other mediums were beginning to claim that they could only produce effects in the dark: Home, though he preferred a dim light, was willing for experimental purposes to work in brightly lit rooms). But Faraday also demanded what would have amounted to a recantation from Home. In any question involving the principles of physics, Faraday believed, 'we should set out with clear ideas of the naturally possible and impossible'. Accordingly, he wanted to know if Home considered the effects natural or supernatural? If Home accepted that they were 'glimpses of natural action not yet reduced to law', that was satisfactory; it would be his duty, and everybody's, 'to develop them, and to aid others in their development'. But if Home wanted to give the credit to spirits, that was another matter. Faraday was not prepared to co-operate unless he would first admit 'the utterly contemptible character both of them and their results, up to the present time, in respect either of yielding information or instruction, or supplying any force or action of the least value to mankind'. As it happened, the letter was never shown to Home. Hearing that Home's wife was dying, Tennant told Faraday that the seance would have to be postponed; and – realising, presumably, that the condition would have been totally unacceptable – he did not resume negotiations later. So the opportunity for what would have been a remarkable confrontation was lost.

The Battle of the Books

On the Continent, as in Britain, orthodox scientists tended to assume that table-turning had been explained by Faraday and Chevreul; and it had been left to a few individual investigators to continue the exploration, among them Victor Hugo, who held many seances. 'The tables tell us most surprising things,' he explained in a letter in 1855; and as they had confirmed a whole system of cosmogony he had been working on for twenty years, 'with magnificent enlargements', he upbraided scientists for their attitude. To ridicule was 'easier than to examine, but it was not scientific'; a scientist who ridiculed possibilities 'is near to being a fool. The unexpected should always be looked for in science.'

It was, however, a scientist who ridiculed possibilities who was unwittingly largely responsible for the breaching of orthodoxy's defences. In 1856 a French lawyer, André Morin, wrote an article speculating on the possibility of mind being able to influence matter; and two years later a member of the Academy of Sciences, G. Mabru, launched a scathing attack on him ('inert matter knocks at your door'), on the mesmerists, and on occultists in general in a massive work, *Les Magnétiseurs Jugés par Eux-mêmes*. It was too massive. If, as Mabru maintained, 'the alleged magnetic trance no more exists than the fluid and the phenomena attributed to somnambulism: they are only pure illusion' – if, as he reiterated, 'there is no animal magnetism, no artificial somnambulism, no magic, no sorcery' – why devote so much space to them? And Mabru was so careless in his selection of facts and so wild in his allegations that he drove other rationalists to present more carefully collected and considered evidence in book form: among them Morin, Alfred Maury, and Guillaume Figuier.

All three of them were sceptics, but not to the point of blind hostility to the mesmerists and spiritists. Maury's contention, in his *La Magie et l'Astrologie* – published, as were the others, in 1860 – was that the phenomena could most easily be explained in terms of mental disorder. The Comtist philosopher Maximilien Littré had suggested this explanation four years earlier, pointing out that astonishing physical effects had often been reported in connection with outbreaks of mass hysteria; Maury, elaborating, propounded the theory that mediums or monks under certain conditions might also possess unusual physical capabilities. It was known, for example, that hysterics could stand for hours on tip-toe apparently without fatigue; and this might help to account for apparent levitations. The stigmata were also a symptom of hysteria, 'in effect a malady', brought on by the hyper-excitability induced after prolonged contemplation. As for such things as visions and the odours of sanctity, they were simply sensory illusions: 'each ecstatic sees what he thinks, what he believes, what he hopes'.

Morin conceded rather more to the occultists. Although he dismissed animal magnetism – like Bertrand, he argued that there was no evidence for any fluid, and that everything could be accounted for in terms of the imagination – he was prepared to accept clairvoyance and thought-transference. A medium, he suggested, might have the power to penetrate the thoughts of others, even picking up thoughts of which others were unaware, thanks to 'a sort of language that he understands instinctively without knowing its principles'. Basically his book was a reasoned appeal for more careful and systematic research.

Figuier's aim, like Salverte's earlier, was to show that events which had been regarded at the time as supernatural could ordinarily be explained in natural terms. But perhaps because of his wide range of interests – he wrote extensively on anthropology, geology and zoology – he was readier than Salverte had been to examine the possibility that 'natural' might have to be stretched to include certain phenomena which had yet to be understood. Past experience, he pointed out, should be a warning; scientists who thought that all nature's secrets had been disclosed were making fools of themselves. There were some phenomena, he felt, which could not be accounted for in terms of the natural laws accepted in his day; including those associated with Angélique Cottin.

In a review of the case in 1854 Jacques Babinet, a physicist who had been on the Academy's investigating committee, had explained that Angélique had eventually been exposed. She had been seen to jerk a small table with a convulsive movement of her knee; and his laboratory assistants had shown that they could move furniture in the way she did by a trick. It was consequently assumed that Angélique had been discredited. But Figuier, reading the evidence about her, was struck by its high quality. Was it really possible, he began to ask himself, that so many people, from the provincial worthies to Tanchou and the great Arago, had all allowed themselves to be taken in by so obvious a trick? The first thing that any investigator would have thought of, after all, was that she was using the muscles of her legs; how could she have survived detection for so long?

Examining Babinet's story of Angélique's exposure, Figuier realised how flimsy it was. She had not been detected by Babinet, or any of her investigators, but by a 'vieillard octogénaire' who, as Babinet admitted, was also 'the most sceptical of men'. And what the octogenarian saw, if indeed he had seen it, might be ascribed to an impatient gesture on the part of Angélique following a two-hour wait during which nothing happened. In any case, what she had been accused of doing could not account for what Babinet had described her as doing earlier. Chairs at the physics lab. where she was tested in Paris had appeared to hurl themselves at the wall, so violently that they were smashed; and on one occasion a chair which had been placed behind the one in which she was to sit, in order to protect two distinguished spectators, was 'drawn along with the propelled chair, and went with it, to arouse from their absent-mindedness the two savants'. On the occasion of her exposure, too, she had earlier while being watched twice overturned 'an immense kitchen table, made out of thick oaken planks of enormous size and weight', which had been laid for dinner with plates and glasses, without anybody being able to detect how she had done it. And Babinet had admitted that what the lab. assistants had been able to do had not compared with Angélique's feats. What it amounted to was that the octogenarian was the only one among a thousand witnesses who claimed to have detected the girl cheating; should his unsubstantiated word, Figuier asked, suffice to annul so many positive observations?

We leave it to our readers to answer that question. We would only say that, supposing that this witness, despite his great age, really had witnessed cheating, the possibility should not be excluded that the earlier phenomena were genuine. One could believe, in fact, that, in the seance in question, without realising the consequences, Angélique Cottin had wanted to supply by a little dexterity the extraordinary faculty which she regretted having lost.

In any case, Figuier pointed out, there had since been reports of another 'electric girl' harassed by similar manifestations, noises, movements of furniture, and clothes bellying out; manifestations which were well-attested, the evidence from respectable citizens showing the care with which they had taken precautions to prevent deception. In cases like this, he felt, it was surely more sensible to accept that a human being might in certain circumstances become charged with, say, electricity, as some fish were; or at any rate, to accept the reality of the phenomena and the honesty and ability of the witnesses, including members of the Academy, and start to look for some other rational explanation.

But this, Figuier had found, was precisely what the 'preconceived disbelievers' (as he called them, to distinguish them from rational sceptics like himself) refused to do. They had learned nothing from their experience with animal magnetism, where they had failed to recognise what was valid in the evidence; and they were now making precisely the same mistake with table-turning, declining to investigate, and thereby showing that 'we have in Paris an intellectual senate, a scientific body *par excellence*, of which the conservative spirit manifests itself by an instinctive aversion to, and incurable terror of, all new discovery'. This attitude was making it impossible for him and others who were actively seeking 'to rebut the partisans of the supernatural' to expose the spiritists. It was no use scientists trying to shelter behind the pronouncements of Faraday and Chevreul. Of course fingertips, pressing down on a table, would begin to exercise a sideways pressure if a table began to turn! But this did not mean that fingertip pressure could account for the movement of heavy tables which could hardly be moved by main force. Scientists must do better than that!

Figuier, though, felt bound to draw the line at the action of mind over matter. That a table might be impelled by some electro-magnetic type of force emanating from human beings was one thing; that tables could do what de Gasparin said they could do, and move without contact – though Figuier did not doubt his 'perfect honour, scientific spirit and wide knowledge, and the good faith of his account' – was manifestly impossible. As for Home, he was simply a prestidigitator cashing in on spiritism's vogue. The higher phenomena of mesmerism, Figuier believed, had also been satisfactorily explained away by Braid's research into hypnosis, which had shown that hypnotised subjects could pick up faint sensory clues and through them provide information which seemed miraculous to onlookers; there was no need to believe that anybody really could 'see' what was happening on the other side of a wall. And where a group of respectable people testified to some miracle such as levitation, in circumstances where trickery were ruled out, there was always the possibility of collective hallucination. Nevertheless his book, along with Morin's and Maury's, reflected a change of attitude; a willingness to accept the possibility that mesmerism and spiritism did not simply represent a recrudescence of superstition: that they deserved scientific study.

In Britain, too, works appeared in the early 1860s presenting the spiritist case sympathetically yet seriously: the first, in 1861, being Robert Dale Owen's *Footfalls on the Boundary of Another World*. Owen had stayed on in America after the failure of his father's New Harmony enterprise in the 1820s, becoming a Congressman and, in 1853, American chargé d'affaires in Naples. His colleague the Brazilian minister there had introduced him to the study of mesmerism and he began, by his own account fortuitously, to witness the movements of objects without physical agency. His curiosity roused, he studied the history of the subject, becoming convinced that 'what by many have been regarded as new and unexampled phenomena are but modern phases of what has ever existed'; and his book provided an introduction to them, with examples taken from a wide range of historical, medical and anthropological sources.

Its title gave the impression that Owen must be more caught up in Spiritualism than in fact he was. *Footfalls* was a sober examination of the evidence for clairvoyance, apparitions, poltergeists and other manifestations, with warnings against credulity on such matters. A dream of the death of a relative at the time the relative was dying, Owen pointed out, could be coincidental; the case for clairvoyance only became strong if there were additional factors, as in a case where a woman had dreamed that her mother had offered her a lock of her father's hair, telling her that he was going to die the next morning; and she had learned later that he had died that day, and that before he had died he had asked for a lock of his hair to be cut off, saying it was to be given to her. On poltergeists, too, Owen's comments were shrewd. What was significant about the weird phenomena, he pointed out, was the unmistakable family likeness; yet in the best known episodes the people concerned had evidently never heard of a poltergeist – for if they had, they surely would have mentioned the fact. In none of the cases, too, had the people concerned anything to gain from the publicity. Ordinarily they had tried desperately to keep the story quiet. What was needed, Owen felt, was more detached, scientific research on the subject: 'we cannot hush it up, if we would; we ought not, if we could. Viewed in its scientific aspect, we might as well interdict the study of electricity.'

Howitt's two-volume *History of the Supernatural*, which appeared two years later, was less critically selective in its use of sources; but it showed even more impressively how enormous was the range of evidence for psychical phenomena, from rappings to translocations. Hume had claimed they were opposed to the experience of mankind: not so – they were 'as old as the hills and as ubiquitous as the ocean'; God's way of communicating with the spirit of man. Home's *Incidents in My Life*, published the same year, proved to be surprisingly restrained and well-documented, though the witnesses were often identified only by their initials – and their titles. But the year's most impressive book, in its modesty and manifest integrity, was Mrs. de Morgan's *From Matter to Spirit*, published pseudonymously, describing her seances with Mrs. Hayden and research which she had undertaken since.

Carefully and unobstrusively – chiefly with friends and domestic servants, one of whom happened to be a medium – Mrs. de Morgan had been exploring the human mechanics of the seance; for example, by observing the effects of introducing sceptics into the group. Hostile scepticism, she found, could inhibit the medium: but detached scepticism was no bar. And occasionally sheer ignorant scepticism seemed to arouse the psychic forces to demonstrate their existence. At a seance with friends an admirer of the daughter of the house contemptuously refused to join the circle, on the ground it was all nonsense. When the raps began, they instructed the sitters to move aside; and the solid, heavy boarding-house-style table, made to seat eight or ten people, began to move on its own, the circle having their hands linked above it, towards the sceptic, until it was 'literally pushing him to the back of the sofa'.

Such research, though in some ways revealing, did not explain what the forces were, and how they were directed. Mrs. de Morgan was prepared to accept that it must be supplied, and to some extent applied, by the people concerned in the seance; and as she felt shocks when the raps came, she assumed that the nerves of the human body were responsible 'if not for the production, at least for the propagation of the sounds'. But she also believed, from her experience, that spirits of the dead must be involved. Her husband, though he accepted the reality of the phenomena, remained unconvinced. 'The physical explanations I have seen are easy, but miserably insufficient', he wrote in his introduction to the book; 'the spirit hypothesis is sufficient, but ponderously difficult'.

In the course of her investigation Mrs. de Morgan had also experimented with mesmerism, occasionally encountering the higher phenomena: a mesmerised boy who had 'felt' a blow which she herself had accidentally received had then shown that he could also distinguish whether what she tasted was sweet or bitter (though only for a short time; he soon lost the faculty); and another mesmerised subject had 'visited' a house belonging to a member of her family, giving her what turned out to be an accurate description of the house's contents, though neither the subject nor Mrs. de Morgan had ever been there. And the first serious attempt to link the phenomena of mesmerism and Spiritualism appeared in 1867: Dr. John Ashburner's *Notes and Studies on the Philosophy of Animal Magnetism and Spiritualism*.

A fashionable London physician, Ashburner had been a sceptic, an admirer of Voltaire and Hume, until convinced in the 1840s by the evidence for animal magnetism – particularly when he found that he could produce the same effects as Scoresby; 'many a time have I made a pass over a comfortable dining-room chair with my hand, and have placed a suspectible young man, or young woman, upon the chair, and the adhesion has been so strong that the person could not move from the chair'. Seances with Mrs. Hayden in 1853 then convinced him that 'manifestations of the presence of unseen intelligences were undeniable'; and when Home resumed giving seances in London after the death of his wife, Ashburner – a neighbour of the Milner-Gibsons, at whose town house they were conducted – satisfied himself that Home's manifestations were genuine, too. His acceptance of spiritualism led to a breach with his friend Elliotson; but while Mrs. Milner-Gibson and some friends, including Home, were staying in Dieppe in 1863 they heard that Elliotson was there. Home took the opportunity to tax him with having neglected to investigate before pronouncing the phenomena fraudulent; and Elliotson accepted the challenge to come to a seance. 'No scepticism could have been more thorough or aggressive,' Home was to recall; but a couple of seances sufficed to convince Elliotson. He and Ashburner were reconciled, leaving the way clear for Ashburner to present his synthesis of Christianity, animal magnetism and Spiritualism. 'We are proposing to show that animal magnetism is neither more or less than the origin of religion,' Ashburner claimed. Human magnetism was 'the highest description of magnetic force'; the source of all health; the way in which God's bounty was transmitted to man. There was no distinction between mind and matter: matter 'is subservient to force, and consequently to mind'; and mind is all-embracing, 'no part of intelligent force is lost in the vast expanse of space'.

The time had also come, Ashburner believed, when it was at last possible scientifically to demonstrate the force involved in animal magnetism and spiritualism. His book was dedicated to John Obadiah Rutter; 'he has his reward, for God has blessed his scientific labours by the discovery of the magnetoscope'. Rutter was an engineer, one of the pioneers in the introduction of gas for domestic cooking and lighting; and while experimenting with a pendulum, he had discovered that the 'bob' reacted differently for different people. There must be a way, he felt, to eliminate the possibility of direct muscular action; and he devised a gadget like a miniature fixed fishing rod, from the end of which the pendulum was suspended over a glass bowl. If the butt end of the rod were touched, the 'bob' would move, and would move differently according to, say, whatever the individual touching it was holding in his hand – even if it were only a homeopathic dose of quinine. Rutter himself was able to start it working simply by placing a crystal on a stand, detached from the pendulum; if the axis of the crystal was changed, the direction in which the 'bob' was moving changed, too.

The magnetoscope, however, failed to live up to Ashburner's expectations. For some people it worked; others could obtain no reaction. Inevitably, a professional had begun to give sittings, claiming that the instrument was, in effect, clairvoyant; and for a time it became a fashionable pastime. But soon there were dissatisfied reports. According to Macaulay, Lord Dufferin went twice, once in disguise, and was given two different readings; and Macaulay himself was indignant when the magnetoscope 'made me out to be a painter – a landscape painter or a historical painter' (though some of his readers might well have agreed with the Bishop of Oxford that the instrument's diagnosis was perceptive). Carpenter attributed its action to a physical cause – vibrations: the magnetoscope was discredited; and Rutter forgotten.

Chapter Twenty-five
The Investigators

HOME – THERE IS ANOTHER PEN-PORTRAIT OF HIM FROM THIS PERIOD, by Princess Metternich: 'fairly tall, slim, well-built, in his dress suit and white tie he looked like a gentleman of the highest social standing. His face was attractive, in its expression of gentle melancholy' – continued to give seances, and to convince doubters. James Hutchinson, for many years Chairman of the London Stock Exchange, described how in a brightly lit room he saw handbells passed from sitter to sitter, by some unseen agency. John Bright brought Samuel Lucas, editor of the *Morning Star*, along with him; and Lucas tried to hold down the table, to the indignation of the spirit-rappers. When he pointed out that he had come to the seance to investigate, the raps asked if a stout gentleman who was present would sit on the table. According to Mrs. Adelaide Senior, the economist's sister-in-law,

the desire was complied with; and instantly the table was not only raised but tossed up, as you would toss a baby in your arms – saying, as plainly as words could have done, 'you tried to prevent our raising the table with nothing upon it, and we will prove to you that we can do it with this additional weight'.

Bright was much impressed as, later, was Ruskin – with Home, as well as with the evidence. But he was not prepared to come out into the open. 'Only fancy Ruskin being converted!' Mrs. S. C. Hall – who with her husband (both edited art magazines) were among Home's most devoted allies – wrote in the summer of 1864; '*but he does not wish it talked about*'. The appearance that year of Browning's *Mr. Sludge the Medium*, which he had not cared to publish so long as his wife lived, helped to explain why he and others, Lytton among them, did not care to make their views known. Sludge' was a piece of rancorous vengeful-thinking,

> ... I cheated when I could,
> Rapped with my toe-joints, set sham hands to work,
> Wrote down names weak in sympathetic ink,
> Rubbed odic lights with ends of phosphor match
> And all the rest ...

Home, however, was on his travels again, returning for a time to the United States, and then visiting France and Russia. Wisely, he chose to treat the verse as if it must have been written about some other medium. And by this time, it could easily have been directed at any one of a number of mediums who had begun to take advantage of the interest that he had aroused. Some continued to give only discreet private seances; but others allowed themselves to be taken up by managers, who arranged for them to appear in halls and theatres on publicised tours, like music-hall performers, as the Davenport brothers were doing in the mid-1860s.

As boys, Ira and William Davenport had been investigated by some Harvard professors in 1857; and to make sure that they could not cheat they had been trussed up with five hundred feet of new rope, the knots being sealed with linen thread, before being put into a cabinet with one of the professors sitting between them, so that he could periodically ensure that they had not released themselves. Yet there had been materialisations outside the cabinet; and when it was opened, some of the rope had wound itself round the professor's neck, which so baffled his colleagues that they published no report.

When the brothers came to England in 1864, they were similarly searched and tied up for a test seance at the home of Dion Boucicault, the knots being fastened with sealing wax; yet – as Boucicault described it – 'while Lord Bury was stooping inside the cabinet, the door being open and the two operators seen to be sealed and bound, a detached hand was clearly observed to descend on him and he started back, remarking that a hand had struck him'. This was confirmed by a *Times* correspondent who was present; what went on in the cabinet, he wrote, could not be observed, but hands and arms were often felt outside it, and sometimes seen, as were materialised forms, human in their appearance. Even the conjuror John Maskelyne, who was relentlessly hostile to the purveyors of 'the so-called Spiritualism' was later to admit that the Davenports had done more than anybody to familiarise the English public in general with Spiritualism by their 'really wonderful feats'; the hole-and-corner seances of most other mediums, he felt, 'where, with darkness or semi-darkness, and a pliant or frequently a devoted assembly, manifestations are occasionally *said* to occur, cannot be compared with the Davenport exhibitions in their effect upon the public mind'.

The Davenports' effect on the public mind, though, was damaging to the prospects of securing scientific recognition for the phenomena which they produced; it was not difficult for Maskelyne and others to reproduce them, in theatres or music halls, thereby suggesting that they might have been elaborate conjuring tricks. Because the brothers sat in a cabinet, too, and consequently could not be seen by the audience, they could not prove that they were not using some ingenious form of trickery. There were, however, a few mediums who, like Home, were prepared to give seances in full light; and it was with one of them that a British scientist took up where de Gasparin, Thury and Hare had left off, ten years before.

Alfred Russel Wallace had been an ardent materialist, a disciple of Voltaire, until as a schoolmaster in the 1840s he had conducted experiments into mesmerism (schoolboys, like domestic servants, were useful subjects, as they were in no position to demand payment). He found a boy who, when mesmerised, could 'taste' or 'smell' the substances which Wallace was tasting or smelling, and who felt pain in the appropriate part of his body when Wallace pinched himself. From this, Wallace was later to recall, he had learned his 'first great lesson in the inquiry into these obscure fields of knowledge: never to accept the disbelief of great men, or their accusations of imposture or of imbecility, as of any weight when opposed to the repeated observations of facts by other men, admittedly sane and honest'. So when he heard that spiritualist phenomena were being obtained in the home of a friend, though he felt bound to express his incredulity, he also felt bound to investigate the facts; and 'the facts beat me'.

The facts, as he observed them, were that a table, too heavy to be moved except by considerable exertion on the part of the assembled company, moved without any such exertion; and that the raps which had been in evidence at the seance continued even when he was alone 'no one present but myself could have made them, and I certainly did not'. When with a sceptical friend he visited a professional medium in London, Mrs. Marshall – the lady Robert Bell had described – they saw a table levitating (his friend slipped underneath, to check) in a brightly-lit room, and a guitar carried round as if by an invisible hand. Objects moved with 'as much reality as the motion of nails towards a magnet', movements which, he felt, were 'not in themselves more improbable or more incomprehensible'. And this gave him the basis of his theory of Spiritualism, which he propounded in 1866; an attempt to reconcile natural and supernatural. There must, he argued, be a spirit force capable of using the body as its instrument. 'Spirit is mind: the brain and nerves are but a magnetic battery and telegraph, by means of which spirit communicates with the outer world.'

Eight years earlier, by his magnanimous gesture in leaving to

Darwin the full credit for the theory of evolution (over which Wallace, if he had published his own version first, as he could have done, could have claimed at least squatter's rights), Wallace had established a reputation for integrity as well as for scientific acumen; and this meant that if he asked fellow-scientists to join him in an investigation, they might appear churlish if they refused. He invited three of them who had openly expressed their hostility to spiritualism to attend seances (a minimum of six, he suggested, as his medium, Miss Nicoll, was not so consistent a performer as Home) : W. B. Carpenter; the physicist Professor John Tyndall, who by his own account had been one of the scientists who had reproached Thackeray for printing Bell's *Cornhill* article; and G. H. Lewes. Carpenter came; heard raps, left; and came no more. Tyndall came; heard even more varied and louder raps; said, 'We know all about these raps. Show us something else; I thought I should see something remarkable'; and seeing no more, came no more. Lewes declined to come, saying that he had 'thoroughly examined' the subject, and had 'forced Mrs. Hayden to avow herself an impostor' which worried Wallace, because he knew that Mrs. Hayden had convinced the shrewd de Morgan; but when he inquired further, he found that the 'avowal' Lewes was referring to was only the one occasion when he had tricked Mrs. Hayden. And Wallace could not get his paper published – even though it was largely historical and theoretical, tactfully omitting the manifestations he had witnessed – in any scientific journal; it eventually appeared in the *Fortnightly Magazine*.

In the meantime, Home had continued to have problems, chiefly financial. After the death of his wife he had been giving public lectures and readings to earn his living, on Dickens' model – he even, for a time, tried to become an actor – until in 1866 his difficulties seemed to be resolved by the appearance of a rich widow, Mrs. Jane Lyon, who offered to adopt him, and to settle twenty-four thousand pounds on him (later raised to sixty thousand pounds) and to make him her heir: all this, as she put it, to render him independent. He was advised by friends, including Robert Chambers, to accept, which he did. In a matter of months, though, he found that Mrs. Lyon had been concerned not to make him independent but to make him dependent upon her. When he declined to accommodate himself to her plans, she did what she had done – he then learned – five times before, revoking the will she had made in his favour and taking him to court to get her money back, claiming that he had deluded her by saying that the spirits had recommended her to give it to him. There was no evidence for this accusation, except her word for it; and her word, as the judge commented at the end of the trial, was utterly untrustworthy. She had made 'innumerable misstatements in many important particulars – misstatements on oath so perservely untrue that they have embarrassed the Court to a great degree, and quite discredited the plaintiff's testimony'. Nevertheless he found in her favour on the ground that the defendant had failed conclusively to prove that the gifts were voluntary, rather than extracted from her by his dominion over her mind; 'for, as I hold Spiritualism to be a delusion, I must necessarily hold the plaintiff to be the victim of delusion, and no amount of evidence will convince me to the contrary'. So Home had to pay back the money, and return to his public readings (which fortunately for him, were extremely well received, by the newspaper critics as well as by audiences).

Before the trial had ended, Home had met Lord Adare, and with him begun on what was to become the first carefully documented sequence of seances. Adare himself knew nothing of Spiritualism; he was simply intrigued by Home, and by the phenomena, as any young army officer and war correspondent – the two categories were not then so clearly defined – might have been. But his father Lord Dunraven (who had been the recipient of Brewster's confidence on the Athenaeum steps) knew something of the subject; he had made an investigation of Mrs. Hayden. He was also a considerable scholar; he had trained and studied astronomy under Rowan Hamilton, and had become one of the foremost archaeologists of the day. When he could, he attended the seances; while he was away, his son's reports took the form of letters to him; and when they were printed for private circulation in 1869, he provided a reasoned introduction.

The composition of the circle at the seances varied; but it included Adare's friend the Master of Lindsay, who although only twenty-one had already begun to establish the reputation which was to lead to a Fellowship of the Royal Society, and the Presidency of the Royal Astronomical Society. It was at a seance which Lindsay attended that Home performed what was to become the most celebrated of his feats, floating out of one window at Ashley House in moonlight and back in at another. As evidence of Home's levitation, however, this account was of less value than most, as it was accomplished in near darkness. More significant were the descriptions of the phenomena which were witnessed time after time at well-lit seances, which were vouched for by the witnesses (Adare sent a copy of the book to each: fifty appended their names to the testimony, and of those who preferred to remain anonymous, none disputed it).

Sometimes Home appeared to be in his ordinary mind: sometimes entranced (when his pronouncements, according to Dunraven, were occasionally striking, but usually vague or trivial). He was often clairvoyant, sometimes appearing to 'travel'. Raps were a standard accompaniment of seances, along with music – sometimes an instrument playing, sometimes just the sound – scents, luminosities, currents of air (on one occasion, pentecostal – a sound as if of a great wind rushing through the room, tongues of flame darting from Home's head, Home talking in an unknown foreign language, and the sound of a bird fluttering above). Materialised hands were seen, and felt; objects moved, or were carried around as if by invisible hands. Sometimes Home levitated; at other times, elongated. Adare's report of one such occasion at the Halls was confirmed by a journalist, H. T. Humphries, who was present.

> Mr. Home was seen by all of us to increase in height to the extent of some eight or ten inches, and then sank to some six or eight inches below his normal stature. Having returned to his usual height, he took Lord Adare and the Master of Lindsay, and placing one beside each post of the folding doors, lay down on the floor, touching the feet of one with his head and the feet of the other with his feet. He was then again elongated, and pushed both Lord Adare and the Master of Lindsay backward along the floor with his head and feet as he was stretched out, his arms and hands remaining motionless by his side.

Hall, who at this point did some measuring, found that Lindsay and Adare had been pushed more than seven feet apart.

While in a trance, Home appeared at times to become incombustible. At a seance in 1868, according to Adare, he stirred the red embers of a fire into flame and 'kneeling down, he placed his face right among the burning coals, moving it about as though bathing it in water'; an account confirmed by the barrister H. D. Jencken who was also present. He was also able to lend his immunity to others. In a letter to Lord Dunraven Mrs. Hall described how, at a seance the following year, Home

> stirred the fire, which was like a red-hot furnace, so as to increase the heat, held his hands over the fire for some time, and finally drew out of the fire with his hand a huge lump of live, burning coal, so large that he held it in *both* hands as he came from the fire place ... Mr. Hall was seated nearly opposite to where I sat; and I saw Mr. Home, after standing for about half a minute at the back of Mr. Hall's chair, deliberately place the lump of burning coal on his head. I have often wondered since why I was not frightened; but I was not, I had perfect faith that he would not be injured. Someone said, 'is it not hot?' Mr. Hall answered, 'Warm, but not hot'. Mr. Home had moved a little away, but returned, still in a trance; he smiled, and seemed quite pleased; and then proceeded to draw up

Mr. Hall's white hair over the red coal; Mr. Home drew the hair into a sort of pyramid, the coal, still red, showing beneath the hair.

Home then handed the coal to Mrs. Hall who, like her husband, found it 'warm' – yet when she bent down to examine it, the heat was so intense that she was obliged to withdraw her face.

The Dialectical Society

Before the Adare sequence was complete, an investigation of a different kind had begun. Early in the new year of 1869, at a meeting of a rationalist debating club, the London Dialectical Society, it was decided to promote an inquiry into 'the phenomena alleged to be spiritual manifestations', and a committee was appointed to undertake it. The committee consisted chiefly of well-known professional men, doctors and barristers, some of them known sceptics – Charles Bradlaugh among them. Wallace was the only established scientist who accepted an invitation to join in the research: Carpenter contented himself with sending a brief exposition of his theory of unconscious cerebration; and Thomas Huxley claimed that although he would be open to conviction, he was not interested.

The committee divided its work into two sections: the collection of oral and written evidence, and tests by six sub-committees of amateur and professional mediums. Two of the committees found nothing worth recording and a third, the one which investigated Home, obtained only a few small raps and movements before he withdrew, pleading ill-health (even Bradlaugh, however, was impressed by the fact that Home had 'afforded the fullest facilities for investigation'). The other three committees obtained results; the most spectacular being a group four-fifths of whose members, to begin with, had believed that the phenomena were created by trickery or involuntary muscular action. They had made a number of stipulations: that no professional mediums should be included in the tests; that the tests should be well lit; that precautions should be taken to eliminate any possibility of fraud through connivance; and that their findings should relate solely to facts, witnessed and accepted by all present, 'palpable to the senses, their reality capable of demonstrative proof'. Out of forty sessions devised in this way, thirty-four were productive, including one in which they had turned the backs of their chairs to a dining-room table, at a distance of nine inches, and then knelt on the chairs.

In this position, their feet were of course turned away from the table, and by no possibility could be placed under it or touch the floor. The hands of each person were extended over the table at about four inches from the surface. Contact, therefore, with any part of the table could not take place without deception. In less than a minute the table, untouched, moved *four* times; at first about *five* inches to one side, then about *twelve* inches to the opposite side.

Even when their hands were withdrawn to the tops of the chairs, a foot from the table, it still moved. The table was carefully examined, turned upside down and taken apart, to satisfy all those present that no machinery had been involved. 'After trial by every detective test they could devise,' they had been convinced that a force was involved 'sufficient to set in motion heavy substances, without contact of material connection of any kind between such substances and the body of any person present'; that sounds could be made in the same way; and that the force was 'frequently directed by intelligence'.

A second group had similar results, and also reported one unusual test. They had asked sceptics to join the seance when it was in full flow, with a view to eliminating the possibility that all those involved might be under some mesmeric influence – as somebody coming in from outside presumably would not be. It had made no difference; the effects had continued. The remaining group, though they had held fewer meetings, felt that the evidence was strong enough to rebut Carpenter's notion that unconscious muscular pressure could have been responsible for the movements they had witnessed.

In all, more than ten witnesses claimed to have seen levitations of people or heavy objects; heard musical instruments playing without being touched; and seen red hot coals held without pain. Eight had been provided by the medium with precise information of a kind that nobody present could have known, and which they had not known themselves but had found on inquiry to be correct. Six had received accurate advance information about future events. There were also examples of objects, flowers or fruit, appearing in a closed room; of visions in crystal balls; and of elongations. The three sub-committee reports, the committee concluded, substantially corroborated each other, appearing to establish certain propositions:

1. That sounds of a very varied character, apparently proceeding from articles of furniture, the floor and walls of the room – the vibrations of which are often distinctly perceptible to the touch – occur, without being produced by muscular action or mechanical contrivance.

2. That movements of heavy bodies take place without mechanical contrivance of any kind or adequate exertion of muscular force by the persons present, and frequently without contact or connection with any person.

3. That these sounds and movement often occur at the times and

in the manner asked for by persons present, and, by means of a simple code of signals, answer questions and spell out coherent communications.

4. That the answers and communications thus obtained are, for the most part, of a commonplace character; but facts are sometimes correctly given which are only known to one of the persons present.

5. That the circumstances under which the phenomena occur are variable – the most prominent fact being that the presence of certain persons seems necessary to their occurrence, and that of others, generally adverse; but this difference does not appear to depend upon any belief or disbelief concerning the phenomena.

6. That, nevertheless, the occurrence of the phenomena is not insured by the presence or absence of such persons respectively.

These findings were later to be dismissed as unscientific because they lacked detailed descriptions of the precautions taken on each separate occasion. It would have been more to the point to say that they revealed the difficulty of finding effective scientific controls when the phenomena being investigated were in defiance of accepted scientific laws. Two letters which were printed among the written evidence submitted to the committee were particularly revealing. One was from Edwin Arnold, disputing the theory that they were supernatural – he preferred to regard them as 'initiatory demonstrations of mental and vital powers not yet comprehended, nor regularly exercised'.

The statement to which I am prepared to attach my name is this: that, conjoined with the rubbish of much ignorance and some deplorable folly and fraud, there is a body of well-established facts, beyond denial and outside any philosophical explanation; which facts promise to open a new world of human enquiry and experience, are in the highest degree interesting, and tend to elevate ideas of the continuity of life and to reconcile, perhaps, the materialist and metaphysician.

The other letter was from Henry Jeffery, unleashing the pent-up irritation which the seances had clearly aroused in him – not surprisingly, as it sometimes took an hour or more for manifestations to begin, and occasionally they did not begin at all. Some of the exhibitions of mediumship, he complained, were attributable to hysteria or deception. The rappings and movements were of no practical value – 'no new thoughts nor fresh expressions of worthy sentiment'. The communications were 'either frivolous or absurd'; the revelations, if from departed spirits, 'for the most part repugnant to minds of high religious and spiritual faculty'. The theories advanced to account for the phenomena were unscientific, contradictory and vague, and the believers in them particularly open to imposture and credulity. Nevertheless Jeffery could not deny that 'several of us have witnessed some remarkable phenomena, which we have not been able to trace to imposture or delusion; and that these, added to the gathered testimony of respectable witnesses, justify our recommendation of the subject to future cautious investigation'.

The Dialectical Society adopted Jeffery's recommendation, making caution the keynote of their own.

Taking into consideration the high character and intelligence of many of the witnesses to the more extraordinary facts, the extent to which their testimony is supported by the report of the sub-committees, and the absence of any proof of imposture or delusion as regards a large proportion of the phenomena; and, further, having regard to the exceptional character of the phenomena, the large number of persons in every grade of society and over the whole civilised world who are more or less influenced by a belief in their supernatural origin, and to the fact that no philosophical explanation of them has yet been arrived at, they deem it incumbent upon them to state their conviction that the subject is worthy of more serious attention than it has hitherto received.

Psychical Research

Chapter Twenty-six
William Crookes

A FEW DAYS AFTER THE REPORT OF THE COMMITTEE AND THE EVIDENCE on which it was based were presented to the Council of the London Dialectical Society in the summer of 1870, the *Athenaeum* revealed that a scientist of international repute was investigating Spiritualism. William Crookes, who had made his name in 1861 with his discovery of the metallic chemical element thallium, was a Fellow of the Royal Society; he was also the editor of the *Quarterly Journal of Science*, and in it he explained the reasons for his inquiry: 'I consider it the duty of scientific men who have learnt exact modes of working to examine phenomena which attract the attention of the public, in order to confirm their genuineness or to explain, if possible, the delusions of the dishonest and to expose the tricks of deceivers'.

By his own account Crookes had originally, 'like other men who thought little of the matter and saw little', taken Spiritualism to be superstition and trickery; he stressed that his aim would be to substitute a strictly scientific appraisal 'for the loose claims of the pseudo-scientific Spiritualists'. They spoke of bodies weighing fifty pounds being lifted up into the air without the intervention of any known force: 'the scientific chemist is accustomed to use a balance which will render sensible a weight so small that it would take ten thousand of them to weigh one grain,' and all he would ask would be for 'this delicately poised balance to move under test conditions'. The Spiritualists spoke of hearing rappings: he would want to record them on a machine. They spoke of whole houses being shaken; he would merely require them, again under test conditions, to start a pendulum swinging – and so on.

Crookes immediately found, however, that test conditions were difficult to maintain. The forces involved had little respect for scientific protocol, as they demonstrated in the first seance with Home; Wallace,

Mrs. Crookes and Miss Douglas being present. It began with a slight tremor of the table. Then

> Mr. A. R. W. was touched. Mrs. Wm. C. felt her knee touched and her dress pulled. Miss D.'s dress was pulled, and I was touched on my right knee as by a heavy hand firmly placed on it.

The table began to tilt, sometimes on one leg, sometimes on two; rising up opposite each person present in succession, as though to indicate that if muscular pressure, conscious or unconscious were involved, they were all involved in it. Eventually the table 'rose completely off the ground, several times', while the gentlemen present examined it, to ensure Home's feet and knees were not responsible, 'until each observer present expressed himself satisfied that the levitation was not produced by mechanical means on the part of the medium or any one else present'.

Crookes was not so naïve as to present such findings to his scientific friends. His preliminary report, published in his journal in the summer of 1871, described only two formal experiments he had undertaken in collaboration with Dr. William Huggins, also a Fellow of the Royal Society, with a barrister, Serjeant Cox, as observer. For each test, an apparatus had been designed to provide a measure of scientific control. One was a wire cage in which a newly-purchased accordion could be placed with its keys at the bottom. While Home was holding the accordion at the top with one hand, his other hand being on the table above – both hands being visible – the accordion began to expand and contract, and then to play notes. Crookes passed an electric current round the cage, to see if it had any effect; the movement and sounds increased in vigour. Sometimes the accordion could be seen floating without visible means of support. And with nobody touching the keys, it played 'a well-known sweet and plaintive melody, which it executed perfectly'. The other gadget was similar to the one Hare had devised, eighteen years earlier: a board attached to a spring balance in such a way that pressure of the fingers by the medium could not move the pointer. Yet when Home touched the board, the pointer began to oscillate. Crookes's account was endorsed by Huggins and by Cox; and he felt justified in claiming that the experiments appeared 'to establish the existence of a new force, in some unknown manner connected with the human organisation'.

Crookes had an additional reason to feel confident; similar results had been obtained by Alexander von Boutlerow, Professor of Chemistry at the University of St. Petersburg, using even more elaborate equipment. Home, Boutlerow reported, had been able to increase the tension on a dynamometer from one hundred to one hundred and fifty pounds, without physical contact. There had also been the familiar accompaniment of side effects. Boutlerow described how he had seen a bell rise up and float around the room:

> As for touches, I have felt them repeatedly and very distinctly during seances with Home, and I have often had objects taken from my hands and transported to other persons present at the seance. A ring was drawn from my finger and again replaced on it; a pencil and handkerchief were taken from me, while Home's hands were resting on the table before our eyes.

Boutlerow's colleague Nicholas Wagner, Professor of Natural History, witnessed the experiments. As he admitted later, he had accepted Boutlerow's invitation 'with the greatest incredulity and disgust of the phenomena', and by his own account behaved to Home with incivility; but he reached 'a single incontestable conviction – that the facts undoubtedly existed'. They could not be accounted for, he insisted, by 'the strange theory of "unconscious cerebration" set forth by Carpenter, which explains absolutely nothing'.

Mrs. Guppy

Crookes's report was not well received. The news of his investigation had been welcomed, with such tributes as 'if men like Mr. Crookes grapple with the subject, taking nothing for granted until it is proved, we shall soon know how much to believe'. What had been expected, though, was a scientific exposition of the grounds for believing nothing. And unluckily for Crookes, an episode had been reported that summer which had whetted the public appetite for a devastating exposure of Spiritualist delusion: the translocation of Mrs. Guppy.

Before her marriage, while she was still Miss Nichol, she had lived with Wallace's sister; it was from her he had acquired some of his early experience of mediumship. At first, it had usually been poltergeist-type activity: objects moved in the house; not, as a rule, at seances, but often in the empty room after a seance was over. Gradually Miss Nichol had begun to exert more direct control, culminating in a seance Wallace described in 1867, where fifteen chrysanthemums, six variegated anemones and other flowers manifested themselves on the table.

Such materialisations were not new. 'Apports', as they came to be called, had occasionally been encountered by the investigators of mesmerism. In his *Recherches Psychologiques sur le Magnétism Vital* in 1839, a doctor who had studied under Du Potet, G. P. Billot, recalled how twenty years earlier he had found a subject who when mesmerised could diagnose what was the matter with his patients, and prescribe for them; and on one occasion, when she had prescribed a flowering herb which was not in season the herb, in flower, had suddenly materialised. He had not cared to disclose this or other similar manifestations, like objects floating in the air, at the time; until in correspondence with Deleuze he had found that Deleuze, too, had encountered examples of apports, but had thought it wise not to publish them ('I have suppressed many things in my works because I considered it was not yet time to disclose them'). By the 1870s the possibility that flowers or anything else could materialise in a seance room was even more repugnant to ordinary common sense; but Mrs. Guppy had worse in store for those who, like Crookes, hoped to convince the public that psychical phenomena were genuine. After her marriage to Guppy they had lived for a time abroad; and she had resumed her mediumship when they returned to London. At eight-thirty on the evening of June 3rd, 1871 she was sitting in the breakfast room of their Highbury home doing the accounts, when to the astonishment of a friend who was with her, she disappeared. A seance was in progress four miles away in Lamb's Conduit Street. It was in the dark; and suddenly (according to the account of one of the sitters) 'somebody called out, "Good God – there is something on my head," simultaneously with a heavy bump on the table, and one or two screams. A match was instantly struck, and there was Mrs. G., who appeared to be in a trance, and perfectly motionless.' She was wearing her loose house-gown, and her account book was still in her hand.

Her disappearance was attested by her friend, by her maid, and by her husband, at the Highbury end; her re-appearance by all the sitters in Lamb's Conduit Street. From the point of view of making an impression, though, it proved unfortunate that it was Mrs. Guppy who had been involved. Describing a seance with her at which she had been levitated in a chair on to the middle of a table, noiselessly and almost instantaneously, Wallace had remarked with awe 'you know Miss N.'s size and weight, and can judge of the force and exertion required'; she was enormous – the biggest woman in London, according to one of the Lamb's Conduit Street sitters. The idea of her floating from her home to the seance was hilarious; and it was delightedly exploited in an article 'Spiritualism and its Recent Converts' in the *Quarterly Review*. The writer did not need to denounce the tale as a fabrication; he simply quoted it, referring to her bulk, and contenting himself with asking a question. If she knew, when she needed to travel, that the spirits would 'save her not merely the fatigue of the journey, but the cost of cabs and railway fares, what on earth, then, has Mrs. Guppy got to do with household accounts?'

The theme of the article was that scientists who let themselves become involved in research into such absurdities were letting their profession down. Obviously Crookes, Huggins and Cox had allowed themselves to be tricked : Home must have been able to attach some device to the musical instrument, and to distract his investigators' attention so that he could put physical pressure on the board, to move the pointer. As it would be objected that nobody worthy of the name 'scientist' would have permitted such elementary deception, the writer had a ready answer; they were not worthy of the name. Crookes, he explained, had made his reputation simply by his discovery of thallium. He had been made an F.R.S.;

> but we speak advisedly when we say that this distinction was conferred on him with considerable hesitation, the ability he displayed in the investigation being purely *technical*. We are advised, on the highest authority, that he is regarded among chemists as a specialist of specialists, being totally destitute of any knowledge of Chemical Philosophy, and utterly untrustworthy as to any inquiry which requires more than technical knowledge for its successful conduct.

As for Huggins, the man was a brewer, and only an amateur astronomer. Although his skill as an observer of the skies was not in question he, too, was clearly a victim of the 'narrowing and perverting influence of a limited specialism'. And to be on the safe side, the writer also derided Cromwell Varley, an electrical engineer who had tested Home some years before, but whose favourable findings had not appeared until they were printed in the Dialectical Society's report. Varley possessed considerable technical knowledge; but 'his scientific attainments are so cheaply estimated by those who are best qualified to judge of them that he has never been admitted to the Royal Society, although he has more than once been a candidate for that honour'.

The article was not signed, but the internal evidence, notably the eulogy of Dr. Carpenter's theory of unconscious cerebration and the reminder that the theory had been endorsed by Faraday, pointed to Carpenter as the likely author; as he was. But to readers who did not know this, such apparently well-documented criticisms must have been persuasive. They were, in fact, sheer invention on Carpenter's part. Varley was an F.R.S.; he had been elected a few months earlier. Although Huggins came from a brewing family, he was not a brewer; and he was an amateur only in the sense that he had been rich enough to build and work in his own observatory; so highly regarded was he by his fellow members of the Royal Society that he was to become its President. As for the notion of Crookes as a narrow specialist, it was the reverse of the truth. Of all the British scientists of the era, Crookes was the most catholic in his interests : alongside his research into physics and chemistry he wrote many papers on how they could be applied, on subjects as diverse as diamonds, wheat-growing and calico-printing. And so far from there being any hesitation in conferring his Fellowship of the Royal Society, he had been elected on first application, at that time an unusual honour for so young a candidate.

Here, then, was an established academic figure – Carpenter was by this time a Fellow of the Royal Society, and Registrar at London University – convicted of deplorable irresponsibility, if not actual dishonesty, about scientific colleagues. Had his attack been on Darwin, Tyndall or Huxley, his reputation would have been irretrievably damaged, unless he had composed a suitably grovelling apology. But as he had erred in orthodoxy's service, he could be forgiven. When Crookes presented the paper he proposed to read on the subject to the Council of the Royal Society, it was returned to him with a request for additional evidence; when he provided the additional evidence, the paper was simply rejected, an unusual snub for a Fellow to receive. And only after Crookes had lodged a formal complaint did the Council pass a mild resolution regretting the statements in the *Quarterly Review* 'because they are incorrect in point of fact, and because the unauthorised publication of the deliberations of the Council is contrary to the usages of the Society'. No attempt was made to rebuke Carpenter, and the British Association for the Advancement of Science showed what they felt by electing him their President for the following year. If he suffered at all, it was only from the sting in the tail of some remarks by Serjeant Cox, whose testimony he had dismissed as worthless. When the *Quarterly* issued a statement that the article had been wrongly attributed to Carpenter, Cox expressed his satisfaction; he had been unwilling to believe, he said, that a man of Carpenter's scientific and professional status, could 'so far forget the gentleman as, in a purely scientific controversy, to be guilty of the mingled mendacity and meanness that pervade the personality of the article in the *Quarterly Review*'.

Charles Darwin

It would be necessary, Crookes realised, to attract more allies; and the conversion of one sceptic in particular would carry more weight than any of his contemporaries: Darwin. Among the few scientists Crookes had been able to interest in his experiments was Darwin's cousin and close friend, Francis Galton – explorer, meteorologist, founder of the principle of eugenics, and influential by virtue of the fact that he was General Secretary of the British Association. After attending three seances, Galton wrote to tell Darwin on March 28th, 1872, he was

> utterly confounded by the results, and very disinclined to discredit them. Crookes is working deliberately and well. There is not the slightest excitement during the sittings, but they are conducted

in an easy chatty way; and though a large part of what occurs might be done, *if the medium were free*, yet I don't see how it can be done, held hand and foot, as is the case.

Three weeks later, finally convinced that it was not a matter of 'vulgar legerdemain', he urged Darwin to investigate for himself, provided that a first-rate medium was at his disposal. Considering that no strain was involved (Darwin suffered from chronic ill-health); considering the possibility that the effects might be genuine; considering that, according to Crookes, Home was willing to put himself at their disposal: 'considering, I say, all these things, will you go into it, and allow me to join?' He felt certain that all that would be needed would be for just the two of them to have a dozen seances with Home.

Darwin agreed. Galton wrote to Home, enclosing Darwin's letter, but there was no reply. The year before, while doing the experiments with Boutlerow, Home had met Julie de Gloumeline, a dedicated Spiritualist, whose spirits told her that he would be her husband. They married that autumn; after the visit to England in 1872, they returned to the Continent. The reason why he had not replied, Crookes explained, was that they had gone to Russia, and would not be back till the following spring. Darwin should await his return, Crookes felt: Home's presence was essential, because 'the experiments were far more successful when he was the medium, than when anyone else was'. But that winter, Home's health deteriorated; he was advised to go south, to the Mediterranean; and he did not come to England again. What promised to be the most remarkable of all the inquiries into his mediumship was never held.

P. P. Alexander

Although Home continued to give the occasional seance for friends, he did no more tests. Apart from his *Lights and Shadows of Spiritualism,* published in 1877 – chiefly concerned to rescue Spiritualism from what he felt were the evil influences to which it was being subjected, including dishonest mediums preying on the public – Home's contribution was limited to exhortations in his correspondence. Effectively his career as a medium was over.

By this time, though – given the premise that Home's mediumistic feats were not *a priori* impossible – the evidence which had accumulated for them was remarkable in both quantity and quality. Even if there were no source other than his own and his wife's books, it would still be formidable, because of the care they both took to give references – particularly in her second volume where, to rebut criticism of the earlier works, she obtained permission to identify many of the witnesses whose anonymity she and Home had earlier felt bound to preserve (Frederic Myers checked the sources after her death, and found them trustworthy). And further accounts were periodically to come to light, confirming and supplementing theirs, such as the notes Crookes made at the time of his experiments. To reject such testimony – there were over a hundred accounts of one single phenomenon, levitation – would be tantamount, Crookes felt, to rejecting 'all human testimony whatsoever'.

There are also some accounts which, though the writers are not now remembered, carry particular conviction because they are so manifestly not the work of credulous witnesses. When Home went to stay for a few days with Dr. Doun in Edinburgh, in 1870, two men had written careful descriptions of seances there: General Boldero and Patrick Proctor Alexander. In a letter to his wife Boldero told how he had been invited with a couple of others to accompany Home to the library. It was not lit, but there was plenty of light coming in through the open door from the landing; enough to see that 'an immense bookcase, that would require at least four men to move, began slowly to come towards us'. Then, Home went into a trance, and began to elongate; inviting Boldero, who could see him plainly, to place his hands on his hips – 'I could feel his flesh stretch and again shrink'. He also picked up a burning coal from a grate in Boldero's presence. Later, in the Boldero household, their piano began to play with the lid closed, while Home was some distance away. Voices were heard; when Home interrupted, talking over them, and Boldero remonstrated with him, Home explained he was simply proving that it could not be ventriloquism on his part.

Patrick Proctor Alexander was an engaging Edinburgh litterateur, the author of commentaries on Carlyle and J. S. Mill; and his commentary is redolent of good sense and pawky Scots humour. He had heard about Home, and took him to be an accomplished conjuror; so when he found that Home was coming to Edinburgh, he persuaded Doun to let him come to a seance, and to bring another sceptic, Dr. Findlater of the Chambers publishing house, the two of them hoping to catch Home up to his tricks in the dark. They were disconcerted, therefore, to find that the seance room was brightly lit, and that there was neither spiritualist mumbo-jumbo nor conjurors' patter. In the half hour they spent waiting for the performance to begin, Home encouraged casual conversation; and even after they had begun 'we contrived to maintain a hilarity, not to say levity, of mood'. The first sign that the forces were in the mood were tremors: the chair of each person was felt to rock 'and – as we Scots says – *dirl* under him'. Still, that might have been done by some trick: and when some of the sitters reported ice-cold blasts of air which Alexander and Findlater did not feel, and to report raps which they did not hear, suspicion returned. Soon, however, louder raps were coming and they were clearly not coming from Home. The table began to move, and then to tilt, Home inviting them to look under it, to ascertain there was no movement of his feet, and no gadgetry. Findlater felt himself touched – a smart stroke on his knee. A woman sitter's chair was jerked forward, jamming her against the table. An accordion began to play on its own: and when the alphabet was called for, raps provided information about dead relatives of some of the sitters.

By Home's standards, it was not a striking seance. Even the accordion played only notes – not a tune. But it was more than enough to convince Alexander (and Findlater, 'not hitherto suspected by his friends of a tendency to undue credulity in any matter') that the results could not possibly have been obtained by sleight-of-hand, unless there had been connivance by his hosts – a notion which 'in my own mind, and I venture to say, that of everyone who had ever had the pleasure of their acquaintance, is disposed of as utterly inadmissible in view of the known and high character of both'. Such was his admiration for the Douns that what happened after a further seance at their house, though Alexander did not witness it himself, actually carried more conviction for him than what he had witnessed, because it happened when Home had already left. While Doun was sitting alone in the seance room, it seemed to him that one of the chairs opposite to him was moving; 'it *was so*; and I could scarcely believe my eyes when I saw it travel slowly across the carpet, and set itself beside my own'. When his wife came into the room and he told her what had happened, she insisted that he must have been under some delusion; as if to contradict her, another chair thereupon left its place, under her eyes, and came across the room towards them.

Similar instances of post-seance effects had been reported before. In his evidence to the Dialectical Society Cromwell Varley recalled that at his first meeting with Home he had been 'too much astonished to be able to feel satisfied'; what rid him of doubt was that when he got back to his house and was alone in his drawing room, he heard rappings there, and the next morning received a letter from Home saying the spirits had reported making them. Even so, had the doctor been the only witness, Alexander admitted, he would have had to accept Mrs. Doun's view, and attribute the doctor's experience to a mental and optical illusion. As it had been seen by a second person, engaged in making a strong sceptical protest, this explanation could not be accepted.

And yet, if it be not accepted, either the thing must be true, or the people reporting of it liars. Personally declining, *in toto*, to take up with this last supposition, I cannot but regard the evidence to the fact as very strong indeed – so strong that I almost think that I *ought* to believe it. Yet, to say sooth, I scarcely *can*; so strong, on the other hand, is the instinctive sceptical recoil from a fact so hitherto unexampled, and in the teeth of all previous experience. Not the less, it is quite certain that on evidence no more conclusive, indeed considerably less so, as tendered to a fact of murder, I should to-morrow hang with these hands, if need be, some half-dozen of my fellow creatures.

It is difficult to convey, without more extensive quotation than the evidence of a single witness would merit, the quiet conviction that a narrative like Alexander's carries. What testimonies of this kind establish beyond question is that Home could not conceivably have obtained his effects by routine trickery. 'When we consider that Home's seances almost always took place in private houses at which he was a guest,' Wallace recalled in his autobiography, 'and with people absolutely above suspicion of collusion with an impostor, and also either in the daytime or in a fully illuminated room, it will be admitted that no form of legerdemain will explain what occurred.' And this was accepted even by some of the leading magicians of the day, little though they can have relished being up-staged. One of the most celebrated of them, Canti, who managed to get into a seance held by Prince Bonaparte without Home's knowledge, testified after it, according to Home, that what he had seen was no trick. T. A. Trollope claimed that another, Bosco, 'utterly scouted' the idea that what Home did could have been done by sleight-of-hand.

The clearest confirmation that Home was not a conjuror, though, comes from the fact that his detractors, who were legion, were unable to produce a single case when he had been detected in trickery. With very few exceptions, people who attended his seances left no recorded doubt about Home's honesty, even if they felt unable to trust their own eyes and ears; and those few who came away with their suspicions still strong were unable to present any concrete evidence. The great bulk of the anti-Home material, which was abundant, was actuated by the malice which prompted 'Mr. Sludge the Medium': as in *Punch*'s 'Spiritual "Hume"-bugs', in 1860.

> Of itself his accordion to play will begin
> (If you won't look too hard at the works hid within)
> Spirit-hands, at his bidding, will come, touch, and go
> (But you mustn't peep under the table, you know)
> Home, Home, great Home
> There's no case like Home.

– which simply displayed the versifier's ignorance of the conditions at the seances. Home was pursued wherever he went by stories of how he rigged his effects: by using a telescopic fishing rod, for example, to hook and move furniture. In some reports it was alleged he had been caught on a Florence roof, fixing up pulleys. After his death, a popular scientific magazine actually published his 'confession'. But when such stories were followed up, by friends who wanted to rebut them or enemies who wanted to exploit them, no source could be traced or, if it were, it was found to be false.

Chapter Twenty-seven

The Mediums

HAD HOME BEEN CONVICTED OF TRICKERY AT ANY TIME IN HIS CAREER it would have been destructive of the credibility of the phenomena; but by the time he retired there were nine or ten other mediums, according to Crookes, who possessed similar psychic powers, even if none had them quite to the same degree. The one ranking next after Home, in Crookes's estimation, was Kate Fox. She had been sent over by the New York banker Charles Livermore on what he regarded as a Spiritualist mission to the English. To Livermore Kate was without doubt 'the most wonderful living medium'. She refused money for seances; her character, he insisted, was irreproachable. Crookes tested her over a period of months; finding, among other things, that her ability to promote rappings was unimpaired since Hydesville days a quarter of a century before. It was only necessary

for her to place her hand on any substance for loud thuds to be heard in it, like a triple pulsation, sometimes loud enough to be heard several rooms off. In this manner I have heard them in a living tree – on a sheet of glass – on a stretched iron wire – on a stretched membrane – on a tambourine – on the roof of a cab – and on the floor of a theatre . . . I have tested them in every way that I could devise, until there has been no escape from the conviction that they were true objective occurrences not produced by trickery or mechanical means.

Kate could also produce materialisations. While Crookes was holding both her hands in one of his, and a pencil in the other, 'a luminous hand came down from the upper part of the room, and after hovering near me for a few seconds, took the pencil from my hand, rapidly wrote on a sheet of paper, threw the pencil down, and then rose over our heads, gradually fading into darkness'. Another witness, Rosamund

Dale Owen, described how objects moved at a distance in a Fox seance, including a musical box which was carried over from a side table: although it had been out of order for months, it began to play.

Perhaps the most impressive tribute to Kate Fox's trustworthiness, however, was the fact that Home, who regarded most of the mediums of the time with deep suspicion – because they insisted on operating in complete darkness, which he feared was a mask for trickery – undertook to be tested jointly with her; and one of these seances was reported in some detail in *The Times*, which had commissioned a special correspondent to investigate the subject. In his report, published on Boxing Day 1872, he made no attempt to disguise his contempt for the 'pseudo-marvel' of Spiritualism. He had to admit, however, that Faraday's apparently conclusive explanation had failed to carry complete conviction; and as there had been no sufficiently impartial and authoritative inquiry (he derided the Dialectical Society's and ignored Crookes's) he had decided to attend seances for that purpose himself.

The first, with Home, produced nothing of interest. At the second, however, with an unnamed medium, a chair climbed on to the table in the dark, and even in the light 'the furniture became quite lively'. He was not satisfied, though; and the third seance, though providing much that was 'curious', was also unconvincing. At the fourth, both Kate Fox and Home were present, in a previously searched and well-lit room. Raps sounded from the walls; the table was rendered alternately 'light' and 'heavy', and eventually levitated; a lath floated around; and an accordion played while he was holding it in one hand. Every opportunity, he emphasised, had been afforded him for examination; and he had found nothing the whole evening, except the unaccountable nature of the phenomena themselves, to suggest imposture. He was not prepared to draw any inferences; 'even with all this, we are not a Spiritualist and do not even believe in a psychic force'. But that the phenomena were real, he was in no doubt.

Like Home, Kate agreed to be tested by Boutlerow in St. Petersburg. The things she was able to do, he reported, were 'sufficient for the most pronounced but *honest* sceptic to cause him to reject ventriloquism, muscular action and every such artificial explanation'. But in 1872 she married H. D. Jencken (according to the *Spiritualist* magazine, some loud raps were heard at the wedding breakfast, and the table on which the wedding cake stood was repeatedly raised from the floor); and thereafter until his death in 1881 her domestic and maternal duties restricted further experiments with Crookes, much to his regret.

Florence Cook: 'Katie King'

Crookes continued his psychical research over the next two years, with Kate Jencken whenever she was available, and with other mediums, such as the American Mrs. Annie Fay, who was able to produce manifestations even when wired up to a galvanometer, a test devised by Cromwell Varley to avoid the need for bonds. As Crookes put it, she was tied with an electric current; the circuit being so arranged that if she tried to cheat, it would be broken. But it was not until the winter of 1874 that he found a potential successor to Home and Kate Fox in Florence Cook.

Two years earlier, while she was working in a London school, the fifteen-year-old Florence had begun to be the centre of disturbances similar to Angélique Cottin's. 'I find a report is spread in Hackney that I am a Spiritualist,' the headmistress wrote to Kate's mother. 'I am sorry to say to you that I am compelled to part with her as a teacher.' A footnote scribbled later on the letter was to explain that this referred to books and pencils flying around, 'chairs following', and 'table rushing without contact'; and as these had happened in school hours the headmistress's concern was understandable. She made it clear, though, in the letter that she did not think Florence was blameworthy. 'I am so fond of Florrie and have such a high opinion of her . . . she is fitted for something far higher and nobler.'

That summer Florence went to the Isle of Wight to participate in a series of experiments with a doctor, John Purdon, and his wife; and while she was with them, there was an early example of the difficulty both of taking adequate precautions and of deciding, if they proved inadequate, whether the disruptive force was physical or psychic. In a letter published in the *Spiritualist*, Purdon described how Florence had been 'locked to the floor by means of straps and rings attached to a canvas jacket, in which she had been laced and sealed', yet his brother had taken a photograph of a spirit face which had appeared at the window of her cabinet. This should have been conclusive; but it 'was rendered utterly worthless as a verification by the fact that on the doors of the cabinet being opened, the medium was found free, the seals having been broken, and the whipcord with which the jacket was laced cut in several places'; the straps also bore marks of some cutting instrument. At first sight, this seemed damning; and Florence's excuse – that a bad spirit had been around – would ordinarily have carried no weight. Florence, however, had one strong point in her favour; no cutting instrument could be found on her, or in the cabinet. The Purdons therefore decided to continue tests, using steel chains to bind her. The manifestations continued. Several times Florence and the chair to which she was bound were levitated on to a table; and once, when Purdon was holding her feet, she elongated to such an extent that his brother-in-law, who was over five feet nine inches in height and had his hands on her shoulders, was hauled up to the ceiling. Florence had never made any attempt to impose on him, Purdon decided; 'she is a wonderful medium and, what is better, is one who is not afraid to show the dark side any more than the light'.

By that autumn Florence was sufficiently sought after to be investigated by a mildly facetious *Daily Telegraph* correspondent. Invited to a seance, he was allowed to examine the cabinet, 'a sort of corner cupboard', and to satisfy himself that it had room enough only for Florence, 'tied round the neck, arms and legs to a chair, in a very uncomfortable and apparently secure manner', to be put into it 'like a pot of jam or a pound of candles', so that she could not reach the aperture at the top. Yet in that aperture three different faces appeared during the seance, though the seals on Florence's bonds remained unbroken.

The following summer the same correspondent described a seance at which a full human form materialised. While Florence was tied up in the cabinet, in a black dress, a tall female figure in white emerged, hands and feet bare, stood like a statue before them, and spoke a few words before retiring. She identified herself as 'Katie King', Florence Cook's 'familiar' or spirit guide. The *Telegraph* correspondent, by this time noticeably less flippant on the subject, saw 'Katie' several time, and took some photographs of her by magnesium light. He was baffled. It could not be Florence, who was still in her black dress, with her boots on, the knots and seals secure. Yet 'Katie King' seemed 'so thoroughly material and flesh-and-blood-like'.

She seemed similarly flesh-and-blood-like to Alexander Aksakov, a relation by marriage of Boutlerow's who had become interested in Spiritualism, and who was on a visit to England that autumn. Invited to a seance by Florence Cook's father, Aksakov was able to satisfy himself that the 'cabinet' was no more than a 'niche' formed by the fireplace and a corner of the room, with a curtain hung across it; and that Florence, in a black dress, was securely tied up in a chair. The seance room was lit by a small lamp. After fifteen minutes 'the curtain was drawn aside sufficiently to show us a human figure standing upright close to the drawn curtain. It was completely clad in white; the face uncovered by the hair enveloped in a white veil; hands and arms were bare. That was *Katie*.' 'Katie' talked for a while, and offered to answer questions.

Taking the hint, I asked her: 'Can't you show me your medium?' She replied: 'Yes, certainly, come here very quickly and have a look!' In that very instant I stood up from my chair, and drew back the curtain. I had only to take five steps to reach the curtain but the white clad figure had disappeared. In front of me, in a dark corner, the figure of the medium, clothed in a black dress, was sitting in an armchair.

He had not been able to see the medium clearly enough, however, to be sure it really was Florence. So when 'Katie' reappeared, and asked him whether he was satisfied, he replied that he was not.

'Then take the lamp with you and go and have a look immediately!' Within a second I stood behind the curtain, holding the lamp in my hand. Every trace of Katie had disappeared. I found myself alone and facing the medium who, in a deep trance, was sitting on a chair, with both her hands bound fast behind her back. The light, shining on the medium's face, started to produce its usual effect, i.e. the medium began to sigh and to awake.

After the seance Aksakov found all the 'bindings, knots and seals' intact; so tightly were Florence's hands bounds together that it was only with difficulty that he could get the scissors under the tapes.

But though 'Katie' might *look* flesh-and-blood-like, the general assumption still was that a spirit form could not *be* material; so that when William Volckman – one of the men who had been concerned in the Dialectical Society's enquiry – grabbed at her as she was walking around at a seance, a few weeks later, and found that she was indeed material, it seemed obvious to him that he had seized the disguised Florence. But Volckman had not, in fact, been able to prove that 'Katie' was Florence. In the scuffle after he seized her (in which he lost part of his beard) she had slipped away to the cabinet; and when the curtains were opened up, she was found still tied up as she had been at the beginning of the seance, the knot still sealed (with the signet ring of the Earl of Caithness); and although a search was made, no white material of the kind 'Katie' had been wearing could be found. The barrister and litterateur Henry Dunphy, who was at the seance, also claimed – describing the way 'Katie' had extricated herself from Volckman's clutches – that 'the figure appeared to lose its feet and legs and to elude the grasp, making for that purpose a movement similar to that of a seal in water'; and this, however improbable it might sound to anybody who did not believe in materialisations (and at this stage, Crookes himself did not believe in them), tied in with the description of materialised hands at Home's seances, which when held would slip mysteriously away. Volckman, too, was not the disinterested truth-seeker he made himself out to be. He was involved with Mrs. Guppy, whom he was later to marry; and Mrs. Guppy was paranoically jealous of Florence. But this was not realised at the time; and the episode was widely assumed to have provided proof that Florence was a cheat.

Florence's reaction was to approach Crookes, who had attended one of her seances; and he agreed to investigate her claims. At a seance a few days later, he had the seance room searched and the doors and windows fastened; Florence herself was searched by, among other ladies, Mrs. Crookes, before being trussed up in a chair, the wax on the knots being sealed with Crookes's signet ring. As before, 'Katie King' apeared in flowing white robes. Crookes had heard the sound of Florence moaning, going into her trance; and while 'Katie King' stood before him he could still distinctly hear the same sound coming from the cabinet. It was good enough evidence, he felt, to proceed with further experiments, in spite of the suspicions she had aroused. And as if in a calculated act of defiance, in the next issue of his magazine he abandoned caution, giving the results of three years of exploration 'into a territory of natural knowledge which offers almost virgin soil to a scientific man'.

He listed thirteen varieties of manifestation he had witnessed. One, movement of heavy bodies with human contact, but without human propulsion, as with fingertip table-turning; generally preceded by currents of air which were not the product of imagination, as he had seen sheets of paper blown around, and a thermometer showed that the temperature lowered several degrees. Two, percussive and other sounds (the popular name of 'raps', he felt, conveyed an erroneous impression; they ranged from delicate ticks to scratchings, twitterings and detonations). Three, alteration in the weight of bodies, as in the test he had described with Home. Four, movement of heavy bodies when the medium was not in contact with them; he had seen this many times as when 'a chair was seen by all present to move slowly up to the table from a far corner, while we were all watching it'. Five, the raising of furniture off the ground without human contact; 'on five separate occasions, a heavy dining-table rose between a few inches and one and a half feet off the floor, under special circumstances which rendered trickery impossible'. Six, levitation of human beings: the most striking occasions had been with Home, but Crookes had also witnessed a chair in which a lady medium was sitting rise off the ground, and the same had happened with children. Seven, miscellaneous movements of small articles: music played on an accordion at a distance; knots tied in handkerchiefs; a fan floating around, fanning the company; a pendulum set in motion 'when enclosed in a glass case firmly cemented to a wall'. Eight, luminous appearances, ranging from points of light to clouds which 'visibly condense to the form of a hand'. Nine, materialised hands; 'I have retained one of these hands in my own, firmly resolved not to let it escape. There was no struggle or effort made to get loose, but it gradually seemed to resolve itself into vapour, and faded in that manner from my grasp'. Ten, 'direct writing', by such hands, visible or invisible. Eleven, phantom forms. Twelve, demonstrations of intelligence not directly attributable to the medium – as in the case of answers to questions which the medium could not have known. And thirteen, translocation: a bell which had been in his library, for example, had appeared in the seance room, though the door into it was locked.

For some reason, Crookes did not mention one of Home's specialities, incombustibility. But when his notes on the inquiry were published later they disclosed how in the last recorded seance Home had taken a coal from the fire and put it on a cambric handkerchief, fanning the coal to white heat with his breath before saying that he was going to burn a very small hole in the handkerchief, which he did, to show the coal really was hot (Crookes tested the handkerchief later, to make sure no chemical had been used).

Some undiscovered process, Crookes felt, must be involved, and he settled for a hypothesis presented by Serjeant Cox of a psychic force

proceeding from, or directly associated with, the human organisation, which, in certain persons, and under certain conditions, can cause motion in heavy bodies, and produce audible and palpable sounds in such bodies, without muscular contact or any material connection between any person present and the heavy body so moved, or on which the sounds are produced.

Like Cox, Crookes felt there was insufficient evidence to identify the source. But *some* intelligence there must be, to answer questions, and provide information, even if it was not always accurate. This was an issue, he thought, that would have to be settled by further research.

By this time Crookes cannot have expected a favourable response; and he did not get it. 'Rational men', Lord Amberley – son of Lord John Russell, and father-to-be of Bertrand Russell – explained in the new year issue of the *Fortnightly* magazine, 'are indisposed to look into evidence by those who betray such hopeless inability to discriminate between adequate and inadequate proof of facts'; a view echoed the following week by the *Lancet*: 'the existence of delusion, and the manner of it being once explained, the subject ceases to possess any interest for educated people'. But there were some educated people who, reading Crookes's account, were disturbed by it. Writing to Lady Derby, Darwin said that had she called on him after he read it, she would have found

a much perplexed man. I cannot disbelieve Mr. Crookes's statement, nor can I believe in his result. It has removed some of my difficulty that the supposed power is not an anomaly, but is common in a lesser degree in various persons. It is also a consolation to reflect that gravity acts at any distance, in some wholly unknown manner, and so may nerve force. Nothing is so difficult to decide as where to draw a line between scepticism and credulity. It was a very long time before scientific men would believe in the fall of aerolites; and this was chiefly owing to so much bad evidence, as in the present case, being mixed up with the good. All sorts of objects were said to have been seen falling from the sky. I very much hope that a number of men, such as Professor Stokes, will be induced to witness Mr. Crookes's experiments.

By this time, too, another force was at work to promote interest: the social and family ties which linked some of the believers to the sceptics. Like Galton, the philologist Hensleigh Wedgwood had been convinced by what he had witnessed at seances. Wedgwood was greatly respected within the circle; a man of such principle that when he had become convinced that oath-taking was incompatible with the religious beliefs he derived from the New Testament, he had given up his post as a London magistrate, remarking 'there is no use in letting eight hundred pounds a year persuade one's conscience' (the equivalent of perhaps eight thousand pounds a year today). In the circle too, there was George Lewes, who was interested in mediums for the opposite reasons, hoping to expose them as frauds. So a seance was arranged at the house of one of Darwin's brothers, Erasmus; and Darwin was invited, along with Galton, Wedgwood, Thomas Huxley's brother George, and Lewes, who brought George Eliot.

By Galton's account, Lewes was troublesome, 'inclined to make jokes and not play the game fairly'; and he and George Eliot soon left. But then things began to happen. 'We had grand fun,' Darwin wrote to tell Thomas Huxley. The medium Charles Williams 'made the chairs, a flute, a bell and a candlestick jump about in my brother's dining room, in a manner that astounded everyone, and took away their breath'. It was in the dark, but George Huxley and Hensleigh Wedgwood 'held the medium's hands and feet on both sides all the time'. Darwin had found it so hot that he had left for an upstairs room 'before all these astounding miracles, or jugglery, took place'. But he had come down to the seance room immediately afterwards, 'and saw all the chairs, etc., on the table which had been lifted over the heads of those sitting round'. It had been a good seance, Galton told him with understandable satisfaction; and it left Darwin uneasy: 'how the medium can possibly do what was done passes my understanding'.

Darwin's account presented Thomas Huxley with a challenge he could hardly afford to refuse. 'That the possibilities of nature are infinite,' he once observed, 'is an aphorism with which I am wont to worry my friends.' Although a devoted admirer of Hume, whose biography he was to write, he felt compelled to reject Hume's opinion of the miraculous; nothing, Huxley insisted, was inconceivable simply because it was contrary to uniform experience, except a contradiction in terms, like 'a round square'. Naturalists were familiar with insects which walked on water; although it was extremely improbable that man could achieve the same feat, 'the limitation of our faculties are such that we never can be in a position to set bounds to the possibilities of nature'. So when Wallace had asked him to witness some seances, he had insisted that he was not antagonistic; he simply was not interested – the excuse which he repeated when invited to participate in the Dialectical Society investigation. But his letter showed his real feelings. 'If anybody could endow me,' he wrote,

> with the faculty of listening to the chatter of old women and curates in the nearest cathedral town, I should decline the privilege, having better things to do . . . the only good that I can see in a demonstration of the truth of 'spiritualism' is to furnish an additional argument against suicide. Better live a crossing-sweeper than die and be made to talk twaddle by a 'medium' hired at a guinea a seance.

Five years almost to the day after he had written that letter, Darwin's account roused Huxley to action; and Williams was hired for a further seance. An attempt was made to obtain results in a lighted room; but when this failed, the Huxley brothers took up their stations one on either side of the medium, each holding a hand (Thomas Huxley preferred to hold a finger) and placing a foot on one of the medium's feet; and the lights were extinguished. There were, however, one or two spots of light, enough for Huxley to see that Williams was capable of moving his head; and when a musical instrument on the table in front of him gave forth sounds, Huxley surmised that the medium had been able to pluck at it with his mouth. Later, after Wedgwood had taken George Huxley's place, things began to happen; an armchair moved up to Wedgwood's leg, and eventually on to the table. In the process, Wedgwood admitted, he had briefly lost contact with the medium's hand, but not for long enough, he felt, to matter. The sitters accepted this – except Huxley. What had happened, he felt sure, was that the medium had somehow managed to distract Wedgwood's attention, enabling him to disengage his foot from control and use it to pull the chair towards him; then, having disengaged his hand, he had been able to lift the chair on to the table. 'My conclusion,' he wrote, 'is that the medium is a cheat and an impostor.' This, his brother agreed, must have been the explanation, hard though it was to believe that the evidence of anyone with 'such perfect bona fides' as Wedgewood's could be so worthless. Darwin's relief was clearly felt. 'The Lord have mercy upon us,' he had remarked in his letter describing the seance he had attended, 'if we have to believe such rubbish.' Huxley's explanation spared him that necessity; 'an enormous weight of evidence would be requisite to make me believe anything beyond mere trickery'.

It had been unfortunate that the tests had not been done with Home; the darkness in which Williams worked made it impossible for him to rebut the imposture charge. He had been accused of deception before, and was later to be accused again. Yet even Home excepted Williams from his general condemnation of mediums who did not work in the light; 'an honest man' and 'one who shrinks from no reasonable tests'. And Huxley's evidence, though it showed laxity on the part of the investigators, provided no positive evidence of imposture on the part of the medium. Even granted that Williams could have freed a hand and a foot, it would still hardly have been possible for him to have hoisted the chair on to the table without Wedgwood's connivance; and what he had done at the earlier seance could not conceivably have been done without the assistance of a confederate. A few days later, too, Crookes and Cox were to test him. In a locked, sealed room, according to Cox, with only the three of them present

an armchair and a heavy oak dining-room chair were brought from the other side of the room, a distance of seven feet from us, and placed *upon* the table at which we were seated. A large china jug, nearly two feet high and weighty, was brought up from the sideboard and placed before us. A heavy musical box was wound up, lifted from the table, and carried round the room, playing the whole time. A handbell was repeatedly taken from the table and rung violently at each corner of the room and up at the ceiling. Asked that it might be brought nearer to me, it was immediately brought from a distant corner of the room, then circled round my head for several minutes, ringing furiously, until I was almost deafened by the noise and begged that it would cease the din; a request refused for some time. My watch was taken from my pocket, wound up, and returned to me.

The value of this experiment, Cox explained, was not in the novelty of the phenomena, which had been repeatedly witnessed, but in the proof which it had provided that conjuring had been impossible; when securely held in that way, no conjuror could perform such tricks unless he had a confederate. And it was no illusion: 'after the experiment had ended, the chairs and jug were upon the table and the furniture of the room displaced'.

Impressive though such an exhibition might be, Crookes naturally preferred to work with a medium who did not insist upon total darkness; and by this time, Florence Cook was showing herself capable of producing materialisations of 'Katie King' in circumstances which left him in no doubt they were genuine. For total conviction, though, he wanted to see Florence and 'Katie' together at the same time. To do this, he realised, he must win the confidence of 'Katie' when she appeared at seances. Gradually she became more co-operative; and on March 12th she offered him the opportunity he had been waiting for, by asking him to go behind the curtain (which served in his house as the cabinet) to help Florence, who had slipped down off the sofa. Crookes went in, passing 'Katie' on his way, and lifted Florence back on to it again. On March 29th 'Katie' told him that the spirit force was now powerful enough for him to see them together, behind the curtain; which he did. The spectacle of the two of them had finally confirmed that 'Katie' could not be Florence in disguise. Not that he had been in any doubt, he insisted; sometimes 'Katie' had appeared six inches taller than Florence; her ears were unpierced, whereas Florence wore earrings; here fingers were longer, her face larger than Florence's; and this last seance, though Florence had a large rough blister on the back of her neck, the bare back of 'Katie's' neck had been smooth both to touch and sight.

Crookes's evidence might be convincing to those who had seen materialisation; but if he still had any hopes of impressing the sceptics, he was quickly disillusioned. In his account of the final seance, he described how 'Katie' had put her arm through his

and the impression conveyed to my mind that it was a living woman by my side, instead of a visitor from the other world, was so strong that the temptation to repeat a recent celebrated experiment became almost irresistible. Feeling, however, that if I had not a spirit, I had at all events a *lady* close to me, I asked her permission to clasp her in my arms, so as to be able to verify the interesting observations which a bold experimentalist has recently somewhat verbosely recorded. Permission was graciously given, and I accordingly did – well, what any gentleman would do in the circumstances. Mr. Volckman will be pleased to know that I can corroborate his statement that the 'ghost' (not 'struggling', however) was as material a being as Miss Cook herself.

To Crookes, this must have seemed the neatest of ripostes, demonstrating how wrong it was 'to draw an important conclusion from an insufficient amount of evidence'. But the notion of Crookes, a respectable married man with a family, embracing a spirit form was risible; and to make matters worse, he described 'Katie' in terms more appropriate to a lover. 'Photography is as inadequate to depict the perfect beauty of Katie's face, as words are powerless to describe her charm of manner,' he claimed; although photography might show her countenance, it could not reproduce 'the brilliant purity of her complexion, or the ever-varying expression of her most mobile features'. Not merely did this make it unnecessary to take the experiments seriously (as Maskelyne put it in his broadside against Spiritualism two years later, 'the "scientist" who writes like this – and clasps the beautiful and substantial spirit in his arms – is much too far gone for "investigation" '), it also left Crookes open to the charge that in his infatuation he had allowed Florence to dupe him – or worse, to seduce him into collusion with her.

Rosina Showers

A more serious blow to Crookes's prospects, though, than the ridicule of his critics was the loss of his medium. In April Florence married Captain Edward Corner; and although seances continued, the following month 'Katie King' announced that she would materialise no more. There were other mediums available, including Mrs. Fay; but she was a professional, and an expensive one to hire. A more promising recruit was Rosina Showers, who had already produced a number of striking materialisations; the daughter of a general, she refused payment for seances. The fact that she fell under suspicion of cheating that summer – a sitter claimed he had seen her pretending to be the spirit, by appearing at the cabinet aperture herself – did not worry Crookes, as he had devised another and simpler test to ensure that the spirit was not the medium in disguise: a bowl of dye, in which the medium dipped her hands. Florence Cook passed the test and even when Rosina Showers did not, he was prepared to reserve judgment because 'the evidence in her favour is *very* strong'; five or six people had declared they had seen Rosina and her spirit 'Florence' at the same time (confusingly, Rosina's spirit guide also identified herself as another 'Florence'). Further seances gave such satisfactory results that his suspicions were lulled until, in the autumn of 1875, Rosina confessed to Mrs Fay that she had been cheating.

Embarrassing though this was, it would not in itself have destroyed Crookes's confidence: a medium who produced genuine results might, after all, be tempted to cheat if the results were not forthcoming. But at this point Crookes made an unwise move; perhaps from kind-heartedness, perhaps to escape humiliation, perhaps both. He arranged a meeting with her to persuade her to give up cheating, promising he would not make the exposure public if she did. Finding out about the meeting Rosina's mother – as Crookes wrote to tell Home – 'put the worst construction on it'. Bound by his promise to Rosina, Crookes could not explain; and, as a result, found himself with 'the reputation of a Don Juan'. The furious Mrs. Showers even forged letters over his name; and one of her friends circulated scandal about him. 'I have worked hard and sacrificed more than anyone would believe for the cause of Spiritualism, and I have met with little but calumny, slander, backbiting and abuse from Spiritualists,' his letter to Home concluded; 'to anyone else I would not take the trouble to make these explanations, but I look upon you as one of the real friends I have, and I would not spare any trouble to retain your friendship and good opinion.' So disgusted was he – he wrote in a further letter – 'that *were it not for the regard we bear to you*, I would cut the whole Spiritual connection, and never read, speak, or think of the subject again'.

Crookes, though, was fortunate. As he was able to obtain a written withdrawal of all the allegations Mrs. Showers had made, he discontinued the legal action which he had begun, thus sparing himself what would certainly have been unpleasant publicity, and enabling him to concentrate once again on his scientific research. 'I am so busy with scientific matters,' he told Home, 'that I have no time to spare for fruitless controversy.' The 'scientific matters' were of profound importance. In April, just after the climax of his seances with Florence Cook, he demonstrated his radiometer, the first fruit of his research with vacuum tubes which, in Sir Cyril Hinshelwood's opinion, 'changed the whole conception of chemistry and physics'. Henceforth he concentrated upon work in this and allied fields. He did not lose his belief in the phenomena, or his trust in the mediums he had originally worked with; but his days as a psychical researcher were over.

Chapter Twenty-eight
Henry Slade

UP TO THIS POINT, ALTHOUGH ACCUSATIONS OF TRICKERY HAD BEEN common, no well-known medium in Britain had been brought to trial for fraud. In the autumn of 1876 two mediums were charged, tried, and found guilty. One of the cases was a minor *cause célèbre* in which the medium, Henry Slade, was convicted in London of practising deception under the Vagrancy Acts, and sentenced to three months' hard labour; when the verdict was upset by a Court of Appeal on a technicality and a fresh prosecution was pending, he managed to escape to the Continent. Coming as this did at the same time as Crookes's humiliation, its effect on psychical research was serious; along with the 'Katie King' affair, it was to be the chief ground for dismissing the whole movement as fraudulent.

The Slade affair, though, was not as simple as looked. A tiresome problem in communicating with the spirits, researchers had found, was the time-consuming nature of the standard 'alphabet and raps' method. Slade was one of the practitioners of new technique: slate-writing. Various methods were used, the commonest being for the medium to take a child's slate, put a crumb of pencil lead on it, and hold it face upwards under the flap of a table, the fingers under, and the thumb on top of the flap; after a few seconds, scraping noises would be heard, and a scrawled message would be found on the slate. 'Dr.' Slade (mediums sometimes accepted the designation, in the same spirit as a conjuror often described himself as 'Professor'; but a medical degree was then easily come by, and Slade may have earned or bought it) was tested in this capacity by one of the investigators of mesmerism in America, Robert Collyer; and Collyer, though he was impressed neither by the messages, which he found often trivial and sometimes ridiculous, nor by Slade's belief that they came from his late wife, satisfied himself that they could not have been produced by any trick. Even when he brought his own slates, and gave Slade no chance either to tamper with them or to substitute his own, the messages continued to appear. 'I am as satisfied on the genuineness of the automatic writing presented by Henry Slade,' Collyer wrote, 'as I am of my own existence, or that the sun gives light.'

Arriving on a visit to England in the summer of 1876, Slade quickly established himself. In August Cox tested Slade on behalf of a Psychological Society which he had founded following the Crookes experiments with Home. Cox was far from credulous – he was as anxious to detect and expose cheats as any sceptic; but he was unable to fault Slade. The room, he reported, was sunlit; and from where he sat he could clearly see below as well as above the surface of the table at which Slade sat, with his hands placed on top of it. First, rappings were heard, turning into 'furious blows' as if of a sledgehammer. Slate-writing followed, with Cox's hand on the slate, and Slade's hand on his (he was holding Slade's other hand); he could actually feel, as well as hear, the pressure on the slate as something was written on it. Although the messages turned out to be trite, Cox was impressed by the fact that the slate was dragged from his grasp at one point, and placed on his head, where the writing continued; the message being, 'Man must not doubt any more, when we can come in this way. J.F. M.D.' – 'J.F.' explaining that he had been the Queen's physician, the John Forbes who had tested and doubted Alexis Didier. A large, heavy armchair then 'rushed forward from the corner of the room', as if wishing to be near the table: and although both Slade's hands were visible, a hand seized and shook Cox's leg. Cox was convinced; but it was the penalty for anybody who had already admitted to a belief in the existence of a psychic force that he ceased henceforth to be regarded as a detached observer. A few days later, however, Slade was tested by Dr. Carter Blake, the former Secretary of the Anthropological Society of Great Britain; and in a meticulous, at times prissy, report he described how the spirit-writing included material known to him which could not have been known to Slade; how the table had levitated, when both his and Slade's hands were on it, and his feet on Slade's; how hands had appeared, casting a shadow in the sunlight on the table and on his waistcoat. Blake had removed his boots, and put them behind him, the better to ensure that he could detect any movement Slade made with his feet; suddenly, the right boot was thrown over his head. To see if the invisible thrower would co-operate, he asked if the other boot could be moved more gently to a chair; but 'before the words were out of my mouth, it was thrown on the table, striking the hands of Dr. Slade and myself, and producing slight excoriation in his case, and ecchymosis in mine'. All this time, Slade's hands were on Blake's, on the table, and Blake's feet on Slade's; 'no possible motion on any part of his body could have produced any of those effects'.

It was time, Professor E. Ray Lankester decided, to call the Spiritualists' bluff. Still in his twenties, but already a Professor of Zoology, he had inherited aggressive scepticism from his father, who had been one of the chief scourgers of Elliotson and the mesmerists. In a letter to *The Times*, published on September 16th, Lankester described how he had seances with Slade and, in the second, had allowed Slade to hold a slate under the table. Before the 'spirit' could begin to write, Lankester had snatched the slate away, and found that the message was already on it; a deception for which he proposed to bring Slade to justice.

The letter drew a brisk correspondence (fear of contempt of court proceedings had not yet inhibited pre-trial controversy), with letters from one of the barristers briefed for the defence, Charles Massey, and from Wallace pointing out that writings sometimes appeared on slates which Slade had not been allowed even to touch; Slade himself also wrote to *The Times* to claim that the spirit-writing had in fact been heard before the slate was snatched away; but this was denied by Lankester and by Horatio Donkin, a physician at the Westminster Hospital who had accompanied him to the seance.

Slade was charged under the Vagrancy Acts, with 'unlawfully using subtle craft, means and devices to deceive and impose upon certain of Her Majesty's subjects' – Lankester, Donkin, and others known to have attended seances, who were to be subpoenaed to give evidence. The first hearing, on October 2nd, was occupied by the evidence of Lankester (his 'heavy-jawed, pig-like face' repelled one critical spectator of the proceedings, Georgina Weldon); and when nearly all the second day's proceedings, too, were given over to Lankester even *The Times*'s court reporter's coverage took on an acerbic tinge. The 'wretched little court', he complained, was 'most inconveniently thronged', and the street outside almost impassable, because of the interest the case had aroused. What Lankester had to say 'amounted to a mere reiteration of the evidence'; and although he had repeatedly been referred to by the prosecution as a skilful observer, Lankester himself had had to admit that he had 'no pretensions to that character'; he could not explain how Slade's tricks were accomplished. All he was prepared to assert with confidence was that they must have *been* tricks, because the celebrated conjuror John Maskelyne had shown how the table had been designed for that purpose. It had specially constructed flaps, movable bars and wedges not found on ordinary tables, but essential to hold the slate, leaving Slade's fingers free to write on it, and to produce the raps.

The table was itself then produced as an exhibit; and Maskelyne was called to give evidence. 'From this point,' *The Times*'s reporter commented, 'the character of the inquiry became absolutely farcical.' Maskelyne proceeded to demonstrate how he thought the trick must have been done, with the aid of a pencil shaped like a thimble; and although defence counsel objected and Mr. Justice Flowers wondered whether a court of law was really a fit place for such a demonstration, Maskelyne, 'undaunted by these protests', continued to 'rattle on with his theme'. The table also gave the prosecution the excuse for the second of their charges. Slade's assistant, who had been prosecuted with him, had given the order and specified how the table was to be constructed; by doing so, he had identified himself as Slade's partner; and consequently the two men could be charged with conspiracy – a useful insurance in case the vagrancy charge should fail in law.

This was a blow to the defence; but soon, there was unexpected compensation. The prosecution had decided to subpoena R. H. Hutton to give evidence; at first sight a clever move, as Hutton was the shrewd, sceptical editor of the *Spectator* ('perfectly fearless', one of his contributors, Harry Quilter, was to describe him, 'so unblemished that during a long life no one ever dared to whisper a word against him'). He could be relied upon to describe whatever he had seen without prevarication; and he did. He had attended seances, he told the court; and though he had his doubts about some of the effects, there were many which he could not account for by sleight-of-hand. For example, a handbell which had been placed on the floor had moved. Had it merely moved along the floor, he could have suspected that Slade had managed to kick it; but it had risen up, floated over the table between him and Slade, and sunk to the floor on the other side. The evidence of the foreman carpenter on whose premises the table had been made also turned out to be embarrassing for the prosecution. The table had been constructed, he confirmed, to a particular specification; but this was to provide greater simplicity – for example, by having one support for each flap, instead of the normal two. It was not easy to see how this could help a conjuror. As for the wedges to which Maskelyne had drawn attention, alleging they were used to make the raps, the carpenter had to admit they had not been in the Slade specification; they had had to be inserted after the table had been made, to compensate for a piece of faulty workmanship.

At this point the prosecution decided to risk no more subpoenas; wisely, as the next witness on their list, Serjeant Cox, was to give evidence for the defence – in writing, as he was indisposed – describing again what he had seen at the Slade seance. But when the defence began to call further witnesses – starting with Wallace, who agreed with Cox that the effects which he had observed could not have been produced by sleight-of-hand – Flowers laid down that he would permit only four; and in his judgment, which followed, he explained why. The court was required to answer only two questions: was what Slade had done an offence? And if so, had Slade committed it? To the first question, the answer was 'Yes' (under the Vagrancy Law, which meant that it was unnecessary to fall back on the conspiracy charge). And in answering the second, Flowers ruled, the evidence of those witnesses who, like Cox and Wallace, had not attended the same seances as Lankester was 'irrelevant'. All the court had to concern itself with was whether Slade had used 'subtle craft' to try to deceive Lankester; and as 'according to the well-known course of nature' there could be no other explanation, Slade must be guilty. 'Considering the great mischiefs likely to result from such practices – mischiefs which those who remember the case of Home, also a professional medium, cannot consider unsubstantial,' Flowers felt that he could not mitigate the punishment the law imposed: three months' hard labour.

Two months later, the Court of Appeal rejected the verdict because the words 'by palmistry or otherwise' had inadvertently been omitted from the indictment; and Lankester announced that he would bring a fresh prosecution. Slade was in an unenviable situation. If he went to the Continent, as he had been invited to do, it would be alleged that he was a fugitive from justice. Before his trial, in fact, when friends had urged him to leave on the ground that it would not be fair, he had refused. Now, he had been shown that the courts not merely would not, but *could* not be fair, because Flowers had made it clear that his verdict had been based on the assumption that spirit-writing was contrary to the laws of nature. If this were the judicial view, Slade could have no hope of escaping conviction. He accordingly left for the Continent, writing to Lankester offering to come back to England to be tested, but only with a safe conduct. Lankester did not reply; and Slade did not return.

The Zöllner Investigation

Had Slade then disappeared from public view, the case would soon have been forgotten. But he was on his way to Germany, following an invitation to come to Leipzig to be tested by Johann Zöllner, Professor of Physics and Astronomy (the two disciplines still often ran in harness). Still in his early forties, Zöllner had already acquired an international reputation. He was not then interested in Spiritualism; but reading about the associated phenomena, he had been struck by the possibility that materialisation and de-materialisation might relate to a project dear to his mind: research which would demonstrate the existence, or at least the likelihood, of a fourth dimension. The mathematical evidence, he believed, was already there. What he needed was experimental verification. Nothing, he thought, could be more convincing than 'the transport of material bodies from a space enclosed on every side'.

To explain why, he offered as an analogy the difficulty which a two-dimensional being would have in visualising a third dimension.

Suppose a plane, a figure of dimensions enclosed by a line on every side; in which is a movable object. By movements only in the plane, that object could not escape from the interior of that two-dimensionally enclosed space, otherwise than by an opening of the line of enclosure. But if the object were capable of a movement in the third dimension, it would need only to be raised perpendicularly to the plane, to be passed over and let down again on the other side of the line. To two-dimensional beings who reasoned on the assumption that *only* such movements were possible as they could intuitively represent to themselves, i.e. only two-dimensional movements, the proceeding just described would seem a miracle. For the body which they suppose to be *completely* enclosed must, at a certain spot, transiently vanish for them, in order suddenly to reappear at another spot.

If he could demonstrate its validity, Zöllner's hypothesis of a fourth dimension would not merely present a reasonably intelligible explanation for phenomena incomprehensible to people accustomed only to three; it would also provide the groundwork for a new conception of physics. He was consequently predisposed in Slade's favour; and therefore, it could be argued, susceptible to Slade's guile. But Zöllner was no innocent. Some of his best work had been done in research into sensory illusions. In any case, he was aware that he would need independent testimony; and he asked some colleagues to collaborate with him.

One of them, Professor Gustav Fechner, the pioneer of psychophysics (which at that time appeared to be on the way to becoming one of the major academic disciplines, though soon it was to split up into specialist segments), already had some experience in the field. In the late 1860s, Baron Reichenbach had made what turned out to be his last efforts to secure scientific support for his theories about sensitives and the odic force; and he had gone to Leipzig to try to convert Fechner, who had been one of his most caustic critics. Reichenbach's sensitive, Mme. Ruf, had fallen ill on the journey, and her psychic powers had diminished; but she was able to deflect a compass needle by making passes over it with her fingers, and this impressed Fechner, because he employed instruments which registered changes in the magnetic field and which would have immediately detected any concealed device. A few other experiments also had promising results; and Fechner had realised that he would have to modify his earlier opinions. But Reichenbach's powers, like his medium's, were failing. He was in his eighties, already worried 'at the thought of having to die without having obtained recognition for his system', and in 1869, as a chastened Fechner recalled, 'such was the tragic fate which actually befell him'.

Also collaborating with Zöllner was Wilhelm Weber, Professor of Physics at Leipzig – and Weber, along with Gauss, had been one of the leading innovators in electro-magnetism, and the inventor of the machine by which Fechner had been able to monitor Mme. Ruf. Wilhelm Scheibner, Professor of Mathematics, also attended; and other colleagues came to some of the seances. In a series of tests in 1877–8 the investigators obtained results which exceeded even Zöllner's hopes. The seances began with the standard slate-writing, and went on to tests with a compass needle which eventually, after some difficulty, Slade managed to cause to oscillate. Poltergeist-type phenomena soon began to be observed. A pen-knife leapt into the air, and fell back with its blade opened. Furniture, out of Slade's reach, began to move around. A wooden screen suddenly split across with a resounding crack (the slate-writing which followed explained 'it was not our intention to do harm. Forgive what has happened'). A string which Zöllner was holding tied itself in knots, without Slade touching it. An accordion played while Scheibner was holding it with one hand, at the end away from the keys. A bell, left standing upright on the floor, began to ring, though nobody was near.

As the experiments proceeded, the manifestations proliferated, as if encouraged by the investigators' favourable reception. A candle lit itself, the spirits explaining 'fire is everywhere', and reminding them that flint could draw a spark. While Zöllner and Weber were watching Slade, Scheibner felt his jacket being unbuttoned; his gold watch was taken out and placed in his hand. The following day a small table suddenly disappeared; later it floated down from the ceiling, giving Zöllner a painful blow on the head. For a decisive proof Zöllner asked Slade if he could arrange for two rings, each carved from a single piece of wood so that there were no joins, to be interlinked. When they were next examined they were not interlinked; but both were wrapped around a table leg, in such a way that they could not be taken off (and could not have been put on) without taking the table to pieces. When asked to leave some memento of itself, the spirit even obliged with the impression of a human foot on some sooted paper.

Zöllner and his colleagues could hardly have had a more comprehensive demonstration of psychic forces at work, especially as Slade had no companion who might have worked as a confederate. And they were not alone in their admiration: Baron Lazar von Hellenbach, who tested Slade in Vienna in 1878, was similarly impressed. When it was pointed out that scientists, however brilliant, might easily be taken in by sleight-of-hand, Slade agreed to demonstrate for the Court conjuror in Berlin, Samuel Bellachini; and in December 1877 Bellachini provided him with a duly witnessed affidavit.

After I had, at the wish of several highly esteemed gentlemen of rank and position, and also for my own interest, tested the physical mediumship of Mr. Slade in a series of sittings by full daylight, as well as in the evening in his room, I must for the sake of the truth hereby certify that the phenomenal occurrences with Mr. Slade have been thoroughly examined by me with the minutest observation and investigation of his surroundings, including the table, and I have not in the smallest degree found anything to be produced by means of prestidigitation or by mechanical apparatus; and that any explanation of the experiments which took place under the circumstances and conditions then obtaining, by any reference to prestidigitation, to be absolutely impossible.

Most of Zöllner's fellow-scientists, though, felt his account was simply ludicrous. Spirit hand unbuttoning jackets, rings wrapping themselves round table legs, footmarks in soot; it was all too much! Either Zöllner and his colleagues must have been duped by a rogue – and Slade, after all, had been convicted as such by an English court – or they must have been suffering from delusions. Rudolf Virchow, the foremost pathologist of his day, had boasted that what he most prided himself on was 'the knowledge of my ignorance'; and in an address on the need for science to avoid making the mistakes of religion in the past, he claimed that he always said to himself, dealing with any new subject, 'now thou must begin again to learn'. But when asked to undertake tests on Slade, Virchow said he would only agree to them if Slade allowed himself to be bound hand and foot. Slade jibbed. He had earlier submitted to such conditions, only to find that it merely encouraged others, still dissatisfied, to try to devise yet more effective bonds. What the investigators were really after was some means of preventing the occurrence of the phenomena, 'instead of being content to witness them'; the object of investigation, Slade contended, ought to be to see whether the phenomena could be produced. To this end he was perfectly willing to be subjected to the same conditions as any other scientific experimenter carrying out tests in full daylight, such as observers to check the movements of his hand and feet. He was not prepared, though, to submit to humiliations of a kind which no scientist would accept. Reasonable though this explanation was, it gave Virchow and others who thought like him the chance to excuse themselves from pursuing the inquiry; and this in turn gave other scientists the chance to dismiss Slade as somebody who would not submit him-self to properly-controlled tests.

William Stainton Moses

There was one other medium from this period whose work cannot be ignored, though it was hardly known by his contemporaries because he refused to give public seances, or to submit to tests. Ordinarily this would have excluded him from serious consideration; but William Stainton Moses was not an ordinary medium. As a young man he had entered the Church of England, working for a time as a curate, until illness had forced him to resign. Then he had begun to teach English at University College School in London, and to give tuition to the children of a physician, Dr. Stanhope Speer. In 1872, when he was thirty-three, he began to have the psychic experiences which were to continue for the next ten years.

For a time they came sporadically, unbidden; as on an occasion in the summer of 1873 described by Cox. Moses had come round to Cox's house to change before they went out to a dinner; and while they were sitting together before leaving – Cox dealing with his correspond-ence, Moses reading *The Times* – the sound of powerful blows came from the dining-room table. It was an old-fashioned, heavy mahogany table, which the combined physical strength of two men hardly sufficed to move; but it began to quiver; then to rock so violently 'as almost to dislocate the big pillar-like legs' (of which there were eight); then to move around. Nothing like this, Moses remarked, had ever happened to him before; and Cox realised that it was an invaluable opportunity to see if they could exercise any control over the force, to obtain move-ments without actual contact.

Accordingly we stood upright, he on one side of the table, I on the other side of it. We stood two feet from it, and held our hands eight inches above it. In one minute it rocked violently. Then it moved over the carpet a distance of seven inches. Then it rose three inches from the floor on the side on which my friend was standing. Then it rose equally on my side. Finally, my friend held his hands four inches over the end of the table, and asked that it would rise and touch his hand three times. It did so; and then, in accordance with the like request, it rose to my hand, held at the other end to the same height above it, and in the same manner.

In time Moses began to acquire some control over the spirit forces, as he believed them to be; helped by his spirit guides. He and the Speers began a long series of seances at which the familiar effects were ob-tained: rappings, table-tiltings and the rest. Luminosities were frequent; globes of light, occasionally taking some particular form. Waves of perfume were a constant accompaniment; 'sometimes the aroma of a flower from the garden is drawn out, intensified and insinuated throughout the house,' he wrote; 'sometimes the odour is like nothing of this earth's production, ethereal, delicate and infinitely delightful'. And a particularly common feature was the translocation of objects. They would appear on the table, though there was no way by which they could get into the seance room. Or they would appear to have been thrown; 'I have more than once been struck on the top of the head by objects as they have been converging on the table; and on one occasion a heavy bronze candlestick, which was brought from the mantelshelf in a room near, struck me a severe blow.' This was later to be confirmed by Charlton Speer, one of Moses' pupils.

The passage of matter through matter was sometimes strikingly demonstrated by bringing from other rooms various articles through closed and bolted doors. Photographs, picture frames, books and other objects were frequently so brought, from rooms on the same floor and from those above as well. How they came through the closed doors I cannot say, except by some process of de-materialisation; but come they certainly did, apparently none the worse for that process, whatever it might have been.

There were also examples of clairvoyance, and some of levitation. 'My sensation was that of being lighter than the air,' Moses wrote. 'There was no pressure on any part of the body; no unconsciousness or entrancement'; the ascent was gradual and steady, 'not unlike being in a lift but without any perceptible sensation of motion other than that of feeling lighter than the atmosphere'.

Moses' chief contribution to the development of Spiritualism, though, was his spirit writing. It was of two kinds, which he distinguished as 'automatic writing', where the medium held a pen or a 'planchette' – a pencil supported by castors above a board, on which the medium placed his fingertips – and his spirit guide wrote through him; or 'psychography', where the writing appeared to be done by the spirits, either invisibly, on slates, or with the disembodied hands familiar from accounts of Home seances.

As recounted in his *Spirit Teaching* (published like his other works under the pseudonym 'M.A. Oxon.') Moses' spirit writing marked a new development. He put the questions; the spirits answered; and their answers, though couched in Bible-ese, were thoughtful and shrewd. When he presented the orthodox Anglican case, 'Imperator' and other spirits worked with considerable skill to wean him from it, taking care not to offend him by attacking Jesus, but arguing that later dogmatic accretions had twisted Jesus's gospel out of recognition. When he objected that their version would not be recognised as Christian by Christians, they went to his heart by expounding orthodoxy's version:

> You have been taught in the creeds of the orthodox churches to believe in a God who was propitiated by the sacrifice on His Son, so far as to allow a favoured few of His children to be admitted to an imagined heaven, where forever and forevermore, with monotonous persistence, their occupation should be singing His praise. The rest of the race, unable to gain admission to this heaven, were consigned to a hell of indescribable torment, perpetual, endless and intolerable.

Did Moses really believe that all the people who failed to qualify for heaven – because they lacked faith, or lived in evil surroundings, or were seduced into sin, or could not understand what was required of them, or had doctrinal objections, or had failed to carry out a prescribed ritual – were everlastingly damned? Put that way, Moses had to admit, 'Imperator's' argument was 'rational and beautiful'. It was certainly coherent and well-expressed, suggesting the possibility that Moses' automatic writing was the vehicle by which certain ideas already in his mind could rise to consciousnesss.

Only in one respect did Moses's evidence appear deficient; his refusal to give test seances. The spirits, he claimed, would not allow him to. Most of the accounts, therefore, were either his own or the Speers'. But as Frederic Myers recalled after Moses's death, he had never heard anyone 'who had even the slightest acquaintance with Mr. Moses impugn his sincerity, his veracity, or his honour' – as numerous testimonies to him confirmed; 'the crassest prejudice,' the barrister Charles Massey claimed, 'has recoiled from even suggesting a doubt of the truth and honesty of Stainton Moses'. Going through the accounts of his seances after his death, too, and checking them against those written independently by the Speers, Myers found them consistent; the hypothesis that Moses might unconsciously have cheated in his trance state, he felt, could be ruled out. If there had been fraud, it could only have been with the Speers' collusion. This was surely inconceivable; apart from the risk they would have run to their reputation, they had nothing to gain from privately participating week after week in bogus seances which could secure them neither fame nor fortune. 'I therefore regard the reported phenomena,' Myers was to conclude, 'as having actually occurred in a genuinely supernatural way.'

Middle East and Far East
Apart from the records of the achievements of the leading mediums

in Europe and America there were also, in this period, many reports making it clear that seance phenomena and the techniques associated with them were to be found in other parts of the world, where they had long pre-dated the new Western version of Spiritualism; in the Moslem countries, in India and in China. The earliest work to draw attention to the parallels was Colonel Charles Churchill's *Mount Lebanon,* based on ten years' experience of the country, published in 1853. He had come greatly to admire the Sheik Bechir, whom he regarded as the best informed of the Druses, and who was an accomplished medium. He would place a jug between two people sitting opposite each other, and after some readings from the Koran, the jug would begin to move around without being touched. More surprising manifestations some-times followed; an egg boiling in a saucepan had sprung suddenly out of the water and been carried a considerable distance. Bechir's ex-planation was that, like Aladdin, he was able to summon Djinns to his assistance. There could be no doubt, Churchill felt, that he sincerely believed in these unseen creatures, resembling disembodied humans, who were 'at the bidding of those who choose to devote themselves earnestly to such intercourse'; a belief universal in the Lebanon, even among the Christians there (who also regraded the psalms as having been written for a divinatory purpose: if they were properly under-stood, he was told, they could 'place the whole world of spirits entirely at men's disposal and invest them, through their medium, with miracu-lous powers'). And Churchill, though he would not commit himself to a belief in Djinns, was in no doubt that some unseen influences must be at work. He could have produced instances of an even more extra-ordinary and unaccountable kind, he claimed; but 'as the ears of Europeans could only be shocked by assertions and statements which they would not fail of holding to be utterly fabulous and ridiculous', he had preferred not to.

A former Secretary to the U.S. Legation in Constantinople, John P. Brown, was less inhibited. In *The Dervishes, or Oriental Spiritualism* he contrasted at length the debased religions of the Western world, which were nothing but 'the outward expression of belief, accompanied by various forms of worship and external ceremonies' – with the noble Spiritualism he had found among the Dervish tribesmen.

European visitors to India often described the magic of the fakirs: men who in the course of their yoga training had reached the stage where they had acquired certain powers, and had then retired from the pursuit of Nirvana to make a living out of them. In his *Recollections of Northern India* 1848 William Buyers had recalled how one of them, summoned to help a friend of his who had lost a pair of gold spectacles, had assembled the friend's servants before producing a small brass pot, which he said would identify the thief; the pot had proceeded to glide across the floor until it stopped in front of one of the servants, who immediately confessed his guilt. Curious about these fakirs, Louis Jacolliot, Chief Justice in French East India in the 1860s, tested some of them under conditions he laid down to prevent trickery. They had to come to his house with no assistants, wearing nothing but a linen slip, and using only such materials as he provided. Some were unable to perform in such conditions; but a few, he found, could move objects without contact. One of them succeeded in lowering one side of a pair of scales by placing a feather on it, though on the other side there was an eighty-kilo weight. And in 1866 Jacolliot had the opportunity to test the most celebrated of the fakirs, Covindasamy. Taken outside to Jacolliot's terrace, Covindasamy was able to cause an 'immense' bronze vase full of water to rock, and then to move to and fro, following Jacolliot's instructions; giving forth, at the same time, noises as if it were being struck by a rod. Covindasamy was also able to levitate himself, in the cross-legged sitting position, to a height of two feet; his only contact with the ground being a thin Ceylon cane of Jacolliot's which could not conceivably have borne his weight. Indoors, Covindasamy could materialise hands which looked and felt human; also flowers. When he left, sounds continued to come from the walls, and within the room. Jacolliot had suspected that he must have been the victim of hallucinations; it was only when he read Crookes's account of his experiments that he realised what he had witnessed might actually have happened.

From the Far East, too, travellers and missionaries frequently reported spiritist practices. The Russian traveller and savant Tsherepanoff described in 1856 how a Tibetan lama traced missing property: after meditation, he placed his hands on a bench, which levitated and floated ahead of him at eye level, to guide him; when it took him to a certain hut, the owner committed suicide, and the goods were found inside. The French missionary Evariste Huc, travelling through China and Tartary in the 1840s, encountered a lama who could fill a vase full of water by prayer (though he admitted that he could not do so when anybody not of his faith was present); and learned that the spirits often replied to questions by rappings, or playing notes on a tambourine. And other missionaries, arriving in China after the first opium war, found divination in widespread use by a variety of techniques, including a version of planchette. In *The Folklore of China*, published in 1870, Nicholas Dennys described the Chinese method, in which the writing was done with the help of a pointed walking-stick shaped like a capital 'T'. The medium balanced the 'T' on his open, face-up palms, leaving the pointer free to trace Chinese characters in the sand-table above which he stood. Dennys did not believe that spirits were responsible for the messages; but observation convinced him that the characters were not being deliberately drawn by the muscular action of the medium.

On his travels Richard Burton, too, had become convinced of the reality of a psychic element. During the Slade trial he had been mentioned as an authority in such matters; and he had written to *The Times*, describing himself as a 'spiritualist without the spirits', to explain that twenty years' experience had convinced him, first that 'perception is possible without the ordinary channels of the seances' and second, 'that I have been in the presence of a force, or a power, call it what you will, evidently and palpably material – if, at least, man be made of matter'.

Rectory Parlour to White House

There were also, in this period, an uncountable number of reports in books, tracts, magazines, newspapers and private correspondence of seances, some planned, some played as a game, in establishments ranging from rural rectories to the White House – where Abraham Lincoln attended one in 1863. Tables moved; a picture of Henry Clay swung on the wall; two candelabra were raised nearly to the ceiling; and there was the usual accompaniment of rappings. But Lincoln shrewdly declined to commit himself. The fact that he had attended a seance would suffice to satisfy the Spiritualists, still numerous among the electorate; but the gently bantering attitude he adopted during the seance (when a bevy of spirits, including former Defence Secretary Henry Knox, Napoleon, Lafayette and Franklin, all gave him contradictory advice on how to run the war, he sardonically commented 'much like my cabinet'), and his assertion after it, that though he had 'seen strange things' he was still not convinced, would reassure the sceptics.

Perhaps recollecting what had happened to Hare, American scientists had shied away from psychical research, and there were few reports of serious investigations in this period; but it was in the United States that spirit photography was first reported and investigated. It initially attracted public notice through a court case in New York in 1869, for which Greeley's *Tribune* could recall no parallel in the annals of criminal jurisprudence. A Broadway photographer, William H. Mumler, was charged with false pretences; with having duped citizens into having their photographs taken by persuading them that he would also bring up the face of some dear one who had died. Mumler ('calm and fathomless' the *Tribune* reporter noted) explained that he had been neither a photographer nor a Spiritualist when, as a young man in Boston, he took some pictures in the house of a photographer friend, and found what appeared to be human figures on them. At first he attributed them to some imperfection either in the plates, or in his technique; but when the figures began to appear frequently, and to be recognised, he had gone into business as a spirit photographer, soon obtaining more work than he could cope with. Among the witnesses who gave evidence on his behalf (his counsel claimed that five hundred respectable people would be prepared to testify that genuine likenesses of some dead relative or friend had been obtained) was the banker Charles Livermore. Livermore had gone to Mumler out of curiosity, taking him to be an accomplished trickster. Mumler had permitted him to supervise all the arrangements and watch the development of the pictures; yet a portrait of Livermore's wife, who had died eight years before, had emerged on the print, and Livermore's friends had admitted it was unmistakably her.

To a Spiritualist there was nothing odd in the camera's ability to pick up what the medium could 'see'. In his evidence on behalf of Mumler, Judge Edmonds tried to explain for the court's benefit how such pictures might be, if not accounted for, at least made less inexplicable. A few days before, he had been trying a case in Brooklyn, in connection with the disposal of a life insurance policy which had been held by a man he had not met or heard of before.

Looking toward that part of the courtroom occupied by the jury, I saw the spirit of the man whose death was the basis of the suit. The spirit told me the circumstances connected with the death; said that the suit was groundless, that the claimant was not entitled to recover from the company, and said that he had committed suicide under certain circumstances. I drew a diagram of the place at which his death occurred, and on showing it to the counsel, was told that it was exact in every particular.

If a spirit could impinge on the human mind in this way, Edmonds argued, it could impose itself on a negative. Impressed by the weight of testimony in Mumler's favour, the judge acquitted him; and in correspondence which followed in the *Tribune* there was a further testimonial which in one respect was even more impressive, as it came from a professional rival. William Slee of Poughkeepsie described how he had challenged Mumler to undertake tests, using Slee's camera and facilities, and allowing Slee and his assistants to develop the pictures. Slee had offered a fifty-dollar reward to any assistant who could find out how Mumler did it, and arranged that he should be watched through a peephole at times when he was left alone. No deception could be detected; yet spirit forms had appeared.

The idea of spirit faces and forms appearing on photographic negatives proved as hard for the public to swallow as materialisation. The human mind might be capable of receiving such impressions; but surely they could not be picked up by any mechanical device? In the phrase that was to become a cliché, 'the camera cannot lie', the assumption was that the spirit portraits must be ingeniously faked, as they easily could be. In 1875 Edward Buguet, who had worked with Kardec and had made a considerable reputation because his spirits were so often adjudged by his sitters to be accurate portraits of their dead friends, rather than just vague blurred forms, pleaded guilty in Paris to fraud, and confessed to having faked the pictures. Although some of those who had been impressed by him – including William Howitt and Stainton Moses, who had tested his work in London – were convinced that he had been blackmailed, or seduced by the promise of a lighter sentence, the fact that he confessed and that he went to jail for a year, was damaging.

But many of the reports of psychic phenomena are of a kind which deception cannot adequately account for: particularly those of family seances, where there was no professional medium or conjuror, and where collusion would have been pointless; why should a family agree, among themselves, to stage bogus seances, week after week, if they had no intention of showing off to other people, or of publishing the faked results? A Devon vicar, the Rev. P. H. Newnham, found that his wife appeared to have a telepathic faculty, and he began in the early 1870s to experiment with the help of automatic writing, using a planchette. He formulated the questions in his mind, and wrote them down: she (or 'Planchette') provided the answers which, he was intrigued to find, were almost always relevant, but irritatingly uninformative. When he craftily asked by what means his thoughts were conveyed to his wife, 'Planchette' replied 'Electro-biology'; to his next question, 'What is electro-biology?' 'Planchette' simply replied, 'No one knows'.

Such experiments were revealing – or, rather, they could have been: as it was, Newnham's record of his seances with his wife were not to be published until years later when he passed them over to the Society for Psychical Research. The chief characteristic of 'Planchette', as he put it, was 'a perfect appreciation of my thoughts, in the queries; but a strange, persistent, almost dogged incapability of seeing my thoughts in the replies'; an imperfection in the psychic communication system which could have made a fascinating subject for research, but only if it could first be established that a psychic communication system existed. And after thirty years of such varied demonstrations that it did exist, in spite of the support of so influential a minority of scientists and of people in Society, it was no nearer gaining acceptance than it had been in the table-turning era a quarter of a century earlier. Orthodox scientists remained as hostile as ever; and as convinced that there was no need for further inquiry.

Chapter Twenty-nine

Retrospect

TWO MAIN ARGUMENTS WERE COMMONLY USED BY SCIENTISTS AND sceptics for refusing to examine the evidence from psychical research: Huxley's contention that the mental phenomena associated with Spiritualism were too silly to merit the attention of busy men; and Carpenter's, that the physical phenomena could all be accounted for by trickery on the part of the mediums and by illusion or hallucination on the part of their dupes.

'Bosh'

That some Spiritualist phenomena were embarrassingly fatuous was conceded by most psychical researchers. Originally it had been the use of raps as a means of communication which excited ridicule; but Robert Chambers had made the point that the most exalted of living persons might be glad in emergency to 'resort to such a mode of telegraphy' – a neat point, as the telegraph was itself a newcomer. A more telling criticism concerned what the raps, or tilts, or spirit-writings actually communicated. The messages were occasionally surprising, in that they provided information to a sitter of a kind which could not have been known to the medium or anybody else at the seance, apparently coming from somebody who was dead; but as a rule they were excruciatingly banal. Even Home, as Elizabeth Barrett Browning had noticed, in his trance state 'talked a great deal of much such twaddle as may be heard in any fifth rate conventicle'. Sydney Dean, a Connecticut congressman, found in the 1850s that when writing, his hand would sometimes be taken over and guided; although he was aware of what was happening, he could exercise no control over what appeared, which occasionally took the hieroglyphic form, produced with the precision of an engravers tool. 'It is an intelligent ego which writes,' Dean insisted,

or else the influence assumes individuality, which practically makes
of the influence a personality. It is *not* myself; of that I am conscious
at every step of the process. I have also traversed the whole field of
the claims for unconscious cerebration, so-called, so far as I am competent to critically examine it, and it fails as a theory on numberless
fronts, when applied to the strange work through me. The easiest
and most natural solution to me is to admit the claims made, i.e.
that it is a discarnate intelligence who writes. But *who*? That is the
question. The names of scholars and thinkers who once lived are
affixed to the most ungrammatical and weakest of *bosh*.

Dean was referring to the fact that the spirit messages so often purported to come from Aristotle, say, or Napoleon. The triviality of what
they had to say was consequently not only embarrassing in itself, but
was also an unwelcome reminder that the lunatic asylums were full of
inmates who had been incarcerated for making the same kind of claim,
and on similarly flimsy grounds; and this bred disillusionment among
those who accepted that the phenomena were genuine, like Horace
Greeley. Greeley had been impressed when the Fox sisters and another
medium provided him with information about his family which
nobody but himself could have known; and in his *Recollections*, published in 1869 – shortly before he made his unsuccessful bid to become
President – he reiterated his belief that 'jugglery' could not have been
the explanation, because in his experience mediums had been clumsy
children without the necessary skill or training, and also because no
conjuror would have dared to inflict such protracted, boring and often
sterile seances on his audience. Yet he had found the whole business
depressing. Spirit communications were 'vague, unreal, shadowy,
trivial'; the information which they provided was rarely of any value;
and Spiritualists were no less bigoted or intolerant than other men.
    Bulwer Lytton reached similar conclusions. He had seen 'astound-
ing' manifestations, along with much rubbish. 'Shakespeare' had come
through on one occasion, and contradicted himself; but when asked
what was Lytton's closest secret he had instantly related it correctly.
After a decade's experience of seances, although he was still convinced
they could be genuine, he felt that their intellectual content was so
meagre that his advice to anybody not of philosophical mind would be
'to trouble his head as little as possible upon the matter'. And spirit
messages could be not merely inaccurate, but deliberately misleading:
even H. D. Jencken had to admit that though the information his wife
Kate Fox provided was often wonderfully accurate, it sometimes became untrustworthy, and remained so for days.
    Why? For Spiritualists who remained Christians there was no prob-

lem: lying spirits had been reported as far back as the Book of Job. In his *Apparitions* in 1873 Newton Crosland suggested another possibility: spirits, too, could be in an evolutionary stage, and the messages purporting to come from great men might be a form of name-dropping adopted by undeveloped, pushful spirits trying to assure themselves of a hearing. Mrs. de Morgan had a simpler proposition: as the spirit messages passed through her medium, who was her maid, were spelled in the way the maid herself spelled, it was reasonable to assume that the content of messages, too, might be affected by the medium's limitations. In any case it could be argued that from a scientific viewpoint the unreliability of the communications was unimportant compared to the simple fact that there was communication on – or so it appeared – a non-material level. Impatience with the content of spirit communications, Harriet Beecher Stowe claimed, was not a valid reason for refusing to investigate them. She had begun to attend seances in the course of a visit to Italy in the 1850s, following the success of *Uncle Tom's Cabin* – every line of which, she said, had been dictated to her 'inner ear by a spirit voice'. But she had remained level-headed on the subject. In her correspondence with George Eliot she recommended Robert Dale Owen's *Footfalls*, because he was one of the few men 'capable of entering into an inquiry of this kind without an utter drowning of common sense'; and she emphasised that she was perfectly aware

of the frivolity and worthlessness of much of the revealings purporting to come from spirits. In my view, the worth or worthlessness of them has nothing to do with the question of fact . . . I reward them simply as I do the phenomena of the Aurora Borealis, or Darwin's studies of natural selection, as curious studies into nature. Besides, I think some day we shall find a law by which all these facts will fall into their places.

The British Spiritualist Andrew Leighton ingeniously contended that the absurd nature of much of the evidence could, in fact, be taken as an indication that there must be something behind it. 'When one surveys the immense quantity of trash,' he wrote,

which is published as veritable communications from the spiritual and celestial sphere, the ignorance, incompetence and inflation of so many of its professors, and the preposterous pretensions which are promulgated in its name, one cannot but acknowledge that Spiritualism must indeed rest upon a wide foundation of indubitable and adamantine facts, to sustain so great a load of garbage and not sink into oblivion, overwhelmed by derision and contempt.

Trickery

The assumption that the physical effects produced by mediums were achieved by conjuring tricks was derived partly from Maskelyne's stage shows, dating from the time when he had demonstrated that he could do whatever Home and the Davenports claimed to be able to do. But T. A. Trollope, who went to watch him, derided his performance as bearing no resemblance to Home's; and Moses pointed out that there was in any case no comparison between what a medium could do alone in a seance room, and what Maskelyne could do only with the help of gadgets and confederates. Maskelyne, he complained, was stooping to illusion

> unworthy of one who passes as so great an artist, and only excusable because he finds it good enough for his purpose in misguiding a credulous public. But were it never so good, what would it prove? Simply that a thing can be imitated when unlimited means of so doing are provided. That is hardly a point which we need to have demonstrated; and if those who lay stress upon it find any comfort in that demonstration they are welcome to it. If, however, they flatter themselves that it extends any further, then they must be advised to commence the study of logic.

Although Maskelyne was willing to be regarded as the man who had shown how the mediums did their tricks, he did not himself share the view that they were necessarily tricksters. 'I have never stated that you cannot produce some manifestations in a genuine manner,' he wrote in 1873 in reply to a group of Spiritualists who had offered him one thousand pounds if he could produce them under seance-room conditions. 'I have done this, or assisted in doing so, myself.' Twelve years later he was to amplify this statement in the *Pall Mall Gazette*. At a seance with no medium present, he recalled, he and a group of friends had produced movements of a table,

> a heavy one – which we could not accomplish afterwards without exerting all the muscular force at our command. I am satisfied there was no trickery here, and equally so that the scientific explanation given by Faraday does not in the slightest account for the phenomenon. I believe, in my own mind, that it must have been some psychic force which passed from our own bodies and neutralised the laws of gravitation.

Maskelyne's objection to Spiritualism, he claimed, was not to the stories about the phenomena, but to the notion that departed spirits had anything to do with them.

Still, it was not disputed that conjuring tricks had been used in seances; and the tendency of the psychical researchers was to divide mediums into two categories: those who could be trusted, and those who could not be trusted. It was a distinction, though, which proved hard to maintain, because experience showed that in the trance state they were not necessarily in control of their actions. The forces which moved them could not be judged 'by the laws of human integrity', Moses warned; 'they do demonstrably enact what must be described as a fraud of which the entranced medium is, or may be, unconscious'. As orthodox scientists did not accept the reality of the trance state – not, at least, of the kind mediums entered – or even of the unconscious mind, this militated against acceptance of the process by which the phenomena were produced; but those who accepted Moses's proposition tended to try to preserve the distinction by applying the term fraudulent only to those mediums who had been found to have planned or carried out some trick when not in the trance state. For others, the issue whether a medium occasionally used trickery was relatively unimportant. There was nothing very wicked in deceiving an audience; this, after all, was what professional conjurors did for a living. For a medium who sometimes could not get his psychic forces working to practise sleight-of-hand was naughty, but understandable. What mattered, surely, was whether the medium, honest or dishonest, could perform in test conditions where sleight-of-hand could be ruled out.

The dilemma was illustrated in the career of Francis Monck. Before his conversion to Spiritualism in 1872 Monck had been a non-conformist preacher; and he had continued to preach his new faith around the country, giving demonstrations of spirit writing and other phenomena. He had been tested several times, with good results; but while Slade was on trial in London, Monck was arrested on the same vagrancy charge in Huddersfield with more positive evidence against him: conjurors' devices had been found in his possession. Like Slade he was sentenced to three months' hard labour; unlike Slade, he served the sentence.

It was easy to assume that Monck had been a cheat all along; particularly as his defence – that he kept the devices so that if necessary he could show audiences how they might be deceived – was unconvincing. Yet not merely had he been tested by experienced investigators; he had more than once given demonstrations of a kind which could not have been accomplished by a conjuring trick. He had, indeed, been the first medium not merely to produce materialised forms, but to remain in full view while he was doing so. On a bright summer's day Wallace and Hensleigh Wedgwood watched what at first appeared to be a faint white patch on his coat, and which spread to become 'a cloudy pillar extending from his shoulder to his feet', eventually assuming the form of a thickly-draped figure, visible for a short time, before being absorbed back into the body of the medium. The Rev. Thomas Colley – later to be more widely known as Archdeacon Colley – made a similar report. From less than a yard away, by the light of a lamp, he had watched spirit forms grow out of Monck's side; at first faces, and then 'a fully-formed figure – in a nebulous condition at first, but growing solider as it issued from the medium', until eventually it left Monck and appeared as 'a separate individuality, two or three feet off, bound to him by a slender attachment of gossamer'.

Commenting on what he had seen, Colley observed that if this was how materialisations came about, it was unfair for 'spirit-grabbers', if they seized a materialised form and found themselves holding the medium, to assume fraud too readily; judgment should be suspended until more was known about 'this subtle chemico-material psychic fabrication'. Epes Sargent, one of the few discriminating American investigators in this period, made the same point in *The Scientific Basis of Spiritualism*, describing how a sceptic had thought up a simple way to combine punishment and exposure, by stabbing a materialised hand with a knife. The immediate result was gratifying: a shriek. But when the medium – Fred Willis, who had continued to practise after his expulsion from Harvard for giving seances – came out of his trance, it was found that his hand was not even scratched.

Episodes of this kind suggested that everyday notions of what constituted fraud were not necessarily relevant in psychical research. Dr. Purdon had acquitted Florence Cook of fraud on the occasion when he found that although her bonds had been cut while she was in her cabinet, there was no knife with which she could have cut them. But in theory at least, if the possibility of apports was accepted, she might have materialised a knife for the purpose, and de-materialised it in time to avoid detection. There was no end to the possible psychic explanations in such cases: evilly-disposed spirits might even materialise conjuring apparatus and 'plant' it on a medium they disliked, to discredit her. But such excuses were destructive of mediumship's credibility; as, indeed, were the phenomena themselves – an affront to common sense, as well as to science. Yet they could not simply be ignored, if respectable citizens continued to report them; and respectable citizens did. In a letter to the magazine *London Society* the barrister, Henry Dunphy, described how hard he had found it

to give in to the idea that solid objects could be conveyed, invisibly, through closed doors, or that heavy furniture could be moved without the interposition of hands. Philosophers will say these things are absolutely impossible; nevertheless it is absolutely certain that they do occur. I have met in the private houses of friends, as witnesses of these phenomena, persons whose testimony would go for a good deal in a court of justice. They have included peers, M.P.s, diplomatists of the highest rank, judges, barristers, physicians, clergymen, members of learned societies, chemists, engineers, journalists and thinkers of all sorts and degrees. They have suggested and carried into effect tests of the most rigid and satisfactory character. The mediums (all non-professional) have been searched before and after seances. The precaution has even been taken of providing them unexpectedly with other apparel. They have been tied; they have been sealed; they have been secured in every cunning and dextrous manner that ingenuity could devise; but no deception has been discovered and no imposture brought to light.

It was a courageous defence, but it was no match for the argument which Carpenter was to produce against it. What would be the reaction, Carpenter asked in a course of lectures he gave in 1877, if it were claimed that a will had been signed in London by somebody who was known to be in Edinburgh at the time? Would any court of law accept that the signatory had been transported by the spirits for the purpose? Of course not! 'Yet there are at the present time numbers of men and women who have so completely surrendered their "common sense" for a dominant prepossession, as to maintain that any such monstrous fiction ought to be believed.'

The higher phenomena of Spiritualism, as they might have been described, wrecked the chances of acceptance of the everyday phenomena – clairvoyance, telepathy, table-tilting; just as the higher phenomena of mesmerism had blocked recognition of the trance state and its everyday phenomena, suggestibility and freedom from pain. Reports of cases, or alleged cases, of fraud contributed to the process; but as Crosland put it, although the discovery of forged banknotes in circulation arouses suspicion, 'we do not conclude therefore that all Bank of England notes are forgeries'. It was not so much the occasional occurrence of fraud that mattered, as the impossibility of accepting any explanation *but* fraud for, say, Mrs. Guppy's translocation. Most of the early psychical researchers, whatever their views, were genuinely anxious that the phenomena should be incorporated into the orthodox scientific framework; that they should cease to be regarded as supernatural, in the colloquial sense of not being bound by natural laws. 'We have only to enlarge our conceptions of the natural,' Chambers told Wallace, 'and all will be well'; and Wallace himself agreed that it was a fallacy to suppose that supernatural events '*invade,* or *subvert,* the laws of nature'. But it was inconceivable that scientists in general could be persuaded that translocations or de-materialisations were natural. The temptation for the researchers, therefore, was to lay down boundary lines beyond which they would neither themselves venture nor accept the reports of those who did venture. 'Mrs. Guppy I don't think I could stand,' Lord Rayleigh wrote in 1874 in connection with some research, 'even in the cause of science.' But no two researchers agreed precisely where the boundary should be drawn. Even Home, who considering the variety of manifestations which he had produced in his time might have been expected to keep an open mind, showed what he thought of 'the asserted phenomena of matter passing through matter' by including it in his *Lights and Shadows* in the section devoted to 'trickery and its exposures'. Other commentators, like the German philosopher Eduard von Hartmann, accepted the mental phenomena, but dismissed all the physical effects as illusions.

Hallucination

The idea that mediums might be illusionists, in the sense of being able to deceive an observer not just by sleight-of-hand but by giving him a hallucination, began to find favour in this period among scientists and sceptics who could not accept that spiritualist phenomena were genuine, but could not bring themselves to believe that colleagues of such eminence and integrity were being taken in merely by conjuring tricks. There must be something more to it, Balfour Stewart, Professor of Physics at Manchester University, decided; and following the publication of Crookes's preliminary report on his research with Home, Stewart wrote to *Nature* in 1871 commending Crookes and his colleagues for their boldness and honesty in describing what they had seen, but saying that he found it difficult to believe they really had seen it. Subjects under the influence of 'electric-biology', he had heard, could be persuaded to believe that water which they were tasting was really wine; might this be the process by which visitors to the seance room 'saw' what they reported?

The following year, Edward Tylor followed up the possibility. Reviewing Tylor's *Primitive Culture,* Wallace had complained that Tylor had rejected even the possibility of so-called supernatural explanations; was it not possible, for example, that werewolves were the product not of myth, but of some mesmeric influence? Tylor agreed that Wallace's theory was plausible: perhaps, he suggested, Wallace was on the track of an explanation not merely for the feats of sorcerers in savage tribes, but also for those of Home and Mrs. Guppy?

It was a shrewd thrust. Of all the explanations of the phenomena, the possibility that the sitters as well as the medium were entranced was the hardest for the psychical researchers to rebut. Some, at least, of the experiences were subjective luminosities, currents of air and even raps were often reported by some sitters and not by others. Nor did Spiritualists dispute that the medium might be in a mesmeric trance state. Moses, in fact, believed that the spirits employed mesmerism; he believed that he himself was sometimes mesmerised by the spirit of Du Potet. And Crookes's reply to Stewart, that the machines he used could not be mesmerised, was convincing only if their evidence was recorded independently. As next to nothing was known about the laws regulating electro-biology, Stewart pointed out, it might be found that it was not the machines which were influenced; only the minds of the investigators watching them.

Replying, Wallace pointed out that in order to put people into a trance state, a hypnotist needed to acquire certain skills which few, if any, mediums had learned; and he had to use certain techniques – passes, or verbal injunctions – which mediums did not employ. Not everybody was susceptible to hypnosis; and those who were, differed in the degree of susceptibility. It was consequently inconceivable that every sitter would have precisely the same delusion at the same time. Nor did sitters behave like people who had been hypnotised; they took notes, made criticisms. If hypnosis were involved, therefore, it bore little resemblance to the kind which Braid had described. But this gave Carpenter his opportunity to resume his onslaught on the psychical researchers. In his *Principles of Mental Physiology* in 1874 he set out to explain away the phenomena in Braid's terms. Most of the physical and mental phenomena, he argued, could quite easily be traced either to hyperacuity of the senses – Braid, he recalled, had shown how a hypnotised boy could unerringly detect which member of a large group had a certain object: a feat accomplished, according to Braid, not by clairvoyance but by hypnotically-stimulated sensory perception improving his sense of smell – or by the increased physical strength which the trance state provided; as on the occasion when one of Braid's subjects, so weak that ordinarily he would not even try to lift twenty pounds, took up a twenty-five pound weight on his little finger, after being assured it was as light as a feather, and 'swing it round his head with the greatest facility'. Most of what had happened at seances could therefore be explained away by a combination of hypnosis and hallucination.

Where tables moved which were ordinarily too heavy to shift, it could be attributed either to the enhanced muscular power of the people touching them, or to 'subjective visual perception produced by mental expectation'. Actual hypnosis was unnecessary; the process by which hallucinations could be induced without it was 'perfectly familiar to all who have carefully studied the phenomena of insanity'. The fact that hundreds of people thought they had witnessed levitations simply indicated that they were victims of a new epidemic delusion. And Carpenter was to develop this thesis in further articles, citing the flagellants, the dancing maniacs, and the St. Médard *convulsionnaires* as earlier examples of the same mental disorder. 'There is nothing too strange to be believed by those who have once surrendered their judgment to the extent of accepting as credible things which common sense tells us are entirely incredible.'

The Materialists

For scientists to accept Carpenter's hypnosis theory required a certain sleight-of-mind, as most of them still did not accept hypnosis. The 'epidemic delusion' notion was more to their taste. But in a sense all these reasons for refusing to accept the evidence for physical phenomena were simply rationalisations. The real reason was simple; even to examine it would imply doubts about the validity of one of the most powerful faiths ever to acquire a hold over man's mind: materialism.

Materialism's chief spokesman was the physicist John Tyndall, a largely self-educated Irishman who had become Professor of the Royal Institution in 1854; being there, as Oliver Lodge put it, 'in a manner the officiating priest, with Faraday a sort of deity'. Tyndall's own pronouncements show that the simple was apt. 'Let us reverently, but honestly, look the question in the face,' he begged the British Association in his Presidential Address in 1874. 'Divorced from matter, where is life to be found? Whatever our *faith* may say, our *knowledge* shows them to be indissolubly joined. Every meal we eat, and every cup we drink, illustrates the mysterious control of mind by matter.' Even if the full story had not yet been told, he continued, because microscopes had yet to be constructed which could tell it, 'by an intellectual necessity I cross the boundary of the experimental evidence, and discern in that Matter which we, in our ignorance of its latent powers, and notwithstanding our professed reverence for its creator, have hitherto covered with opprobrium, the promise and potency of all terrestrial life.'

Tyndall's words make it easy to understand why Crookes's researches were brushed aside. When Lord Rayleigh had begun to take an interest in them, he was shocked by the attitude of his fellow members of the Royal Society. Surely, he urged, the possible existence of mind independent of matter 'must be far more important than any scientific discovery could be . . . or rather, would be the most important scientific discovery'. He might as well have expected the College of Cardinals to investigate dispassionately evidence pointing to the conclusion that Jesus was a myth. To Tyndall, materialism was a religion. He even denounced Spiritualism in biblical terms, as 'intellectual whoredom'. A miracle, he claimed, could be defined as an invasion of the law of the conservation of energy; as to create or annihilate matter 'would be deemed on all hands a miracle', it followed that Spiritualism must be spurious; 'surely no baser delusion has ever obtained dominance over the weak mind of man'. So he urged his fellow-scientists actively to propagate the materialist doctrine, as he was constantly doing himself in popular journals, in order to encourage 'a strong and resolute enthusiasm', in which science would find a useful ally.

The majority of scientists were moving towards Tyndall's belief. So materialistic had they become in their attitudes, William James lamented, that they mistrusted the intrusion of any subjective element into their calculations; 'many persons nowadays seem to think that any conclusion must be very scientific if the arguments in favour of it are all derived from the twitching of frogs' legs, especially if the frogs are decapitated; and that on the other hand any doctrine chiefly vouched for by the feelings of human beings, with heads on their shoulders, must be benighted and superstitious'. And inevitably they were still more mistrustful of phenomena which behaved even more unpredictably than human beings. 'A man trained in physical inquiry,' as Patrick Proctor Alexander observed, 'who everywhere postulates constancy in the relation of cause and effect, may naturally be a little impatient when asked to consider phenomena of which inconstancy is expressly asserted, so that under seemingly identical conditions, the result may occur or not.' And there was no section of the scientific Establishment able or willing to do battle with materialism. A few psychologists had been investigating how the unconscious mind acted, independently of consciousness – Oliver Wendell Holmes in America, Myers in Britain, von Hartmann in Germany; and this was providing at least the foundation for a study of mediumship, hypnotism, divination, and other subjects hitherto under the interdict. But psychology was still not accepted as an academic discipline, the excuse – as Cox, himself the author of a manual on the subject, complained – being that it was too 'immaterial, intangible'. It had not even rounded the first marker buoy on the course to acceptance: the right to a hearing at meetings of the British Association for the Advancement of Science.

Anthropologists were just ahead of psychologists in the queue for admission; and it was from them, in this period, that the idea of a psychic or spirit force might have received its most powerful backing. The middle of the nineteenth century was the period when they began to collect and collate the mass of material from tribal communities, the first comprehensive survey appearing in 1871: Edward Tylor's *Primitive Culture*, a comparative anatomy of savage (as they were then described) customs. It showed how remarkably consistent the belief was in magic and divination, everywhere; particularly the assumption that there was a spirit world, and that it was possible to communicate with it for such purposes as divination and magic. But as Wallace grumbled, reviewing the book, 'all narratives tending to prove that anything which goes under the general term supernatural really exists in fact, are either entirely omitted or just mentioned in such a manner as to imply that they are necessarily impostures or delusions, and therefore unworthy of discussion'. Could it not be, Wallace suggested, that 'the uniformity of *belief* is due in great part to the uniformity of the underlying *facts*?' And he cited the experiments of Crookes and others as possible confirmation. Tylor was a shrewd and relatively open-minded man, who in different circumstances might have been prepared to examine the evidence in favour of the reality of magic and divination. But he was not free to do so. If he had taken them seriously in his book, not merely would it have been ignored or ridiculed by the scientific Establishment; he would have jeopardised anthropology's prospects of qualifying in Britain, as it had in Germany, as an accepted academic discipline. Tylor at least posed the question whether there was anything in 'the whole monstrous farrago', as he described it, of magical beliefs and practices before dismissing them; but most anthropologists took for granted that they were superstitions, of interest only for the light they might throw on the mentality of the savages. They were rarely interested even in that, Cox complained; at their Institute, they devoted 'long debates to the shape of man's skull; not a word or thought to the structure of his mind'.

Church and State

If materialism had been the creed only of the scientists, they could hardly have guided public opinion along Tyndall's lines. But a profound change had come over people's opinions on the supernatural. 'At present,' W. E. H. Lecky observed in his *History of Rationalism* in 1865,

> nearly all educated men receive an account of a miracle taking place in their own day with an absolute and even derisive incredulity which dispenses with all examination of the evidence. Although they may be entirely unable to give a satisfactory explanation of some phenomena that have taken place, they never on that account dream of ascribing them to supernatural agency, such an hypothesis being, as they believe, altogether beyond the range of reasonable discussion.

That Lecky was not exaggerating can be seen in the attitude of the Bench. 'I blush for the land of a Bacon or a Newton,' William Paget Wood, soon to become Lord Chancellor, told an audience soon after Spiritualist seances began in Britain, 'where such absurdities are tolerated'; and in the Lyon v. Home and Lankester v. Slade cases, the judges admitted they were basing their verdicts on materalist principles. Materialism had even taken root among churchmen, particularly in the Church of England. With a few exceptions, such as Richard Whately,

Archbishop of Dublin, they rejected Spiritualism, not because they thought of it as diabolic, except in the colloquial sense, but because by this time they repudiated the miraculous element in their religion. For some years past theologians had been purging the gospels of their miraculous element in the variety of ingenious ways which were later to be listed and categorised by J. M. Thompson in his *Miracles in the New Testament*: by the 'rationalist method', which attributed miracles to the fact that events originally accepted as natural had become transmuted in the telling; by the 'mythological method', which revealed how stories had been inserted to show that prophecies had been faithfully fulfilled; by the 'literary method', which explored the corruption of texts as they passed through the hands of successive scribes; or by the 'symbolic method', illustrating how episodes had been invented or twisted in the ecclesiastical interests of the writer. With such devices it was easy for theologians quietly to jettison the New Testament miracles, without having to accept the atheistic propositon that they had been deliberately faked by Jesus or his disciples to delude the ignorant. The feeding of the five thousand, for example, was variously explained by the sharing out of food already brought; by the arrival of an unexpected gift sent by wealthy sympathisers; by the provision of supplies through the agency of a secret society; or by confusion with the earlier story of manna in the wilderness. Every miracle could have, and most did have, several explanations of this kind, relieving Christianity from the need to have another bruising contest with orthodox science. Spiritualism, with its clear implication that the theologians had been selling the gospel writers short, was consequently unwelcome.

It was equally unwelcome to those traditionalists who accepted the miracles of the Old and New Testaments, but thought of them as events from far away and long ago. The revised gospel according to Robert Dale Owen and William Howitt claimed that man had now rediscovered the forces which had been responsible for biblical prophecies and miracles; a theme taken up enthusiastically by the writers of Spiritualist tracts, who began to put the old miracles into categories – spirit writings, materialisations, levitations – to emphasise the similarity with those of seances. Quoting one such survey which showed that Spiritualism was 'but a fresh, full influx of the same spirit power', John Farmer, the editor of *Light*, echoed Howitt's claim that the angels were simply spirits. Not merely could the Bible be interpreted in spiritualist terms, he argued; it could not reasonably be interpreted in any other terms. Stainton Moses, citing 'the odour of sanctity', as an example, took the proposition a stage further. As in his experience no seance passed 'without perfumes being showered upon us, or perfumed waves of air being wafted around', such manifestations were clearly associated with mediumship, rather than with holiness. The only reason why they had come to be identified with saintly monks and nuns was that

> they gave themselves the best conditions – seclusion, prayer, fasting; and the odour of sanctity became a well known occurrence among them. Only they named it badly. There was no particular sanctity about them, or about us now – frequently the reverse. The perfume had nothing to do with sanctity. It was a phenomena of mediumship which was rife then, and which exists now, perhaps more frequently than we know.

And in his *Spirit Teachings* Moses went on to advocate mediumship, rather than observances, as the path to the knowledge of God's will.

Nor was it only Christian Spiritualists who took advantage of historical parallels. The writings of the neo-Platonists were becoming familiar again from such works as F. D. Maurice's *Moral and Mental Philosophy*; and Wallace, who moved from Voltairean agnosticism to Spiritualism without embracing Christianity on the way, was understandably gratified to find that this leap had a respectable ancestry. In his book on miracles he was to cite Iamblichus, to show the similarities.

> Often at the moment of inspiration, or when the afflatus has subsided, a fiery appearance is seen – the entering or departing power. Those who are skilled in this wisdom can tell by the character of this glory the rank of the divinity who has seized for the time the reins of the mystic's soul, and guides it as he will. Sometimes the body of the man is violently agitated, sometimes it is rigid and motionless. In some instances sweet music is heard, in others, discordant and fearful sounds. The person of the subject has been known to dilate and tower to a superhuman height, in other cases, it has been lifted into the air. Frequently, not merely the ordinary exercise of reason, but sensation and animal life would appear to have been suspended; and the subject of the afflatus has not felt the application of fire; has been pierced with spits, cut with knives, and not been sensible to pain.

This aspect of Spiritualism disturbed the Vatican. Miracles attributed to the intervention of an angel or saint were still regarded as essential to the maintenance of the Church's hold over the faithful; and although most of them were by this time of healing – a trend which was beginning to be reinforced by the growing reputation of Lourdes following the visions there of Bernadette Soubirous in 1858 – reports of traditional miracles such as levitations did not cease. In 1855 Maria

of Monte San Savino was seen floating two feet in the air in a kneeling
position, with her arms outstretched, for an hour: 'I placed my hand
under her knees,' a patient of Dr. A. Imbert Gourbeyre told him; 'and
I was able to lift her up; she did not weigh more than a feather. I blew
upon her, and her body swung about slowly in the air like a leaf waving
in the breeze.' That Spiritualists with no claim to sanctity should claim
to be able to levitate was a threat to the Church's monopoly of the
supernatural; Spiritualist ideas and practices were condemned as 'a
scandal against moral purity'. Had Home agreed to submit to monastic
discipline when he entered the Church, as he was urged to do, his
feats might have been acclaimed as miraculous; but as he had gone on
his own (or his spirits') way he had been expelled from Rome in 1864
for practising sorcery, on the assumption that if the manifestations were
genuine, they must be diabolic.

This was a subject upon which Cardinal Manning was particularly
vehement. Nothing could be more sinister as a sign of the times, he
told the author W. H. Mallock, than Spiritualist seances; they were a
revival of black magic. Manning 'went on to assert, as a fact supported
by ample evidence, that the devil at such meetings assumed a corporeal
form – sometimes that of a man, sometimes that of a beautiful and
seductive woman; the result being frequent births, in the prosaic
world around us, of terrible hybrid creatures, half diabolic in nature,
though wholly human in form'; a theme on which Manning elaborated
in such plain language that Mallock could hardly believe his ears, and
could not bring himself to set it down in print.

For a few Protestants the argument ran along similar lines, the battle
being joined over whether the spirits who rapped or moved furniture
were, or were not, diabolic; but for the majority, this was irrelevant. In
Britain, F. Sitwell claimed in a study of mesmerism in 1853, they had
'come well-nigh to disbelieve and deny the possibilities of any *present*
spiritual manifestation'; an assertion endorsed in the *Edinburgh
Review* in 1862, with the explanation that although Protestants were
bound to believe that God could do anything he chose, what he chose
to do was to work by and through the rules which he himself laid down;
he never acted 'unless in and through what they call the laws of nature'.
The ordinary churchgoer, particularly if he were an Episcopalian, no
longer believed in levitation, or in ever-full cruses of oil, or even in
angels. Florence Nightingale's comment that the story of Balaam's ass
was 'fit only to be told to asses' reflected the increasingly common attitude that the Old Testament should be respected only as myth; and
those who had come to accept this view did not want to have to take
Genesis seriously again. Still less did the Episcopalian want the even
tenor of his religious habits – family prayers, grace before meals, church
on Sunday – disrupted by the intervention of spirit forces with, ap-

parently, unrestricted powers and erratic habits. Unless convinced by personal experience he was likely to continue to believe what happened at seances was the result of trickery; especially as it carried the comforting implication that the same was probably true of the miracles of Rome.

The hostility of Christians, though, was mild compared to that of rationalists. The disciples of Comte and J. S. Mill felt that Spiritualism represented a recrudescence of all they most feared and hated; and they reacted according to temperament. Browning developed an obsessive loathing of Spiritualists. 'I have seen him stamping on the floor,' Frances Power Cobbe noted in 1860, 'in a frenzy of rage at the way some believers and mediums were deceiving Mrs. Browning.' After attending a seance, Samuel Butler simply shut his mind to what he had witnessed: 'Granted that wonderful spirit forms have been seen and touched and then disappeared, and that there has been no delusion, no trickery. Well, *I don't care*. I get along quite nicely as I am'; and although he later admitted to Wallace that he was being childish, he stuck by his refusal to investigate further. George Lewes derided Spiritualism as 'a delusion so gross, a doctrine so absurd, and a practice so base and debasing', that he would have felt justified in ignoring it altogether had it not been a good example of people's lack of appreciation of the true nature of evidence. That Spiritualism could inspire revulsion even in the most balanced of individuals is shown in the correspondence of George Eliot – though admittedly she may have been influenced by her relationship with Lewes. She was not without some experience of the phenomena: 'in all that she called her best writing there was a "not herself" which took possession of her', she told John Cross, whom she married after Lewes's death; 'she felt her own personality to be merely the instrument through which the spirit, as it were, was acting'. Yet she could tell Harriet Beecher Stowe in 1869 that Spiritualism in Britain was regarded 'either as a degrading folly, imbecile in the estimate of evidence, or else as impudent imposture'; and though she was obviously a little shaken by Mrs. Stowe's quiet insistence that it could not so lightly be dismissed, in a further letter three years later, she could still say of Home, 'I could not choose to enter a room where he held a seance. He is an object of moral disgust to me, and nothing of late reported by Mr. Crookes, Lord Lindsay and the rest carries conviction to my mind that Mr. H. is not simply an impostor.'

Inevitably this coloured the selection of what she accepted as evidence; for example, she unhesitatingly accepted Brewster's version of the early Home seances, though it conflicted with the recollections of everybody else present (except Brougham, who declined to comment; which, it seems fair to suggest, he would hardly have done if he believed his friend was in the right). And this was to be one of the common characteristics of materialist attitudes: a willingness to reject the evidence for psychical phenomena on the flimsiest of pretexts. Only people who remained in ignorance of what psychical research had accomplished, von Hartmann claimed, could 'persist in an absolute denial of all such phenomena', in particular of divination; he lamented, though, that it was easy for them to remain in ignorance if they did not want to become acquainted with the facts, because the facts were rarely published in scientific journals. And lay journals, though they occasionally published unbiased (or more often, baffled) accounts of seances, were predominantly hostile: Spiritualism, *The Times* asserted after the Slade trial, 'is, of course, an imposture or a delusion'. There was also a continuing tendency among the writers of popular scientific medical works to invent natural explanations of a kind even harder to swallow than the possibility of some psychic force at work. As it was 'well known', the American writer William Hammond asserted in a study of Spiritualism in 1876, 'that a piece of spongy platinum becomes incandescent where a current of hydrogen is allowed to impinge upon it', it was consequently reasonable to suppose that Home had employed this method when playing with fire, with the help of 'a small reservoir of hydrogen'. Similarly, 'it would have been very easy for Mr. Home to place a layer of asbestos cloth under the burning coals on Mr. Hall's head and Mr. Lindsay's hand'. The notion that Crookes, of all people, could have mistaken platinum for coal, or that Lindsay would not have noticed if an asbestos cloth had been inserted between his hand and the red hot piece of coal, was ludicrous; yet it passed into common currency.

In such an atmosphere the only people who could be convinced by the results of research, if positive, were the researchers themselves. In the whole period there appears to have been only one well-known academic figure in Britain who was prepared without personal experience to accept the evidence: James Challis, Palmerian Professor of Astronomy at Cambridge, who as early as 1862 had said that he found the written testimony to the phenomena so abundant, from so many places, 'that either the facts must be admitted to be such as are reported, or the possibility of certifying facts by human testimony must be given up'. Ordinarily the reaction to reports of investigations which accepted the phenonema was simple incredulity. When the Dialectical Society was beginning its inquiry one of its members, Dr. J. Dixon, warned that if it should affirm the facts in question, 'the majority of your society and of outsiders will, unless they belie all precedent, add the committee to their list of "dupes", "victims" and "fools".' They did. A favourable report at best prompted suggestions that a case had been made for the subject to be 'properly' investigated. But this

only led to the repetition, in various forms, of the experience of the
Fox sisters in Rochester, where the findings of three successive committees had been rejected by the very people who had appointed them.

How could it be otherwise, when the prevailing assumption was that,
say, levitation was a physical impossibility, as Faraday had insisted,
and as Lord Amberley reiterated; 'when we are told of human bodies
floating unsupported in the air, the assertion is irreconcilable with a
well-known law?' It was useless, Alexander complained, to point out
that on the same argument scientists might claim that iron could not
be lifted into the air by a magnet; they simply claimed that as levitation
was impossible and absurd, 'there can be no evidence to prove it –
such is the easy formula with which they kick aside the subject'. As a
result, when a scientist undertook to investigate, it was ordinarily
with a view to discrediting the phenomena; 'and should a man of scientific distinction, after much care and pains bestowed, announce himself convinced of their genuineness, it is considered that this does not in
the least accredit the phenomena, but merely discredits the inquirer'.
Nor did the standing of the investigator make any difference. What
would scientists say, Alexander asked, if they heard that Huxley had
undertaken research, and had been impressed?

Probably that Professor Huxley, though indeed a very clever person,
had despite all his deep precautions, been hoaxed by a cleverer man
than he. But suppose it is beyond question shown, when the detail of
the matter was given, that Professor Huxley in his scientific experiment had eliminated every possible or conceivable source of error,
what would *then* be said by the wise men? Such of them as once for
all *would not* believe, on the strength of their fundamental axiom,
laid down and stuck to, that the thing could not possibly be true,
was incredible, monstrous etc., might perhaps be capable of insinua-
ting against Professor Huxley a charge of *collusion* with Mr. Home.
Or, possibly some brother might say, pointing to his own wise head,
and shaking it with a look of melancholy sagacity: 'Ah, poor fellow.
Poor Huxley! But he was always a little . . . , you understand?'

When a few months later the report had appeared of the investigation of Home by Crookes – less well known, but better qualified than
Huxley to undertake it – this was precisely what happened.

Understandably, therefore, scientists to protect their reputations
tended to hold aloof; and had they contented themselves with expressing their repugnance for the subject, the worst that could have been
said of them was that they had been cowardly. But a few of them, who
could not resist investigating in the hope of discrediting the phenomena,
behaved in ways which, as scientists, they would ordinarily have been

the first to censure. Some, like Faraday and Chevreul, performed experiments which had no real relation to the phenomena they were purporting to duplicate. Others, like Carpenter and Huxley, went to single seances and then either seized upon the excuse that little had happened, and refused to come again, or invented hypotheses to explain away what they had witnessed. Usually, they refused to accept the possibility that, as Moses put it, 'whatever disturbs the mind of the psychic is likely to prevent the occurrences or, at least, seriously to impair the power of any manifestations'; as Galton admitted to Darwin, they were 'usually so disagreeable, opinionated and obstructive, and have so little patience, that the seances rarely succeed with them'. Occasionally they deliberately set out to trick the medium, as Lewes had done. In *Fragments of Science for Unscientific People,* Tyndall actually boasted that he had surreptitiously shaken the floor under the table with his feet, in order to enjoy the spectacle of the other sitters deluding themselves that he would be converted by such a good demonstration of spirit power. What the irascible Tyndall would have said if a Spiritualist had secretly upset one of his experiments in a similar way can be imagined.

The most unpleasant feature of all was the willingness of the scientific Establishment to condone smear tactics against the psychical researchers; a campaign in which Carpenter took the lead. His academic standing meant that his frequent contributions to the lay press appeared to carry the Establishment's *nihil obstat*; and his glib, self-confident style made them appear well informed, though he was in reality a chronic distortionist, incapable of arguing the case on its merits without falling back on verbal sleight-of-hand.

The technique he adopted was significant not just for its influence at the time, but because it was to breed a swarm of imitators. The arguments he put forward sounded reasonable and were backed by evidence. But the arguments were rationalisations, and the evidence selected and if necessary twisted to fit the needs of his case for the prosecution. A typical sample was to be found in 1876 in the *Contemporary Review,* one of the journals of opinion which proliferated at this time, and were influential because philosophers and poets and scientists thronged their pages; their existence enabled Carpenter to preach to the influential minority which constituted the British ruling class, and to repeat his main themes with appropriate variations in different journals. The Spiritualists, he explained, were 'led by the influence of a strong prepossession to believe in the creations of their own visual imagination'. A whole party of believers 'will affirm that they saw Mr. Home float out of one window and in at another, whilst a single honest sceptic declares that Mr. Home was sitting in his chair all the time'; and what this showed was that 'the honest testimony of any number of individuals, on one side, if given under a prepossession, is of no more weight than that of a single adverse critic – if so much'. There could be no doubt about the episode to which Carpenter was referring: the occasion when Home had performed the feat for Adare and Lindsay. And as the report of the seance had said that there had been another witness, Carpenter's clear innuendo was that his account had been suppressed. But it had not been suppressed. The witness, Captain Wynne, promptly wrote to Home to reiterate that it was non-sense to suggest that it had been either hallucination or humbug: 'the fact of your having gone out of the window, and in at the other, I can swear to'.

Carpenter rarely defended himself when detected in such decep-tions unless he could put the blame on somebody else. In one of the appendices to the published version of some lectures he had given on mesmerism and Spiritualism he printed Mrs. Culver's 'exposure' of the Fox sisters; when it was pointed out to him that her account had been shown to be a fabrication, Carpenter explained that his source was Maskelyne, who in a broadside against the Spiritualists had asked why they never mentioned the Culver document. But there was neither re-traction nor apology for Carpenter's final stroke. In an article in *Nineteenth Century* – yet another new journal of opinion – in 1877, he was rash enough to attack Crookes's work on vacuum tubes, insinuat-ing that Crookes's psychical researches reflected his inadequacies as a scientist; and Crookes had no difficulty in showing that he had merely displayed his ignorance. Carpenter did not have to wait long for his revenge. When Home's *Lights and Shadows of Spiritualism* was pub-lished Mrs. Crookes wrote sadly to Home to point out the awkward position in which his denunciation of fraudulent mediums had placed her husband: 'I can assure you it is the best weapon Dr. Carpenter and his class have ever had, for of course it is looked upon as a complete exposure of the whole subject by the biggest impostor of the lot.' So it proved. In *Fraser's Magazine,* Carpenter lavished praise on Home for his belated conversion and went on to accuse Crookes, who could now be regarded as one of Home's dupes, of having given the medium Mrs. Fay a testimonial to the effect that she had been tested by mem-bers of the Royal Society, and that they had satisfied themselves that her manifestations were genuine. Crookes had in fact received a letter from America after Mrs. Fay's return there, asking him if certain hostile rumours about her were well founded; and he had guardedly replied that he had no reason to doubt her honesty. But he had made no reference to tests by members of the Royal Society in the letter, nor was it in any sense a testimonial. Those embroideries simply reflected Carpenter's malice.

If Carpenter's scientific papers were of 'the slovenly nature of his published utterances on Spiritualism,' Moses despairingly asked, 'where did he get his scientific reputation?' The answer was that he was valued as an energetic defender of the materialist faith. Ironically, he was not a materialist himself – or so he claimed in a letter which the recipient passed on to Madame Home, who was to include it in her biography of her husband; he was even, he insisted, prepared to accept the possibility of the existence and of the influence of the spirits of the dead. He was simply a professional sceptic, in the Brewster tradition, catering for the prejudices of his fellow-scientists, knowing that he could be sure of their support because they would believe he had the right ends in view, even if the means he employed were underhand.

Again, the analogy of the Inquisition presented itself. 'Half-truths can, we know, be made so specious,' Moses observed, commenting on Carpenter's article in *Fraser's Magazine*:

they can be so manipulated, that decent people will turn away and, knowing the only side that it suits critics to present, will think that Spiritualists are a mere crew of evil-doers. That is the modern rack and faggot. We don't burn people now; we set public opinion against them by means such as those used in the article under notice, and the arch-priests and kings are the Carpenters of science who have run away with the cast-off clothes of mediaeval priestcraft, and wear them with an arrogant dogmatism worthy of their original owners.

All over Europe, and in America, the same pattern of rancorous hostility was to be found. 'The reaction against the movement,' Nicolaus Wagner wrote, reporting on some experiments in St. Petersburg, designed to repeat those of Zöllner with Slade,

runs its course with the same violence as every fanatical opposition. If 'blind faith' is the motive power of religious fanaticism, so also is the direction of the contrary movement determined by a force which is quite as illogical – 'blind scepticism'. In the one and the other the cause is the same – feeling, passionately excited, and resisting every cool, matter-of-fact objective consideration ... Impelled by this antipathy even the strongest understanding is blind; it seeks support from, and attaches itself to, such strangely childish arguments and suppositions as to any sound thinking and unprejudiced person are in the highest degree, absurd.

Tyndall, Alexander recalled, had once complained that preconceived notions could 'vitiate to an extraordinary degree the testimony of even veracious people'. If the preconceived notion should chance to be a so-called 'scientific one', Alexander observed, the danger was not thereby diminished; the history of Science in this context having been 'a mean record of the perfect *rabies* of unfairness thus induced'.

The Society for Psychical Research

Chapter Thirty

Exploring the Unseen World

THERE WAS, HOWEVER, AN ACADEMIC COTERIE IN EXISTENCE AT THE time which though composed neither of scientists nor of spiritualists was deeply concerned with the phenomena. In about the year 1873, Myers was later to recall,

> at the crest, as one may say, of perhaps the highest wave of material-ism which has ever swept over these shores – it became the con-viction of a small group of Cambridge friends that the deep questions thus at issue must be fought out in a way more thorough than the champions either of religion or of materialism had yet suggested. Our attitudes of mind were in some ways different; but to myself, at least, it seemed that no adequate attempt had yet been made even to determine whether anything could be learnt as to the unseen world or no; for that if anything were knowable about such a world in such fashion that Science could adopt and maintain that know-ledge, it must be discovered by no analysis of tradition, and by no manipulation of metaphysics, but simply by experiment and ob-servation – simply by the application to phenomena within us and around us of precisely the same methods of deliberate, dispassionate, exact inquiry which have built up our actual knowledge of the world which we can touch and see.

There was more than a hint of intellectual arrogance in this retro-spective manifesto; the Cambridge friends were not the originators of 'deliberate dispassionate exact inquiry' in this field. Still, their influ-ence was to become decisive in shaping the course it was to take. The group had as its nucleus three Fellows of Trinity, two of them Fellows no longer – to be a Fellow it was necessary to avow acceptance of the doctrines of the Church of England; and Henry Sidgwick and Myers were not the men to disguise their doubts in order to keep their places. Sidgwick had been appointed a Lecturer in the Moral Sciences; his *Methods of Ethics*, published in 1874 when he was thirty-six years of age, established him among the leading academic philosophers of the period. Myers, five years younger – 'a profound connoisseur of classical antiquity, an essayist delicate and penetrating, a poet of high inspiration', as the Swiss psychologist Theodore Flournoy described him – chose to become an Inspector of Schools under the new Education Act.

The shared doubts of Sidgwick and Myers had drawn them together, and in 1871 on an evening walk Myers asked his companion

> whether he thought that when Tradition, Intuition, Metaphysic, had failed to solve the riddle of the Universe, there was still a chance that from any actual observable phenomena – ghosts, spirits, whatsoever there might be – some valid knowledge might be drawn as to a World Unseen. Already, it seemed, he had thought that this was possible; steadily, though in no sanguine fashion, he indicated some last grounds of hope; and from that night onwards I resolved to pursue this quest, if it might be, at his side.

They were joined in the quest by Edmund Gurney, four years Myers's junior, who became a Fellow of Trinity in 1872, and who so impressed George Eliot when she met him there the following year that for days, according to her biographer Oscar Browning, she could think of nothing else; 'she afterwards discovered that his mind was as beautiful as his face', and perhaps used him as the model for her Daniel Deronda.

For a while Myers investigated on his own, becoming convinced that the phenomena were, or at least could be, genuine. At a seance with Charles Williams in 1873 a large hand materialised which Myers seized and held in his, feeling it diminish in size until it was no bigger than a baby's, before it melted away altogether. He was at the seance with Darwin, the following January; in May, with Gurney, he met Stainton Moses, and was greatly impressed by his account of his mediumship; and that summer, with Sidgwick and Gurney, he started up an informal investigatory association, its members including Lord Rayleigh and his brother-in-law, Arthur Balfour, who had just become a Conservative M.P. Another of the Balfour sisters, Eleanor, married Sidgwick in 1875, and worked with the group. The Sidgwicks had several test seances with Slade in 1876, remaining unimpressed and suspicious as little happened apart from some trivial slate messages. Myers had more luck with Slade; a handbell floated around, and the table rose high in the air 'apparently untouched by anyone'.

Shortly before Slade's trial, the group realised from reports of the proceedings of the British Association that they had an ally in the scientist's camp: William Barrett, Professor of Physics at the Royal College of Science in Dublin. Barrett had a friend with whom he used to stay in the country in Ireland who had been experimenting with mesmerism, using the village children as his subjects; and watching some of the tests Barrett found that in a mesmeric trance, one girl had a remarkable range of perception. Making sure that the girl could not see what was happening, he got his friend to perform a number of actions, Barrett observing the girl's reactions. 'If he placed his hand over the lighted lamp, the girl instantly withdrew hers, as if in pain; if he tasted salt or sugar, corresponding expressions of dislike and approval were indicated by the girl.' Carpenter had accepted the existence of heightened sensory perception under hypnosis; but this, Barrett felt, was not enough to account for what he had witnessed. There must be some rapport; some 'community of sensation', as he described it. And 'not only sensations, but also ideas or emotions occurring in the operator appear to be reproduced in the subject without the intervention of any sign, or visible or audible communication'. Sometimes the subject would pick up what was 'not always a clear image, but one that could not fail to be recognised as a more or less distorted reflection of my own thought'.

Barrett's paper was not printed; had Wallace not happened to be chairman of the committee responsible for vetting the papers, it would not even have been read. ('The discussions of the British Association,' Lankester complained in one of his letters to *The Times* in reference to the Slade case, 'have been degraded by the introduction of the subject of Spiritualism.') With Crookes no longer involved, psychical research languished. Serjeant Cox's Psychological Society, one of whose aims was to carry out 'a laborious and long-continued series of experiments' failed to produce results; its chief activities were lectures, most of them given by Cox himself; and when he died in 1879, the Society was wound up. It seemed for a time that the Cambridge group might also fade away. The Sidgwicks had meagre results from their investigations; after a visit to the United States in 1879 Myers got married the following spring, and for a while his attention was distracted.

Barrett's interest in the subject, however, had not subsided; and his curiosity was further roused by a pastime imported to Britain from the United States. In the mid-1870s living rooms there had become the scene of a craze almost comparable to table-turning: 'the willing game'. One of the group would leave the room while the others decided on an object he was to be willed to find, or an action he was to be willed to carry out. On his return, with the rest of the group concentrating on what he was to find or do, he would surprisingly often (and often surprisingly quickly) perform as required; particularly if his hand or shoulder were held, or lightly touched, by one of the group. The obvious explanation, collusion between some of the players, had to be ruled out because everybody in his turn was 'it' – the percipient – and would know in his own case that he had touched the object or performed the act without prompting.

Inevitably, Carpenter's theory of unconscious muscular pressure was resurrected; the percipient must be picking up clues from the pressure, or lack of it, on his hand or shoulder. But this could hardly account for the percipient, say, selecting one type of flower from a bunch in a vase, or putting his forefinger to his nose rather than to his ear. In 1875, when the craze was at its height, a writer in the *Detroit Review of Medicine* admitted that there were features which the hypothesis was inadequate to explain; could it be, he speculated, that some form of thought-transference was involved? And when the willing game found its way across the Atlantic, a few individuals began to experiment to try to find out whether it was the 'willing' or some other force that was at work; among them, the Rev. A. M. Creery of Buxton. Playing the game with four of his daughters and a young maidservant, Creery discovered that they could do better than simply pick out objects, or perform actions. They were able to guess, not quite consistently but remarkably frequently, whatever the group of people willing them was concentrating upon: the names of towns, or of people; cards drawn from a pack; even lines of poetry. Knowing of Barrett's interest in the subject Creery contacted him; Barrett came to investigate; and he was sufficiently impressed by what he saw to write a short report for *Nature* in the summer of 1881.

That winter, Barrett stayed a night in London with Dawson Rogers, a leading figure in the British National Association of Spiritualists, founded five years before with the aim of, among other things, conducting psychical research. As an avowedly Spiritualist body, though, it had difficulty in attracting outside support; and Rogers suggested it was time to form another society 'on lines which would be likely to attract some of the best minds which had hitherto held aloof from the pursuit of the inquiry'. Barrett agreed, and called a meeting in London early in January 1882 to consider the project. The Cambridge group showed no great enthusiasm, but Myers and Gurney agreed to serve provided that Sidgwick would agree to be President. He accepted; and the Society was formally launched on February 20th.

Controversy was later to arise over who could justly claim to be the founder of the Society: the Spiritualists, who provided the initial impulse and the majority of its members in the early stages; the Cambridge group, to whom its foundation was later credited; or Barrett, who believed it was his idea. In fact all three were necessary for its existence: the Spiritualists, for the initial impulse and the early support; Barrett, for the academic link without which the Cambridge group would have held aloof; and the Cambridge group, for the academic and social contacts without which the Society could not have hoped to attract the kind of members it needed if it were to establish itself as a scientific institution. From the start this was its aim; the Spiritualists self-effacingly allowed their beliefs to be kept discreetly in the background.

It had been widely felt, the Society's manifesto claimed, that the time was opportune for an investigation of psychical phenomena. From the testimony of many eminent witnesses 'there appears to be, amidst much delusion and deception, an important body of remarkable phenomena, which are *prima facie* inexplicable on any generally recognised hypothesis, and which, if incontestably established, would be of the highest possible value'. Hitherto investigation had been undertaken by individual effort; the Society had been founded to enable research to be organised on a broader basis. To this end there would be five investigating committees. The first would examine 'the extent of any influence which may be exerted by one mind upon another, apart from any generally recognised mode of perception'. The second would investigate 'hypnotism, and the forms of so-called mesmeric trance, with its alleged insensitivity to pain'. The third was to carry out a critical revision of Reichenbach's researches to discover whether there were 'sensitives' and whether they 'possess any power of perception beyond a highly exalted sensibility of the recognised sensory organs'. The fourth would investigate 'any reports, resting on strong testimony, regarding apparitions at the moment of death, or otherwise, or regarding disturbances in houses reputed to be haunted'. And the fifth was to examine 'the various physical phenomena commonly called Spiritualistic; with an attempt to discover their causes and general laws'. A sixth committee would be responsible for collecting and collating all the existing historical material relevant to the Society's work.

The Society's expressed aims showed that it would be following the lead of the Cambridge group, rather than of the Spiritualists. The *physical* phenomena of Spiritualism were to be investigated, because they could be subjected to scientific tests; the non-physical aspects were discreetly left unmentioned. And from the start the group, with Sidgwick as President and Myers and Gurney as Joint Hon. Secretaries (Gurney was also editor of the *Proceedings*) provided the drive. They had private means sufficient to enable them to work without payment and to subsidise the Society's activities. And their academic and social background helped them to recruit the kind of men they needed to lend their work intellectual and scientific respectability. How difficult this was likely to be can be gauged from a lecture given in 1883 by Sir William Thomson – the future Lord Kelvin, already one of the leading figures in the British scientific Establishment. Discussing the possibility that there were additional senses, he instanced perception of changes in temperature as a sixth, and surmised that there might be a seventh, some kind of perception of magnetic fields. But he was careful to add that he was in no way supporting 'that wretched superstition of animal magnetism, table-turning and spiritualism, and mesmerism and clairvoyance and spirit-rapping, of which we have heard so much'. Clairvoyance and the like, he insisted, were 'the result of bad observation mostly; somewhat mixed up, however, with the effects of wilful imposture, acting on an innocent, trusting mind'. Kelvin's scepticism was later to become something of a joke; he declared heavier than air flying machines to be a physical impossibility, and dismissed X-rays as a hoax. But in the 1880s his views were widely shared. Any scientist who became identified with psychical research ran the risk of being ridiculed, or worse, as Crookes had been. Nevertheless within four years the Society numbered Barrett, Crookes, Oliver Lodge, Rayleigh, Balfour Stewart (won over from his earlier scepticism), J. J. Thomson, J. Venn, F.R.S., and Wallace among its members; along with many other notabilities, including two bishops, William Ewart Gladstone, Arthur Balfour, John Ruskin, Lord Tennyson and G. F. Watts. Alone of those scientists who had been closely identified with psychical research in the 1870s, Huggins, though he took a sympathetic interest, did not become a member (years later his wife – previously his observatory assistant, whom he had married shortly after his involvement in Crookes's experiments – claimed that it was she who had kept him 'clear of the Spiritualist set', because she thought it would waste his time and perhaps endanger his health).

Donkin's Law

At the time of the foundation of the Society, some of its members had joined Barrett in his tests of the Creery children: the investigation to which, in Myers' opinion, 'we owed our conviction of the possibility of genuine thought-transference between persons in a normal state'. The 'genuine' label was required to distinguish it from another kind of thought-transference which had attracted attention: a refinement of Carpenter's unconscious cerebration. Carpenter had retired (with a C.B. in recognition of his services); but his ideas had been adapted and exploited in what was coming to be known as 'Cumberlandism'. Stuart Cumberland described himself as a professional thought-reader; but he insisted that his remarkable ability to tell people what they were thinking about was derived from his ability to pick up clues from their behaviour. Neither he nor anybody else, he claimed, could 'look into the mind of another and see by "mental picture reading" what is going on therein, any more than he can see through a stone wall or into the middle of next week'; his method was to get at a person's thoughts by observing his muscular tensions, and watching his facial expressions.

Cumberland, though, was a professional who had brought his method to a fine art. The Creery children could not have such expertness. In any case the investigators, only too well aware of the kind of criticisms which would be levelled at them, had taken care to ensure in some of their experiments that information could not be conveyed to the children through the ordinary sensory channels. A variety of experiments had been undertaken by the Sidgwicks, Myers, Gurney and Balfour Stewart; and Barrett had tested the daughters by taking them one by one to another room before choosing the object which they were to be willed to get, and then willing them to get the object before they returned to the room where the group was sitting, and to bring it in with them. On other occasions all the members of the family had been excluded, only the investigators being present; yet still the girls had succeeded. One of them had named the card pulled from a full pack nine times out of fourteen, and it was difficult to imagine – as Myers put it – how the investigators could have 'unconsciously carried, say, the two of diamonds written on our foreheads'. And as at different times each of the investigators individually carried out successful tests in which he alone knew the answers, 'the trick, if trick there was, must have been one in which they, or one of them, *actively shared*'. This, at least, was the view of a statistician to whom they had sent the results of the tests. The odds against their having been achieved by chance, he replied were 999999999999999999999999999999999999999 to one; figures which, he observed, 'more impressively than any words' pointed to thought-transference, unless there had been collusion on the part of those concerned.

On the strength of this endorsement Barrett, Gurney and Myers had no hesitation in presenting their result in the *Nineteenth Century* magazine for July 1882. Surely nobody was going to say that they might all have participated in a fraud? But this was precisely what Horatio Donkin, Lankester's supporter at the Slade trial, suggested in the magazine's next issue. Common sense, he argued, 'demands that every known mode of explanation of facts should be exhausted before the possibility of an unknown mode is considered'. One known mode of explanation had not been exhausted: collusion between the investigators and the children. It was no use the investigators standing on their dignity and protesting their good faith; 'in all scientific inquiries the good faith of individuals concerned should form no part of the data on which the conclusion is to rest'.

Donkin's Law – as it might well have come to be known, so often was it to be restated – was an early intimation to the Society that it could not expect preferential treatment simply on account of the academic and social standing of its members. Yet carried to its logical conclusion it would have rendered all psychical research nugatory, because even if precautions were taken to ensure that the investigators as well as the subjects were watched for collusion, who would guard the guards? If a sufficient number of different tests were carried out by a sufficient number of reliable investigators, producing confirmatory results, surely it could no longer be seriously claimed that they could all be in collusion? So the experiments with the Creery children were continued. They were brought to Cambridge, there to be tested by Myers and Gurney as well as Barrett, in conditions which ruled out family collusion; and though the results fluctuated, there were some spectacular successes. When cards were drawn from a pack, the children would be right once in every three or four guesses, though by chance expectation they should have been right only once in every fifty-two. And some good results were obtained by Barrett, when the Creery children were on a visit to Dublin later in the year.

The Guthrie Experiments

If the requirements of Donkin's Law were to be convincingly met, it was desirable for the Society to be able to cite independent confirmation of thought-transference from other sources. It was provided early in 1883 by Malcolm Guthrie, a partner in the chief drapery establishment in Liverpool, and in his spare time a magistrate and a student of philosophy, who had written some learned critiques of the theories of Herbert Spencer. He had heard that two of the showroom assistants had won the reputation of being thought-readers; and his interest aroused by a magazine article on the subject, he decided to test them, asking James Birchall, the Hon. Secretary of the Liverpool Literary and Philosophical Society, to act as an independent assessor.

Although neither of them had any previous experience of, or even interest in, the subject, their experiments were carefully devised and strictly controlled. At their own request – they found it easier to 'see' – the girls were blindfolded; but as an additional precaution the objects which they were to guess were kept out of their range of vision. At first contact was maintained between investigator and percipient by a light touch of hands; but in the course of the experiments it was found that this made no significant difference to the results. In the first 'no contact' trial, 'Miss J.' described a half-crown as 'like a flat button ... bright ... no particular colour'; the four of spades as 'a card ... four of clubs' (it was later found she did not know the difference between clubs and spades); an egg as 'looks remarkably like an egg'; a penholder with an inverted thimble on the end as 'a column with something bellshaped turned down on it'; and a small gold ear-ring as 'round and bright . . . yellow . . . with loop to hang it by'.

Guthrie reported the results of these trials to the Society, and Myers and Gurney decided to go up to Liverpool that autumn to investigate on their own account. Preparing for their arrival, Guthrie was disconcerted to find that the girls seemed to have lost their clairvoyant power; and he decided to try them out on community of sensation – in this case, taste. Could they tell what he or his colleagues were tasting? As Myers and Gurney found, they could. In one test on 'Miss E.' the results were:

Substance	Guess
Carbonate of soda	Nothing tasted
Cloves	Cloves
Citric acid	Salt
Acid juju	'Pear drop'
Candied ginger	'Something sweet and hot'
Home-made noyau	Salt
Bitter aloes	'Bitter'

There were also experiments with drawings, some of which were even more successful. In one test with six drawings, made with 'Miss E.', the results were

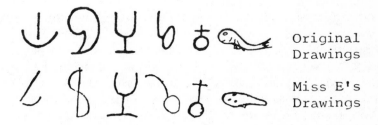

Original Drawings

Miss E's Drawings

In 1884 Guthrie tried another variety of community of sensation: pain. In one run of twenty trials, in which the investigators (several took part) pricked or pinched themselves, the percipient 'felt' the pain in the corresponding part of her own anatomy seven times, and tentatively guessed it correctly a further seven times. Other guesses were close to the mark; and only twice could she offer no guess at all.

Guthrie, however, was not a scientist, and he realised that this might be held against him by critics of his experiments. As a member of the governing body of the University College of Liverpool, he had been concerned in the establishment of a Chair of Physics there in 1881; and at the age of thirty, Oliver Lodge had arrived from London to take up the post. Lodge had immediately embarked on the researches which were to win him a Fellowship of the Royal Society in 1887, and an international reputation; but, always mindful of his responsibility to the city which had adopted him, he was ready to lend a hand with any local projects which might advance scientific understanding. When Guthrie appealed to him 'to come and witness, and within limits modify, the experiments in such a way as would satisfy me of their genuineness and perfect good faith', he agreed to attend; at first as a witness, and then as investigator.

Lodge was soon convinced of 'the transparent honesty of all concerned'; but he was also aware that this testimonial would not count as evidence to people who had not been present. In his report to the Society for Psychical Research in the summer of 1884, he stressed the care he had taken to make the experiments fraud-proof.

He was under no illusions about his ability to detect sleight-of-hand: 'I am perfectly sure,' he admitted, 'that a conjuror could impose on me, possibly even to the extent of making me think he was not imposing on me.' But conjurors need to set up their acts; if he controlled the tests, Lodge felt, and could vary them at will, he would be able to prevent or detect trickery. For example, he brought the objects which were to be used in the tests, and ensured that nobody except himself could know what they were until the tests were complete. If there were collusion, it could only be between him and the percipients.

As in earlier experiments the results were mixed, but the number of hits was out of all proportion to chance expectation. One test with both percipients was particularly instructive. Lodge had a paper with a square on one side, a cross on the other, arranging the test so that 'Miss E.' would be facing the side with the cross and 'Miss R.' facing the side with the square. Soon, 'Miss R.' said she seemed to be 'seeing' two things, and did not know what to draw. When told to draw what she had seen, she first drew the square, and then the cross inside it, adding, 'I don't know what made me put it inside.' Similarly when he asked two people who were acting as thought-transferers – the 'agents', as they were coming to be described – to concentrate not on the same object, but on two different objects, the percipient managed to draw both objects correctly.

Lodge was careful to insist that though he used the term 'thought-transference', this did not imply he held any theory on the subject. 'How the transfer takes place, or whether there is any transfer at all, or what is the physical reality underlying the terms "mind", "consciousness", "impression", and the like; and whether this thing we call mind is located in the person, or in the space around him, or in both, or neither; whether indeed the term location, as applied to mind, is utter nonsense and simply meaningless – concerning all these things I am absolutely blank, and have no hypothesis whatsoever.' For the Society, though, the important point was that he had been convinced of the reality of the phenomena. In theory, at least, if a sufficient number of Guthries could be found to set up such trials, there was no reason why scientists should not be convinced in the way Lodge had been. And over the next two years the Society received the results of seventeen batches of trials conducted, for simplicity, with the percipient simply guessing which suit – spades, hearts, diamonds or clubs – would next be turned up. In ten of them, a thousand or more tests were made (to reduce the possibility of chance fluctuation); and the odds against the end result of the tests being obtained by chance was worked out at about a thousand million to one.

Here, then, was the psychical reseachers' answer to Donkin. The experiments which he had dismissed because they depended upon the reliability of the investigators were being carried out again and again, on the Continent as well as in Britain, on different subjects, with different investigators, and with broadly similar results. Yet there was a snag, as Lodge had warned in his report. The experiments would be described as objective only in the sense that certain precautions were taken to prevent deception, conscious or unconscious. But in the tests themselves, the subjective element could not be eliminated. Creery had made this clear to them from the start:

When the children were in good humour, and excited by the wonderful nature of their successful guessing, they very seldom made a mistake. I have seen seventeen cards, chosen by myself, named right in succession, without any mistake. We soon found that a great deal depended on the steadiness with which the ideas were kept before the minds of 'the thinkers', and upon the energy with which they willed the ideas to pass. Our worst experiments before strangers have invariably been when the company was dull and undemonstrative; and we are all convinced that when mistakes are made the fault rests, for the most part, with the thinkers rather than with the thought-readers.

But the thought-readers also needed to be kept attuned. 'The Creery children had their most startling successes at first, when the affair was a surprise and an amusement, or later, at short or seemingly casual trials,' Myers observed. 'The decline set in with their sense that the experiments had become matters of weighty importance to us, and of

L*

somewhat prolonged strain and tediousness to them.' The results they had obtained with Barrett in Dublin, though still well above chance level, showed a distinct falling off when compared with earlier experiments; so that by the end of the year 'they could not do, under the easiest conditions, what they could do under the most stringent in 1881'. If they had been cheating, their investigators' report pointed out, the girls could have been expected to become *more* proficient; in fact, they could not even produce results in casual games with no controls at all.

Guthrie had experienced the same frustrations when, after he had arranged for Myers and Gurney to come to Liverpool, his girl percipients lost their power – if the tests had not been switched to tasting, 'our visitors would have gone away disappointed'; and his final report to the Society expressed his own disappointment. There had been a decline in the success rate; he had found difficulty in continuing to act as agent, as it seemed to make him unwell; one of the girls had left to get married. As the vivacity had gone out of the trials, they would be terminated.

Had the experimenting with the Creery girls also ceased at this point they would still be regarded as the most valuable allies the Society had found. But the tests continued; in 1888, the girls were caught cheating; and they confessed that for some time they had been using a code. When they were in sight of each other, they would signal – say, by an upward look for hearts, downwards for diamonds. Where they could hear each other, they would scrape their feet, cough, or make other such sounds. The signals had originally been used, they claimed, only on occasions when experiments were unsuccessful, and they 'feared that visitors would be disappointed'; in many trials such collusion had not been possible. 'But of course,' Gurney sadly admitted, 'the recent detection must throw discredit on the results of all previous trials in which one or more of the sisters shared in the agency.' He might have added that to sceptics, and even to some members of the Society, doubt would be cast not only on the results of all the tests in which the girls had taken part, but also on the competence of the investigators to conduct experiments of any kind.

Chapter Thirty-one

Phantasms

SHORTLY AFTER BARRETT HAD READ HIS PAPER ON THOUGHT-TRANS-
ference to the British Association in 1876, Dr. R. Angus Smith, F.R.S.,
had written to him to suggest that if the action of mind upon mind
could be proved by experiment 'it would be a discovery that would
make all other discoveries seem trifles', and to remind him that there
was another well-attested source of examples: visions of people who
were dying seen by friends or relatives at a distance. As joint Hon.
Secretaries of the Society for Psychical Research, Myers and Gurney
were soon impressed by the quantity of evidence for such visions and
also, as they noted in the first volume of the Society's *Proceedings*, by
its harmonious nature, 'the similarities of unlooked-for detail which
bind the phenomena together into distinct groups, the very similarity
which make the accounts of them monotonous reading, give the
strength of a faggot to the dispersed unities which it looked as if the
mere dead weight of uninquiring incredulity might easily break'.

After they had produced a 'sighting shot' in the *Fortnightly* in
March 1883, explaining the nature of the research, the Council agreed
to their preparing a book on the subject with the assistance of Frank
Podmore, a young civil servant who had joined the Society. Gurney
did most of the work. The fact that stories had been vouched for by
earlier writers was not enough, he felt (though he was half inclined to
make an exception in the case of Robert Dale Owen). He, or some
other member of the Society, must personally check each account.
This – Alan Gauld has estimated in his account of the Society's early
years – entailed writing anything up to fifty or sixty letters a day, in
his own hand, to elicit the details he required; in particular, corrobora-
tion by all those who might remember the episode under investigation.
From the mass of evidence which he accumulated he weeded out everything which could reasonably be attributed to natural causes – dreams,
say, about the death of a soldier killed in a campaign – or which

lacked precision. But this still left some seven hundred accounts which, he felt, merited inclusion.

Phantasms of the Living appeared in 1886 – the archaic term 'phantasms' having been adopted, Myers explained in his introduction, because 'although etymologically a mere variant of phantom, it has been less often used, and has not become so closely involved with *visual* impressions alone'. And as it happened, of the cases of visual impressions none was so striking as one where clairaudience was involved. It was described by 'A.Z.', a member of the landed gentry; according to Gurney, a man 'as far removed as possible from superstition' who had furnished the evidence but desired that his identity should not be disclosed. Returning home one evening with his wife, he had met one of the tenant farmers on his estate; they had talked for a while, and the man had asked him to drop in later that evening, an invitation he had declined. That night, around ten, he was reading in his breakfast room,

> when I distinctly heard the front gate opened and shut again with a clap, and footsteps advancing at a run up the drive. When opposite the window, the steps changed to sharp and distinct on gravel to dull and less clear on the grass slip below the window, and at the same time I was conscious that someone or something stood close to me outside, only the thin shutter and a sheet of glass dividing us. I could hear the quick panting laboured breathing of the messenger, or whatever it was, as if trying to recover breath before speaking. Had he been attracted by the light through the shutter? Suddenly, like a gunshot, inside, outside, and all around, there broke out the most appalling shriek – a prolonged wail ... of my fright and horror I can say nothing – increased tenfold when I walked into the dining room and found my wife sitting quietly at her work close to the window, in the same line and distant only ten or twelve feet from the corresponding window in the breakfast room. *She had heard nothing.*

'A.Z.' was too shaken to go outside, but the following morning there was no trace of footsteps on the snow. Later, he heard that his tenant had committed suicide; the consequence, it transpired, of an unhappy love affair. He had taken prussic acid; and at the inquest, his groom described how he had heard him scream as he died. All this happened, 'A.Z.' discovered, 'as near as I can ascertain, at the exact time when I had been so much alarmed at my own home' – though his home was far too distant for the sound of the scream to have carried.

But Gurney did not waste much space on dramatic episodes of this kind. He was clearly anxious to show that they were a small part of a great range of psychic impressions, transmitted not only by 'seeing' and 'hearing', but through 'smelling' (one of his informants remembered an occasion when he had been thinking of violets, in a place where he had a romantic recollection of them; his wife suddenly remarked that it was very curious, but she felt that she could smell violets, even though it was November). There were also examples where none of the five senses was involved; the percipient simply felt alarmed about somebody, without being able to account for it.

A. Skirving, foreman of the masons who worked in Winchester Cathedral, recalled how at work one day he had suddenly felt an intense urge to go home, which made him uneasy, as he did not want to lose the money, or to incur his wife's ridicule. Eventually he could resist it no longer. When he reached his house his wife's sister, answering the door, asked him how he knew? His wife had been run over by a cab, and seriously injured; and had been calling for him piteously. When she saw him she calmed down, and recovered. As the incident had taken place thirty years before, the account would hardly have qualified for inclusion had not Gurney been impressed by the writer. 'I am not a scholar as I left school when twelve years of age, and I therefore hope you will forgive all sins against composition and grammar,' Skirving remarked. 'This short narrative has only one merit; it is strictly true.' And though Skirving's wife was dead Gurney, when he went to check, had it vouched for by his sister-in-law, who remembered the incident well.

The perception of danger could come in stranger ways; the most striking – literally – being the experience of the wife of the artist Arthur Severn. One morning in 1880 she had woken up in her bedroom in her room by Coniston Water,

feeling that I had had a hard blow on my mouth, and with a distinct sense that I had been cut and was bleeding under my upper lip, and seized my pocket-handkerchief, and held it (in a little pushed lump) to the part, as I sat up in bed, and after a few seconds, when I removed it, I was astonished not to see any blood, and only then realised it was impossible anything could have struck me there, as I lay fast asleep in bed, and so I thought it was only a dream.

Looking at her watch, she found it was seven; and as her husband was not in the room, she assumed he had gone out for a sail. He had. When he came in for breakfast,

I noticed that he rather purposely sat farther away from me than usual, and every now and then put his pocket-handkerchief furtively up to his lip, in the very way I had done. I said, 'Arthur, why are you doing that?' and added a little anxiously 'I know you've hurt yourself! But I'll tell you why afterwards.' He said, 'Well, when I was sailing a sudden squall came, throwing the tiller suddenly round, and it struck me a bad blow in the mouth under the upper lip, and it has been bleeding a good deal and won't stop.' I then said 'Have you any idea what o'clock it was when it happened?' and he answered 'it must have been about seven'.

Arthur Severn confirmed the story.

To include an experience of this kind under the label of 'phantasms' was to stretch the concept to breaking point; but this did not worry Gurney or Myers, as they wanted to get rid of the 'ghoulies and ghosties' image and to establish sensory messages as simply another branch of communication, by telepathy – the term which Myers had coined as an alternative to thought-transference (party because *tele*, at a distance, and *pathos*, feeling, came closer to representing the 'auditory, tactile and even purely ideational and emotional impressions' which were sometimes involved; partly because the association of the term thought-transference with mesmerism had 'distinctly damaged its chance of scientific recognition'). Unlike phantasms, the term telepathy caught on, acquiring colloquial status; and the book was, in a sense, its manifesto. Under certain conditions, the authors contended, telepathic communication established itself by impinging on one of the senses; most frequently in dreams. For example: arriving to stay in London William Warburton, Canon of Winchester, found that his host, his brother, was at a party. Sitting up waiting for him to return, Warburton fell into a doze; and in a dream, saw his brother come out of a drawing room, catch his foot on a stair, and fall. Half-an-hour later his brother arrived back and explained he had just had a narrow escape from breaking his neck; 'coming out of the ballroom, I caught my foot and tumbled full length down the stairs'. Recalling the story, Warburton surmised that as his brother might well have been reproaching himself at the time for not getting back in time to receive his guest, 'the chances are he was thinking of me'.

It was not only actual or potential danger which could be communicated. Sometimes a frightening thought, or dream, could be picked up by a percipient. Miss Mason described how in the summer of 1878 she had been staying at Oban, and went to see the Falls of Lora, which are caused by the tide rushing down between two seawater lochs. Below are whirlpools, and she began to wonder whether anybody who fell in could be sucked down, fancying what would happen if friends fell in and she was faced with the decision whether to try to save them. Thinking of the falls a week later, when she had left Oban and gone back to the place where she had left her maid, she could not sleep because of the anxiety for some friends who were in trouble; and this became mixed up with her mental picture of the falls. The following morning her maid, who had neither been to Oban nor heard of the falls, described how every time she had fallen asleep she had had a weird dream of 'water rushing over the rocks, and the most dreadful whirlpools' and of standing on high rocks, 'trying to save people out of them with ropes'. And, 'it was not a waterfall of the river', she added, 'it was a *waterfall of the sea*'.

The Rev. A. B. McDougall of Hemel Hempstead provided the oddest case history of a telepathic dream. Staying with friends in Manchester early in the new year of 1882 he woke to find a rat in his bed, and informed his host. The same morning a cousin of his, staying at his Hemel Hempstead home and sleeping in his room, came down to breakfast to tell the company of a dream she had had 'in which a rat appeared to be eating the extremities of my unfortunate self'. 'We always said "E." was a witch,' McDougall's mother wrote to tell him, having had a letter from him describing what had happened in Manchester. 'She always knew about everything almost before it took place.'

A few individuals, the evidence suggested, were 'witches' in this sense, being periodically gifted with second sight. Sometimes it would provide a warning; but often, according to J. G. Keulemans, what was 'seen' appeared to be of no significance. One day in 1882 he had suddenly had a mind's eye picture of a little wicker basket containing eggs of different sizes and colours. Two hours later, at lunch, he was reminded of his vision by the sight of eggs on the table, and mentioned it. His wife thereupon brought up the basket he had 'seen', with the remaining eggs in it; and he later learned from his mother-in-law, who had sent them, that she had put them in the basket, thinking of him, at the time the vision of them came into his mind. Keulemans explained to Gurney that he had made a study of these visions. They were spontaneous, but always preceded by a strange sensation; and they were always, when he was able to check them, accurate down to minute details.

As well as numerous examples of straightforward telepathy, clairvoyance or prevision, *Phantasms* gave several examples of travelling clairvoyance; including one from Newnham, the clergyman who had carried out the tests of his wife's psychic powers with the help of a ouija board. Some thirty years before, when still unmarried (and a sceptic), he had dreamed that he saw her ascending some stairs; he had run after her and put his arms around her waist. Waking up, he noted the time – ten o'clock; and the next morning sent her an account of his dream. Crossing his letter came one from her in which she asked whether he had been thinking of her, around ten? 'As I was going upstairs to bed, I distinctly heard your footsteps on the stairs and felt your arms around my waist.'

There were also some reports of induced travelling clairvoyance. John Moule recalled how he had told a girl whom he knew to have psychic powers that he would try to 'visit' her, some day, at a time when he would not know where she would be, or what she would be doing. If she noticed anything strange, she should make a note of it. A couple of months later he tried the experiment; felt he had 'expended energy', as he put it; and then fell asleep. In a dream, he watched the girl coming down some kitchen stairs; when she saw him she cried 'Oh! Mr. Moule!' and fainted. Assuming this was simply a dream, he thought no more about it; but three weeks later the girl told Moule's wife how she had fainted when she had 'seen' Moule sitting in her kitchen. And when Moule told her his recollections of the kitchen from his dream, they tallied exactly with the actual kitchen.

It was characteristic of Gurney that though he felt certain Moule was a careful and honest witness, he was not prepared to attach much weight to the account because the girl had been warned in advance of the experiment. As she had since died, too, she could not confirm the story. More convincing evidence came from the Rev. C. Godfrey of Eastbourne who only a few months earlier, in 1886, had read about travelling clairvoyance and decided to try to 'visit' a friend. Without telling her, he tried when he went to bed one night to 'translate himself' – spiritually – into her company, and to attract her attention; and that night he dreamed that the experiment had worked. It had: the next day she described to him how she had seen him standing by a window, but he had gradually faded from her view. Podmore, who investigated the case, suggested that Godfrey should try again. A fortnight later, he reported that he had decided to make his presence felt both by voice and by touch, by visualising placing his hand on Mrs. W.'s head. Again, he dreamed that he had succeeded; again, he had. By Mrs. W.'s account, she had been aroused by a voice saying 'wake' and the feeling that a hand was resting on the side of her head, and she had seen the misty face and form of Godfrey.

There were two obvious openings for critics of *Phantasms*, one of which Gurney attempted to counter in the book. Could chance coincidence be responsible? To test the possibility, he had conducted a primitive poll, asking five thousand people whether they had ever had 'a vivid impression of seeing or being touched by a human being, or of hearing a voice or sound which suggested a human presence when no one was there'. Only twenty-one people replied that they had. If this sample was representative, then the odds against anybody having a hallucination about seeing or being touched by a human being at the time that human being was on the point of death were far too high for chance to account for the number of occasions when such hallucinations had been reported. And although Gurney's statistical apparatus could be challenged, the coincidence explanation could not seriously be sustained in the light of the evidence from the much more elaborate 'census of hallucinations' conducted in Britain and other countries three years later; provided such evidence could be relied upon.

But should it be relied upon? In the *Nineteenth Century* a Scots lawyer, A. T. Innes, pointed out that although there was plenty of evidence of psychic visitations after the event, there was a lack of documentary evidence written and attested before it became known that, say, the 'visitor' had died. Still, even though written evidence of this kind had rarely been preserved, Gurney and Myers felt that the accumulated mass of testimony was amply sufficient to prove 'the ability of one mind to impress or be impressed by another mind, otherwise than through the recognised channels of sense'. Allowing for the occasional hoaxer (who in any case would tend to give himself away later to enjoy his joke), and for all the other possibilities of error, it was difficult to put any other interpretation on the mass of facts vouched for by people of all ages, especially as so many of them had nothing to gain from recounting their stories and took care that their identities were not disclosed. *Phantasms of the Living* was, and remains, a notable landmark in psychical research; to pass to it from even the ablest of its predecessors, as Gauld has remarked, 'is like passing from a medieval bestiary or herbal to Linnaeus's *Systema Naturae*'.

Chapter Thirty-two

Hypnotism

ALTHOUGH THE PSYCHICAL RESEARCHERS COULD CONGRATULATE THEM-
selves on their progress, as measured by the results of such experiments
as Barrett's and Guthrie's and by the publication of *Phantasms*, they
could not claim to have made any breach in orthodoxy's defences.
They had shown convincing evidence that spontaneous telepathic communication existed, and that it could be induced; but the induced kind
had not been sufficiently reliable for the experiments to be conclusive.
The need now was to find some means whereby communication could
be laid on at will, for the benefit of sceptics. And there was an obvious
potential ally in mesmerism, which in its new guise, hypnotism, had
suddenly established itself as a clinical reality.

Liébeault and Richet

In spite of the fact that it had a supporter in Carpenter – and a
reluctant convert in the *Lancet*, which in 1870 (Wakley had died in
1862) had abandoned its virulently antagonistic campaign – hypnotism had made little progress in Britain. But in 1860 Braid had been
invited to send a paper to the French Academy, where it was read
by the surgeon Professor Velpeau; and though Braid did not live to
enjoy the prestige of being a prophet with honour outside his own
country – he died three days later – his ideas became better known on
the Continent than they were in Britain. And among those who had
been present at the Academy meeting was a country doctor, A. A.
Liébeault, who returned to his practice near Nancy determined to see
if he could treat patients by Braid's method.

In the first major textbook on hypnosis in the English language
J. Milne Bramwell was to recall how he had paid a visit to Liébeault,
and been impressed by his ability and integrity. He worked hard –
by that time he was in his late sixties, but he was often in the saddle

making his rounds by two a.m.; some of his colleagues thought him mad, but the poor called him 'the good father'.

In order to find subjects Liébeault took advantage of the parsimonious character of the French peasant. His patients had absolute confidence in him, but they had been accustomed to be treated in the ordinary manner. He therefore said to them, 'if you wish me to treat you with drugs, I will do so, but you will have to pay me as formerly. On the other hand, if you allow me to hypnotise you, I will do it for nothing.'

Liébeault's method was simple: he quietly suggested to his patients that they were ready to go to sleep, and when they sank into the trance, he made further quiet suggestions designed to remove their symptoms. The method was so successful that patients began to arrive from afar. It does not seem to have occurred to him to use hypnosis for any other purpose than the treatment of everyday disorders; his treatise *Du Sommeil et des Etats Analogues*, published in 1886, made no reference to higher phenomena. But they began to break through. In 1868 'Mlle. B.' was brought to him by her parents to be treated for a nervous condition which she had contracted while teaching at a school in Coblenz. Mlle. B., Liébeault found, was a medium, who could do automatic writing at great speed, quite unconscious of what she was putting down; she could even engage in conversation while she did it. One morning the urge came upon her; and when she deciphered what she had written it told her that a friend of hers at Coblenz, Margaret, had died. Mlle. B. wrote to the school, not mentioning the reason, but assuming that if Margaret were dead, she would be told in the school's reply. Margaret, it transpired, had died at the time Mlle. B. was writing.

Liébeault regarded the episode as no more than a curiosity; and as he had remained unknown, except to his patients (according to Bramwell only a single copy of his book had been sold), the story attracted no attention. Nor did Charles Richet's experience at the Hôtel Dieu in Paris, where he worked as a physiologist, and used the opportunity to experiment with the patients, as Du Potet had half a century before. Richet found that he could hypnotise some of them; and though he was sceptical about the higher phenomena, he asked a hypnotised subject whether she could name a friend of his whom he was thinking about. She spelled out 'H ... E ... I cannot "see" the third ... R ... N'. The name of his friend was Hearn; and the odds against the patient getting it right by chance, Richet estimated, were two hundred thousand to one. As he was later to recall, though, hypnosis in the 1870s was still associated with 'mystery and magic'. The account he wrote

of his investigations in 1875 began with the admission that it needed
some courage even to use the term 'somnambulism'; and he discreetly
avoided the subject of the still more suspect higher phenomena.

Hansen and Heidenhain

The man who was responsible for beginning the process whereby
hypnotism was switched from the supernatural to the natural was given
little credit for the achievement at the time, and has since been forgotten. Carl Hansen, a Dane, made his living as a travelling showman,
giving the kind of performance that stage hypnotists do to this day:
relying on his ability to put a few volunteers into a trance and then
getting them to behave like dogs, dowagers or drunks for the amusement of the audience. He would also demonstrate their immunity to
pain. The stock reaction of the medical profession was still, as it had
been for a century, that the volunteers were 'planted', and that Hansen
was only pretending to pinch them or burn them. But one of his acts
was less easy to account for. He would suggest to an entranced subject
that his body was absolutely rigid; and in this condition the body
could be stretched out like a plank between two chairs, head on one,
heels on the other. Hansen would then invite members of the audience
to come forward and test the rigidity of the horizontal figure by striking it in the belly, or sitting on it, to prove for themselves that a kind
of living equivalent of *rigor mortis* had been induced. Naturally this
aroused the curiosity of doctors; and Hansen was occasionally asked
to demonstrate for them. The collective scepticism of the assembled
group might prevail; Hansen would be unable to get any results, and
the doctors would return to their homes congratulating themselves on
how they had rumbled him. But when he did get results, the scepticism
of some members of his audience was likely to be shaken. The sight
of a portly colleague, Dr. A., stretched out between two chairs and
being pounded by his friends could not be satisfactorily accounted for
on accepted physiological theories; nor was it easy for a group of
doctors who knew each other well to accept that when Dr. B., normally
reserved, went down on his hands and knees and began mewing like
a cat, and lapping up a saucer of milk, that he was in collusion with
the mesmerist. What could Dr. B. conceivably get out of it?

When Hansen gave a demonstration in Breslau in 1879, among his
audience was Rudolf Heidenhain, Professor of Physiology, who had
shared the general assumption that collusion was responsible for the
effects. Collusion, Heidenhain realised, did not satisfactorily account
for the spectacle he now witnessed. Surely there must be some way in
which he could set up an experiment which would preclude any possibility that the subject was co-operating with the hypnotist? The only
way, he decided, was to persuade somebody on whose honesty he could

rely absolutely to act as the subject, in order to see whether the hypnotist could make him do things under hypnosis which he would not ordinarily do for love or money. His younger brother volunteered.

A glass containing ink was given him, with the request to drink some beer. Without the least hesitation he began to drink the ink. He also, on being told to do so, thrust his hand into a burning light; and with scissors so unmercifully cut off his whiskers, which he had assiduously cultivated for a year, that on awakening he was greatly enraged.

Heidenhain's treatise setting out the results of his investigation appeared in 1880. In the introduction to the English edition G. J. Romanes recalled that if the facts then stated had been presented by any ordinary observer, they would have been 'at once dismissed, and rightly dismissed, as much too improbable for acceptance'; but Heidenhain happened to have a national – among his medical colleagues, international – reputation. He was careful, too, to present his findings in a form which orthodoxy could assimilate, presenting hypnosis as a physiological process, and describing it in suitably impressive clinical jargon as 'an inhibition of the action of the ganglion cells of the cerebral cortex, induced by continued weak stimulation of other nerves'; in other words, as a neurological rather than a psychological condition.

Charcot

Although this was a help towards establishing hypnosis as natural, rather than occult, there was a catch. As the existence of the trance state had been so strenuously denied for so long, medical scientists did not know quite what to do with it now that they had it. But at this point they were rescued by Jean-Martin Charcot, Professor at the Salpêtrière in Paris. He, too, had been experimenting with 'Braidism'; and he had found that patients who were being treated for hysteria reacted with extraordinary consistency, their trances following the same pattern, the 'three stages' of lethargy, catalepsy, and somnambulism. To Charcot, the significance appeared obvious. Hypnosis – a state of 'neuro-muscular hyper-excitability', induced by 'peripheral mechanical stimulation' – was simply hystero-epilepsy, artificially induced. A notorious symptom of hysteria, for example, had been the 'rainbow'; the patient's body would stiffen in the form of an arc, only the head and the heels remaining on the ground. Endlessly, his patients demonstrated the symptom when put into a hypnotic trance – as anybody was welcome to witness: Charcot's *Leçons du Mardi* at the Salpêtrière became famous, 'the huge amphitheatre filled to the last place with a multicoloured audience drawn from *tout Paris*,' Axel Munthe recalled in *The Story of San Michele*; 'authors, journalists, leading actors and actresses, fashionable *demi-mondaines*, all full of morbid curiosity to witness the startling phenomena of hypnotism'. Munthe's tale of how he became disillusioned with Charcot, and tried unsuccessfully to rescue one of the hysterics from his clutches, reads like one of his flights of fancy; but his description of the manic atmosphere of hysteria and fraud at the exhibitions tallies with contemporary accounts.

In ordinary circumstances Charcot's showmanship would have aroused the anger, or the derision, of medical scientists. But the exhibitions, and the explanations which he provided for them to the Academy in 1882, happened to provide orthodoxy with precisely what it had needed. Charcot had not merely confirmed that the hypnotic trance was a neurological condition, as Heidenhain had claimed; he had also shown that it was a disordered condition. And if hypnosis were simply induced hystero-epilepsy, medical science need hardly concern itself further with the subject, except perhaps for the purpose of investigating hysteria itself. There was no need for doctors to learn how to hypnotise, for what doctor in his senses would want to induce hystero-epilepsy? Better still, Charcot's theory would finally dispose of mesmerism, old-style. Its essential charlatanry, and the gullibility of those who had believed in animal magnetism – let alone the higher phenomena – had surely been established. The ghost of Mesmer was finally laid.

The Nancy School

Or was it? In 1882 Liébeault had cured a patient whom Hippolyte Bernheim, Professor at Nancy, had treated for years without success by orthodox methods. Expecting to find and expose a charlatan Bernheim visited Liébeault, and was immediately won over, accepting the reality of and the benefits from hypnotherapy, and introducing it in his own hospital. What Bernheim witnessed bore no resemblance to the antics at the Salpêtrière; and it was manifestly ludicrous to claim that all the thousands of patients who had testified to the success of Liébeault's method had been suffering from hysteria. The idea that the trance state was induced by 'peripheral muscular stimulation', could also be dismissed; for years, Liébeault had been inducing it by simple suggestion.

So the battle was joined between the Nancy School, as it became known, and the Salpêtrière. For a while, they had in common a desire to divest hypnotism of any association with animal magnetism, and particularly with the higher phenomena. But in 1883 Liébeault, emboldened by the new celebrity he had won as a result of Bernheim's conversion, published his oddly-named *Etude sur le Zoomagnetisme*; and in it he admitted that they had occurred in his experience. 'I can no longer deny that certain phenomena are due to the action of one organism on another, without any conscious intervention of the subject under experiment.' He was under no illusions that his local reputation would make scientists elsewhere believe him; but 'we invite the true friends of science,' he wrote, ' – those who, being independent, do not believe in the infallibility of academicians – we invite them to verify our experiments'. They would find, he thought, that 'animal magnetism is more complex than has been believed'.·

These were hardly the words of a man who had glibly deluded himself into belief in thought-transference. Nor was his frank admission that he had not been sufficiently careful in the case of Mlle. B. Although he had ascertained that the letter which disclosed the death of her friend had a Coblenz postmark,

> I have since regretted that I did not, in the interest of science, ask the family to go with me to the telegraph office, to make sure that they had not received a telegram during the morning of February 7th. Science ought not to have any bashfulness; truth has no fear of being seen. I have only a moral proof of the truth of the fact; that is, the honour of the family, which always seemed to me to be above suspicion.

Janet and Ochorowicz

Nothing could have suited Charcot better than that the Nancy School's reputation should be compromised by Liébeault's defection to the ranks of the mesmerists. But soon, Charcot was confronted with a maverick in his own camp. In 1885 his newly-formed *Société de Psychologie Physiologique*, whose name disclosed its founder's preconceptions, heard a paper written by one of his students, a young lecturer in philosophy and psychology (the two disciplines had not yet split apart), Pierre Janet. Janet had been to Le Havre to witness some experiments by a local doctor, J. H. A. Gibert, on one of his patients. 'Mme. B.' was a stolid peasant woman, but subject to occasional spontaneous attacks of somnambulism, a disorder which the Salpêtrière School considered to be a symptom of hysteria, and therefore treatable by hypnosis. In the course of treatment, Gibert found he could hypnotise her by simple pressure on her hand – 'peripheral muscular stimulation'. But he had been disconcerted to find that this method worked only when he concentrated on what he was doing. When he was preoccupied with other matters, 'the trance did not supervene'. Inducing hypnosis, therefore, could not just be a mechanical exercise. And what was even more disturbing, Gibert found that when he was giving his full attention to what he was doing, there was no need to touch Mme. B.'s hand. He could induce the trance simply by *thinking* he would induce it; as Janet, investigating, had been able to confirm.

Apart from the obligatory few remarks from Charcot as chairman, Janet's paper was received in silence. It was an uncomfortable moment, for Janet could hardly be lying; yet if he were telling the truth, then the ugly spectre of the higher phenomena had returned to haunt the Salpêtrière. There remained one possibility: hyperacuity of one of Mme. B.'s senses. With the acceptance of hypnotism, there had been a need for a parallel hypothesis to account naturally for the higher phenomena, and hyperacuity was clearly the most promising. In 1881 Romanes, Galton and Lankester had tested a 'thought-reader' who had claimed he did not know what the force was which led him consistently to find some hidden object; and their verdict, published in *Nature*, was that he did it by 'muscle-reading'. Although the hypothesis was challenged by Barrett on the strength of his tests with the Creery children – 'after making the most extravagant allowance for the existence of some persons of a muscular sense of preternatural acuteness, there still remains a large residuum of facts wholly unaccounted for' – it was presented the following year as a fully-fledged theory by the New York neurologist George M. Beard, who claimed that he had shown how 'a well-trained operator may find so small an object as a pea or a pin by connecting his finger with the finger of the subject'. And confirmation was lent to the theory by Cumberland – by this time internationally known; in 1884, he had a season in Paris. Although understandably reluctant to disclose how he managed to read people's thoughts, he continued to insist that no psychic element was involved.

With Mme. B., however, this interpretation presented problems. She was clearly not 'a well-trained operator', on the Cumberland model; except in the trance state she had no thought-reading ability. And no contact of fingers was required, when she was in a trance, for her thought-reading to succeed. Could it be that one of her other senses was responsible? So Janet went back to Le Havre, with his brother Jules, to carry out further tests with Gibert's help; and they were joined there by Myers and by Dr. Julian Ochorowicz, an assistant professor of philosophy and psychology at the University of Lemburg.

Although Ochorowicz came to enjoy an international reputation for his psychological researches, his name is not now remembered. It deserves to be, as the early autobiographical part of his *De la Suggestion Mentale* is the most revealing of all the works of the period about the problems which confronted researchers, as their findings lured them or goaded them out of the safe harbour which materialism provided. He enjoyed none of the keen pleasure which an investigator experiences when his experimental findings illustrate and confirm his hunches. Instead, he was continually being compelled to revise his beliefs, and remodel his theories, to accommodate the unwelcome facts which those experimental findings disclosed.

Ochorowicz had been only nineteen when his first essay on psychological method was published in Leipzig, and still in his twenties when he received his Lemburg appointment; orthodox enough not merely to reject the possibility of thought-transference, but to dismiss it as a subject unworthy of research. But hypnosis intrigued him; and in the course of his research he came across a boy who when entranced could recognise who had touched him behind his back. Trying to find out which of the five senses was being employed, Ochorowicz tested him with a book, and found that the boy could read from it when it was held out of his sight, so long as Ochorowicz kept his eyes on the text. Sometimes he could read even when the book was closed, if he were given some clue to the passage.

This provided Ochorowicz with the clue he himself needed. The boy must be using aided recall; in the trance state, he must be remembering what he had read earlier. When the boy mentioned something which was in his mesmerist's mind at the time, Ochorowicz thought 'coincidence'. Even when, contemptuously, Ochorowicz agreed to a table-rapping session, and the raps correctly described the contents of an envelope – a photograph of a man of twenty-three – Ochorowicz told himself that the envelope looked as if it might have a photograph in it; that a man was a likely subject of a photograph; and that he must himself have given the man's age away by pausing at the twenty-third rap. He assumed there must be deception because he was himself a skilled prestidigitator, and knew the tricks of the trade; not as used in the halls, but as demonstrable by a psychologist who enjoys showing his pupils how easy it is to distract their attention, to make them think they have seen what they have not seen, or to make them give away the contents of a sealed envelope by apparently innocent questions. And where trickery could not be the explanation, hyperacuity of vision or hearing or of the other senses always sufficed him. At Lemburg, he had a subject who when mesmerised would obey suggestions which he made mentally, even though she had her eyes bandaged and her ears plugged. She must, he decided, have exceptional sensitivity to the gestures which he was making behind her back. Perhaps the currents of air they set up enabled her to register minute changes of temperature? Or could it be that her sense of smell enabled her to detect his gestures, because they would waft towards her the odour of his tobacco?

Groping for a natural solution, Ochorowicz studied the work of other researchers in the same field; and it brought him no comfort.

Dr. Baréty of Nice showed him how a hypnotised subject could 'feel' his way towards a hidden object as if being drawn to it by a magnet. 'I exist only in my fingers which, however, work without me,' the subject assured Ochorowicz. 'The more I reason, the less do I succeed.' When Richet published the positive results of some card-guessing experiments in 1885 Ochorowicz, trying them out for himself, obtained similar results. If ordinary men and women could score better than chance in such tests, he surmised, hypnotisable people ought to do better still. He tried one under hypnosis, and her success rate went so far beyond chance expectation that he was almost compelled to accept that thought-transference existed. The subject could not have cheated. He knew that he had not cheated – not consciously. Was it perhaps possible, though, that in some way they had been *un*consciously deceiving themselves?

There could hardly be a better illustration of the resistance which researchers put up to acceptance of any psychic content in hypnosis. In growing desperation, Ochorowicz longed for some, *any* hypothesis which could bridge the growing fissure between what he had experimentally proved as real, and what he was prepared to accept as theoretically possible. Was there some form of concordance between minds – 'a transmission, *always indirect*, of vibrations produced by the thought itself' – on the analogy of the newly-discovered telephone? But a series of experiments with a woman who, when hypnotised, was able to follow his thoughts, obey his mental orders (often irascibly), and feel his pain if he pinched himself, finally convinced him that 'neither chance, nor coincidence, nor suggestion by attitude or gesture, nor any other possible cause of error' could explain the facts: thought and feeling must actually be transferable.

If the results of his own experiments were confirmed by those of Janet, Ochorowicz realised, it would destroy the pretensions of the Salpêtrière School, which had been 'boasting of itself as the legitimate successor of animal magnetism, deceased'; and though it would not re-establish the case for animal magnetism, it would point to the existence of some unknown force at work. The tests at Le Havre were accordingly arranged to eliminate the possibility that Mme. B. could be picking up sensory clues, and to preclude the possibility of collusion between her and any of the investigators. Either Janet or Gibert did the hypnotising, the others monitoring – so that if there was collusion all of them would have to be involved. It was not enough for the hypnotist and Mme. B. to be in different rooms; they must be in different establishments, up to half a mile apart, and there must be no way in which either she or those observing her would know when the hypnotist was operating. The hypnotist would note the time when he began to try to induce the trance state; the others would note the time

when Mme. B. became entranced. In twenty-five trials, the times coincided on eighteen occasions, and there were four further partially
successful experiments. Not only would Mme. B. become entranced;
on coming out of her trance, she would do what she had been told to
do, mentally, while she was in it. And Janet established that if the
hypnotist put Mme. B. into a trance, and then pinched himself, she
would react as if she herself was being pinched in the same place. In
ordinary circumstances Mme. B. reacted only to the hypnotist; but the
Janet brothers found that either of them could influence her. In one
experiment, while Pierre remained with her, Jules went to another
room and made a severe burn on his arm. As Pierre Janet described
it, Mme. B. began crying out wildly:

> I had great difficulty in restraining her. She had hold of her right
> arm above the wrist and complained of suffering greatly there. Now,
> I did not know exactly the spot at which my brother had intended
> to make the burn. *It was at that part*. When Mme. B. was awakened,
> I noticed with astonishment that she still held her right wrist and
> complained of suffering greatly therein, though she knew not why.

No longer, Ochorowicz realised, could he hope to reconcile what he
had observed with any of the theories of sensory hyperacuity yet advanced, including his own. In his *Mental Suggestion*, when it was
published the following year, he described how he left Le Havre with
profound emotion – 'I had at last witnessed the extraordinary phenomenon of action at a distance, which upsets all currently received
opinions'. This did not mean, he insisted, that what they had witnessed
could not be fitted into the framework of science; but it did mean that
science would need to enlarge its conceptions. It would also have to
allow for a greater element of uncertainty. It had worried him that a
hypnotised subject should be able to enjoy a run of correct guesses,
explaining that he could 'see' the cards; yet then begin to get them
hopelessly wrong, though still 'seeing' them. This was just the kind of
thing which would bring the research, and the researchers, into disrepute. But was it really so inexplicable? Perhaps thought-transference
was subject to the same kind of blocks as hearing. 'One does not hear
if deaf; one does not hear if there is too much noise; one does not hear
when one is absorbed in thought.' And although much remained to
be explored, enough was known, he felt, to help to account for, if not
fully to explain, a great deal of what previously had been dismissed as
superstition.

The Le Havre series was the most carefully controlled and attested
of those carried out under hypnosis; but it was only one of many.
Experiments continued with 'Léonie', as Mme. B. of Le Havre came

to be called; and periodically she would produce more striking results. Asked by Janet to 'travel' to Paris in her trance, to 'visit' Richet, she told him 'it is burning'; and later, 'But, M. Janet, I assure you it is burning'. That morning, Richet's Paris laboratory had caught fire and been gutted. Richet himself found other subjects with the same faculty. At his bidding 'Alice' would describe the country house of anybody who came to visit him. She told Dr. P. Rondeau, among other things, about 'someone looking at the clock whose shoulder is visible. A large painting of a landscape; between the town and the sea something pointed, a tower, or the roof of a church.' Dr. Rondeau confirmed that at his home he had a statue of Penelope, looking over her shoulder towards a clock; and a Canaletto with water in the foreground and the church of San Giorgio in the background. Perhaps the most remarkable of 'Alice's' guesses was wrong. Richet had asked a friend of his to do some drawings, which he placed between layers of paper in sealed envelopes, and shuffled, so that he himself would not know which envelope contained which drawing. 'Alice' was occasionally able to give an accurate description, but she was not consistent; and one of her mistakes was a sketch of a picture frame, which she thought was of a French soldier in uniform. Told of this guess, the artist explained that the frame contained a picture of himself, dressed in precisely the uniform which she had described.

From all over France reports came in to journals of medicine and psychology of a similar nature; including one where the information had been solicited in order to provide some clues about a crime. In the *Revue Philosophique* in 1889 Dr. Dufay of Blois described how 'Maria', who had been observed to have clairvoyant powers, was hypnotised and given a packet containing a small piece of a necktie which a prisoner had used to strangle himself in jail. She proceeded to describe to Dufay and the examining magistrate how the prisoner had murdered another man with a hatchet (which they already knew); and then told them where they would find the hatchet (which they had not known). In subsequent tests Maria also was able to tell from articles owned by the prisoners, concealed in packets, what crime each of them had been jailed for.

In 1889, too, confirmation of the Le Havre results came from Liébeault, who had been experimenting along similar lines to Janet. He wrote instructions to a hypnotised subject on a piece of paper: for example, 'Mademoiselle, on waking, will see her black hat transformed into a red one'. When the girl came out of her trance,

without a moment's hesitation she fixed her eyes upon the hat, and with a burst of laughter exclaimed that it was not her hat, she would have none of it. It was the same shape certainly, but this farce had lasted long enough – we really must give her back her own ... we had to press her for some time before she would say what change had come over her hat; surely we were making fun of her. At last she said, 'You can see for yourselves that it is red'.

She had to be assured that it would presently resume its usual colour, as if by a conjuring trick, before she would accept it as hers. Later, when Liébeault realised that such a test did not entirely eliminate the possibility that his subject had been picking up other sensory clues, he arranged for her to be watched while, unbeknown to her, he hid in the garden. From there he hypnotised her successfully, though the process took him twenty minutes (a colleague succeeded in eight).

A few German scientists, too, had become interested; and in 1888 a report was published of a careful series of experiments by Dr. Albert von Schrenck-Notzing. Schrenck-Notzing had become interested when, passing a house where he knew one of the daughters of the family who had the reputation of being psychic, he stood under her window willing her to wake up and think of him; and later, he found she had woken up and told the friend who was sharing her room that she had 'seen' his face. After studying hypnosis at the Salpêtrière and at Nancy, Schrenck-Notzing embarked on experiments with a subject, 'Lina', along the same lines as Guthrie's in Liverpool. In her trance 'Lina' would react when, standing behind her, he pricked himself with a pin; express in dumb show appropriate feelings when he ate something sweet, or sour; obey orders he gave her mentally; and reproduce sketches he drew. The philosopher Carl du Prel, Director of a Society for Scientific Psychology and author of *The Philosophy of Mysticism*, attended many of the tests, and vouched for the precautions taken to prevent 'Lina' from acquiring the information through any of the ordinary sensory channels. In one test, witnesses were invited to bring a book; when placed on top of her head and opened at random she was able, even though with obvious difficulty, to 'read' from it.

The Critics

Yet all this evidence – and there was more from other countries, notably from Russia – failed to make any impression upon orthodox scientists, for reasons which Richet foresaw in his introduction to Ochorowicz's *Mental Suggestion*. The most notable thing about Ochorowicz, Richet thought, was his 'resolute, unflagging determination to weigh all objections, to put away all causes of bad faith, whether conscious or unconscious, to take note of all the difficulties of the problem, sometimes magnifying them, and not to be content until every possible cause of illusion has been removed'; nobody could fail to recognise his sincerity, his perseverance, and his passionate love of truth. 'And yet I do not think,' Richet went on,

> that his book, strong as it is in proofs, will convince all, or even many persons. I know too well (from my own experience) how difficult it is *to believe what we have seen* when it does not accord with the general tenor of our thoughts, with the commonplaces that underlie all our knowledge. A fortnight ago I witnessed such-and-such an astonishing fact, and I was convinced. Today I toss my head and begin to doubt. Six months hence I shall no longer believe it at all. This is a curious anomaly of our minds. To produce conviction it is not enough that a fact is proven logically and experimentally; it is necessary, furthermore, that we – so to speak – become intellectually habituated to it. If it clashes with our routine it is rejected, spurned.

Richet's prediction was fulfilled. Charcot's explanation of hypnosis had been acceptable because, in the form he presented it, it could be fitted relatively painlessly into the existing framework of medical science. The assimilation process, in fact, had been remarkably rapid. Only a few weeks before Charcot presented his case to the Academy in 1882, the whole subject was so suspect from its links with occultism that the S.P.R. committee appointed to research into it was asked to investigate the 'so-called' mesmeric trance, with its 'alleged' insensibility to pain. Within four years, so well established was the reality of the trance state that Arthur Desjardins of the Academy had opened a campaign to restrict the practice of hypnotism to members of the medical profession, making it a criminal offence for anybody else. 'In psychology, physiology and medicine,' William James wryly commented,

> wherever a debate between the mystics and the scientifics has been once for all decided, it is the mystics who have usually proved to be right about the *facts*, while the scientifics have the better of it in respect to the theories. The most recent and flagrant example of this is 'animal magnetism', whose facts were stoutly dismissed as a pack of lies by academic medical science the world over, until the non-mystical theory of 'hypnotic suggestion' was found for them – when they were admitted to be so excessively and dangerously common that special penal laws, forsooth, must be passed to keep all persons unequipped with medical diplomas from taking part in their production.

The excuse for Desjardins's campaign sounded plausible. If, as

Charcot had claimed, hypnosis was induced hysteria, it would obviously be risky to allow unqualified persons to experiment with it. But what was even more remarkable than the speed with which hypnosis had been accepted, following Charcot's demonstration, was that within four years his theory had been so comprehensively demolished that even his Salpêtrière disciples had abandoned it. For as soon as research into hypnosis had been given the tacit sanction of an Academy hearing, a torrent of reports began to flow in from doctors and others who had been quietly experimenting with hypnosis; and the overwhelming majority of them indicated that it was the Nancy School's interpretation, not the Salpêtrière's, which was correct. Patients did not have to be hysterics to be hypnotisable. The process by which hypnosis was induced was psychological, not physiological. And suggestion under hypnosis could safely be used to remove some symptoms of physical illness. The Salpêtrière patients had behaved in the way they did, not because it was the natural course of hypnosis, but because, as hysterics, they needed to call attention to themselves. Consciously or unconsciously they had realised that the way to bask in Charcot's favour was to perform according to his design.

The Nancy School's alternative, however, though endorsed by most researchers, was unacceptable to scientists. As Janet observed, Charcot's doctrine had been

clear, definite, and easy to study; it seemed to bring animal magnetism within the limits of physiology, and that looked like scientific progress. What was it that the School of Nancy put in place of this fine dream? A few vague assertions on suggestibility and credulity that could not be discussed without going into the new studies of psychology. And psychology, considered a confused mixture of literature and ethics, had no standing in the school of medicine.

Charcot's disciples were quick to seize the advantage this gave them. They could not rebut the overwhelming evidence in favour of the Nancy School's interpretations; but they could and did claim that they had examined it, sorted out what was scientific (and therefore acceptable) from the mass of unscientific data, and incorporated it in their wider, better-attested Salpêtrière scheme. In their preface to their *Animal Magnetism*, in 1888, Alfred Binet and Charles Féré presented a historical survey of the subject, derived from Charcot's ideas. They singled out for respectful comment those researchers who, like Bertrand and Braid, had taken a physiological stance; and ignored those who, like Elliotson and Esdaile, had strayed. Liébeault, they conceded, had been conscientious, but he was muddled and unsystematic; his work 'would never have been accepted without the labours of Charcot and his pupils, who re-established the study of hypnotism, simply by giving an accurate description of the physical characteristics of some of the nervous states designated by that name'. The operative word was 'accepted'. Binet and Féré simply accepted whatever suited them from the techniques Liébeault had pioneered, and the theories Bernheim based on them; contriving subtly to leave the impression that they had been known at the Salpêtrière all along.

Using such means, the Salpêtrière was able to retain credibility, so that by 1890 it had become the fashion – a British student disciple of Braid, Dr. Augustus Nicoll, complained – to speak of Charcot as if he represented the entire theory of hypnotism; 'as if he had originated, discovered and founded the science'. But to maintain its reputation, the Salpêtrière had to dissociate itself firmly from any taint of mesmerism, old-style. Binet and Féré (or their publisher) felt compelled to call their book *Animal Magnetism* because that term, often still abbreviated simply to 'magnetism', was still in common colloquial use in France, where 'hypnotism' had not yet established itself. But they were careful to insist that true animal magnetism and hypnotism were synonymous; it was simply that animal magnetism had unfortunately become mixed up with the spurious higher phenomena 'which have always compromised the cause of these fruitful studies'.

Anxious though they were to reject the higher phenomena, thought-transference presented them with a problem. Charcot had carried out a number of tests for it with hypnosis, including one where a subject would be told that there was a portrait on a card, when in fact the card was blank. It would then be shuffled with a dozen other blank cards, and the subject, on being aroused, would be asked to run his eye over them, without being told why. When he came to the card with the 'portrait', he would recognise it immediately. So extensive was the evidence from this kind of test that Binet and Féré could not attempt to dispute it. Instead, they resorted to the explanation pioneered by Morin and Carpenter: hyperacuity of the senses. The suggested hallucinatory image of a portrait, they explained, had not remained in the subject's brain 'in a vague and floating state'. It had been associated in his brain with some external mark on that particular card; 'a dot, for instance, or a raised spot'.

The ability of hypnotised subjects to recognise such guide-marks was one of several explanations along similar lines. 'Cumberlandism' was the most often cited, because of Cumberland's claim that he read thoughts without using any psychic aid. But Cumberland was a professional whose skills had been developed by long practice; the subjects used by the hypnotists were amateurs, and some of them were performing feats of a kind Cumberland did not attempt. So fresh versions of hyperacuity of the senses had to be presented to account for them, until the concept began to be stretched to the point of lunacy. Having a subject who could pick out a named card from a new pack lying on a table without turning them over, Dr. C. Sauvaire explained that this must be because her improved keenness of vision under hypnosis enabled her to see through cards in the same way as an ordinary individual might be able to see through them by holding them up to the light. Dr. Taguet of Bordeaux had a patient who held up a piece of cardboard in front of her and 'read' a book held behind her back; such was her hyperacuity of vision, he suggested, she was able to use cardboard as other people used mirrors. And in the *Revue Philosophique* a correspondent explained the Le Havre results by auditory hypersensitivity. In her somnambulist state, he argued, Mme. B. could tell when she was being hypnotised, because she could hear the change in the blood flow through Dr. Gibert's arteries when he began to concentrate upon her ('I find it hard to believe,' Myers was content mildly to comment, 'that a peasant woman is sent to sleep by "the sound of a gong" in the arteries of an elderly physician at a distance of half a mile').

Another hypothesis, which Binet and Féré endorsed, was that a thought – a mental representation, for example, of a word or a letter –

cannot occur without a corresponding movement in the muscles which serve for the articulation of this word or letter. This movement, constituting external speech, is not generally considered as such, since it may remain unperceived by the individual in whom it occurs. Yet such a movement is visible enough to be rapidly understood by certain subjects, as we have observed for ourselves.

The subject, in other words, was able to pick up thoughts by a process comparable to lip-reading by the deaf. But an alternative idea was to find more favour, because it explained why hypnotised subjects could sometimes tell what the hypnotist was thinking even when they could not see him. Thought, the proposition was, must be accompanied by verbalisations. The hypnotist might be unaware of it, but the sound would reach the somnambulist's sharpened hearing. A hypnotised subject, asked how she read Dr. Bourdon's mind, told him, 'I heard you think it'; and this prompted him to offer the theory that 'the imperceptible noise made by the larynx in forming the words corresponding to the thought is caught by the keen ear of the subject' – and even the fact that the subject could read his mind when he was a quarter of a mile away did not disconcert him. The Danish psychologist Alfred Lehmann, after experiments which he and his colleague Dr. F. C. Hansen conducted, claimed they had actually proved that hypnotised subjects were picking up the 'unconscious whispering' of the hypnotist, although 'no movement of the lips was visible, and a bystander could not hear any sounds'. And this, they suggested, was the real explanation of the results of the thought-transference tests reported by the Society for Psychical Research.

As it happened, Sidgwick had been aware of the possibility that hyperacuity of hearing might be held to account for some of the cases of thought-transference, and had taken precautions to prevent it. Examining Lehmann and Hansen's statistical apparatus he found that they had botched it; the figures did not in fact show what was claimed. They had also asserted that the number '0' had been guessed by the percipient more often than chance when the number '7' was in the agent's mind, or vice-versa; obviously, they argued, the explanation was that even somebody with hyperacuity of hearing could easily confuse a whispered 'zero' with 'seven'. Even if this particular error *had* occurred significantly often, Sidgwick pointed out, it would have done nothing to support their hypothesis, because nobody in Britain thought of '0' as 'zero', let alone whispered it that way; the English term was 'nought'. But as scientists tended to read only scientific periodicals, which in turn tended to quote only experiments like Lehmann's, misinterpretations of this kind tended to be perpetuated even when they had been so comprehensively demolished in a journal devoted to psychical research. In 1898 the American magazine *Science* carried an article by Professor E. B. Titchener of Cornell claiming that 'no scientific-minded psychologist believes in telepathy', and citing Lehmann's 'brilliant demonstration of unconscious whispering'. When William James protested that Titchener could not have read Sidgwick's rebuttal, Titchener blandly claimed that he had, but that he had not been convinced by Sidgwick's reasoning. James thereupon quoted a letter in which Lehmann himself, as a result of Sidgwick's reasoning, had backed down. Yet Titchener still refused to concede defeat, extricating himself from his embarrassment by accusing James of introducing an acerbic note into what had been a scientific discussion.

In general, the evidence for hyperacuity presented in this period was speculative, and often bizarre. As Gurney had pointed out, it often did not disprove thought-transference, but simply left it out of account. Similar evidence presented in favour of psychic phenomena would certainly have been dismissed out of hand. But Binet and Féré's conclusion – that as every change in the mind is accompanied by physical changes, 'and consequently by modifications of colour, of temperature, or secretion, etc., we shall not push the hypothesis too far if we admit that excessively sensitive subjects are capable of feeling these thermic or secretory modifications' – happened to suit the temper of the times; it was easy for scientists to welcome their claim that thought-reading could be 'reduced to the reading of involuntary signs'.

In much the same way, Charcot and his followers were able to shrug off evidence which confronted them which suggested that some hypnotised patients had physical capabilities which could not easily be naturally accounted for. One of them would occasionally suddenly be jerked upwards 'as if by a spring', her whole body rising from the ground as she was thrust up into the air, again and again. Another could perform prodigies of agility, leaping on to furniture, then flinging himself backwards, and landing in the rainbow position, touching the ground with head and heels only; or he would revolve with 'the most amazing swiftness'. There were obvious similarities with the St. Médard *convulsionnaires* – and with isolated cases reported afterwards. In 1811 a scientific conference in Orleans had heard how Adelaide Lefebvre, when mesmerised, could not only 'see with her belly' but would spin round rapidly and then jump six or seven feet in the air. While the mesmerist Lafontaine was in England, he had encountered a patient who could hop around the room almost as if she were floating, landing among ornaments, cups and glasses without breaking or even upsetting them. In a medical textbook in 1868 Dr. Pierre Jousset had described similar feats. But they could just be contained in the super-human, rather than the supernatural, category if 'muscular hyper-excitability' were invoked as the explanation.

The Stigmata

Hyperacuity and hyper-excitability might be gratefully accepted at the Salpêtrière, and even at Nancy; but if such remarkable natural manifestations resulted from them they would need to be explored further, Binet and Féré urged, so that they could be explained, rather than 'relegated to the occult sciences'. But this was the last thing that orthodox medical scientists wanted. They had welcomed Charcot's explanation because it had appeared to settle the issue, rendering further research unnecessary, except perhaps in lunatic asylums. Reports of experiments with hypnosis were welcomed only if they provided fresh confirmation that phenomena formerly attributed to divine or diabolic intervention could be re-classified as symptomatic of mental disturbance. 'Stigmatisations, invulnerabilities, instantaneous cures, inspired discourses, and demoniacal possessions,' as James observed, 'the records of which were shelved in our libraries but yesterday in the alcove headed "Superstitions", now, under the brand new title of "cases of hystero-epilepsy" are republished, re-observed, and reported with an even too credulous avidity.' The idea that some individuals had a dual – or as Myers called it, 'multiplex' – personality, hitherto scouted, became acceptable (*Dr. Jekyll and Mr. Hyde*, published in 1886, reflected the lay public's growing awareness of the idea of split personality). Even automatic writing, suspect through its association with Spiritualism, became tolerable when Janet and others showed it could be induced by suggestion under hypnosis, to demonstrate that it was nothing to do with spirits.

The re-classification of phenomena which had previously been regarded as divine was particularly welcome. In the 1860s the stigmata which had appeared on the body of a Catholic girl, Louise Lateau, from the Mons region, had attracted international attention. Her wounds, and her claim that she had found that she did not require to eat any food in order to live, were investigated and pronounced genuine by Catholic doctors; but a doctor sent to examine her on behalf of the Belgian Medical Association counter-claimed that he had discovered a secret cache of food in her apartment, which she must have been using; and if she could cheat in that way, she could hardly be trusted in other ways. The controversy, however, had remained at that level; either she was a cheat, Virchow insisted, or the stigmata were miraculous – which in his view simply meant that she must be a cheat.

But there was another possibility: automatism. Might there not be automatic symptoms, like automatic writing? If there were, they might be induced under hypnosis. In 1873 Dr. M. H. Biggs, practising in San Francisco, met a girl who became cataleptic every Friday, with her arms outstretched as if she was being crucified; marks as of nails appeared in her hands and feet, and a wound in her side. Her piety had made her a favourite of the Archbishop there; but Biggs, convinced that it was simply 'automagnetisation' began to experiment on his patients, mesmerising them and suggesting that the sign of the cross would appear on them. In 1879 he found a Californian girl who was a good subject. The suggestion at first only made her feel itchy on her chest, where he planned that the cross was to appear; but on the following Friday, 'there, to my utter astonishment, was a pink cross'; and it continued to appear on subsequent Fridays. Later, in Lima, he was able to produce a similar cross on a girl's arm.

As soon as hypnosis won recognition, it became possible to cite case histories of this kind without risk of arousing scientists' incredulity; and as it happened, both the Salpêtrière and Nancy could claim them in support of their own theories. Bernheim insisted that they illustrated the extraordinary power of suggestion in the trance state; he was able to find a subject who could actually duplicate under hypnosis the stigmata of Louise Lateau. In the Salpêtrière, the stigmata were taken to be just another symptom of hystero-epilepsy – the version which proved most acceptable to science. 'As so often happens,' – William James, again, commented in his *Principles of Psychology* – 'a fact is denied until a welcome interpretation comes of it. Then it is admitted readily enough; and evidence judged quite insufficient to back a claim so long as the Church had an interest in making it, proves to be quite sufficient for modern scientific enlightenment'.

The experimenters, however, did not content themselves with using hypnosis to induce bleeding. They found that they could also produce artificial blisters, by suggesting to a hypnotised patient that he was being burned. In 1890 the *Revue de l'Hypnotisme* described how a boy who had been hypnotised was informed that when he awoke, he would feel cold; 'you will go and warm yourself at the stove, and you will burn your forearm on the line which I have traced out. This will hurt you: a redness will appear on your arm; it will swell and blisters will form.' On waking, the boy obeyed the suggestion; his forearm came in contact with the stove; he uttered a cry of pain; a redness appeared a few minutes later, and the following day a blister had formed. Yet the stove had not been lit.

Even more revealing, in relation to the treatment of illnesses, were experiments carried out by the Belgian psychologist Professor J. R. L. Delboeuf; not a member of the medical profession, but a man who had become convinced by personal study of mesmerism's importance. A meticulous researcher, he recognised the importance of controlled experiments; and when with a patient's consent he made two small burns on his skin, Delboeuf was able by suggestion under hypnosis to make one of them become inflamed and painful, yet block those symptoms in the other. The healing process, Delboeuf went on to satisfy himself, could be speeded up by suggestion in this way. This was a finding that was decidedly less congenial to the medical profession. Its implication was that doctors ought to learn and practise the craft of the hypnotist, which was not what they had bargained for.

There remained the prospect that psychologists – still, at that time, being recruited from such sources as the School of Moral Sciences at Cambridge University, as well as from hospitals and laboratories – would go their own way, investigating hypnotism independently of medicine and, in the process, continuing to engage in psychical research. This seemed at least a possibility when a conference of psychologists was held in Paris in 1889, with Richet – who had just been appointed Professor of Physiology: these faculties, too, were still not completely segregated – as General Secretary, and about two hundred members attending. Hypnosis was one of the four aspects of psychology deemed important enough to have a section to itself in the morning sessions, and among those who were involved were many of the leading psychical researchers: Sidgwick, Mrs. Sidgwick and Myers from Britain; Delboeuf – elected Chairman – from Belgium; Ochorowicz from Poland; William James from America. The way the tide was running against the Salpêtrière was immediately apparent. Those present had been summoned to a 'Congress of Physiological Psychology' under Charcot's presidency; but Charcot could not attend, owing to ill-health, and in his absence it was decided to change its name to 'The International Congress of Experimental Psychology'; an almost brutal repudiation of what he stood for. Reports of research into thought-transference, too, were presented and deliberated upon as if it were an integral feature of academic psychology.

But this acceptance was already threatened. Many of the hypnotists either were reluctant to admit the possibility of thought-transference, or felt that it was too risky to allow it to jeopardise the prospects for further recognition of their craft. In his *Hypnotism*, published in 1890 in Berlin and in an English version later the same year, Albert Moll presented what was to become the standard case against the higher phenomena. He had investigated thought-transference, but only with the intention of proving that it could always be accounted for by hyper-acuity of the senses. He had taken elaborate pains to ensure that in his experiments there could be no transfer of sensory impressions, hoping to show that this would banish thought-transference. In tests in which a hypnotised subject was asked to find a playing card, say, in a pack, or one of a dozen identical glasses of water, the object was ordinarily magnetised by 'passes' made over it; to ensure that its identity was not disclosed by minute changes of temperature, resulting from the passes, Moll kept the objects under a sheet of glass. He was honest enough to admit, however, that some subjects had been able to detect which glass of water, or which card, had been magnetised. And although he did succeed, to his own satisfaction, in fooling a subject by pretending a card was magnetised – as he had hoped, the subject could not pick out the card which *had* been magnetised – she could, and did, find the card which he had *pretended* was magnetised, which left open the possibility of thought-transference unaided by magnetisation. But these results did not shake Moll's conviction that a natural explanation would be found. In the past, he claimed, controls had been insufficiently rigorous. He had found only one series of experiments in which the controls could not be faulted: Guthrie's, in Liverpool. But even in these, Moll was 'subjectively convinced that some sources of error were overlooked, and that suggestion was somehow or other called into play'.

Moll at least was prepared to urge the need for further research along these lines. The indifference of science to such matters, he complained, had 'always been the mainstay of charlatanism'. But increasingly, hypnotists had been seeking to dissociate themselves from mesmerism. Mesmerism was so completely contradicted by Braid, August Forel, Professor of Psychiatry at Zurich, claimed, 'that it were vain to waste any more time on the subject', especially as the higher phenomena could not be genuine, being contrary to the law of conservation of energy. A few hypnotists continued researching, notably the young physicist Dr. G. B. Ermacora in Italy. With two cousins – Angelina Carazzoni acting as agent; four-year-old Maria as recipient – he experimented with thought-transmission while Maria was in a trance, or asleep; finding that in her dreams or trances she could pick up messages from Angelina – identifying, say, a picture which Angelina had in mind. But such research became less common.

There was a revival, however, in the 1890s of the ideas of Reichenbach; in particular his claim that sensitives could 'feel' the approach of a magnet, or 'see' light streaming from a magnet's pole. Charcot and his disciples had found that some hysterics had similar reactions; and the committee set up by the S.P.R. to pursue Reichenbach's researches had obtained some initially promising results. Although the results were never consistent, or could be attributed to hyperacuity of one of the senses, a few hypnotists continued to try to devise experiments which would demonstrate, and perhaps even measure, the capacity of a 'sensitive' not just to detect magnetic forces, but perhaps also to divine the nature of objects brought close to them. And from their work evolved the theory of 'externalisation of sensibility'; the capacity of the body to obtain information from its surroundings as if through some invisible antennae. The presence of this faculty could be demonstrated in various ways: ordinarily by bringing a substance gradually up to a hypnotised subject to gauge when he reacted – and how he reacted. As the mesmerists half a century earlier had found, there would often be, say, a pursing of the lips if the substance were alum (even, Dr. J. B. Luys reported, signs of drunkenness if the phial which he brought close to the subject contained brandy).

Some of the experiments were carefully designed and carried out: notably those of Dr. Paul Joire (who found that hypnotised subjects could sense the approach of a pencil behind their backs even when the skin area had been so effectively anaesthetised by suggestion that they felt nothing when the pencil actually touched them) and of Colonel Albert de Rochas, Administrator of the French Polytechnic, whose book on the subject, *L'Extériorisation de la Sensibilité*, created a mild sensation when it was published. But increasingly, acceptance of evidence in this suspect area was frowned upon by orthodox hypnotists, as they now came to regard themselves. Some of them bluntly asserted that they had never come across the higher phenomena, in any form. Bernheim claimed that he had tried to induce thought-transference, without any success; and Bramwell, though he was a member of the S.P.R. and undertook some experiments for it, was later to write that he had seen 'nothing, absolutely nothing, which might be fairly considered as affording even the slightest evidence for the existence of telepathy, or any of the so-called occult phenomena'.

Why should practitioners as open-minded as Bernheim and Bramwell never have encountered thought-transference, where other hypnotists had found that it often occurred spontaneously, and in some subjects could easily be induced? In *The Law of Psychic Phenomena*, the American investigator Thomas Jay Hudson was to offer an ingenious explanatory hypothesis. The early mesmerists, he pointed out, and a few of the later ones, used elaborate 'passes', concentrating on the subject to put him into his trance. But Braid, with his use of a bright object to induce the trance state, and Bernheim, who used simple suggestion, did not attempt to establish real rapport. There was consequently less two-way traffic; and this, Hudson suggested, might block the development of mental communication. The fact that hypnosis on Braid's model was not conducive to the appearance of thought-transference should not, therefore, be regarded as casting doubt on the evidence for it from other sources which, Hudson felt, was more than sufficient to show that 'there is inherent in mankind the power to communicate thoughts to others independently of objective means of communication'. Telepathy, he concluded, was 'as thoroughly established as any fact in nature'.

Orthodox hypnotists disagreed. 'We have still with us the spiritists, the stage hypnotists, the living magnets, the mahatmas, the belated psychical researchers, and the ghost-seers,' Ernest Hart lamented the same year; but, thanks to Charcot, they were 'only the stunted remnants, the vestigial and atrophied traces, indicating the later stages of ages of development in which we have outgrown the period when such follies were the almost universal heritage of mankind'.

Hart was the editor of the *British Medical Journal*, the organ of the British Medical Association, which had just belatedly recognised hypnosis after an inquiry by a committee. Its members had reported that not merely had they satisfied themselves of the genuineness of the hypnotic state; they were of the opinion that hypnotism could be an effective therapeutic agent in 'relieving pain, procuring sleep, and relieving many functional ailments'. This was too much for the profession to swallow. At the annual meeting of the B.M.A. in 1892, to which the report was presented, it was referred back for further consideration. When it came up again the following year, along with impressive details of the results of research carried out in Paris and Nancy as well as in Britain, a motion was proposed that the committee should be thanked for their services, and their report received. Only received; not accepted. The resolution was carried.

Chapter Thirty-three

Slate-writers

In view of the interest which Home's career and Crookes's investigations had aroused, the committee which the S.P.R. set up to investigate 'the various physical phenomena called spiritualistic' could have been expected to become the most important of all. It was not: chiefly because the members of the Cambridge group had become disillusioned with physical mediumship even before the Society was founded. Sidgwick and his wife had wasted a great deal of time at what had usually been extremely boring, and often unproductive, seances; and though Myers had encountered a few impressive displays he, too, had tended to be affected by his friends' doubts.

These doubts were reinforced by reports of exposures of fraudulent mediums, which periodically were publicised in the newspapers. Usually they followed the pattern established by Volckmann when he seized 'Katie King'; and one, in particular, was very damaging to Spiritualist claims. Sir George Sitwell went with a friend, Carl von Buch, to one of Florence Corner's seances; and while Sitwell seized and held 'Marie' – 'Katie King's' spirit successor – von Buch pulled aside the curtain to reveal the medium's empty chair and discarded clothes. Although Florence's supporters could claim that this was not conscious deception on her part – in her trance state, she might be acting out the spirit role – to anybody believing he had seen a material-ised being this was still deception, conscious or unconscious. To be on the safe side the committee studying the physical phenomena decided not to have any dealings with professional mediums; but amateurs who offered their services were unable to produce any worth-while mani-festations, and the committee soon ceased to function.

In 1884, however, an *ad hoc* inquiry was undertaken into the physical phenomena reported in connection with Mme. Blavatsky, who a few years earlier had founded the Theosophical movement, with headquarters in India. Preliminary tests by members of the

Society had been sufficiently promising for them to recommend further research; and Sidgwick, who had been impressed, delegated it to Richard Hodgson. A young lawyer from Australia, Hodgson had come to England hoping to launch himself on an academic career, but had failed to obtain the necessary first class honours (he had been top of the seconds in a year when no man had been awarded a first – though to his mortification, two women had). Hodgson had studied under Sidgwick, and had been a member of the Cambridge psychical research society; the trip to India was consolatory, and in view of his inexperience he might have been expected to be cautious. His report, however, describing a system of fraud worked by Mme. Blavatsky, bluntly pronounced that 'none of the phenomena were genuine'.

As Mme. Blavatsky made no secret of her readiness to use whatever means would help to serve the ends of Theosophy, there might have been some excuse for the verdict; but the report revealed that Hodgson had approached the inquiry from the standpoint of a prosecutor, ready to accept evidence even from suspect sources so long as they were hostile. To the Cambridge group, however, in their growing disenchantment with the physical phenomena, the report was welcome, and it was published in the Society's *Journal* in 1885. Barrett, perturbed, urged caution; in a paper read to the Society the following year, though he conceded that much of the testimony for the physical phenomena justified the contempt with which scientists regarded it, he cited the reports of de Gasparin, the Dialectical Society's number one committee, and Crookes as showing how regrettable it would be if 'this contempt is hastily extended to the *whole* of the testimony'. The Cambridge group's reaction was immediate: at the next meeting Mrs. Sidgwick countered with a paper displaying her contempt for the whole of the testimony. Although she insisted that she did not disbelieve in the physical phenomena, she made it clear that they could best be explained by deception and illusion.

Recalling how she had been to seances with Kate Fox-Jencken, and had at first been impressed by a spirit message which had appeared on a piece of paper at a time when the medium's hands were in full view, Mrs. Sidgwick described how she had decided it might have been written by the medium's foot; and later sessions had been unproductive. There was no mention in the paper of the tests which Mrs. Jencken had undergone in various places, among them one in 1883 in St. Petersburg, where Alexander Aksakov, reported that she had produced rappings, touches, luminosities, and movements of objects without contact. Nor did Mrs. Sidgwick cite any other of the numerous testimonials Mrs. Jencken had collected. Instead, she preferred to hark back to the verdict of the Buffalo professors, thirty-five years earlier, which apparently she had only recently heard about. Having herself found that Mrs. Jencken could not produce raps when clasped round the knees, or standing on a hassock, Mrs. Sidgwick felt safe in accepting the Buffalo professors' explanation; apparently unaware that it had long since been rejected as irrelevant because even if it could account for the kind of straightforward raps which were the commonplace of seances, it could not explain the great variety of reported sounds which bore no resemblance to the popping of joints, from the 'falling knitting needles' described by Augustus de Morgan to the battery of miscellaneous noises listed by Crookes. By similarly ignoring in this way whatever did not fit in with her thesis, Mrs. Sidgwick was able to reach the conclusion that 'by far the larger part of the testimony put forward as affording solid ground for a belief in them, which I have been able to examine, is of such a nature as to justify the contempt with which scientific men generally regard it'. And among the 'alleged' mediums (the Sidgwicks always used the qualification) she dismissed was William Eglinton. Twice, she claimed, he had been detected in fraud; she herself had had only unproductive seances with him; and she had 'no hesitation in attributing the performances to clever conjuring tricks'.

Eglinton and Davey

Eglinton was the medium in Britain at the time who had shown most promise of becoming a worthy successor to Home. Unlike Slade, he did not insist on his own (or his spirits') terms for tests; he allowed investigators to take whatever precautions against deception they considered necessary. What this could entail was related by Barrett in a description of a seance in 1878 attended by Myers, Wallace and Wedgwood. Eglinton had to remove his coat and waistcoat and put on a jacket Wedgwood provided. His shirt was stitched tightly round his wrists, and to the jacket sleeve; and he was asked to sit in a chair in a corner of the room, his hands behind his back, his thumbs tied together, the two sleeves stitched together and attached to a nail in the woodwork which was itself nailed to the wall. Yet while he was in full view, by gaslight, witnesses heard rappings all round them, and saw objects moving in ways for which Eglinton could not have been physically responsible without detaching himself from his fastenings.

On occasion, Eglinton was reported as levitating. Hoping to expose him, the conjuror Harry Kellar went to one of his seances in 1882 and found himself borne aloft, trying to hold on to Eglinton; an experience which Kellar admitted at the time he could not account for. But ordinarily Eglinton's seances consisted mainly of obtaining spirit messages on slates. Unlike Slade, he would allow the investigators to bring their own slates and retain possession of them; and the messages might contain information which he could not have known in advance – the investigator was at liberty to choose a line from a book taken at random, and it would appear on the slate. Among those whom Eglinton impressed, apart from such seasoned researchers as Barrett, was Gladstone, who had a seance with him in the autumn of 1884 and complained after it that scientists were 'too often indisposed to give any attention to matters which seem to conflict with their established modes of thought. Indeed, they not infrequently attempt to deny that into which they have never inquired, not sufficiently realising the fact that there may be forces in nature of which they know nothing'.

Understandably, therefore, the Spiritualists in the S.P.R. were outraged at what they regarded as Mrs. Sidgwick's ill-informed, uncalled-for assault on Eglinton's integrity. They were able to produce plausible reasons for discounting the evidence that he had been caught cheating; and they enlisted the support of 'Professor Hoffman' – the conjuror Angelo Lewis – who had had a dozen sessions with him; although many were unproductive, and in others Lewis had suspected sleight-of-hand, he had to admit that even the cleverest conjuror in the world could not, 'in the same conditions, use trickery in the wholesale way necessary to produce all these phenomena'. A biography of Eglinton, too, written by J. S. Farmer, the editor of a Spiritualist journal, though it contained some self-evident hagiography, included also a considerable volume of testimony to the medium's powers. But with the Cambridge group in control of the Society and its publications, the Spiritualists were in no position to obtain any retraction from Mrs. Sidgwick; and several resigned.

Mrs. Sidgwick, however, had not been quite so casual in her research as she had appeared to be. A year earlier, irritated by Hodgson's report on Mme. Blavatsky, a correspondent had remarked in the *Journal* how ridiculous it had been to send Hodgson to India when Eglinton was at hand in Britain. She had taken the hint. In the autumn of 1886 a series of accounts by Hodgson of sessions with Eglinton, and a critical commentary on the evidence in his favour, began to appear in the *Journal*, revealing the source of her criticisms. As with Mme. Blavatsky, Hodgson had clearly considered that his task was simply to show how the tricks were performed; and as he was unable to detect Eglinton in deception, he concentrated on those aspects of the medium's performances which pointed to the likelihood of his being a conjuror, in particular the frequent distractions: coughs, which might mask the sound of slates being unlocked from each other; shufflings of the feet; interruptions to go to the door and receive messages; and so on.

Hodgson's account was so transparently one-sided that it would have carried little weight, except among sceptics; but he was joined by an unexpected and, as things turned out, invaluable ally. A young member of the Society, S. J. Davey, had been to Eglinton and had written enthusiastic accounts of what he had witnessed. One of the slate messages had intimated that he too, had psychic powers; he had begun to experiment; and he found that spirit writing had indeed appeared for him on slates. To his chagrin, however, he then came to suspect that he might have been taken in by a practical joke, played on him by friends. Later visits to Eglinton proving less satisfactory, he decided to see what he could do by way of conjuring of the kind that Hodgson was describing. In a series of articles and letters in the *Journal*, Davey revealed just how easy it had been to deceive sitters; the sitters themselves admitting that they had allowed their attention to be distracted by ludicrously simple diversions while he substituted prepared slates for the ones they had seen to be blank, or wrote on blank slates. They had believed that he could not possibly have deceived them; he had, and had shown them how.

The Seybert Commission

At this point, any residue of uneasiness that the Cambridge group might have experienced at the split in the Society, and the consequent defections, was removed by a report from the United States. An American Society for Psychical Research had been set up in Boston following a visit there by Barrett in the autumn of 1884, with William James, by this time running a psycho-physical laboratory in Harvard, as its nerve centre; but James was busy on a variety of projects, and before the new society had settled down to research it became known that an *ad hoc* team had already embarked on an investigation of mediumship in Philadelphia. A Spiritualist, Henry Seybert, had offered a legacy sufficient to support a Chair of Philosophy on condition that the University there would set up a committee to investigate 'all systems of Morals, Religion and Philosophy which assume to represent the Truth, and particularly modern Spiritualism'; and a Commission had been appointed. Although its members claimed to be free from prejudice on the subject, only one, the acting Chairman Dr. Horace Howard Furness, admitted to any predeliction in favour, and that no more than a 'leaning'. And as Furness also sadly admitted, his usefulness as an investigator was limited by the fact that he was very deaf.

A number of local mediums offered their services; and although none of them was able to produce any phenomena of a kind that would impress the commission, in one respect their performances were collectively impressive. A few resorted to trickery; but the others frankly and ruefully admitted that the spirits were declining to co-operate. This could not be attributed to the precautions which the commission had taken to prevent sleight-of-hand, because on the advice of a Spiritualist they had agreed not to behave inquisitorially, in case that should have an inhibitory effect. The way they put it – 'even the very spirit of investigation, or of incredulity, seems to exercise a chilling effect, and prevents a successful manifestation' – may have been intended as sarcastic; but it could also be read as respectful of the continually reiterated claim of mediums about the effects of scepticism.

The commission also invited the two most celebrated mediums in America to demonstrate: Margaret Fox, who had become Mrs. Fox-Kane; and Henry Slade. Mrs. Fox-Kane had no difficulty in producing raps, which intimated that they came from the spirit of Seybert. Sometimes they were heard apparently coming from the table, even when she was not touching it; and Furness, who with her permission had put his hands on her feet, reported that though he could feel 'an unusual pulsation', he was certain that the feet did not move. But the raps were not sufficiently detached from the vicinity of the medium, and the messages not sufficiently explicit, to carry conviction. After two seances Margaret herself admitted that they were unsatisfactory, and withdrew.

Slade arrived in Philadelphia early in the new year of 1885. His reputation, temporarily damaged by the London trial eight years before, had been restored first by Zöllner's testimonial and then, after his return to New York, by a report from Frederick Powell, a member of the American Society of Magicians, who had sittings with him in 1881–2. According to Harry Houdini (not ordinarily a reliable source in this context, as he detested Spiritualists; but he was unlikely to have invented a story redounding to a medium's credit) Powell witnessed movements of furniture at a distance; a slate was snatched from his grasp, and carried around; a matchbox de-materialised; and the chair in which he was sitting levitated. Though convinced there must be trickery Powell could not detect it; he could only surmise that a foot was being used, 'though I did not actually see Slade use his foot to do the lifting'.

Slade was able to produce spirit writing on slates for the Seybert commission. Sometimes, when the spirits were answering questions put to them, the messages were clumsy and rude; but at other times they were quite legible and literate, and after several seances he returned to New York so well satisfied with his demonstration that he wrote to thank the commission for their treatment of him, which he thought had been entirely fair and courteous, and to express his willingness to return, should further demonstration be required. Yet in their report, the commission bluntly stated that the manifestations they had witnessed were 'fraudulent throughout'. Slade, they were sure, had obtained his results by substituting duplicate slates, on which he had already written spirit messages (distracting observers' attention while substituting the duplicates); by scratching with a fingernail, to imitate the spirits; by shifting chairs with his feet; and by using 'manual dexterity' to play an accordion with one hand.

Why, if the tricks they had seen were 'almost puerile in their legerdemain', had they allowed Slade to leave with the impression that he had convinced them, or at least made them take slate-writing seriously? According to Coleman Sellers, who had taken on the role of prosecuting attorney, they had agreed beforehand not to intervene, because they had been warned that if they deviated in the slightest degree from the conditions imposed by Slade he would 'pack up his traps and clear out'. The method they had adopted was to allow him full liberty to cheat, and to show no sign if they caught him. One member, peeking under the table, had seen that Slade's foot had been removed from its slipper. Another had seen that a supposedly clean slate had writing on it – though Slade, apparently realising he had been detected, had hurriedly cleaned it off. But by agreement these rules were not pointed out until the post-mortems which the members of the commission held after seances; so Slade was never actually caught red-handed.

Some of his effects, too, at the time had seemed unaccountable. Once he had held two slates, one of them cleaned, behind the head of one of the investigators; when the question was put 'will the spirits endeavour to write on the slate thus held?' the sound of writing and a rap, signifying 'yes', were heard, and the message on the slate was 'Yes, we will try'. It was 'one of the neatest things he did', Furness thought; an inspired guess if he had prepared the slate in advance. Even Sellers could detect no substitution. In the circumstances, the commission realised that it would be unwise to denounce Slade until they could reassure themselves that everything he did could be duplicated by sleight-of-hand. Harry Kellar, one of the best known conjurors of the day, happened to be in Philadelphia; and a few days later he gave three members of the commission a demonstration of slate-writing which, they found, was 'far more remarkable than any which we have witnessed with mediums', including messages in various languages. Later, Kellar showed one of the commission's members how he did it; and although in deference to the interests of his profession this was not made public at the time, the members of the commission felt that it constituted sufficient proof that Slade was a conjuror, and nothing more.

Over thirty years later Kellar, having retired, felt at liberty to disclose how he had done the slate-writing. He told Hereward Carrington that he had had a trap-door constructed under the seance table, and employed an assistant in the room below – an explanation echoed by Houdini. But this method would only have been possible for a professional magician. Slade gave seances wherever he happened to be, in private houses or hotel rooms; there could be no question of his having trapdoors cut wherever he went – and if he had, he would soon have been exposed. The reliance on Kellar's testimony was consequently dishonest – at least on the part of the member of the commission who was let into the secret. So far from discrediting Slade, it could have been held to be in his favour.

Before they published their report the members of the commission decided that it would be wise to insure themselves against criticism of a different nature: that they had not taken into account the available evidence from Europe. No attempt was made to enlist the help of the Society for Psychical Research; instead the commission's Secretary, Professor George Fullerton, was despatched to Germany in 1886 to bring back information about the Zöllner experiments with Slade, nine years before. In view of the committee's findings, Fullerton did not feel there was any need even to pretend to be dispassionate in his quest. His personal view of Spiritualism was that it represented 'the melancholy spectacle of gross fraud, perpetrated on an uncritical portion of the community'. In Germany, he contented himself with seeking out evidence which would show that Zöllner and his associates had been in that uncritical portion; calling first upon Wilhelm Wundt, Professor of Psycho-physiology at the University of Leipzig, the most trenchant critic of Spiritualism and everything associated with it (he was to dismiss 'this so-called telepathy' and 'similar aberrations').

Wundt, Fullerton reported, had claimed to have been at 'two or three' seances with Slade: the conditions for observation had been unsatisfactory, as he had not been permitted to look under the table; and he had seen nothing that could not be explained by juggling. Whether or not this was what Wundt actually told Fullerton, it was very different from what he had written soon after the Zöllner experiments. In an open letter to Professor Hermann Ulrici of Halle, one of the academics who had declared in Slade's favour, Wundt had disagreed with him – but on the ground that spiritualistic phenomena ran counter to the presupposition of a universal causality; 'whence is the scientific investigator to get courage and perseverance for his work, if the laws of nature, according to the prospect you open, are approaching a point where they shall be done away with?' In Wundt's description of the Slade seance – he had only attended one – he did not attempt to disguise that he and his colleagues had witnessed phenomena which they could not account for in terms of jugglery. 'Throughout almost the entire seance,' he recalled, 'the door of the room was in violent commotion, such as gusts of wind might create; this explanation, however, had to be excluded, since on that afternoon the air was perfectly still.' His colleagues had occasionally felt thrusts against their legs, and the slates which they held in their hands were

violently pushed away. 'At the end of the "sitting" we arose; Mr.
Slade laid his hands upon ours and first lifted the table several inches
from the floor, then let it suddenly fall again.' And it was not being
lifted by Slade; 'it was clearly perceptible that the table was raised by
a central force from beneath'. Although Wundt felt certain it must be
a trick, 'If you ask me now,' he wrote, 'whether I am in a condition
to express a conjecture as to how these experiments were performed,
I answer, No.'

By the time of Fullerton's visit Wundt's recollection of the seance
had certainly undergone a change. He went on to deride those who,
like Ulrici, had been impressed by Slade. Zöllner, he thought, had not
been in his right mind. Zöllner had in fact become touchy, his friends
admitted, resentful of what he felt were the unfair criticisms to which
he had been subjected; but there had been no suggestion that he was
mentally unstable, and both Weber and Baron Hellenbach insisted
that he had remained perfectly sane until the day of his death, from
a stroke. But Weber's indignation at the smear on his old friend
allowed Fullerton to dismiss him as 'extremely excitable': Scheibner,
he found, was less certain in his mind about the validity of the Slade
phenomena than he had been at the time; and as for Fechner, he
suffered from eye-trouble. Thus it would appear, Fullerton concluded,

> that of the four eminent men whose names have made famous the
> investigation there is reason to believe one, Zöllner, was of unsound
> mind at the time, and anxious for experimental verification of an
> already accepted hypothesis; another, Fechner, was partly blind,
> and believed because of Zöllner's observations; a third, Scheibner,
> was also afflicted with defective vision, and not entirely satisfied in
> his own mind as to the phenomena; and a fourth, Weber, was ad-
> vanced in age, and did not even recognise the disabilities of his
> associates. Not one of these men had ever had experiences of this
> sort before, nor was any one of them acquainted with the ordinary
> possibilities of deception.

The Seybert commission report, therefore, was far from being a
detached survey carried out in a scientific spirit. But the members of
the commission were men of standing in the academic world, and they
said what orthodoxy wanted to hear; so when the report was published
in 1887 it was widely held to be a devastating exposure not only of
Spiritualism and the mediums who were exploiting it, but of Zöllner's
experiments, too. Myers, who reviewed it in the *Proceedings* of the
S.P.R., could reasonably have been critical of the fact that no attempt
had been made by the commission to obtain the Society's advice.
Instead he praised the report, with its 'revelations of vulgar, unblush-

ing fraud, such as must make the ears of honest believers to tingle', for having swept away so much crude imposture. He went on innocently to assume that the university would use 'so ample a bequest' to investigate 'certain perplexing phenomena which do admittedly occur, but which need not be interpreted in the Spiritualistic sense' – such as automatic writing. The university had no intention of squandering so ample a bequest in so futile a pursuit. The report provided just the excuse it needed to abstain from further psychical research.

The Seybert commission and Davey had effectively disposed of slate-writing as a serious contender for recognition by psychical researchers; but they had not disposed of psychic phenomena – as Davey admitted. Although he had come to believe that the spirit writing which had appeared on his slates was a practical joke, he apparently had no proof that his friends had done it; and in the course of his conjuring tricks, thought-transference sometimes appeared to intrude. In a session with a man he did not know, he had asked him to think of a number; Davey himself wrote down '98' which turned out to be correct. 'This may have been merely a coincidence,' he admitted; 'but the fact that I have had several similar experiences with other investigators led me to think that there might be something in the nature of thought-reading in it.' Davey, therefore, was not disputing the possibility that there might be some form of communication between individuals which had not been satisfactorily accounted for; he was simply casting doubt on the trustworthiness of slate-writing as a test. It was an issue that was never settled. Some Spiritualists remained convinced that Slade and Eglinton were genuine; some repudiated them as tricksters; some, like Charles Massey, thought they were both. Slade, he was sure, could do things in a seance which no conjuror could do; yet he might use sleight-of-hand in another seance, or even the same seance, 'with an almost infantile audacity and naïveté'.

Massey was more impressed by the occasional side-effects of seances than by the slate-writing itself. On one occasion he had seen a chair 'picked up and placed at my side, by my sudden request, at a distance of five measured feet, with a clear space from Slade'. On another, when Slade's chair had moved, Massey had asked if his could be moved, too; and he had immediately felt it move back. Whatever was responsible for the movement, it could not have been Slade, who was in full view. With both Eglinton and Slade, evidence of this kind was more convincing than their slate-writing; particularly as the phenomena were occasionally reported as continuing after the seance had ended. When the Rev. John Page Hopps, editor of a religious magazine, brought his own slate along to a seance the spirits intimated their disapproval by refusing to put any message on it; but as if sensing his suspicion, they said they would provide him with a different form of proof of their existence. On his way home, the slate suddenly shivered into splinters: 'how, I know not'.

But such testimonials had no chance of impressing members of the S.P.R. who accepted Davey's account and the report of the Seybert commission, both of which consolidated Hodgson's position in the Society. If Davey had been able to dupe sitters with his amateurish conjuring tricks, was it not reasonable to assume that Slade and Eglinton, with their greater experience, could find ways to produce the movements of furniture, too? And certainly, Hodgson could claim, Davey had made one thing very clear: all the accumulated evidence from and about slate-writing must now be dismissed as 'worthless'.

Chapter Thirty-four
Mrs. Piper

IN 1888 SPIRITUALISM SUFFERED A FURTHER HUMILIATION, MORE injurious to its public image than any so far. A quarrel had developed between Leah, the eldest of the Fox sisters, and Margaret and Kate. Their husbands had died; they were in their fifties, their mediumistic powers in decline; they had taken to drink; and Leah had tried to bring them under control. In the autumn of 1888 the rumour began to circulate in New York that Margaret was going to admit that she was a cheat; and as part of what turned out to be a well-orchestrated promotion campaign she confessed at a meeting that she made the raps with her joints, giving a demonstration. As Kate was present, and made no protest, it could be assumed that she was in agreement with her sister; and a letter she wrote shortly afterwards explained why. They had been penniless; the venture had made one thousand five hundred dollars. Now, she felt, she could perhaps again make a living – by proving her sister's confession to have been spurious. A few days later, Margaret herself retracted it. Desperate for money, she had agreed to collaborate with the *New York World* and Reuben Davenport to give 'the death-blow to Spiritualism' – the title under which Davenport's book on the subject was now published.

Even if Margaret had not retracted her confession, anybody with even a slight acquaintance with her history could have seen that it was spurious; it made no attempt to account for most of the phenomena which had come to be associated with her and her sister, and with mediumship in general. But the fact that she had revealed herself as a liar, and that Kate had abetted her, was finally destructive of Spiritualims's prospects of being taken seriously by scientists. Naturally this caused the Cambridge group no concern. On the contrary, they could congratulate themselves on their wisdom in having purged the Society of Spiritualists. Now, they could concentrate upon what they had come to regard as their main line of inquiry: telepathy.

'It is an obvious fact,' Myers had written in 1884, 'but it is neverthe-less a fact which we must repeat as often as possible, that in no way can psychical research be better aided than by constant and varied ex-periments on thought-transference in every form.' Even clairvoyance came to be discounted. By the 1890s, according to Podmore in his follow-up of *Phantasms*, it was losing its original wider meaning of a faculty by which the subjects were enabled to ascertain facts not within human knowledge, including those which were in people's minds; the evidence for a faculty of perceiving things – as distinct from thoughts – psychically, was so small, Podmore thought, that it hardly deserved separate consideration. It was the existence of telepathy, the Cambridge group believed, that they had come nearest to demonstrating with the Guthrie experiments; their only serious defect having been that the percipients had lost their power. Research with hypnosis had produced abundant confirmatory evidence; but as hypnosis was again suspect, further work along these lines would be unlikely to promote their cause. What was needed was somebody, anybody, who could obtain information otherwise than through the five senses, and be able to demonstrate that faculty continually under test conditions. And William James had found her, in Leonora Piper.

A Boston housewife, Mrs. Piper had discovered she had psychic powers in the same way that shamans had traditionally found them: she had begun to slide off into spontaneous trances. After one of them, a judge from Cambridge, Mass., long a Spiritualist, informed her that she had passed him the most remarkable spirit message he had ever received; and people began to press her to give seances. Reluctantly, she consented to do so for members of her family and friends; and one of them happened to be William James's mother-in-law.

James was not at first impressed by what his mother-in-law told him. He was of the Cambridge group's way of thinking about Spiritualism; and the fact that Mrs. Piper claimed to have as a spirit 'control' a French doctor, 'Phinuit', aroused his suspicions. A visit to her, how-ever, convinced him that by whatever means the information reached her, she must either be genuine or by some chance have acquired an astonishing fund of knowledge about his wife's family. Further visits, as he reported to the S.P.R., soon led him 'absolutely to reject the latter explanation, and to believe that she has supernormal powers'. The most convincing things Mrs. Piper told him, he found, were either very intimate or very trivial. He could not publish the intimacies; but among the trivia were such pieces of correct information as that he and his wife had lost a rug; that he had put down his cat with ether (she even described the manner of the cat's death); and that his wife had received a letter from an aunt, warning her against mediums – Mrs. Piper con-tributing 'most amusing criticisms, full of *traits vifs*, of that excellent woman's character'. Insignificant as these appeared, James observed, the accumulation of them had an irresistible effect. 'Taking everything I know of Mrs. Piper into account, the result is to make me feel as absolutely certain as I am of any personal fact in the world that she knows things in her trances which she cannot possibly have heard in her waking state.'

James's numerous commitments, however, had prevented him from doing as much as he would have liked for the American S.P.R.; and it lacked an equivalent of the Cambridge group in Britain to get it moving – and to keep it financed. The Cambridge group, too, must have been uneasy about Mrs. Piper's Spiritualism. The obvious solution was to despatch Hodgson, who was available for such an enterprise, to take over the American Society and run it as a branch of the S.P.R.; and, in the process, to investigate Mrs. Piper. By his own admission he began his inquiry when he arrived in 1887 on the assumption that she 'obtained her information previously by ordinary means, such as inquiries by confederates'. In his first sitting with her, however, she gave him a wealth of information about his family in Australia which it was difficult even for Hodgson to attribute to the activity of her agents; not just names of members of his family but intimate childhood details, such as his cousin Fred's skill at leapfrog, and the convulsions he had suffered before his death. Nevertheless Hodgson persevered, sending at least fifty people who were strangers to Mrs. Piper to sittings with her, taking care she should not know whom she was going to see, and having her watched to ensure she could not brief confederates. But though at times she could not enter a trance, and at other times 'Phinuit' turned out to be inaccurate, the accumulation of testimony to her ability to provide sitters with information about them and their families and friends eventually convinced even Hodgson. 'As my investigations have proceeded,' he admitted, 'I have been more and more strengthened in the conviction that Mrs. Piper's trance is a genuine abnormal state, and that the waking normal Mrs. Piper has no direct knowledge whatever of the sayings and doings of her trance personality. That she exhibits supernormal phenomena in the trance state I have no doubt.'

In 1889 Mrs. Piper was invited to England to be tested by Lodge, at his Liverpool home, and by Myers at Cambridge. They took elaborate precautions to ensure that she could not be provided with material of any kind by confederates; Mrs. Piper raising no objection because, as she told Lodge, she was disturbed by what she regarded as an abnormal mental condition, and hoped her investigators would be able to throw some light on it. At no stage in the tests did they find any reason for mistrust; her attitude was 'natural, uninquisitive, ladylike and straightforward,' Lodge reported; 'her whole demeanour struck everyone who became intimate with her as utterly beyond and above suspicion'.

Following earlier reports of her capabilities it had been suggested by members of the S.P.R. that if she did not get her results from paid agents, she might be obtaining them by 'fishing' – 'the utilisation of trivial indications, of every intimation, audible, tactile, muscular and of little shades of manner too indefinable to name', as Lodge described the process, explaining that he had been on the watch for it; 'all these excited in the sitter by skilful guesses and well-directed shots, and their nutriment extracted with superhuman cunning'. Sometimes, he found, 'Phinuit' did fish around, floundering, groping, making mistakes. But at other times he simply poured out a flow of information of a kind which even the most protracted fishing could hardly have trawled up (in a letter to Lodge, James was later to say it was actually sensible, if fishing began, for the sitters to take the bait; 'for it often happens if you give a name, or some small fact, for the lack of which he is brought to a standstill, that he will then start off with a copious flow').

A local doctor, though, brought in by Lodge for a sitting, determinedly made no contribution, except grunting noises regardless of whether 'Phinuit' was on the right or the wrong tack. Yet 'Phinuit' told him that he had four children, one a little lame girl, aged thirteen, 'a little daisy' with dark eyes, talent for music, and a curious little mark, or scar, over the left eye; that he also had a boy who should be sent to school for his good; that he drank hot water when he had indigestion; and that he had recently had a bad experience, when he 'nearly slipped out once on the water'. All these were correct – he and his wife had been discussing whether the boy should go to school; and that summer, he had been in a dangerous yachting accident – except that his daughter was not lame. In the second sitting with him, however, 'Phinuit' called the daughter Daisy (which was in fact her name) and said it was a friend of hers who was the lame one: Daisy was deaf – which was correct.

If Mrs. Piper were a genuine medium, another question remained to be answered. Did she obtain her information from the spirit world, or by thought-reading? In more than forty cases, Lodge found, she provided information of which the sitter had no conscious knowledge, but on inquiry found to be correct. In some of them, too, this could not be attributed simply to a lapse of memory, as there seemed to be no way in which the sitter could have known. An instance which personally impressed Lodge was when he handed a gold watch to Mrs. Piper while she was in a trance, and was told that it belonged to an uncle. Lodge had in fact just received the watch from an uncle that morning, not knowing it was coming. Another uncle, 'Phinuit' went on, had owned the watch before; and he gave a description of the brothers as boys, how they had owned a gun and a snakeskin, and how they had been in scrapes; once they had nearly been drowned; once they had killed a cat. Lodge knew nothing of this; his uncle, too, he found, had forgotten most of the details. It was only when they communicated with another uncle, still living, that they received confirmation that 'Phinuit' had been accurate.

Did this mean, then, that 'Phinuit' could be accepted on his own terms, as the spirit of a Frenchman who had lived years before? Certainly, Lodge emphasised, he emerged as a distinct personality; 'you are speaking no longer to a lady but to a man, an old man, a medical man'. But whether he was a man who had actually existed, Lodge did not know – and did not greatly care; 'it would be interesting to have the fact ascertained, if possible', but he could not see that it would much affect the question of the genuineness of the information. Hodgson, however, *did* care. When Mrs. Piper went back to America he embarked on an investigation which was to culminate in 'Phinuit' himself confessing that his name was not 'Phinuit' at all, but 'Scliville', and he was not even sure about that. No evidence was found that 'Scliville' had existed; and the medical knowledge he displayed, Hodgson suggested, could be attributed to clairvoyance or thought-transference. In this case, 'Phinuit' might be a hidden personality within Mrs. Piper, with access to her unconscious memories, and to the thoughts of sitters. 'Phinuit' himself admitted that he used psychometry; objects, he claimed, brought him into relation with people, living or dead, who had handled them. This, Hodgson thought, might help to explain how Mrs. Piper obtained her knowledge, without recourse to the hypothesis of spirits.

> Where the sitter knows the circumstances connected with the object, the associations will probably form a specially vivid cluster of experiences in his mind, conscious or subconscious, owing to the very presence of the object within the field of his perception; and this may help 'Phinuit' to discover and disentangle these associations by direct thought-transference. Where, on the other hand, the sitter is ignorant of the circumstances connected with the object, it may, at any rate, form a sort of *point de repère*, enabling 'Phinuit' to get telepathically, through the mind of the sitter, at the mind of the distant living person from whom the object was obtained and who knows of its associations.

The fact that Lodge's uncle had not remembered the episodes 'Phinuit' had referred to, in other words, did not necessarily mean that the medium was obtaining them from the spirit of the dead brother. Mrs. Piper might be picking them up telepathically from the memory of Lodge's other uncle, still living.

Later, 'Phinuit/Scliville' went into retirement. A new control began to take over in Mrs. Piper's trances: 'George Pellew'. There could be no doubt that 'G.P.' had existed: Hodgson had known him before his death in an accident, shortly before he began to communicate. When other sitters were brought in who had known him, 'G.P.' always recognised them, and spoke to them much as he had done in his lifetime, rarely making a mistake. Telepathy, Hodgson began to feel, was no longer a tenable hypothesis; or, rather, it had to be so stretched, to explain not only the range of information which 'G.P.' supplied, but also the way that the personalities of the deceased communicators kept breaking through to identify themselves to sitters, that 'we reach a conception which goes as far as the "spirit" hypothesis itself'.

Spiritism was not what the Cambridge group had hoped for. It was not that they any longer doubted Mrs. Piper. Hodgson had convinced them; writing to Wallace in 1890, Myers described his report on Mrs. Piper as 'the best thing we have yet published, it has converted *Podmore*, among other people'. During Hodgson's absence in the United States, Podmore emerged as the Society's hard-core sceptic, and also as its most prolific chronicler; and in his *Studies in Psychical Research*, published in 1897, he began to display what was soon to become an obsessional mistrust of any psychical research which had not been conducted with the strictest of controls – which ruled out almost all research done before he and Hodgson came on the scene. But though he was contemptuous about 'Phinuit', he accepted that Mrs. Piper had psychic powers. And Mrs. Piper fulfilled most of the Cambridge specifications, being reasonably consistent in her ability to produce information from what appeared to be a psychic source, and retaining her powers even after prolonged tests. The spiritist element, however, and in particular the slippery 'Phinuit', destroyed any chance there might have been of convincing orthodox scientists that psychic communication existed. James's colleague Hugo Muensterberg, Professor of Psychology at Harvard, laid down the natural law in an article in the *Atlantic Monthly* in 1899, ruling out telepathy on *a priori* grounds; 'the psychologist insists that every perception of occurrences outside one's own body and every influence beyond one's own organism must be intermediated by an uninterrupted chain of physical processes'. It was no use saying, Muensterberg asserted, that it was narrow and stubborn to reject a fact because it did not fit into the scientific system of the time. This argument was wrong, and dangerous, because the psychical researchers were not really dealing in science.

The question is not whether the substance of the real world is spiritual; it is only whether departed spirits enter into communication with living men by mediums and by incantation. The scientist does not admit a compromise: with regard to this he flatly denies the possibility. Of course he does not say that all the claims are founded on fraud. He does not deny that sincere persons have frequently believed through hallucinations, and still others through illusions, that they saw the apparitions of departed friends and heard their voices. The psychologist has no dearth of explanations for this product of the psychophysical mechanism. In the same way, he need not doubt that many of the mediums really believe themselves to be under the control of departed souls; for this also exactly fits many well-known facts of nervous disturbance. But the facts as they are claimed do not exist, and never will exist, and no debate makes the situation better.

From India to Mars

As Muensterberg admitted, he had not himself attempted to undertake any psychical research; but his thesis was lent support by another Professor of Psychology, who had : Theodore Flournoy, of Geneva. In 1894 Flournoy had accepted a colleague's invitation to attend some seances with a non-professional medium, 'Hélène Smith', who in her trance states 'saw' or 'heard' deceased relatives of sitters, described them accurately, and passed on messages from or about them, usually by raps on the table. To Flournoy's astonishment, she was able to give him information about events which had occurred in his family before he was born; and he decided to find out how she did it. Soon, he ruled out conscious deception. Hélène was 'a beautiful woman of about thirty years of age, tall, vigorous, of a fresh healthy complexion, with hair and eyes almost black, of an open and intelligent countenance which at once evoked sympathy'; and the good impression he formed of her was at once confirmed when he made inquiries, and found that she was 'of model bearing and irreproachable moral character', having worked for years for a business firm in which her ability and integrity had led to her being promoted to a position of considerable responsibility. But Flournoy had read about Mrs. Piper; and he realised that Hélène in her trance state became – or was controlled by – different personalities who might not have her strict moral code.

Their machinations fascinated him. To judge from the notes of seances provided by earlier investigators, they had struggled for possession of her like furies, the benevolent 'Victor Hugo' having been ousted by the malevolent 'Leopold', who to express his bad temper thought nothing of pulling Hélène's chair from under her so that she fell to the floor. The idea that these were real spirits, Flournoy quickly became convinced, was preposterous. They must be personifications of forces in her own mind. 'Take any individual having, in her subconscious, memories, scruples, emotional tendencies, and put into her head spiritistic leanings,' he explained,

> even though she may not be of a very impressionable or suggestible temperament, or inclined to the mental disintegration which the general public calls the mediumistic faculty, nevertheless it will not be long before her subliminal elements group themselves and arrange themselves according to the 'personal' form to which all consciousness tends, and which discloses itself outwardly by communications which have the appearance of coming directly from discarnate spirits.

In her seances with Flournoy, Hélène began to go into even deeper trance states in which she no longer provided simple information about sitters' dead relatives. She described her own past 'lives': as the wife of a Hindu prince, five hundred years earlier; as Marie Antoinette; and as an observer of life on Mars. Flournoy decided to follow up the information she provided to find how much, if any, of it was accurate; and the title of the book in which he described the results of this quest, *From India to the Planet Mars,* might have suggested that he had been impressed. Not so: most of her descriptions, he found, could most easily be explained as 'dream fictions, fantastic subdivisions of her hypnoid consciousness'. Her description of Mars, for example, with its horseless carriages, houses with roof fountains, and people identical with the earth's inhabitants except that both sexes wore a uniform costume, was 'childishly puerile, insignificant in all aspects save as a psychological curiosity'.

The 'Hindu cycle', however, was a different matter. It was possible to check Hélène's fantasy with historical records; and they showed that she had a real knowledge, if not an entirely accurate one, of the languages and customs of the people at the time she described. Nor could this be accounted for by a knowledge of the standard works on the subject. She related, for example, how in 1401 she had received a declaration of love from her husband, Prince Sivrouka Nayaka (with whom, to his amusement, she identified Flournoy). Orientalists he consulted knew of no such person: it was an unlikely name, he was assured, for a Hindu. But researching on his own account, Flournoy eventually came across a rare old six-volume history of India by de Marlés; and in it he read of a fortress, constructed in 1401 by a Jain prince, Sivrouka Nayaka.

'At last,' Flournoy wrote, 'with what a beating heart did I fasten my eyes on that irrefutable historic evidence that my preceding incarnation, under the beautiful skies of India, was not a myth! I felt new life in my veins . . .' Flournoy, though, was joking. When he told his orientalist colleagues of his discovery, they pooh-poohed it, on the ground that de Marlés was not a trustworthy source. Perhaps, then, it was the passage in his book which had furnished Hélène's subliminal memory? Hélène herself declined to believe she could have read, and forgotten having read, de Marlés; and Flournoy had to admit that the idea of her having seen the passage in so old and rare a work was 'a trifle absurd'. But the remote possibility remained that she had read it, or heard about it, and forgotten it, remained; and Flournoy decided that 'cryptomnesia', as it was coming to be known – 'the reappearance of memories profoundly buried beneath the normal waking state' – must be accepted as the answer because, 'though there is scarcely any choice, extravagance for extravagance, I still prefer the hypothesis which only invokes natural possibilities to that which appeals to occult causes'.

Between the period of Flournoy's initial investigations into Hélène and the publication of his account of them, however, he had seen, and been convinced by, the physical phenomena demonstrated by Eusapia Palladino. He was no longer a sceptic; he was prepared even to accept that Hélène herself displayed occasional clairvoyance. But his hypothesis to explain Hélène's visions of the past, that it was cryptomnesia rather than psychical retrocognition, was seized upon by sceptics. Many cases similar to Hélène's were to be reported, and investigated, often with similar results. Embedded in flights of fantasy or of uncheckable material there would be clear intimations that the medium had 'seen' some historical episode; and when checked, the accuracy of her vision would be confirmed. But it was never possible to prove that the medium had not taken the information from a book, or perhaps from overhearing a description of the scene while she was a child, and then forgotten it. Cryptomnesia became scepticism's standby to strip retrocognition of any psychic content.

Chapter Thirty-five
Eusapia Palladino

ALTHOUGH A FEW MEDIUMS HAD CONTINUED TO PRODUCE PHYSICAL phenomena in conditions which appeared to preclude deception, the general opinion even among psychical researchers had been inclining towards the admission that they must be either fraudulent or hallucinatory – the view put forward by von Hartmann in his *Philosophy of the Unconscious,* published in Germany in 1868 and in England in 1884. Only Aksakov attempted a rebuttal, groping towards a theory which would embrace the physical as well as the mental psychical phenomena. The problem, he admitted, for any intelligent observer was 'firstly the obviously *automatic* character of so-called Spiritualist manifestations and secondly the frequent falsity – shameless and conspicuous – of their intellectual content'; and after years of experimenting with them, he himself had begun to wonder if he might not after all have been the victim of some fearful illusion. But illusion, he had realised, simply could not account for much of what he had experienced; and he had instead settled for the belief that mediumistic phenomena were produced not by the spirits of the dead but by the unconscious action of the living, through some force which 'can overstep the bounds of the body and can exert, either within or without the body, activities of a physical, nay even of a plastic, kind', a force for which he suggested the name telekinesis.

Among those not involved in psychical research, however, it was commonly assumed that the physical phenomena, and indeed spiritism, had been totally discredited – as an aside in an article written in 1888 by Cesare Lombroso, Professor of Psychiatry at the University of Turin, revealed. He was by this time publicly recognised as the founder of a new branch of science, criminology; and he described good-humouredly the opposition which his theories provoked in the academic world, which 'still laughs at criminal anthropology', as it still laughed at hypnotism. 'Who knows,' he mused, 'that I and my friends who laugh at spiritism are not also in error?' Although he was clearly being facetious, his challenge was taken up by Ercole Chiaia. In an open letter in a Rome journal, he asked Lombroso to come to Naples to investigate the spiritist phenomena produced at a seance by Eusapia Palladino.

Chiaia and Lombroso

Chiaia had won an enviable reputation in Neapolitan circles for integrity. Expelled by the Bourbons for his opinions, his academic career disrupted, he had joined Garibaldi, and become a cavalry officer. But what he had to tell about Eusapia sounded ridiculous. She was from the humblest class of society, thirty years old, illiterate; 'neither fascinating nor irresistible', yet endowed with the power which 'attracts to her the articles of furniture which surround her, lifts them up, holds them suspended in the air like Mahomet's coffin, and makes them come down again with undulatory movements, as if they were obeying her will'. She could increase or decrease the weight of objects, and produce raps on walls and luminosities. If a layer of clay was placed at a distance from her, she could imprint on it the image of a hand or a face. 'This woman rises in the air, no matter what bands tie her down. She seems to lie upon the empty air as on a couch, contrary to all the laws of gravity; she plays on musical instruments – organs, bells, tambourines – as if they had been touched by her hands or moved by the breath of invisible gnomes.' She could increase her stature by as much as four inches; and while her limbs were being held, other limbs could be seen coming into view: 'when this woman is bound, a third arm is seen, and nobody knows where it comes from'.

It required great courage – as Lombroso was to recall in a tribute to Chiaia after his death in 1905 – to become the apostle of ideas which at the time were ridiculed in Italy. And fear of that ridicule made Lombroso himself reluctant to meet the challenge. One thing alone prompted him to investigate. Treating a patient, a girl from one of the most aristocratic families in Italy, for hystero-epilepsy, he had been compelled to recognise that there were forces at work which he did not understand; she could 'read' with her eyes shut. But 'if ever there was an individual in the world opposed to spiritism, it was me'. Lombroso was a materialist, a disciple of Comte; and he had successfully demonstrated that certain nervous disorders had simple physiological causes. How delighted those academic colleagues who resented his success would be if they heard he was attending seances! His friends, too, begged him to have nothing to do with Eusapia, as it would ruin his only recently established reputation; and he could not blame them, for he himself felt that if the phenomena were genuine, they would appear to negate 'one of the most precious fruits of our culture, reprieved by so sore a conflict from the clutches of superstition and prejudice'.

For nearly three years, he hesitated; but he finally decided that it would be cowardly to shirk the investigation simply to preserve his reputation and his peace of mind. With three psychiatrist colleagues he investigated Eusapia; and they found that the facts were as Chiaia had stated them. Eusapia could move objects at a distance; levitate furniture (and herself); cause musical instruments to sound (though she could not produce tunes in the way Home had done); and make psychic imprints in clay. 'I am quite ashamed and grieved,' Lombroso wrote to a friend after the tests, 'at having opposed with so much tenacity the possibility of the so-called spiritist facts. I say the facts, because I am still opposed to the theory. But the facts exist, and I boast of being a slave to facts.'

Lombroso was also a slave, though unaware of it, to his preconceptions about the interpretation of the facts. He still assumed, as did his colleagues, that Eusapia must be suffering from a mental disorder. Entering her trance she commonly had tremors, sometimes convulsions: she might sob, or laugh maniacally. In the trance, or coming out of it, she made overt sexual overtures to any of the sitters who caught her fancy. And if the trance deepened, she became possessed (by 'John King', who held sway as the chief spirit control in Europe; sometimes he talked to her, sometimes through her). It was consequently easy for the psychiatrists to present a diagnosis along approved Salpêtrière lines: Eusapia was a victim of hystero-epilepsy – the cause of the strange manifestations'.

The Milan Experiments

The diagnosis did not satisfy the physicist Ermacora. In a paper 'Spiritist Facts and Hasty Hypotheses' he pointed out courteously but firmly that if the facts were as related by Lombroso, they could not be contained in any psychiatric strait-jacket; they had significant implications for other branches of science. Aksakov, who had founded a German review of psychic studies, decided to set up a fresh investigation; and he managed to gather together in Milan a group of an academic standing hitherto unmatched for such an inquiry. As well as Lombroso and Ermacora, there were Giovanni Schiaparelli, director of the Milan observatory and the outstanding astronomer of his generation; Giuseppe Gerosa, Professor of Physics; Angelo Brofferio, Professor of Philosophy; Carl du Prel; and Richet. They carried out a series of test seances, some in near darkness but others well lit; and when it was light enough to observe Eusapia's movements, and to see that her feet were securely held down to the floor, they saw the table in front of her rise 'as though fixed to the medium's hands', a dynamometer to which it had been linked up registering an upwards 'pull' of over seven pounds. On such occasions, they recorded, the table, after making lateral movements,

finally rises altogether with its four feet horizontally in the air, generally to a height of four to eight inches but, in exceptional circumstances, to twenty-four or twenty-eight inches; then it falls back on to all four feet simultaneously. It often remains in the air for several seconds and while there makes certain undulatory movements, during which the four feet of the table can be examined.

Photographs of reasonable quality showed the table in the air. The only snag, as the investigators had to admit, was that they also showed Eusapia's skirt had bellied out (just as Angélique Cottin's had) as if being puffed by a draught, to touch the table leg. There was no question of the skirt hiding a support strong enough to do the lifting; but they would have preferred to eliminate any such source of suspicion.

As well as the levitations, objects out of Eusapia's reach were displaced; chairs would begin to move, as if inquisitive about what was happening, and anxious to get closer to the action. When a heavy chair moved in this way, Schiaparelli rose and put it back in its place; 'he had scarcely sat down again when the chair came towards him a second time'. In darkness the phenomena were even more spectacular. While Eusapia's hands and feet were held chairs were transported on to the table in front of her; luminosities appeared, including what looked like hands; there were breaths of air, and 'touchings produced by a mysterious hand'. Schiaparelli's glasses were taken off his nose. Knots were tied, and untied, in pieces of string. Twice, while Lombroso and Richet were holding her, Eusapia was gently lifted up in her chair and deposited on the table. Once, though her hands were held, she was found when the light was turned up to be wearing a coat belonging to one of the investigators.

Had Eusapia been able to produce phenomena only in the dark, it would have been impossible to rule out deception; but so many effects had been witnessed in good light, which she could not have produced by any artifice, that the committee felt bound to put on record what had happened in darkness, too. 'We recognise that from the point of view of exact science our experiments leave much to be desired,' they concluded. 'Nevertheless, what we have seen and ascertained is sufficient to prove to us that these phenomena are well worthy of the attention of scientists.'

The findings were greeted by a torrent of ridicule in the scientific and popular journals; the critics preferring to accept the verdict of a casual observer who claimed that it was all sleight-of-hand. But only one member of the committee refused to sign the report: Richet, who after being convinced had begun to have doubts. As a physiologist by training he had been of the Faraday/Carpenter persuasion, taking for granted that table-turning and other such phenomena were the product of unconscious muscular pressure; and although he admitted that he could not ascribe what he had witnessed in Milan to deception, he nevertheless felt that 'conclusive and indisputable proof that there was no fraud on Eusapia's part, no illusion on our part, is wanting'. More research, he felt, was required.

By this time there was no lack of investigators anxious, on the strength of the Milan evidence, to undertake it. That winter Eusapia went to Rome, there to be tested by Ochorowicz and M. de Siemeradski. A piano placed out of her reach played notes at de Siemeradski's behest; a glass, half full of water, placed out of reach of all the sitters, 'was carried by an unknown power to the lips of Ochorowicz, Eusapia, and another person, who all drank of it'. And in the new year of 1894 Ochorowicz brought Eusapia to Warsaw, where she was put through an exhaustive series of forty seances. The same phenomena were reported as those which had been recorded in Milan. One of the investigators attempted a classification: partial or total levitations of a table; movements of objects not touched by the medium (a tambourine had floated, playing, above their heads; an electric lamp had been switched on at a distance); touchings by hands (usually invisible, but on occasion seen, and apparently materialised); sounds (rappings, notes on instruments); levitation of the medium; luminosities; written matter appearing on paper or tablets; a cold wind; externalisation of the medium's sensibility; and clairvoyance.

There was some diversity of opinion among the Warsaw investigators; partly because there were twenty-three of them, partly because it became clear that given a chance to try to cheat, by distracting their attention and freeing a hand or a foot, Eusapia would take it. One of Ochorowicz's friends, convinced that she must be cheating but unable to discover how, suggested that they should 'give the medium free rein, in order to discover her method'; but all they discovered was that Eusapia's attempts at deception were so clumsy and obvious that they could not conceivably account for what they had witnessed. Her explanation for her behaviour was that in her trance state she did not know what she was doing, and she might be picking up some malign influence; but this impressed Ochorowicz less than the fact that some of the most successful seances had been held in light good enough for observers to make sure that her hands and feet were securely held, and still the manifestations continued. At the end of the series only three of the observers thought that fraud was a satisfactory explanation; three were doubtful; and seventeen were satisfied that what they had witnessed could not have been accomplished by mechanical means alone.

Among the majority was Ochorowicz. Characteristically, he had doubted the reality of the physical phenomena; but finding that he and his wife were able to examine Eusapia as she floated beside them, passing their hands round her to make sure that she was not being lifted by invisible wires, he was finally convinced. 'When I remember that I branded as a fool the fearless investigator Crookes because he had the courage to assert the reality of the physical phenomena, I am ashamed.'

So, by this time, was Richet. He might doubt himself; but he found it hard to doubt Ochorowicz. In the summer of 1894 he invited Ochorowicz, Myers and Lodge to be his guests on Roubaud, an island he owned near Hyères in the south of France, where they could test Eusapia at their leisure; confident that she could have no confederate, as they were the only inhabitants apart from the lighthouse keeper. The phenomena which had been reported in Milan and Warsaw were repeated. While Eusapia was being held, a musical box began to play 'and then visibly approached, being seen both by Myers and Lodge coming through the air, and settled on our table against Myers's chest'; there were bangings, and luminosities; the investigators were touched, and even shaken. Sometimes it looked to them as if Eusapia might be using physical means to cause an object to move; she would make movements as if tugging something towards her, and a writing-desk in the corner would respond, tilting towards her. But it was easy to check that there was no wire, or thread. When the accordion played, too, Lodge observed that the fingers of the medium were 'moving in a thoroughly appropriate manner; the process reminds one of the twitching of a dog's legs when he is supposed to be dreaming that he is chasing a hare. It is as if Eusapia were dreaming that she is fingering an instrument, and dreaming it so vividly that the instrument is actually played.'

Mme. d'Esperance

'There is *no doubt* as to this business,' Lodge wrote to re-assure William James; adding jocularly, 'we are all plunged into the grossest superstition'. To the Sidgwicks, this was disconcerting. In 1887 an attempt had been made to revive the Society's committee on physical phenomena; but it had done little more than collect a few reports of earlier seances, including some which Myers found when he was allowed to inspect the originals of letters quoted in Mme. Home's biography of her husband. These were published in the *Journal* and the *Proceedings* in 1889, along with Crookes's notes of some of his seances with Home. But in 1890 a medium who had given promise of producing

good results for the Society's investigators was found to be a prestidigitator; and two years later the reputation of physical mediums took
another blow when Mme. d'Esperance, the most respected medium in
Europe, was given the same treatment by a sceptic that Sitwell had
meted out to Florence Cook-Corner.

By her own account, Mme. d'Esperance had suffered a troubled
childhood, 'seeing' people who were not there and nearly being put
into a lunatic asylum as a result; but she had survived to develop her
powers. In 1876 she had been tested in Manchester by a young student,
William Oxley, who had the simple but ingenious idea of ensuring
that there really was a materialised form not by the standard method
of tying the medium up or fastening her to the wall inside her cabinet,
but by putting plaster casts on the wrists and above the ankles of the
materialised figure, 'Yolande', outside it, so that 'Yolande' could not
get out of them except by de-materialising; a test which 'Yolande'
passed. Oxley had also satisfied himself that Mme. d'Esperance could
materialise flowers, and perform other such feats.

Mme. d'Esperance had also impressed Boutlerow and Aksakov;
leading Aksakov to formulate a theory to try to account for some
past 'exposures'. The medium, he found, while sitting in her chair,
could 'feel' the sensations that 'Yolande' felt: if 'Yolande' was touched
on the shoulder, Mme. d'Esperance felt a touch on her own shoulder.
Could it be, Aksakov asked himself, that the medium and the materialised being were, though separate, one? In that case, if somebody
grabbed a materialisation and it turned out that there was no medium
in the 'cabinet',

it is not yet a proof of fraud on the medium's part. According to our
hypothesis, what could happen if we detain the medium's double
by force, when it is materialised to such a degree that nothing but
an invisible simulacre of the medium remains in the seat behind the
curtain? It is obvious that the simulacre – that small portion, fluid
and ethereal – will be immediately absorbed into the already com-
pactly materialised form, which lacks nothing (of being the medium)
but that invisible remainder.

In 1893, when Mme. d'Esperance was giving a seance in Helsingfors,
'Yolande' was seized in that way by one of the sitters, who triumphantly
demonstrated that the 'materialised' form was in fact the medium. Her
supporters pointed out that no trace could be found, after the confusion,
of the fabrics which 'Yolande' had been wearing; the implication being
that they, at least, must have de-materialised – the same defence had
been made in the case of Florence Cook, but with Mme. d'Esperance
it carried more weight because nobody who knew her could conceive

of her being involved in a deliberate fraud. Of all the books written by mediums her *Shadow Land*, written after her recovery from a nervous breakdown brought on by the Helsingfors episode, was the most impressive; it had no false notes. Even Alfred Lehmann, who was not disposed to be charitable about Spiritualism and could not accept Aksakov's theory, thought that she must have been unaware of any deception, his assumption being that she played out the part of 'Yolande' in a trance. At the time, however, Mme. d'Esperance's 'exposure' was taken to be simply another episode in the protracted history of Spiritualistic frauds, and as such a warning to the Society to avoid entanglement.

If both Myers and Lodge had been convinced that Eusapia was genuine, however, it would be difficult to convince the members of the S.P.R. that there was nothing worth investigating; and if there had to be an investigation, the Sidgwicks felt it would be wise to reconnoitre for themselves. They went to France and attended seances with her. With one of them on either side of Eusapia, holding her hands (and Ochorowicz her feet) they experienced for themselves the touches and nudges, and they saw objects moving around, a melon and a small table being lifted over from behind them and placed on the seance table in their midst.

If it were difficult for the Sidgwicks to believe in what they had witnessed, it was impossible for Hodgson. His experiences with Mrs. Piper had not taught him humility; and in the Society's *Journal* for April 1895 he explained to the investigators just how they had been cheated. Eusapia's convulsive movements were designed to disguise the fact that she was getting the investigators on either side of her to loose hold of her hands, or get them both to hold the same hand, or even to hold a dummy hand. Levitations and movements of objects could then be effected with the help of straps on her shoulders or upper arms, 'with hooks or other forms of clip appendages which she might have attached unnoticed to the table'. Or, attached to her knee there might have been a steel rod 'or a folded umbrella-like or other expansible object'. Systematically, Hodgson went through the reports of the seances, to show how the investigators could have been duped by such methods.

With exemplary patience, Myers replied in similar detail. Did Hodgson seriously think that he could mistake Eusapia's 'small, perspiring, quivering sharp-nailed hand' for Lodge's 'massive, steady, round-nailed hand'? Careful searches had ensured that there had been no steel rods, or appendages: so even if she had managed to free both hands, or both feet, she still could not have displaced objects at a distance without getting up and leaving her place; and as they could actually see her, this was manifestly impossible. Lodge and Richet also answered Hodgson's objections; but the most effective reply came from Ochorowicz. He had had the most prolonged experience of Eusapia – over seventy seances in all. The idea that she could have been using gadgets could be dismissed, he pointed out, because when she had stayed with him in Poland she and her effects had often been searched, and she had been provided with special clothes to wear for seances. In any case, Ochorowicz had found, Eusapia tried deception – 'reflex fraud' as he called it – only in 'bad' seances; by which he meant seances which lacked sufficient light to facilitate control. Even then, it was usually possible to detect her tricks because they were 'invariably of an infantile character'. And as some of the seances in Warsaw, and those at Roubaud, had been 'good', with plenty of light, if Eusapia had cheated in any of the ways Hodgson suggested she would immediately have been caught.

The Cambridge Experiments

There was only one way to settle the issue, the investigators agreed; Eusapia must be brought to England, where Hodgson and others could test her for themselves. That summer she came to Cambridge, to stay with the Myers'. With them she quickly felt at home; at preliminary seances, the table in front of her rose off the floor on several occasions, and she herself levitated. The formal seances which followed, however, were less successful. Effects could only be obtained in darkness or in such dim light that although objects moved at a distance from her, and sitters felt themselves being touched, they could not feel confident that Eusapia was being securely enough held to be unable to free one of her hands.

Yet one of the investigators was impressed. Joseph John Thomson – Cavendish Professor of Experimental Physics at Cambridge and already involved in the work which was to lead him, less than two years later, to formulate his theory of electrons – had watched Eglinton perform, and been unconvinced; but Eusapia produced phenomena he was unable to account for. 'Chairs came down on the table with a bang; the table rose in the air – at any rate the end near me did. We were hit on the back, and dug in the ribs, and this went on for several minutes.' Admittedly this was in the dark; but to be able to do anything with her hands, Eusapia would have had to extricate them from him and from Rayleigh, who was on the other side of her, and leave them holding each other's hands. In sufficient light for him to be able to see, too, Thomson saw a curtain belly out 'like a sail full of wind' – not in the way it would have moved if it had been physically pulled; he had been careful, too, to satisfy himself that there was no attachment by which it *could* have been physically pulled.

If sleight-of-hand was used, Thomson had to admit – and he as-

sumed it must be – he had been unable to detect it. Nor could
Maskelyne, who was invited to Cambridge to attend a seance with his
son. In a newspaper article in the *Daily Chronicle* Maskelyne described
how Eusapia – 'a sallow faced woman, far from beautiful, with dark
eyes and hair. Her general appearance was that of the usual cunning,
oily-countenanced spirit medium' – had produced rappings, levitations
of the table, and movements of objects. A wicker table which had been
behind her was found deposited upside down on the table in front of
her; both he and his son had felt 'slaps and pokes'; and a hand had been
seen which could not have been a dummy. Yet Maskelyne had to admit they had been unable to catch her cheating. All he could suggest
was that she might have been able to do her tricks – as he remained
convinced they were – by being able to free her hands without him or
his son detecting it; or, in the case of the wicker table, that she had
managed to lean over backwards, while her hands were still held, to
pick it up in her mouth, and hurl it forward over her head. There
could hardly have been a more abject confession of failure to catch
her out, yet it was presented by the *Chronicle* as a triumphant exposure;
an editorial boasted that it had ended the pretensions of the medium
and put the finishing touch, 'shall we say, to the humiliation of the little
European clique of scientific dupes'.

In the course of his article Maskelyne mentioned an explanation
which had been put forward, to him quite unacceptable, that the movements of objects, raps and nudges were produced by 'prolongations':
phantom protuberances which emanated from the medium's body, but
were not ordinarily visible. Although materialised hands and even
bodies were by this time familiar, the idea of 'pseudopods', as these
psychic extensions were coming to be known, had not attracted much
attention since it had been referred to by Chiaia in his challenge to
Lombroso; but it was lent some support by two of the Cambridge observers. During the fifteen years of her marriage Mrs. Myers had not
taken a very active part in psychical research. At one of the seances,
however, while her husband and Alice Johnson, the S.P.R.'s Secretary,
were holding Eusapia's hands, she was given the job of holding the
medium's feet; and from her position on the floor, she was able to see
Eusapia quite clearly outlined against the ceiling, which was reflecting
the light from a candle in the room. While the others reported that
they had felt touches and nudges, she saw what looked like 'two long
simultaneous prolongations', as she described them in her notes, 'like
neck of swan'. One of them prodded her husband in the back; the
other, which appeared to circle round towards Alice Johnson, went
out of her range of vision. She also reported 'a kind of stump', linked
to Eusapia 'by a narrower neck, coming out from about the hips or
flank', to strike her husband. And his sister-in-law, the wife of the ex-

plorer H. M. Stanley, said that she too had seen what appeared to be a hand growing out of Eusapia's back. As Mrs. Myers helped Eusapia to undress after seances, she was able to satisfy herself that there was no artificial limb, or gadgetry of any kind.

If it had been only Mrs. Myers and Mrs. Stanley who had reported pseudopods, it could reasonably have been attributed to their amateur status. But phantom limbs, or prolongations, had been noted not only with Eusapia, but on earlier occasions. At seances with Home, though the hand which would appear carrying objects or writing notes was ordinarily disembodied, one observer had noted that it had appeared to be attached to him (a circumstance which Podmore was later to treat as suspicious). At a time when both of Moses' arms were plainly visible resting on the table, Dr. Speer had seen what looked like another shadowy arm emerging as if from one of his elbows. And after a seance with Florence Cook-Corner, while Mrs. Crookes was holding her hands, Crookes traced from a materialised hand back along her arm, finding that it seemed to be 'a projection from Mrs. Corner's shoulder'.

Any prospect that this line of inquiry might be pursued at Cambridge, however, was removed by the arrival from America of Hodgson. The seances had been set up primarily for his benefit; and he proceeded to take charge. What followed was farcical. After a succession of 'bad' seances, in Ochorowicz's sense of the term, control was relaxed; ostensibly to encourage Eusapia, but also to see if she would try to cheat by freeing a hand or a leg. She did. Hodgson felt he had been vindicated; the Sidgwicks and even Myers agreed with him. Terminating the seances, they reported unanimously 'that systematic fraud had been used from first to last, and that there was no adequate reason to suppose any supernormal agency whatever'.

The verdict revealed how far the Cambridge group had been infected by scepticism about the physical phenomena. It was not as if Eusapia's cheating had been unexpected. Following the experiments with Richet, Lodge had written in his report to the S.P.R. that he thought 'it not unlikely that she employed deception half-somnambulistically'; he would expect her to, 'if undue latitude were given'; and Ochorowicz had actually described *how* she cheated, if she could. After attending one of the Cambridge sessions, too, Lodge had warned that he had observed her attempting deception, not necessarily consciously. All that the Cambridge group had found, Richet complained, was that Eusapia had behaved just as they had been warned she would behave, if allowed to. Ochorowicz agreed. To claim that Eusapia was trying to cheat simply because she disengaged her hand, he reiterated, was absurd; it was a natural reflex movement. And even if her gestures made it appear she was using it to reinforce the psychic power, this was precisely what believers in 'Cumberlandism' should expect – their hypothesis being that the hand automatically tended to follow the impulse of the thought.

The real test, the Continental researchers agreed, was whether Eusapia could continue to produce results in conditions which made trickery impossible. Following the Cambridge visit she was brought to Colonel de Rochas's home at Agnélas, to be investigated by a team which included the experienced psychical researcher Dr. Xavier Dariex, editor of the *Annales des Sciences Psychiques*; the psychologist Paul Joire; Count de Gramont, a Doctor of Science; Joseph Maxwell, who was shortly to become attorney general for the Bordeaux region, and had a medical as well as a legal training; and Professor Sabatier, a physiologist. Their experience confirmed that of earlier observers. At one seance Eusapia levitated, still seated in her chair, until her feet were at the level of the table top, and her hands were pulled out of the clutches of the investigators seated on either side of her. She also passed a test devised by de Gramont to try to introduce better scientific control into the proceedings. By making passes up and down with her hands on either side of one of a pair of scales used for weighing letters, she was able to get it to lower, as if a weight were being put on it; the witnesses satisfying themselves that no thread or hair was being used.

When the results of the Agnélas series became known, a member of the S.P.R. asked if a summary of them would be included in the *Proceedings* or the *Journal*. Myers replied that this 'might more fitly be left to some other organ'; and in the *Journal* for April 1896 Sidgwick reminded members that it was not the practice of the Society 'to direct attention to the performances of any so-called "medium" who had been proved guilty of systematic fraud'; accordingly 'I propose to ignore her performances for the future, as I ignore those of other persons engaged in the same mischievous trade'. Not 'we' – simply '*I* propose to ignore . . .'

The French Experiments

There was nothing for it, Richet realised, but to leave the S.P.R. to go its own way, and to concentrate on persuading French scientists and savants to investigate Eusapia. And over the next two years, several of them were to leave accounts of seances which they had attended; among them Emile Boirac, later to become Rector of the Dijon Academy. Boirac had been a sceptic until a few years earlier when, holidaying at Amélie-les-Bains, he heard that a local group had been claiming to pick up spirit communications by table-turning; and he had decided to investigate. While all their hands were in the air above the table, he had sarcastically beckoned to it; 'and to my great surprise, the table glided along the floor in my direction, and each time my hands renewed their beckoning the gliding recommenced'. Suspecting that some machinery must have been employed, he tried the same experiment in his own house, drawing a circle round the table within which the group were not allowed to place their feet, and employing a friend to check that they all their hands were in the air above the table; but still it moved. He was consequently not unprepared for Eusapia; but what he witnessed staggered him. There were touches; objects moved at a distance; a curtain bellied out 'as though moved by a tempest'; a zither was snatched from the hands of one of the sitters and borne across to Eusapia. While the seance was in progress, Boirac took the opportunity thoroughly to search the room, and behind the curtain; but he could find nothing.

Up to this point the French scientific Establishment had held aloof. But there was one member of it, Richet realised, who was susceptible: Camille Flammarion, founder of the Juvisy Observatory and the best-known French astronomer of his day owing to the facility with which he presented the subject to the public in readable books. Flammarion had been interested in spiritism from the age of nineteen, when he had joined Kardec's society; five years later, in 1866, he had written *Des Forces Naturelles Inconnues* – describing those forces as 'psychic', a term which he was later to claim he had coined. Chiefly interested in clairvoyance and thought-transference, he had remained sceptical about the physical phenomena – on one occasion nearly landing himself in trouble in Naples for being too overtly inquisitive about the composition of the liquefied blood of St. Januarius. Whatever doubts Flammarion had about Eusapia, though, they were quickly removed. He had been dubious about her insistence on having a 'cabinet', but it turned out to be only some light curtains drawn across a corner of the seance room; she would sit in front of it, and observers could at any time satisfy themselves that there was nobody, and no gadgetry, behind it. Her justification was that some manifestations needed the total darkness it provided; and Flammarion, though he suspected this was simply a rationalisation she had picked up somewhere, realised that it would be unscientific to scoff in view of the fact that 'he who would seek to make photographs without a dark chamber would cloud over his plate and obtain nothing'. So when in 1897 he was invited to attend a seance with Eusapia at the house of a friend, he contented himself with thoroughly inspecting the seance room, and insisting that his host's wife undressed Eusapia and searched her clothes.

Taking charge of her left hand and leg, with the equally sceptical Guillaume de Fontenay taking charge on the other side, Flammarion sat back to wait; and within three minutes, in the full light shed by a kerosene lamp, he saw the table begin to move,

balancing itself, and rising sometimes to the right, sometimes to the left. A minute afterwards it is *lifted entirely from the floor*, to a height of about nine inches, and remains there two seconds . . . so then it seems that an object can be lifted, in opposition to the law of gravity, without the contact of the hands which have just been acting upon it.

A side table approached, and appeared to try to climb on to the seance table; the cabinet curtain bellied out; objects began to move round; a musical box started to play. Both de Fontenay and Flammarion were pummelled and pinched; and they found that a 'spirit head' had been moulded in a tray of putty, its features closely resembling Eusapia's.

Although he had entire trust in his friends, Flammarion was not to be satisfied that the phenomena were genuine until he had brought Eusapia to Paris to be tested in his own home, where he could establish for himself 'that the hypothesis of a confederate is inadmissible, and ought to be entirely eliminated'. Among those who came as witnesses, as well as Richet and de Rochas, was the playwright Victorien Sardou. While he was holding Eusapia, in light enough to see what was happening, he felt 'the rubbing of a hard body which was trying to climb upon me' which turned out to be a violin; 'after an unsuccessful effort to climb higher than my knee, this apparently living creature fell with a bang upon the floor'. Jules Clarétie, director of the *Théâtre français* and, like Sardou, a member of the *Académie française*, had a book snatched from him by disembodied fingers; and while he was holding Eusapia, a small table approached 'with sufficient force to make me recoil, draw in my shoulders, and try to push back my chair to let this moving piece of furniture pass'. It seemed to try, 'like a living thing, to struggle between the table and me'.

In December 1898 Richet at last managed to talk Myers into abandoning the Sidgwicks' policy, and consenting to attend a further two seances with Eusapia. Flournoy was also present, confident after his experience with Hélène that he would have no difficulty in finding some flaw. For ten years, he later admitted, he had been hoping to expose the tricks such mediums used: but following the seances with Eusapia he had to admit that the hope had been shattered: 'I was struck, and my arm squeezed as though by a large hand which gave an invisible pinch', the medium being in full view at the time; and the conditions of control left no room for doubt, 'unless we are to distrust the combined testimony of sight, hearing and touch, as well as that modicum of critical sense and astuteness in the possession of which every person of ordinary intelligence prides himself'. The only alternative was to accept the proposition that there were secret doors in Richet's establishment, and that Richet and his assistants were 'the wicked aiders and abettors of the farce enacted by this charming Neapolitan lady'. If collusion of that kind were ruled out there could be no question of deception, because a conjuror would have had to prepare the room in advance. As Flournoy had been careful to check that no such preparation had been made, he could confidently assert that there was 'not a conjuror living who could produce the same manifestations under the same conditions of control'.

Myers, too, was re-converted. It had not been easy to persuade him to come to France; but what he saw when he came finally banished his doubts. In light better than he could remember at any previous seance, so that he could see every detail of her, 'every finger', he saw many of the usual manifestations, and experienced some new ones. A hand grasped his, behind the curtain; and when a zither emerged from a window recess out of Eusapia's reach and floated over Myers on to the table, a phantom shape, coming from behind the curtain, played some notes on it.

Crookes and Richet

It remained to try to re-convert the Society for Psychical Research: and here, Richet could count on another powerful ally. Crookes's research into vacuum tubes and allied subjects had rendered his orthodox status unassailable; in 1897 he had been knighted; in 1898, he was belatedly elected President of the British Association. In his Presidental Address he remarked that there was one issue which had not yet enlisted the interest of the majority of scientists; but he felt that to ignore it would be an act of cowardice.

To stop short in any research that bids far to widen the gates of knowledge, to recoil from fear of difficulty or adverse criticism, is to bring reproach on science. There is nothing for the investigator to do but to go straight on, 'to explore up and down, inch by inch, with the taper his reason', to follow the light wherever it may lead, even should it at times resemble a will-o'-the-wisp. I have nothing to retract. I adhere to my already published statements. Indeed I might add much thereto. I regret only a certain crudity in those early expositions which, no doubt justly, militated against their acceptance by the scientific world.

Crookes thought he could now detect signs of coherence among the elusive phenomena; an advance largely due to the Society for Psychical Research, 'of which I have also this year the honour to be President'. In this capacity he took the chair at an S.P.R. meeting in the new year of 1899, at which Richet read a paper, 'On the conditions of certainty'. Like most members of the Society, Richet recalled, he

had been a sceptic about the physical phenomena, setting them down
to illusion or faulty observation.

Nay, in my servile respect for the classical tradition I mocked at
what was called *spiritism*; and after reading the astounding statements which Mr. Crookes had published, I allowed myself – and
here do I publicly beg his pardon for it – to laugh at them as heartily
as almost every one else was doing. How could I suppose that the
savant who has discovered thallium and the radiometer, and foreshadowed the Röntgen rays, could commit gross and inexplicable
blunders, and allow himself to be duped for years by tricks which a
child could have exposed?

Eventually, Richet went on, Aksakov had persuaded him to go to
Milan, for the experiments there; and at the time they had fully convinced him.

But at this point a remarkable psychological phenomenon made itself
felt; a phenomenon deserving of all your attention. Observe that
we are now dealing with observed facts which are nevertheless
absurd; which are in contradiction with facts of daily observation;
which are denied not by science only, but by the whole of humanity
– facts which are rapid and fugitive, which take place in semi-darkness, and almost by surprise; with no proof except the testimony of
our senses, which we know to be often fallible. After we have witnessed such facts, everything concurs to make us doubt them. Now,
at the moment when these facts take place they seem to us certain,
and we are willing to proclaim them openly; but when we return to
ourself, when we feel the irresistible influence of our environment,
when our friends all laugh at our credulity – then we are almost
disarmed, and we begin to doubt. May it not all have been an illusion? May I not have been grossly deceived? ... And then, as the
moment of the experiment becomes more remote, that experiment
which once seemed so conclusive gets to seem more and more uncertain, and we end by letting ourselves be persuaded that we have
been the victims of a trick.

Thus it had been in connection with Eusapia, Richet recalled. A fortnight after the Milan experiments he had persuaded himself that it
had all been fraud and illusion. Members of the Society had also experienced such 'oscillation'; and he and they might again do so. The
prejudices of the world 'hold us in so strong a grasp that we can
scarcely free ourselves completely. *Certainty does not follow on
demonstration; it follows on habit.*'

So it proved. When a translation of Richet's paper was published in the Society's *Proceedings*, Myers added a footnote to the effect that the seances the previous December had to him appeared conclusive, but that Hodgson had made it clear that his opinion was in no way modified; and Hodgson was by this time editor of the *Proceedings* and the *Journal*. He dismissed the evidence of Richet and Myers as worthless, reiterating his conviction that Eusapia was 'a trickster from beginning to end'; and nearly ten years were to go by before the next report on Eusapia by members of the Society was to appear in any of its publications.

Psychical Research in Decline

Chapter Thirty-six
Andrew Lang

THE CHIEF ADVERSARIES OF PSYCHICAL RESEARCH HAD BEEN PHYSI-
cists and physiologists. By the turn of the century they were being reinforced by two groups who were establishing themselves as academic
disciplines: anthropologists and psychologists.

Anthropology came of age in Britain in 1895, when Edward Tylor was
given the first Chair in the subject at Oxford; a remarkable achievement, as he had had no academic training. His mind was not entirely
closed: 'magic has not its origins in fraud,' he had conceded in his
Primitive Culture, 'and seems seldom practised as an utter imposture'.
And he had been a little disturbed by the implications of spiritualism.
'The issue raised by the comparison of savage, barbaric and civilised
spiritualism,' he had written,

> is this: do the Red Indian medicine man, the Tatar necromancer,
> the Highland ghost-seer, and the Boston medium share the possession
> of a belief and knowledge of the highest truth and import which,
> nevertheless, the great intellectual movement of the last two cen-
> turies has simply thrown aside as worthless? Is what we are habitu-
> ally boasting of and calling new enlightenment, then, in fact a decay
> of knowledge? If so, this is a truly remarkable case of degeneration
> and the savages on whom some ethnographers look as degenerate
> from a higher civilisation may turn on their accusers and charge
> them with having fallen from the high level of savage knowledge.

As Tylor was a materialist, and an evolutionist, he replied to his own
question by saying that magic was an elaborate and systematic pseudo-
science, 'a sincere but fallacious system of philosophy'. At least, though,
he had put the issue in the form of a question. In the first volume of
The Golden Bough, in 1890, James Frazer felt no need for such caution;
and he proceeded to demonstrate the utter absurdity of magic. It was

derived, he asserted, from two principles: 'first, that like produces like, or that an effect resembles its cause; and second, that things which have once been in contact with each other continue to act on each other at a distance after the physical contact has been severed'. After providing examples of 'homeopathic magic' (such as making images of somebody and sticking pins into them), and 'contagious magic' (such as collecting and burning somebody's nail-parings), Frazer explained that savages, in their ignorance, had clearly come to them by misapplying an association of ideas; 'in short, magic is a spurious system of natural law as well as a fallacious guide of conduct; it is a false science as well as an abortive art'.

There could hardly have been a more misleading summary of either the theory or the practice of tribal magic. Homeopathic and contagious practices were indeed widespread, but they were not fundamental; on the contrary, both were aids to divination and magic – much as psychometry now is to a clairvoyant. But owing to the success of *The Golden Bough* Frazer, though his technique of making arbitrary selections in this way from the mass of anthropological data and building shaky theories on them did not commend itself to some of his colleagues, was the most influential anthropologist for the informed reading public in Britain; and it came to be widely assumed that magic need not be taken seriously.

There was, however, an alternative hypothesis, put forward in 1896 by M. Lefébure in France, and the following year by Andrew Lang in Britain. If the shaman was thought of as a medium, Lefébure argued, capable of putting himself into a trance, it would not be surprising 'to see him animate what he touches with a life borrowed from his own, like a European medium'. In that case, magic would have a valid foundation in reality.

Whether or not he saw Lefébure's article, Lang had been moving towards a similar hypothesis. He had long since made his name as poet, classical scholar, historian, biographer and journalist – 'an overwhelming confluence of specialities', as G. K. Chesterton put it. He was also, for Rider Haggard, 'one of the sweetest-natured and highest-minded of men, whom it has ever been my privilege to know' – though Haggard admitted that some people had been put off by 'a certain obtrusive honesty which will out, and an indifferent off-handedness of manner'. From an early interest in folklore and myth, Lang had gone on to steep himself in anthropology; not even his reverence for Tylor could reconcile him to what he regarded as Tylor's mistaken views about divination and magic, and he hardly troubled to conceal his contempt for Frazer. Lang was by instinct sceptical; Spiritualism in particular repelled him – 'at least as impious, as absurd, as odious to taste and sentiment as it is insane in the eyes of reason'; and again, later, 'a word of the worst associations, inextricably entangled with fraud, bad logic, and the blindest credulity'. But he could not deny that many of the phenomena associated with it had been reported from every part of the world in every age – and were still being reported; a study of Spiritualist ideas and practices in China by John L. Nevius, who had worked there as a missionary for nearly forty years before his death in 1893, had just been published. Although belief in such phenomena had declined, Lang suspected that this might not be, as Lecky had thought, due to growing enlightenment. It was not before the advance of reason that they had vanished, he argued, but 'before a kind of sentiment, or instinct, or feeling that events contradictory of normal experience seem ridiculous or incredible'. And in his *Cock Lane and Common Sense* in 1894 he had taken a fresh look at some of the stories from the past, suggesting that there was a need for re-examination of the evidence.

It riled Lang that anthropologists continued not merely to ignore the subject but, in their new-found academic robes, to affect to despise it. 'Anthropology adopts the airs of her elder sisters among the scientists,' he lamented in *The Making of Religion* in 1898, 'and is as severe as they to the Cinderella of the family, psychical research. She must murmur of her fairies among the cinders of the hearth, while they go forth to the ball, and dance with provincial mayors at the festivities of the British Association.' This struck Lang as misguided, as well as unfair. There was a mass of material about divination, magic and other related matters, particularly from tribal communities; yet when he came to investigate the subject, not one work by an anthropologist had he been able to find on it in the English language, and only one meagre tract in German. Tylor's question, he urged, needed to be re-opened – and also re-phrased; 'have the Red Indian, the Tatar, the Highland seer, and the Boston medium (the least reputable of the menagerie) observed, and reasoned wildly with, and counterfeited, and darkened with imposture, certain genuine by-products of the human faculty, which do not *prima facie* deserve to be thrown aside?'

The reported phenomena fell into regular groups, Lang observed, 'like the symptoms of a disease'. Was it a disease of observation? If it were it would still be of undeniable psychological interest. And if it were not, its importance could hardly be overestimated. It was not necessary to accept individual reports, still less the explanations put forward to account for what was witnessed; but it was absurd to ignore phenomena – rappings, luminosities, movement of objects without contact – which had been reported from all times and places. Admittedly they could be faked: 'but that ignorant modern knaves should feign precisely the same raps, lights and movements as the most remote and unsophisticated barbarian, and as the educated neo-Platonists of the fourth century after Christ, is certainly noteworthy'. And if it could be demonstrated that any of the effects which had been dismissed as supernatural could be reproduced, this would put an entirely different complexion on savage beliefs.

As if in answer to Lang's plea, evidence that one of the effects was genuine began to reach the S.P.R. at this time, in the form of reports of investigations of fire walking. The stock explanation of fire-walking and fire handling had been that it was, as the American sceptic William Hammond described it, jugglery: 'for many centuries, preparations for making the skin and clothing incombustible have been known'; but the evidence from Dr. Hocken and Colonel Gudgeon in Polynesia disposed of that explanation. The evidence, however, made no difference; most anthropologists simply ignored it. Until Pierre Staintyves's *La Force Magique* appeared just before the first world war broke out, Lang lacked support; except, guardely, from Mary Kingsley. She had gone to Africa with *The Golden Bough* as her Bible, but had soon realised her mistake. In a talk to the S.P.R. in 1899 she tried to remove common misconceptions, such as that savages worshipped material objects: the heathen in his blindness bowing down to wood and stone. Savages, she insisted, did nothing of the kind. Their assumption was that objects could be infused by spirit forces – fetishism. And though she declined to concern herself with the issue of whether or not the spirit forces were real, she felt that the African witch doctor was not, as Frazer thought him, insane. His nervous system might be more sensitive; 'or, as one might say, the African mind may be a more perfect photographic plate on which the spirit world can print itself.' But in 1900 Mary Kingsley went out to South Africa as a nurse in the Boer war, and died there.

Divination

Perhaps the most significant evidence linking past and present, Lang felt, were certain techniques of divination. Scrying had been used in every era, all over the world; and Lang, though inclined to doubt whether people could really 'see' distant or future events in a glass or crystal ball, had conducted some experiments with a scryer who satisfied him that she could correctly describe people or places unknown to her, though known to witnesses who were present. This, he assumed, must be thought-transference. But he conceded that there must be something more to it, because the scryer occasionally correctly described things which had not been in the questioner's mind.

But how could people be persuaded to take scrying seriously? The crystal ball had a fun-fair connotation. And dowsing, which Lang also surveyed – divination by means of implements like a pendulum or a forked hazel twig – was similarly suspect. As Edward R. Pease had observed in the S.P.R.'s *Proceedings* in 1884, it had long been regarded as a 'comparatively harmless superstition that preys only on men's pockets and does not imperil their liberty or their lives'. Pease felt there was a *prima facie* case for more research; and at Sidgwick's request, it had been undertaken in Ireland by William Barrett.

'At first sight,' Barrett wrote in his report in 1897,

> few subjects appear to be so unworthy of serious notice and so utterly beneath scientific investigation as that of the divining rod. That any one with the smallest scientific training should think it worth his while to devote a considerable amount of time and labour to an inquiry into the alleged evidence on behalf of the rod, will appear to my scientific friends about as sensible as if he spent his time investigating fortune-telling or any other relic of superstitious folly.

Barrett himself had shared the prejudice: he had accepted the task with reluctance 'and even repugnance', hoping that in a few weeks he would be able to relegate it

> Into a limbo, large and broad, since called
> The Paradise of fools.

Still, as he had felt bound to study the subject carefully, he had given up part of two summer vacations to reading all he could find about its history; and he had examined the record of professional diviners, being particularly impressed by one of them, John Mullins. Mullins's achievements were well attested, notably by the Waterford Bacon Factory, whose managers had earlier wasted money on getting expert advice from geologists and having boreholes sunk through hard rock, one of them to a depth of over a thousand feet. Sent for in 1889 from his Wiltshire home, Mullins walked over the site until suddenly, at a spot only a few feet from the main borehole, the forked twig twisted so violently it broke in his hands. They would find an abundant supply of water, he assured them, at between eighty and ninety feet. The Irish Geological Society had asked a local geologist to hold a watching brief; he reported that when a new borehole was sunk to Mullins's specification water was found at the point and depth indicated, from a small fissure in the otherwise hard rock. The result was a well of excellent water, yielding up to five thousand gallons an hour.

From this and other case histories, past and present, Barrett was forced to admit that this form of divination was not, as he had assumed, simply a matter of the dowser having a shrewd eye for the terrain, enabling him to pick up natural indications of underground water (like a darker shade of vegetation), the divining rod having no more significance than a professional conjuror's wand. Some instinct, or faculty, Barrett felt, must be involved. He admitted that he could not prove that dowsers did better than geologists, because there were no reliable statistics; and in tests in artificial conditions dowsers' results were usually poor. But a few had had remarkably consistent records; and the subject, he urged, would repay further investigation.

Members of the Society, however, if they accepted dowsing at all, usually did so on the basis of Chevreul's hypothesis of unconscious muscular action. Barrett accepted this too; but his contention that the muscular action was translating some undiscovered instinct into visual language was unwelcome. The first paper on the subject read to the Society in 1884 had explained that the divining rod was

> always held in a position of extreme tension, and at the same time of unstable equilibrium. Light muscular contractions produce violent and startling effects. It would seem, therefore, that the action of the rod may be caused by unconscious movements of the diviner's hands, due possibly to a sensation of chill on reaching water-bearing spots or, possibly, merely to an unwritten practical science of the surface signs of hidden water.

If this were the explanation, then it was for psychologists and neuro-logists, rather than psychical researchers, to follow it up. But there was a further snag. The divining rod did not necessarily behave as if it were merely responding to muscular action, conscious or unconscious. Even Edward Tylor had admitted as much. Out of curiosity he had accompanied a dowser on an expedition; and in a report for *Nature* Tylor described how, to his astonishment, he had found that the rod worked for him, too. 'I noticed,' he added, 'when I allowed my attention to stray, the rod would from time to time move in my hands in a way so lifelike than an uneducated person might well suppose the movement to be spontaneous.' This was getting perilously close to psycho-kinesis which, being an educated person, Tylor could not accept. At least he had been open-minded enough to admit and report the rod's movement; to most scientists, such antics were an indication that the whole process was spurious. Barrett's findings were ignored. When in 1897 a Local Government Board employed a dowser, *Nature* published a denunciation: 'it is depressing to think that there exist not only private persons, but public bodies, who put more trust in the wild assertions of charlatans than in the mature conclusions of science'.

Poltergeists

By this time the stock rationalist argument was that ghosts, if they were seen at all, were hallucinations. Lang agreed; a ghost 'gives the impression of the presence of a real person, in flesh, blood and usually clothes. No such person in flesh, blood and clothes is actually there. So far, at least, every ghost is an hallucination.' But simply to leave it at that, Lang felt, would be to ignore the evidence. Why should different people see the same hallucination at different times in the same place? And if by hallucination the sceptics implied it was all in the eye of the beholder, how could they account for associated physical effects; as in a case of a 'mild but pertinacious' haunting experienced by friends of his in their Hammersmith home for twenty years? Ordinarily only sounds would be heard: knockings, footsteps, sighs. But sometimes when Mrs. Rokeby approached a door, the handle would turn and it would open, though nobody was there (Lang had once seen this happen for himself); and occasionally she would feel her hair being pulled. They had lived five years in the house before Mrs. Rokeby had seen the ghost: a woman in grey who entered the room, stood there for a moment, and then dissolved. Nobody else saw the woman but herself at the time, and she and her husband kept it a secret; but later, two domestic servants saw the grey lady, one of them leaving their service as a result.

The poltergeist-type ghost, Lang realised, offered better opportunities for research than the traditional castle spectre, partly because it was usually more persistent, partly because even if the spirit were an hallucination (if it were visible at all) the physical manifestations could not be dimissed as the product of over-heated imagination. And by the end of the century, many more poltergeists had been reported, investigated, and described in great detail, all over the world. They followed a remarkably consistent pattern, nearly always being centred around a girl or boy, often emotionally disturbed. Usually the child was suspected of being the cause of the trouble, until it became clear objects were being moved or thrown around in ways for which it could not be held responsible. Poltergeists were rarely seen, but occasionally heard; in Clarendon, Quebec, in 1889 the poltergeist claimed to be the devil, argued, and muttered obscenities. It also abstracted objects; an ink-stand would periodically disappear from the house, to be found later in an outbuilding (the local minister, who had been sceptical, changed his mind when it de-materialised while he was watching it).

Another frequently reported characteristic was that moving objects did not obey the laws of gravity. In the case of 'der Spuk von Resau' a clergyman, Dr. Müller, who had been called in to exorcise it, described how he had watched missiles – in this case, potatoes, turnips and other vegetables – flying around corners, more slowly than if they had been thrown by human hand. Sometimes they would seem to be arrested in mid-flight. A Georgia poltergeist which began operations in 1879 not only broke furniture and caused objects to float, but disrupted dinners by throwing the food about (occasionally, according to the report in the local paper, inflicting painful scalds; one of the few reported instances of people getting hurt). Spoons, too, were broken, or suddenly twisted out of shape in the diners' hands.

One of the reported poltergeists had actually been subjected to scientific testing. At the first psychological Congress in Paris Dr. Xavier Dariex described how the year before, following disturbances in his empty study at night, he had invited some colleagues to undertake an experiment with him by which every night, in the presence of the investigators, the study was locked and sealed, with elaborate precautions to prevent the intrusion even of a length of wire; not to be opened up until the investigators had satisfied themselves the following morning that the seal was still affixed to the keyhole. On eight of the ten nights nothing happened; but on the third night two chairs had been overturned, one on its side, the other on its back; and the same thing happened again on the tenth and last night. Testifying, Dariex and his witnesses agreed that the force

> does not appear to us to be in conformity with any ordinary explanation; and without wishing to prejudge in any way the precise character of this force and draw positive conclusions, we are inclined to think that the phenomena are of a psychic order.

Here, then, was a type of psychic manifestation for which there was an abundance of evidence. 'I am not ashamed to confess,' William James told the S.P.R. in his Presidential Address in 1896, 'that in my own case, although my *judgment* remains deliberately suspended, my *feeling* towards the way in which the physical phenomena of mediumship should be approached has received from ghost and disturbance-stories a distinctly charitable lurch.' Scientists might keep saying 'such things are simply impossible'; but with such a multiplication of stories, and with no natural explanation, it was foolish to ignore them.

> In all these, if memory does not deceive me, material objects are said to have been witnessed, by many persons, moving through the air in broad daylight. Often the objects were multitudinous – in some cases they were stones showered through windows and down chimneys. More than once it was noted that they fell gently and touched the ground without shock. Apart from the exceptionality of the repeated occurrences, their mutual resemblance suggests a natural type, and I confess that until these records, and others like them, are positively explained away, I cannot feel (in spite of such vast amounts of detected fraud) as if the case against physical mediumship itself as a freak of nature were definitely closed.

Realising the opportunity which poltergeists could provide for an investigation, Sidgwick had entrusted it to Frank Podmore. In the S.P.R.'s early years Podmore had been the willing work-horse, overshadowed by Hodgson; but his *Apparitions and Thought-Transference*, an 1894 follow-up of *Phantasms*, showed that he was capable of making a shrewd as well as a thorough appraisal of the evidence. Like Lang, he had been struck by the way in which some of the phenomena which were being reported, notably by the French investigators of hypnosis, might help to explain the past; and as an example, he cited a case described by Dr. J. Gibotteau in the *Annales des Sciences Psychiques*. Gibotteau had been astonished to find that one of his patients, 'Bertha J.', had the power to 'will' people walking along a pavement to stumble, or to turn off in one direction or another. She could also transmit impressions to him: when he felt a sudden spasm of uneasiness, or saw a luminosity on his bedroom wall, he would tell himself, 'This is one of Bertha's tricks!'; and when they next met, she would boast that she had indeed been responsible. 'Many of the alleged wonders of witchcraft and ancient magic in general,' Podmore suggested, 'when disentangled from the accretions formed round them by popular myth and superstition, present a marked resemblance to some of the facts recorded in this book.'

Unluckily for Podmore, *Nature* sent his book for review to the young H. G. Wells; and Wells contemptuously dismissed it. People who claimed to be able to produce the alleged phenomena, he pointed out, were usually 'from a social level below that of the investigators' – as in the Guthrie tests; the implication being that the girls, on the make, had been in collusion to dupe their employer. How could anybody take such evidence seriously? 'The persuasion is unavoidable that the ordinary psychical investigator is endowed with a considerable faculty of belief'; and this, Wells thought, was dangerous, because the general public would not be content with telepathy: any general recognition of the evidence for it would be taken to mean 'the recognition of ghosts, witchcraft, miracles, and the pretensions of many a shabby-genteel Cagliostro'.

There were already signs, in the book, that Podmore was anxious to establish himself as a no-nonsense psychical investigator, whom nobody could thus accuse of wanting to believe. It may have been Wells's review which set him on the road towards scepticism – as his report on poltergeists, when it was published in 1896, was to reveal, in spite of the fact that the eleven cases he described presented most of the usual poltergeist features. At the home of Joe White, a Worksop horse dealer, furniture had begun to move, kitchen equipment to fly around, and ornaments to fall off the mantelpiece, until White sent for a doctor, and went out himself to fetch Police Constable Higgs.

Whilst they were alone in the kitchen, standing near the door, a glass jar flew out of the cupboard into the yard; a tumbler also fell from the chest of drawers in the kitchen, when only Higgs was near it, Both then went into the inner room, and found the chest of drawers there turned up on end and smashed.

On their return to the kitchen they found the doctor, two neighbours and a girl, Rose, who was staying in the house,

and all saw a cream jug, which Rose had just placed on the bin, fly four feet up in the air and smash on the floor. Dr. Lloyd and Mrs. White then entered, and in the presence of all these witnesses a basin was seen to rise slowly from the bin – no person being near it except Dr. Lloyd and Higgs. It touched the ceiling, and then suddenly fell to the floor and was smashed.

Further disturbances followed during the next few days. A clock which had not struck for eighteen months began to strike again, and when they went to look at it, they found it had floated some distance to the floor, though the nail it had hung from was still firmly in the wall. Pictures moved; a candlestick flew over to where a visiting Salvation Army woman was standing, and she fled in terror. Only when the girl, Rose, left the house did the disturbances cease.

At the time, Podmore had been entirely convinced both of the veracity of the witnesses whom he interrogated and of the impossibility of any trickery accounting for the movements. The objects, he observed,

do not appear to have been thrown, but in some manner borne, or wafted, across the room; for though they fell on a stone floor fifteen or sixteen feet distant, they were often unbroken and were rarely shivered. And it is impossible to reconcile the account given of the movement of some other objects, variously described as 'jerky', 'twirling', and 'turning over and over', with the supposition that the objects depended on any fixed support, or were in any way suspended.

Even where children had confessed to deception, Podmore warned, this should not necessarily be accepted because such confessions might have been extorted by threats. Besides, the actual explanations of how the tricks had been done were 'for the most part, as in the Cock Lane case, ludicrously inadequate to the effects'. In some cases, therefore, 'we are driven to assume a conjunction of extraordinary cunning on the part of one of the actors in the drama, with imbecile stupidity on the part of the rest; or to surmise that the thing vouched for may actually have been due to the operation of some supernatural agency'.

Podmore's aim, however, in emphasising the difficulty of finding any natural explanation which would cover the facts, was the same as David Hume's in citing St. Médard. No matter how strong and consistent the evidence, Podmore believed, it was still not strong enough to overturn the basic proposition that such things did not happen. In almost all the cases, he pointed out, a child or an adolescent was involved; in eight out of the eleven cases investigated the child had a history of ill-health or abnormality; and as in four of the cases the child had on occasion used trickery, there was strong ground 'for assuming trickery as the true and sufficient explanation in all eleven cases'. Where it had been established that the child had not been present at some of the manifestations, and could not be held responsible for them, then there must have been a confederate. And where cheating could be ruled out – in one case Podmore had satisfied himself that no gadgetry was involved when a picture moved along the wall, before returning, when commanded to do so in the name of the Trinity, to its old position – 'I think it not impossible that the whole movement was imaginary'.

Podmore's interpretation was immediately challenged in a carefully argued letter from a member of the S.P.R., Lt.-Col. G. L. Taylor. What Podmore had done, Taylor pointed out, was take whatever evidence suited his thesis, and explain away whatever did not suit it as reporting error, deception or hallucination. But the reporting errors he had cited were trivial, of a kind which always occurred when several people described the same event; Podmore had himself accepted in several instances that deception could not have been used; and if hallucination were responsible, people would surely 'see' what they expected to see, whereas a characteristic of poltergeist hauntings was that people who knew nothing about them reported what they had *not* expected to see, like objects floating. A more reasonable hypothesis, Taylor thought, was that poltergeist phenomena were of the same species as spiritualist manifestations: telekinetic energy directed by some intelligence through a medium. If so, the fact that the disturbances were usually related to some central figure, a girl or a boy, 'no longer appears a suspicious circumstance, but becomes explanatory'.

Podmore was unrepentant; in his 1897 *Studies in Psychical Research* he elaborated upon his new scepticism. On the strength of Hodgson's evidence he was still prepared to accept that Mrs. Piper had some supernormal powers; nor could he deny that 'coming events in some sort cast their shadows before' – the evidence from dreams was too strong to be explained away by coincidence. But he ruled out the physical phenomena, discrediting them by showing all the possible means of deception, and emphasising that the medium need not necessarily be in pursuit of money or fame; there was such a thing as disinterested deception, for the pleasure, say, that she might get from the exclusive knowledge that she was a successful hoaxer. Investigators, too, were apt to become emotionally involved in the success of their experiments. It followed that results could not be accepted unless they were achieved under conditions of such strict control that virtually all past experiments in history could be set aside. Only one physical medium survived his scrutiny: to his obvious chagrin he could find no trustworthy evidence against Home.

Whether Podmore realised it or not, and from the evidence of the books which were to pour from his pen over the next few years, he was deficient in insight, the reason for his hostility to the physical evidence – and indeed, to evidence even for telepathy unless it was most rigorously tested – was that he hoped to have himself recognised as a detached, scientific, no-nonsense commentator on psychic affairs. But he overdid it. As Wallace observed, Podmore's method suffered from a fundamental defect: it ignored J. S. Mill's dictum that 'an argument is not answered until it is answered at its best'. Although he refused to accept well-attested evidence simply because the investigator had failed to list all the precautions he had taken against fraud, Podmore had no hesitation in accepting any allegations of fraud, even from writers whose motives were suspect – like J. W. Truesdell, whose *The Bottom Facts Concerning the Science of Spiritualism* had been published in New York ten years earlier, purporting to expose Spiritualist practices; a work so puerile that had it been written in defence of spiritualism, Podmore would have mocked it, if he had condescended to notice it at all.

This was not simply a quirk of Podmore's. His typescript had been read by the Sidgwicks who, he claimed, were 'in complete agreement as to the attitude of mind in which the questions here discussed should be approached'. It was an attitude of mind which by this time permeated the Society; signing the application form of a prospective member in 1896 Wallace told her that 'the majority of the active members are so absurdly and illogically sceptical that you will not find much instruction'; and a few years later, even William James had to admit, reflecting on Sidgwick, that 'the liberal heart which he possessed had to work with an intellect which acted destructively on almost every particular object of belief that was offered to its acceptance'. The effect on psychical research was also destructive. In effect, it represented the canonisation of David Hume. Without actually committing themselves to the proposition that the physical phenomena were *a priori* impossible, the Sidgwicks and Podmore demanded standards of evidence to prove their existence, which could not be met.

Spirit Photography

Of the developments out of Spiritualism, there was one which Lang would not touch. Spirit photography reeked of fraud. In whatever guise they appeared, the spirit features or forms which appeared on photographs *looked* spurious. If they were no more than misty patches, they could easily be attributed to poor plates or faulty developing; yet paradoxically the clearer they were – the more closely they resembled some dead parent or child – the more suspicion they aroused, because the popular notion of a departed spirit was not of some solid-looking being, but of a wraith. Naturally, too, the closer the resemblance to a loved one, the greater the boost to the reputation of the photographer, the better his prospects for future commissions and profits, and the greater the temptation to cheat – as some photographers had admitted doing. As the photographic process in dark rooms was particularly conducive to fraud, the evidence in spirit photography's favour was viewed by psychical researchers with scepticism.

Nevertheless there had been one report of an investigation which it was hard to dismiss out of hand as it had been conducted by J. Traill Taylor, a member of the Council of the Photographic Society of Great Britain, and well known in that circle for his research into chemistry and optics. He had scoffed at the notion that spirit forms could appear on photographic plates; but he was aware that things which could not be seen by the human eye could be photographed – certain types of light, for example; and though he was sure some trickery was being used, he was not prepared to rule out spirit photography as inherently impossible. To settle the issue he decided to make the necessary arrangements for testing a medium 'and exposing the fraud, should it prove to be such, instead of pooh-poohing it as insensate because we do not understand how it can be otherwise'.

Taylor described the results of his experiments in a paper which he read to the London and Provincial Photographic Association in 1893. He had obtained the services of David Duguid, a Scots medium with an hitherto unblemished reputation, whose presence in a studio was reputedly enough to produce spirit forms on photographic plates. The camera was Taylor's, and the plates were ordered from reputable dealers, remaining unopened until the tests. Witnesses were invited to watch for irregularities: clergymen, scientists, merchants. But Taylor's most ingenious control was a second camera, monitoring the one he was using, and providing 'a binocular stereoscopic check'. While Taylor took the pictures he took care to ensure that Duguid, though present, did nothing (once, when asked what he was thinking about, Duguid replied that his thoughts 'had been mainly concentrated upon his chances of securing a corner seat in a smoking carriage that night from Euston to Glasgow'). Sometimes Taylor let the witnesses take the photographs to see whether that made any difference. Yet in spite of every precaution 'abnormal appearances' – as he cautiously described them to his audience – appeared on some of the plates when they were developed.

> The psychic figures behaved badly. Some were in focus, others were not so; some were lighted from the right while the sitter was so from the left; some were comely, as the dame I shall show on the screen, others not so; some monopolised the major portion of the plate, quite obliterating the material sitters; others were as if an atrociously badly vignetted portrait, or one cut oval out of a photograph with a can-opener, or equally badly clipped out, were held up behind the sitter. But here is the point – not one of those figures which came out so strongly in the negative was visible in any form or shape to me during the time of exposure in the camera, and I vouch in the strongest manner for the fact that no one whatever had an opportunity of tampering with any plate anterior to its being placed in the dark slide or immediately preceding development. Pictorially they are vile, but how came they there?

The stereoscopic camera had afforded Tayor a clue. 'It is due to the psychic entities to say that whatever was produced on one half of the stereoscopic plates was reproduced on the other, alike good or bad in definition.' But careful examination revealed that although the sitters were stereoscopic in both pictures, 'the psychic figure was absolutely flat'; and in one, the psychic figure was a little displaced compared to the other, at least a millimetre higher. Granted the possibility of spirit forms – or whatever they were ('are they,' Taylor speculated, 'crystallisations of thought?') – this evidence was revealing. The camera was not 'taking' the forms. They appeared on the plate as if they were beside or behind the sitter, but only in the same way that a dirty fingerprint on the plate would have appeared. They 'had not been formed by lens,' Taylor concluded: and consequently 'the psychic image might be produced without a camera'.

Taylor's account was impressive, not simply for showing the care with which the tests had been conducted, but also for the ring of honesty in his presentation – comparable to Patrick Proctor Alexander's commentary on Home. But it made no impact. To most psychical researchers spirits of any kind were disturbing; but spirits of the dead appearing on photographic plates were as unwelcome as gate-crashers at a funeral feast.

Materialism

By 1900 psychical research, of the kind that Sidgwick and Myers had hoped to establish as a scientific discipline, had lost its way. The S.P.R. was still investigating, still collecting material; and outside it, individuals and groups were functioning – in the 1890s there was a revival of Hermetic occultism with the setting up of the Order of the Golden Dawn, whose members undertook experiments of the kind W. B. Yeats was to describe in his autobiography. But hypnotism was in the psychiatrists' strait-jacket, and Spiritualism, at least so far as scientists were concerned, was discredited. In his survey of Christian mysticism in 1899 W. R. Inge, later Dean of St. Paul's, refused even to include it, deriding the phenomena as 'ridiculous fables' and denouncing the psychical researchers for 'breaking down the middle wall between matter and spirit' in a way that was not scientific, merely 'a hankering after the beggarly elements of the later neo-Platonism'. In the same year Hugo Muensterberg, Professor of Psychology at Harvard, insisted that Spiritualism *was* mysticism – 'mysticism's most repulsive claim'; and agreed with Inge that the phenomena 'do not exist and never will exist'. It did not matter how much evidence the psychical researchers produced for telepathy, Edmund Parish claimed in his *Hallucinations and Illusions*: coincidence or some other natural explanation would always account for the results of card-guessing. And Joseph Jastrow, Professor of Psychology at Wisconsin University – a disciple of Carpenter, who was emerging as the most vocal of the critics of psychical research – agreed. 'My admiration of Hamlet is somewhat dulled,' he wrote in an essay on the subject in 1901, 'by reason of that ill-advised remark to Horatio about there being more things in heaven and earth than are dreamed of in our philosophies'; a contention, Jastrow claimed, which he would disapprove of even if it were valid, because of the encouragement it had given to the occultists. The belief in thought-transference was part of

a complex conglomerate, in which imperfectly recognised modes of sense-action, hyperesthesia and hysteria, fraud, conscious and unconscious, chance, collusion, similarity of mental processes, and expectant interest in presentiments and a belief in their significance, nervousness and ill-health, illusions of memory, hallucinations, suggestion, contagion and other elements enter into the composition; while defective observation, falsification of memory, forgetfulness of details, bias and prepossession, suggestion from others, lack of training and of a proper investigative temperament, further invalidate and confuse the records of what is supposed to have been observed.

Chapter Thirty-seven
Cross-correspondences

LANG HAD ARRIVED ON THE SCENE TOO LATE. WHAT HE HAD TRIED TO DO was important; to show that almost all the psychical phenomena had a long and well-attested pedigree, and that they could be regarded not as occult or supernatural, in the derogatory sense of those terms, but as awaiting explanation. This was very much what the Cambridge group had hoped to do; but without being fully aware of it the Sidgwicks, Hodgson and Podmore had struck most of what had originally been accepted as psychic phenomena off the Society's visiting list. When Sidgwick died in 1900 the only issues which the active members could feel safe in investigating were telepathy and precognition. Even clairvoyance was disregarded, Podmore relegating it to what amounted to an appendix in his 1897 book.

If he had a fresh chance to introduce scientists to the study of psychic phenomena, Crookes told the British Association in his Presidential Address, 'I should choose a starting point different from that of old. It would be well to begin with telepathy; with the fundamental law, as I believe it to be, that thoughts and images may be transferred from one mind to another without the agency of recognised organs of sense.' Already research in the S.P.R. was concentrating largely on seeking to prove that telepathy existed – in the U.S. as well as in Britain. Ten years earlier, Thomas Jay Hudson noted in 1902, everything had been attributed to clairvoyance or the spirits; now, telepathy was thought to explain everything.

The research produced some striking confirmatory evidence for telepathy, helped by the use of automatic writing by mediums. The method commonly used had been suggested by Kardec: anybody who could induce a trance state need simply sit relaxed, pen in hand, until the spirits took over. Moses had found he did not even have to sit idle; he could be thinking, or even reading, while his pen was taking down the spirit messages. And although Janet and Myers had argued it was not necessary to think in terms of spirits – the writer's subliminal self, or one of his selves, might be responsible for the messages – this made no difference to the method. Some members of the S.P.R. became accustomed to use it not merely, as they hoped, to open up telepathic communication, but also because it meant that a written record was available to them after each seance; among them Mrs. A. W. Verrall, a lecturer at Newnham College, Cambridge, and a member of the S.P.R. Council.

'I do not look at the paper,' Mrs. Verrall was to explain,

I perceive a word or two, but never understand whether it makes sense with what goes before . . . I have tried more than once to reproduce from memory what has just been written, but I have never been able to give more than a word or two and I have no impression as to the general sense, if there has been any.

Looking at what she had written on December 11th, 1901, Mrs. Verrall found:

The trivial helps, gives confidence. Frost and a candle in the dim light. Marmontel, he was reading on a sofa or in bed – there was only a candle's light. She will surely remember this. The book was lent, not his own – he talked about it

– typical of the spasmodic elliptical nature of such communications. Baffled, Mrs Verrall wrote to Mrs Sidgwick, asking her if 'Marmontel' meant anything to her. Then, on the 17th, she found she had brought up the name again:

I wanted to write. Marmontel is right. It was a French book, a memoir I think. Passy may help, souvenirs de Passy, or Fleury. Marmontel was not on the cover – the book was bound and was lent – two volumes in old-fashioned binding and print.

A few days later Mrs. Verrall saw an advertisement for Marmontel's *Moral Tales* – the first time she had consciously heard of him. The following March she met a friend, Mr. Marsh, who told her he had been reading Marmontel's *Memoirs* which he had taken out of the London Library and brought to Paris, where he had read it by candle light on the evening of February 20th, in bed, and on the 21st, lying between two chairs. In the book there was a description of an episode at Passy, connected with a story in which Fleury played an important part. There were minor discrepancies: Marmontel's name, though not on the cover, was on the spine; Marsh had only one of three volumes;

o

and the weather, though cold, was not frosty. But the resemblances were striking, particularly as Marsh said that he ordinarily read by electric light. And the fact that the automatic writing had predated the event could be confirmed by the date on the letter Mrs. Sidgwick had written in reply to Mrs. Verrall's request for information about Marmontel.

After Myers's death in 1901, messages began to appear from time to time in automatic scripts which seemed as if they might have been from him – sometimes purporting actually to come from him. They came not only through Mrs. Verrall, but also through Mrs. Piper, in Boston, and 'Mrs. Holland' – a pseudonym which Rudyard Kipling's sister Mrs. Fleming, who lived in India, used because her husband and family disapproved of such activities. The scripts found their way to the S.P.R. where eventually they gave the Secretary, Alice Johnson, the idea that they might be part of a scheme by which Myers, in conjunction with Sidgwick and Gurney, who had also begun to communicate, were sending messages in an elaborate code designed to prove the reality of spirit communication. To each automatist, the information would be so fragmentary and strange as to be meaningless; but pieced together, it would carry information of a kind which could only have come from Myers, or one of the others, or all three.

The pursuit was endlessly fascinating, and threw up many indications of the kind the investigators were looking for. On February 26th, 1907, Mrs. Piper got 'Morehead (or some such word); Laurel'. On March 17th, Mrs. Verrall got 'Alexander's tomb . . . laurel leaves'. On March 27th, Mrs Holland got 'Darkness, light and shadow, Alexander Moor's head'; and there were similar fragments. Not until two years later did another automatist, Mrs. Willett, come up with 'Laurentian tombs, Dawn and Twilight'; providing the essential clue. The scattered scripts had been hovering around the theme of the tomb of Lorenzo the Magnificent, adorned with his emblem, the laurel, and with the two figures representing dawn and twilight. For it was also the tomb of Alexander the Moor, whose corpse had been secretly placed there after he had been murdered.

That automatists in different parts of the world, with no possibility of inter-communication, should produce cross-correspondence of this kind – and this was only one of many – was certainly remarkable. But that they should occupy so much of the S.P.R.'s attention and so much space in the *Proceedings* was ironic, considering that Sidgwick, Gurney and Myers had been largely responsible for ousting the Spiritualists from the Society, and then for some years ignoring their activities. Week after week journals like *Light* in Britain and its counterparts elsewhere reported manifestations, but it was only the occasional exposure of a medium which made news outside Spiritualist circles; and the growing tendency of Spiritualists to regard themselves as a religious sect, reflected in the introduction of churches and pastors, helped to remove them still further from any contact with psychical research. Yet here were the spirits of Sidgwick, Myers and Gurney – or communicators in their image, behaving in life-like fashion – absorbing the attention of some of the Society's leading members, to the exclusion of other forms of research.

Some of the information transmitted through the automatists, admittedly, could be ascribed to telepathy – or clairvoyance. 'Myers' gave Mrs. Holland, who did not know the Verralls, an accurate description of their Cambridge dining-room, correct except in describing a water filter as a bust. This might sound like clairvoyance; but when the script was read to a friend of Mrs. Verrall he admitted that he too had thought there was a bust in her dining-room, which suggested that Mrs. Holland might have picked up somebody's mental picture of the room. There were also occasional flashes of precognition: a reference to the sinking of the *Lusitania* occurred in scripts a year before it happened, before the first world war had even broken out. And there were several examples of the automatists writing fluently in languages they did not know. But though the pursuit of the cross-references went on for years, becoming ever more complex as allusions and puns were found which had not at first been suspected, it proved in the end a fruitless enterprise – except, possibly, in providing material which psychical researchers, perhaps with the benefit of improved understanding of such communications, might later work over again more productively. All the cross-correspondences could reasonably be held to have demonstrated was that if Sidgwick, Gurney and Myers were indeed trying to communicate, they were finding it extremely difficult – as, indeed, their messages often intimated: 'Myers' complained that it was as if he were 'standing behind a sheet of frosted glass – which blurs sight and deadens sound – dictating feebly – to a reluctant and somewhat obtuse secretary. A feeling of terrible impotence burdens me . . .'

A feeling of impotence also burdened the S.P.R. in this period. Individual members continued to undertake research along lines which interested them, and some of it was impressive; William Barrett investigated poltergeist outbreaks anew, and provided a useful analysis of their commoner features. In general, though, the S.P.R. – with Mrs. Sidgwick the quietly dominating influence in the Council, and Podmore putting out book after book largely devoted to disparaging the work of earlier researchers – did little of importance until, in 1909, it sponsored a fresh investigation of Eusapia Palladino; an investigation which was authorised at the cost of abandoning Sidgwick's cherished principle that the Society ought not to concern itself with any medium who had been caught cheating, and which was to show just how unwise adherence to that principle had been.

Chapter Thirty-eight
Eusapia Palladino (2)

Flammarion and Maxwell

On the Continent of Europe, too, psychical research languished in the early years of the century, in spite of Flammarion's bold effort in 1900 to provide a successor to *Phantasms,* using some of Gurney's material but concentrating on providing similar examples of telepathy and pre-cognition from French sources. He was much less thorough than Gurney, being inclined to use good stories which he had heard from people he believed he could rely on without checking to make sure the stories were accurate; but for most of his episodes he gave names and addresses, so that sceptical critics could have followed them up. His standpoint was roughly the same as Andrew Lang's. There were two enemies of progress, he claimed, credulity and incredulity: 'Let us deny nothing, let us assert nothing, let us observe impartially'; and in general he lived up to this injunction, though like Lang he found it hard to stomach the higher phenomena of spiritualism. Kardec's quiet com-munication with the spirit world was one thing; 'noises, movement of tables', he was to write a few years later,

> raps, replies to questions asked, are really childish, puerile, vulgar, often ridiculous, and rather resemble the pranks of mischievous boys rather than serious *bona fide* actions. It is impossible not to notice this. Why should the souls of the dead amuse themselves in this way? The supposition seems almost absurd.

Yet he had tested Eusapia; and he could not deny that the physical phenomena in her case were genuine. Nor could Joseph Maxwell, whose *Metapsychical Phenomena* ('metapsychical', coined by Richet as preferable to 'supernormal', remained in favour until overtaken by 'paranormal') was and remains the most convincing single account of psychical research at this time.

Introducing the author to British readers, Lodge said he had been deputy attorney general in Bordeaux, but when at the age of thirty he had ceased to be sceptical about psychical phenomena he had taken the trouble to graduate in medicine, as well as law, the better to qualify as a researcher; a very different attitude, Lodge observed, from that of people who went into psychical research looking for a faith. Maxwell explained that he did not believe in the supernatural, or in miracles. He assumed that the phenomena he had observed were real, natural; although he could not account for them, he was 'inclined to think that they are produced by some force within ourselves'. He described his research in detail, with one omission: he would not, he said, specify all the precautions he had taken against fraud. It would be a waste of time, he felt, because past experience had shown that there was no way in which a psychical researcher could demonstrate that he had made his experiments fraud-proof. It was more important, he had decided, to verify the phenomena again and again in different circumstances with different mediums, if possible amateurs, in such a way that he could satisfy himself that no deception was involved – dark seances being 'absolutely worthless'.

When by sight and touch, I make sure of the absence of contact between the experimenters and the article which is displaced, I have sufficient reasons for excluding the hypothesis of fraud. When I measure the distance between the objects before and after the displacement, I have also sufficient reason for excluding the hypothesis of the illusion of my senses. If this right be refused me, I should really like to know how any fact whatever can be observed. No one is more convinced than myself of the frailty of our impressions and the relativity of our perceptions; nevertheless there must be some way of perceiving a phenomenon in order to submit it to impartial investigation.

'Illusion' could not be used to discredit psychical research in general, Maxwell pointed out, without undermining the whole foundations of science. But it could be used to discredit an individual's research – such as his own; 'in vain might I plead that I am persuaded of the regularity of my perceptions, in vain assert that I observe no tendency to illusion in myself: my testimony would remain none the less suspect'. Therefore he was not going to affirm the objective reality of what he had seen. He was merely going to affirm that it was what he had *believed* he had seen, and to invite those who cared to challenge his credibility to do the same experiments, using the same techniques, and see for themselves. 'To criticise without experience is unreasonable, and I recognise no competence in those judges whose decisions are made without preliminary information.'

It is difficult in Maxwell's case, as in some others, to transmit the flavour of integrity which his work conveys, because it emerges from his meticulous attention to detail; ranging from the recording of changes of temperature during seances to studies of the effect of fatigue or of mood on performances – the harmony of a group, he found, being of great importance. He refused to dramatise his own part; successful though some of his own researches had been, he admitted that none had been so revealing as those of de Rochas with Eusapia which he had attended as an observer. Other mediums had provided him with more startling variations of telekinesis, but not levitations; except one, whom he could not quite trust. To de Rochas's account, Maxwell was able to add a description of some informal occasions at Agnélas where the effects had been even more striking than at the formal seances; one in particular:

It was, I think, about five o'clock in the afternoon; at all events it was broad daylight in the Agnélas drawing room. We were standing round the table; Eusapia took my hand and held it in her left, resting her right hand on the right-hand corner of the table. The table was raised to the level of our foreheads; that is to say, the top of the table was raised to a height of about five feet from the floor.

Such an experience, Maxwell felt, was particularly convincing, because it was utterly impossible for Eusapia to have raised so heavy a table by muscular effort, even if she had a hold of it; and as it was daylight, she could not have used hooks and wires, or other such devices.

Morselli

From time to time similar accounts had continued to appear in journals such as the *Annales des Sciences Psychiques,* showing that Eusapia was continuing to produce her familiar effects; but following her rejection by the S.P.R. it was easy for orthodox scientists to dismiss them. In 1907, however, a report appeared in the *Annales* which could not easily be ignored, because its author was the psychologist and neurologist Professor Enrico Morselli. Morselli had long been regarded as a pillar of materialist rectitude; 'one of the foremost leaders of Italian science,' Flournoy described him, 'whose professional studies and philosophic tendencies hardly predispose him to tolerate any infringements of known biological laws'. He had in fact been Italy's foremost campaigner against the Spiritualists: so vehement in his denunciations that he had been excluded from witnessing the Milan experiments, for fear his rancorous scepticism might inhibit Eusapia's performances. In 1901, however, he had managed to attend a seance without her knowing; and having modified his attitude, managed to secure her co-operation in a series of over twenty tests. Striking though the results were, they did not make so much of an impression as a second series, in 1906. Both were described in the *Annales* and in Morselli's *Psicologia e Spiritismo*: and more succinctly and entertainingly by Luigi Barzini, the editor of the Milan *Corriere della Sera*.

'I confess,' Barzini admitted, 'that I assisted at these seances with the object of unmasking fraud and trickery' – to that end, he had the premises thoroughly searched, and Eusapia stripped – 'and that, on the contrary, I have ended by being convinced of the reality of some of the phenomena.' While he and Morselli were holding Eusapia's hands and feet, in sufficient light to see what was happening, a chair edged up towards Morselli and nestled against him; 'after having made him this little visit it returned to its place by jerks, as it had come'. A trumpet floated down on to the table. The curtain was blown out like a sail, though there was nothing behind it (once, putting his hand to the curtain, Barzini felt a face; nose, cheeks, teeth). A metronome started up on its own, exciting surprise; 'doubtless feeling flattered, it arrived on the table, just in front of its master, and began cheerily to beat time'. Two vertical rods had been attached to Eusapia's chair to hold some frames, in connection with tests to detect if there were radiations; while Eusapia's hands were on the table, Barzini saw the knots being 'patiently undone, before our eyes'; the liberated frames then raised themselves, and disappeared behind the curtain.

With eye-witness backing of this kind, it was not difficult for Morselli to dispose of the idea that Eusapia could be using sleight-of-hand; but the possibility of illusion or hallucination was harder to dismiss. In an attempt to provide irrefutable evidence, a variety of gadgets had been introduced at seances designed to render it impossible for Eusapia to deceive the witnesses (it had been suggested she might be using some form of hypnosis), or for the witnesses to deceive themselves. A clockwork mechanism was brought in, sealed inside a bell glass, and Eusapia was asked to try to activate it: the key by which it was ordinarily started being shut up inside a sealed box. While she was being held in her chair, Eusapia managed to get the mechanism to start. But when the investigators examined it, they found that the seals had been torn off the bell glass and the lid of the box had been ripped off.

It might not be quite what Morselli had been hoping for, but spontaneous effects of that kind carried their own type of conviction, at least to anybody who had observed them. He had clung to the belief that the phenomena must be the product of deception. Now, he was convinced that the phenomena of physical mediumship attributed to Eusapia are in the great majority of cases real, authentic, genuine; that in the now innumerable series of her 'spiritistic' manifestations there may be an admixture of some spurious phenomena, sometimes also naïve and puerile attempts at deception on her part, and illusions or errors of appreciation on the part of the sitters; but on the whole the phenomena produced by Eusapia have – for a calm scientist, an impartial observer, a competent student of psychology – an objective existence and a positive consistency equal to those attained by and verified and accepted in accordance with the rules of the experimental method.

Later in that year, following a triumphal tour of Italy, Eusapia was at last accorded the honour of a formal investigation in her home city, in which the rules of the experimental method were even more closely applied, with monitoring equipment designed to work independently of the investigators. The mechanical aids operated better, on this occasion; and the usual phenomena were observed, including the growth of a pseudopod. One witness, while holding Eusapia's right hand and looking to make sure her left hand was also secure, saw what seemed to be another arm appear; it 'seemed to come out of the shoulder,' he reported, 'and then return and melt into the body again'; Professor Filipo Bottazzi, Director of the Naples Physiological Institute, who had set up the investigation, was convinced; the results, he felt, finally eliminated 'the slightest trace of suspicion about the genuineness of the phenomena'.

The Sorbonne Trials

Bottazzi was being over-optimistic: neither the French nor the British were likely to be impressed by trials in Italy, let alone in Naples. But French scientists had been conducting their own tests investigation in Paris, the most carefully planned and carried out of any so far: forty-three seances, spaced out over four years, from 1905 to 1908. They had been organised by Jules Courtier, Professor of Psychology at the Sorbonne; and among those participating were Gilbert Ballet, Henri Bergson, Pierre and Marie Curie, Jean-Baptiste Perrin, and Richet – all Professors at the University of Paris; Jacques-Arsène d'Arsonval, director of the Laboratory of Biological Physics; and M. Youriévitch, General Secretary of the *Institut Général Psychologique*. A more formidable research team could hardly have been assembled.

From the start, the investigators aimed to reduce the subjective element to a minimum. The usual precautions to prevent deception were supplemented by an elaborate system of monitoring instruments not merely designed to record any physical intervention, but also remote-controlled, from a separate laboratory, to ensure that the observers were not subjected to hypnotic influences, or whatever illusions might generate in the seance chamber. Eusapia's chair was suspended on a weighing machine; the tables were wired up so that movements, and their source, could be registered; every sound, every comment, was recorded; and the tests were conducted in electric light, so arranged that it was indirect, and could be varied according to need.

At the conclusion of the tests Courtier, who like most of the observers had been a sceptic, reported that Eusapia had been able to produce raps at a distance from herself, sometimes by striking mock blows, sometimes by touching somebody, the raps echoing her gestures. The table in front of her had moved when her feet were being held, and her hands withdrawn from it. First, two table legs, then three, rose, even when one of the investigators actually sat on it. Then the table levitated, all four legs off the floor, while Eusapia's feet were controlled and her hands were resting on the heads of witnesses on each side of her; and remained for a few seconds floating about thirty centimetres above the floor. When the group stood holding hands above it, the table hoisted itself so high that its legs almost came out of the sheaths which had been designed to prevent any interference with them; its movements being recorded by the group of observers, and by the recording machines in the other room. And what impressed the physicists was that although there was no way by which she could have physically moved the table without being detected, the balance registered figures which conformed to what would have been expected if she *had* been physically lifting it – 'as if the fulcrum of the force were in the subject herself'. Whatever the force might be, it was coming from her.

Other manifestations followed the usual pattern. The curtain bellied out towards Eusapia, when she called it. Saucers and boxes were thrown on to the floor at a distance; or on to the seance table. A zither sounded, as if it were being played. Investigators were touched, or pinched; their hair was pulled; the knots in their cravats were untied. Luminosities were seen, sometimes in the shape of a hand, sometimes like limbs in silhouette. A basin of wet clay, designed to receive psychic impressions, was transported to the table; the stool on which it had rested began to try to climb up on to Pierre Curie. When nobody was touching it a pencil broke; so did one of the tubes carrying information to the other room. A small three-legged table, placed out of her reach and connected with a monitoring apparatus designed to detect any physical contact, moved towards or away from her at her bidding, before sailing over Pierre Curie's shoulder and gently coming to rest on the top of the seance table ('it made a pretty curve,' he commented). And when it was placed on a balance, Eusapia was able to increase or decrease its weight. 'I must confess that these spirit phenomena intrigue me a great deal,' Curie had written in 1894; there were aspects of them, he felt, which 'touch closely on physics'. But while the experiments with Eusapia were in progress, he was killed in a street accident.

The Conjurors

The Sorbonne investigators declined formally to endorse Eusapia; they contented themselves with giving the results of their work. But even before their report appeared Flammarion, who had witnessed some of the tests, was arguing that levitation should no longer be any more in question than the attraction of iron by a magnet. Unless it was going to be alleged that the Paris investigators were all in collusion with Eusapia to rig the results, it was hard to think what further proofs she could conceivably be required to give to convince the scientific world that the phenomena were genuine. The Society for Psychical Research was consequently in an embarrassing position. In his *Modern Spiritualism*, published in 1902, Podmore had dismissed the physical phenomena as a discredited branch of legerdemain; and though by the rules of the Society he spoke only for himself, he had become its chief spokesman in the eyes of the public. In any case the Society was still bound by the Sidgwick convention.

Paradoxically, it was the fact that Eusapia was again suspected of trying to cheat in the Sorbonne experiments which gave the Society the excuse to go back on its principle. A nail had been found where no nail should have been, which she might have tried to use to influence one of the instruments; and – a more serious charge – she had been seen using what looked like a hair to move objects. As it happened, though, when the report appeared it coincided with an account from Ochorowicz of tests he had made on another medium, Stanislawa Tomczyk, whom he had seen using what at first he had assumed to be a thread, in the same way. He had, however, been forced to the conclusion – because, among other things, she could 'push' with it as well as 'pull' – that it must have been a materialisation of the force which she was projecting; 'an unknown force oozing from her hands, which acts at a distance, and which can be concentrated upon a point chosen at will'. Had the Paris investigators known of this hypothesis, they might have been less disposed to suspect Eusapia, as it tied up with their own discovery that the force which levitated the table came from her.

Otherwise, Eusapia had been detected in nothing more heinous than occasionally freeing her hands from her neighbours' control. Still, the fact that she had been accused gave the S.P.R. Council a way out of their difficulty. It was no longer possible, as Eleanor Sidgwick herself admitted, to maintain 'an obstinate attitude of incredulity'. But they could, to save face, set up a different kind of inquiry. To defend himself from the charge that he had never personally investigated the phenomena which he rejected, Muensterberg had claimed that it was only because he 'should be the last man to see through the scheme and discover the trick'; the investigators should be conjurors, not psychologists. The S.P.R. now took his hint: Eusapia, it was decided, should be investigated 'by persons specially practised in the investigation of mediumistic physical phenomena, who had themselves detected trickery in other cases' – the society's equivalent of a Fraud Squad. The chosen investigating trio were the Hon. Everard Feilding, Hereward Carrington, and Wortley Baggally. Feilding, son of the Earl of Denbigh and Hon. Sec. to the Society, was by his own account a complete sceptic; and he had already distinguished himself as a fraud detector. In *The Physical Phenomena of Spiritualism*, published the year before, Carrington had devoted over three hundred of its four hundred pages to the most detailed analysis which had yet appeared of fraudulent mediumship, how it operated and how it could be exposed. And Baggally, a practised conjuror, claimed to have investigated almost every medium in Britain since Home without finding one who was genuine.

It had constantly been said, Feilding observed, that 'no one is easier to deceive than a man of science'; and although this might be unfair, he thought it entirely reasonable if Eusapia really was a conjuror, as he assumed, that she should be investigated not by experts in physics or psychology but by experts in legerdemain. In Naples he and Carrington (Baggally arrived a few days later) made their preparations with care, ensuring that Eusapia had no prior access to the seance room, and themselves purchasing any objects such as musical instruments which would be required to move or play at a distance; but they allowed her to have her 'cabinet' – a curtain to stretch across a corner of the room, behind which the objects could be placed on a small stand. She was also permitted to bring her own seance table, provided they could give it a thorough examination. And only the two of them, along with a British note-taker hired locally from a travel agency, were present when the first seance with her was held.

There was one significant difference between their method and their predecessors'. The emphasis was not just on the phenomena, but also on the controls they were applying to the medium. Every time there was a rap, or a movement, each of the investigators involved in holding Eusapia would note it and at the same time confirm that he was holding her correctly; either by looking at her hands and feet, or, if it were too dark to see clearly (they assumed she would prefer darkness) by feeling that it really was her hand, or foot, that he was holding; not somebody else's, or a false hand or foot. And their descriptions both of what they saw and of their controls were given out loud, so that they could be taken down in shorthand; when written up they would provide rather more than the usual memory-jog.

From the start, the phenomena were just as they had so often been described: levitations; curtains billowing out; raps and bangs; musical instruments giving off sounds; furniture and other objects moving; touchings and graspings; hands becoming visible, also 'objects more or less like heads'; luminosities; a cold breeze (which appeared to issue from a scar on the medium's brow – 'perhaps of all the phenomena,' Feilding commented, 'this, by reason of its very simplicity, appears one of the most preposterous'); and – though only in a single instance – the untying of knots.

At first, though they could not dispute that Eusapia was producing the effects, Feilding and Carrington assumed that they would soon be able to find explanations for them. If her skirts billowed out (as, like Angélique Cottin's, they still sometimes did), it might be because some gadget was concealed. But they could find no gadget concealed. Gradually they eliminated all the possibilities of deception until, at the sixth seance, their resistance had collapsed. 'For the first time,' Feilding wrote, 'I find that my mind, from which the stream of events has hitherto run off like rain from a mackintosh, is at last beginning to be capable of absorbing them. For the first time, I have the absolute conviction that our observation is not mistaken.'

Baggally, though, having just arrived, was still toying with the idea that there must be some apparatus. It would be an interesting problem for a manufacturer, Feilding sardonically mused, to devise an apparatus capable of producing such a succession of manifestations, including a variety of materialised faces and hands; of such dimensions that it could be concealed about a somewhat stout and elderly lady parading herself for inspection on a chair in her underwear, and later seated in a tight plain gown; and of such a nature as to enable her to actuate it while held visibly hand and foot by two practised conjurors, in such a way as to deceive them, though they were on the look-out for just such a trick.

They had expected that Eusapia might make difficulties about accepting controls, and on occasion she did; her mood varied, and some days she would object to them. But the security of the controls, they found – as Ochorowicz had – did not unfavourably affect the production of the phenomena; 'on the contrary', Feilding noted, 'it was on the nights when she was in the best humour, and consequently when our precautions were most complete and the light was strongest, that the phenomena were the most numerous'. Unless they were all three of them unconsciously deluding themselves (and also deluding occasional visitors: Professor Bottazzi; a doctor, invited to examine Eusapia's physiological reactions; and two English ladies, who were able to give

Eusapia a more thorough search than the investigators could decently apply) many of the effects could not conceivably be accounted for by any form of conjuring. As for the possibility of hallucination, how could it account for effects which continued when Eusapia was not there? A bell, for example, hanging from a cord, which began to ring?

Their consternation, as this dawned on them, emerged from the notes which were written up by the shorthand taker, and their appended observations following each seance; particularly from Feilding's wry commentary. He took a humorously masochistic pleasure in recalling the 'invincible conceit' which he had brought with him to Naples. In retrospect he felt that the third seance was crucial. Eusapia insisted on near darkness: the phenomena seemed less impressive than on the first two; her investigators could detect her trying to extricate her feet and hands out of their control. In their comments after the seance, they naturally concentrated on these efforts to deceive them. It was only when they read the shorthand taker's notes of what they had described during the seance that they realised how few of the phenomena which they had been reporting could be accounted for by her cheating: 'all the more remarkable manifestations had receded in our memory, driven back by the certainty that the medium had been detected in fraud'. Re-reading the account of this third seance a few months later, Feilding expressed his satisfaction that, unfair though he now realised it had been to Eusapia, it existed 'as a record of our critical, indeed hostile, state of mind'. Clearly the often reiterated criticism of psychical researchers, that they *wanted* to believe, could not have applied to them. On the contrary, although the first two seances had impressed them, they had been puzzled and irritated rather than convinced – conviction being after all, 'an emotional and not an intellectual process'. The ordinary effect, as Feilding put it

of the sudden confrontation of a fairly balanced mind with a merely bizarre fact is a reaction; the mind rejects it, refuses to consider it. And the more bizarre the fact, the stronger the reaction. If the possessor of such a mind were, for example, in the course of a walk down Piccadilly, to see a policeman levitated across a motor omnibus, no permanent impression as to the mutability of the laws of gravitation affecting policemen would remain with him. The emotional certainty produced by his long continued previous experience that policemen do not do such things would be stronger than any degree of intellectual certainty that this particular policeman did, and would presently efface it; and so it was with ourselves. Tables, we knew, or thought we knew, do not go into the air by themselves; curtains do not bulge out without some mechanical agency; and although we saw them do so, we still refused to believe that they did. We preferred to believe that we had been deceived in some way unknown; that we had been hallucinated, or had wrongly observed. We doubted our senses rather than our experience; were guided, in fact, by our emotions rather than our observation.

The U.S. experiments

There was no more convincing description, from this period, of a conversion. Although not so traumatic an experience as a change of religious faith, in one respect it was more uncomfortable; Feilding had nothing to gain. On the contrary, by admitting it he would suffer the equivalent of an endorsement to his licence as a researcher, losing his hitherto unblemished record of scepticism. Only if Eusapia managed to win over orthodoxy would he hope to recover respect; and this prospect was immediately dashed by what happened when, at Carrington's invitation, she sailed for America in November 1909 to be tested there.

The leading members of the American Society for Psychical Research had tended to share the British view of the physical phenomena – and of Eusapia. 'It is pleasant,' William James had told the British S.P.R. in his Presidential address in 1896, 'to turn from phenomena of the dark-sitting and rat-hole type (with their tragi-comic suggestion that the whole order of nature might possibly be overturned in one's own head, by the way one imagined oneself, on a certain occasion, to be holding a tricky peasant woman's feet) to the "calm air of delightful studies",' – studies like telepathy. James was no longer so active; he died in 1910. But his successor as the dominant personality in the Society, James Hyslop – a former Professor of Ethics and Logic in Columbia University – was even more hostile. He had written to congratulate his S.P.R. colleagues in Cambridge for their exposure of Eusapia; in his 1906 *Enigmas of Psychical Research* he had dismissed materialisations, and even rappings, as the product either of hallucination or fraud; and as he assumed that Carrington was simply cashing in on a conjuring act, he refused to co-operate.

Some of the seances were successful. A conjurer, M. Howard, who had earlier exposed a number of bogus mediums, expressed his conviction that Eusapia really had levitated a table. At John Hopkins University a physicist who had arranged to have a spy-hole into the 'cabinet' was able to see what he described as a 'black object', sometimes pointed, sometimes rounded, reaching out as if from Eusapia's back to move the stand behind her. But just before Christmas, when she was being tested by Muensterberg, she was caught using her foot by a man who had insinuated himself into the cabinet; and the following spring a conjuror, Joseph Rinn, concealed himself at Jastrow's instigation under the seance table, and she was caught again. 'Palladino is exposed by noted scientists as expert trickster', the *Boston Herald*'s headline ran; and Muensterberg, in the *Metropolitan Magazine*, and Jastrow, in *Collier's*, gave detailed descriptions of how the exposures had been accomplished. Muensterberg had felt touches on his arm and a pull at his sleeve before Eusapia suddenly screamed.

What had happened? Neither she nor Mr. Carrington had the slightest idea that a man was lying flat on the floor and had succeeded in slipping noiselessly like a snail below the curtain into the cabinet. I had told him that I expected wires stretched out from her body and he looked out for them. What a surprise when he saw that she had simply freed her foot from her shoe and with an athletic backward movement of the leg was reaching out and fishing with her toes for the guitar and the table in the cabinet. And then, lying on the floor, he grasped her foot and caught her heel with a firm hand, and she responded with the wild scream which indicated that she knew at last she was trapped and her glory shattered.

Eusapia made no attempt to deny that if she was given the opportunity to cheat, in her trances, she might take it – particularly if that was what witnesses wanted; 'they think of tricks, nothing but tricks; they put their mind on the tricks and I automatically respond'. Yet in the light of what had been discovered in the course of the European investigations, it was far from certain that what had been described as 'feet' were Eusapia's feet. Neither Muensterberg nor Jastrow would have taken the 'pseudopod' hypothesis seriously; and their assistants were unlikely even to have heard about it. But given the possibility that she could produce psychic elongations, the experiments were simply not designed to distinguish between them and her arms and feet. Muensterberg actually stretched physical credibility in his description.

Her achievement was splendid. She had lifted her unshod foot to the height of my arm when she touched me under the cover of the curtain, without changing in the least the position of her body. When her foot played thumb and fingers the game was also neat throughout.

By this time a fat, elderly lady, Eusapia would have had to be a contortionist, as well as a conjuror, of genius to be capable of sliding a foot back round or under her chair, behind a curtain, and up as high as Muensterberg's arm, to use her toes to pull at his sleeve, without any movement of her body – her hands being held. And Rinn's description, which Jastrow quoted in *Collier's*, was similarly unsatisfactory. To account for the curtain behind her bellying out, Rinn claimed that she kicked it; an inadequate explanation, given the position in which she was sitting in a chair in front of it. Even if her feet were left free – as they deliberately were, Jastrow explained, the better to find how she used them – it was difficult to see how without moving from her chair she could have stretched one of them back far enough to pick up the table from behind the curtain and then, by juggling (or so Rinn assumed) with her big toe, to make it appear to be 'floating in the air'. And for some of Eusapia's tricks Rinn still had no explanation half a century later, when he came to write his memoirs; such as the draught apparently emanating from her forehead which lowered the temperature on a thermometer by four degrees F. Muensterberg suggested that Eusapia had a kind of balloon under her armpit connected with a rubber tube extending through her hair to the forehead. Failing this, they could only assume she must be blowing upwards, deflecting her breath with her fingers. 'It seems incredible,' Rinn mused, 'that for twenty-five years she has been able to fool scientists with such a simple trick.'

It was indeed incredible. How careful European scientists had been not to allow themselves to be duped in such ways is obvious from the reports of inquiry after inquiry. By allowing Eusapia to cheat, and then claiming that this showed how she had obtained all her effects in the past, Muensterberg and Jastrow had simply displayed their ignorance. Even a casual study of the records would have shown them that what Eusapia had done, and been seen to do, and been recorded by instruments while doing, could not have been done by freeing a leg or an arm. Eusapia had done nothing, Carrington protested, which she had not been detected doing many times in earlier tests. He had warned the investigators what would happen, yet they had allowed it to happen; 'it would be difficult to imagine a more inconclusive and superficial examination'. But there was no point in her staying in America if the investigations were to be on this level; and she returned to Italy. Either because her confidence had been eroded, or advancing age, or both, her powers began to desert her. When that autumn Feilding returned to Naples to do further tests with her, 'everything was different'; the cheating was there, but few of the phenomena.

Yet even in this short series of tests, unsatisfactory though they were, Eusapia managed to impress the Russian psychical researcher, Count Perovsky-Petrovo-Solovovo. He was an experienced investigator, having carried out protracted tests with a materialising medium, Sambor, in Russia; and though he had been greatly impressed at the time, he had become a prey to doubts later, and written so dismissively about the physical phenomena that Lodge had felt compelled to reply with a gentle warning in the *Proceedings* against too facile an acceptance of the *a priori* case against them. Petrovo-Solovovo agreed with Feilding that the seances had been unsatisfactory. But when, as Feilding had done in the earlier series, he went back over his notes, he could not help admitting that in one of the seances, in reasonable light, touches had been felt; a table in the 'cabinet' had overturned; and an object had moved for some distance along the floor, in spite of the fact that there was 'very satisfactory' control of Eusapia's hands and feet.

At least we repeatedly said so at the time, and I wrote so in my notes the day after. I think in such incidents, it could be the impression felt at the time of the occurrences (I am speaking of experienced enquirers only) which must really count – not the one produced by subsequent unfavourable circumstances.

But Petrovo-Solovovo's reservations made less impression than the fact that Feilding appeared to have been disillusioned. Coupled with the reports from America, it helped to confirm the impression that Eusapia had been finally discredited; and although she was to live on until 1920, she was not again to be taken seriously, let alone investigated, by scientists.

The Unknown Guest

The exposure (as it came to be regarded) of Eusapia marks the end of the phase of psychical research which had begun with Crookes's experiments with Home. Not merely had she been discredited; the discredit operated retrospectively, wiping out the results of all previous research carried out with her as the medium. It was useless to argue, as Richet did after her death, that 'there have perhaps never been so many different, sceptical and scrupulous investigators into the work of any medium, or more minute investigations'. The argument in fact rebounded because if so many different, sceptical and scrupulous investigators had all let themselves be fooled, as was now assumed, then the investigators of Home, the Fox sisters, and all the other physical mediums had presumably been duped, too. And from this it was a further easy step to the assumption that *all* psychical research had been discredited. Physical mediumship had been closely bound up with clairvoyance and thought-transference; the whole gamut, so far as orthodox science was concerned, could surely henceforth be ignored.

So it came about that the research results which had been accumulating in the early years of the century were, in effect, wiped out. Yet they were impressive. Eusapia was far from being the only medium capable of producing the physical phenomena; several others had been tested, two of them in prolonged and careful experiments: Stanislawa Tomczyk, whose telekinetic abilities Ochorowicz described in careful detail in the *Annals of Psychical Science* in 1909; and 'Eva C.'. 'Eva C.' was Marthe Beraud; 'a very intelligent and lively young lady', Richet found her, when he went to Algiers to investigate her in 1905, attracted there by the news that she could not only produce materialisations almost as a matter of course, but also produce them in full view of the investigators. 'A kind of liquid paste or jelly,' as Richet was to describe it, 'emerges from the mouth or the breast of Marthe, which organises itself by degrees, acquiring the shape of a face or a limb'; and he coined for it the term 'ectoplasm'.

These materialisations are usually gradual, beginning by a rudimentary shape, complete forms and human faces only appearing later on. At first these formations are often very imperfect. Sometimes they show no relief, looking more like flat images than bodies, so that in spite of oneself, one is inclined to imagine some fraud, since what appears seems to be the materialisation of a semblance, and not of a being. But in some cases the materialisation is perfect. At the Villa Carmen I saw a fully organised form rise from the floor. At first it was only a white, opaque spot like a handkerchief lying on the ground before the curtain, then this handkerchief quickly assumed the form of a human head level with the floor and a few moments later it rose up in a straight line and became a small man enveloped in a kind of white burnous, who took two or three halting steps in front of the curtain and then sank to the floor and disappeared as if through a trap-door. But there was no trap-door.

The 'trap-door' allegation was put about by a former coachman employed by the villa owners, who had been sacked for theft, and who claimed he had played the part of 'Bien Boa' in the white burnous – an allegation which inspection of the seance room floor promptly refuted, but did not dispose of. It was also to be claimed that Marthe had confessed that she had cheated. But it was hard to see how she could have cheated in the series of experiments she went on to do with Mme. Juliette Bisson and Schrenck-Notzing, who introduced the most stringent precautions ever taken against fraud.

As Marthe's psychic powers were largely limited to materialisation, and as her investigators were chiefly concerned to study ectoplasm, their precautions were mainly designed to ensure that she could bring nothing with her into the seances. For Mme. Bisson, Marthe could simply work with no clothes on: when Schrenck-Notzing was invigilating, or when other scientists, Richet among them, were invited as witnesses, she would be undressed beforehand by Mme. Bisson and put into a close-fitting garment resembling a strait-jacket. It was, however, suggested that even these precautions were insufficient, as she might be 'ruminating' and 'regurgitating' – swallowing muslin, say, and vomiting it up. Schrenck-Notzing protested that the muslin could hardly, after such treatment, form itself into the kind of faces and forms which they saw and photographed. Still, for the sake of the record they took further precautions, which Richet described.

Her hair, armpits, nose, mouth and knees were examined; in some cases even examination *per rectum et vaginam* was resorted to. As the materialised substance frequently comes from her mouth, syrup of bilberries was administered, whose deep colouring powers are well known, but notwithstanding this, the extruded forms were absolutely white. Experimental rigour was even pushed to the point of giving her an emetic before a seance.

Yet not once, in over four years of experiments, was Marthe detected in any attempt at trickery. If there were trickery, then, it could only have been through the complicity of the investigators; and, as Mme. Bisson asked, what would have been the point? Her *Phénomènes Dits de Matérialisation,* when it appeared just before the first world war, was a sober record of protracted and often tedious research, conducted in private. There was no money in it for the investigators and little enough for the medium; certainly far less than she could have earned displaying her powers on the halls. And there was no kudos; such research attracted only mockery, if it were noticed at all. At the end of it, Mme. Bisson claimed no more than that all doubt had been removed from her mind : 'the medium, in the trance state, externalises a certain substance, which can present diverse forms'. Schrenck-Notzing elaborated a little: 'by an unknown biological process, there comes from the body of the medium, a material, at first semi-fluid, which possesses some of the properties of a living substance, notably that of the power of change or movement, and of the assumption of definite forms'.

Apart from these investigations into the physical phenomena, other branches of psychical research had continued to provide positive results. The work of the Society for Psychical Research in Britain and in the United States had, admittedly, been unproductive compared with previous years, largely because so much of the activity had been concentrated upon the cross-correspondences. Yet even if it were accepted that they did not provide conclusive evidence for the continued posthumous intervention by founder members of the Society, this, it could be argued, actually strengthened the evidence for telepathy, because nothing else could account for the extraordinary interlinking of subject matter in the scripts of automatic writers as far apart as Boston, Calcutta and London – in much the same way as the rejection of 'Phinuit' and the other spirit guides as bogus strengthened, rather than weakened, the presumption that Mrs. Piper must have telepathic powers. The evidence for telepathy was strong enough to convince the man who was to become the most influential psychologist in the humanist tradition of Myers and James: William McDougall, doctor and anthropologist, later Professor of Psychology at Harvard. It was of such a nature, he wrote in his *Body and Mind* in 1911, 'as to compel the assent of any competent person who studies it impartially'. Bergson agreed. In his presidential address to the S.P.R. in 1913 he said that after weighing it, he had felt compelled to accept telepathy not just on scientific but on historical grounds, for the same reason that he felt compelled to accept the reality of the defeat of the Spanish Armada; 'my belief is not the physical certainty that I have of the law of the fall of bodies; but it is at least all the certainty that we obtain in a historical or judicial matter'.

The only type of psychical research whose results showed a marked falling-off, in the early years of the twentieth century, were experiments with hypnotically induced thought-transference, community of sensation and externalisation of sensibility. Partly this could be accounted for by the fact that there were far fewer experimenters, owing to the spread of the belief that Braid, Charcot and Bernheim between them had purged hypnotism of animal magnetism, dispelling the myth of the higher phenomena. Although a few individuals like Boirac continued to demonstrate that they could hypnotise subjects from a distance, and will them to take certain actions, the fact that such claims were more rarely encountered made it easy for critics to claim that the requirement of stricter controls had made it less easy to fake the results. And where the results of experiments in other branches of research could not easily be dismissed, because of the prestige of the investigator – as in the case of the trials of dowsers carried out by Armand Viré, Professor of Geology at the Paris museum, and read by d'Arsonval to the Academy in 1913 – they could simply be ignored.

'Baffling'

There was no shortage, in the early years of the century, of reported spontaneous psychical phenomena; the most celebrated case being the Versailles adventure, as it came to be known, of Charlotte Moberly, Principal of St. Hugh's College, Oxford, and her colleague Eleanor Jourdain, who while visiting the Petit Trianon 'saw' scenes which they later came to believe were a kind of psychic play-back of an episode from 1789 – thereby starting up a controversy which has grumbled on ever since. But it was clear that such reports, even when linked to the continuing research, were making no impression. In 1909, the year before he died, William James recalled how Sidgwick, a year before *his* death, had recognised what little progress had been made towards the original objective of the S.P.R.: the elucidation of the mysteries which they had come together to investigate. Sidgwick had said that if anybody at the outset had forecast that after twenty years he would be in the same state of doubt he had started with, he would have deemed the prophecy incredible. James admitted that his own experience had been similar; after twenty-five years, 'I am theoretically no "further" than I was at the beginning; and I confess that at times I have been tempted to believe that the creator has eternally intended this department of nature to remain *baffling*, to prompt our curiosities and hopes and suspicions all in equal measure'. Another illuminating comment on this issue came from Maurice Maeterlinck, playwright and philosopher, who was awarded the Nobel Prize for literature in 1911. In *The Unknown Guest*, published in 1914, he speculated about

the strange, inconsistent, whimsical and disconcerting character of the unknown entity within us that seems to live on nothing but nondescript fare borrowed from worlds to which our intelligence as yet has no access. It lives under our reason, in a sort of invisible and perhaps external palace, like a casual guest dropped from another planet, whose interests, ideas, habits, passions have naught in common with ours. If it seems to have notions on the hereafter that are infinitely wider and more precise than those which we possess, it has only very vague notions on the practical needs of our existence. It ignores us for years, absorbed no doubt with the numberless relations which it maintains with all the mysteries of the universe; and when suddenly it remembers us, thinking apparently to please us, it makes an enormous, miraculous, but at the same time, clumsy and superfluous movement which upsets all that we believed we knew, without teaching us anything. Is it making fun of us, is it jesting, is it amusing itself, is it facetious, teasing, arch, or simply sleepy, bewildered, inconsistent, absent-minded? It readily performs the most glamorous feats of sleight-of-hand, provided that we can derive no profit from them. It lifts up tables, moves the heaviest articles, produces flowers and hair, sets strings vibrating, gives life to inanimate objects and passes through solid matter, conjures up ghosts, subjugates time and space, creates light; but all, it seems, on one condition, that its performances should be without rhyme or reason, and keep to the province of supernaturally vain and puerile recreations.

In retrospect, Maeterlinck's words can be read as a valediction. By the outbreak of the first world war the psychical researchers had exhausted the possibilities open to them. They had not failed to produce theories; but the theories had not been of a kind which would command attention, let alone acceptance. And the 'nondescript facts' discovered in the course of the 'puerile recreations' could be dismissed with derision by the sceptics, by this time in possession of most of the commanding heights of Academe.

The researchers had tried hard to remedy this deficiency; chiefly with the help of analogies. The simplest was with magnetism. Magnetism, too, influenced objects without contact; and although the force was constant, its action might appear erratic. Mediums, Boirac suggested, could accumulate and release the psychic force, though it passed through ordinary people unnoticed; 'it follows as a general rule that the effects of the force will appear to be rare and exceptional, though its action may be constant and regular.'

At this point, though, the theorists had run into a problem: how to account for the fact that the impersonal, constant force whose existence they were postulating behaved in such a personal fashion. Leaving preconceptions aside, the Spiritualists had a plausible case. There was an abundance of evidence pointing to communication by the dead with the living; the cross-correspondences were beginning to convert even some of the S.P.R.'s chronic doubters. The way in which psychokinesis operated in the seance room or in poltergeist outbreaks, too, was easier to account for in terms of spirit activity than in terms of any impersonal force, even if it were activated by the medium. Spirit photography and materialisations were similarly difficult to explain except in spirit terms. Lombroso – who, having moved across the board from scepticism to Spiritualism, was impatient with laggards – cited examples of the absurdity of clinging to 'natural' explanations in his *After Death, What?* shortly before his own death in 1909. Morselli, he recalled, 'in the rashness of his anti-spiritism', had claimed that Eusapia must have obtained her information about sitters' relations not from the spirits but by thought-reading; but to Morselli's horror, Eusapia had actually materialised his own mother, who playfully bit him instead of kissing him, and mocked his baldness. She also conjured up Professor E. Bozzano's dead wife, whom Bozzano had loathed, and who further established her identity by speaking in her own Genoese dialect, of which Eusapia was ignorant.

The spiritist case, though, was in some respects unconvincing. Many of the phenomena could as easily, or more easily, be explained by the hypothesis that the subliminal mind of the medium or the sitters was at work. When it was suggested that a dowser should be regarded as a medium, rather than as a clairvoyant, a view held by Wallace, he was mocked by Lodge: 'Does he suppose a deceased person comes and bobs the stick?' In any case, spiritism suffered from the fatal disadvantage that it raised too many hackles. It might be possible to persuade orthodox scientists to listen to the case for the existence of an undiscovered psychic force; there was no chance whatsoever of persuading them to listen if they thought they were being asked to believe that it was operated by spirits.

In theory, the way out of this dilemma would have been to concentrate exclusively on the phenomena. Many misunderstandings could have been averted, Carrington argued, 'if the question were rightly considered as a question of *facts* and not a question of the *interpretation* of facts'. But in practice, the formidable accumulation of facts had failed to make any impact on orthodoxy, for a reason which Robert Chambers had grasped: 'a novelty, however true, if there be no received truths with which it can be shown in harmonious relation, has little chance of a favourable hearing' – a sentiment echoed by Charles Massey in the introduction to his translation of du Prel's *Philosophy of Mysticism*: 'when we see *how* a thing can have happened, we are much more likely to give a fair hearing to evidence that it *has* happened; and thus an explanatory hypothesis is hardly less necessary for the reception of facts of a certain character, than are facts of the support of a hypothesis'.

The psychical researchers, therefore, felt they had to put forward theories of a kind which, if they could persuade a materialist to examine them, would compel him to try to rebut them, rather than simply to look round for the waste-paper-basket. To explain Eusapia's powers, for example, Morselli suggested that a medium must have 'the faculty of externalising a force capable of plastically moulding in space the figures produced in her imagination', in such a manner as 'to give birth to teleplastic phantoms, or materialisations, whose substance is provided by the medium, and whose appearance is shaped by the spectators' – this last point permitting Morselli to escape from spiritism; the ectoplasm, he was suggesting, might be provided by the medium, but it was moulded into its materialised form by the imagination of the sitters. This force could also, Richet suggested, impregnate objects. Just as a magnet seems inert until its energy is disclosed by the proximity of a piece of iron, 'the ring long worn by an individual might accumulate properties characteristic of the wearer which it had not when it left the jeweller's hands'. This could also account for those hauntings which were linked with specific places. Citing the analogy of objects left on a photographic plate (or even on a plain sheet of glass) leaving a trace which might not be revealed until long after, Barrett surmised that 'some kind of *local imprint*, on material structures of places, has been left by past events occurring to certain persons who, when on earth, lived or were closely connected with that particular locality; an echo or phantom of these events becoming perceptible to those now living who happened to be endowed with some special psychic sensitiveness'.

But how to account for perception at a distance? 'We think with our brains, as we see with our eyes, as we hear with our ears, but it is not our brain which thinks any more than it is our eyes which see,' Flammarion proclaimed. 'What would you say of a person who congratulated a telescope on seeing the canals of Mars so well? The eye is an organ, and so is the brain.' On this theory it was possible to account for the higher phenomena of mesmerism, eyeless vision and thought-transference. To onlookers, perception might appear to be 'through some bizarre corporeal channel, as the knee or the stomach', Myers pointed out; but the hypnotised subject would simply be perceiving in a 'wholly supernormal fashion'. And though this would obviously be hard to swallow, a few physicists were beginning to feel that Tyndall-style materialism was a strait-jacket. In his presidential address to the S.P.R. in 1897 Crookes recalled the proposition of the astronomer Roger Boscovitch in the eighteenth century that atoms 'are mere centres of forces or powers, not particles of matter', extending 'so to say, throughout the whole of the solar system, yet always retaining their own centre of force'; an idea which had attracted Faraday. Perhaps, Crookes suggested, there were 'centres of intellect, will, energy and power, each mutually penetrable, whilst at the same time permeating what we call space, but each centre retaining its own individuality, persistence of self, and memory'; though whether these centres were associated with atoms remained unknown. If this hypothesis were accepted, there need no longer be any materialist limit to the reach of human perception. Flammarion carried the idea further. As early as 1865 he had rejected the materialism of his time, insisting that matter and energy would be found to be interchangeable, and in his *Mysterious Psychic Forces* in 1907 he argued that the 'magic substance' was really immaterial, and

unknowable in its essence. We see and touch only its condensations, its aggregations, its arrangements; that is to say, forms produced by movement. Matter, force, life, thought, are all one. In reality, there is only one principle in the universe and it is at once intelligence, force and matter, embracing all that is and all that possibly can be. That which we call matter is only a form of motion. At the basis of all is force, dynamism, and universal mind, or spirit.

It was also desirable, the pyschical researchers had realised, to find some biological and anthropological hypothesis to account for the strange ways in which the phenomena manifested themselves to human beings. Research with hypnosis had given a clue. 'If a vague suggestion, say of *danger*, is conveyed to several hypnotised patients, to be developed after their awakening,' Myers had reported in 1891, 'each will realise the hallucinatory danger in a different way: voice of enemies – smell of fire – sight of a wild beast advancing', and later, in his *Human Personality*, he fused this in with an idea thrown out by Prince Peter Kropotkin in the *Nineteenth Century* magazine: that the five senses had been preceded in evolutionary terms by a less specialised sense, or senses, working through less specialised organs of perception.

Might it be, Myers suggested, that psychic information came to man through the sixth, unspecialised (and as yet unrecognised) sense; but to reach consciousness, it worked through one of the specialist senses – through man's hands, say, in dowsing; through his sight, in scrying; through his hearing, in clairaudience; and so on. When these 'motor-automatisms' were surveyed together, 'their essential analogy will be recognised beneath much diversity of form. They will be seen to be messages from the subliminal self; endeavours, conscious or unconscious, of submerged traits of our personality to present, to ordinary waking thought, fragments of knowledge which no ordinary waking thought could attain.' And to the question why, if man had once enjoyed the benefits of a sixth sense, he should have lost them on his evolutionary journey, Flournoy had an answer. The unspecialised sense, he maintained, had not developed to the point where it was a reliable guide; and in the short term, man's evolutionary needs might have produced more specialised and, for his immediate purposes, more efficient devices.

For example; our four members of flesh and blood, sweeping the space around us, could be but a more economic expedient invented by nature, a machine wrought in the course of a better-adapted evolution, to obtain at the least expense the same useful effects as this vague, primordial, spherical power. Thus supplanted or transformed, these powers would thereafter manifest themselves only very exceptionally in certain states, or with abnormal individuals, as an atavistic reappearance of a mode of acting long fallen into disuse because it is really very imperfect, and it necessitates, without any advantage, an expenditure of vital energy far greater than the ordinary use of arms and limbs.

Here, then, was a reply to Tylor's question why the Red Indian medicine man and the Tatar necromancer should have had access to powers which civilised man had lost. And taken as a whole the available evidence, Lombroso could claim, was not inconsistent; it resembled a continent submerged by the ocean so that the only traces of it were islands, isolated and apparently without connection, but to the expert eye 'seen to coalesce in one immense and compact body of land, though the shallow mob laughs at the seemingly audacious hypothesis of the geographer'.

The psychic hypothesis, however, was too audacious – or, rather, too embarrassing – to be acceptable. The scientific Establishment's readiness to accept Einstein's theories showed that it was capable of absorbing startling propositions if they added a new dimension to science; but not if they undermined it. If even telepathy alone were admitted, the German philosopher Friedrick Jodl warned in his textbook of psychology in 1903, it would 'indicate the presence of a crack in the very foundations of all our views on nature'. It would not just be a matter of revising the scientific textbooks. Many of them would simply have to be thrown away because, as Ochorowicz had realised, they had simply not taken psychic phenomena into account; 'a multitude of facts hitherto inadmissible may – nay, must – henceforward be examined seriously' – among them clairvoyant diagnosis, mass hysteria, hallucinations, community of sensation, dream telepathy, divination 'and sundry facts recorded in the history of civilisation and credited to demons, oracles, sorcerers, obsessed persons etc.' It would not be a case of clearing out the old lumber room to get rid of myth and superstition, as Darwin had acceptably done; it would entail bringing much of the junk back, and re-furnishing the scientific household with it. Psychical phenomena, Hyslop observed, were associated with theories which science supposed had been banished. Science had become accustomed to clearing up residual facts in its own domain, 'but it is loath to admit the existence of facts that limit that domain, or demand the acceptance of a larger than the ordinary world'; and it had made so many conquests by ignoring the existence of spirit that it would go to great lengths to keep them out.

Nor was it only scientists who would be threatened. For churchmen, too, admission of the reality of psychical phenomena would have uncomfortable implications, as William James made clear in the conclusion to his Giffard Lectures, later published as *The Varieties of Religious Experience*. It must have seemed to his audiences, he realised, that he was chiefly bent 'on rehabilitating the element of feeling in religion and subordinating its intellectual part'; and it had indeed been his intention to stress the importance of trance inspiration. In his own day, it was neglected or dismissed as psychopathic. Yet

you will in point of fact hardly find a religious leader of any kind in whose life there is no record of automatisms. I speak not merely of savage priests and prophets, whose followers regard automatic utterance and action as by itself tantamount to inspiration; I speak of leaders of thought and subjects of intellectualised experience. St. Paul had his visions, his ecstasies, his gift of tongues, small as was the importance he attached to the latter. The whole array of Christian saints and heresiarchs, including the greatest, the Bernards, the Loyolas, the Luthers, the Foxes, the Wesleys, had their visions, voices, rapt conditions, guiding impressions, and 'openings'. They had these things because they had exalted sensibility and to such things, persons of exalted sensibility are liable.

Not only would man's past have to be re-examined; acceptance of the reality of psychical phenomena must also be expected to exercise a profound effect on man's future. Telepathy, the Scottish theologian Henry Drummond claimed in his 1894 Lowell lectures on 'the Ascent of Man' was 'theoretically the next stage in the evolution of language'; it was there to be used, as soon as man qualified himself to make use of it – just as the means to communicate by telegraph, electricity, had always been there to be used, if he had known how. 'May it not be that that which delays the power to transport and drive one's thought as thought, to whatever spot one wills, is not the fact that the possibility is withheld by nature, but that the hour is not quite come – that the instrument is not yet fully ripe?' And Drummond later expanded this idea into his theory of the evolution of evolution – nature 'gravitating from the pursuit of survival towards the pursuit of quality', a notion which attracted Barrett. Telepathy, he felt,

furnishes the prospect of a far more perfect interchange of thought than by the clumsy mechanism of speech. It affords a rational basis for prayer and inspiration, and gives us a distant glimpse of the possibility of communion without language, not only between men of various races and tongues, but between every sentient creature, which if not attainable here may await us all in that future state when we shall 'know even as we are known'.

The reason that telepathy and telekinesis were unacceptable, then, was not just that scientists could not fit them into the prevailing set of assumptions: it was that they did not *want* to fit them in. Nor did the great majority of churchmen, or rationalists, or the Establishment in general, the members of which, whatever their professed faiths might be, tended to be materialist at the same instinctive level as that at which other superstitions had formerly thrived. That their antipathy was not rational was clear from the arguments they ordinarily resorted to, which were beginning to look increasingly threadbare. To decline to study the phenomena on the ground that they were so anomalous, for example, was unscientific; as Myers pointed out, it was precisely through the study of anomalies that scientists had made advances, because 'the more bizarre and trivial the phenomena, the greater the chance of their directing us to some law which has been overlooked'. To argue that the results of psychical research were unworthy of scientific study because 'there is no scientific fact' – as E. Duclaux, Director of the Pasteur Institute, claimed in 1901 – 'except a fact which can be reproduced at will' was also absurd. As Richet pointed out, it would place a wholly unjustified limitation on science's boundaries. If positive results had been obtained in any other kind of experimental work which continually, even if not consistently, ran at odds of over a thousand to one (and sometimes much higher) compared to chance expectation, they would be accepted without question: why not with telepathy? Besides, scientists no longer denied the existence of meteorites, though nobody claimed to be able to foresee where they would fall.

Nor could scientists reasonably try to excuse themselves, as Huxley had done, by claiming they were not interested in the subject. If the facts were as stated, the scientist would have to be interested, whatever his speciality. The sceptical Babinet, mocking the table-turners in the early 1850s, had in fact disposed of that argument in advance when he admitted that if anyone could release an object from the force of gravity without mechanical means, he would have bettered Newton's performance; and the equally sceptical Professor Pouchet had made the same point in 1893 in connection with telepathy. To show that one brain could influence another at a distance would imply that there was 'an influence, a nervous vibration diffusing itself without a material conductor', a proposition which Pouchet declined to believe possible. But he, too, had added: 'Find it for us, good people, show it us, and your name shall be greater in immortality than that of Newton'. Sceptics, therefore, had to fall back on the argument that the phenomena witnessed were the product of deception or hallucination; and neither proposition was easy to sustain.

Hallucination

The idea that witnesses at a seance might be collectively hallucinated had been periodically revived after Carpenter had expounded it in his articles; notably in 1890 by the author Hamilton Aidé, to account for what he felt were the otherwise unaccountable phenomena he had encountered at a seance with Home in Nice some years before. Aidé had been prejudiced against Home before they met, and had taken an immediate dislike to him when they were introduced. But when he heard that his friend Alphonse Karr, who was the editor of *Figaro*, 'one of the most hard-headed, the wittiest, and the most sceptical men in France', was going to a seance, he felt that between them they might have some fun exposing the tricks. It had come as a surprise to them to find the room was well lit – twenty candles round the wall, and a lamp on the table. The furniture was sparse; there were no cloths covering or hiding anything; and careful examination revealed no trace of wires or gadgets. But a heavy armchair had suddenly run violently from one side of the room towards them; and when a table began to oscillate Aidé and Karr, who could see clearly under as well as over it, had both noted that when it rose on one of its claws, the lamp and pencils which were on it, though they slid around over the surface, did not fall off. Eventually the table rose off the floor to a height of over three feet, enabling Karr to get under it and grovel around, looking for some explanation, without success. It remained suspended in the air for two or three minutes, with everybody's hands visible on top of it. Nine people were present, Aidé recalled; all gentlemen and ladies of untarnished repute. Yet this, he felt, was beside the point. Suppose all of them (including himself) had been scoundrels; could their eyes have deceived them? Of one thing he was certain, it was no conjuring trick. Had they witnessed a phenomenal exhibition of a force which reversed the laws of nature? 'Or were we deluded? Hypnotised, as it is now called, into believing we saw what we did not actually see?'

The hypothesis had the advantage that it could be related to the discovery that, as Myers put it, 'a hypnotised subject is easily hallucinated; if he is told to see a non-existent dog he sees a dog'. Admittedly there was still a difficulty; there was no evidence that mediums used, or even could use, hypnotism; but the possibility remained that they might have a hypnotic faculty which enabled them to dispense with the ordinary preliminaries of passes or suggestions; perhaps, as Carpenter had suggested and, as Gustave le Bon claimed in *The Crowd* in 1903, people at seances became victims of collective hallucinations. But there were serious objections to the idea. Why should collective hallucinations of this kind be reported only from seances? If they were so common, they would surely be more often observed at other gatherings. And if mediums had some hypnotic power, they would be unlikely to waste it on seances; they would be much more likely to exploit it commercially, as they would presumably be able to do. In any case, the monitoring of the Sorbonne tests on Eusapia, in a room separate from the seance, virtually eliminated the possibility that her investigators had all been hallucinated; and in his survey of the evidence for the S.P.R.'s *Proceedings* in 1909 Petrovo-Solovovo, though conceding hallucination might occur, held that it could not explain all the unaccountable phenomena so far reported.

Fraud

The criticism most frequently used to discredit the results of psychical research, though, was still that they were too contaminated by fraud to be relied upon. But on the evidence from the reports of the investigations it was a charge which could not seriously be sustained. There were fraudulent mediums, as there would always be fraudulent mediums; but they did not as a rule submit themselves for testing, and if they did, they were soon detected by members of the Society for Psychical Research, some of whom were notoriously more interested in exposing fraud than in obtaining positive results. And those researchers who were looking for positive results took the most elaborate precautions against fraud, for the obvious reason that they would be made to look extremely foolish if they allowed themselves to be duped. Fear of being tricked, Richet was to recall, was 'my chief, and even only anxiety throughout my experiments'. The reports of the experiments with Eusapia, particularly, showed just how much time and trouble were expended in making them fraud-proof. If the results reported were obtained by deception, it could only have been with the collusion of her investigators; and the notion that a hundred or more of the best-known scientists and savants in Europe were prepared to co-operate in such an international swindle was ludicrous.

The charge of false pretences could, however, reasonably be sustained against some of the committed sceptics, such as Muensterberg and Jastrow. Their reports of their investigations of Eusapia revealed the extent they were prepared to go to fudge the evidence in support of their materialist faith. Jastrow's 'The Case of Paladino' in the *American Review of Reviews* in 1910 was a representative sample. In his earlier *Collier's* article he had reported his 'exposure' of Eusapia; in the *Review* he purported to describe her previous career of deception in Europe. To anybody who had no knowledge of the subject it must have seemed a devastating revelation of past infamy. But Jastrow had simply borrowed Carpenter's technique. He devoted most of the article to what Eusapia's critics had written, without admitting that only one of them, Hodgson, had even pretended to investigate her. Moll and Dessoir, whose opinions he cited, had attended only a few seances; other critics had not even seen her perform. The dozen or so reports by teams of scientists and psychologists Jastrow simply ignored, dismissing them in a footnote about the 'extravagant accounts' of Lombroso, Flammarion and others. The results of his own experiments, Jastrow blandly explained, had made it unnecessary to pay any further attention to them – a ruse which allowed him to denounce Eusapia, of all people, for not having submitted herself to tests; 'it cannot be too strongly emphasised that if those who profess to influence physical objects were willing to submit to the experimental rules of the laboratory, the investigation would be a matter of minutes and not of years'.

Jastrow went on to present what was to become the stock explanation for the easy way in which Eusapia and others had been able to pull the ectoplasm over the psychical researchers' eyes. The distorting influence on their perceptions, he claimed,

lies in the psychology of belief. Were there not some strong pull urging one on to the acceptance of the effects as transcending known experience, we should not be so ready to overlook or scantily attend to the requirements of the premises. It is the attraction of conclusions, often subconscious and subtle, as well as slight and seemingly feeble, that throws reasoning out of its orbit . . . they sustain life and make life worth living.

Nothing could have been further from the truth. The great majority of the psychical researchers had been sceptics, or at least sceptical, when they began their research. Most of them, so far from wanting to believe, had been deeply disturbed by what they found; and most of them remained a prey to doubt, continually groping for natural explanations. It would have been nearer to the mark to say that it was the reasoning of the sceptics which was thrown out of its orbit, by their need to *dis*believe. As Hyslop – himself, ironically, frequently blinkered by his own preconceptions – put it, the materialist

will have nothing but his 'natural' even if he has to change the meaning of his terms to preserve an apparent consistency. That is to say, he is ready to usurp cover of the new by extending the meaning of 'nature' and 'matter', already strained beyond endurance, while he clings to the implications of their traditional import long after they have lost their validity. There is no elasticity of mind too great for his audacity, and he gloats like a conqueror over his imaginary triumphs, which are concessions of territory in all but name.

Nor was it only scientists who regarded this kind of treatment of the evidence as defensible. Anatole France's biography of Joan of Arc was designed to strip her story of its supernatural element; to present her as a peasant girl, honest but credulous and a little deranged, who had been exploited by unscrupulous courtiers and priests. Andrew Lang, by this time in his late sixties, was stung to action. He went to Paris to comb through the archives which Anatole France had used; and in his own biography of Joan, published in 1910, Lang was able to show how France had systematically rigged the evidence to fit his thesis. As the Sorbonne historian Louis Cazamian noted when he came to review the controversy on the five hundredth anniversary of Joan's death, a substantial proportion of France's impressive-looking collection of source references purporting to justify his statements was shown by Lang to be irrelevant: 'if authority can be found at all for a statement, it is not the passage quoted; this very often does not bear any relation to the theme'. Sometimes the source, when it was looked up, would actually be found to sustain conclusions opposed to France's. Yet when France came to revise the book, though he corrected a few of the errors Lang had found, he lightly dismissed Lang's 'praiseworthy scruples' as if they were pedantry.

'We recognise that mood,' Cazamian charitably remarked. 'It may seem dry, but at bottom an imaginative ardour suffuses it; in its essence

P

it is a passion, and it is a faith.' Like the Inquisitors of old, sceptics were not looking for truth; they thought they were already in possession of it, and anything which did not suit their preconceptions was ignored. In 1912 Muensterberg, hearing of the exploits of the medium and healer Edgar Cayce, went to Kentucky to see him, telling him, 'I have come here to expose you'. When he was unable to catch Cayce out, the baffled Muensterberg said that he would need to investigate further before passing judgment; but he never returned to undertake the investigation.

It is not possible even to guess how often this happened; or how often individuals who admitted to having had some psychic experience refused to make it public, for fear of the consequences. Myers lamented that valuable evidence had been lost to the S.P.R. in this way, citing the case of a Fellow of the Royal College of Physicians with a striking instance of clairvoyance which he would not allow to be used. Scientific progress would be impossible, he agreed, if everybody behaved as he did; but he did not dare face the risk of the professional injury he would suffer if he were believed to defend 'opinions at variance with general scientific belief'.

If Anatole France, Muensterberg and Jastrow could use such tactics, it was Hodgson, Podmore and other members of the S.P.R. who taught them how. In the early years of the century Podmore poured out books dealing with psychical research, past and present, in which he displayed an obsessive determination to cast suspicion on the evidence in favour of psychical phenomena. Had he regarded the case for telepathy or precognition as unproven, this would have been understandable; but the fact that he had come to accept them did not prevent him from leaving the impression that earlier research had been largely in the hands of dupes and knaves. Podmore also excelled at producing weird 'natural' explanations. In his *Naturalisation of the Supernatural* – published in 1908: he committed suicide two years later – he even took seriously a suggestion that the stones dropped in a poltergeist outbreak were the seeds of fruit being dropped by bats. As for levitations, he simply declined to credit them; they must, he assumed, be the result of fraud or hallucination – as Mrs. Sidgwick (though she claimed to keep an open mind) and Hyslop would have agreed. So far from providing a counterweight to the sceptics, the Society in this period might almost have been described as their ally.

By contrast, the record of those psychical researchers who were chiefly concerned with investigation for its own sake, rather than to expose fraud, was strikingly free from any suggestion of dishonesty. Nor should this have been surprising; had they not been men of integrity they would not have continued to undertake psychical research.

The prejudice against it in academic institutions remained strong: the attitude in some of them, Maxwell found, was

similar to that of the ecclesiastical authorities in the Middle Ages. The novelty of a thing frightens them. They treat independent scientific thought as the inquisitors treated free thought in days gone by. Like their prototypes of other times, they have the same intolerance, the same hate for schism and heresy. Their accumulated errors ought to make them cautious; but no! If they no longer make a pariah of the arch-heretic or schismatic, if they no longer deliver him up to the executioner, they treat him with the same relative vigour. They ex-communicate him, in their fashion, and cast him out of sane healthy humanity as a degenerate, a mystic.

In academic terms, therefore, the psychical researchers had nothing to gain; and in material terms, as Flammarion observed, it was 'labour without reward'. And by a melancholy irony, the more immaculately their experiments were designed, the more suspect the researchers became if the results were positive; for if fraud on the part of the medium could be ruled out because of the precautions taken, the only explanation, to anybody who felt that the phenomena were spurious, was collusion between the researcher and the medium. And where the medium was young and attractive, like Florence Cook, the motive seemed obvious. But even supposing that Crookes had been the most susceptible of men, what point would there have been in faking the results of his tests with Florence? He would have left himself open to exposure, or to blackmail; and all to no purpose because positive results brought no kudos. If he had faked tests with a medium to give *negative* results, that indeed would have advanced his career; he would have been hailed as the great exposer of deception. Nor can it seriously be suggested that because if he could demonstrate telekinesis, say, he would win the enduring fame that Babinet had foretold, Crookes had a motive to fake his results. He must have known, none better, that orthodoxy would never accept results which could not be duplicated. As for the notion that he, like the other psychical researchers, was a little cracked – that 'great wits are sure to madness near allied' – how, in that case, could he have carried on his orthodox researches with such resounding success, and become President of the Royal Society in 1913? And how could Richet have won the Nobel Prize, as he did that year, for his work on allergic reactions?

But by 1914, orthodoxy was in no mood to accept the possibility that such men as Crookes or Richet could have been scientific in their psychical research. Physicists might be moving away from Tyndall-style materialism, but they could not stomach the bizarre manifestations of the seance room. With rare exceptions such as McDougall, psychologists had become generally hostile; one of Jastrow's aims, 'the dissociation of the term psychology from the undesirable and irrelevant connotations of psychical research', had virtually been accomplished. Whatever anthropologists might think of Sir James Frazer (he was knighted in 1914) in other respects, they tended to share the views he had expressed the year before in *The Belief in Immortality* that mediumship was hystero-epilepsy, and spiritism a menace to society. For a scientist to interest himself in psychical research was consequently to incur a stigma, in some cases a lasting one. Future generations of students in Germany were to learn that Zöllner had had a brilliant career until he had allowed himself to be caught up in charlatanry, which had unhinged his mind; and the scientific reputations of Lombroso, Crookes, Lodge and Flammarion were similarly besmirched.

Aksakov had suffered his share of obloquy; but in the concluding passage of his reply to von Hartmann's *Philosophy of the Unconscious*, he offered an apologia.

> One last word. In the decline of life I ask myself sometimes, 'Have I in truth done well to have devoted so much time and toil and money to the study and the publication of facts in this domain? Have I not wasted my existence, with no result to justify all my pains?' Yet always I seem to hear the same reply: 'A life on earth can have no higher aspiration than to demonstrate the transcendental nature of man's being; to prove that he is called to a destiny loftier than the existence which he knows.' I cannot then regret that I have devoted my whole life to the pursuit of this aim; although it be by methods which science shuns or spurns – methods which I hold far trustier than any other which science has to show. And if it be in the end my lot to have laid one stone of that temple of the spirit, built up from century to century by men true of heart – this will be the highest, and the only, recompense which ever I strove to gain.

The first world war did not entirely disrupt psychical research; one of the most carefully organised and illuminating of all the investigations into the physical phenomena was to be carried out during it by a lecturer in engineering in Belfast, W. J. Crawford. But in Britain, and on the Continent, little could be done; and the massive upsurge of demand for mediums who could console the bereaved by bringing them in contact again with loved ones killed in the trenches tended to concentrate attention on this aspect of the phenomena – and all too often on the frauds, or alleged frauds, associated with it. By the time peace returned, all prospect of psychical research establishing itself as an academic discipline had vanished.

Yet paradoxically, it was to be in a university department that a new era was to begin. McDougall, who had succeeded Muensterberg as Professor of Psychology at Harvard, decided in 1927 to move to Duke University; he appointed, as one of his assistants, Dr. J. B. Rhine; and it was to be Rhine's research first into telepathy, and later into clairvoyance, precognition and psychokinesis, that was to lead to a revival of interest in parapsychology (as it was coming to be called), and to the resumption of the long and often bitter struggle to obtain scientific recognition and acceptance; the campaign which is still in progress today.

Acknowledgments

I HAVE HAD MUCH PATIENT ASSISTANCE FROM THE BRITISH LIBRARY and the New York Library; from A. W. Wesencraft, who has been looking after the Harry Price collection in the library of the University of London; from Paul Beard and the College of Psychic Studies; as always, from the London Library; and from many members of the Society for Psychical Research – the Secretary, Miss E. O'Keeffe; the former Librarian, Mrs Barry; and the acting Librarian, Leslie Price. Renée Haynes and Rosalind Heywood have often helped with advice; and like everybody who delves into the history of psychic phenomena, I owe much to Dr. E. J. Dingwall's pioneering research – rare though it has been to find myself in agreement with his interpretations of the historical evidence.

My thanks, too, to those who have read and commented on sections of the book – Paul Beard, Professor Norman Cohn, Dr. Rosemary Delbridge, Dr. Alan Gauld, Renée Haynes, Arthur Koestler, Elisabeth Morse, Leslie Price, Pat Williams, and Professor Peter Worsley; to Bill Grundy and Anita Gregory, who read it in its entirety and saved me from errors and obscurities; to Raye Farr, who looked after my research needs in the U.S.; and to Bernard Levin, who not merely took the proofs away with him on holiday, but actually – as his opprobrious marginal comments and corrections revealed – found the time to read them.

Charles Wintour's idea of 'Mind and Matter' notes in the *Evening Standard*, which he hatched with John Metcalf, has provided a constant stimulus to ferret out historical examples of paranormal phenomena: and I am grateful to many readers of the paper for putting me on the track of sources which otherwise I would have missed.

There are three people to whom I owe a special debt, for letting me air my opinions at them. Michael Sayers is chiefly interested in the Hermetic tradition, and what has stemmed from it; and if I have avoided this aspect in the book, it is partly in the knowledge that he is much better equipped to write about it than I will ever be. Tony

Bloomfield has been the generous host on many an agreeable occasion when the subject has been under discussion. And Arthur Koestler has helped in many ways; through his books, particularly in bringing physics and paraphysics within reach of the lay mind; and through the ideas thrown out in his perennially stimulating company.

Source references

THE NAMES AND WORDS IN BRACKETS REFER TO THE WORDS AND names to be looked up in the relevant page of the text. Where the author is named in the text, brackets are dispensed with. Where the source is listed in the Bibliography, only the date of the edition I have consulted is given here. References for biblical and other familiar classical sources have been omitted.

(p) stands for the familiar *passim*. I have used it both in cases where the material in the text refers to the book or article as a whole, or where the scattered sources can conveniently be found indexed.

Proc.s SPR and *SPR Jnl.* refer to the Society for Psychical Research's *Proceedings* and *Journal*.

INTRODUCTION

Page
7 Renan, 1964, 45.
9 Myers, 1903, i, xxii.
  Thomson, *The Forseeable Future*, 1955, 157–9.
10 Eysenck, 1957, 131–2.
  New Scientist, 15 September 1956.
12 Koestler, 1974, 78.
13 Flournoy, 1901, 381.
  De Morgan, 1882, Preface.
14 Wells, 1894, 121.
  Salverte, 1846, Introduction.
15 Richet, 1923, Introduction.

CHAPTER ONE: BELIEFS AND PRACTICES

20 Saintyves, 1914, 20–1.
  Codrington, 1891, 191–2.
21 de Vesme, 1931, 15.
  Callaway, 1869, 338.
  Lang, 1898, 92.

Codrington, 1891, 192.
Shooter, 1857, 167.
22 de Vesme, 1931, 15.
Evans-Pritchard, 1937, 167, 192.
23 Reynolds, 1963, 118.
Swettenham, 1896, 207.
Seligman, 1910, 654.
Melland, 1923, 222–30.
Hodgson, 1847, 170.
Skeat, 1900, 535–7.
24 (Bastian) Oesterreich, 1930, 237.
(Shaw) Wilson, 1856, 211.
25 (Lejeune) Lambert, 1955, 20–1.
Howitt, 1904, 388.
Tylor, 1871, i, 131.
Lang, 1899, 187.
de Vesme, 1931, 159.
Eliade, 1964 (p).

CHAPTER TWO: NATURAL OR SUPERNATURAL

26 (Pané) Pinkerton, 1808, vii, 144.
27 (Hernandez) Wilson, *Proc.s SPR* 1949, 353.
Cieza, 1864, 415–18.
(Lejeune) Lambert, 1955.
(Brebeuf), Lambert, 1955, 22–3.
28 (Regnard) Pinkerton, 1804, i, 181.
(Scheffer) Lang, 1898, 78.
(Henry) Lambert, 1955, 27.
29 Darwin, 1845, 458.
Melland, 1923, 286–7.
Lang, 1898, 47–8.
Brinton, 1896, 309.
30 (Boilat) de Vesme, 1931, 112–13; 211–12.
31 Trilles, 1914, 200–9.
Leslie, 1875, 45–56.
32 Leslie, 1875, 192–3.
de Vesme, 1931, 119.
(Schultz) de Vesme, 1931, 108–9.
33 Sinel, 1927, 84.
Van Der Post, 1958, 124, 238–40.
Gibier, 1889, 67–8.
34 Swettenham, 1896, 206.
Harbinger of Light, August 1914.
Rose, 1957, 50–1.

35 Rose, 1957, 206–7, 277.
    (clairvoyance) Man, 1932, 28; Eliade, 1964 (p).
    Endicott, 1970, 21.
36 McKenzie, 1935, 231.
    (Denny) Lambert, 1955, 38–9.
    (Bogoraz) Oesterreich, 1930, 137.
37 (Weston) de Vesme, 1931, 139.
    Callaway, 1869, 331.
    Melland, 1923, 229.
    (Brigham) Long, 1954, 69.
    Van Der Post, 1958, 190–5.
38 (Papetard) Imbert-Gourbeyre, 1873, ii, 246.
    (Le Roy) 1923, 228.
    Kellar, 1893, 80.
    (Furst) Andrews, 1974, 363.
39 ('insulating') Frazer, 1890, iii, 307–8.
    (Gudgeon/Hocken) *Proc.s SPR*, 1901, 4–10.
40 Howitt, 1863, i, 398.

CHAPTER THREE: FROM SHAMAN TO PRIEST

43 Benedict, 1952, 93–4.
44 Junod, 1927, ii, 538.
    (papyrus) Lang, 1898, 188.

CHAPTER FOUR: THE OLD TESTAMENT

46 Leach, 1969, 34.
49 Stobart, 1926, 146.
50 Eliade, 1960, 88.

CHAPTER FIVE: GREECE

52 Dodds, 1971, 189–90.
53 Levi, 1913, 132.
54 Myers, 1921, 1.
55 Parke, 1967, 101.

CHAPTER SIX: ROME

66 Bruce, 1886, 251.

CHAPTER SEVEN: THE NEW TESTAMENT

76 Field, 1960 (p).

CHAPTER EIGHT: THE EARLY FATHERS

80 Johnson, 1976, 49–50.

Chapter Nine: The Middle Ages

84 (Lambertini) Haynes, 1970, 109–15.
85 (Dante) Lombroso, 1909, 33; Flammarion, 1922, ii, 331.
Froissart, 1855, ii, 126.
(Bingen) Hyslop, 1906, 100–2.
(Giraldus) Thurston, 1953, 6.
86 (Sommeln) Summers, 1962, 69.
St. Patrick, 1887, 35–9.
87 Lecky, 1865, i, 153.
Tylor, 1871, i, 151.
Leroy, 1928, 11–12, 48, 186.
88 (stigmata) Thurston, 1952, 54–5.
(magic) Summers, 1962, 118; Dodds, 1971, 219; Cohn, 1975, 147–63.
89 (Demons) Cohn, 1975, 167; Kieckhefer, 1976, 104.
90 (Psellus) Laver, 1952, 45.
(Catharine) Butler, 1895, 200.
91 (Catharine) Butler, 117, 134; Underhill, 1925, 155; Leroy, 1931, 15.
(Joan) Lang, 1908, 42–7.
92 (Joan) Lang, 1908, 60–109, 265.

Chapter Ten: Alchemy

95 (Hermetic tracts) Yates, 1964 (p).
96 (Hermetic tracts) Yates, 1964 (p); Salverte, 1846, i, 181.
97 (Agrippa) Morley, 1856, 217; Yates, 1964, 130.
98 (Paracelsus) Podmore, 1908, 8; Morley, 1856, 221.
99 (Nostradamus) Laver, 1952 (p); Forman, 1940, 185.
100 (Louis) Laver, 1952, 145–50.
(Dee) French, 1972 (p).

Chapter Eleven: Miracles

102 (Cabalists) Yates, 1864 (p).
Thurston, 1954, 9.
103 (Teresa) Thurston, 1952, 9–26; Leroy, 1928, 163–4.
Teresa, 1870, 144; Underhill, 1911, 449–50.
104 (Neri) Leroy, 1928, 67.
(Joseph) Haynes, 1970, 34–5.
105 (Joseph) Leroy, 1928, 90–102.
106 (Joseph) Dingwall, 1947, 9–27; Thurston, 1952, 16–27.
Leroy, 1928, 149.
107 (Neri) Thurston, 1952, 152.
(Maria) Thurston, 1952 (p).
108 Thurston, 1952 (p).

109 (Lollards) Thomas, 1971, 51.
  Hobbes, 1946, 40.
110 (Weyer) Veith, *Hysteria*, 1965, 108–11.
  (Casaubon) Thomas, 1971, 145, 270.
  Walton, 1640, 24–5.
  Hobbes, 1651, 243.
  Evelyn, 8 October 1672.
111 (prayer) Thomas, 1971, 113–29; Ochorowitz, 1891, 150; Underhill,
  1925, 233; Stobart, 1925, 174; Thomas, 1971, 145–6; *Light*,
  Spring 1976.
112 Burton, 1808, 296.
  Thomas, 1971, 248–9.

CHAPTER TWELVE: WITCHCRAFT

113 Cohn, 1975, 238.
114 (Françoise) Leroy, 1928, 13.
  (levitations) Lang, 1894, 89–100; 295–6.
115 (Loudun) Binet/Féré, 1888, 59; Leroy, 1928, 16; Huxley, 1952 (p).
116 (Salem) Upham, 1867, 296–300; Calef, 1861, 75–6; Mather, 1862
  (p).
  (St Médard) Matthieu, 1864 (p).
117 (St Médard) Knox, 1950, 372–88.
  (Namur) 'ABV' 1887 (p); Dingwall, 1947, 182.

CHAPTER THIRTEEN: GHOSTS

118 Lavater, 1572 (p).
  Spectator, July 1711.
120 (Montalambert) Lang, 1894, 110–13.
  (Perreaud) Owen, 1964, 237.
121 Glanvil, 1689, 322–36; Boyle, 1744, v, 44.
122 (Scot; Chamberlain) Thurston, 1953, 134, 171.
  (Wesley) Wright, 1917 (p).
123 (Cock Lane) Lang, 1889, 219–20; Grant, 1965 (p); de Morgan,
  1863, 25.
126 Boswell, 1949, i, 251; ii, 167, 213, 381.

CHAPTER FOURTEEN: SECOND SIGHT

127 Aubrey, 1857, 207.
  Martin, 1820, 181–7.
128 Johnson, 1925, 160–3.
  Sully, 1856, iv, 109–10; Jung–Stilling, 1834 (p).
129 Saint–Simon, 1829, v, 120.
130 (dowsing) Chevreul, 1854, 42–65; Barrett, 1897, 12.
  (Swedenborg) Wilkinson, 1849 (p); Mayo, 1851, 46–7.

132 Kant, 1900, appendix ii, iv; Broad, 1953, 116–55.

CHAPTER FIFTEEN: THE GROWTH OF SCEPTICISM

135   (Lambertini) Haynes, 1970 (p).
136   (Joseph) Thurston, 1952, 17.
       (Liguori) Leroy, 1928, 113–16, 151, 174.
137   Thomas, 1971, 643.
       Lecky, 1865, 171.
       Woolston, 1727–9, 19.
138–9 Hume, *Enquiries*, 1902, 86–101.
140   (meteorites) Flammarion, 1922, i, 320; Voltaire, 1824, 295–6;
       Zoellner, 1882, 115.

CHAPTER SIXTEEN: FRANZ MESMER

141 Mesmer, 1948, 8, 39–55; Goldsmith, 1934, 21.
142 (Seifert) Ochorowicz, 1891, 260–1.
     Mesmer, 1779 (p).
143 Franklin, Commission *Report*, 1837 (p).
144 Jussieu, 1884, 31–78.
     Chastenet de Puysegur, 1786 (p).
145 (Petetin) Foissac, 1837, 295; Mayo, 1851, 108–10; Dingwall, 1967,
     i, 20–8.
146 Deleuze, 1812 (p).
147 (German hypnotists), Moser, in Dingwall, 1967, ii, 101–202.
     (Swedish hypnotists) Bjelfvenstam, in Dingwall, 1967, ii, 203–46.
148 (Russian hypnotists) Zielinski, in Dingwall, 1967, iii, 1–103.
149 Deleuze, 1850 (p); Ochorowicz, 1891, 300–1.
150 (Faria) Figuier, 1860, iii, 288; Dingwall, 1947, i, 34–40.
151 (De Bruno) Ochorowicz, 1891, 129–30, 264.

CHAPTER SEVENTEEN: THE SECOND INQUIRY

152   Du Potet, 1838 (p).
       (Bertrand), 1823, 1826 (p).
153–5 (French hypnotists) Dingwall, 1967 (p); Podmore, 1809, 88;
       Ochorowicz, 1891, 107–18, 263–9; Foissac, 1837, 283; Hus-
       son, 1836, xxix; Du Potet, 1838, 18–19; Deleuze, 1850, 58–62,
       90, 194–6.
156   Dupau, 1826, 206; Dingwall, 1967, i, 43–72.
157   Foissac, 1837 (p); Husson, 1836, 118.
158   (Report) Husson, 1836, 172; Newnham, 1845, 244; Braid, 1843,
       xii; Figuier, 1860, iv, 287.
       (German scientists); Dingwall, 1967, ii, 118–29; Schopenhauer,
       1909, 75–6.

159   Jung-Stilling, 1832, ix, 43–4; Goethe, 1897, i, 433.
160   Carlyon, 1836, i, 219–20.
161   (Cazotte) Jung-Stilling, 1832, 157–69; Figuier, 1860, iv, 137; Gregory, 1851, 504–5; d'Oberkirch, 1852, iii, 301–18.
      (Paine) Underhill, 1911, 79, 294.
162   (Zschokke) Howitt, 1863, i, 96.
      Young, *Autobiography*, 1898, 350.
163   (Kahn) Crowe, 1852, 433.
      Durbin, 1800 (p).
      Heaton, 1820 (p).
164   (Ontario) Lambert, 1955, 63.

CHAPTER EIGHTEEN: COUNTER-ATTACK

165   (surgery) Foissac, 1837, 208; Podmore, 1909, 111; Dingwall, 1967, i, 83.
166   (inquiry) Burdin/Dubois, 1841, 511; Binet/Féré, 1887, 42–9; Dingwall, 1967, i, 89–90.
167   (Pigeaire) *Lancet*, 18 August 1838; Binet/Féré, 1887, 50–2; Dingwall, 1967, i, 116–25.
      Bell, 1792, 65.
      (Chenevix) Colquhoun, 1836, ii, 186; *Zoist*, 1943, i, 88.
168   Du Potet, 1838, 3.
      Creevey, ii, 331.
      Elliotson, 1840, 664–84.
169   Elliotson, 1840 (p).
      Brodie, *Quarterly*, April 1838.
170   *Lancet*, 1838 (p); Sprigge, 1897, 444–9.
171   Lafontaine, 1866, i, 45–9; Zorab, in Dingwall, 1967, ii, 8–15; Ochorowicz, 1891, 146–7, 270.
      Braid, 1843, 1–37; 1852, 10.
172–3 Salverte, 1846 (p).
174   (sceptics) Bruce, 1886, 85; Podmore, 1909, 112; Burdin/Dubois, 1841, 633–4.

CHAPTER NINETEEN: THE ZOIST

175   (Elliotson) Wilson, *Dickens*, 188; Johnson, *Dickens*, 346, Foster, 1911, 329.
176   *Lancet*, 8 July, 28 December 1848.
      Elliotson, 1846 (p).
176–7 Esdaile, 1846 (p); 1852 (p); *Zoist*, 1843, i, 83; Bramwell, 1956, 10; *Zoist*, 1849, vi, 114–5.
177   (Laycock) *Zoist*, 1845, iii, 478; 1846, iv, 81.
178   (Buckley) *Zoist*, 1849, vi, 99, 380–4; Gregory, 1851, 141, 353.
      Newnham, 1845, i, 317.

179 (Church) Binet/Féré, 1887, 54–5.
Sandby, 1944, 167–85.
Townshend, 1844 (p).

180 Scoresby, 1849 (p).
Esdaile, 1852, 124–5.

181–3 (Didier) Teste, 1843, 133–4; Newnham, 1845, 244; 1849, 34;
Zoist, 1849, vi, 417; Forbes, 1845, 18; Gregory, 1851, 473;
Delaage, 1856, 122–3, 150–2; Rogers, 1856, 292; Mayo, 1851,
162–3; *Proc.s SPR*, 1898–9, xiv, 373–81.

183–4 Reichenbach, 1846 (p).
(research) Tardy, 1785, 28; Figuier, 1860, iii, 258; Moser, in
Dingwall, 1967, ii, 175; Bjelfvenstam, in Dingwall, 1967, ii,
215–66.

184–6 (Cottin) Figuier, 1860, iv, (p); de Rochas, 1896, 437–41.

187 *Gazette*, 2 February 1849; Wallace, 1881, 230.

CHAPTER TWENTY: MID-CENTURY

188 Martineau, 1845, vii.
(Arnold) Newnham, 1845, 419.

189 Bennett, 1851 (p).

189–91 Gregory, 1851 (p).

191–2 Mayo, 1851 (p).

192 Braid, 1852, 71–81.

192–3 (United States) Grimes, 1851, 44, 120; Collyer, 1871, 50–73;
Carpenter, 1874, 550–1; Angoff, in Dingwall, 1968, iv (p);
Brown, 1970, 32.

194 Carpenter, 1848, 754–6.
Zoist, 1847, iv, 517.
(Hall) *Zoist*, 1851, ix, 88; *Lancet*, 1 March 1851.
Esdaile, 1852, 257; Bramwell, 1956, 20–1.

CHAPTER TWENTY-ONE: THE FORERUNNERS

199–201 (Seeress) Kerner, 1845 (p); Howitt, 1863, i, 43–85; Moser, in
Dingwall, 1967, ii, 161–72.
(Werner) Podmore, 1902, i, 104; Moser, in Dingwall, 1967, ii,
150–4.

202 Ricard, 1840, 168.
(Cahagnet) *Zoist*, 1850, viii, 71; Podmore, 1902, i, 81–110;
1909, i, 203–4; Dingwall, 1967, i, 210–41.

203 Townshend, 1840, ii.
(United States) Angoff, 1968, 31–8; Brown, 1970, 73.

CHAPTER TWENTY-TWO: THE PSYCHIC CLOUD

204–6 (Fox sisters) Capron, 1855 (p); Brown, 1870, 102–17.

206 (U.S. mediums) Britten, 1875, 27; Doyle, 1926, 30–2.
206–7 (Phelps) Mahan, 1875, 111–14; Thurston, 1915, 12–13; Brown, 1970, 135.
209 ('exposure') Wallace, 1878, 27; Doyle, 1926, i, 83.
209–10 Edmonds, 1858, 1875 (p); *N.Y. Tribune*, 1 July 1859; *N.Y. Herald*, 6 Aug 1853; Lang, 1896, 88–90; Podmore, 1902, i, 227; Anspacher, 1952, 175.
211 (Willis) Doyle, 1926, i, 143–4.
(Edmonds) Doyle, 1926, i, 132; Podmore, 1902, i, 227; Brown, 1970, 157, 113–20.
211–14 (Hayden) Stone, 1852 (p); Brewster, 1869, 255; de Morgan, 1863 (p); Podmore, 1902, ii, 5; Wyndham, 1937, 27; Doyle, 1926, i, 151.
Godfrey, 1853 (p).
Gillson, 1853 (p).
(Victoria) Longford, *Victoria*, 1964, 339.
Brewster, 1869, 254–9.
215 Macaulay, 1909, 559–60.
Brewster, 1869, 254.
Wilberforce, 1881, ii, 425.

CHAPTER TWENTY-THREE: TABLE-TURNING TESTED

216 (demonstration) *Times*, 13 June 1853.
(Humboldt) Reichenbach, 1968, xiii.
Faraday, 1870, 207.
217 *Times*, 2 July.
(controversy) Owen, 1861, 74.
218 Bunsen memoirs; Brewster, 1869, 254–5.
(Bersot) Grasset, 1910, 12–13.
219 De Gasparin, 1854 (p); Lang, 1894, 310; Podmore, 1897, 43.
220 Thury, *Les Tables Tournantes*, 1855 (p); Flammarion, 1907, 359–69.
221–2 Hare, 1855 (p); Wallace, 1896, 90; Podmore, 1902, i, 334; Brown, 1970, 159.
222–3 Chevreul, 1854 (p); Flammarion, 1900, 223–4; Faraday, 1970, ii, 309.
222–3 (split) *Zoist*, April-July 1853; Grimes, 1860, 7; Dods, 1854, 27; Buchanan, 1893, 3–10; Carpenter, 1853, 508.
224 (Foucault) Sudre, 1960, 33.

CHAPTER TWENTY-FOUR: DANIEL DUNGLAS HOME

225–6 (early career) Home, 1863, 1–61; 1890, 95.
227 Browning, 1897, ii, 99.
(seances) Brewster, 1869, 254–5; Home, 1888, 38; Miller, 1957, 317.

228 Brewster, 1869, 257; Home, 1863, i, Appendix.
229 (lionised) Home, 1888, 37; Burton, 1948, 103–23.
230 (London) Home, 1863, i, 103; 1888, 162.
231 Weld, 1865, 179–81.
232 (Faraday) Home, 1888, 144–6; Wallace, 1896, 94; Crookes, 1874, 4, 24.
　　Faraday, 1870, ii, 446; Home, 1890, 214.
　　Hugo, 1921, 190; Sudre, 117–18.
233 Mabru, 1858, 356, 380–2, 483.
　　Maury, 1860, 383, 408.
　　Morin, 1860, 183, 271.
　　Dingwall, 1967, i, 228–54.
234 (Cottin) Figuier, 1860, iv (p); *Revue des deux mondes*, 15 May 1854; Flammarion, 1907, 227, 307–10.
236–7 Owen, 1861 (p).
237 De Morgan, 1863, 1–26.
238 Ashburner, 1867 (p).
239 Rutter, 1851 (p).
　　(magnetoscope) Wallace, 1896, 85; Carpenter, 1877, 46.

CHAPTER TWENTY-FIVE: THE INVESTIGATORS

240 (witnesses) Home, 1863, 173–4; 1888, 213–17; Burton, 1948, 160–1.
241 (Davenports) Nichols, 1964 (p); *Times*, 30 September, 1864; Maskelyne, 1876, 65.
242–3 Wallace, 1896 (p); 1905, ii, 278–82.
244–5 (Lyon; Adare) Home, 252–90; Adare, 1869 (p).
246–9 Dialectical Society Report, 1869 (p).

CHAPTER TWENTY-SIX: WILLIAM CROOKES

253–4 Crookes, 1874 (p).
　　Quarterly Journal of Science, 1870–1.
255 (Russian tests) Home, 1888, 367–8; 1890, 341–5.
　　Wallace, 1896, 168; Podmore, 1902, ii, 65–7.
256 Billot, 1839, 6; Dingwall, 1967, i, 221–2.
　　(Guppy) Britten, 1884, 162; Podmore, 1902, ii, 81; Wallace, 1905, ii, 292–3; Brown, 1970, 10–11.
257–8 Carpenter, *Quarterly*, October 1871; Lodge, 1931, 140; Fournier, 1923, 211; Anspacher, 1952, x.
　　Crookes, 1874, 73.
　　Cox, 1871, 56.
259 (Galton) Pearson, 1914, i, 63–6.
　　(Home) *Proc.s SPR*, 1964, 41–4 (Home did in fact come back for a few days in 1973, but there were no further experiments).

260 Crookes, *Quarterly Journal of Science*, January 1874.
   (Doun), Home, 1890, 293.
261 Alexander, 1871 (p).
262 Wallace, 1905, ii, 287.
   Home, 1890, 13, 221.
   Punch, 18 August 1860.
263 (stories) Home, 1890, 201; Podmore, 1902, ii, 230; 1910, 45;
   Proc.s SPR, 1924, 317; Wyndham, 1937, 85; Dingwall, 1947.

CHAPTER TWENTY-SEVEN: THE MEDIUMS

264–5 Crookes, *Quarterly Journal of Science*, October 1871, January
   1874.
   (Fox) Doyle, 1926, i, 95–9.
266–8 (Florence) *Spiritualist*, 12 March 1875; *Proc.s SPR*, 1964 (p);
   Telegraph, 10 October 1872, 12 August 1873; Podmore, 1902,
   ii, 103; Dunphy, 1874, xxv, 175.
269 Crookes, 1874 (p).
270 (incombustibility) *Proc.s SPR*, 1890, 98.
   Cox, 1871, 8, 49.
   Lancet, 10 January 1874.
271 Darwin, 1903, iii, 187–8.
   (Galton) Pearson, 1924, ii, 66.
272 Huxley, 1902, 197–8; Wallace, 1896, xix.
273 (Williams) Huxley, 1900, i, 419–23; Darwin, 1903, iii, 187–8;
   Pearson, 1924, ii, 66.
   Cox, 1879, ii, 444; Podmore, 1902, ii, 111; *Proc.s SPR*, 1964,
   44–6.
274–5 Crookes, 1874, 102–7; Maskelyne, 1876, 145; *Proc.s SPR* 1964,
   63–123.
275–6 (Rosina) Dunphy, 1874, xxv, 55; Home, 1888, 296; Fournier,
   1923, 174; *Proc.s SPR*, 1964, 105–23.

CHAPTER TWENTY–EIGHT: HENRY SLADE

277 (Slade) *Times*, 3 October, 1876; Moses, 1882, 19; Podmore,
   1902, 204–22.
278 Collyer, 1876, 4.
   (Slade) Moses, 1882, 67.
279–81 (prosecution) *Times*, 18 September–1 November 1876.
   Weldon, 1881 (p).
281–4 (German inquiry) Zollner, 1882 (p); Reichenbach, 1976,
   Introduction.
285 (Moses) Myers, 1893, 259–73, 347–8; Lillie, 1894, 74–5.
286–7 (Spirit Teaching) Moses, 1949 (p); Myers 1894, 248; Gauld,
   1968, 218.

288   Churchill, 1853 (p).
       Brown, 1868, 6.
289   Buyers, 1848, 375.
       Jacolliot, 1884, 208–67.
       (Tsherepanoff) Figuier, 1861, iv, 263–4.
       Huc, 1928, 264–7.
       Dennys, 1870, 56–7.
290   Burton, *Times*, 13 November 1876.
       (Lincoln) Sandberg, 1940, iii, 543.
291   (Mumler) Britten, 1884, 473; Wallace, 1896, 248; Doyle, 1924,
           ii, 121–3.
       (Newnham) Gurney, 1886, i, 163.

CHAPTER TWENTY-NINE: RETROSPECT

293   (Chambers) Home, 1888, 9.
       (Browning) Howlett, *Elizabeth Barrett Browning*, 1953, 283.
294   (Dean) Nevius, 1897, 219.
       Greeley, 1869, 234–41.
       Lytton, 1913, ii, 42–50.
       (Jencken) Wallace, 1905, ii, 301; Thurston, 1928, 27.
295   Crosland, 1873, 19.
       De Morgan, 1863, 19–24.
       Stowe, 1889, 464–5.
       (Leighton) Thurston, 1928, 15.
296   Trollope, 1887, 390.
       Moses, 1882, 60.
       Pall Mall Gazette, 20 April 1885.
297   Moses, 1880, 30–1.
       (Monck) *Times*, 28 October, 14 November 1876; 7 February
           1877; Oxley, 1899, 7.
298   (Monck) Adshead, 1877 (p); *Spectator*, 7 October 1877; Moses,
           1882, 36, 78; Wallace, 1905, ii, 330–1; Colley, 1877 (p);
           Doyle, 1926, i, 316; *Annals of Psychic Science*, December
           1905.
       (Willis) Sargent, 1881, 198.
299   Dunphy, 1874, xxv, 175.
       Carpenter, 1877, 57–8.
       Wallace, 1896, 38; 1905, ii, 285–6.
300   Rayleigh, *Proc.s SPR*, 1964, 57.
       Home, 1877, 57.
       Hartmann, 1884, i, 106.
       Nature, 27 July, 1871.
       (werewolves) *Academy*, 15 February, 1872; *Nature*, 29 February
           1872.
       (Stewart) *Nature*, 27 July 1871; 7 March 1872.

301–2 Carpenter, 1874, 606–7, 632; 1877, 4.
302   Lodge, 1931, 75.
       Tyndall, 1874 (p).
       Rayleigh, 1968, 65.
303   (James) Sargent, 1881, 139–40.
       Alexander, 1871, 75.
       Cox, 1880, 1–2.
304   Wallace, *Academy*, 15 February 1872.
       Tylor, 1871, i, 120.
       Cox, 1879, i, 1.
       (materialism) Rymer, 1857 (p).
305   Thompson, 1911 (p).
       Farmer, 1881, 79.
306   (Moses) Thurston, 1952, 226.
       Wallace, 1881, 229.
307   (Imbert Gourbeyre) Leroy, 1928, 127.
       Mallock, 1920, 99–100.
       (Nightingale) Pickering, *Creative Malady*, 1974, 157.
308   Cobbe, 1894, ii, 15.
       Wallace, 1905, ii, 296.
       Lewes, 1860, 293.
       Eliot, 1885, ii, 93, 154–5.
309   Von Hartmann, 1884, 108–9.
       Hammond, 1876, 98.
       (Challis) Crookes, 1874, 32.
       LDS Report, 1869, 243–5.
310   Faraday, 1859, 479.
       Alexander, 1871, 38, 81–8.
311   (sceptics) Wallace, 1896, 279–80; (Galton) *Proc.s SPR*, 1964, 42;
       Tyndall, 1892, i, 447–52; Carpenter, *Contemporary Review*,
       January 1876.
312   (innuendoes) Carpenter, 1876; 1877, 150; *19th Century*, March
       1877; *Frasers*, November, 1877; (Crookes) Fournier, 1923,
       254; *Proc.s SPR*, 1964, 121–2; *Human Nature*, December
       1887.
313   Moses, 1877, 5.
       Home, 1888, 309.
       Moses, 1877, 14.
       Zollner, 1882, 133–4.
314   Alexander, 1871, 89–90.

CHAPTER THIRTY: EXPLORING THE UNSEEN WORLD

317   Myers, 1903, i, 7.
318   Flournoy, 1911, 48.

(trio) Gauld, 1968, 103, 175.
(Slade) *Proc.s SPR*, 1891–2, 268.
319 Barrett, *Proc.s SPR*, 1882–3 (p).
Times, 15 September, 1876.
(Crookes) *Quarterly Journal of Science*, January 1874.
320 (willing game) Gauld, 1968, 137.
(SPR) *Proc.s SPR*, 1972, 341.
Barrett, *Proc.s SPR*, 1924, 280–1.
321 (manifesto) Gauld, 1968, 138.
322 (Kelvin) Thomson, 1910, ii, 798, 1125.
(Huggins) Montefiore, 1931, 29–30.
(Creery) Gurney, 1886, i, 26.
323 Cumberland, 1888, 316–7; *Proc.s SPR*, 1882–3, 4; *SPR Jnl.*,
   February 1884, 10–11.
(Creery) *Nature*, 7 July, 1881.
Donkin, 1882, 131.
324 (Creery) *Proc.s SPR*, 1882–3, 70–8.
325–7 (Guthrie/Lodge) *Proc.s SPR*, 1884–5 (p); Lodge, in *Nature*, 12
   June, 1884; 1931, 274; Gurney, 1886, i, 31–2; Podmore, 1894,
   35.
327–8 (Creery) Myers, *Proc.s SPR*, 1882–3, 43; Gurney, 1886, i, 28–30;
   Proc.s SPR, 1882–5 (p); 1888–9, 269–70.

CHAPTER THIRTY-ONE: PHANTASMS

329 Barrett, 1920, 141.
Proc.s SPR, 1882, 118.
330–5 Gurney, 1886 (p).
335 (census) *Proc.s SPR*, 1894 (p).
19th Century, August 1887.
Gauld, 1968, 153–99.

CHAPTER THIRTY-TWO: HYPNOTISM

336 *Lancet*, 11 June 1870.
(Braid) Maury, 1860, 427.
336–8 Liébeault, 1894 (p); Bramwell, 1956, 30–3; Gurney, 1896, i,
   293; Richet, *Proc.s SPR*, 1898, 153.
338–9 (Hansen) Bjelfvenstam, in Dingwall, 1967, ii, 242–5.
Heidenhain, 1888 (p).
339–40 Charcot, 1887, iii (p); Forel, 1906, 58; Munthe, 1935, 287–313.
340–1 (Nancy) Bernheim, 1917, vii; Bramwell, 1956, 30–2; Gurney,
   1886, i, 293; Joire, 1916, 125–7.
341–5 (Le Havre) Ochorowicz, 1891, 81–97; *Revue Philosophique*,
   February 1886; Dingwall, 1967, i, 264–9; *Nature*, 23 June, 7
   July; Nicholl, 1890, 57; Hart, 1893, 154; Zielinski, in
   Dingwall, 1968, iii, 108–30.

346   Richet, 1931, 130; *Proc.s SPR*, 1888–9 (p).
        (Dufay) Boirac, 1908, 242.
347   Liébeault, 1889, 295; *Proc.s SPR*, 1891–2, 291.
        ('Lina') *Proc.s SPR*, 1891–2, 3–23; Moser, in Dingwall, 1967, ii,
        180–95.
348   (assimilation) Ochorowicz, 1891, 298–9; James, 1960, 28.
349   (reports) Gurney, *Proc.s SPR*, 1884, 60; Munthe, 1935, 305;
        Dingwall, 1967, i, 257–62.
        Janet, 1925, 28–9.
349–50 Binet/Féré, 1888, (p); Nicholl, 1890, 34.
351   (sceptics) Moll, 1890, 101; *Revue*, December 1886; Myers,
        Proc.s SPR, 1886–7, 535–6; Binet/Féré, 1888, 64–5; Nicholl,
        1890, 58; (Lehmann) *Proc.s SPR* 1896–7, 298; *SPR Jnl.*,
        October 1899.
353   (physical effects) Helot, 1897, 175–6; Lafontaine, 1866, i, 285;
        Leroy, 1928, 30, 159–60; Dingwall, 1967, i, 34.
353–4   (stigmata) Binet/Féré, 1888, 60; James, 1961, 28; (Lateau)
        Hammond, 1876, 350; (Biggs) Moll, 1890, 116; Myers,
        Proc.s SPR, 1891–2, 339–41; James, 1901, ii, 612.
355   (blisters) Nicholl, 1890, 69; (Delboeuf) Bramwell, 1956, 83–4.
355–6   (Congress), *Proc.s SPR*, 1889–90 (p).
356   Moll, 1890 (p).
        Forel, 1906, 50–1.
357   Ermacora, *Proc.s SPR*, 1895, 235.
        (Reichenbach) Binet/Féré, 1888, 296; *Proc.s SPR*, 1883, 230;
        Hart, 1893, 79; Bramwell, 1956, 141–3.
        Joire, 1916, 14.
        Bernheim, 1890, x.
        Bramwell, 1956, 142.
358   Hudson, 1902, 75, 177.
        Hart, 1893, 28–9.
        (BMA) Bramwell, 1956, 36–7.

CHAPTER THIRTY-THREE: SLATE-WRITERS

359   Myers, *Proc.s SPR*, 1889–90, 669–7.
        ('exposures') Gauld, 1968, 105; *Telegraph*, 13 January 1880;
        Proc.s SPR, 1964, 80–1.
359–60 (Blavatsky) *SPR Jnl.*, October, November 1885; Gauld, 1968,
        200; Sinnett, 1881, 56–82; Sidgwick, 1906, 385; (Report)
        SPR Jnl., April 1885; *Proc.s SPR*, 1885 (p); Waterman, 1963
        (p); Aksakov, 1901, 193–9.
361   Sidgwick, *SPR Jnl.*, June 1886; *Proc.s SPR*, 1886–7, 381–404.
361–2   (Eglinton) *Proc.s SPR*, 1886–7, 36–7, 411; *SPR Jnl.*, July,
        August, October 1896, Doyle, 1926, ii, 42.

363 (Davey) *Proc.s SPR*, 1886–7, 405–95; Gauld, 1968, 204–5.
363–9 (Seybert) Report, 1920 (p); Houdini, 1924, 88–93; (Kellar) *Annals*, 1910, 309; (German inquiry) Tischner, 1925, 21; Wundt, 1879, 577; Doyle, 1924, ii, 34–6; *Proc.s SPR*, 1886–7, 80, 94–5, 412; 1888–9, 260–3; (Hopps) Moses, 1882, 72.

CHAPTER THIRTY-FOUR: MRS PIPER

370 (Foxes) Doyle, 1926, 102; Rinn, 1954, 5; Gauld, 1968, 25.
371 Myers, *Proc.s SPR*, 1884, 217.
(Piper) Allen, 1967, 283–5; *Proc.s SPR*, 1989–90, 651–9.
372–4 Lodge, *Proc.s SPR*, 1889–90 (p).
Hodgson, *Proc.s SPR*, 1892, 56–7.
375 (Myers) Merchant, *Wallace*, 1916, ii, 202–3.
Podmore, 1897 (p).
(Cambridge), Gauld, 1968, 346.
Muensterberg, 1899, 253.
376–8 Flournoy, 1901 (p).

CHAPTER THIRTY-FIVE: EUSAPIA PALLADINO

379 Aksakov, 1906, 110; *Proc.s SPR*, 1888–90, 666–7.
379–81 (Eusapia) Lombroso, 1909 (p); Carrington, 1909, 28; Flammarion, 1907, 137–8; *Annals*, 1905.
381–3 (Eusapia) *Annales*, 1893 (p); Richet, 1923, 413–17; de Rochas, 1896 (p); Flammarion, 1907, 162–72.
384 (Eusapia) *Revue de l'Hypnotisme*, July–December, 1894; de Rochas, 1896, 138; Richet, 1923, 412–17; Joire, 1916, 453–4; Gauld, 1968, 221–9; Jolly, *Lodge*, 103–4.
385 D'Esperance, 1897 (p); Oxley, 1899, 13–16; Richet, 1923, 443–79.
386 (D'Esperance) Schrenk-Notzing, 1920, 5; Doyle, 1926, ii, 25.
(Sidgwicks) Gauld, 1968, 229–31.
387 Hodgson, *SPR Jnl.* April, November 1895.
387–90 (Cambridge) Gauld, 1968, 234–41; Thomson, 1936, 150–1; *Chronicle*, 29 October, 1895; Podmore, 1910, 45; (Speer), Burton, 1948, 80; (Crookes) *Proc.s SPR*, 1964, 67; *SPR Jnl.*, November 1894, April 1985; Jolly, *Lodge*, 1974, 105–6 *Annales*, 1896 (p); de Rochas, 1896 (p); Flammarion, 1907, 173; Joire, 1909, 454.
390–3 (France) Boirac, 1908, 311–26; Flammarion, 1900, viii; 1907, 63–101; de Fontenay, 1898 (p); Flournoy, 1911, 244; (Myers) Gauld, 1968, 240–2.
393–5 (Crookes/Richet) *Proc.s SPR*, 1898–9, 152–7; *SPR Jnl.* January, December 1898; Gauld, 1968, 242.

CHAPTER THIRTY-SIX: ANDREW LANG

399   Tylor, 1871, 134–41.
       Frazer, 1890, 52.
400   Lefebure, 1896, 145.
       Chesterton, *Literature*, 13 November 1901.
       de Cocq, Lang, 1968, 27.
401   Lang, 1894, 13–23; 1898, 6, 47–9.
402   Lang, 1894, 35; 1876, 87–8; 1901, 277; 1898, 8–9, 94.
       (fire-walk) *Proc.s SPR*, 1900–1, 2–15.
       Kingsley, 1892, 20.
       Proc.s SPR, 1899, 331–3.
403   Barrett, 1897, (p).
404   (divining rod) *SPR Jnl.*, February 1884; *Nature*, 17 May, 1883;
       10 June 1897.
405   (poltergeists) Lang, 1899, vi, 196; 1894, 1899, 196; Dupouy,
       1898, 20; Lambert, 1955, 405; Thurston, 1953, 93.
406   (Dariex) Joire, 1916, 426–30; *SPR Jnl.*, September 1926; *Proc.s
       SPR*, 1891–2; (James) Murphy/Ballou, 1960, 62–3.
407   Podmore, 1894 (p).
       Wells, *Nature*, 6 December 1894.
408   Podmore, 1896 (p).
409   Taylor, *SPR Jnl.*, October 1896.
410   Wallace, *Proc.s SPR*, 1898–9, 375.
       Podmore, 1897, Preface.
       (Wallace) Marchant, 1916, 204.
       (Sidgwick) Murphy/Ballou, 1960, 309.
411–12 Taylor, *British Jnl. of Photography*, 17 March 1893.
413   Yeats, 1926, 322.
       Inge, 1899, ix.
       Muensterberg, 1899, 278.
       Parish, 1897, 301.
       Jastrow, 1901, 42–3.

CHAPTER THIRTY–SEVEN: CROSS-CORRESPONDENCES

414   Crookes, 1898, 2.
       Hudson, 1902, 242.
       (research) Sudre, 1960, 13–14.
415–18 Verrall, *Proc.s SPR*, 1906, 417.
       (cross-correspondences) *Proc.s SPR*, 1911–14 (p); Heywood,
       1959, 69–85; Owen, 1964, 121.

CHAPTER THIRTY-EIGHT: EUSAPIA PALLADINO (2)

419   Flammarion, 1900, viii, 41; 1907, 441.

420–1   Maxwell, 1905 (p).
422–3   (Morselli) *Annales*, 1907 (p); *Proc.s SPR*, 1908–9, 516; (Barzini) Lombroso, 1909, 192; Oesterreich, 1923, 88.
423–5   (Sorbonne) *Annals*, 1909 (p); *Proc.s SPR*, 1909, 570–90; Reid, Curie, 1974, 146.
425   (Flammarion), Grasset, 1910, 346.
        Podmore, 1902, ii, 354.
        Tomczyk, *Proc.s SPR*, 1909, 577; *Annals*, 1909 (p).
426   Muensterberg, 1889, 259.
        (Naples) *Proc.s SPR*, 1909, 306–19.
426–9   Feilding, 1963 (p).
429   James, Murphy/Ballou, 1960, 61.
        Hyslop, 1906, 337.
429–30 Carrington, 1954 (p); Dingwall, 1950, 210–12; Rinn, 1954, 190; Schrenck-Notzing, 1920, 9–10; *Colliers*, 14 May 1910; Houdini, 1924, 53.
431   (Naples) *Proc.s SPR*, 1911, 57.
        Perovsky, *Proc.s SPR*, 1911, 57–9; 447–54.

CHAPTER THIRTY-NINE: THE UNKNOWN GUEST

433   Richet, 1923, 421.
434–5   ('Eva') Richet, 1923, 438–70; Schrenck-Notzing, 1920 (p); *Annals*, 1905 (p); (precautions) Richet, 1923, 510; Bisson, 1914, 311; Doyle, 1926, ii, 101.
        McDougall, 1911, 349.
436   Bergson, *Proc.s SPR*, 1913, 159–61.
        ('falling-off') Osty, 1913, 26; Richet, 1923, 230; *Proc.s SPR*, 1918, 166, 731.
        Moberly/Jourdain, *An Adventure*, 1911.
        (James) Murphy/Ballou, 1960, 310.
437   Maeterlinck, 1914, 142.
438   Boirac, 1918, 331.
        Lombroso, 1909, 197–8.
        (Lodge) Barrett/Westerman, 1926, 269.
        Carrington, 1907, 321.
439   Chambers, *Proc.s SPR*, 1886–7, 41–2.
        (Morselli) Flournoy, 1911, 261.
        Richet, 1923, 569.
        Barrett, 1911, 197.
        Flammarion, 1900, Introduction.
440   Myers, 1903, 197.
        Crookes, *Proc.s SPR*, 1897, 343.
        Flammarion, 1907, 429.
        Myers, *Proc.s SPR*, 1891–2, 312.

441   Myers, 1903, 1, 222.
Flournoy, 1901, 377–8.
Lombroso, 1909, Preface.
442   (Jodl) Tischner, 1925, 21.
Hyslop, 1906, 3–4.
James, 1960, 457, 478.
443   Drummond, 1894, 234; 1902, 110–11.
Barrett, 1911, 68–9.
(anomalies) Flammarion, 1907, 438; Richet, 1923, 134–5.
444   (sceptics) *Annales*, 1908, 220; Boirac, 1918, 223.
444–5 (hallucination) Aidé, *19th Century*, April 1890; Myers, 1903, i, 189; le Bon, 1903, 49; Podmore, 1897, 121, 431.
446   Richet, 1923, 592.
Jastrow, *Review of Reviews*, 1910, 74–82.
447   Hyslop, 1906, 5.
(Joan) Lang, 1910 (p); Cazamian, 1931, 10–16.
448   (Cayce) Moss, Thelma, *The Probability of the Impossible*, 1977, 260–4.
Myers, 1903, i, 280.
Podmore, 1908, 169.
449   Maxwell, 1905, 394.
450   Jastrow, 101, 47.
Frazer, 1913, i, 15.
Aksakov, *Proc.s SPR*, 1889–90, 674.

POSTSCRIPT

'There is a general lack of historical continuity in modern parapsychological literature', Carlos Alvarado observed in the *SPR Journal* in 1982. 'Many discussions of specific aspects of psi research give the impression that nothing has been done on the topic before the work of the last couple of decades'. I plan to give due credit to the authors who have been the exceptions, Alvarado himself among them, in the final volume of the trilogy of which *Natural and Supernatural* is the first. I have not made any changes here, however, to the original text, apart from correcting a few literals.

Bibliography

A few of the titles have been shortened. The place and date of publication refer to the edition consulted; where it is not the first edition, its place and date follow in brackets.

'A.B.V.', *Les Convulsionnaires de Namur*, Namur, 1887.

Abbott, David P., *Behind the Scenes with the Mediums*, Chicago, 1908.

Abercrombie, John, *Inquiries Concerning Intellectual Powers*, London, 1840.

Adare, Lord, *Experiences with D. D. Home*, London, 1869.

Adshead, W. P., *Dr. Monck in Derbyshire*, London, 1877.

Aidé, Hamilton, 'Was I hypnotised?', *Nineteenth Century*, April 1890.

Aksakov, Alexander, 'Experiences with Mme. Fox-Jencken', *Annales des Science Psychiques*, 1901, xi, 193 ff.

Aksakov, Alexander, *Animisme et Spiritisme*, Paris, 1906.

Alexander, Patrick P., *Spiritualism*, Edinburgh, 1871.

Allen, Gay, *William James*, London, 1967.

Amberley, Lord, 'Experiences of Spiritualism', *Fortnightly*, Jan. 1st, 1874.

Andrews, George, (ed.) *Drugs and Magic*, London, 1974.

Angoff, Allan, 'Hypnotism in the U.S.A.', in Dingwall, 1968, iv.

Angoff, Allan, and Diana Barth, *Parapsychology and Anthropology*, New York, 1974.

Anspacher, Louis, *Challenge of the Unknown*, London, 1952.

'Anti-Satan', *The Testers Tested*, London, 1853.

Apuleius, Lucius, 'A Discourse on Magic', *Works*, London, 1899.

Apuleius, Lucius, *The Golden Ass* (ed. Graves), London, 1950.

Aristotle, *Works* (ed. W. Ross), Oxford, 1931.

Arnold, Matthew, *Literature and Dogma*, Michigan, 1968.

Ashburner, John, *A Series of Essays*, London, 1859.

Ashburner, John, *Notes and Studies in Animal Magnetism and Spiritualism*, London, 1867.

Ashby, Robert, *Guidebook for the Study of Psychical Research*, London, 1972.

Aubrey, John, 'Accurate Account of Second-Sighted Men', *Misc. Scotica*, iii.

Aubrey, John, *Miscellanies*, London, 1857.

Azam, C. M., *Hypnotisme et Double Conscience*, Paris, 1893.

Barnum, P. T., *Humbugs of the World*, London, 1866 (N.Y., 1865).

Barrett, William, *On the So-called Divining Rod*, London, 1897.

Barrett, William, *On the Threshold of a New World*, London, 1908.

Barrett, William, *Psychical Research*, London, 1911.

Barrett, William, *On the Threshold of the Unseen* (as revised 1908), London, 1920.

Barrett, William, E. Gurney and F. Myers, 'Thought-reading', *Nineteenth Century*, June 1882.

Barrett, William and T. Westerman, *The Divining Rod*, London, 1926.

Beard, G. M., *The Study of Trance, Muscle-Reading*, New York, 1882.

Beattie, John, *Other Cultures*, London, 1964.

Beattie, John, and J. Middleton (eds.), *Spirit Mediumship and Society in Africa*, London, 1969.

Beecher, Charles, *A Review of the 'Spiritual Manifestations'*, New York, 1853.

Bell, J., *The General and Particular Principles of Animal Electricity and Magnetism*, London, 1792.

[Bell, Robert], 'Stranger than Fiction', *Cornhill*, August 1960.

Benedict, Ruth, *Patterns of Culture*, London, 1952.

Bennett, John H., *The Mesmeric Mania of 1851*, Edinburgh, 1851.

Bergasse, M., *Considerations sur le Magnétisme Animal*, Paris, 1784.

Bernheim, Hippolyte, *Suggestive Therapeutics*, Edinburgh, 1890.

Bernheim, Hippolyte, *Automatisme et Suggestion*, Paris, 1917.

Bernheim, Hippolyte, *Hypnosis*, London, 1965.

Bertrand, Alexandre, *Traité du Somnambulisme*, Paris, 1823.

Bertrand, Alexandre, *Du Magnétisme Animal*, Paris, 1826.

Besterman, Theodore, *Crystal-Gazing, London*, 1924.

Bevan, Edwyn, *Sybils and Seers*, London, 1928.

Billot, G. P., *Recherches Psychologiques sur le Magnétisme Vital*, Paris, 1839.

Binet, Alfred, and Charles Féré, *Animal Magnetism*, London, 1888 (Paris, 1877).

Bisson, Juliette, *Les Phénomènes Dits de Matérialisation*, Paris, 1914.

Bjelfvenstam, Eric, 'Hypnotism in Scandinavia', in Dingwall, 1967, ii.

Boirac, Emile, *The Psychology of the Future*, New York, 1918 (Paris, 1908).

Bossier, A. K., 'ESP among African Priest-Diviners', in Poynton, 1975.

Boswell, James, *Samuel Johnson*, London, 1949.

Bouché-Leclerc, *Divination dans l'Antiquité*, Paris, 1879 (4 vols.).

Boulting, William, *Giordano Bruno*, London, 1929.

Boyle, Robert, *Works*, London, 1744.

Bozzano, Ernesto, *Discarnate Influences on Human Life*, London, 1938.

Brackett, E. A., *Materialised Apparitions*, London, 1910.

Braid, James, *Neurypnology*, London, 1843 (with additional material, 1899).

Braid, James, *Magic, Witchcraft, Animal Magnetism*, London, 1852.

Bramwell, J. Milne, *Hypnotism*, New York, 1956 (London, 1903).

Brewster, Sir David, *Letters on Natural Magic*, London, 1832.

Brewster, Margaret (Mrs. Gordon), *The Home Life of Sir D. Brewster*, Edinburgh, 1869.

Brinton, Daniel, *The Myths of the New World*, Philadelphia, 1896.

Britten, Emma Hardinge, *History of Modern American Spiritualism*, New York, 1870.

Britten, Emma Hardinge, *Nineteenth Century Miracles*, New York, 1884.

Broad, C. D., *Religion, Philosophy and Psychical Research*, London, 1953.

Broad, C. D., *Lectures on Psychical Research*, London, 1962.

Brodie, Benjamin, 'Animal Magnetism', *Quarterly*, April, 1838.

Brown, John P., *The Dervishes, or Oriental Spiritualism*, London, 1868.

Brown, Slater, *The Heyday of Spiritualism*, New York, 1970.

Browning, Elizabeth Barrett, *Letters*, London, 1897.

Browning, Oscar, *George Eliot*, London, 1890.

Bruce, Alexander, *The Miraculous Element in the Gospels*, London, 1886.

Buchanan, Joseph Rodes, *Outlines of Lectures on the Neurological System of Anthropology*, Cincinnati, 1854.

Buchanan, Joseph Rodes, *Manual of Psychometry*, Boston, 1893.

Burdin, C., and E. F. Dubois, *Histoire Académique de Magnétisme Animal*, Paris, 1841.

Burton, Isabel, *Sir Richard F. Burton* (2 vols.), London, 1893.

Burton, Jean, *Heyday of a Wizard*, London, 1948.

Bushnell, Horace, *Nature and the Supernatural*, New York, 1859.

Butler, Josephine, *Catharine of Siena*, London, 1895.

Buyers, William, *Recollections of Northern India*, London, 1848.

Bywater, John, *The Mystery Solved*, Rochester (N.Y.), 1852.

Cahagnet, Louis, *Magnétisme* (3 vols.), Paris, 1848.

Calef, Robert (ed.), *Salem Witchcraft*, Salem, 1861.

Callaway, Henry, *The Religious System of the Amazulu*, Cape Town, 1868.

Calmet, Augustine, *The Phantom World* (2 vols.), London, 1850 (Paris, 1746).

Campbell, G. D., 'The Supernatural', *Edinburgh Review*, Oct. 1862.

Capron, E. W., *Modern Spiritualism*, Boston, 1855.

Carlyon, Clement, *Early Years and Late Reflections*, London, 1836.

Carpenter, W. B., *Principles of Human Physiology*, London, 1846.

Carpenter, W. B., 'Electro-biology and Mesmerism', *Quarterly*, Oct. 1853.

Carpenter, W. B., 'Spiritualism and its Recent Converts', *Quarterly*, Oct. 1871.

Carpenter, W. B., 'Epidemic Delusions', *Science Lectures for the People*, 3rd s. 1871.

Carpenter, W. B., *Principles of Mental Physiology*, London, 1874.

Carpenter, W. B., 'On Fallacies in Relation to the Supernatural', *Contemporary Review*, Jan. 1876.

Carpenter, W. B., *Mesmerism, Spiritualism, etc.*, London, 1877.

Carpenter, W. B., 'The Radiometer', *Nineteenth Century*, March 1877.

Carpenter, W. B., 'Psychological Curiosities of Spiritualism', *Fraser's*, Nov. 1877.

Carrington, Hereward, *The Physical Phenomena of Spiritualism*, London, 1920 (New York, 1907).

Carrington, Hereward, *Eusapia Palladino*, New York, 1909.

Carrington, Hereward, *Personal Experiences in Spiritualism*, London, 1913.

Carrington, Hereward, *The American Seances with Eusapia Palladino*, New York, 1954.

Carrington, Hereward and Nandor Fodor, *The Story of the Poltergeist*, London, 1953.

Case, Shirley, *Experience with the Supernatural in Early Christian Times*, New York, 1929.

Castaneda, Carlos, *The Teachings of Don Juan*, Los Angeles, 1971.

Castiglione, Arturo, *Adventures of the Mind*, London, 1947.

Cazamian, Louis, *Andrew Lang and the Maid of France*, Oxford, 1931.

Charcot, J. M., *Clinical Lectures* (3 vols.), London, 1887.

Chastenet de Puységur, A. M. J., *Mémoir du Magnétisme Animal*, Lyon, 1786.

Chastenet de Puységur, A. M. J., *Mémoires pour Servir à l'Histoire du Magnétisme Animal*, Paris, 1809.

Chastenet de Puységur, *Recherches sur l'Homme dans l'Etat de Somnambulisme*, Paris, 1811.

Chevreul, Michel Eugène, *De la Baguette Divinatoire et des Tables Tournantes*, Paris, 1854.

Churchill, Charles, *Mt. Lebanon*, London, 1853.
CIBA, *ESP: a CIBA Foundation Symposium*, New York, 1966.
Cicero, *On Divination*, London, 1876.
Cieza de Leon, *Travels in Peru* (ed. Markham), London, 1864.
Clarke, Edward H., *Visions*, Boston, 1878.
Close, F., *The Testers Tested, or Table-Moving not Diabolical*, London, 1853.
Cobbe, Frances Power, *Life* (2 vols.), London, 1894.
Cocq, Antonius de, *Andrew Lang*, Tilberg, 1968.
Codrington, R. H., *The Melanesians*, Oxford, 1891.
Cohn, Norman, *Europe's Inner Demons*, London, 1975.
Colley, Thomas, *Later Phases of Materialisation*, London, 1877.
Collyer, Robert H., *Mysteries of the Vital Element*, London, 1871.
Collyer, Robert H., *Automatic Writing*, London, 1876.
Colquhoun, J. C., *Isis Revelata* (2 vols.), London, 1836.
Colquhoun, J. C., *An History of Magic, Witchcraft and Animal Magnetism*, London, 1851.
Comet, Charles, *La Verité*, Paris, 1860.
Cox, Edward, *Spiritualism Answered by Science*, London, 1871.
Cox, Edward, *What am I?*, London, 1873.
Cox, Edward, *The Mechanism of Man* (2 vols.), London, 1879.
Cox, Edward, 'The Claims of Psychology', *Proceedings of the Psychological Society*, 1880.
Crawford, J. R., *Witchcraft and Sorcery in Rhodesia*, Oxford, 1967.
Crawford, W. J., *The Reality of Psychic Phenomena*, London, 1916.
Crehan, Joseph, 'St. Augustine and Psychical Research', *The Christian Parapsychologist*, Dec. 1976.
Crookes, William, *Psychic Force and Modern Spiritualism*, London, 1871.
Crookes, William, Articles in *Quarterly Journal of Science*, 1871-78.
Crookes, William, *Researches in the Phenomena of Spiritualism*, London, 1874.
Crookes, William, 'Another Lesson from the Radiometer', *Nineteenth Century*, July 1877.
Crosland, Newton, *Apparitions*, London, 1873.
Cross, R. Nicol, *Socrates*, London, 1914.
Crow, W. B., *A History of Magic*, London, 1968.
Crowe, Catherine, *The Night Side of Nature*, London, 1852.
Crowell, Dr. Eugene, *The Identity of Primitive Christianity and Modern Spiritualism* (2 vols.), New York, 1874.
Cumberland, Stuart, *A Thought-Reader's Thoughts*, London, 1888.
Cumberland, Stuart, *Spiritualism – the Inside Truth*, London, 1919.
Czaplicka, M., *Aboriginal Siberia*, Oxford, 1914.
Danville, Gaston, *Magnétisme et Spiritisme*, Paris, 1908.

Darnton, Robert, *Mesmerism and the End of the Enlightenment in France*, Cambridge (Mass.), 1968.

Darwin, Charles, *Journal*, London, 1845.

Darwin, Charles, *More Letters* (ed. F. Darwin) (2 vols.), London, 1903.

Davenport, Reuben B., *The Death-Blow to Spiritualism*, New York, 1888.

Davies, Charles M., *Mystic London*, London, 1875.

Davies, T. W., *Magic, Divination and Demonology*, London, 1898.

Defoe, Daniel, *A System of Magick*, London, 1728.

Delaage, Henri, *Le Sommeil Magnétique*, Paris, 1856.

Deleuze, J. P. F., *A Critical Study of Animal Magnetism*, London, 1816 (Paris, 1812).

Deleuze, J. P. F., *Histoire Critique du Magnétisme Animal* (2 vols.), Paris, 1819.

Deleuze, J. P. F., *Practical Instruction in Animal Magnetism*, London, 1850 (Paris, 1825).

Delitzsch, Franz, *A System of Biblical Psychology*, Edinburgh, 1857.

de Morgan, Mrs. ('C.D.'), *From Matter to Spirit*, London, 1863.

de Morgan, Mrs. ('C.D.'), *Memoir of Augustus de Morgan*, London, 1882.

Dennett, John, *Voyages*, London, 1826.

Dennys, N. B., *The Folklore of China*, London, 1870.

Denton, William, and Elizabeth Denton, *The Soul of Things*, Wellesley (Mass.), 1888.

D'Eslon, Charles, *Observations sur les Deux Rapports du Magnétisme Animal*, Paris, 1784.

D'Esperance, E., *Shadow Land*, London, 1897.

Devereux, George, *Mohave Ethnopsychiatry*, New York, 1961.

Dibdin, R. W., 'Table-Turning' (1853), in *Reply to the Quarterly Review on Spiritualism*, London, 1871.

Dingwall, Eric J., *Ghosts and Spirits in the Ancient World*, London, 1930.

Dingwall, Eric J., *Some Human Oddities*, London, 1947.

Dingwall, Eric J., *Very Peculiar People*, London, 1950.

Dingwall, Eric J., *The Critic's Dilemma*, London, 1966.

Dingwall, Eric J., *Abnormal Hypnotic Phenomena* (4 vols.), London, 1967–8.

Dingwall, Eric J. and John Langdon Davies, *The Unknown – is it Nearer?*, London, 1956.

Dixon, Jacob, *Hygienic Clairvoyance*, London, 1859.

Dodds, E. R., *The Greeks and the Irrational*, Berkeley, 1951.

Dodds, E. R., *Pagan and Christian in an Age of Anxiety*, Cambridge, 1965.

Dodds, E. R., *Supernormal Phenomena in Classical Antiquity*, London, 1971.

Dods, John Bovee, *Spirit Manifestations Examined*, New York, 1853.

Dods, John Bovee, *The Philosophy of Mesmerism*, London, 1876 (N.Y., 1950).

Dods, John Bovee, *Lectures on Animal Magnetism*, London, 1876.

Donkin, Horatio, 'A Note on Thought-Reading', *Nineteenth Century*, Aug. 1882.

Donkin, Horatio, 'Miracles and Medium-Craft', *Fortnightly*, Aug. 1883.

Doolittle, Justus, *Social Life of the Chinese* (2 vols.), London, 1866.

Douglas, Alfred, *Extra Sensory Powers*, London, 1976.

Doyle, Conan, *The History of Spiritualism*, London, 1926.

Driesch, Hans, *Psychical Research* (ed. Besterman), London, 1933.

Drummond, Henry, *The Lowell Lectures on the Ascent of Man*, London, 1894.

Drummond, Henry, *Natural Law in the Spiritual World*, London, 1902.

Dunne, J. W., *An Experiment with Time*, London, 1927.

Dunphy, Henry, 'Modern Mysteries', *London Society*, 1874 (Vols. xxv, xxvi).

Dupau, J. A., *Lettres sur le Magnétisme Animal*, Paris, 1826.

Du Potet de Sennevoy, J. D., *An Introduction to the Study of Animal Magnetism*, London, 1838.

Du Potet de Sennevoy, J. D., *La Magie Dévoilée*, Paris, 1893.

Dupouy, Edmond, *Sciences Occultes et Physiologie Psychique*, Paris, 1898.

Du Prel, Carl, *The Philosophy of Mysticism* (ed. C. C. Massey), London, 1889 (Leipzig, 1885).

Durbin, Henry, *A Narrative of Some Extraordinary Things . . .* Bristol, 1800.

Ebon, Martin, 'A History of Parapsychology', in Mitchell, 1976.

Edmonds, John Worth, *Spiritual Tracts*, New York, 1858.

Edmonds, John Worth, *Letters and Tracts on Spiritualism* (ed. J. Burns), London, 1875.

Elbé, Louis, *Future Life*, London, 1919.

Eliade, Mircea, *Myths, Dreams and Mysteries*, London, 1960.

Eliade, Mircea, *Shamanism*, New York, 1964 (Paris, 1951).

Eliade, Mircea, *From Primitives to Zen*, London, 1967.

Eliot, George, *Life* (2 vols., ed. J. W. Cross), Edinburgh, 1885.

Eliot, George, *Letters* (7 vols.), London, 1956.

Ellenberger, Henri F., *The Discovery of the Unconscious*, New York, 1970.

Elliotson, John, *Human Physiology*, London, 1840.

Elliotson, John, *Harveian Oration*, London, 1846.

Elliott, G. Maurice, *The Bible in Psychic History*, London, 1959.

Ellis, William, *Polynesian Researches*, London, 1832.

Endicott, Kirk, *An Analysis of Malay Magic*, Oxford, 1970.

Ennemoser, Joseph, *The History of Magic*, London, 1893 (Munich, 1843).

Esdaile, James, *Report of the Committee on Surgical Operations by Dr. Esdaile*, Calcutta, 1846.

Esdaile, James, *Mesmerism in India*, London, 1846.

Esdaile, James, *Natural and Mesmeric Clairvoyance*, London, 1852.

Evans, Henry, *The Old and the New Magic*, Chicago, 1906.

Evans-Pritchard, E. E., *Witchcraft among the Azande*, Oxford, 1937.

Evans-Pritchard, E. E., *Nuer Religion*, Oxford, 1956.

Eysenck, Hans, *Sense and Nonsense in Psychology*, London, 1957.

Fahnestock, William, *Statuvolism, or Artificial Somnambulism*, Chicago, 1871.

Faraday, Michael, 'Experimental Investigation of Table-Moving', *Athenaeum*, July 2nd, 1853.

Faraday, Michael, *Experimental Researches in Chemistry*, London, 1859.

Faraday, Michael, *Life and Letters* (ed. Bence Jones), London, 1870.

Farmer, Hugh, *A Dissertation on Miracles*, London, 1771.

Farmer, John S., *A New Basis for Belief in Immortality*, London, 1881.

Farmer, John S., *Twixt Two Worlds*, London, 1886.

Feilding, Everard, *Sittings with Eusapia Palladino*, New York, 1963.

Field, Margaret J., *Search for Security*, London, 1960.

Field, Margaret J., 'Spirit Possession in Ghana', in Beattie/Middleton, 1969.

Field, Margaret J., *Angels and Ministers of Grace*, London, 1971.

Figuier, Guillaume, *Histoire du Merveilleux* (4 vols.), Paris, 1860.

Fitzpatrick, W. J., *Memoirs of Richard Whately*, London, 1864.

Flammarion, Camille, *The Unknown*, New York, 1900 (Paris, 1900).

Flammarion, Camille, *Mysterious Psychic Forces*, Boston, 1907 (Paris, 1907).

Flammarion, Camille, *Death and its Mystery* (3 vols.), London, 1922 (Paris, 1921).

Flournoy, Theodore, *From India to the Planet Mars*, New York, 1901 (Paris, 1900).

Flournoy, Theodore, *Spiritism and Psychology*, New York, 1911 (Paris, 1911).

Foissac, P., *Rapports sur le Magnétisme Animal*, Paris, 1833.

Foissac, P., *Abstract of Report on Magnetic Experiments*, Philadelphia, 1837.

de Fontenay, Guillaume, *A propos d'Eusapia Palladino*, Paris, 1898.

de Fontenay, Guillaume, *Comptes Rendues d'Eusapia Palladino*, Paris, 1908

Forbes, John, *Illustrations of Modern Mesmerism*, London, 1845.

Forel, August, *Hypnotism*, London, 1906 (Paris, 1889).

Forman, Henry J., *The Story of Prophecy*, New York, 1940.

Fornell, E. W., *The Unhappy Medium*, Austin (Texas), 1964.

Forster, John, *Charles Dickens* (2 vols.), London, 1911.

Fort, L., *Lo!*, London, 1931.

Fournier d'Albe, E. E., *New Light on Immortality*, London, 1908.

Fournier d'Albe, E. E., *The Life of Sir William Crookes*, London, 1923.

Franklin, Benjamin (*et al.*), *Animal Magnetism: Report of the Commissioners*, Philadelphia, 1837.

Frazer, James, *The Golden Bough* (vols. 1–2), London, 1913 (1890).

Frazer, James, *The Belief in Immortality*, London, 1913.

Frazer, John, *A Brief Discourse Concerning the Second Sight*, Edinburgh, 1707.

French, Peter J., *John Dee*, London, 1972.

Frobenius, Leo, *The Voice of Africa* (2 vols.), London, 1913.

Froissart, *Chronicles* (2 vols.), London, 1855.

Funk, Isaac K., *The Widow's Mite, and Other Psychic Phenomena*, New York, 1904.

Furst, Peter T. (ed.), *Flesh of the Gods*, London, 1972 (New York, 1972).

Gardner, Martin, *Fads and Fallacies in the Name of Science*, New York, 1957 (1952).

Gardner, P., *The Religious Experience of St. Paul*, London, 1911.

Garstin, E. J. Langford, *Theurgy*, London, 1930.

Gasparin, Agenor de, *A Treatise on Turning Tables* (2 vols.), London, 1857 (Paris, 1854).

Gauld, Alan, *The Founders of Psychical Research*, London, 1968.

Geley, Gustave, *Clairvoyance and Materialisation*, London, 1927.

Gelfand, Michael, *Witch Doctor*, London, 1964.

Gerloff, Hans, *The Crisis in Parapsychology*, London, 1965.

Gibier, Paul, *Le Spiritisme*, Paris, 1889.

Gillson, E., *Table-Turning*, London, 1853.

Glanvil, Joseph, *Sadducismus Triumphatus*, London, 1689.

Glendinning, A., *The Veil Lifted*, London, 1894.

Godfrey, N. S., *Table-Turning Tested*, London, 1853.

Godwin, William, *Lives of the Necromancers*, London, 1834.

Goethe, J. W., *Autobiography*, London, 1897.

Goldenweiser, Alexander, *Early Civilisations*, London, 1923.

Goldsmith, Margaret, *Franz Anton Mesmer*, London, 1934.

Goldsmith, Oliver, *The Mystery Revealed*, London, 1762.

Görres, J.–J., *The Stigmata*, London, 1883.

Grant, Douglas, *The Cock Lane Ghost*, London, 1965.

Grasset, Joseph, *The Marvels Beyond Science*, New York, 1910 (Paris, 1907).

Greeley, Horace, *Recollections*, New York, 1869.

Green, Roger L., *Andrew Lang*, London, 1962.

Gregory, William, *Letters . . . on Animal Magnetism*, London, 1851.

Grimes, J. S., *Electrical-Psychology*, Boston, 1851.

Grimes, J. S. and Leo Miller, *Great Discussion on Spiritualism*, Boston, 1860.

Gurney, Edmund, and F. Myers, 'Transferred Impressions and Telepathy', *Fortnightly*, March 1883.

Gurney, Edmund, F. Myers and F. Podmore, *Phantasms of the Living*, London, 1886.

Haddock, Joseph W., *Somnolism and Psychism*, London, 1851.

Hall, G. Stanley, *Founders of Modern Psychology*, New York, 1912.

Hall, T. Spencer, *Mesmeric Experiences*, London, 1845.

Hall, Trevor, *The Spiritualists*, London, 1962.

Hall, Trevor, *New Light on Old Ghosts*, London, 1965.

Halliday, W. R., *Greek Divination*, London, 1913.

Hammond, William, *Spiritualism and Allied Causes of Nervous Derangement*, New York, 1876.

Hansel, C. E. M., *E.S.P.: a Scientific Evaluation*, New York, 1966.

Hare, Robert, *Lecture on Spiritualism*, Philadelphia, 1855.

Hare, Robert, *Experimental Investigation: the Spirit Manifestations*, New York, 1858.

Harner, Michael J. (ed.), *Hallucinogens and Shamanism*, Oxford, 1973.

Hart, Ernest, *Hypnotism, Mesmerism and the New Witchcraft*, London, 1893.

Hartmann, Eduard von, *Philosophy of the Unconscious* (3 vols.), London, 1884 (Berlin, 1868).

Haynes, Renée, *The Hidden Springs*, London, 1961.

Haynes, Renée, *Philosopher King*, London, 1970.

Heaton, James, *The Extraordinary Affliction . . . of a Little Boy*, Plymouth, 1820.

Heidenhain, Rudolf, *Hypnotism or Animal Magnetism?*, London, 1888 (1880).

Hélot, Charles, *Névroses et Possessions Diaboliques*, Paris, 1897.

Herodotus, *History* (4 vols., ed. Rawlinson), London, 1880.

Heysinger, I. W., *Spirit and Matter Before the Bar of Science*, London, 1910.

Heywood, Rosalind, *The Sixth Sense*, London, 1959.

Hill, J. Arthur, *New Evidence in Psychical Research*, London, 1911.

Hobbes, Thomas, *Leviathan*, Oxford, 1946 (1651).

Hodgson, B. H., *On the Aborigines of India*, Calcutta, 1847.

Hollander, Bernard, *Hypnotism and Suggestion*, London, 1910.

Holmes, Oliver Wendell, *Mechanism in Thought and Morals,* London, 1871.
Holroyd, Stuart, *Psi and the Consciousness Explosion,* London, 1976.
Home, Daniel Dunglas, *Incidents in My Life,* London, 1863.
Home, Daniel Dunglas, *Lights and Shadows of Spiritualism,* London, 1877.
Home, Julie, *D. D. Home,* London, 1888.
Home, Julie, *The Gift of D. D. Home,* London, 1890.
Houdini, Harry, *The Unmasking of Robert-Houdin,* London, 1909.
Houdini, Harry, *A Magician Among the Spirits,* London and New York, 1924.
Houghton, Georgiana, *Chronicles of the Photographs of Spiritual Beings,* London, 1882.
Howitt, A. W., *The Native Tribes of S.E. Australia,* London, 1904.
Howitt, Ann, *The Pioneers of the Spiritual Reformation,* London, 1883.
Howitt, William, *The History of the Supernatural* (2 vols.), London, 1863.
Huc, Evariste, *Travels in Tartary, 1884–6,* London, 1928 (1850).
Hudson, Thomas Jay, *The Law of Psychic Phenomena,* London, 1902 (Chicago, 1893).
Hugo, Victor, *Correspondence* (3 vols.), Paris, 1898.
Hume, David, *Essays* (2 vols.), London, 1875.
Hunt, Chandos, *A Treatise on Organic Magnetism,* London, 1876.
Husson, H. M., *Report on the Magnetical Experiments,* Boston, 1836 (Paris, 1831).
Huxley, Aldous, *The Devils of Loudun,* London, 1952.
Huxley, T. H., *David Hume,* London, 1879.
Huxley, T. H., *Life and Letters* (2 vols., ed. L. Huxley) London, 1900.
Huxley, T. H., *Science and Christian Tradition,* London, 1902.
Hyslop, James, *Enigmas of Psychical Research,* London, 1906.
Iamblichus, *The Mysteries,* London, 1895.
Iamblichus, *Theurgia,* New York, 1911.
Imbert-Gourbeyre, A., *Les Stigmatisées* (2 vols.), Paris, 1873.
Inge, W. R., *Christian Mysticism,* London, 1899.
Innes, Taylor, 'Where are the Letters?', *Nineteenth Century,* Aug. 1887.
'Insulanus, Theophilus' (Donald Macleod), 'A Treatise on the Second Sight', *Misc. Scotica,* Glasgow, 1820.
Jacolliot, Louis, *Occult Science in India,* London, 1884 (Paris, 1875).
James, William, *The Principles of Psychology,* London, 1901 (New York, 1890).
James, William, *The Varieties of Religious Experience,* London, 1975 (New York, 1902).
James, William, *Collected Essays,* London, 1920.

James, William, *On Psychical Research* (ed. Gardner Murphy and Robert O. Ballou), London, 1961.

Janet, Pierre, *Principles of Psychotherapy*, London, 1926.

Jarvis, I. C. and Joseph Agassi, 'The Problem of the Rationality of Magic', in *Brit. Jnl. Sociology*, March 1967.

Jastrow, Joseph, 'The Problems of "Psychic Research",' in *Harper's New Monthly*, June 1889.

Jastrow, Joseph, *Fact and Fable in Psychology*, London, 1901 (New York, 1900).

Jastrow, Joseph, 'The Unmasking of Paladino', *Collier's*, May 14th, 1910.

Jastrow, Joseph, 'The Case of Paladino', *American Review of Reviews*, July 1910.

Jastrow, Morris, *Aspects of Religious Belief and Practice in Babylonia and Assyria*, New York, 1911.

Johnson, Paul, *A History of Christianity*, London, 1976.

Johnson, Raynor C., *Psychical Research*, London, 1955.

Johnson, Samuel, *A Journey to the Western Islands of Scotland*, London, 1925 (1775).

Joire, Paul, *Psychical and Supernormal Phenomena*, London, 1916 (Paris, 1909).

Jones, H. Bence, *On Animal Electricity*, London, 1852.

Jones, John, *The Natural and Supernatural*, London, 1861.

Jung-Stilling, Heinrich, *Life of Jung-Stilling* (2 vols.), London, 1835.

Jung-Stilling, Johann, *Theory of Pneumatology Concerning Presentiments, Visions and Apparitions*, London, 1834.

Junod, Henri A., *The Life of a South African Tribe* (2 vols.), London, 1927.

Jussieu, Laurent de, *Rapport de l'Un des Commissaires . . . du Magnétisme Animal*, Paris, 1884.

Kant, Immanuel, *Dreams of a Spirit Seer*, London, 1900.

Kardec, Allan, *Le Livre des Esprits*, Paris, 1862.

Kellar, Harry, 'High-caste Indian Magic', in *North American Review*, Jan. 1893.

Kerner, Justinus, *The Seeress of Prevorst*, London, 1845 (Stuttgart, 1829).

Kidd, Dudley, *The Essential Kafir*, London, 1904.

Kieckhefer, Richard, *European Witch Trials*, London, 1976.

King, George, *Experiments with Dr. Slade*, London, 1876.

King, John H., *The Supernatural* (2 vols.), New York, 1892.

King, William, *John Locke* (2 vols.), London, 1830.

Kingsley, Mary, *Travels in West Africa*, London, 1897.

Knox, Ronald, *Enthusiasm*, Oxford, 1950.

Koestler, Arthur, *The Roots of Coincidence*, London, 1972.

Krige, E. J. and J. D. Krige, *The Realm of a Rain-Queen*, Oxford, 1947.

Kroeber, A. L., *Anthropology*, London, 1923.

Kuhn, Thomas S., *The Structure of Scientific Revolutions*, Chicago, 1970 (1962).

Lafontaine, Charles, *Memoires d'un Magnétiseur* (2 vols.), Paris, 1866.

Lambert, R. S., *Exploring the Supernatural*, London, 1955.

Lang, Andrew, *Myth, Ritual and Religion* (2 vols.), London, 1887.

Lang, Andrew, *Cock Lane and Common Sense*, London, 1894.

Lang, Andrew, *Modern Mythology*, London, 1897.

Lang, Andrew, *The Book of Dreams and Ghosts*, London, 1899 (1897).

Lang, Andrew, *The Making of Religion*, London, 1898.

Lang, Andrew, *Magic and Religion*, London, 1901.

Lang, Andrew, *The Maid of France*, London, 1908.

Lang, Andrew, *Concerning Andrew Lang* (the Andrew Lang Lectures, 1927–37), Oxford, 1949.

Langton, Edward, *Essentials of Demonology*, London, 1949.

Laplace, Pierre, *A Philosophical Essay on Probabilities*, New York, 1902 (1812–20).

Lapponi, Joseph, *Hypnotism and Spiritism*, London, 1906.

Laubscher, B. J. F., 'Psi in Traditional Basuto Culture', in Poynton, 1975.

Lavater, Lewes, *Of Ghosts*, Oxford, 1929 (1572).

Laver, James, *Nostradamus*, London, 1952.

Le Bon, Gustave, *The Crowd*, London, 1903.

Lecky, W. E. H., *History of the Rise and Influence of Rationalism in Europe*, London, 1865.

Lee, Edwin, *Animal Magnetism*, London, 1849.

Lee, F. G., *Glimpses of the Supernatural* (2 vols.), London, 1875.

Lefébure, E., 'Les Origines de Fetichisme', *Mélasine*, 1896, viii, 145ff.

Lenormant, François, *Chaldean Magic*, London, 1877.

Leppo, Luciano, 'Italy' in Dingwall, 1967, iii.

Le Roy, Alexander, *The Religion of the Primitive*, London, 1923 (Paris, 1909).

Leroy, Olivier, *La Raison Primitive*, Paris, 1927.

Leroy, Olivier, *Levitation*, London, 1928 (Paris, 1928).

Leroy, Olivier, *Les Hommes Salamandres*, Paris, 1931.

Leslie, David, *Among the Zulus*, Edinburgh, 1875.

Levi, Eliphas, *The History of Magic*, London, 1913.

Lévi-Strauss, Claude, *Structural Anthropology*, London, 1968 (Paris, 1958).

Lewes, George H., 'Seeing is Believing . . .', *Blackwoods*, Oct. 1860.

Lewes, George H., *The History of Philosophy* (2 vols.) London, 1867.

Lewis, Ioan, *Ecstatic Religion*, London, 1971.

Lewis, Ioan, 'The Anthropologist's Encounter with the Supernatural', in Angoff/Barth, 1974.

Liébeault, A. A., *Du Sommeil et des Etats Analogues*, Paris, 1866.

Liébeault, A. A., *Etude sur le Zoomagnetisme*, Paris, 1883.

Liébeault, A. A., *Le Sommeil Provoqué*, Paris, 1889.

Lillie, Arthur, *Modern Mystics and Modern Magic*, London, 1894.

Lodge, Oliver, *Past Years*, London, 1931.

Lombroso, Cesare, *After Death, What?*, London, 1909.

Long, Max Freedom, *The Secret Science Behind Miracles*, Vista, Cal., 1954 (1948).

Lowe, J. E., *Magic in Greek and Latin Literature*, Oxford, 1929.

Lowell, Percival, *Occult Japan*, Boston, 1895.

Lowie, W. H., *Primitive Religion*, London, 1925.

Lytton, Earl of, *Life of Edward Buller, first Lord Lytton* (2 vols.), London, 1913.

'M.A. Oxon', see Moses, Stainton.

Mabru, G., *Les Magnétiseurs Jugés par Eux-mémes*, Paris, 1858.

Mabru, G., *Le Siècle et la Patrie devant la Verité*, Paris, 1859.

Macaulay, Thomas Babington, *Life and Letters* (ed. Geo. Trevelyan), London, 1909.

McCabe, Joseph, *Spiritualism*, London, 1920.

McCormick, G. D. ('Richard Deacon'), *John Dee*, London, 1968.

McCreery, Charles, *Science, Philosophy and ESP*, London, 1967.

McCreery, Charles, *Psychical Phenomena and the Physical World*, London, 1973.

McDougall, William, *Body and Mind*, London, 1911.

Mackay, Charles, *Memoirs of Extraordinary Popular Delusions*, London, 1956 (1841).

Mackenzie, D. R., *The Spirit-Ridden Konde*, London, 1925.

MacNish, Robert, *The Philosophy of Sleep*, Glasgow, 1830.

Maeterlinck, Maurice, *The Unknown Guest*, London, 1914.

Mahan, Asa, *The Phenomena of Spiritualism*, London, 1875.

Malinowski, Bronislaw, 'Magic, Science and Religion', in Needham, 1925.

Mallock, W. H., *Memoirs*, London, 1920.

Man, E. H., *On the Aboriginal Inhabitants of the Andaman Islands*, London, 1932 (1885).

Marchant, James, *Alfred Russel Wallace* (2 vols.), London, 1916.

Marett, R. R., *The Threshold of Religion*, London, 1914.

Marett, R. R., *Tylor*, London, 1936.

Mariner, William, *An Account of the Natives of the Tonga Islands*, London, 1817.

Markham, Clements R., *Cuzco*, London, 1856.

Martin, Martin, 'History of Second Sight', *Misc. Scotica*, iii.

Marwick, Max (ed.), *Witchcraft and Sorcery*, London, 1970.

Maskelyne, J. N., *Modern Spiritualism*, London, 1876.

Mather, Cotton, *The Wonders of the Invisible World*, London, 1862 (Boston, 1693).

Mathieu, P.-F., *Histoire des Miracules et des Convulsionnaires de St. Médard*, Paris, 1864.

Maury, L.-F. Alfred, *La Magie et l'Astrologie*, Paris, 1860.

Mauss, Marcel, *A General Theory of Magic*, London, 1972 (Paris, 1950).

Maxwell, Joseph, *Metapsychical Phenomena*, London, 1905 (Paris, 1903).

Mayo, Herbert, *Letters on the Truths Contained in the Popular Superstitions*, London, 1851.

Medhurst, R. G., *Crookes and the Spirit World*, London, 1972.

Melland, Frank, *In Witchbound Africa*, London, 1923.

Mercer, J. E., *Alchemy*, London, 1921.

Mesmer, Franz Anton, *Mesmerism*, London, 1948 (trans. of *Mémoires sur la Découverte du Magnétisme Animal*, Paris, 1779).

Middleton, John (ed.), *Magic, Witchcraft and Curing*, New York, 1967.

Miller, Betty, 'The Seance at Ealing', *Cornhill*, 1957–8, clxix, 317ff.

de Mirville, J. E., *Pneumatologie. Des Esprits et leurs Manifestations Diverses* (7 vols.), Paris, 1853–4.

Miscellanea Scotica, Glasgow, 1820.

Mitchell, Edgar D., *Psychic Exploration*, New York, 1976 (1974).

Moberly, C. A. and E. F. Jourdain, *An Adventure*, London, 1955 (1911).

Moll, Albert, *Hypnotism*, London, 1890 (Berlin, 1890).

Monardes, Nicolas, *Joyful News out of the New Found World*, New York, 1925 (Seville 1569).

Montefiore, John, *Sir William Huggins*, London, 1931.

Montgomery, C. W., 'St. Augustine's Attitude to Psychic Phenomena', *Hibbert Journal*, Oct. 1926.

Moor, Edward, *Bealings Bells*, Woodbridge, 1841.

Morin, A. S., *Du Magnétisme et des Science Occultes*, Paris, 1860.

Morley, Henry, *Cornelius Agrippa* (2 vols.), London, 1856.

Moser, Liselotte, 'Hypnotism in Germany', in Dingwall, 1967, ii.

Moses, Stainton ('M.A. Oxon'), *The Slade Case*, London, 1877.

Moses, Stainton ('M.A. Oxon'), *Carpenterian Criticism*, London, 1877.

Moses, Stainton ('M.A. Oxon'), *Higher Aspects of Spiritualism*, London, 1880.

Moses, Stainton ('M.A. Oxon'), *Psychography*, London, 1882.

Moses, Stainton ('M.A. Oxon'), *Spirit Teachings*, London, 1949 (1883).

Moss, Thelma, *The Probability of the Impossible*, London, 1977.

Muensterberg, Hugo, *Psychology and Life*, London, 1899.

Muensterberg, Hugo, 'Report on a Sitting with Eusapia Palladino', *Metropolitan*, Feb. 1910.

Muir, Sir W., *Life of Mohammed*, Edinburgh, 1923.

Munthe, Axel, *The Story of San Michele*, London, 1935 (1929).

Murchison, Carl, *The Case For and Against Psychical Belief*, Clark Univ., Worcester, Mass., 1927.

Murphy, Gardner, *Challenge of Psychical Research*, London, 1961 (New York, 1961).

Murray, Gilbert, *Five Stages in Greek Religion*, London, 1935.

Myers, Frederic W. H., *Essays Classical and Modern*, London, 1921 (2 vols., 1883).

Myers, Frederic W. H., *Human Personality and its Survival after Bodily Death* (2 vols.), London, 1903.

Nadel, S. F., *Nupe Religion*, London, 1954.

Nassau, Robert, *Fetichism in West Africa*, London, 1904.

Needham, Joseph, *Science, Religion and Reality*, London, 1925.

Nelson, Geoffrey K., *Spiritualism and Society*, London, 1969.

Nevius, John L., *Demon Possession*, London, 1897.

Newnham, William, *Human Magnetism*, London, 1845.

Nichols, T. L., *The Brothers Davenport*, London, 1964.

Nicoll, Augustus, *Hypnotism*, London, 1890.

d'Oberkirch, Henriette, *Memoirs*, London, 1852.

Ochorowicz, Julian, *Mental Suggestion*, New York, 1891 (Paris, 1887).

Olcott, Henry S., *People from Another World*, Hartford, 1875.

Osterreich, T. K., *Occultism and Modern Science*, London, 1923 (Dresden, 1921).

Osterreich, T. K., *Possession*, London, 1930 (1921).

Osty, E., *Lucidité et Intuition*, Paris, 1913.

Osty, E., *Supernormal Faculties in Man*, London, 1923 (Paris, 1923).

Ould, F., *The Wonders of the Saints*, London, 1919.

Owen, A. R. G., *Can We Explain the Poltergeist?*, New York, 1964.

Owen, Robert, *The Future of the Human Race*, London, 1853.

Owen, Robert Dale, *Footfalls on the Boundary of Another World*, London, 1861.

Owen, Robert Dale, *The Debatable Land*, New York, 1874.

Oxley, William, *Materialisations and their Alleged Exposure*, Manchester, 1899.

Panati, Charles, *Supersenses*, London, 1975.

Panati, Charles (ed.), *The Geller Papers*, Boston, 1976.

Paracelsus, *Selected Writings* (ed. Jacobi), London, 1951.

Parish, Edmund, *Hallucinations and Illusions*, London, 1897.

Park, George, 'Divination and its Social Contexts', in Middleton, 1967.

Parke, H. W., *Greek Oracles*, London, 1967.

Parke, H. W., *The Oracles of Zeus*, Oxford, 1967.

Pastrovici, Angelo, *St. Joseph of Copertino*, London, 1918.

Paton, Lewis, *Spiritism and the Cult of the Dead in Antiquity*, London, 1921.

Pearsall, Ronald, *The Table-Rappers*, London, 1972.

Pearson, Karl, *Francis Galton: Life and Letters* (4 vols.), Cambridge, 1914.

Pététin, J. H. D., *Mémoires sur . . . le Somnambulisme*, Lyon, 1787.

Philostratus, *Apollonius of Tyana*, London, 1809.

Pinkerton, J., *Voyages* (17 vols.), London, 1804–14.

Plato, *Dialogues* (ed. Whewell), London, 1860.

Plotinus, *Works* (ed. Guthrie), London, 1918.

Plotinus, *The Enneads*, London, 1962.

Podmore, Frank, *Apparitions and Thought-Transference*, London, 1894.

Podmore, Frank, *Studies in Psychical Research*, London, 1897.

Podmore, Frank, *Modern Spiritualism* (2 vols.), London, 1902.

Podmore, Frank, *The Naturalisation of the Supernatural*, London, 1908.

Podmore, Frank, *Mesmerism and Christian Science*, London, 1909.

Poyen, C., *A Letter to Col. Stone on Animal Magnetism*, Boston, 1837.

Poynton, J. C. (ed.), *Parapsychology in South Africa*, Johannesburg, 1975.

Pratt, John Gaither, *Parapsychology*, London, 1964.

Price, George R., 'Science and the Supernatural', *Science*, Aug. 26th, 1955.

Price, Harry, *Fifty Years of Psychical Research*, London, 1939.

[Prince, W. F.] *Noted Witnesses for Psychic Occurrences*, Boston, 1928.

Prince, W. F., *The Enchanted Boundary*, Boston, 1930.

Puthoff, Harold and Russell Targ, 'A Perceptual Channel for Information Transfer over Kilometre Distances', *Procs. of the Inst. Elect. E. Engineers*, March 1976.

Puységur (see Chastenet de Puységur).

Randall, John, *Parapsychology and the Nature of Life*, London, 1975.

Rapport des Commissaires . . . du Magnétisme Animal, Paris, 1784.

Rapport des Commissaires de la Société Royale de Médécine du Magnétisme Animal, Paris, 1784.

Rayleigh, Lord, *Life of J. W. Strutt, 3rd Baron Rayleigh*, Wisconsin, 1968.

Read, Carveth, *Man and His Superstitions*, Cambridge, 1925.

Receuil des Pièces les Plus Interessantes Pour et Contre le Magnétisme

Animal (12 vols.) Lyon, 1785.

Redgrove, H. S. and I. M. L. Redgrove, *J. B. Van Helmont*, London, 1922.

Reginald-Omez, Fr., *Psychical Phenomena*, London, 1959.

Reichenbach, Carl von, *Abstract of Researches on Magnetism* (ed. Gregory), London, 1846.

Reichenbach, Carl von, *The Odic Force* (ed. O'Byrne), London, 1976.

Renan, Ernest, *The Life of Jesus*, New York, 1964 (Paris, 1863).

Reynolds, Barrie, *Magic, Divination and Witchcraft Among the Barotse*, London, 1963.

Rhine, J. B., *Extra-Sensory Perception*, Boston, 1934.

Rhine, J. B., *The Reach of the Mind*, New York, 1966 (1947).

Rhine, J. B. and J. G. Pratt, *Parapsychology*, Oxford, 1957.

Rhine, Louisa, *E.S.P. in Life and Lab.*, New York, 1967.

Rhine, Louisa, *Mind over Matter*, London, 1970 (New York, 1970).

Richet, Charles, *Thirty Years of Psychical Research*, London, 1923 (Paris, 1922).

Richet, Charles, *Our Sixth Sense*, London, 1930 (Paris, 1927).

Rinn, Joseph, *Searchlight on Psychical Research*, London, 1954.

Robert-Houdin, J. E., *Memoirs*, London, 1859.

de Rochas, Albert, *L'Extériorisation de la Sensibilité*, Paris, 1895.

de Rochas, Albert, *L'Extériorisation de la Motricité*, Paris, 1896.

Rogers, Samuel, *Table-Talk*, London, 1856.

Rogo, D. Scott, *Parapsychology*, New York, 1975.

Rose, H. J., 'Divination', *Encyclopedia of Religion and Ethics* (ed. Hastings) Edinburgh, 1911.

Rose, Ronald, *Living Magic*, London, 1957.

Rose, Ronald, *South Seas Magic*, London, 1959.

Rutter, J. O. N., *Magnetoid Currents*, London, 1851.

Rymer, J. S., *Spirit Manifestations*, London, 1857.

St. Patrick, *Writings*, London, 1887.

Saint-Simon, Claude Henri de, *Mémoires* (vol. 5), Paris, 1829.

St. Theresa of Avila, *Life*, London, 1870.

Saintyves, P., *La Force Magique*, Paris, 1914.

Salter, W. H., *Trance Mediumship*, London, 1950.

Salverte, Eusebe, *The Occult Sciences* (2 vols., ed. Thomson), London, 1846 (Paris, 1829).

Samson, G. W., *Physical Media in Spiritual Manifestations*, Philadelphia, 1869.

Sandberg, Carl, *Lincoln, the War Years*, New York, 1940.

Sandby, George, *Mesmerism and its Opponents*, London, 1848 (1944).

Sardina, Maurice, *Where Houdini was Wrong*, London, 1950 (Paris, 1947).

Sargent, Epes, *Does Matter Do It All?*, Boston, 1876.

Sargent, Epes, *The Scientific Basis of Spiritualism,* Boston, 1881.

Scheffer, Joannes, *History of the Lapps,* Oxford, 1674.

Schmeidler, Gertrude (ed.), *Extra-sensory Perception,* New York, 1969.

Schopenhauer, Arthur, *The World as Will and Idea,* London, 1909 (1819).

Schrenck-Notzing, Albert von, *Phenomena of Materialisation,* London, 1920 (Munich, 1914).

Scoresby, W., *Zoistic Magnetism,* London, 1849.

Scot, Reginald, *The Discoverie of Witchcraft,* Arundel, 1964 (1584).

Scott, Walter, *Letters on Demonology,* London, 1831.

Seligman, C. G., *The Melanesians,* Cambridge, 1910.

Seligman, Kurt, *Magic, Supernaturalism and Religion,* London, 1971.

Seybert Committee, Report of, Philadelphia, 1920 (1887).

Shah, Idries, *Oriental Magic,* London, 1968.

Shooter, Joseph, *The Kafirs of Natal,* London, 1857.

Sidgwick, Henry, *A Memoir* (ed. Arthur and E. M. Sidgwick), London, 1901.

Silva Mello, A. da, *Mysteries and Realities,* London, 1960.

Sinel, Joseph, *The Sixth Sense,* London, 1927.

Sinnett, A. P., *The Occult World,* London, 1881.

Sitwell, F., *What is Mesmerism?,* London, 1862 (1853).

Sitwell, Sacheverell, *Poltergeists,* London, 1940.

Skeat, William, *Malay Magic,* London, 1900.

Smythies, J. R., *Science and ESP,* London, 1967.

Spence, Lewis, *Second Sight,* London, 1951.

Spicer, Henry, *Sights and Sounds,* London, 1853.

Sprigge, S. S., *Thomas Wakley,* London, 1897.

Stanley, Arthur P., *Canterbury Historical Memorials,* London, 1883.

Stephen, Leslie, *History of English Thought in the Eighteenth Century,* London, 1881.

Stobart, Mrs. St. Clair, *Torchbearers of Spiritualism,* London, 1925.

Stobart, Mrs. St. Clair, *Ancient Lights, or the Bible, the Church and Psychic Science,* London, 1926.

Stone, G. W., *An Exposition . . . of Spirit Manifestations,* London, 1852.

Stowe, Harriet Beecher, *Life* (ed. Stowe), London, 1889.

Sudre, René, *Treatise on Parapsychology,* London, 1960 (Paris, 1956).

Suetonius, *The Twelve Caesars* (ed. R. Graves), London, 1957.

Sully, Maximilien de, *Memoirs,* London, 1856 (1634).

Summers, Montague, *The Physical Phenomena of Mysticism,* London, 1962.

Swettenham, Frank, *Malay Sketches,* London, 1896.

Tabori, Paul, *Companions of the Unseen,* London, 1968.

Tardy de Montravel, *Essai sur la Théorie du Somnambulisme Magnétique,* Paris, 1785.

Taylor, John, *Superminds*, London, 1975.

Teste, Alphonse, *A Practical Manual of Animal Magnetism*, London, 1843.

Thomas, Keith, *Religion and the Decline of Magic*, London, 1971.

Thomas, Northcote, W., *Thought Transference*, London, 1905.

Thompson, J. M., *Miracles in the New Testament*, London, 1911.

Thomson, J. J., *Recollections and Reflections*, London, 1936.

Thorndyke, Lynn, *A History of Magic* (2 vols.), London, 1923.

Thouless, R. H., *From Anecdote to Experiment in Psychical Research*, London, 1972.

Thurston, Herbert, *Modern Spiritualism*, London, 1928.

Thurston, Herbert, *The Physical Phenomena of Mysticism*, London, 1952.

Thurston, Herbert, *Ghosts and Poltergeists*, London, 1953.

Tischner, Rudolf, *Telepathy and Clairvoyance*, London, 1925 (Munich, 1921).

Townshend, Chauncy, *Facts in Mesmerism*, London, 1844.

Trilles, H., *Fleurs Noires et Ames Blanches*, Lille, 1914.

Trollope, Thomas Augustus, *What I Remember*, London, 1887.

Truesdell, John W., *The Bottom Facts of Spiritualism*, New York, 1887.

Tuckett, Ivor, *Evidence for the Supernatural*, London, 1932 (1911).

Tylor, Edward B., *Primitive Culture* (2 vols.), London, 1871.

Tyndall, John, *Fragments of Science for Unscientific People*, London, 1871.

Tyndall, John, *Address Delivered Before the British Association*, London, 1874.

Tyrrell, G. N. M., *Apparitions*, London, 1942.

Tyrrell, G. N. M., *Science and Psychical Phenomena*, London, 1938.

Tyrrell, G. N. M., *The Personality of Man*, London, 1946.

Underhill, Evelyn, *Mysticism*, London, 1911.

Underhill, Evelyn, *The Mystics of the Church*, London, 1925.

Upham, C. W., *Salem Witchcraft* (2 vols.), Boston, 1867.

Van Der Post, L., *The Lost World of Kalahari*, London, 1958.

Vernant, J. P., *et al.*, *Divination et Rationalité*, Paris, 1974.

de Vesme, Caesar, *Primitive Man*, London, 1931.

Voltaire, *A Philosophical Dictionary*, London, 1824 (1764).

Wallace, Alfred Russel, 'Physical Science and Philosophy', *Academy*, Feb. 15th, 1872.

Wallace, Alfred Russel, 'Psychological Curiosities of Scepticism', *Fraser's* Dec. 1877.

Wallace, Alfred Russel, *On Miracles and Modern Spiritualism*, London, 1896 (1875).

Wallace, Alfred Russel, *My Life* (2 vols.), London, 1905.

Walmsley, D. M., *Anton Mesmer*, London, 1967.

Ward, Henshaw, *Charles Darwin*, London, 1927.

Ward, W., *A View of the Hindoos* (2 vols.), London, 1817.

Wasson, R. G., *Soma*, New York, 1968.

Waterman, Adlai, *Obituary: The 'Hodgson Report' on Mme. Blavatsky*, Madras, 1963.

Watson, Lyall, *Supernature*, London, 1973.

Webster, Hutton, *Magic: a Sociological Survey*, Stanford, 1948.

Weld, Charles Richard, *Last Winter in Rome*, London, 1865.

Weldon, Georgina, *Death Blow to Spiritualism – Or Is It?*, London, 1881.

Wells, H. G., 'Peculiarities of Psychical Research', *Nature*, Dec. 6th, 1894.

Welton, Thomas, *Jacob's Rod*, London, 1870 (1693).

Westfall, Richard, *Science and Religion in Seventeenth Century England*, Yale, 1958.

White, Rhea A., and Laura Dale, *Parapsychology: sources of Information*, Metuchen (N.J.), 1973.

Whyte, Lancelot, *The Unconscious Before Freud*, London, 1962.

Wiedemann, Alfred, *Religion of the Ancient Egyptians*, London, 1897.

Wiesinger, Alois, *Occult Phenomena in the Light of Theology*, London, 1957.

Wilberforce, Reginald, *Life of Samuel Wilberforce* (3 vols.), London, 1881.

Wilhelm, John L., *The Search for Superman*, New York, 1976.

Wilson, Colin, *The Occult*, London, 1973.

Wilson, Daniel, *Satanic Agency Not Connected with Table-Turning*, London, 1853.

Wilson, Forrest, *Crusader in Crinoline* (Harriet Beecher Stowe), London, 1942.

Wilson, J. L., *Western Africa*, London, 1856.

Windstedt, Richard, *The Malay Magician*, London, 1951.

Winter, George, *Animal Magnetism*, London, 1801.

Wissler, Clark, *The American Indians*, New York, 1917.

Wolff, Joseph, *Travels and Adventures*, London, 1860.

Woolston, Thomas, *Six Discourses on the Miracles of our Saviour*, London, 1727–9.

Wundt, Wilhelm, 'Spiritualism as a Scientific Question', *Popular Science Monthly*, Sept. 1879.

Wright, Dudley, *The Epworth Phenomena*, London, 1917.

Wyndham, Horace, *Mr. Sludge, the Medium*, London, 1937.

Yates, Frances A., *Giordano Bruno and the Hermetic Tradition*, London, 1964.

Yates, Frances A., *The Rosicrucian Enlightenment*, London, 1975 (1972).

Yeats, W. B., *Autobiographies*, London, 1926.
Young, Julian, *A Memoir of Charles Mayne Young*, London, 1871.
Zielinski, Ludmila, 'Hypnotism in Russia and Poland', in Dingwall, 1968, iii.
Zöllner, Johann, *Transcendental Physics*, London, 1882 (Leipsic, 1879).
Zorab, G., *Bibliography of Parapsychology*, New York, 1957.
Zorab, George, 'Hypnotism in Belgium and the Netherlands', in Dingwall, 1967, ii.

Periodicals

U.S. *American Review of Reviews, Atlantic, Collier's, Harper's New Monthly, Journal of the American Society for Psychical Research, Journal of Parapsychology Metropolitan, North American Review, Popular Science Monthly, Proceedings of the Institute of Electrical and Electronics Engineers, Proceedings of the Parapsychological Association, Science.*

Britain. *Academy, Annals of Psychical Science, Athenaeum, Blackwoods, British Journal of Sociology, Borderland, British Spiritual Telegraph, Christian Parapsychologist, Contemporary Review, Cornhill, Edinburgh Review, Fortnightly, Fraser's Magazine, Hibbert Journal, Human Nature, Journal of the Royal Anthropological Institute, Journal of the Society for Psychical Research, Lancet, Light, Literature, London Society, Nature, Nineteenth Century, Pall Mall Gazette, Proceedings of the Psychological Society of Great Britain, Proceedings of the Society for Psychical Research, Quarterly Journal of Science, Quarterly Review, Reader, Spiritualist, Zoist.*

France. *Annales des Science Psychiques, Mélasine, Revue Philosophique.*

Australia. *Melbourne Harbinger of Light.*

Index